Judge Thelton Henderson: Breaking New Ground

JUDGE THELTON HENDERSON:
BREAKING NEW GROUND

by
Richard B. Kuhns

TWELVE TABLES PRESS
XII

▥

www.twelvetablespress.com

P.O. Box 568
Northport, New York 11768

© 2017 Twelve Tables Press
All Rights Reserved

Library of Congress Cataloging-in-Publication Data

Name: Richard B. Kuhns, author
Title: Judge Thelton Henderson: Breaking New Ground
Description: Northport, New York: Twelve Tables Press, 2017
Subjects: 1. Law — United States 2. History/Judges 3. Biography
Classification: LCC## (Print)/LCC (ebook)
LC record available at https://lccn.loc.gov
ISBN 978-1-946074-00-3 (hardcover)

Twelve Tables Press, LLC
P.O. Box 568
Northport, New York 11768
Telephone (631) 241-1148
Fax (631) 754-1913
www.twelvetablespress.com

Printed in the United States of America

For Mary

Contents

Dolphins, Vietnam Veterans, and Johnny Spain

Institutional Reform Litigation and the Limits of Judicial Power: California Prisons and an East Palo Alto School District

Judge Henderson's Judicial Activism and His Judicial Restraint: Two Examples (with Two Ninth Circuit Reversals and Two Supreme Court Vindications)

Coda

Appendices

Acknowledgments

Dozens of people have contributed to this project. I am especially grateful to Judge Thelton Henderson and my wife, Mary Quigley. Thelton has spent many hours with me — talking about his life and his important cases and reading early drafts of the manuscript. Mary has read every word too many times; she has offered invaluable suggestions; and her patience knows no limits.

Many of Thelton's law clerks are included in the list of names that follows, but four deserve special mention for their help and support: Michael Chu, Karen Kramer, John Lewis, and Jonathan Rowe.

Others who have made this book possible include Maria Alaniz, Fred Alvarez, Barbara Babcock, Leroy Bobbitt, Hyla Bondaroff, Harry Bremond, Barbara Brenner, Dustin Brown, Matt Cate, Shelley Cavalieri, Mort Cohen, Judge LaDoris Cordell, John Doar, Troy Duster, Russ Ellis, Nnamdi Ezeife, Bob Fastov, Jack Friedenthal, Emily Galvin, Abby Ginzberg, Bob Gnaizda, Alan Goldstein, Bob & Colleen Haas, Kelsey Helland, Shane Henry, Jon Hirschoff, Justice Martin Jenkins, Jim Johnson, Leonade Jones, Robert Keller, Ian Keye, Peter Kuhns, Bruce La Pierre, Brian Landsberg. Elizabeth Letcher, Bayless Manning, Leah McGarrigle, Skye McNeill, Sam Miller, Mark Mlawer, Sara Neufeld, Owen O'Donnell, David Oppenheimer, Hank Organ, Judge Marilyn Patel, Melinda Pilling, Jim Quigley, Mae Quinn, Dru Ramey, Cliff Rechtschaffen, Judge James Redden, Ian Rick, Dennis Riorden, Sandy Rosen, Mark Rosenbaum, John Rosenberg, Laura Rosenbury, Kyla Rowe, Sarah Ruby, Roy Schmidt, Carol Sharp, Barbara Slenkin-Slater, Mark Smallwood, Erma Smith, Margo Smith, Don Specter, Anjali Srinivasan, Ed Steinman, Kent Syverud, Dan Tarlock, Jim Thomas, Savala Trepczynski Mike Wald, Judge James Ware, Dick Wasserstrom, and Ron Yank.

Thanks also to the organizers of and participants in the University of California at Berkeley Law School symposium honoring Judge Henderson's thirty years on the federal bench: Ariana Ceja, Judge LaDoris Cordell, Holly Doremus, Richard Drury, Dean Christopher Edley Jr., Karen Kramer, David Oppenheimer, Cliff Rechtschaffen, Brad Seligman, Judge William Orrick Jr., Jonathan Simon, Deborah Sivas, Paul Sonn, Norman Spaulding, Ed Swanson, Judge Myron Thompson, Leti Volpp, and Robert Weisberg.

Finally, for making this book come to life, thanks to Carol McGeehan, to Steve Errick and Twelve Tables Press, to Jay Tidmarsh, and to my very talented stepdaughter, artist, and graphic designer, Skye McNeill. Skye designed both cover and its jacket. Her portrait of Judge Henderson appears on the back of the jacket. The three drawings on the left side of the portrait represent, from top to bottom, Thelton's and my friendship, Thelton's brief movie career (discussed in Chapter Nine) and Thelton's decision to loan a Justice Department car to Dr. Martin Luther King (discussed in Chapter 5).

Permissions

Visit Author Website at www.twelvetablespressauthorsite.com for additional photos and information about the book and Judge Thelton Henderson.

The author gratefully acknowledges permission to reprint excerpts from the following:

Jack Bass, Unlikely Heroes (1981), reprinted with permission of Jack Bass.

Thelton Henderson, The Honorable Thelton E. Henderson: Making a Difference, the Federal Judiciary and Civil Rights in the United States, 1933–2002, an interview conducted by Leah McGarrigle in 2001 and 2002, Regional Oral History Office, The Bancroft Library, University of California, Berkeley (2005), reprinted with permission of the Regents of the University of California and the Bancroft Library.

Thelton Henderson, Keynote Address: Confronting the Crisis in California Prisons, 43 U.S.F. L. Rev. 1 (2008), reprinted with permission of the University of San Francisco Law Review.

Richard Kuhns, Three Stories and a Brief Comment about Institutional Reform Litigation, 13 Berkeley J. Afr.-Am. L. & Pol'y, 218 (2011), reprinted with permission of the Regents of the University of California.

Sonia Sotomayor, Raising the Bar: Latino and Latina Presence in the Judiciary and the Struggle for Representation: A Latina Judge's Voice, 13 Berkeley La Raza L.J. 87 (2002), reprinted with permission of the Regents of the University of California.

Jack B. Weinstein, The Role of Judges in a Government of, by, and for the People: Notes for the Fifty-Eighth Cardozo Lecture, 30 Cardozo L. Rev. 1 (2008), reprinted with permission of the Cardozo Law Review and Judge Jack B. Weinstein.

Introduction

I met Thelton Henderson in the summer of 1966. He had just been hired to run a legal services office in East Palo Alto, California, and I was about to begin my third year at Stanford Law School. For the next two and a half years, I worked with Thelton at the legal services office, first as a student volunteer and then as a young lawyer. He was my mentor, and he was and continues to be a close friend. Thelton presided at my marriage to Mary Quigley in 2002. To everyone's delight except mine, he managed to confuse a wedding ceremony with a roast. I've threatened to use this book as payback; but except for getting in a couple of jabs about Thelton's early fishing prowess, I'll have to wait for another occasion to get my revenge.

Throughout the years, as I learned more about Thelton's life before I met him and his later accomplishments as a lawyer, an academic, and finally a United States District Court judge, I became convinced that he had a compelling story to tell. I urged him to write about his experiences on a number of occasions; and although he was initially attracted to the idea, it eventually became apparent that somebody else would have told the story.

Lawyer and film maker Abby Ginzberg stepped into the breach. Her documentary, *Soul of Justice: Thelton Henderson's American Journey*, tells about Thelton's early life and career as a lawyer and then focuses on three highlights of his judicial career: saving dolphins from needless slaughter by tuna fishers, protecting inmates at Pelican Bay State Prison from cruel and inhumane treatment, and contending with the constitutional issues raised by California's anti–affirmative action initiative, Proposition 209. Soul of Justice was the immediate inspiration for this book.

My friendship with Thelton has provided a unique opportunity to explore matters with him in often great depth. In addition, the relative contemporaneity of the accounts in this book may provide insights and perspectives that, but for the book, would not be readily available later. On the other hand, later accounts may benefit more from the hindsight of history; and my friendship with Thelton raises at least the appearance, if not the reality, of bias. As the text in Chapter Two suggests with respect to judging, the most that one can do to eradicate this latter problem is to try — as I have here — to be aware of and to compensate for one's biases. Whether I have succeeded or not, the many awards and accolades that Thelton has received are strong evidence that the very positive portrait of him presented here is much more a function of his character than of my bias.

Part One

Thelton Henderson and the Process of Judicial Decision Making

Chapter One

Introducing Thelton Henderson

From the poverty of South Central Los Angeles[1] to the federal district court bench, Thelton Henderson has spent his entire career breaking new ground. He was one of only two black students in his class at Boalt Hall, the University of California, Berkeley School of Law. After graduating, he was the first black Justice Department lawyer in the South during the 1960s. He later ran one of the first federally funded legal services offices, and at Stanford University he created one of the nation's first minority admissions programs for law students. President Jimmy Carter appointed him to the United States District Court, Northern District of California in 1980; and in 1990 he became the first black chief judge of that district. As a jurist, he has issued a number of significant, often controversial decisions. In two long-lasting cases, he has held that the treatment of inmates in the California prison system violates the Eighth Amendment ban on cruel and unusual punishment; and he has placed the entire California prison medical system under federal receivership. He has issued rulings protecting the rights of Vietnam veterans suffering from the effects of Agent Orange; and in a courageous and sound decision (later reversed), he held that Proposition 209, California's anti–affirmative action initiative, was probably unconstitutional. He has ruled on numerous civil rights and environmental issues, the most notable of which are his decisions protecting dolphins from needless slaughter by the tuna fishing industry. Indeed, Judge Henderson is responsible for the integrity of the "dolphin safe" label on canned tuna.

---

1. South Central (officially South Los Angeles since 1993) is a relatively impoverished area to the south and west of downtown Los Angeles. Until recently, South Central was predominantly black and now is predominantly Latino. In 1992 when it was still predominantly black, South Central was the site of the riots that followed the acquittal of four white police officers, who had beaten Rodney King.

Thelton Henderson is easygoing and nonconfrontational, but he has not shied away from difficulty or controversy. His months in the South with the Justice Department were fraught with danger and tension. At Stanford, he was not merely the person hired to develop the law school's minority admissions program. Rather, as he well knew, the question whether Stanford Law School would have an enduring minority admissions program was — at least for the short term — dependent upon his success. Had he failed, Stanford at best would have been a follower, not a leader, in creating opportunities for minority students in the law. And as a judge, Thelton Henderson has stood firmly against political forces — including calls for his impeachment in the wake of his Proposition 209 ruling — to interpret the law in a reasoned, dispassionate manner.

Thelton Henderson has devoted most of his professional life to public service — and not only as a Justice Department and legal aid lawyer, an educator, and a judge. He has served as a board member of various public interest organizations and foundations, and in public addresses he has exhorted law students to commit themselves to public interest law. In 1985, he — along with the late Judge Leon Higgenbotham of the Third Circuit Court of Appeals and the late Julius Chambers, former Director-Counsel of the National Association for the Advancement of Colored People (NAACP) Legal Defense Fund — participated in a Carnegie Corporation-sponsored trip to South Africa to meet with black lawyers and leaders who were fighting apartheid. Later Judge Henderson made similar trips to other countries, including Bolivia, Egypt, and Panama. Frequently people he met abroad would come to the United States to observe our legal system, and Judge Henderson would then have an opportunity to renew old friendships. One such friendship is with Richard Goldstone, who established South Africa's Truth and Reconciliation Commission and later became a member of the South African Supreme Court and the first prosecutor of Serbian war crimes.

Despite his busy schedule on the federal bench, Judge Henderson has found time to sit as a volunteer state judge in drug diversion programs, first in Oakland and more recently in San Francisco. The San Francisco program, like other "drug courts,"[2] provides an alternative to criminal conviction for first-time drug offenders who successfully complete a rigorous agenda that includes community service, education, job training, employment, and multiple contacts each week with social workers. Every few weeks — or sometimes more often — the

---

2. Drug courts have enjoyed increasing popularity throughout the country. However, how they operate, how successful they are in preventing recidivism, and whether they adequately protect defendants' rights can vary from court to court. Thus, they are not without controversy. Indeed, there is a growing literature that is extremely critical of drug courts.

defendants appear in drug court, which has all of the trappings of a regular court — robed judge, bailiff, court reporter, prosecutors, and defense counsel, as well as the social workers, who have been monitoring the defendants. Prior to the open court session, the judge will have met with the prosecutors, defense lawyers, and social workers to discuss each case on the day's docket and to share observations and suggestions about each defendant's needs. Then, in open court, the defendants will be called one by one, and the prosecutor will report on their progress. Depending on that report, the judge will offer words of encouragement or warning, perhaps impose some new conditions, and set a future court date. The process is time consuming for all participants, but the recidivism rate for individuals who complete drug court programs can be substantially lower than the recidivism rate of those who proceed through the normal criminal process.

Here is Judge Henderson's description of one drug court hearing in Oakland:

> The last hearing was a young kid who had been remanded by another judge in the program. . . . [H]e wasn't doing things right. . . . [Y]ou're supposed to bring proof of your seeking employment, or if you're employed you're supposed to bring pay stubs and you're supposed to be tested for drugs weekly, and he just . . . wasn't showing up for this. . . . [T]he other judge said, "Well, I don't want to terminate you from this program, and I'm going to send you to jail for three days to show you what's awaiting you if you flunk this program. . . . If you flunk, you go back into the system, and that drug bust, they prosecute you, and you'll probably end up going to jail." So he was coming back from jail, and he was in prison garb, and there was a black man, an elderly — elderly, now, I think he was younger [laughs] than I was — but there was an older black man sitting in the audience. I didn't know who he was. The kid's attorney was a public defender, and I was talking to the kid and I said, "You know, we're very concerned about whether you're right for this program." He said, "I'm right for it." "Well, let's go over this." "Yes, I know, well, I had transportation problems, that's why I was late." And we talked about that.
>
> Then finally — I was going to let him out, but I was going to make him think he had to talk me into it, and I was being gruff. And his attorney said, "Well, his grandfather is here." This man stood up, and talked about the rough life this kid had had, his father had abandoned him and his grandfather had stepped up and was ready to try to take care of him. It was very, very touching, and I talked to him a long time. I actually did something we don't usually do, let him come in and they hugged and he said, "I'm here for you," and "Listen to the judge." You know, it gives me hope that if we work with this kid right, get some resources, and help his grandfather, that we can help this kid. That's fulfilling. That's fulfilling.

I used to feel that we could save every kid I came in touch with. Now I feel if I help this kid and a few others in this program, I've really done something. So that's what I'm trying to do and that's why I've volunteered my time to work in this program. I think hopefully I can make a difference. I've been able to talk to them, I've been able to draw upon . . . my experiences in South Central L.A. and Jefferson High. And they sense it. I think it's important that I'm not just an abstract judge who's coming down on them but someone who can let them know, "I understand that, and I had some of those same experiences. Let me prove it to you."

Particularly in recent years, Judge Henderson has received recognition from a number of organizations for his work as a lawyer and judge. For example, he was the 2000 recipient of the Anti-Defamation League's Pearlstein Civil Rights Award. In 2004, he received the Bernard E. Witkin Medal from the California Bar Association, and in 2005 the American Inns of Court presented him with the Lewis F. Powell, Jr. Award for Professionalism and Ethics. Boalt Hall renamed its justice center "Thelton E. Henderson Center for Social Justice" in 2006. That same year, Judge Henderson was the keynote speaker at the prestigious American Law Institute. In 2008, Judge Henderson was named University of California (Berkeley) alumnus of the year, and in 2013, he received the American Bar Association's Thurgood Marshall Award.

Neither the awards nor the achievements that preceded them have altered Judge Henderson's unassuming, humble character. Throughout his life, he has remained soft-spoken and unpretentious. He has never sought prestige or leadership roles; yet because of his hard work, quick mind, and easygoing personality, he has repeatedly found himself in leadership positions — class president in junior high school; captain of athletic teams from grade school through high school; chief judge of his court — and, most important, empathetic and caring authority figure for young drug defendants; mentor to dozens of young lawyers, many of whom have served as his clerks; and role model and inspiration for countless others. In short, Thelton Henderson is a man who has made a difference.

Chapter Two

Judge Henderson and the Art of Judging[1]

Judges make factual findings and apply the law to the facts. For many cases, the process is relatively straightforward and uncontroversial. For others — including Judge Henderson's cases discussed in later chapters — there may be serious disputes about the facts or how the law should apply to the facts. And if a case is politically sensitive, the result, regardless of its legal merit, is likely to generate criticism. The critics — including dissenting judges and justices — may claim that personal preference or ideology has trumped the rule of law.

When Judge Henderson first assumed the bench in 1980, he had a very non-political, idealistic notion about his role that he hoped would place him above such criticism. "I really knew how I wanted to be perceived . . . : the fairest, squarest-shooting judge in the universe . . . cutting the case right down the middle, when I thought I saw where the middle was." That notion of judging, however, was short lived:

> I very quickly realized that that's not what was happening. My colleagues, most of whom were more conservative than I, weren't cutting it down the middle, and indeed, now I know, nor should they necessarily have done so.

But why should Judge Henderson and his colleagues not try to cut it down the middle? Is that not the epitome of fairness for which all judges should strive?

---

1. If you are not a lawyer or law student or if you have not studied courts, you might want to read Appendix A at this point. It provides an introduction to the judicial process, including brief discussions of the distinct roles of trial and appellate courts, the important distinction between fact and law, and the significance of precedent.

The answers to these questions — as well as a full appreciation of Judge Henderson's decisions and the ability to cut through the hyperbolic rhetoric associated with controversial cases — require an understanding of the nature of judicial decision making.

The Nature of Judging: Politics or Principle — or Both?

The conception of judicial decision making, popular in the nineteenth century and still given voice today, is that judges simply apply rules enshrined in the law to the controversies before them; they do not — or at least should not — let their personal preferences or ideologies influence their decisions. When US Supreme Court Chief Justice John Roberts appeared before the Senate Judiciary Committee at his confirmation hearing, he echoed this view by analogizing judging to umpiring a baseball game: "Judges are like umpires. Umpires don't make the rules, they apply them."[2] In other words, just as a ball is either fair or foul or a runner is safe or out, there are objectively correct answers to legal disputes. And while judges, like umpires, may occasionally err, good judges and good umpires know the rules and make correct decisions most of the time.

Legal realists in the early twentieth century maintained that such a formalistic view of judging was at odds with reality. More recently, some political scientists have made a cottage industry out of producing empirical studies that demonstrate the impact of politics or ideology on judicial decision making.

The legal realists' and the political scientists' insights are not surprising, and Chief Justice Roberts must have known that his analogy was inapt.[3] Baseball is a closed system. Most of its rules are relatively specific and apply to an extremely limited and well-anticipated set of human actions. By contrast, provisions of the Constitution, legal principles derived from cases, and often even statutes are not as specific and precise as the rules governing baseball. Moreover, no set of legal rules can anticipate with any degree of certainty the varied factual contexts within which lawsuits arise. A simple reading of majority, concurring, and dissenting Supreme Court opinions readily demonstrates that there are not objective, predetermined rules for judging as there are for umpiring. In any given case where there are multiple opinions, one may agree more with one

---

2. At her confirmation hearing, Justice Sonia Sotomayor also maintained that "[t]he task of a judge is not to make the law, it is to apply the law."

3. Chapter Nineteen discusses why Chief Justice Roberts — and Justice Sotomayor, see footnote 2 supra — may have chosen to characterize the nature of judging as they did at their confirmation hearings.

than the other(s); but it is rarely, if ever, possible to say that one justice's view is objectively right or another's view is objectively wrong.

On the other hand, Chief Justice Roberts' baseball analogy may have been more apt than he intended it to be. When he first made the analogy, he did not specify what aspect of umpiring he had in mind, but a bit later in his testimony he stated, "[I]t's my job to call balls and strikes." And calling balls and strikes is arguably different from calling runners safe or out or calling balls fair or foul. As former baseball player Hugh Chance related to his son, Kincaid, in David James Duncan's novel, The Brothers K:

> The strike zone that matters, the only one we've got to work with really, is the one locked up inside the skull of the plate ump. And that, m'boy, is why it's no rectangle, no well-defined shape, no sort of plate wide knee-high armpit-low configuration at all. A strike zone is a damned *illusion* is what it is, Kade. It's a *figment*. It's a geometrical wil-o'-the-wisp perched on a twig inside the ump's law-abiding little brain.

But, of course, that is not what the Chief Justice meant.

The reality is that, unlike the rules of baseball, legal rules and principles alone often do not provide judges with sufficient guidance for much of their work. How should a judge decide whether a particular action, say a police search, is "reasonable" in the absence of a specific precedent addressing that question? Or how should a judge decide whether to invoke an extreme remedy such as appointing a receiver to oversee an institution or ordering a reduction in a state's prison population? There may be some general principles that offer guidance, but ultimately the judges in these and myriad other situations will have to rely on their own senses of what is just. And if judges rely on their own senses of what is just, it is not surprising to learn that they do so in light of their political and ideological perspectives. Indeed, judges are no different from the rest of us in that, when there is no clear-cut, objectively correct answer, they bring their own understanding, knowledge, experience, and values to decision making. That is not good or bad; it is inevitable. At most, they — and we — can try to be aware of and compensate for our biases and our unfamiliarity with new situations.

Nonetheless, Supreme Court Justice Antonin Scalia repeatedly stated that his conservative views did not affect his decision making. Professor Erwin Chemerinsky reports that a federal court of appeals judge who heard one of these statements "rolled her eyes and said, 'What nonsense.'" Chemerinsky adds:

> [T]he statements are indeed nonsense. In deciding whether diversity in the classroom is a compelling government interest, how can a judge's own views and experience not matter? In deciding whether recounting ballots in the Florida presidential election violated equal protection, does anyone

believe that the five-four decision was not composed along ideological lines? More generally, what neutral methodology, free of a judge's views, exists to help decide what is reasonable? Reasonableness issues arise in countless areas of constitutional law, from the Fourth Amendment to Equal Protection, and as with the preceding issues, require judgment calls that inescapably are influenced by — if not based on — a judge's own views and experiences.

The pernicious aspect of Justice Scalia's claim is that it denies a basic truth about judging. Was he simply afraid to be candid with the American public and even his own colleagues, or was there a deeper problem? We want judges to be wise, but how can they be wise if they are self-delusional about a critical part of their decision making?

Because each of us has a unique set of background experiences, we are bound to see issues differently and sometimes have disagreements about what is a proper decision. Supreme Court Justice Sonia Sotomayor captured this reality in a speech to Berkeley law students in 2001, when she was a member of the Second Circuit Court of Appeals. One sentence from that speech — her "wise Latina" statement ("I would hope that a wise Latina woman with the richness of her experiences would more often than not reach a better conclusion than a white male who hasn't lived that life") — received widespread publicity and a flood of criticism from conservatives after President Obama nominated her to the Supreme Court in 2009. For example, former House Speaker Newt Gingrich labeled Sotomayor a racist, and Andrew McCartthy in the National Review maintained, "Judge Sotomayor is unabashed in claiming license to judge, and, indeed, to make law, in accordance with her feelings and politics, which are decidedly leftist." However, despite the bombast, Justice Sotomayor's speech — including the "wise Latina" sentence taken in context — is an eloquent description of the inevitable truth that personal experience affects judging:

> While recognizing the potential effect of individual experiences on perception, [I] . . . nevertheless believe[] that judges must transcend their personal sympathies and prejudices and aspire to achieve a greater degree of fairness and integrity based on the reason of the law. . . . [However], I wonder whether achieving that goal is possible in all or even in most cases. . . . Whatever the reasons why we may have different perspectives, either as some theorists suggest because of our cultural experience or as others postulate because we have basic differences in logic and reasoning,. . . I accept the thesis of a law school classmate, Professor Steven Carter of Yale Law School,. . . that in any group of human beings there is a diversity of opinion because there is both a diversity of experience and of thought. . . .

... No one person ... will speak in a female or people of color voice. I need not remind you that Clarence Thomas represents a part but not the whole of African-American thoughts on many subjects. Yet, ... I further accept that our experiences as women and people of color affect our decisions. The aspiration to impartiality is just that — it's an aspiration because it denies the fact that we are by our decisions making different choices than others. ...

Whether born from experience or inherent physiological or cultural differences, ... our gender and national origins ... will make a difference in our judging. Justice O'Connor has often been cited as saying that a wise old man and a wise old woman will reach the same conclusion in deciding cases. ... I'm ... not so sure that I agree with that statement. First, as [Harvard Law School] Professor Martha Minnow has noted, there can never be a universal definition of wise. Second, I would hope that a wise Latina woman with the richness of her experiences would more often than not reach a better conclusion than a white male who hasn't lived that life.

However, to understand takes time and effort, something that not all people are willing to give. For others, their experiences limit their ability to understand the experiences of others. Others simply do not care. ... Personal experiences affect the facts that judges choose to see. My hope is that I will take the good from my experiences and extrapolate them further into areas with which I am unfamiliar. I simply do not know exactly what that difference will be in my judging. But I accept there will be some based on my gender and my Latin heritage.

Justice Sotomayor, like all other judges, has faced and will continue to face criticism from those who disagree with particular decisions. But there will be few, if any, instances where one can say that she reached an objectively incorrect result or that experience, politics, and ideology affected her views but not the views of those who disagree with her. Indeed, just as Democratic appointees to the Supreme Court, including Justice Sotomayor, have tended to be relatively liberal in their rulings, Republican appointees — for example, Chief Justice Roberts, with his elitist, conservative background, and Justice Scalia, with his somewhat less elitist but equally conservative credentials — have not surprisingly tended to take conservative positions on the issues before them.

On the other hand, as Justice Sotomayor suggested in the first sentence of the preceding excerpt from her Berkeley speech, judging is not *all* about politics and ideology. There are rules and standards to apply. Constitutional and statutory language, though often vague, provides at least some contours for decision making. Another constraint stems from the fact that courts have little power to enforce their mandates — a subject explored more fully in Chapter Thirteen. Courts' strength ultimately comes from the respect with which they are held in the community. In addition, as noted in Appendix A, the requirement that lower courts adhere to precedent, the principle of stare decisis, and the tradition of offering reasoned bases for decisions all act as limitations on free-wheeling decision making. The socialization of legal training, where law students are taught to "think like a lawyer" and too often urged to put aside their personal views in analyzing problems, may inhibit their willingness to give priority to matters of politics and ideology. Finally, for some judges, the fear of reversal by a higher court and the desire for respect among judicial colleagues may act as constraints. After all, a decision based on a judge's personal preference is unlikely to bring any direct benefit to the judge.

The extent to which judicial decision making is a matter of individual ideology and the extent to which it is an effort to apply the law in a principled, neutral way will vary depending on the court, the case, the specificity of the law, and the individual judge. Because of the requirement of precedent, trial courts are more constrained than appellate courts by legal norms. For many cases, the law is relatively clear, and at least once the facts are settled, the resolution is easy. Other cases, for which there may not be clear precedent, provide greater opportunity for judges to shape the law to fit their ideologies. Finally, regardless of the court or the case, some judges are more willing than others to push the envelope to advance personal ideologies.

The Exercise of Discretion in Determining and Applying the Law

Reasonable people can disagree about the extent to which judges should or in fact do rule on the basis of politics and ideology. One thing, however, is clear. A critical part of judicial decision making is exercising discretion — that is, using judgment to choose among two or more plausible interpretations of the law or its application in a particular case. For a variety of reasons, judges often *must* exercise discretion in deciding cases. The legal standard may be inherently vague, which is particularly true of constitutional mandates; there may be conflicting precedents; the legislature or a higher court may have intentionally created a multifactored test rather than a bright-line rule; or prior decision makers, be they courts, legislators, or constitution drafters, may not have anticipated the particular situation that is the subject of litigation. In each of these contexts, there is likely to be no clearly right or wrong answer; and yet, judges must resolve the dispute. They must, in short, exercise discretion.

There is no litmus test for the exercise of discretion in these situations. Some might argue that judges should strive to put aside their personal preferences, whereas others might claim that judges should be free to promote their own agendas within the bounds of legal discretion. The dichotomy, however, is largely a false one. All would agree that judges should be wise in the exercise of their discretion; and for any judge, wisdom encompasses the accumulated knowledge and experience of a lifetime. And that knowledge and experience obviously includes ideological predilections, values, and beliefs, which will necessarily affect any judge's view of what is wise and correct in a particular situation. Controversial decisions, of course, will be subject to criticism — and because they are controversial, perhaps more likely to be reversed on appeal by judges whose values and priorities may be somewhat different. The fact remains, however, that the exercise of discretion is an integral and legitimate part of the judicial decision-making process. In this important sense, judging is truly an art.

Judge Henderson and the Exercise of Discretion

When Judge Henderson characterized his more conservative colleagues as not "cutting it down the middle," he acknowledged that they were "going toward their beliefs of what fairness is, what justice is, to the extent that their discretion allowed them to do so." He then added:

> And so that's what I do now. One of the things I ask my clerks[4] regularly when we have a tough case is, "What is my range of discretion? What do the cases say I can do with my discretion without abusing that discretion?" And once I find the range, I go as far as . . . my predisposition, [my] liberal tendencies will allow me to go.

In many respects, Judge Henderson's theory of judging reflects that of another great champion of civil rights, Skelly Wright. Before being appointed to the Court of Appeals for the District of Columbia in 1962, Wright served as a federal district court judge in Louisiana, where he became socially ostracized for issuing orders to end segregation in the New Orleans public schools. In a

---

4. A federal district judge has two (or in the case of the chief judge, three) law clerks. Most often they are recent law school graduates who serve for one or two years. Occasionally, however, judges will have "permanent" clerks, who serve for longer periods of time. Judicial clerkships, especially for federal courts and some state supreme courts, are prestigious, highly competitive positions.

1979 interview, Judge Wright "acknowledged that his sympathies supported his actions as a judge." However, as Wright elaborated:

> [My sympathies weren't what] made me do what I did in New Orleans. I did it because the Supreme Court had said it, and there wasn't any way out except subterfuge. Other judges were using subterfuge to get around the Supreme Court, delays and so on, but I grew up around federal courts and had respect for them, and I tried to carry on tradition. . . . But I think the key in all of this is doing justice within the law. You have to stay within the law, but you can press against the law in all directions to do what you perceive to be justice. And sometimes you can press too far, and it might be counterproductive. But just as long as you stay within the law, and really not go overboard and disregard the law, I think it's justified to do what's right. . . .
>
> I guess I'm an activist, but I want to do what's right. When I get a case, I look at it and the first thing I think of automatically is what's right, what should be done — and then you look at the law to see whether or not you can do it. That might invert the process of how you should arrive at a decision, of whether you should look at the law first, but [with me] it developed through making decisions, which involves resolving problems. . . . And I am less patient than other judges with law that won't permit what I conceive to be fair. Now there's a legitimate criticism of that, because what's fair and just to X may not be fair and just to Y — in perfect good faith on both sides. But if you don't take it to extremes, I think it's good to come out with a fair and just result and then look for law to support it.

Jack Bass, whose book *Unlikely Heroes* contains the interview with Judge Wright, added:

> Such candor about deciding cases might shock many lawyers and law professors, but Wright's reflections after thirty years on the bench are less likely to surprise his fellow judges who understand that the discretion given them in exercising judgment allows *and requires* more than the mechanical application of the law.

Critics of liberal jurists may claim that Judges Henderson and Wright — particularly the latter by first asking what is right and then attempting to justify that result with the law — are manipulating the judiciary in furtherance of a political agenda. Such a charge, however, misperceives an important reality: After hearing a case, a judge almost always will have at least some inkling both of what seems right and, as a result of preliminary research, of what the rough contours of the law may be. The process of refining those inklings almost always goes on simultaneously. Indeed, it would be a feat of incredible mental gymnastics to suspend one's beliefs and values — that is, to forego completely thinking about the justice of the case — as one considered the legal parameters that must govern the decision. Thus, whether judges think about what seems right before they complete their legal research is basically irrelevant. What both Judge Henderson and Judge Wright are describing is a process of decision making that takes into account their fundamental values; and that is what all judges inevitably do, be they liberal or conservative.

More important, neither Judge Henderson nor Judge Wright was describing or recommending an approach that put ideology above the law. Judge Wright emphasized that one had to "stay within the law," and Judge Henderson stressed that he was committed to deciding cases within the range of discretion established by the law: "What is my range of discretion? What do the cases say I can do with my discretion without abusing that discretion?"

An example of the limits of discretion — and one that has been particularly painful for Judge Henderson — is in the area of criminal sentencing. In the mid-1970s, there was a national movement for sentencing reform fueled by two separate interest groups — those (predominantly liberal) who believed that there was unfair disparity in sentencing and those (predominantly conservative) who believed that too many criminal sentences were too lenient. The result of this reform movement generally was to limit judicial discretion in sentencing and to create more severe sentences. In the federal system, the mandatory "Federal Sentencing Guidelines" took effect in 1987.[5] Judge Henderson has characterized the Guidelines as both "unfairly punitive" and as disproportionate: "I saw heads of drug conspiracies getting lighter sentences than the mules [i.e., couriers employed by drug organizations]." Although Judge Henderson was not reluctant to impose stiff sentences on privileged individuals who abused their power and other major offenders, he often chafed at sentences the Guidelines required for relatively minor offenders.

Despite Judge Henderson's antipathy for the harshness of the Guidelines, criminal defense lawyers regarded him as a tough sentencer. One likely explanation for this apparent anomaly is that, despite his personal feelings, he took the Guidelines very seriously. To deviate from the standard sentencing range, the Guidelines required the judge to find specific aggravating or mitigating factors. Regardless of how sympathetic the defendant might be, Judge Henderson would not find a mitigating factor in the absence of adequate proof. And if the prosecutor established an aggravating factor, Judge Henderson felt compelled to take that into account in sentencing.

---

5. A 2005 Supreme Court decision, United States v. Booker, had the effect of making the Guidelines advisory.

The Agony of Discretion:
Judge Henderson's Epiphany

Although Judge Henderson disliked the severity of the Federal Sentencing Guidelines, he was never comfortable with the greater sentencing discretion that he enjoyed before their adoption. In those days, as Judge Henderson explained:

[A] typical argument would be, [first from defense counsel, "The defendant's three bank robbery convictions are] really a drug problem. You ought to give him six months and then send him to . . . some rehabilitation." The prosecutor [would respond,] "Oh no, Judge. The next time he'll have a real gun and kill somebody. Sentence him to five years for each of those, tack them on, that's fifteen years." And I could have done either of those [or anything in between]. . . . That was a responsibility I wasn't emotionally ready for. Eventually, it was so emotional that I had to take extra shirts. When I got off the bench, I was drenching wet just from the anxiety of having that kind of dominion over someone's life.

In the first year or two of his judgeship, many of Judge Henderson's criminal cases involved white-collar defendants, most of whom were white. Well coached by their attorneys, they expressed appropriate remorse, which Judge Henderson took into account in sentencing. As the 1980s progressed, the Reagan Justice Department focused less on white-collar crime and more on welfare fraud and drugs. As a result, a greater number of criminal defendants appearing before Judge Henderson were poor people of color; and they often appeared to be less contrite about their malfeasance.

One such case relatively early in Judge Henderson's judicial career involved a black woman convicted of welfare fraud. Despite her crime, she was clearly needy, and Judge Henderson was predisposed to be lenient, at least if she would show some remorse or acknowledge her wrongdoing. However, unlike the typical white-collar criminal, she was defiant. At the urging of her attorney, who seemed frustrated with her lack of contrition, Judge Henderson adjourned the court proceedings and invited the woman and her attorney into his chambers in the hope that he could coax her into saying the "right" things. But she was unmoved.

At that point, Judge Henderson had an epiphany of sorts. When he first became a lawyer, his uncle Lemuel, who had had numerous encounters with the law, boasted that he would never have to go to jail again. He believed, Judge Henderson recalled, that the criminal justice system was a game and that with Thelton representing him, he had a free pass. There was no doubt in his mind that Thelton, as one of his own, would come to his aid.

To some extent, Lemuel's expectations were understandable. The rituals of the courtroom — including the expectation of remorse at sentencing — give courtroom proceedings the aura of a game. More important, it is common to expect more from those with whom one identifies, particularly when they appear to be people with connections.

Judge Henderson believed that the welfare fraud defendant's reluctance to express remorse was not merely an idiosyncratic character trait. Rather, with the words of his uncle Lemuel in mind, he assumed her defiance was the manifestation of expectations and frustrations rooted in race and poverty. Indeed, her expectations could have been understandably stronger than those of Lemuel. A black attorney might not always be able to manipulate the system for a black client, but surely a black *judge* could do so. And her frustrations may have been even more deeply rooted in race and poverty than Lemuel's expectations. She may have been fed up with the cumbersome, sometimes demeaning process of dealing with the social services bureaucracy; she may have believed that her crime was insignificant in comparison to those of wealthier individuals who defraud the government of millions of dollars; and having been buffeted by poverty and the welfare system, she may have felt that defiance was the last bastion of human dignity. She may have expressed that defiance to any judge, regardless of race; but as Judge Henderson intuited, it was particularly galling for her to be expected to kowtow to a black judge.

From that day forward, Judge Henderson thought of his uncle Lemuel whenever he had to sentence a black defendant. When during a sentencing hearing he saw an older black woman sitting in the courtroom, he surmised that she might be the defendant's mother, and he thought of his mother, Wanzie. He felt a tension between his role as a judge and his role as a black man with insights about race and poverty probably not shared by many of his fellow jurists. And when he heard statements of remorse and contrition, he wondered if they were real and why, in any event, they should make a difference.

Despite — or perhaps because of — his discomfort with criminal sentencing, Judge Henderson made sure that in his courtroom sentencing was not merely a ritualistic game. As former law clerk Jonathan Rowe relates:

> [C]riminal sentencing day [in Judge Henderson's court was] absolutely riveting. Sadly, most of the convicted defendants were young black men, and Thelton would glare at them throughout the hearing like he knew them personally.
>
> [If y]ou've seen criminal sentencings[, t]here's a ritual. First, the probation officer speaks — unemotionally, clinically, but nonetheless incredibly damningly — about the scuzzy reality of the convicted man's actual life. Next, in an even quieter tone, the prosecutor respectfully, but still

meaningfully, declines to "allocute." In other words, he's leaving it up to the judge, because the appalling facts of the case speak for themselves.

Then, more theatrically, the defense attorney does his duty, by bringing up the three best things he can say about his client — but the very meagerness of these "best" things actually damns his client more than anything, convincing everyone the jury was right to convict in the first place.

Finally the judge asks if the defendant wishes to speak on his own behalf. Sullenly, the defendant shakes his head no, the judge issues the sentence, and everyone moves on.

Except in Thelton Henderson's courtroom. Because again, Thelton was a little too real to let it all go down without comment.

First Thelton let the defendant know that the black man sentencing him had grown up in Watts.[6] Then he'd order the defendant to look back at the two or three ladies behind the bar, who were inevitably the only spectators at the hearing. "I've never met your grandmother, or your mother or your sister, or whoever those nice ladies are, but I know that today I'm sentencing THEM, not you. Because THEY care about you, far more than you care about yourself."

Thelton would let THAT sink in, and then he'd really get down and dirty with the poor dude. By the time he was done explaining how much better he understood the guy's bad choices in life than the guy himself had ever understood them, the guy had to be wishing he could just get sentenced by some bland white judge, like most felons draw.

. . . I spent five years as a federal prosecutor, and twenty years in private practice, doing some criminal defense. I've seen at least 1,000 sentencings. But I never, ever saw one anywhere near as compelling, and powerful — and always fair and just — as a Thelton Henderson sentencing.

Judges with senior status are permitted to opt out of hearing certain types of cases. When Judge Henderson assumed that status in 1997, he immediately took advantage of the opportunity to decline criminal cases. New York Federal

---

6. Judge Henderson actually grew up north of Watts, which is a community in the southeast corner of South Central Los Angeles. Watts was the epicenter of the 1965 riots, which spread into much of South Central. Indeed, Thelton's mother, Wanzie, who still lived in the house where she had raised Thelton, told her son that she could see rioting from her living room window during the Watts riots. Because Watts was close to and demographically similar to the area where Thelton was raised and because Watts for years was — and perhaps still is — a more familiar name than South Central to people unacquainted with Los Angeles' geography, Thelton, after 1965, would sometimes describe himself as being from Watts.

District Court Judge Jack B. Weinstein took a similar position when he became a senior judge:

> I have taken my name out of the wheel for drug cases. . . . This resolution leaves me uncomfortable since it shifts the "dirty work" to other judges. At the moment, however, I simply cannot sentence another impoverished person whose destruction has no discernable impact on the drug trade. . . . I am a tired old judge who has temporarily filled his quota of remorselessness.

Procedural and Remedial Discretion

All courts have some degree of procedural discretion. For example, with only very limited exceptions, the Supreme Court has freedom to decide which cases it will decide, and courts of appeals have the discretion to decide whether to reconsider — that is to decide *en banc* — decisions of three judge panels. The greatest procedural discretion, however, resides in the trial courts. Trial judges have discretion to decide such matters as how quickly cases proceed, the extent of pretrial discovery, whether to allow intervention by those who claim an interest in a particular suit, whether to appoint panels of experts, whether to admit or exclude probative but potentially prejudicial evidence, and whether and how to sanction attorneys and litigants who misbehave. Particularly in complex class action lawsuits, discretionary decisions about procedural matters may have a significant impact on the outcome. For example, in Kraszewski v. State Farm General Ins. Co., Judge Henderson approved a $157 million settlement in plaintiffs' favor. He was able to do so only because he had previously made the procedural ruling that the named plaintiffs were entitled to represent the entire class of women discriminated against by State Farm in California.

Trial judges also have substantial discretion in deciding how to fashion and ensure compliance with remedial orders. For example, if an institutional entity is subject to a court order, what specific obligations should the order place on what individuals? Should the court require periodic reports or court hearings to ensure continuing compliance with the order? Should the court appoint a monitor or special master; and if so, what specifically should that person's obligations be? Should individuals who violate remedial orders be held in contempt? Judge Henderson has dealt with these types of issues repeatedly, most notably in his prison cases (Chapters Fifteen to Seventeen) and the case dealing with rights of children with disabilities in the Ravenswood School District in East Palo Alto, California (Chapter Eighteen). His remedial decisions are an integral part of the stories of those cases.

Most trial judges' procedural and remedial decisions are not subject to appellate review or may be reviewed only for abuses of discretion. Thus, it is particularly important that trial judges exercise their discretion in these areas wisely.

Fact-Finding

Although appellate judges typically apply law rather than determine facts, trial judges frequently act as fact finders. There is no right to a jury trial in pretrial proceedings, where factual issues may determine matters, such as the admissibility of evidence, the right to discover information from an opponent, or even whether to proceed to a full-blown trial. In civil cases, the right to jury trial is limited to actions for monetary damages; it does not apply, for example, to proceedings for injunctions or declarations that a law is unenforceable. Finally, in cases in which there is a right to jury trial, criminal defendants and civil litigants can and often do waive that right.

In any lawsuit, the development of a strong factual record begins with the attorneys who examine and cross-examine witnesses and present various documents and exhibits. They must not only discover and set forth the evidence, but they must also marshal it to tell a convincing story to the fact finder. And when the fact finder is a judge, the strength of the judge's decision will depend in part on how well the judge's opinion manifests those same skills in providing a compelling factual account. Although a judge's factual findings will not be reversed as long as there is evidence to support them, a strong factual record can have an impact on an appellate court's interpretation of the law. If the legal standard has some flexibility — for example, if it uses imprecise terms such as "cruel and unusual punishment" or if it is a balancing test that weighs burdens and benefits — the strength (or weakness) of the factual record may be determinative.

Two of Judge Henderson's cases illustrate the importance of lawyers' and judges' attention to facts. Madrid v. Gomez (Chapter Fifteen) held that conditions at Pelican Bay State Prison violated the Eighth Amendment ban on cruel and unusual punishment. Judge Henderson's opinion contains eighty-five pages of detailed factual findings. The record was so compelling that the state did not bother to appeal. The other case, Spain v. Rushen (Chapter Twelve), raised the question of the extent to which shackling Johnny Spain throughout his murder trial interfered with his due process right to assist with his defense. At Judge Henderson's request, Magistrate Judge Joan Brennan conducted a hearing on that issue and made extensive findings of fact. Judge Henderson incorporated those findings into his decision granting Johnny Spain's writ of habeas corpus. The detailed findings by Judge Brennan were critical to the Ninth Circuit's affirmance.

A recent Supreme Court case, Crawford v. Marion County Election Bd., illustrates the same point from a different perspective. The Court affirmed lower court decisions upholding an Indiana statute requiring individuals to present a government-issued photo identification card when voting in person. Justice Souter, in a dissenting opinion joined by two other justices, detailed the burdens on would-be voters — particularly the elderly, the homeless, and individuals with disabilities — that, in his view, made the statute unconstitutional. Some of the facts upon which Justice Souter relied, however, were not part of the official court record. In his opinion announcing the Court's judgment, Justice Stevens observed, "Supposition based on extensive internet research is not an adequate substitute for admissible evidence subject to cross-examination in constitutional adjudication."

If the plaintiffs in *Crawford* had presented detailed evidence supporting Justice Souter's factual assumptions, and if the trial judge had set forth that evidence in a compelling manner, the result in *Crawford* may well have been different. Comments by District Judge Sarah Evans Baker in her opinion rejecting plaintiffs' claims and by Court of Appeals Judge Richard Posner in his opinion affirming the decision support this hypothesis:

Judge Baker:

> [O]ur task . . . has been impeded . . . by the haphazard, "shot gun" approach utilized by the attorneys. . . . Plaintiffs made no apparent effort to match individual plaintiffs to specific claims. . . . What the court faced, as a result, was the gargantuan task of sorting through the hodge-podge of individual plaintiffs, their claim, and their evidence and then trying to make sense of it all.

And Judge Posner:

> [T]here is something remarkable about the plaintiffs considered as a whole. . . . [Some] have photo IDs and so are not affected by the law and [others] . . . have no photo IDs but have not said they would vote if they did and so are, as far as we can tell, unaffected by the law. There thus are no plaintiffs who the law will deter from voting. No doubt there are at least a few such people in Indiana, but . . . the sponsors of this litigation [have been unable] to find any such person to join as plaintiff. . . .

The Malleability of "Facts": Discretion in Fact-Finding

Just as judges inevitably bring their background and experience to bear in interpreting and applying law, trial judges — like jurors and, for that matter, all of us — necessarily evaluate evidence and draw factual conclusions in light of the prism of personal experience. And sometimes that means individuals reach different conclusions after examining the same evidence. Did O. J. Simpson murder his wife and Ron Goldman? Did the four police officers who beat Rodney King use excessive force? Did Clarence Thomas sexually harass Anita Hill, as she claimed? Despite what some called overwhelming evidence of guilt, juries acquitted the defendants in the first two examples. In confirming Clarence Thomas as a justice of Supreme Court, the Senate implicitly rejected the sexual harassment charge, but there is substantial evidence to support it.

Background and experience are particularly important in evaluating the credibility of witnesses, as Judge Henderson makes clear in this story from his early days on the bench:

> When I was a very new judge . . ., on any given day six, seven, eight, nine of us would eat in [the judges'] lunchroom; and we'd talk shop. . . . [O]ne of my colleagues was in . . . [an] employment discrimination trial. . . . [H]e'd come in and we'd say, "How's the trial going?" and he'd give us a brief report. . . .
>
> One or two weeks into the trial . . . he came in and said, "Oh, it's getting interesting now. The plaintiffs testified today. . . . They were black plaintiffs, and they were testifying that there was rampant discrimination in the locker room where they dress to go to work and to go home. They were saying that there were many events of painting the 'n' word on their lockers and hanging monkeys and gorillas from their lockers and all kinds of racial insults."
>
> And he said to my astonishment, "I just don't believe that. Their testimony is incredible. People don't act like that." And my mouth fell open and I said, "My Gosh, they do! I grew up hearing my father and my uncles, who were poor black workers, telling stories about that kind of behavior. It does happen."
>
> . . . This is a fine person, who's still a friend of mine who just had a different life experience that led him to believe that. And I found myself saying, "Thank God that this honest, well-meaning man doesn't represent the view of all of the federal judiciary, that we have others with a different view who have insights that his rather privileged background didn't allow him." That's one of the arguments I would make for the need for diversity on the bench.

In addition to evaluating credibility, judges acting as fact finders (like anyone making factual assessments) have to decide how much weight to give evidence and what inferences — including inferences of intent or state of mind — to draw from circumstantial evidence. And like the credibility issue raised by Judge Henderson's colleague, resolving factual questions is a process that involves exercising discretion — that is, drawing upon one's background, personal experiences, and judgment to reconstruct (in the face of inevitable uncertainty) what probably happened. For example, when young Thelton, a talented

skater and the only black at a roller-skating rink, observe⟨...⟩ him
(Chapter Three), what should he have inferred that they w⟨...⟩ t he
was an accomplished skater, or that he was an out-of-pl⟨...⟩ a
white environment? Similarly, when evidence before Judg⟨...⟩ b-
lished that prison guards placed an inmate into a vat of scald⟨...⟩ r
Fifteen), what inference should he have drawn about their int⟨...⟩

Although the law governing a case will often be relatively ⟨...⟩
trials, as well as many pretrial issues, require these kinds of factu⟨...⟩
And since a trial court's factual findings are not likely to be sub⟨...⟩
on appeal, the wise evaluation of evidence is a critical part of a tri⟨...⟩

The Art of Great Judging

But what is the *wise* evaluation of evidence or *wise* judging in genera⟨...⟩
distinguishes a great judge from a poor or only mediocre one?

A comprehensive answer to these questions would require an entire⟨...⟩
Moreover, regardless of how thorough one tried to be, there undoub⟨...⟩
would be criticism from some who regarded the conclusions as inconsis⟨...⟩
with their views of the world and their personal political and policy preferenc⟨...⟩
Indeed, some might claim that the task is impossible, that judicial greatness –
at least without the hindsight of history — is only in the eye of the beholder.

Recognizing these difficulties and without making any effort to be thorough,
one can nonetheless make several claims about great judging that should (but
probably will not) be relatively free from controversy.

First, being well versed in the law is, of course, essential. Greatness, however,
does *not* come merely from mastering the intricacies of even complex laws and
legal principles. It takes no special talent for a well-trained lawyer to understand
the requirements and the limits of the law. And when the law is precise, a judge
should have no more difficulty applying it to a given set of facts than a baseball
umpire has in calling a ball fair or foul. Rather, greatness resides in how judges
use the discretion that is an inevitable part of their decision-making processes.

Second, because judges are called upon to exercise their discretion in a wide
array of situations, judges with broad ranges of experiences are probably more
likely to achieve greatness than judges with relatively narrow, sheltered backgrounds. Breadth of experience, however, is neither a sufficient nor a necessary
condition of greatness.

Third, regardless of their backgrounds, judges must exercise their discretion
in situations about which they have, at best, only imperfect, limited personal
knowledge or understanding. Thus, to exercise discretion wisely, judges with
both broad and sheltered backgrounds must be ever curious, inquiring, and
willing to learn. Without these traits, greatness is impossible.

Fourth, and probably most important, a great judge must have the ability to channel curiosity and learning in a way that overcomes personal biases that might otherwise affect discretionary decision making. That requires initially a keen awareness of the limitations of one's own experience and insights, but it also requires empathy — that is, an ability to rise above one's limitations; an ability to see and understand the perspectives of those whose lives or situations may be unfamiliar. As Alabama Federal District Judge Myron Thompson suggested at a symposium honoring Judge Henderson's thirty years on the bench, a great judge must have

> the ability not to discriminate,. . . the ability to . . . transcend yourself. . . . It's that expansion outside yourself. . . . It means that you're there to be open-minded and to hear about other people who are unlike you.

Similarly, Justice Sotomayor spoke of the importance of empathy in her 2001 "wise Latina" speech:

> I am reminded each day that I render decisions that affect people concretely and that I owe them constant and complete vigilance in checking my assumptions, presumptions and perspectives and ensuring that to the extent that my limited abilities and capabilities permit me, that I reevaluate them and change as circumstances and the cases before me requires.

And Federal District Judge Jack Weinstein has identified empathy, along with law and facts, as one of the "three elements of a just decision":

> Some judges and lawyers seem to ignore the passageway to the heart and spirit of the law. Up in high towers, many look for the bottom financial line or the rigid imposition of technical niceties, ignoring the effect of their work on individuals' well being. . . .
>
> Powerful stories of human tragedy have echoed in my court through the years: women damaged by their mothers' ingestion of DES [diethylstilbestrol, a synthetic estrogen], who are now unable to have children of their own; Vietnam veterans, frightened by the effects of herbicides on their progeny; men struck down by dreaded lung cancers because, when they were still teenagers, they were exposed to asbestos while building the ships with which we won a war; persons sufferings from AIDS because of tainted blood used in transfusions; and mothers driven to become drug couriers by cruel traffickers and poverty. To see those who live such stories is to understand why the law must be sensitive to human needs.
>
> We must try to bridge the gap between us and those who need us. We must try to open a dialogue between the heart of the law and the hearts of those who seek justice from us. . . .

Inside the courtrooms and the law offices, it is essential that we try to humanize our work. Given our increasingly complex legal system, lawyers and the judiciary run the risk of becoming dangerously divorced from the real world of individuals. We ought not to permit that distance between ourselves and the public to widen through lack of communication and understanding. . . .

Leading appellate judges and law professors have described the legal function as performed almost exclusively through bookish research and cogitation. But this description is not complete [especially] for trial lawyers and district judges who must observe and deal with real people — people who are sometimes irrational, but always unique, interesting, and important.

Often what people need most is a hearing, a forum, a sense that we understand their fears, needs and aspirations.

Empathy, Compassion, and the Rule of Law

Judge Weinstein's description of empathy, unlike the brief quotations from Justice Sotomayor and Judge Thompson, emphasizes having a sense of compassion for those who are unlike us, for those whose perspectives we need to try to understand. Developing a sense of compassion for those who are different and unfamiliar may enhance, if not be critical to, a thorough understanding of their perspectives.

Psychologists and other scholars debate the relationship among cognitive empathy (a rational understanding of others' perspectives), emotional empathy (putting oneself as much as possible into the shoes of others and feeling their emotions with them), and compassion (having feelings *for* rather than *with* others). For example, can cognitive empathy and emotional empathy be independent of each other, or are they necessarily intertwined? Is compassion necessary for emotional empathy, or does emotional empathy lead to compassion? Fascinating as these questions are, they are beside the point here. Empathy — as described by Justice Sotomayor and Judges Thompson and Weinstein — is first and foremost a deep understanding of the perspectives of others. As used here, empathy is that understanding, which may include or be accompanied by emotional empathy or compassion.

What begins or appears to begin as a purely cognitive understanding may generate a strong emotional pull, but such an emotional pull should not dictate a case's outcome. Appropriately, Justice Sotomayor, Judge Thompson, and Judge Weinstein do not suggest that empathy should be a substitute for the rule of law or for reasoned decision making. Rather, empathy enhances understanding, which is critical to the wise exercise of discretion *within the parameters of the law.*

This is not to say, however, that empathy will not or should not affect judicial decision making. As noted previously, judges inevitably rely on their own understanding, knowledge, experience, and values in exercising their discretion. And part of their understanding is the empathy that they have (or lack) with the litigants. For example, to the extent that judges have discretion in sentencing, Judge Weinstein's empathy with "mothers driven to become drug couriers by cruel traffickers and poverty" may lead him to give a mother/courier a lighter sentence than a judge without such empathy would give. However, if the young mother were being tried without a jury and if the evidence of her guilt were clear, Judge Weinstein's legal obligation, despite his empathy, would be to find her guilty.

Within the areas where judges exercise discretion, empathy is not, or at least should not be, a one-way street. Judges' personal knowledge and experience will often be insufficient to appreciate fully the perspectives of any of the parties to a lawsuit. Thus, in a large drug conspiracy trial Judge Weinstein, as he presumably would acknowledge, should try to have empathy not only with "mothers driven to become drug couriers," but also with the "cruel traffickers," who drove them to that fate. Similarly, in a lawsuit challenging a vague environmental regulation, a judge should try to understand the perspectives of both the environmentalists and those whose economic interests could be adversely affected by the regulation.

Even empathetic judges will have had different experiences and will have different degrees of understanding. As a result, they may reach different conclusions about the same issue. Nonetheless, an empathetic understanding of the litigants and their perspectives is the most that one can hope for both to minimize the risk that judges will let their own narrow predispositions bias their decision making and also to help ensure that judges exercise their discretion wisely.

The Unwarranted Attack on Empathy

In recent years, empathy has received undeserved, bad press from conservative commentators, politicians, and even academics. These attacks on empathy did not surface in 1991 when supporters of Justice Clarence Thomas maintained at his confirmation hearing that he would have empathy with poor blacks. Nor did they materialize in 2006 when Justice Samuel Alito at his confirmation hearing spoke of how his background gave him empathy with victims of discrimination. Rather, they appeared to begin in response to a 2007 speech by then candidate Barack Obama to Planned Parenthood. In discussing qualifications for judicial candidates, Obama said:

We need somebody who's got the heart, the empathy, to recognize what it's like to be a young teenage mom. The empathy to understand what it's like to be poor, or African American, or gay, or disabled, or old. And that's the criteria by which I'm going to be selecting judges.

Empathy, the critics claim (or at least imply), is a liberal value that promotes placing personal preference above the rule of law. Personal preference, of course, is the opposite of empathy. Nonetheless, the critics' misconception of empathy predominated the discussion when President Obama selected Sonia Sotomayor for the Supreme Court. For example, the *Wall Street Journal* derisively referred to her as "the 'empathy' nominee":

> In making Sonia Sotomayor his first nominee for the Supreme Court yesterday, President Obama appears to have found the ideal match for his view that personal experience and cultural identity are the better part of judicial wisdom.
>
> This isn't a jurisprudence that the Founding Fathers would recognize, but it is the creative view that has dominated law schools since the 1970s and from which both the President and Judge Sotomayor emerged. In the President's now-famous word, judging should be shaped by "empathy" as much or more than by reason. In this sense, Judge Sotomayor would be a thoroughly modern justice, one for whom the law is a voyage of personal identity.

Despite the *Wall Street Journal's* hyperbole, President Obama's views were not inconsistent with the traditional demands of reasoned decision making. In announcing his nomination of Justice Sotomayor for the Supreme Court, President Obama specifically recognized that judges are

> to approach decisions without any particular ideology or agenda, but rather a commitment to impartial justice, a respect for precedent, and a determination to faithfully apply the law to the facts at hand.

Moreover, President Obama's concern with empathy was not a reflection of some relatively recent fad in legal education. Indeed, Judge Weinstein, who taught at Columbia Law School for almost the entire last half of the twentieth century, has observed that "because [empathy] is invisible and almost never explicitly acknowledged in law schools, it is hard to know when we have adequately dealt with it." And when President Obama spoke of empathy, he invoked Chief Justice Oliver Wendell Holmes' famous 1881 statement that "the life of the law has not been logic; it has been experience." According to Holmes:

> It is something to show that the consistency of a system requires a particular result, but it is not all. The life of the law has not been logic; it has been

experience. The felt necessities of the time, intuitions of public policy, avowed or unconscious, even the prejudices which judges share with their fellow-men, have had a good deal more to do than syllogism in determining the rules by which men should be governed.

In other words, the law does not exist in a vacuum. Judges shape the law in light of their perceptions of the "necessities of the time," their "intuitions of public policy," and, to the extent that they lack empathy, their own prejudices.

President Obama elaborated on the Holmes' "life of the law" statement in a manner that evokes the language of Judges Thompson and Weinstein:

> [It is] experience being tested by obstacles and barriers, by hardship and misfortune, experience insisting, persisting, and ultimately overcoming those barriers. It is experience that can give a person a common touch and sense of compassion, an understanding of how the world works and how ordinary people live.

That "understanding," that empathy is not a license to ignore the law. Rather, as suggested earlier, it is vital to wise decision making in those many areas in which the law entrusts judges with discretion. The only alternatives are to deny the reality of discretion or to advance alternative, inevitably less humane criteria for its exercise.

Judge Henderson's Empathy and the Limits of Discretion

As Judge Myron Thompson explained at the symposium honoring Judge Henderson, part of the latter's "stellar legacy" is his empathy with those in the prison system — an empathy that extends both to inmates and to prison guards. But Judge Henderson's empathy stretches much further. It embraces a hearing impaired U.P.S. driver who did not understand his rights (Chapter Nine), veterans subjected to Agent Orange in Vietnam (Chapter Eleven), and gays discriminated against by the Defense Department in the early 1980s (Chapter Twenty), to name only a few. And Judge Henderson, himself, has never been an inmate or a prison guard; he is not hearing impaired; he was never in combat, much less subjected to Agent Orange; and he is not gay. However, he has had a wide range of experiences; he is inquisitive; and as California Court of Appeal Justice Martin Jenkins has said, he is "self-effacing [and] humble . . . all of the time" — all of which undoubtedly help him understand and relate to other people and their perspectives.

To get a sense of Judge Henderson's empathy and its limits, consider Madrid v. Gomez (Chapter Fifteen). In *Madrid,* Judge Henderson held that the conditions of confinement at Pelican Bay State Prison in northern California violated the inmates' Eighth Amendment right to be free from cruel and unusual punishment. Conditions of confinement, particularly for prisoners who are disruptive, will inevitably be harsh; and there is no bright-line test for determining when the Eighth Amendment threshold has been passed. At the same time, though, Judge Henderson's discretion was not unlimited. There are general guidelines from existing case law that give content to the concept of cruel and unusual punishment, and neither Judge Henderson nor any other judge is free to ignore evidence.

The record of prisoner abuse at Pelican Bay was so horrific that Judge Henderson was acting well within the range of appropriate judicial discretion to reach the conclusion he reached. Indeed, a contrary holding might have been considered an abuse of discretion. Or, to put the matter somewhat differently, given the record of abuse, it would have taken a great deal of empathy with the prison guards and virtually no empathy with the inmates to understand the evidence in a way that would have led to the opposite result.

Not surprisingly, Judge Henderson's opinion demonstrated his empathy with the prisoners in the detailed descriptions of their suffering. At the same time, it also demonstrated his empathy with the prison guards. Judge Henderson repeatedly acknowledged that their job was dangerous and difficult; and when their actions injured prisoners, he gave the guards the benefit of the doubt about their intentions.

One of the contentious issues in *Madrid* was whether the Secure Housing Unit (SHU), where inmates spend weeks and sometimes years in extreme isolation, should be closed. In other words, did the psychological injury (and sometimes resulting self-inflicted physical injury) caused by confinement in the SHU constitute cruel and unusual punishment? Judge Henderson placed some limited restrictions on the use of the SHU, but he refused to close it.

In light of recent, renewed criticism of the SHU, I asked Judge Henderson in 2014 if he regretted not having closed the unit. His reply began with an emphatic "No." "I thought about closing the SHU." he continued. "I searched the record — and I had one of my clerks search too — with the specific purpose of finding evidence that would justify that result. But the plaintiffs didn't make the case. The evidence just wasn't there, and I had to follow the evidence."

The fact that Judge Henderson made special efforts to look for a justification to close the SHU suggests that his empathy with the inmates tilted him toward wanting to take that action. Ultimately, though, he understood that his discretion was limited by the evidence.

Judge Henderson's approach to civil rights cases provides another example of the limits of discretion to act with empathy. Because of his civil rights background and his exposure to segregation and racial discrimination, Judge Henderson with little effort can empathize with individuals who have been subjected to racial and gender discrimination. And, as Judge Henderson's story about the testimony of racist graffiti in the locker room illustrates, his experiences may make him better able than some of his colleagues to evaluate wisely evidence of discrimination. However, Judge Henderson's empathy affects his judging only in so far as the law and the facts, as he understands them, give him discretion:

> To the extent there's a case there . . ., I . . . use my discretion to push enforcement of rights as far as I think I can properly do it. But it's not an automatic. I can point to dozens . . . of cases where I've ruled against civil rights plaintiffs. Sometimes they don't make their case. I will even go further. Sometimes very bad and lazy employees do the race thing and run to court, and they don't have a leg to stand on. Nobody has wronged them and I so find. So it's not automatic. I look at the merits. You've got to make your case. You don't automatically win when you come into Thelton Henderson's court. If you have a strong case, I'll push it; and I'll use my discretion to try to right the wrongs that I have found, but I have to first find those wrongs, and I don't always do that.

Judge Henderson's willingness to empathize with others and his commitment to the rule of law, like anyone's important characteristics and values, are in some large measure the product of a lifetime of daily experiences and influences. Thus, to appreciate Thelton Henderson, the judge, one must try to understand Thelton Henderson, the person. The next several chapters trace Judge Henderson's path from South Central to his appointment to the federal bench. Much of the story — particularly Judge Henderson's time with the Justice Department — is fascinating in its own right. The broader purpose, though, is to provide insights into Thelton Henderson's character, his values, and some of the people and events that helped to make him who he is. His humility, his leadership abilities, his sense of moral outrage when pressed too far, his good humor, the lesson he learned from Attorney General Robert Kennedy about always being prepared, and his successful effort to institutionalize a minority admissions program at Stanford Law School are all part of the story of his prejudicial life, and they all have parallels in his career as a judge.

Part Two

Path to the Bench

Chapter Three

The Early Years

Wanzie

Wanzie Henderson gave birth to her only child, Thelton, on November 28, 1933 in Shreveport, Louisiana. Wanzie was one of nine children born to Estelle and Fred Edgar Herring, who had come to Shreveport from Bude, Mississippi. Eugene Henderson, Wanzie's husband and Thelton's father, had grown up in Texas.

For blacks in the South in the first third of the twentieth century, Wanzie and Eugene had fairly substantial educations. Eugene had completed high school. Wanzie, the more motivated and driven of the two, had begun working full time as a maid after the eighth grade. Eugene made his living as a janitor. Except for a brief time during World War II when they were both able to secure jobs in the defense industry, these were their life-time occupations.

When Thelton was three, his grandmother, Estelle, decided that the family should join John and Lemuel, two of Wanzie's younger brothers, in California. John and Lemuel had left Shreveport for Los Angeles when they were still teenagers, and in their letters home, they lauded the virtues of California — more opportunity and less discrimination. Estelle, like Wanzie by that time, was separated from her husband. The two of them, Thelton, Thelton's uncle Fred, and three aunts packed all of their belongings in a truck and — like the Joads in John Steinbeck's Grapes of Wrath — headed for the promised land.

Upon their arrival in Los Angeles, the Herring–Henderson clan rented a small house on 53rd Street. During the next three years, they moved twice, first to 756 E. 52nd Street and then 1207 E. 27th Street. All three areas were predominantly black.

During the early years in California, Wanzie worked as a maid "in service," — that is, as a live-in housekeeper. She was able to come home only one weekend a month, so Estelle had primary responsibility for Thelton's day-to-day care.

However, even in her absence, Wanzie was committed to the proposition that Thelton would be a success, and she did everything in her power to further her goal. To the extent that she was able, she ensured that Thelton had a variety of experiences; and although Thelton did not fully appreciate it at the time, she was grooming him to feel comfortable in white and integrated environments, as well as the black environment of their first homes and neighborhoods.

Despite Wanzie's meager salary and regular contributions to the Herring–Henderson household, she managed to save enough money during the first few years to purchase a house. When Thelton was seven or eight, he and his mother moved to 219 E. 43rd Street. The new neighborhood was more prosperous than the old ones, and it was integrated. Wanzie continued to clean houses, but she no longer lived "in service."

Wanzie's and Thelton's new house was only a few doors from an African Methodist Episcopal (AME) church, where Thelton had his first exposure to organized religion. Wanzie — unlike her mother, Estelle, who was an avid churchgoer — did not belong to any congregation. The strict social code (e.g., no dancing, no movies, restricted dating) of the church she attended as a youth had soured her on religion. Nonetheless, she believed it was important for her son to have some knowledge of Christianity and Biblical stories. Thus, for several years Wanzie insisted that Thelton attend Sunday School at the AME Church. Except for that brief experience and occasional visits with Estelle to her church, organized religion did not play a role in Thelton's youth, as it has not in his adult life.

Thelton's 43rd Street neighborhood — like his integrated school, Trinity Street Grammar — quickly became predominantly black. A new neighborhood junior high school, George Washington Carver, had just been completed when Thelton was ready to enter seventh grade. However, Wanzie arranged for Thelton to attend the predominantly white — and better — John Adams Junior High School.

Wanzie had similar plans for Thelton's high school education, but Thelton balked and ultimately prevailed. The issue was athletics. In order to prevent high school coaches from recruiting students for their sports teams, the school district had a rule that students could not compete against their neighborhood high school. That meant that if Thelton wanted to be on the high school football team, which he did, he would have to go to his "neighborhood" school, the all-black Jefferson High. Having taken algebra and geometry in junior high school, Thelton was more advanced than most of his Jefferson classmates.

Soon after the move to E. 43rd Street, Wanzie bought a piano and arranged for Thelton to take lessons. Nobody else in the family played a musical instrument, and Thelton had not asked for the piano. Rather, the piano was Wanzie's idea — part of her effort (perhaps influenced by what she had observed while working "in service") to ensure that her son would have a well-rounded education. Thelton claims that he was never a very good piano player; but he enjoyed the lessons, which he continued until he lost access to the piano in high school.

Losing the piano was indirectly the result of a decision Wanzie made at about the same time she bought the piano. She had begun a correspondence with her estranged husband, and before long Eugene moved from Shreveport to South Central and rented a nearby apartment. By the time Thelton was in sixth grade, his father and mother had reconciled and Eugene had moved in with them. The relationship between Wanzie and Eugene was rocky at best. Eugene was verbally abusive to both Wanzie and her son. When Thelton was in tenth grade, Eugene — in what Thelton refers to as the "spaghetti incident" — threw his spaghetti dinner against the wall. That was the final straw for Wanzie, who left the house with Thelton that evening.

Estelle arranged for Wanzie and Thelton to stay with a Mrs. Hall, a member of Estelle's congregation. The new accommodations were in a poorer part of South Central — near Ross Snyder Playground and only a few blocks from Jefferson High School. Wanzie and Thelton remained with Mrs. Hall for a little over a year — until Wanzie was able to hire a lawyer, who obtained a divorce for Wanzie and a court order removing Eugene from the E. 43rd Street house. When Wanzie and Thelton returned home, they discovered that Eugene had sold the piano.

Thelton was never close to his father, even when they were living together; and his uncles Lemuel and John were seldom around — probably a good thing, as they tended to live at the edge of the law. Thelton's uncle Fred would occasionally take Thelton fishing at the San Pedro pier, but Fred lived in another part of town. And when Fred and Thelton were together — even on their fishing outings, they rarely spoke to each other. Thelton's only significant adult male role model was Bill James. Bill had married Thelton's Aunt Ziporah, one of Wanzie's sisters who made the trip from Shreveport to Los Angeles. Bill occasionally bought Thelton books and took him to sporting events. He taught Thelton how to tie a tie. "He was like a parent," Thelton recalls. "He talked to me about girls. He tried to educate me." But Bill and Ziporah had their own family, so his influence on Thelton, as significant as it was, was necessarily limited.

Wanzie was the mainstay in Thelton's life. Both her love and her high expectations did much to shape his early years. Thelton knew that he was "the apple of her eye" and that she expected him to "be somebody." Despite her roots, Wanzie did not have a southern accent, and she insisted that Thelton use proper grammar and diction. While Thelton's friends frequently wore scruffy jeans and t-shirts, Wanzie made sure Thelton regularly appeared in white corduroys or khakis and a clean shirt.

Reading

Growing up in the 1930s and 1940s, Thelton exhibited the same easygoing, hardworking traits that have characterized his professional career. Thus, one might expect that the numerous friendships and accolades of his adult life would have their counterpart in his youth. In one area—athletics—that expectation is accurate. Otherwise, Thelton was usually an outsider.

Thelton's natural shyness, the lack of male role models, Wanzie's efforts to make him stand above his peers, and the reality of racial discrimination all combined to make Thelton somewhat isolated from his classmates. He was never at ease socially with girls, even after he had become a high school football star:

> [Jefferson High School] was the hippest school. Guys could dance . . . and I couldn't dance. I didn't date. I didn't know how to talk to girls.
>
> . . . [W]hen I finally did learn how to slow dance—I could just slow dance or do some sort of two-step—I'd start dancing and say something like, "Gee, do your homework today?" She'd say, "Yes." And that was it. That was my whole line—my whole rap! [laughter] And then, like five hours later, this dance would end and it just was awful. I would see the other guys and they'd be talking and I'd say, "What could they be saying?" I couldn't even imagine what the conversation was.

Thelton's classmates made fun of his dress; and because of his speech, he was seldom fully comfortable with his black peers. Indeed, the black teens with whom he hung out when he was living at Mrs. Hall's house would tease him about the way he spoke—using a mock British accent to parody his proper diction and grammar.

In both elementary and junior high school, Thelton's association with white classmates inevitably brought him face to face with discrimination. Once in grade school Thelton went to a roller-skating rink with a group of white children. As he was skating around the rink, he noticed that just about everyone was watching him. At first, Thelton thought he was the subject of attention because of his skating—not an unreasonable assumption, since he had mastered roller-skating on the streets with clip-on skates. Eventually, though, he realized that the stares were not because of his skating but because he was the only black person at the rink.

Another incident of discrimination occurred during Thelton's junior high years. The Deputy Auxiliary Police (DAP) was a youth organization sponsored by the police department, and it was "cool" to be one of the DAPs. On a school day afternoon, Thelton and half a dozen of his white friends went to the police precinct closest to John Adams Junior High to become members of DAP. The officer on duty took one look at Thelton and suggested that he join the DAP in his own neighborhood. When Thelton did not immediately take the hint, the officer made it clear that Thelton was unwelcome.

Thelton's vivid memory of these two incidents years after their occurrence is testimony to their impact on him, but they pale in comparison to the discrimination that Thelton faced from the parents of his classmates. While Thelton had good relationships with his fellow students and participated fully in academic and extracurricular activities at Adams, he gradually began to realize that he was excluded from much of the Adams social life. He simply was not invited to the parties that his white peers attended. He shared only part of the life of his classmates.

While still in grade school, Thelton became acquainted with the public library. This, perhaps surprisingly, was not one of Wanzie's initiatives. There was no tradition of reading out loud in the family; and except for the few books that Bill James brought to Thelton and a family Bible, which Estelle read silently, there was no reading material at home as he was growing up. Probably because of loneliness, Thelton has surmised in later life, he would regularly check out books from the library, bring them home, and read on the living room floor. Left to his own devices, most of the books were about sports; but whenever a teacher would mention a book—even in passing—Thelton would find it at the library and read it. In ways that Thelton could not have understood at the time, his immersion in books was excellent preparation for the rigors of college and law school.

"Speedball"

Perhaps in part from a sense of wanting to belong but primarily because it was the way he approached any endeavor, Thelton, a.k.a. "Speedball," took athletics seriously. And his hard work, coupled with his natural ability and his speed, paid off. He excelled at kick-ball in grade school, baseball in junior high and high school, and football in high school. He was always the fastest member of his teams—hence the moniker "Speedball." At Jefferson High School, Thelton was a starting half-back on the football team. Los Angeles Times sportswriter John de la Vega described him as a "terrific breakaway artist[]," and in his senior year, Thelton was selected to be a member of the All-League first team football squad. However, it was not just his speed and his athletic prowess that made Thelton an important member of his teams. Despite his shyness, both his teammates and coaches saw leadership qualities in his soft-spoken, good-humored manner. Thelton was the captain of his kick-ball team, his junior high baseball team, and his high school baseball and football teams.

For Thelton, athletics was an outlet at least as important as reading. Indeed, he credits his involvement in team sports with saving him from being a complete outsider:

> It was exciting to be on a good football team. I think what was more important to me was the camaraderie of team sports. I mean, my teammates were very important to me and that's the thing I valued most. It was a plus that we were good and won championships, but it was more hanging out with them and talking about that than it was saying, "Here I am, look at me." That was the way I looked at it. . . .
>
> I remember we had what we called dance night. One night a week—maybe a Thursday—they would play records at the school gym. You'd go and guys would be dancing. I didn't know how to dance. And I'd go, and I could hang out with the team. And I was even cool because—just being cool and not dancing was sort of cool in that sense if you didn't know I didn't know how to dance. That's how I survived in this thing, really being out of the loop in every meaningful way, but being in the loop and standing there talking about sports and being part of it.
>
> . . . [I]t was sports that saved me.

Chapter Four

College, the Army, and Law School

Thelton's discipline, reading, decent grades, and athletic ability led to a football scholarship at the University of California, Berkeley (Cal). In some ways, though, Thelton was unprepared for Berkeley. Jefferson High School did not have a strong college preparatory program, and Thelton had never taken an essay examination. Most Jefferson students, if they continued their educations at all, went to local community colleges. Thelton's vague plan was to follow that traditional course — until Isaac McClelland, a Berkeley alumnus and one of the few black teachers at Jefferson High, approached him after football practice and began talking to him about applying to Berkeley. Because of his football successes, Thelton had had inquiries from several schools, including College (now University) of the Pacific, Oregon, Oregon State, Arizona, and the University of Washington. Thelton, however, was particularly intrigued by Isaac McClelland's suggestion. At the time Thelton did not know of Berkeley's stellar academic reputation, but he was well aware of Cal's then outstanding football teams and its legendary coach, Pappy Waldorf. With Isaac McClelland's help, Thelton filled out his application form. He was admitted on the condition that he successfully complete two courses in summer school before beginning the fall semester — a requirement that turned out to be a substantial benefit.

Undergraduate Days

Thelton arrived at Berkeley in June of 1951. He took up residence at the Tyrone House for Men, a rooming house where most of the black athletes lived and one of the few places near the campus that was available to blacks in the largely segregated Berkeley.[1] Thelton's two summer school courses were History of Western Civilization and Geology.

Although he studied hard and was "determined to succeed," Thelton almost flunked his first examination in Western Civilization:

> I remember to this day, the first question was, "Give the significance of Napoleon's blockade of the English Coast." I got a D- on the exam. . . . [M]y professor . . . had a note in the blue book which said "Come see me." I went in, and he was a kindly man, and he said, "You know, I should have given you an F because you didn't answer the question. I wrote the book and it's clear to me you studied." I didn't know how to take an essay exam. I had never done it in my life and so I started writing, "Napoleon was born here, and he was short, and he did this —." That was the only way I knew how to relate to the information.

The professor arranged for his teaching assistant to tutor Thelton. The teaching assistant showed Thelton the A papers; and

> all of a sudden I said, "Oh, that's what you do with all this information."

With this insight, Thelton improved his performance in Western Civilization, and he never had difficulty with grades again.

Once the fall semester began, Thelton divided his time between studies and football. Because of his speed, he made the varsity team his freshman year; but Thelton's football career at Cal was short lived. In one of the early games his sophomore year, Thelton received a severe knee injury. As he was being carried from the field, Earl Warren, then California governor and shortly thereafter US Supreme Court Chief Justice, walked beside the stretcher offering words of encouragement. Thelton's injury kept him in the hospital for six weeks, and the long recuperation period forced him to drop out of school for the semester. Because he never fully regained his speed, he decided to abandon football. As Thelton, who had been one of smaller players on the team, observed:

> [T]here's room in football for a big slow guy, and there's room in football for a little fast guy, and there's no room in football for a little slow guy! [chuckles] I wasn't slow but I was slower.

Thelton retained his athletic scholarship by serving as manager for the football team the following semester and by playing baseball in his last two years of college.

---

1. The University Housing office, which listed rental units in the area, participated in the segregation by indicating which landlords would not rent to blacks.

Despite the fact that he was an excellent player, baseball was always somewhat "alienating" — undoubtedly in large measure because the baseball environment was more racist than the football environment. Jackie Robinson had broken the major league color barrier only a few years earlier in 1947; and during the two seasons that Thelton played baseball for Cal, he was the only black on the team. He encountered racial epithets from opposing teams' players and fans and even racist remarks from his own head coach. On the opening day of practice in his first season, the coach tried to rally his players by telling them they were good enough to have a great season, to beat powerhouse U.S.C. They just needed to stay alert and to be in shape. Then, to emphasize the last point, the coach ordered the players to take two laps around the field and shouted, "Last one back is a nigger baby!" Thelton was dumbfounded, but his best friend on the team, Donny Walker, nudged him and said, "Come on, let's run." That was the end of the incident. The racism, however, was not limited to players, the coach, and fans:

> I remember — this was my second season — there was a company that had a pitching machine, which is quite common now but was a new idea then, and they wanted to film it. They brought it to the stadium and coach mentioned it. And so, they wanted to have some pictures. I think it was a newsreel. They were going to show how this worked and people were going to hit. So the guy said, "Okay, let's get your top hitter up and hit at the ball." That was me, and I stepped up. He said, "Well — " He saw I batted right-handed and he said, "Let's see, we need a left-handed hitter." You know, I knew what that was. He wasn't going to show his pitching machine with a black hitting.

Even off the field, Thelton's association with baseball exposed him to discrimination. He and his teammate, Donny Walker, hoped to become roommates. However, because Donny was white and Thelton was black — or perhaps only because Thelton was black, they could not find a landlord who would rent to them. Nonetheless, at least in retrospect, baseball had one huge advantage over football. It was less time consuming, and that meant Thelton had more time to devote to his classes. He never found his course work easy, but his diligent study led to good grades and admission to several honor societies.

The decision to go to law school had its seeds in Wanzie's determination that Thelton should "be somebody." In the 1940s and 1950s, the typical "successful" black man might be a teacher, government bureaucrat, or probation officer. It was clear to Thelton, though, that "being somebody" meant more than that; it meant being a doctor or a lawyer. Nobody in Thelton's family was a doctor or a lawyer. Indeed, Thelton was the first member of his family to attend college, where a few science courses convinced him that he was not destined to become a doctor. So with no role models and no clear idea of what lawyers did but with

Wanzie's vision of his future, Thelton applied and was admitted to UC Berkeley's Boalt Hall, one of the top law schools in the country.

"The Honorable Henderson"

The semester that Thelton missed because of his football injury postponed his graduation from June, 1955, to the following January. Thelton planned to begin law school the next fall, but the draft board intervened. Although he had been classified 4-F (not acceptable for military service) as a result of his knee injury, the draft board happened to be located near the baseball stadium, and some of the draft board employees were baseball fans. They had seen Thelton in action on the field and considered him fit for military service. Without any notification or a physical examination, he was reclassified 1-A (available immediately for military service). Several months after graduation, he was drafted into the army, where he spent the next two years.

Thelton's stint with the army was uneventful—except for one incident, which (unbeknownst to anyone at the time) foreshadowed his judgeship. Thelton and the other privates had signed a roster, and one of the sergeants was calling roll from the roster. Suddenly the sergeant stopped and hollered out, "O.k, who's the wise ass?" No response. And then, "O.k, who's 'The Honorable Henderson'? Step out here!" Eventually Thelton thinking that the "Henderson" might be referring to him, identified himself. And it turned out that he was the subject of the sergeant's wrath. In signing the roster, he had inadvertently made the "l" and "t" in Thelton look like a capital "H." He had, in the sergeant's view, called himself "The Hon. Henderson."

The "Dozens Cousins"[2]

Although Boalt Hall had deferred Thelton's admission, it had not deferred his scholarship. After getting out of the army, Thelton had to work for a year in order to afford law school. He obtained a job at Systems Development Corporation in Santa Monica, where he met Russ Ellis and, through Russ, Troy Duster. The three of them, all successful black professionals, ended up living in Berkeley—Troy as a sociology professor at Cal; Russ first as a behavioral sciences professor in the architecture school and then Vice Chancellor for Undergraduate Education at Cal; and Thelton as a lawyer and then federal judge sitting in

---

2. The dozens is a contest of verbal insults common in black communities. Typically the insults are about the adversary's mother.

San Francisco. For years, Russ and Troy have been Thelton's best friends. All guitar players, they found comradery in their music and billed themselves as the "Dozens Cousins." Much more importantly, they have supported each other and shared their experiences as successful black men making their way in a predominantly white society.

Boalt Hall (1959–1962)

On December 1, 1955, just over a month before Thelton received his undergraduate degree, Rosa Parks, a black seamstress and department store worker, refused a bus driver's order to relinquish her seat to a white rider. The ensuing Montgomery, Alabama, bus boycott awakened racial consciousness throughout the country. By the time Thelton returned to Berkeley for law school in the fall of 1959, the community was less segregated and considerably more race conscious. Thelton had no difficulty finding living accommodations. The legal profession, though, remained largely segregated; and Boalt Hall, like other major law schools, was a bastion of white America. Thelton was one of only two blacks in his class, and law firms coming to Boalt to interview prospective young lawyers refused to interview blacks.

While pursuing his legal studies, Thelton was active in the African American Association (AAA), a group organized by Donald Warden, a black student in the class ahead of him. Each week AAA members would meet at Warden's home in Oakland to discuss a book about the black experience that they had selected the week before. Initially, the AAA was limited to Berkeley students, but eventually other blacks in the community joined. Participants included Huey Newton and Bobby Seale, cofounders in 1966 of the Black Panther Party, and future congressman and Oakland mayor Ron Dellums.

The nascent civil rights movement continued to grow as Thelton progressed through law school. The first lunch counter sit-in occurred in Greensboro, North Carolina, on February 1, 1960. The following year the Congress on Racial Equality (CORE) began the Southern freedom rides, which were designed to integrate interstate buses and public transportation facilities. By 1961, boycotts, demonstrations, and sit-ins had become common throughout the South. In the fall of 1960, the CORE chapter at UC Berkeley and the Ad Hoc Committee to End Racial Discrimination picketed local businesses that were thought to discriminate.

Except for his participation in the AAA, Thelton did not become involved in civil rights activities during law school. As fellow law student Henry Ramsey put it years later, "Thelton wasn't going to jump up on a soap box. That just wasn't his personality." Moreover, Thelton's studies, a brief marriage, and his newborn son, Geoff, were more than enough to keep him occupied. Thelton's plan upon graduation was to follow the traditional path for black attorneys—find an established black lawyer from whom he could rent space, assist with some of the lawyer's routine cases, and eventually develop a practice of his own.

The undoing of that plan began with a telephone call in the spring of 1962 (a few weeks before Thelton was to graduate) to William Prosser, the law school's dean, from John Doar. Doar was a Boalt alumnus and, at the time, First Assistant in the Civil Rights Division of the Justice Department. The Civil Rights Division was deeply involved in voter registration litigation in the South, and Doar was calling to see if Prosser could recommend a young black lawyer to him.[3] Prosser recommended Thelton, who flew to Washington for an interview. The Justice Department decided to offer Thelton a job; and without hesitation, he accepted.

After graduating in June, Thelton spent the next two months studying for the California Bar Examination. Having completed that two-and-a-half-day ordeal in late August, he put his affairs in order, packed his belongings in his Volkswagen Beetle, and headed east. On September 10, 1962, the Supreme Court affirmed James Meredith's right to attend the University of Mississippi. The ensuing effort to enroll Meredith became a national news story, to which Thelton listened with interest on his car radio as he drove across the country.

---

3. At the time the Civil Rights Division had one black lawyer, Maceo Hubbard. Hubbard worked in Washington and was not involved in the Southern voter registration litigation.

Chapter Five

The Justice Department

When Thelton arrived in Washington, DC, he found a room in a building on what was then an all black section of Massachusetts Avenue. After a few weeks of training, Thelton was dispatched to the South, where — except for brief trips back to Washington to report to his superiors, John Doar, Burke Marshall (head of the Civil Rights Division), and Attorney General Robert Kennedy — he spent his entire Justice Department time.

The assignment to the South thrust Thelton into the midst of a somewhat schizophrenic official response to the burgeoning civil rights movement. On the one hand, both President John Kennedy and his brother Robert, the Attorney General, seemed genuinely committed to the principle of equal rights. By the time Thelton joined the Department, the Civil Rights Division was actively investigating and litigating cases in which blacks were prevented from registering to vote; and only a few short weeks before Thelton arrived in the South, President Kennedy called up federal troops to ensure that James Meredith could enroll in the University of Mississippi. On the other hand, the South at that time was predominantly Democratic, and Southern white Democrats were an important part of President Kennedy's political base. There was no mention of civil rights in President Kennedy's inaugural address, and as civil rights era historian Taylor Branch reports about the James Meredith incident:

> To protect the racial sensibilities of Mississippi, [President Kennedy] stripped Negro soldiers out of the military units at Ole Miss. Like [Mississippi] Governor [Ross] Barnett, he went out of his way to avoid mentioning that Meredith was a Negro. The President and his brother ignored most of Governor Barnett's slanderous accusations, and in fact they asked the best legal minds in the Justice Department to find a way *not* to collect the contempt fines imposed on Barnett and [Lieutenant Governor Paul] Johnson [for their refusal to obey court orders to permit Meredith to register at Ole Miss]. There might have been persuasive tactical reasons, as they did

not want to renew the constitutional crisis, but such small steps consistently beckoned the Administration to minimize both the significance and the racial texture of the Ole Miss crisis.

Although the Kennedy Administration embraced the cause of voter registration, it refused publicly and even privately to support the more activist aspects of the civil rights movement. Indeed, the Kennedy Administration seemed more concerned with trying to prevent civil rights activists from rocking the boat than it was with redressing the grievances of those who were intimidated and physically abused by the segregationists. Civil Rights Division lawyers were frequently assigned to monitor meetings, protests, and demonstrations, but their role was clear: They were only observers; they were not to become actively involved. For example, at an October 7, 1963 voter registration effort in Selma, Richard Wasserstrom, a Civil Rights Division lawyer, sought permission to escort Student Nonviolent Coordinating Committee (SNCC) workers, who wanted to bring water and sandwiches to the long lines of people waiting to register. Burke Marshall, head of the Civil Rights Division, denied Wasserstrom's request. When the SNCC workers tried to deliver the sandwiches, Sheriff Jim Clark's posse clubbed them. Three days later the SNCC workers were convicted of criminal provocation.

As Thelton later recalled, "I found myself too often in the role of a notetaker . . . recording atrocities. . . . I became a collector of civil rights atrocities." And typically nothing was done. Thelton elaborated:

> I was naive in the sense that I thought that if you found a wrong you would go about correcting it. I later learned that this wasn't necessarily so. My effectiveness seemed to end at the point of finding the wrong. . . .

> I was working with [FBI agents], and I can remember pointing . . . things out and asking them to photograph it and document it. They were cooperative in the sense that they never said no. But the FBI that you and I hear about was never there, in terms of digging in and really getting it and doing a workman-like job. They would take a picture, but I think our banks would be nonexistent if they pursued bank robbers like they pursued civil rights cases. I presume that they had no interest in it. I would again just presume that their directions come from above. At no place above them did anyone have any interest in developing a system of investigation and pursuing it with the vigor that they pursued other areas. It was very bad.

Even the picture taking left something to be desired. On October 7, 1963, the FBI was filming the voter registration drive in Selma. However, when Sheriff Jim Clark's posse attacked and beat SNCC workers, Thelton observed the FBI cameras pan to the upper stories of nearby buildings.

According to Taylor Branch, the FBI's "neglect of logical, urgent investigative leads drove [Thelton's Justice Department supervisor, John] Doar[,] to despair," and Richard Wasserstrom maintained that the FBI "couldn't be relied on to do anything." In Selma, Wasserstron recalled, if you asked an agent to investigate, the agent would go to Sheriff Jim Clark, who would say he didn't know anything. "And that was it." The Department would write detailed instructions for the FBI, but it didn't have much impact. The FBI was an "obstructive force."

In 1964, after Thelton had left the Justice Department, he made similar but much milder criticisms of the FBI during an interview published in *New University Thought*. Despite the journal's obscurity, publication of the article led to FBI interviews with Thelton and to at least four internal FBI memoranda, in two of which the Bureau's head, J. Edgar Hoover, is quoted as saying "Make him put up or shut up."

"Thelton"

One of Thelton's first assignments was a voter registration case in Shreveport, Louisiana, the city of his birth; and it was there that he learned something about the probable origin of his name. The Hendersons had planned to name Thelton "Eugene," after his father; but at the time of Thelton's birth, one of the hospital nurses said, "You know, Thelton would be a nice name." The nurse did not elaborate, but Wanzie liked the name. Her son became Thelton Eugene Henderson.

Thelton never encountered another "Thelton" until he was pouring over the list of registered voters in Shreveport. There he discovered a "Thelton" who was probably about the same age as the nurse that had attended Wanzie — perhaps a spouse, or boy friend, or relative. Like the nurse, he was white; and he was in law enforcement.

In all likelihood, Thelton Henderson is named after a white Louisiana police officer.

Preparation

On one of his early trips back to Washington, Thelton learned a lesson that has served him well throughout his professional life. As he related in his *Oral History* in 2005:

> One morning they had a staff meeting with [Attorney General Robert] Kennedy and the higher-ups in the Justice Department. They called me to that meeting. I went, and I thought I was fairly well-prepped, and I did a

little paper on the demographics of the black community in Birmingham. And [Kennedy] asked a few questions, and I didn't have the answers. And I remember he sort of pushed the paper at me and said, "Well, go do some work, come back when you have all the information." It was very gentle, but I was devastated. . . . I went out and just knew everything there was possible to know for the next meeting. . . . That was [over] forty years ago and I have not forgotten it.

Since that time, both as a lawyer and later as a judge, Thelton has always been thoroughly prepared; and he expects the same of those who are working for him:

I use [the Kennedy story] as an example with my law clerks, especially when they're new. They can come in and not really hit the books like I want them to, and I tell that little story to gently make the point that you really do have to be prepared when you come in here. And then that's a lasting lesson.

The Evolution from Voter Registration Lawyer to Valued Resource

Thelton's first assignments were voter registration cases, which involved detailed, tedious pouring through voter registration records and finding and interviewing blacks who had been denied the right to register. Soon, however, Thelton's job took on a new aspect. As the only black Justice Department lawyer in the South, Thelton had a unique opportunity to interact with the black civil rights leaders, and frequently his duties included keeping tabs and reporting on their activities. Initially, the civil rights leaders were wary of Thelton because of his Justice Department credentials, but over time Thelton gained their trust — the turning point being the occasion that Thelton said to Dr. Martin Luther King Jr. in the presence of King's associates Fred Shuttlesworth and James Bevel, "You really shouldn't tell me anything that you don't want Bobby Kennedy to know." That act of candor cemented his relationship with the civil rights community. At the same time, it gave him access to more information than he otherwise would have had, thereby making him a more valuable resource for the Justice Department. As Thelton explained several years after his Justice Department experience:

Looking back on it I'm sure that this eventually became my major job. . . . [M]y main value came to be that I was trusted by the civil rights people and that I was a good source of information and also a good sounding board. . . . I had a good sense of what was going on.

Three Realities: Segregation, Danger, and Role Conflict

Throughout his time in the South, three pervasive realities had a forceful impact on Thelton. The first was segregation, which Thelton confronted on a daily basis for the first time in his life. Brown v. Board of Education, the Civil Rights Division's voter registration cases, and various demonstrations, including the freedom rides and lunch counter sit-ins, had begun to loosen the grip of Jim Crow on the South, but progress was slow and spotty. In the early 1960s, segregation was still the order of the day. Thelton could not stay in the same hotels and motels occupied by his white Justice Department colleagues. And although he undoubtedly would have been welcomed into the homes of many black families, he could not stay with them because of the mandated "neutrality" for Justice Department lawyers. On one occasion Thelton rented space at a black funeral parlor in Jackson, Mississippi. The smell of formaldehyde permeated the room. Another time, a Justice Department colleague arranged for Thelton to stay at a black motel in Shreveport, but the accommodations were less than ideal. "[T]o give you an idea of the flavor of it," Thelton reported, "they rented by the hour." The only integrated facilities available to Thelton were the military bases throughout the South, and they were where he usually stayed—except when his assignments took him to Birmingham, Alabama.

A. G. Gaston was a successful black Birmingham businessman, and one of his enterprises was the Gaston Motel. When Thelton was in Birmingham he stayed at the Gaston Motel, as did Martin Luther King and other black civil rights leaders. Thus, the reality of segregation thrust Thelton into close contact with individuals whose activities he was supposed to only observe, and this contact in turn contributed to the two other daily realities for Thelton: danger and role conflict.

Bombings were not uncommon, particularly in Birmingham. Because the Gaston Motel was a hub of civil rights activity, it was the target of a bombing shortly after midnight on May 12, 1963. That same night, another bomb exploded at the home of the Rev. A. D. King, Martin Luther King's younger brother. The bombings were almost certainly a response by the Ku Klux Klan to the announcement that civil rights leaders and the Birmingham business community had reached an agreement that called for, among other things, the "desegregation of lunch counters, rest rooms, fitting rooms and drinking fountains" and the "upgrading and hiring of Negroes on a nondiscriminatory basis throughout the industrial community."

There is no reason to believe that Thelton was an intended victim of the motel bombing; however, the bomb was placed in an alley immediately outside the room that Thelton vacated the previous morning[1] for a brief trip to Washington. Thelton returned to Birmingham almost immediately to investigate the bombing of A. D. King's home. Although he had escaped injury, danger and vigilance were a constant part of his life.

Staying with civil rights leaders at the Gaston Motel also contributed to the role conflict — actually multiple role conflicts — that Thelton faced daily. First, there was the obvious conflict between Thelton's living and socializing with the black civil rights community and, at the same time, not being able (because of his Justice Department role) to be anything more than a peripheral part of that community. Second, although Thelton was an attorney for the Justice Department, segregation inevitably limited his contacts and relationships with his Justice Department colleagues. He was both part of the Justice Department and at the same time apart from the Department.

Third, Thelton was sympathetic with the goals and many of the tactics of the civil rights activists; but because of the mandated Justice Department neutrality, he could not act on his political and moral beliefs. This problem, of course, also existed for white Justice Department lawyers, but they at least had not only a common purpose but a comradery they could share on a daily basis. Thelton, by contrast, was significantly isolated from both the Justice Department community and the civil rights community. In addition, as a black man and a Kennedy Justice Department observer he was doubly an outsider in the eyes of the Southern white power structure. This isolation increased the tension between wanting to be a good Justice Department lawyer and wanting to further the objectives of the civil rights movement. Thelton sometimes felt guilty for not doing enough for the movement; and at the same time, he felt guilty because his Justice Department credentials gave him a kind of immunity not available to the civil rights workers, who were constantly risking their lives and livelihoods.

Finally, and most important, there was the conflict between Thelton the lawyer and Thelton the black man. Thelton was valuable to the Justice Department as a lawyer, but he was even more valuable because of the color of his skin. As a graduating law student, Thelton was genuinely excited about the prospect of being a Justice Department lawyer; but he perhaps had an inkling of this last conflict from the outset. In April 1962, he wrote jokingly to his friend, Russ Ellis:

---

1. The bomb was very close to Martin Luther King's room as well; but he, like Thelton, had vacated his room before the bomb exploded.

[A]fter I more or less accepted, they informed me they wanted a "bright young Negro lawyer with a northern legal education" to work with the Civil Rights Division, investigating and litigating <u>voting cases</u> in the South. (This is lawyer talk meaning they want some black fool to go down to Georgia and get shot in the head "for his people.")

Arrests (Segregation, Danger, and Role Conflict)

In the segregated South, any black person was potentially subject to arrest for no reason — or at least no legally sufficient reason — and, once arrested, potentially subject to physical abuse. Thelton, however, had the equivalent of a get-out-of-jail-free card: his Justice Department identification. But should he use it?

A small lunch counter sit-in involving only three students in Jackson, Mississippi on May 28, 1963 mushroomed over the next few days into a series of large demonstrations and massive arrests. The Justice Department ordered Thelton and John Doar to Jackson to be observers. On June 1, local civil rights leader Medgar Evers and NAACP National Director Roy Wilkins were arrested picketing Woolworth's, the site of the earlier sit-in. Thelton was arrested for no reason as he was walking toward Woolworth's to observe the demonstration. On this occasion, as on several others when he was arrested, Thelton did not hesitate to show his Justice Department identification, and he was immediately released. According to one report, the arresting officer started trembling at the sight of Thelton's credentials.

James Bevel, one of Martin Luther King's associates, regularly teased Thelton "about how much danger he was willing to face as an ordinary Negro before invoking his official status." That teasing coupled with Thelton's own misgivings about receiving special treatment had frightening consequences when he was arrested, allegedly for speeding, at dusk in a small Mississippi town:

> To the best of my knowledge I was not speeding, [as] I was very aware of speeding problems. Anyway, I was stopped by this policeman for speeding and taken to this little combination City Hall, grocery store, fire department, police station. . . . The chief of police, the nastiest guy I think I've ever met, told me to show him my driver's license. I pulled my license out of my wallet. It was in a little plastic thing like a credit card holder and I held it out. He took a nightstick and hit me with a tremendous crash on the hand and said, "Take it out of the god damn thing. What do you think this is?. . . [A]t the same time I saw this deputy . . . circle behind me and pull out his club, and I said to myself, "Oh God, this guy's going to come up and crack me over the head from the rear."

To avoid a clubbing from the deputy, Thelton responded briefly and politely to the police chief's continued provocations. However, when he answered one question with a "yeh" instead of a "Yes, sir!" the chief wrapped his knuckles again.

Thelton's hand was permanently disfigured by those blows, but the ordeal was not over. After searching the car, the police chief said, "O.K., take him off." A man who had been playing checkers with the police chief got in the front passenger seat of Thelton's car, and the chief told Thelton to get behind the wheel. The two deputies got in a police car behind Thelton and ordered him to begin to drive.

[W]e drove an awfully long way and nothing made sense at that point. . . . I thought jail should be around the corner. . . . I was really convinced that I was going to be one of those people who just disappears and [is] dug up years later.

In fact, they were driving to the county seat, which was about thirty miles away.

Well, I was never happier to see a jail. So we get to the jail and they drop me off; and they go back in the police car; and I get pushed around by some big — really Rod Steiger played him perfect[ly] in "In the Heat of the Night"; really he looked like him and he was built like him and everything — started pushing me around again. "O.K., get over there" with a hard jab, and you just couldn't move fast enough; and so then they show me this cell with vomit over in the corner, filthy mat, and I said to myself, "I'll make my point in some other jail.". . . I had no communication; they weren't going to let me make a call; I didn't know how long I was going to stay there. I just couldn't see it, so I pulled out my I.D. and it kind of puzzled this guy who was dull-normal at best, and he ran across the street to the sheriff. And I always delight in telling this story, and it's a true one. The sheriff came over and looked at the I.D. "Hmmm" and asked me a few questions, and my hand was bleeding [from the earlier incident]. . . . And he turned around and gave this [Rod Steiger look-a-like] guy a whack on the arm with his club for hitting me. WHACK! "You leave this man alone.". . . There was some kind of fine for $60, which I had to pay; and I didn't have the money. . . . He said, "Mr. Henderson, with credentials like that we'll treat you like any self-respecting white man. When you get back to Washington, you send us that money now, ya hear?" And I said, "Yes, sir." I got back to Washington and borrowed the money from John Doar [and] sent it in. . . . I knew I'd be back there, and I didn't want to have this traffic thing out against me. That was it,. . . [a] very, very frightening thing.

The Jackson, Mississippi Concert (Role Conflict)

Following his brief arrest on June 1, 1963, Thelton remained in Jackson for the next ten days. After spending the evening of June 10 with Medgar Evers at a black social club, he left for Washington in the morning. That evening President Kennedy delivered his first (and only) major civil rights address in which he proposed what became the Civil Rights Act of 1964. Shortly after midnight back in Jackson Byron De La Beckwith assassinated Medgar Evers, who had just returned home from a meeting and was walking to his front door.

Only a few days earlier, Evers — along with a cast of celebrities that included Harry Belafonte and Lena Horne — participated in a large rally to raise bail money for the hundreds of demonstrators that had been arrested. Thelton attended the rally in his capacity as Justice Department observer, and he witnessed long lines of poor black students and laborers march across the stage to make contributions they could ill afford to the cause of freedom. He was so moved by the spectacle that he left his seat and joined the line of donors waiting to walk across the stage. He wanted "to make a display," "to say 'I'm with you.'" Then, just as he was approaching the stage, Thelton's Justice Department persona took over. He left the line.

"I Got My Hat in Forest, Mississippi" (Segregation and Danger)

For Thelton, racial isolation and fear reached their zenith in Forest, Mississippi, a town of (at the time) some 3,000 people located forty-five miles east of Jackson. Forest was the home of segregationist Sen. James Eastland, but Thelton's only contact with Forest was a telephone booth at a closed gas station across the street from the police station and fire department.

It was a hot summer night. Thelton and Jim Thomas,[2] a black law student and summer intern with the Justice Department, were traveling to Jackson when they came to Forest, Mississippi. Thelton was supposed to check in with John Doar before the end of the day, so he and Jim turned left into a gas station with a double phone booth. Jim remained in the car; and Thelton made his

---

2. Jim Thomas graduated from Yale Law School in 1964. After law school, he joined the Civil Rights Division of the Justice Department. Later he became Dean of Admissions at Yale Law School, a position he held for many years.

call, which he thought would last only a few minutes. When the conversation began, there were several firemen in uniform across the street at the fire house. As the conversation continued, a police car passed the phone booth several times.

> Finally, this '56 Chevy ... convertible ... drove up and two young kids get out, ... about 20, tough looking kids. They get out and they walk by my car. ... [O]ne stands by the car and another one comes to the phone booth. ... I figure they're just making a call, and all of a sudden I get this feeling, you know, like someone staring at you. ... I turn around and this guy's just standing in the other phone booth, looking at me. I don't know what to say. If I tell John Doar, he's in Washington. ... [T]hat's not going to help worth a damn. ... [H]e has called the FBI for me before, but I'm in Forest, Mississippi, and this is really Klan country. ... [T]here's nothing he could do, so I don't mention it to John. An old man walks up, 50ish, and he stands around looking. ... [A]nother car drives up. ...

Jim, of course, was not distracted by a telephone conversation. He observed the entire scene developing. He later told Thelton he was so frightened that he almost drove off and left Thelton alone (something that Thelton is confident Jim never would have done).

After twenty to thirty minutes, Thelton completed his call to John Doar.

> I get in the car. ... [T]here's a police car parked across the street, and there's a double yellow line on the highway we've been driving down. I know ... from my experience not to go across that double line. ... So we go the way from which we came [for a short distance, circle around, and] get back on the highway [heading toward Jackson]. ... The block [where we had been] was packed with people. A taxi had just driven up. ... [T]he call had gone out. ... [T]he first two guys weren't going to take us on. They didn't know whether we had guns or what. ... There were 50 people there if there were any, and the taxi driver shouted when we drove by. ... [He] jumped in the car, but ... I had a running start. ... I floorboarded it. No one could have caught us. ... Jim and [I are] convinced that if we had stayed there another five or even two minutes more and gotten cornered by that crowd, we would have been in bad trouble.

As they were driving away, Thelton and Jim composed a song. The lyrics and melody are long forgotten, but the title has remained as vivid in Thelton's and Jim's memories as that almost disastrous incident at the telephone booth: "I Got My Hat in [i.e., I got my hat and left] Forest, Mississippi."

"The Flight to Birmingham" (Segregation and Danger)

SNCC had been trying with little success to register voters in Selma, Alabama, since early 1963. The voter registration office was open only two days a month, and local officials tended to show up late, take long lunch breaks, and leave early. Sheriff Jim Clark and his posse harassed and intimidated both civil rights workers and would-be registrants. The few blacks who were able to meet with a registrar were likely to flunk the literacy test regardless of their level of education.

To bring attention to the situation, SNCC organized a "Freedom Day" voter registration drive on October 7, 1963. Hundreds of blacks stood in line all day at the Dallas County Court House. According to rules established by Sheriff Clark, anyone who left the line for any purpose could not return to the same spot. When SNCC workers tried to bring food and drink to those in line, Clark barred their way under the guise of preventing them from molesting the crowd. According to the *New York Times*, "By the end of the day, fewer than 40 had been processed," and only those who passed the literacy test would be registered to vote.

James Baldwin, the writer, was in Selma to support the Freedom Day registration effort. Thelton had come from Birmingham and taken up residence at nearby Craig Air Force base a few days earlier so he could be an observer for the Justice Department. Sometime in the afternoon of Freedom Day, Thelton learned that Baldwin, whom Thelton had recently met in Birmingham, was the subject of a death threat. When Thelton relayed the information to Baldwin, they decided that Baldwin should leave town. Baldwin, however, had come to Selma with his brother, David, in a bright red Ford, which, they feared, would be easily recognized. In the hope of avoiding detection, Thelton offered to drive the Baldwins to Birmingham.

That evening Thelton left Selma with James and David Baldwin as his passengers. They made a brief detour to Craig Air Base, where Thelton said, "I have to stop for something." He left the car briefly and returned with a duffle bag. As they were traveling to Birmingham, James Baldwin talked about how ironic it was that he was seeking refuge in Birmingham, which, because of all its bombings, he had considered the most dangerous city in the South. As they drove, he vowed to write a story about the trip. It would be called "The Flight to Birmingham."

James Baldwin never wrote that story, but he did relate it orally. Several months after Freedom Day, Thelton attended a speech that Baldwin gave in Washington, DC. Thelton let some of Baldwin's associates know he was there, and during the speech Baldwin called Thelton to the stage. With Thelton standing beside him, James Baldwin told the story of how Thelton saved his life — but the story had an interesting twist. Baldwin explained that he felt safe after Thelton had stopped at the military base and returned with a duffle bag full of weapons.

Thelton never told Baldwin that he had been staying at the base and that the duffle bag contained only his dirty laundry.

Martin Luther King and the Car (Segregation, Danger, and Role Conflict)

One week after the flight to Birmingham, the realities of segregation, danger, and role conflict came together for Thelton in a seemingly innocuous but in fact extremely powerful manner. On the evening of October 15, 1963, Thelton — not having a choice of accommodations because of segregation — returned to his room at Birmingham's Gaston Motel. As Thelton was getting out of his car, Rev. Nelson "Fireball" Smith, one of Martin Luther King's associates, approached him to ask if he would drive Dr. King to Selma, where King was scheduled to give a speech. Thelton was initially reluctant. He knew that the police sometimes followed him, and he thought it would be inconsistent with his Justice Department role to be chauffeuring Dr. King to meetings.

Rev. Smith and Dr. King continued to press Thelton, explaining that the car they had planned to use had a bad tire and might not make it to Selma. That mattered to Thelton, for as he well knew, Dr. King's life would be in serious jeopardy if he were found stranded on a dark country road at night in Alabama. Thelton loaned his car to Rev. Smith, who drove Dr. King to Selma.

State police followed the car, saw that the driver was black, checked the car's license number, and learned that it had been rented by the Justice Department. They, of course, knew that Thelton was a black Justice Department lawyer; and they may have known from their surveillance activities that Thelton had recently driven the car to the Gaston Motel, from which they saw it depart. In any event, the next morning Governor George Wallace charged that Thelton had driven Dr. King to Selma. When the Justice Department inquired about Wallace's charge, Thelton truthfully denied it without volunteering anything about having loaned the car to Rev. Smith. The Justice Department then issued a statement denying any involvement with Dr. King's transportation.

At that point, strong political forces came into play. Because the white South was an important constituency for President Kennedy, it was crucial that the Justice Department avoid the appearance of taking sides in the civil rights struggle. Moreover, much of the South — and particularly Alabama — had been recently on the defensive. Sheriff Jim Clark's treatment of the voter registration movement in Selma had received national publicity, and there was continuing national news coverage of a Birmingham church bombing that killed four young black girls only a month earlier. Linking the Justice Department with Dr. King was an opportunity for the segregationists to change the focus and take the offensive.

Thelton returned to Washington briefly and then took some vacation time in California. Meanwhile, the story continued to grow. Two separate state grand juries were convened, and the Justice Department's alleged collusion with Dr. King became major news throughout the South.

The Justice Department stuck with its initial denial until early November when Thelton, who had been staying with Wanzie in Los Angeles, acknowledged to John Doar that he had loaned the car to Rev. Smith and Dr. King. At that point, Thelton submitted and the Justice Department accepted his resignation. Burke Marshall, head of the Civil Rights Division, publicly apologized to the state of Alabama.

Despite Thelton's resignation under a cloud of recriminations, his actions were understandable. First, it was quite reasonable for him initially to regard the car story as inconsequential. He was not personally involved with assisting Dr. King; he merely made his car available to him and Rev. Smith. Second, it is hard to imagine how, even for Southern segregationists, loaning the car could be more newsworthy and more of a state law enforcement priority than the death of four girls in a church bombing. Finally, and most important, Dr. King's safety was at stake.

Except for his continued strong belief that loaning the car to Rev. Smith was the right thing to do, Thelton has not embraced these explanations. Rather, he has unhesitatingly acknowledged that his initial statement was misleading and that he should have been completely candid from the outset.

It is doubtful, however, that candor would have saved his job. Thelton had violated the Justice Department's neutrality rule; and to the segregationists, it probably would have mattered little whether Thelton drove Dr. King to Selma or merely loaned him the car. They would have tried to make an issue of the incident in either case. Given the Kennedy Administration's timidity and its obsession with not alienating the South, it seems likely that Thelton would have been a sacrificial lamb.

Even if that conclusion is wrong, Thelton at the very least was putting his Justice Department employment at risk when he loaned the car to Dr. King (and when he drove James Baldwin to Birmingham a week earlier). He may have minimized the risk in his own mind, but he certainly knew it was there. Both his stepping away from the stage at the Jackson, Mississippi concert earlier in the year and his initial reluctance when Rev. Smith asked him to drive Dr. King to Selma demonstrate that Thelton was well aware of his professional role. And he must have known that even if the risk was small, the stakes were enormous.

The possibility of losing one's first law job after only a year, particularly when it is a prestigious position with the Justice Department, could be economically, emotionally, and professionally devastating.

In Jackson, when the issue was expressing comradery with civil rights demonstrators and contributing a small amount to their bail fund, Thelton's professional persona took over, as it should have. However, when lives were at stake, Thelton had no qualms about making the right decision even though it was inconsistent with his professional obligation as a neutral observer.

Looking Back

In retrospect, the remarkable thing about Thelton Henderson's Justice Department service, despite its ignominious ending, was his strength of character in incredibly difficult circumstances. Young and politically naive, he was forced to deal with the realities of segregation, danger, and conflict without any role model or guidebook. As John Doar summarized, Thelton was sent to Birmingham to be the Justice Department's "eyes and ears"; and he was "under constant and steady pressure from the Dr. King lieutenants for why . . . the Justice Department [wasn't doing] more. He was alone down there without sufficient support." According to historian Taylor Branch, "In a time when the world wasn't accustomed to having black professionals, [Thelton] was a little bit of all the worlds that were colliding — the movement, the segregated South, the federal government."

Chapter Six

Law Practice, Legal Services, and Academia

Soon after Thelton resigned from the Justice Department, he went to Washington, DC, where he planned to write about his experiences in the South. The writing, however, came slowly; and by February Thelton had exhausted his meager savings. He returned to Berkeley as he had come to Washington initially — in his Volkswagen Beetle with all of his belongings. In Berkeley, he rented a room for $35 per month in one of the houses where he had lived as an undergraduate.

With the emergence of increasingly radical leaders, such as Stokely Carmichael, Huey Newton, Bobby Seale, and Eldridge Cleaver, the next several years were turbulent times for the civil rights movement. During this period, the Dozens Cousins — Thelton, Troy Duster, and Russ Ellis — became particularly close. Although they were all engaged in various ways in the civil rights activity, none of them was entirely comfortable with the Black Panthers and other advocates of black power. "We were," Troy has remarked, "poster children for the non-threatening black male." At the same time, because of their professional positions, they were interacting on a daily basis with whites, many of whom, as Troy put it, "think you're there for the wrong reason." Each of them had to deal with these realities in his own way, but they found support and encouragement from sharing their experiences with each other. For Thelton, the most reserved of the three, the friendships with Troy and Russ have been especially important.

Private Practice

To support himself in the initial weeks after his return to California, Thelton began making court appearances for Donald Warden. Warden was Thelton's law school friend who had founded the African American Association and who by early 1965 had a thriving, storefront solo practice on Adeline Street in Oakland.[1] By the late spring, the two of them and another lawyer, Bill Holliman, formed a partnership: Henderson, Holliman, & Warden. The partnership was a financial success, but Thelton sensed he was not growing as a lawyer. The cases, many of which involved minor criminal charges, tended to be straightforward; and Thelton was not learning any of the skills necessary for more complex litigation.

As he was thinking about looking for a new job, Thelton had a chance meeting with another friend from law school, Rod Duncan. Later an Alameda County Superior Court judge, Duncan was then practicing law in Oakland with Fitzsimmons & Petris (F & P). As a result of that contact, Thelton accepted a position with F & P in late 1964. Because he felt bad about abandoning Donald Warden and Bill Holliman so quickly, Thelton left behind his share of the partnership and made no effort to take any clients with him to F & P. The new firm had only four lawyers — Ed Fitzsimmons; Nick Petris, a state legislator; Rod Duncan; and now Thelton. The legal work, however, was more complex and diversified and, as a result, more satisfying.

Because of Thelton's experience with criminal law, he handled all of F & P's relatively few criminal cases — one of which gave him some notoriety. The defendant was a half-brother of one of F & P's business clients. According to Thelton:

> [H]e was accused of killing a police informant in a bar in the Hispanic part of L.A. And the prosecutor, when I went down to talk to him, was so convinced that this was a gangland type of slaying of one of their informers, he wouldn't give me any kind of deal. At that point I probably would have recommended certainly that he accept a manslaughter — who knows about second degree murder. But he wouldn't even offer anything. That — just plead out first degree. And of course I couldn't do that, so we went to trial, and I convinced the jury, as I was convinced at the time, that this was self-defense. Now the consequence of that was that it was fairly big news in the Hispanic community, and I sort of got a reputation as being a really hotshot lawyer who could get you off if you had a charge against you.

That victory brought more criminal cases — including those of clearly guilty defendants — to Thelton, who recognized that he "could have had a . . . rather successful criminal defense practice." However, he did not relish the idea of being a criminal defense lawyer. Thelton, of course, knew and appreciated that

---

1. Warden later changed his name to Khalid al-Masour, became an attorney and advisor to Saudi billionaires, and was the subject of thoroughly debunked right wing meme claiming that he had funded Barack Obama's legal education at Harvard.

even the clearly guilty were entitled to zealous representation by competent counsel, and he provided that representation to his clients. Still, Thelton did not want to be "just a mouthpiece" for "real criminals."

So that affected me, and in a sense it may be why I'm not a good criminal defense lawyer . . . I had no taste for it at that level.

In the spring of 1966, Thelton received a call from a Peace Corps recruiter. When Thelton expressed interest, the Peace Corps flew him to Washington, DC for interviews and a language aptitude test, on which he did well. Thelton was informally offered the job as head of the Peace Corps in the Cameroons, and he resigned from F & P. Weeks then passed without any word from the Peace Corps. When Thelton called to inquire about the situation, he was told that there was some unresolved concern about the Martin Luther King car incident. More time elapsed with no word from the Peace Corps, and Thelton needed to earn a living. He felt it would have been awkward to try to return to F & P, but Rod Duncan suggested a new possibility. Across the San Francisco Bay in San Mateo County, Sy Rosenthal had just been named executive director of a legal services program. He was looking for attorneys to hire.

The East Bayshore Neighborhood Legal Center

Gideon v. Wainwright, a 1963 Supreme Court case, held that the Sixth and Fourteenth Amendments required judges to appoint lawyers for indigent criminal defendants charged with serious crimes. *Gideon*, however, had no impact on poor people with "civil" legal problems — for example, abusive spouses, family break-up and custody issues, and disputes with landlords, creditors, or welfare officials. For these matters, individuals who could not afford to hire a lawyer had to turn to legal aid societies, typically sponsored by local bar associations. Legal aid societies existed throughout the country, but for the most part they were woefully understaffed and often did little more than provide names of private attorneys who might be willing to give a free initial consultation.

All of that changed (at least a bit) with the 1965 enactment of the Legal Services Program as part of President Lyndon Johnson's War on Poverty. Administered by the Office of Economic Opportunity (OEO), the Legal Services Program provided funds for offices with full-time lawyers and support staff to serve poor communities. The goal was not merely to meet the noncriminal legal needs of individuals who happened to come into a legal services office, but also to use the law as a means of empowering poor people to make decisions for themselves about their legal needs and priorities in their communities. The law was to be a tool for raising people out of poverty, and the people themselves were to decide how to use that tool. Poor people from the community were members of the boards of directors of the local legal services agencies, and they had a voice in hiring and policy decisions.

An early recipient of an OEO grant for a legal services program was the San Mateo County Legal Aid Society, which planned to open four offices. One office was to be in East Palo Alto, an economically depressed, predominantly black neighborhood across the freeway from the considerably wealthier Palo Alto and Stanford University. The East Palo Alto office, scheduled to open in the fall of 1966, would have one full-time attorney, a receptionist, and a secretary.

During the summer of 1966, a small group of Stanford law students with the assistance of Professor Jack Friedenthal and the approval of the Legal Aid Society Board of Directors devised and implemented a program to augment the services provided by the East Palo Alto office.[2] Stanford received a grant to hire a recent graduate to serve as a second attorney in the office[3] and to supervise volunteer Stanford law students, who would assist with the caseload.[4]

Racial identity was very much a part of the politics and culture of East Palo Alto. In the late 1960s, a local shopping center was renamed the Nairobi Village Shopping Center; and two community leaders, Bob Hoover and Gertrude Wilks, were instrumental in establishing Nairobi College and the Nairobi Elementary and High Schools. Hoover, Wilks, and other leaders — including Everlyn Wallace, a member of the Legal Aid Society Board of Directors — were adamant that they should have a black attorney to represent their interests. The full board agreed. Sy Rosenthal, the executive director, hired Thelton, who opened the East Bayshore Neighborhood Legal Center in October 1966. The office was located in a small run-down strip mall that included two bars (the 3J's Barbeque and Mickey's Blue Room), a barber shop, and Bill's Smoke Shop, which had no smokes but considerable gambling activity in the back room. The parking area at the front of the mall was a magnet for unemployed young black

---

2. I was one of those Stanford students. I first met Thelton at a Legal Aid Society Board of Directors meetings in the summer of 1966.

3. The plan called for Stanford to hire a "Teaching Fellow" each June to work in the East Palo Alto office for eighteen months. During the first six months, the Teaching Fellow would study for, take, and (hopefully) pass the California Bar Exam and, in the meantime, learn the ropes from the outgoing Teaching Fellow. I graduated from law school in June, 1967 and was the second Stanford Teaching Fellow in East Palo Alto.

4. The students did not receive academic credit for their work in East Palo Alto, but the Stanford Teaching Fellow and Jack Friedenthal co-taught a poverty law course that was available to them. Although clinical law courses are now common fare in law schools, that was not the case in 1966. Stanford's program was the first effort at Stanford and one of the early efforts nationally to integrate actual law practice and academic study.

men. On more than one occasion in the first months of the office's existence, Thelton insisted on escorting the white Stanford lawyer and white Stanford students to their cars.[5]

Everlyn Wallace, the community representative on the Legal Aid Society Board, apparently considered the Stanford program so uncontroversial that she had not bothered to say anything about it to her East Palo Alto constituency. Thus, when the office opened, community leaders were shocked to find Thelton, their black attorney, in the midst of a sea of white Stanford students and a white Stanford lawyer. It was not what they had envisioned, and over the next few months a number of community leaders called for an end to the Stanford presence at the East Bayshore Neighborhood Legal Center.

Although the initial objections to the Stanford program were framed in terms of race, it quickly became apparent that race alone was not the predominant — or at least not the only — issue. Even without the Stanford students, Thelton was surrounded by a white secretary and a white receptionist, Gelsie Becks, to whom the community did not object. Indeed, community leaders — including Gelsie's husband, Ed Becks — urged Thelton to hire Gelsie. As Thelton later learned, the community leaders wanted to be able to get information about what was happening in the office from someone they trusted.

One underlying substantive concern about the Stanford program related to the office's clients and probably had at least as much to do with age and gender as race. From the outset, over a third of the caseload involved women with domestic issues (divorce, domestic violence, child custody), and there was a sense that many of them would feel uncomfortable talking about their personal lives with young, white, predominantly male Stanford law students.[6]

A more pervasive concern stemmed from the prior relationships between East Palo Alto and Stanford. In 1968 when an interviewer asked Thelton to compare the racial situation in the South with that in the North, he said, "What's happening here is just as evil as down there. It's just that it's done in a different

---

5. From time to time, I encountered "Hey, Whitey" taunts as I entered or left the office, but there was only one occasion on which I was seriously frightened: April 5, 1968. I arrived at the office before 8 a.m., and Thelton was already there. He was devastated. Martin Luther King had been assassinated the night before. Later in the morning Thelton, Bob Fastov (a classmate and another lawyer in the office), and I walked several blocks to a nearby church for a memorial service. Along the way groups of blacks would shout and swear and threaten us. Even in his grief Thelton offered calm words of reassurance, and Bob and I stoically followed his lead. I am convinced that we remained safe only because we were with Thelton.

6. Roy Schmidt, the first Stanford attorney, was a young, white male. Of the first group of approximately 15 Stanford students, all were white and in their early twenties. Only two, Lisa Anderson and Vicki Popkin, were female.

way. Whereas [Alabama Governor George] Wallace would say, 'I'm going to stand in the schoolhouse door before I'm going to let you integrate the schools,' here they say, 'Let's sit down and talk about it and hold a study.'" That statement captures perfectly what Stanford University had done — albeit presumably with benign intent — to East Palo Alto: Over the years, the citizens of East Palo Alto had been guinea pigs for a variety of Stanford studies, which had enhanced the reputations of the university researchers but had done little to improve the lot of the people studied. Given that background, it is understandable that East Palo Alto community leaders objected to what they saw as just another Stanford experiment.

In retrospect, it is clear that the students developing the Stanford component of the legal services program should have been sensitive to the bad feelings that Stanford had generated in East Palo Alto. However, they naively believed that their presentations to the Legal Aid Society Board of Directors, with its East Palo Alto community representative, were sufficient to lay the groundwork for the Stanford participation. Just as the community was shocked to see its new legal services office populated by Stanford students, the Stanford students and their advisor, Jack Friedenthal, were shocked by the community's initial reaction to the Stanford presence.

As a result of the poor communications between the Stanford law students and the East Palo Alto community leaders, one of Thelton's first tasks was completely unexpected. He, of course, wanted to be responsive to the community leaders, but he discovered almost immediately that a single attorney could not begin to meet the legal needs of poor people in East Palo Alto. He — along with Jack Friedenthal — spent many hours in the first few months of the office's existence explaining to local leaders and groups why Stanford's participation was an asset. As a result of those efforts and the quality legal representation provided by Roy Schmidt, the first Stanford attorney, the criticisms eventually abated, and the Stanford program became an integral part of the East Bayshore Neighborhood Legal Center.

Some Stanford Law School faculty members had wondered whether there would be enough legal work to justify a second attorney in the East Palo Alto office. It soon became apparent, however, that even with the Stanford contribution, the office's resources were insufficient to meet the community needs. There were not enough lawyers; and because part of the OEO vision was to hire people from the community to staff the office, it was difficult to find (and adequately compensate) a trained legal secretary.[7] Thelton typically would be in

---

7. During its second year of operation, the office was fortunate to hire some very competent staff, including Andrea Bobbitt, the wife of Stanford law student Leroy Bobbitt (later a successful entertainment attorney in Los Angeles), and Jeanette Taylor. When

the office by 7 a.m. typing his own letters on an old manual typewriter. In those days, it was customary with business letters to place below the signature the initials of the letter writer (in capitals) and then, after a colon, the initials (in lower case) of the secretary who typed the letter. When Thelton typed his own letters, he would end them with TEH:me. Readers presumably would assume that the "me" was his secretary, but Thelton knew that the "me" was he.

In less than eighteen months, the office had expanded to three full-time attorneys (plus the Stanford attorney and another attorney, who handled domestic dispute cases for all four Legal Aid Society offices) and a second full-time secretary. Thanks to the vision of Read Ambler, a Stanford law student and later a Santa Clara County Superior Court Judge, the East Bayshore Neighborhood Legal Center was able to accommodate the expansion without changing its location. In late 1966 and early 1967, Read prepared a design and then supervised Thelton, Roy Schmidt, and the Stanford students in constructing several offices in the back half of the rental space, which had been only an empty shell when the office first opened.

After the renovation, Thelton occupied a large office at the rear of the building. It was comfortable, but it had one drawback. Cooks at the 3J's Barbeque, the establishment immediately to the west in the small shopping mall, occasionally threw rotting chickens in the area behind Thelton's office. When the stench was unbearable, Thelton became not only chief attorney but also head groundskeeper.

Even with the added resources, the office was struggling to meet the client demand. Moreover, merely responding to a client's immediate problem — for example, fighting an eviction, stopping a wage garnishment, or filing for bankruptcy — did little more than provide temporary band-aid relief. The discrete legal problems that brought clients to the office were frequently only symptomatic of more serious, intransigent problems associated with poverty and powerlessness. Fighting and even winning the same legal battles over and over again rarely had an impact on the underlying structure that contributed to the problems.

The goal of using the legal system to empower poor people was at risk of becoming lost in the mass of immediate problems that clients brought through the door. This dilemma quickly became a familiar one to legal services offices throughout the country: How much time does one spend in a reactive mode dealing with relatively simple individual cases (which, of course, were of critical importance to individual clients)? And how much time does one spend on "law reform" — that is, working with the larger community on economic development issues and identifying legal problems to attack by seeking legislative

---

Thelton was appointed to the federal district court, he asked Jeanette to be his secretary; and she stayed with him until she retired.

relief and by initiating complex, time-consuming cases that ultimately will affect large numbers of poor people?

The East Bayshore Neighborhood Legal Center tried to do everything. In addition to his early arrival at the office, Thelton spent countless evenings working with community groups interested in economic development and education reform. Nobody, however, had anticipated how great the individual client demand would be. Ultimately, the unrelenting press of individual cases tended to overwhelm law reform efforts.

Stanford Law School

Stanford Law School graduated its first African American student, Sallyanne Payton, in 1968. That was seventy-five years after Stanford hired its first law professors, forty-five years after the American Bar Association accredited the law school, and forty-four years after the law school began its three-year professional program. And Sallyanne was not at Stanford Law School because of any effort to recruit minority law students. Rather, she was simply a student with stellar academic credentials who happened to be black.

During her final year of law school, Sallyanne, along with several other students, devoted considerable time and effort to encouraging Stanford Law School to increase its minority enrollment. Some lobbied the administration to create a specific minority admissions program; others persuaded the law school to send them to recruit minority undergraduates at institutions in southern California and the South. They were all vocal about their frustration with the law school's abysmal record in attracting minorities; and at least in part because of their initiative, several faculty members began to press the administration to increase minority admissions. In addition, since some of the students were volunteering at the East Bayshore Neighborhood Legal Center, Thelton heard their frustrations and learned that Sallyanne was about to become the first black graduate in the law school's history. He too became interested in urging Stanford to do more.

The law school administration's initial public responses to the student and faculty demands were at best tepid, in large measure because the administrators perceived several other law schools' hastily conceived minority admissions programs as disasters: Under-qualified students were admitted and not given adequate support. Either they flunked out; or if they were retained and graduated, they failed bar examinations in disproportionate numbers. Nonetheless, three key administrators—Dean Bayless Manning, Associate Dean Keith Mann, and Assistant Dean Robert Keller—were quietly working to develop a minority admissions program for the law school. The focus was on black,

Chicano, and Native Americans. At the time, they were perceived to be the most disadvantaged groups.

As a result of these student, faculty, and administration efforts, Thelton began to have conversations with Dean Manning about minority admissions at the law school. In the summer of 1968, Thelton accepted a half-time position at Stanford Law School as "Coordinator of Special Programs" and continued half-time at the legal services office. It soon became apparent, however, that Thelton had two full-time jobs, not two half-time jobs. By early 1969, he was at Stanford full-time with the title Assistant Dean for Student Affairs.

The Stanford plan was to recruit and admit minority students whose academic records alone would not necessarily have gotten them into Stanford and to have some of those students — the ones with promise but less than outstanding academic credentials — complete their first year of law school in two years. Requiring some minority students to spread their first year of law school over two years had potential advantages that, it was hoped, would avoid the problems that other law schools had encountered with their minority admissions programs. Students would have time (and could be required) to take undergraduate courses to supplement their earlier education. Moreover, since no student could flunk out of law school before completing the first-year curriculum, students who did not do well after their first year of the two-year program could leave the law school in good standing. Finally, students who did well could accelerate their studies and, if they went to summer school, graduate in the normal three years.

On the other hand, the notion that minority students admitted pursuant to Stanford's new program should take only half of the regular law school curriculum in their first year had two significant failings. First, there was the obvious risk that minority students would be labeled as second-class citizens of the law school. Second, the two-year first year was too blunt an instrument for accomplishing the remedial objectives with which the Stanford administrators were so concerned.

Minority students whom one might expect to succeed at Stanford Law School fall into three general categories. First, there are students such as Sallyanne Payton, who would be admitted to Stanford regardless of their minority status. Second, there are students whose grade point average and law school aptitude test (LSAT) place them just below the cut-off for admission. Third, there are individuals from disadvantaged backgrounds and inferior educational systems but with strong academic potential. Students in the first category are not likely to need academic assistance; and because Stanford is so selective in its admissions, the same is true for students in the second category. However, students in these two categories are most likely to be in demand by other law schools with minority admissions programs. If Stanford wanted to ensure that it would have a solid nucleus of minority students, and, more importantly, if Stanford was serious about having a significant impact on the legal education of minorities, it would have to seek students in the third category. It would, in short, have to reach out to a more diverse minority population. And just as Thelton benefited from tutoring in college because he had never taken an essay examination in high school, some of these students might require tutoring, and other assistance. Yet, they might not — and it turns out they did not — need the slow introduction to law school originally contemplated by the Stanford administrators. According to Bob Keller, one of the initiators of the two-year first-year program, Thelton's ability and hard work made the program unnecessary. After three years, it was abandoned. Minority enrollment nonetheless flourished, and minority students distinguished themselves — both during law school and after graduation.

Thelton's recruiting efforts were an important part of the success of Stanford's minority admissions program.[8] He did not confine himself to seeking out "safe" minority students with solid academic backgrounds. Instead, he took risks with people in whom he saw potential. Perhaps because of his own disadvantaged background and academic success, Thelton had an uncanny ability to identify individuals who could succeed at Stanford. At the same time, Thelton's own life story was an inspiring role model for the students.

Recruiting, however, was only part of the story. In one of his first years at Stanford, Thelton persuaded several professors teaching first-year courses to give mid-semester examinations (a relatively rare occurrence in law schools, at least at that time) in order to provide early feedback to the minority students without singling them out for special treatment. That additional feedback reduced one of the perceived needs for the two-year program. Thelton also convinced the admissions committee to acknowledge the generally accepted cultural bias of the LSAT by awarding additional points to minority applicants. Another of Thelton's innovations was to persuade the law school to hire a recent graduate "teaching fellow," whose primary responsibility would be tutoring minority students. Most important, though, was Thelton's own personal commitment to supporting minority students once they arrived at Stanford. Particularly in the early years of the program, when there were only a few minority students and no minority (or female) faculty members,[9] Thelton's mentoring was invaluable even for minority students who had strong academic records.

---

8. Thelton recalled that for the 1968 entering law school class there had been only 17 minority applicants.

9. In 1972, Barbara Babcock became the first female member of the law faculty and William Gould became the first minority faculty member.

One of those students was Leonade Jones. Thelton had not recruited her, and she first met Thelton after she arrived at the law school in the fall of 1969 — only one year after Sallyanne Payton had graduated. As Leonade put it:

> My personal belief is that recruitment is only part of increasing minority enrollment. The big work comes after admission and throughout the three years you are in law school. In my case, five African-American students entered the class and three finished. . . . Judge Henderson helped to create a supportive environment for us pioneers. He was a mentor, coach, safety net, and friend.
>
> Harry Bremond [, a prominent black attorney in Palo Alto,] . . . hosted barbeques and picnics at his home for minority students at Stanford Law School because he was a good friend and colleague of Thelton Henderson. I doubt that that would have happened without Thelton's friendship.

Leonade graduated with degrees in both law and business and for many years was treasurer of the Washington Post Company. She describes Thelton as being "very instrumental" in getting her through Stanford and the bar examination.

Other students recruited and mentored by Thelton — nine of whom eventually became judges — are similarly effusive in their praise. LaDoris Cordell, who went from Stanford Law School to the state court bench to Vice Provost at Stanford, credits Thelton with getting her to Stanford and providing invaluable support not only in law school but also when she was a judge.[10] James Ware calls Thelton "one of my heroes." Ware began law school in the four-year program and successfully lobbied Thelton to become a full-time three-year student. According to Ware, "Thelton provided a feeling of security. Knowing there was a place to go was very reassuring." Thelton introduced Ware to the black legal community, gave him support and encouragement in law school, and helped get him a position with a small but prestigious Palo Alto law firm. Appointed to the federal bench in 1990, Ware became chief judge of Thelton's court, the Federal District Court for the Northern District of California, in 2011.

"Dean Henderson Is Here Now"

Thelton's duties at Stanford were not limited to his dealing with minority students. He taught several courses, including Criminal Procedure with Professor John Kaplan, a Juvenile Defense Clinic with Professor Mike Wald, and a

---

10. From 1978 to 1982, LaDoris Cordell was Thelton's successor as assistant dean for Student Affairs at Stanford Law School.

Defense of the Criminally Insane seminar with the psychiatrist Don Lundy. In addition, as Assistant Dean for Student Affairs, he dealt with student organizations, the law student dormitory, and day-to-day problems of student life.

In his early years at Stanford, white students were sometimes surprised to learn that their Dean of Students was black. On one of these occasions, a student entered Thelton's office, saw him sitting at the desk and asked, "Is Dean Henderson in?"

> Thelton peered slowly at him over his glasses, and told the student to have a seat, and said matter-of-factly, "Dean Henderson will be with you shortly." Thelton returned to his work, completed another five minutes of whatever he was doing, then looked up and said, "Dean Henderson is here now."

Troy Duster, who related this story in the Introduction to Thelton's *Oral History*, observed:

> While it is undeniably true that extraordinary things happen to ordinary people, it is also true that extraordinary people seem to convert "ordinary happenings" into events of significant moment. . . . In this little vignette, one can discern the interlacing of wit and humor with a latent but fierce tone of serious purpose. It was an 'ordinary moment' in some ways, but that moment surely seared itself into the student's experience. Extraordinary people can make ordinary moments memorable.

Thelton's most extraordinary contribution to Stanford, though, was his creation of the minority admissions program. When he arrived at Stanford, Thelton had no experience with law school administration; and at most law schools, minority admissions programs were nonexistent or in their infancy. Just as Thelton had no role models or play book for his unique position with the Justice Department, he had no established path to follow at Stanford. Moreover, perhaps in part because of the perceived failures of nascent minority admissions programs at other schools, the faculty had a decidedly mixed reaction to the notion that Stanford Law School should even have such a program. Indeed, Thelton's early success in attracting minority students led two faculty members to approach him and urge him to slow down.

Although all of Thelton's previous jobs had lasted less than two years, he realized from the outset that this pattern would have to change. Stanford Law School had no tradition of educating or even trying to attract minority students, and it seemed implausible that a year or two of recruiting minority students would bring about lasting change. In Thelton's mind, success at Stanford meant ensuring that the law school was committed to sustaining a minority student population into the future. His goal was "to institutionalize" the minority admissions program, "to have it take roots," and he succeeded. When he left

Stanford in the fall of 1977, the minority enrollment at the law school was above 20%, a figure that has grown over the years.

Thelton is justifiably proud of that achievement, as he is of the relationships that he has maintained with the students he admitted to Stanford. As Thelton related to Leah McGarrigle in the summer of 2001:

> I have remained friends with all of these students and we keep in touch.
>
> I had a wonderful, wonderful meeting this . . . spring. . . . A student that I admitted who was in the Chicano law student association — I won't mention his name — who had a tough time, he was from New York. I remember one of the more dramatic days I had at Stanford. He came to me crying, and he wanted to quit school. He said, "You know, I'm tough. I was in a gang in New York, and handle myself, but I just can't handle this.
>
> . . . [We] went out, I forget the place, there was a popular student hangout, went out, bought a pitcher of beer, . . . and we talked, and I talked him into staying in school. It happened one more time the next year. But he went through and he called me early in the year and said, "I'm coming out for my twenty-fifth class reunion, and I want to get together with you." I never felt prouder. He is a successful attorney, he has a son that he wants to go to Stanford. You know, just powerful. I've never felt more pleased with something I've done than seeing him sitting where you're sitting, and then going out to lunch and hearing about his family. So it was some good memories from that, I made some wonderful friends among those students. It was a good program.

Rosen, Remcho, & Henderson

Thelton had moved from Berkeley to East Palo Alto soon after he began working at the East Bayshore Neighborhood Legal Center and then from East Palo Alto to Palo Alto when he took the position at Stanford. In 1976, while still at Stanford but with the minority admissions program firmly established, Thelton moved back to Berkeley, where he purchased a house. The occasion for the move was his son, Geoff, who was about to enter high school. Just as Thelton's junior high peers were white, Geoff lived in a predominantly white environment in Palo Alto; and like his father before him, Geoff was beginning to be excluded from some of the junior high school social activities. As Thelton put it, "I thought I just don't want that to happen to my son, so I thought Berkeley would be a much more nourishing community for a kid like Geoff."

At the same time that he was making his move to Berkeley, Thelton began thinking about leaving Stanford and returning to law practice. Private practice was his preference — except for one daunting problem: Money. Thelton had just invested what savings he had in his Berkeley house, and it often takes several years for a new firm to generate a profit. Additionally, Thelton was put off by the traditional model of charging high fees for the work of young associates; and he did not want to have to select clients on the basis of their ability to pay. Instead, he wanted to do public interest work, to represent clients, for example, with discrimination or civil liberties claims. Those kinds of cases could be financially rewarding, but probably not in the short term. The payoff would come in attorneys' fees agreed to in a settlement or awarded by the court to the victorious party.

Thelton began to put out feelers to friends and some public interest law organizations including California Rural Legal Assistance and Public Advocates, Inc. in San Francisco. As a result of those inquiries, Drucilla Ramey, then an attorney with Mexican American Legal Defense and Education Fund, put Thelton in touch with her boss, Sandy Rosen, who had expressed an interest in private practice similar to Thelton's.

Dru Ramey got Thelton and Sandy together with NAACP Legal Defense Fund lawyer Bill Turner, who had also expressed an interest in private practice. However, Bill eventually decided to stay with the Legal Defense Fund. Dru then recruited Joe Remcho, an ACLU attorney. Crediting Dru as their founder, Sandy, Joe, and Thelton established the law firm Rosen, Remcho, & Henderson in 1976.

Thelton remained at Stanford on a half-time basis until the middle of 1977; and beginning in 1978, he taught Civil Procedure and Administrative Law at Golden Gate Law School in San Francisco. The new partners had agreed that Thelton's income from both of these positions would go to the firm to help secure its financial stability in the early months. That was a wise, but perhaps unnecessary security blanket. Rosen, Remcho, & Henderson quickly developed a reputation for excellence and had no trouble attracting clients. Most of Thelton's work for the firm involved litigating cases in federal court on behalf of individuals victimized by sexual and racial discrimination in the workplace.

Chapter Seven

Appointment to the Bench

In October 1978, President Jimmy Carter signed the Omnibus Judgeship Act, which created 152 new federal judgeships. Thelton had not previously considered the possibility of trying to become a judge. However, at the prodding of his law partners, he reluctantly wrote for an application form, which he received in early January 1979. A few days later, he received a form letter from Sam Williams, an old boyhood friend and at the time head of California's Judicial Nominating Commission for federal judges. The typed "Mr. Henderson" in the heading was crossed out, and in its place Williams had written "Thelton." The letter stated that Thelton's name had been brought to the Commission's attention and invited him to apply for a judgeship. After further encouragement from his law partners and discussions with his family and friends, Thelton submitted his application. He was applying for a federal district court judgeship in California, which is in the Ninth Circuit.

Two factors persuaded Thelton that he might be a realistic candidate. First, as a result of his work with Rosen, Remcho, & Henderson, he was one of the very few black lawyers in California with a predominantly federal practice.[1] Second, President Jimmy Carter had pledged to increase the numbers of minority and female federal judges — a commitment that he fulfilled:

> When President Carter took office, six women had been appointed to lifetime federal judgeships in our nation's history. Carter appointed forty women in four years. Similarly, while thirty-three ethnic minorities (blacks,

---

1. After having been a federal judge for more than thirty years, Thelton has observed only moderate changes in the racial makeup of the lawyers appearing before him. Although it is not uncommon today for members of racial minorities to make federal court appearances on minor matters or to assist senior lawyers litigating major cases, lead counsel in major cases continue to be almost exclusively white.

Hispanics, and Asians) had been appointed prior to the Carter administration, fifty-five ethnic minorities were seated during his four-year tenure.

The Federal Judiciary and the Appointment Process

Most federal lawsuits begin in the district courts, and the losing party can appeal to the circuit court of appeals. The losing party in the court of appeals can request the Supreme Court to review the case. The Supreme Court, however, has the resources to hear only a very few cases each year. Typically, the Supreme Court chooses cases either because the issues appear to have some overriding importance or because there are conflicting circuit court of appeals decisions.

Because the Supreme Court has the ultimate say in the cases it chooses to decide and because the circuit courts of appeals are the courts of last resort for most cases that are appealed, people typically think of the Supreme Court as the most powerful and prestigious, followed by the circuit courts of appeals, followed by the district courts. This ranking is reflected both in the compensation for judges of the three different levels of courts and in the political controversy that judicial appointments sometimes generate. Supreme Court justices are the highest paid federal judges, and their appointments typically arouse the most widespread political interest.

Another indication of the ranking is the relative influence of the president and the senate in selecting judges. Formally, the president nominates and the senate votes whether to confirm the nine justices of the Supreme Court and judges of the courts of appeals and the district courts. Presidents (or at least their close advisors) are actively involved in the selection process for Supreme Court justices; however, in nominating lower court judges, presidents have often deferred to the recommendation of senators from the state within which the judge will be sitting. Traditionally, the deference has been greatest with respect to district court judges.

There are three important nuances to this description of power and politics. First, the extent to which the appointment of district court and court of appeals judges creates national political controversy can vary widely. President George W. Bush's determination to appoint ideologically right wing lower court judges led to filibusters, a threat by the Republicans to end filibusters for judicial appointments ("the nuclear option"), and finally a compromise of sorts. After Republicans had used the filibuster even more extensively against President Barack Obama's judicial and executive nominees, the Democratic majority in the senate adopted the nuclear option. By contrast, in the late 1970s the nomination and confirmation of lower court judges brought virtually no national attention. In California, the real decision maker for district court judgeships was Democratic Senator Alan Cranston, who — like Democratic President Jimmy Carter — was committed to increasing the number of women and minority judges. When Cranston recommended individuals for the district court, President Carter followed the recommendations; and the Democratic-controlled senate confirmed Carter's nominations.

Second, even when there is little national political controversy over judicial appointments to the district courts and courts of appeals, the process is very political. Although federal judges are underpaid in comparison to what lawyers in large firms make, the power and prestige of a life-time appointment to the federal bench has an allure for many. The competition can be fierce, and one must have political connections with the real decision makers, be they the senator(s) in one's home state or others to whom a president may from time to time look for advice.

Third, and most important, the district courts, despite their lesser political status, have a huge impact on the administration of justice. There is no appeal in the vast majority of district court cases. Moreover, when there is an appeal, the review is typically limited to questions of law, not facts;[2] and the binding nature of a district court's factual findings can be a powerful tool. For example, detailed factual findings may make a compelling case for the correctness of the district judge's legal conclusion; and if there is some uncertainty in the law, factual findings that can accommodate more than one underlying legal theory may make the district judge's decision virtually unassailable. Thus, in some senses the district courts are the most powerful and the most important of the federal courts — a point that Professor Tony Amsterdam made simply and eloquently with a story he told when Thelton was sworn in as a Federal District Judge:

> One of the office boys at the N.A.A.C.P. Legal Defense Fund in New York got into an altercation with a policeman and got busted, and the policeman took him off to the hoosegow, and this fellow got himself a legal aid lawyer and was out in an hour-and-a-half and back at work that afternoon. And when Jack Greenberg, the director-counsel of the Legal Defense Fund, learned about this, he called George into his office and said, "George, gee, I'm really glad you're here, you're out and everything worked out fine, but, George, I got a question to ask you: George, why did you get a legal aid lawyer? We have thirty-five lawyers in this office. We handled more cases in the Supreme Court of the United States last year than anybody but the Solicitor General of the United States. The five lawyers who

---

2. The fact/law dichotomy is discussed more fully in Appendix A.

are on the top of this office have handled more cases in the Supreme Court of the United States than any other five lawyers in history. We have a staff of graduates from the Harvard Law School, the Yale Law School" — this went on for about twenty minutes — "and you go and get yourself a legal aid lawyer. Now, George, I just want to ask you why you did that?"

George thought for a moment and he said, "Mr Greenberg,. . . I didn't mean that to be an insult. I really didn't. I hope you won't take it that way. But, honestly, Mr. Greenberg, I didn't want to go to the Supreme Court. I just wanted to get out of jail."

. . . I think that says it all about the level at which justice is primarily demanding and primarily dispensed in this country.

The Selection Committee for California District Court Judges

When Jimmy Carter was running for president, one of his campaign goals was to reduce patronage in the judicial selection process. Less than a month after taking office in 1977, he established a Judicial Nominating Commission to recommend judges for the circuit courts of appeals on the basis of merit; and he urged senators to create similar commissions to make recommendations for district court judgeships.

That same year Senator Cranston, acting jointly with California's conservative Republican senator, S. I. Hayakawa, created a nine person, bipartisan Federal Judicial Selection Committee to seek out and recommend candidates for judicial openings on California's federal district courts. The Committee consisted of four Democrats appointed by Senator Cranston, two Republicans appointed by Senator Hayakawa, and three individuals appointed by the State Bar Association. Initially Cranston made all of the recommendations from the Committee's lists, but in 1979 Hayakawa threatened to remove his appointees from the Committee and oppose all of Cranston's recommendations unless he was given a greater role in the appointment process. Eventually the two senators reached an agreement in late 1979 whereby Hayakawa would be permitted to make the recommendation for every fourth district court judgeship. Usually, though, the Committee reached a consensus on its list of candidates, and Hayakawa did not exercise his prerogative. As a matter of practice, the Committee gave its list to Senator Cranston, and he made the recommendations to President Carter. Hayakawa was known as "Sleeping Sam" for falling asleep on the floor of the senate. Perhaps he also slept through his opportunities to participate in the judicial appointment process.

The Committee included four people that Thelton knew well: Tony Amsterdam, Vilma Martinez, Bob Gnaizda, and Sam Williams. Amsterdam was a member of the Stanford law faculty, and Martinez was head of the Mexican American Legal Defense and Education Fund in San Francisco. Gnaizda had been a founder of both California Rural Legal Assistance, one of the most successful legal services programs in the country, and Public Advocates, a San Francisco public interest law firm. Williams, the Committee Chairman and the first black president of the California Bar Association, was Thelton's friend and classmate from grade and junior high schools.

Although the Committee had no directive to make recommendations that would diversify the bench, Senator Cranston encouraged the Committee to seek minority and female candidates. According to Bob Gnaizda, some Committee members — including Williams, Martinez and himself — made this a high priority, but not, he stressed, at the expense of other qualifications. In an effort to develop a strong and diverse candidate pool, the Committee aggressively sought out individuals who they thought might not apply on their own. Part of that effort was the form letter that Thelton received.

There are four federal district courts in California — the Northern, which includes the San Francisco Bay area, the Central, the Eastern, and the Southern. The Committee's practice was to consider only individuals who lived in the district where a judicial vacancy occurred, which for Thelton was the district court for the Northern District of California.

"I Made Every Mistake I Could Possibly Make"

Competition for federal judgeships is often intense. Typically, individuals who want to join the federal bench seek advice and support from influential lawyers, judges, and political figures. Indeed, since becoming a judge Thelton has received multiple requests for advice and support whenever there is federal judgeship opening. In 1978, however, Thelton did not realize how political the process was. Reflecting back on that period, he said, "I made every mistake I could possibly make."

> I filled out my application, I mailed it in, and I kept working. I didn't talk to a single judge, I didn't talk to a single attorney. I didn't even call my good friend Sammy Williams with whom I grew up to say, "Hey, can you help me?" I didn't call my good friend Tony Amsterdam. I didn't call my good friend Bob Gnaizda. . . . I was . . . so naive.

Despite his passivity, the Selection Committee asked Thelton to come for an interview. As he sat in the waiting room, he recognized other candidates, whom he described as "much more prominent [and] active politically than I." When it was Thelton's turn to meet with the Committee, the interview went smoothly — except for an exchange with one of the Republican members:

> He said, "Well, I see from your resume here you've done lot of civil rights and public interest. That's essentially all you've done. And a federal judgeship requires — you know, we have antitrust, we have corporate interests, and I have to say, I'm a bit worried whether you can be fair to these kinds of interests, given your background."
>
> It sort of nettled me, and I said . . . fairly pointedly, "Well, my experience in court is that most of the judges come from that background and I sometimes feel they are unfair to me and my clients from their corporate [perspective] — and I assure you that I can be at least as fair to them."

At that point, Bob Gnaizda interrupted and changed the subject.

After seeing the competition and making what he considered a faux pas in the interview, Thelton believed he was out of the running for a federal judgeship. Others, however, may have seen the interview incident differently. The Committee, after all, was trying to identify qualified minority and female candidates, and any serious effort to bring racial and gender diversity to the bench would necessarily require selecting candidates with nontraditional backgrounds. In the late 1970s, there were very few minority and female partners in large firms, where the most sophisticated corporate and antitrust practice occurred. More important, as Bob Gnaizda and other public interest lawyers on the committee certainly knew, the intricate regulatory framework governing such matters as employment law, Social Security, Medicaid, and Medicare — matters with which public interest lawyers deal regularly — can be at least as demanding and complex as the laws with which business lawyers deal. Finally, and most important, Thelton's supposed faux pas illustrates a great strength of his character. Despite his usual quiet, affable demeanor, Thelton has what Troy Duster has described as "clear standards and limits and a sense of moral outrage." Thelton's somewhat sarcastic expression of that moral outrage was fully justified and, indeed, may have enured to his benefit. It is inevitable that candidates for judgeships will be better versed in some areas of the law than others. There is no reason to believe that lawyers with a civil rights and public interest background will be less "fair" in ascertaining and applying the law than lawyers with a corporate or antitrust background.

Resigned to the notion that he would not become a federal judge, Thelton returned to work and devoted his full attention to his cases. He heard nothing more from the Selection Committee, but in May he read in the paper that the Committee had forwarded his name as one of five recommended individuals to

Senator Cranston. In addition to Thelton, the list included two white males, an Hispanic (Robert Aguilar), and a woman (Marilyn Patel).

Enlisting Support

Thelton's renewed hope for becoming a federal judge suffered a setback almost as quickly as it arose. At the time, there was only one opening on the district court for the Northern District of California, and Senator Cranston almost immediately recommended Robert Aguilar to President Carter. However, as Thelton knew, there would be two additional vacancies on the Northen District bench within the next few months. District Judge Lloyd Burke was retiring, and District Judge Cecil Poole was being elevated to the Ninth Circuit. For the first time, Thelton took a serious interest in trying to enlist support for his candidacy, but for some potential backers he was much too late. John George, an undergraduate roommate and at the time member of the Alameda County Board of Supervisors, was committed to another candidate. So was Nick Petris, the powerful state senator with whom Thelton had practiced law in the mid 1960s.

The impetus for Thelton's decision to become active in pursuing the judgeship was his learning that some politically influential black lawyers and politicians were lobbying against him. Their claim was that he was not sufficiently a member of the black community: He had two white law partners; his office was on Montgomery Street, in the heart of the San Francisco financial district; and at the time he was married to a white woman.

Despite the rhetoric about his blackness, the campaign against Thelton probably had more to do with politics than race. Because Thelton had not previously sought support for the judgeship, he had the appearance of being a stealth candidate. The announcement of his name undoubtedly surprised many black leaders, who were already committed to other candidates. In any event, the opposition was real. Prominent blacks lobbied both Senator Cranston and Sam Williams. Years later Sam Williams confided to Thelton that he responded by saying, "Don't worry; I'll take care of this" and then did nothing.

Perhaps because of the opposition to Thelton, Senator Cranston decided not to limit his choices for the two upcoming judgeships to the four remaining names on the list. The Selection Committee reopened its process. Its new recommendations included Thelton, Marilyn Patel, and two new black candidates: Don McCullum, an Alameda County Superior Court judge, NAACP leader, and prominent member of the East Bay Democratic Club; and Henry Ramsey, one of Thelton's friends, who was a former Berkeley City Councilman, and later an Alameda County Superior Court judge and dean of Howard University Law School.

In the meantime, Thelton focused his efforts to enlist backers on the community of public interest lawyers, where he garnered support from blacks and Hispanics, as well as whites. For example, in a lengthy letter to Senator Cranston, Mike Baller of the Mexican American Legal Defense and Education Fund specifically addressed and debunked the notion that Thelton was "insufficiently devoted to civil rights causes or to the civil rights of minority communities." In addition, Thelton obtained support from some of his Stanford friends, including Professor Robert Gerard, who had been a fund-raiser for Senator Cranston, Professor William Gould, and LaDoris Cordell, whom Thelton had recruited when he was establishing Stanford's minority admissions program. LaDoris became a de facto campaign manager; and because one of her friends and classmates, Conway Collis, worked for Senator Cranston, she was able occasionally to provide Thelton with inside information.

An important, perhaps critical, endorsement came from Colleen and Bob Haas. Colleen had been a law student at Stanford in the early 1970s, when Thelton was Assistant Dean. After law school, she worked with criminal defense attorney Charles Garry. Her husband, Bob, an heir to the Levi Strauss family fortune, was a respected Levi Strauss executive and later Chairman of the Board. The Haases were generous supporters of Senator Cranston, and Colleen wrote to him expressing strong support for Thelton.

> . . . He possesses, as you must already know, outstanding academic and intellectual qualifications. It is, however, his qualities of character, his demeanor and his unquestionable personal integrity which I feel most strongly suit him for the judicial role.
>
> Thelton is a quiet man rather than a "political" one. That fact should not obscure his firm sense of principle and morality nor his great compassion and sensitivity for his fellow man. The federal judiciary could only be enhanced by his selection.
>
> Many thanks for your consideration. Bob joins me in sending our warmest personal regards.

Late one evening in mid-January 1980, LaDoris called Thelton to tell him that she had heard from Senator Cranston's office that tomorrow the Senator would recommend Thelton and Marilyn Patel for the two vacancies on the district court.

The Last Hurdle

The next morning Marilyn Patel called Thelton to tell him that she had been selected for one of the vacancies. Thelton had heard nothing from Senator Cranston's office, but later in the morning he received a call requesting that he meet with the Senator that afternoon. Thelton assumed there must still be some unresolved issue, and the only thing he could think of was the Martin Luther King car incident. Thelton immediately got in touch with his former Justice Department colleague and supervisor, John Doar, and asked him if he would call Senator Cranston and say something to put the car incident in perspective. Doar agreed, and Thelton waited nervously for his meeting.

At the meeting, Senator Cranston asked about the car incident, and Thelton explained what had happened.

> Then [Senator Cranston] said . . ., "Well we got a call from John Doar today," and something to the effect, "I would trust that man with my life," in terms of his integrity. "And he said that I needed to understand the time there, and if I deprived you of a judgeship because of that, I would never forgive myself." And I thought, okay, this has to be helpful. So we went on a bit, and then finally he said, "Okay, well, I'm satisfied, you're going to be our next federal judge."

Wanzie

Thelton left the meeting and went directly to a telephone booth, where he called Wanzie in Los Angeles to tell her the good news:

> ". . . I just met with Senator Cranston and I'm going to be a federal judge." And my mother said, "Oh gee, that's nice. Did I tell you about your cousin Ronny?" [laughter] That's my family, and I said, "No, you didn't." So we talked about family matters and then I was thoroughly disgusted. [laughter] I had just called with the biggest news of my life, and then, you know, after about ten minutes, maybe fifteen, at this point I have no interest in what we're talking about. So then I say, "Well, I better be going home now. I'm standing on the corner in a phone booth."
>
> Then she said, "Okay, but let me get this straight, you're going to be a judge, you said, is that like a traffic judge?" And I said, "No, Mother, it's different," and hung up.

Several months later, after Thelton's investiture, he took Wanzie to see his stately, oak paneled courtroom. "Oh," she exclaimed, "You're a *real* judge!"

The Final Steps

President Carter nominated Thelton for the federal district court bench in May 1980. After Thelton made a brief, pro forma appearance before the Senate

Judiciary Committee on June 10, the full senate confirmed his nomination on June 26, 1980.

At his investiture five weeks later, friends and colleagues spoke of Thelton's past and of their hopes and expectations for his future. Troy Duster retold the story of one of Thelton's arrests and how that might have an impact on his decision making as a judge:

> ... The ideal role of today's federal judge is to interpret the law ... for rich and poor alike. But ... we know that experience shapes interpretation. ...
>
> ... [When he was working for the Justice Department, Thelton] would observe how law enforcement was being handled. Every now and again, he'd hang around a demonstration and be arrested. ... At a certain point, of course, he would flash is badge and say, "Department of Justice.". ...
>
> But he realized that if he waited longer, he would learn more. And so he waited longer and learned a bit more. Until one night he waited a bit too long, and a sheriff's deputy in rural Alabama left a scar on his hand where a bone was broken.
>
> I don't suggest that this experience is a requirement to sit on the federal bench. I do suggest that the bench is greatly enriched today by this appointment of a man who would take himself down the road to that experience so that justice might better be served.

Sandy Rosen, one of his law partners, spoke of Thelton's "commensurate skills, his diverse and interesting background, his tender character, and yet, his firmness and hardheaded realism." Joe Remcho, Thelton's other law partner, said:

> All of us in our office will miss him greatly. We will miss his talent, his energy, dedication; we will miss his wisdom, his common sense; we will miss his role as conciliator and as a peacemaker; and we will miss his humor, his consideration and his patience. But we know that it is precisely ... because of those qualities that he is moving on. ...

And Tony Amsterdam, Thelton's colleague from Stanford Law School, provided this assessment of Thelton's character:

> He is the outstanding demonstration ... of ... [the] proposition ... that a person who does good things can also be a good person. Not just sometimes. Not deep down inside of him in some hard shell. Not with embarrassment. Not to some people, but not to other people. But can be a good person all the time, unashamedly, to everybody, without hiding it, without trying, without effort.
>
> There is a line from A.E. Houseman, something about a mind too unhappy to be kind. I sometimes think ... many ... lawyers and others ... who have devoted themselves to doing important works of good ... are in

that boat; that when we see the injustices, the inequalities, the [miseries] of the world, to which Thelton is fully sensitive, they make us unhappy and they make us too unhappy to be kind. Fight. Yes, [we] will fight. But it is a fight. And very often it is a losing fight. And in the fight, [we] get bitter.

Well, that has not happened to Thelton Henderson. . . .

. . . [I]n all [that he has done] . . . he [has] . . . recognized that he had, not simply responsibility to programs, but a responsibility to people. . . .

When he was in charge of the minority program, he was also a counselor to students. He never forgot he was a counselor to students. And whenever he was out in the field, in the legal services office, he was running a program. It wasn't the program. It was the client. It was the student out there in the office that mattered to Thelton. He managed to do the program. He managed to implement the idea. He managed to advance the ball, but he never lost sight of the people.

. . . [W]hat Thelton has touched in us has left lingering behind a touch not only of wisdom, but a touch of joy; a feeling that a human being can be not only wise, perceptive, active, dynamic, but also happy, and shed a little bit of happiness on the folks around him.

Amsterdam then told the story about the NAACP Legal Defense Fund office boy to illustrate the importance of trial lawyers and trial courts, and he concluded:

The court to which Thelton goes, the court of first impression, is also a court on the front line. It is a court that stands, to all of us, for what the legal system means to the people. If anybody deserves to be on a court like that, and will grace it, it is Thelton Henderson.

Chapter Eight

Rashomon[1]

Hearing Thelton talk about his life makes one wonder why he has not yet won the lottery. Time and again he attributes his successes and achievements to luck, to being in the right place at the right time. But for having a mother with high expectations, he would have spent more time in the streets and less time studying when he was growing up. But for the fortuity of his athletic ability, he would have been a complete outsider among his peers in Los Angeles. But for Isaac McClelland's support, he never would have gotten to Berkeley. But for the initiative of his Western Civilization professor, he would not have successfully completed his courses during the first summer at Berkeley. But for his football injury, he would not have had the academic record that got him admitted to Boalt Hall. But for John Doar's telephone call to Dean Prosser, he never would have worked for the Justice Department. But for the fact that he happened to be available when Stanford Law School decided to become serious about minority admissions, he never would have had the opportunity to create a minority admissions program. And but for all of these things, a form letter from Sam Williams, and another telephone call from John Doar, he never would have been a federal judge.

There is some truth to this narrative of chance and coincidence. Virtually all achievement depends partially on good fortune, and Thelton's rise from the poverty of South Central to a federal judgeship is no exception. However, like

---

1. Akira Kurosawa's award-winning 1950 film, Rashomon, is the story of a samurai's death and his wife's possible rape — told from the perspective of four different individuals. Each person's narrative conflicts with the others in significant details. Some of the discrepancies may be the result of deliberate lying, but other differences are almost certainly a reflection of the reality that each of us interprets and remembers events in the context of our own unique prisms of experience. There is some truth in each version, but any ultimate truth is only in the eye of the moviegoer.

Rashomon, the story of Thelton's life depends very much on the perspective of the storyteller.

Thelton's perspective downplays facts that even he will acknowledge when pressed: He was not simply an outstanding athlete but the captain of his sports teams from grade school through college. His peers and coaches, who repeatedly selected him for that honor, must have recognized his intelligence, dedication, and leadership ability. Thelton was always a conscientious student who received good grades. Isaac McClelland and Dean Prosser had to have helped Thelton because they saw his potential to succeed. John Doar had to have been similarly impressed with Thelton, first to hire him and then to place him in the incredibly difficult position of being the Justice Department's eyes and ears in the South in 1963. The Judicial Selection Committee and Senator Cranston had to be impressed with Thelton's intelligence and integrity to recommend him for a federal judgeship.

These realities are parts of a counter-narrative — a narrative about which there is substantial consensus among Thelton's friends, colleagues, and law clerks. It includes Troy Duster's description of Thelton's wit and firm resolve:

> At a personal level, Thelton is easygoing, affable, flexible, congenial, and possessed of a laugh that is so infectious and so deeply resonant that those within range find themselves smiling. To this add a mischievous teasing style, somewhat in the tradition of Shakespeare's Falstaff. Even when Falstaff was seemingly bested by his peers in some sparring verbal one-upmanship, he was always able to find his way back on top with a cleverly humorous turn of the phrase. The affability and flexibility are real [and] wide ranging. . . . But when he has extended himself, and an attorney in his courtroom crosses a line, the fiercely uncompromising part emerges . . . . [A] stony, steel-like resolve catches many a foe off guard.

The counter-narrative also includes John Doar's accolades to Senator Cranston and former law clerk Sam Miller's characterization of Thelton as "very forceful and brilliant." He is, Miller continued, "an incredible model of integrity and humility." "The surest sign of Thelton's genuine humility," former law clerk Jonathan Rowe adds, "was the extremely high regard in which he was held by the courthouse staff — the regular people who suffered untold muddled and miscellaneous indignities from the other, more arrogant judges, but never from Thelton." And, of course, it is that humility that leads Thelton to attribute so much to chance.

Former Federal District Court Judge Martin Jenkins — now a justice on the California Court of Appeal — captured Thelton's sense of humility in a reminiscence about his first encounter with Thelton and their later becoming colleagues. Jenkins met Thelton in 1980, Thelton's first year on the bench and

Jenkins' final year of law school. One of Jenkins' professors had suggested that he talk to Thelton about career opportunities and the possibility of becoming a judge. Thelton spent nearly four hours with Jenkins, a fact of which Jenkins is particularly appreciative given his personal knowledge of the demands on a first-year federal judge:

> [T]he first year is almost like a train wreck every day. You come on and there are 350 cases waiting for you. . . . I don't imagine that even if there are judges that would have made time for me that they would have made as much time and conveyed a deep sense of genuineness, genuinely caring about what would happen to me, what the range of possibilities were, and communicating that. It was almost like the dictates of the job didn't exist. I was the focus. That's . . . a basic tenet of Thelton Henderson. You meet him. His focus is completely upon you. . . . That comes out of his humanity. He doesn't have an ego. I know he does. I know psychologists would say he obviously does, but it's not manifested in the way most of us think about ego. It's never manifested in a way that elevates him over others in a job where that's what happens every day. People stand up when you walk into the courtroom. No one really tells you the truth once you get this job and you put that black robe on. . . . [M]ost of the people you come in contact with, other than family members,. . . [pay] deference to the position, and [there is] a sort of polite convention about how you deal with members of the judiciary. So it's very easy to lose perspective in these jobs. Most of us do from time to time. I've never seen any evidence that he does. That basic, self-effacing, humble, tremendous sense of humanity is just with him all the time. That to me is part of his genius.

Similar testimonials could fill many pages, but the most compelling evidence of Thelton's character is his performance on the bench. In discussing why the Selection Committee forwarded Thelton's name to Senator Cranston, Bob Gnaizda explained that Thelton is "highly intelligent," "well versed in the law," and someone who members of the Committee believed had "the courage to stand up for social justice" in the face of strong political opposition. As a judge, Thelton has exhibited all of these qualities, but what is most notable is how thoroughly he has fulfilled the hope that in his courtroom social justice would not become the victim of political expediency. He has made politically unpopular decisions, including those defending affirmative action and upholding the rights of prisoners. When Thelton wrote to California Governor and former "Terminator" actor Arnold Schwarzenegger threatening to place the entire California prison medical system in receivership — a step that he eventually took, lawyers warned that the governor should take him seriously. Criminal defense attorney Cristina Arguedas said, "He will be immune to the governor's legendary Hollywood celebrity charm. He cares a lot about the state prison system — he has been working on it for more than a decade. And he is an expert on the subject." Former Boalt Hall law professor Stephen Barnett agreed: "The governor will find that Judge Henderson cannot be terminated."

Part Three

Judge Thelton Henderson

Chapter Nine

On and Off the Bench

Life inevitably changes when one becomes a federal judge. Lawyers who have cases before a judge — or who anticipate the possibility of having cases in the future — tend to behave with great deference toward the judge, both inside and outside the courtroom. Out of respect for both the person and the office, all but a judge's closest nonlawyer friends are likely — at least at the outset — to use more formal terms of address. At social gatherings, conversations may be more subdued and less racy than they were before. Recreational drug use that may have occurred openly in the past is likely to be no longer visible.

These and other small signs of deference and respect, the physical trappings of the courtroom, and the acknowledged authority to make decisions that will have a profound impact on other people's well-being constitute the inevitably rarified environment in which federal judges spend much of their time. Thus, it is not surprising that some judges seem to be out of touch with the day-to-day lives of ordinary people or that some become obsessed with their power and arrogant about the correctness of their views.[1]

Especially in the early years of his judicial career, Judge Henderson acknowledged being treated outside the courtroom with a formality to which he was unaccustomed and with which he tended to be uncomfortable. However, neither that treatment nor the prestige of the office has altered Judge Henderson's compassion and humility. As Supreme Court Justice (and former Ninth Circuit Judge) Anthony Kennedy put it, "Sometimes when people go on the bench, it changes them and not always for the better. It didn't change Thelton."

---

1. Whether elitism, egotism, and arrogance result from the way judges react to their environment or whether people with those characteristics tend, perhaps disproportionately, to seek judicial office is a topic I will leave to others.

The Beginning

After Judge Henderson had been serving on the federal bench for thirty years, LaDoris Cordell asked him about his training to become a judge ("absolutely none") and his early days on the bench. Here are portions of his recorded answers:

They have a judges' school for federal judges, but it's given periodically. When I took the bench the judges' school was about four month away because they have to wait for enough new judges to make it worthwhile. So by the time the judges' school came along, I was judging, and I felt I didn't need the school. So I never attended. I kept on judging and learning the techniques. The coolest technique I learned was, when I had a problem on the bench, I would say, "Oh, looks like it's time for a break, counsel." And run down the hall [to then Chief Judge Robert Peckham and say,] What do I do?" That's sort of the way I learned to do it. . . .

I remember my first day. [Judge] Cecil Poole . . . was my mentor, one of my mentors, and he wisely told me, "Don't get on the bench with something hard. Do a case management conference, where you just talk about the progress of the case." So that's what I did. The first day I had a number of case management conferences, and a script, and I was plenty nervous. But I was able to do that. I didn't have to rule on anything. I just had to sort of frown at the right time and do the things that judge's do, and when I didn't have an answer, just say, "hmm, o.k." You know, those things work well. So the first day was that. The following Monday I decided I was going to hear my first motions . . . I was ready, and I peppered [the lawyers] with a lot of questions, took the motion under submission, and figured it out with my wonderful law clerks.

. . . Two things [were the most difficult for me early on]. . . . I remember I had a [temporary restraining order] motion against the Navy, the Alameda Naval Station, and . . . I was being asked to enjoin the Navy. I said to my clerk, "Can I enjoin the Navy?!" That was hard to realize all this power I had. That was hard to get used to. . . .

But the really hardest thing for me was sentencing. . . . I found myself sentencing people to jail for really long times.

Judge Henderson quickly became aware of both the breadth of his power and its severe limits, as he struggled to enforce lawful orders against such diverse defendants as the Department of Veterans Affairs, state prison officials, and a recalcitrant school superintendent in East Palo Alto, California. (Ensuing chapters document those struggles.) But he never became comfortable with criminal sentencing.

Latent Racism

Judge Cecil Poole, the first black ever to serve on the Northern District bench, was appointed to that position by President Gerald Ford in 1976. By the time Judge Henderson assumed the bench in the summer of 1980, Judge Poole was sitting on the Ninth Circuit. For a number of years, Judge Henderson remained the only black judge on the Northern District court.

Despite Judge Poole's prior service on federal district court, Judge Henderson, in his early months on the bench, frequently encountered the latent racism of attorneys appearing before him. For example, on one occasion Judge Henderson had scheduled a settlement conference in his chambers — where he, of course, would not be wearing his robe. When the attorneys were ushered into the chambers, one of them looked around and asked, "Where's the judge?"

On another occasion, a lawyer defending against a racial discrimination charge asked Judge Henderson to recuse himself because he was black. Judge Henderson responded by pointing out that the case would then necessarily go to a white judge. Yes, the attorney agreed. After all, that was the point of the motion. And why, Judge Henderson asked, did the lawyer think that only a white judge could fairly resolve a dispute between a black employee and a white employer? Needless to say, Judge Henderson did not recuse himself.

A similar situation arose in a disability rights lawsuit when defense counsel asked Judge Henderson to dismiss for cause (i.e., bias) a juror with disabilities. Judge Henderson asked the lawyer if he would make a similar motion to disqualify a black juror in a racial discrimination suit. "Absolutely," the lawyer said. "Wrong answer," Judge Henderson responded. "Motion denied."

Chief Judge and Senior Status

In 1990, after ten years on the bench, Judge Henderson became the first black chief judge of any district court in the Ninth Circuit. Elevation to the status of chief judge is based on seniority, but the title is not merely an honorific. The chief judge is the principal administrative officer of the court with responsibility for such diverse matters as budgets, special programs, the annual retreat, and, of course, attending and speaking at numerous meetings as the public face of the court. The added responsibilities, however, do not come with new powers. Federal judges are — and tend to view themselves as at least — equals among equals. Each judge has a vote, and judges tend to have strong personalities. Being chief, Judge Henderson has remarked, is "like herding cats."

Judge Henderson was initially reluctant to take the position. He enjoyed working on his cases much more than he liked administrative tasks, but the decision was about more than whether to take on administrative duties. There was a large symbolic value in being the first black chief judge in the Ninth Circuit. In the position of chief, Judge Henderson could be a role model and inspiration for minorities. Realizing this, he acceded to the entreaties of his friends and colleagues from across the country who urged him to take the position.

For the first time in his life, Judge Henderson had a role model — former Chief Judge Robert Peckham, who had done much to streamline the operations of the court and who had the foresight to obtain an able administrative assistant, Kumi Okamoto. As Judge Henderson put it, she "comes with the job," and her institutional memory and competence made her "invaluable." And as Judge Henderson eventually learned, her position was unique, at least among the Ninth Circuit district courts:

> I made a dreadful mistake, because I took her for granted. I went to a meeting at the Ninth Circuit of chief judges and some of the other chief judges were complaining about the work load and all, and I said, "Well, gee, don't you give that to your administrative assistant?" And they said, "What administrative assistant?". . . [I]t was the first time I realized that everybody doesn't have one. . . . Bob Peckham,. . . in some way that I still don't know the history of . . ., was able to get this special slot for our court. Most other courts don't have . . . a Kumi.

Not surprisingly, Judge Henderson had a modest view of his own role as chief judge:

> I felt like a captain on a big ship. . . . [I]t's well-oiled, it's clean, it's modern, and all I want to do is keep that baby from running into an iceberg. I just want to keep it going the way Bob Peckham had run it. . . . I thought we had a forward-looking court, an innovative court, and I simply wanted to keep it that way. And in addition, carry out the will of the court — I tried to be a consensus judge. I negotiated with Washington on behalf of the court to get us money and resources. So that was what I saw my job as, as chief judge.

Judge Henderson did all of that, and, at the same time, he used his tenure as chief judge to leave his distinctive mark on the court. He greatly expanded the programs — begun by Judge Peckham — for Alternative Dispute Resolution, a cheaper, more efficient mechanism for settling legal claims; he instituted a program to help ensure that indigent claimants could get legal representation; and he took steps to integrate magistrate judges into the daily life of the court.

District courts include both federal district judges, such as Judge Henderson, who are appointed by the president, and magistrate judges, who are appointed by the district courts. Magistrate judges perform all of the functions of district court judges; however, magistrate judges do not have life-time tenure, and often their decisions are recommendations that a district court judge must review. When Judge Henderson became chief, magistrate judges were not permitted to use the judges' lunchroom or the judges' elevator; and they were not allowed to attend retreats or judges' meetings. All of that changed during his tenure as chief judge.

Judge Henderson's term as chief judge ended in 1997. When he stepped down as chief, he assumed senior status,[2] a position that in essence allows him to work for free. Had Judge Henderson retired from the bench, he would have received his existing salary and benefits for the rest of his life. By taking senior status, a judge agrees do at least one-fourth of the work of active judges, and in return the senior judge receives cost-of-living increases. Since taking senior status, Judge Henderson has maintained an active, but somewhat reduced caseload. The reduced caseload, however, has not been a slow step toward retirement. Rather, it has permitted him to devote time he otherwise would not have had to several long-running, complex cases, including two prison suits — one monitoring prison conditions at Pelican Bay State Prison and the other dealing with the California prison medical system, which he has placed in receivership. For Judge Henderson, senior status is only a title.

Being Prepared

The courtroom that Judge Henderson has occupied for most of his judicial career is a cavernous, oak-paneled space with a two story high ceiling and a marble backdrop behind a large, elevated bench. It was clearly designed to emphasize the authority of the law and the dominance of the judge. For nonlawyers and inexperienced attorneys, the setting can be quite intimidating. Judge Henderson, however, maintains a low-key, welcoming environment.

Lawyers who have appeared before Judge Henderson, regardless of whether they were on the winning or losing side, acknowledge his fairness, compassion, knowledge, and commitment to the rule of law. Undoubtedly part of the reason for the praise stems from the lesson Judge Henderson learned from his first encounter with Robert Kennedy at the Justice Department: Always be thoroughly prepared. Judge Henderson never goes on the bench without having a grasp of the issues he knows will arise. In addition, he often has a prepared script of questions or opening remarks to set the tone for the hearing that is about to ensue. However, he never reads from the script. Instead, he looks directly at the attorneys and their clients as he delivers his remarks. And when the circumstances

---

2. To qualify for senior status, a judge must be at least sixty-five years old, and the judge's age and years of service on the bench must equal at least eighty.

warrant it, he will abandon his script altogether, as this incident related by former law clerk Jonathan Rowe demonstrates:

> Like any judge, Thelton worried most about cases in areas where he had never practiced, like maritime law or patent law, because he wasn't as confident his great common sense would allow him to figure out which side was bullshitting, as he did easily in most other cases.
>
> We had one huge patent case, with lawyers from fancy firms in New York on both sides, but their papers were always total gobbledygook (because, as I later learned, patent lawyers aren't really litigators). So for one motion, I wrote out five questions to which Thelton ABSOLUTELY NEEDED to know the answer, in order to even know what was at stake in the motion.
>
> Motion day comes, and two pasty-faced guys get up in their tight Eastern suits, dandruff flying — truly, they looked like two stuffed birds who'd been dead about five years each — and start droning on about intellectual property rights. Half an hour into the hearing, I'm hand-signaling prayers to Thelton to ask at least ONE of the questions I wrote out for him. He nods at me, but he never says a word. Back in chambers after the 90-minute hearing, he can tell I'm a little miffed.
>
> "Sorry I didn't ask your questions," Thelton says. "I just didn't think they'd help me rule."
>
> "Why not?" I protest, feeling defensive. "They were good questions."
>
> "Yes, they were," Thelton concedes, "but anything those guys said wasn't going to help us — and besides, if I'd seemed the least bit *interested*, we'd still be out there."

Being Firm but Compassionate

Despite Judge Henderson's generally easygoing manner, he has always dealt firmly with lawyers who are unprepared or who try to take advantage of him or abuse the legal process — and often, because of his general good nature, an offending attorney would not sense what was happening until it was too late. For example, Judge Henderson might admonish an attorney not to mention a particular fact in the presence of the jury or not to pursue a particular argument. If the attorney persisted, Judge Henderson would say to Barbara Slenkin-Slater, his deputy clerk (whom he regularly teased about wearing sneakers in the courtroom), "Get ready to run for the marshal. If this attorney says that one more time, I want him removed from the courtroom." And if that warning were not sufficient, Barbara Slenkin-Slater would get the marshal, who would take the attorney from the courtroom and place him in a holding cell. Typically, Judge Henderson would either remain calm throughout the process or not express any anger or frustration until the moment of taking disciplinary action. As a result, one of his clerks characterized him as a person with "no middle gears."

Judge Henderson's compassion and a rare expression of anger — as well as his sense of humor — were on display in an incident that Jonathan Rowe recalls from his clerkship in the early 1980s. Rowe labels his remembrance "The Lawyer Without a Dime," and it happened on what Rowe refers to as "Manic Monday," that is, motion day, when sometimes dozens of lawyers "are stacked up in our courtroom, like planes at an overcrowded airport, awaiting permission to take off." The motions are often mundane, and frequently law firms send their newest, least experienced attorneys to present the arguments. The process is much too boring for an eager young clerk:

> So the parade of semi-coherent idiots, blathering on about their tedious motions, proceeds way too slowly. Since Thelton is a major HUMANIST, who sympathizes with these dolts because, unlike most judges, he still recalls when he was a struggling young lawyer who was seldom afforded respect, Thelton courteously affords these bozos way MORE than a full day in court. Frankly, I'm half-dozing.
>
> But then our phlegmatic bailiff calls a dispositive motion in a case where we have literally received ZERO papers from plaintiff's counsel. Zippola. Since this is very rare, I perk up.
>
> The smarmy big-firm defense lawyer ticks off his main points, makes one quick snide comment about how "it's hard to anticipate plaintiff's arguments, since no brief was filed," and sits.
>
> Up stands the rumpled plaintiff's lawyer, who looks like he slept on the street in the Tenderloin. But he's still got the silver tongue that once made his friends say: "you should go to law school," so he launches into a litany of excuses for not filing a brief. He just moved his offices, so although he concedes the defense timely served the motion three weeks ago, he didn't actually SEE the motion till last Thursday. He started to draft a brief, but he missed his bus. Or his puppy ate his research. I can't remember which. Maybe both. The more he talked, the worse it got.
>
> Finally, Thelton interrupts this farce, and demands: "Do you have a dime?"
>
> "Uh, why, yes, I do," plaintiff's counsel says, fumbling in his pocket.
>
> "So even if you had no office," Thelton SHOUTS, "why couldn't you go outside and use that dime to call my clerk and ask for an adjournment of THIS MOTION?"
>
> Without waiting for an answer, Thelton storms off the bench. Everyone in the courtroom is stunned, because Thelton NEVER shouts. Like Dagwood's

dog in the old *Blondie* comics, I scramble after my master, aping his angry *mien*. But I'm truly scared. I've NEVER seen Thelton angry. In full fury he stalks through the door to chambers I hold open for him. I close the door, turn—and Thelton immediately laughs, slaps me on the shoulder and breaks into his trademark huge grin. "That'll make all those lawyers out there think twice about messing with me."

But that is not quite the end of the story:

> [T]he most important thing . . . is, of course, Thelton ultimately adjourned the motion for a week in order to give the guy without a dime a chance to file a brief. Because Thelton always valued ensuring that justice was served far more than exercising power.

Judge Henderson does not recall this specific instance of faux temper. However, he readily admits to having developed a similar strategy. When he knows that a lawyer has not filed the appropriate papers or suspects that a lawyer will beg for an extension of time to do something that should have done earlier, Judge Henderson will make a point of calling that lawyer's case first. This maximizes the opportunity for other attorneys, who are waiting for their cases to be called, to witness Judge Henderson's expression of displeasure, and hopefully to "think twice about messing with me."

Looking Out for the Unrepresented

Although he has little patience for unprepared lawyers, Judge Henderson will be solicitous of attorneys whose floundering, he senses, is the result of inexperience or nerves. And if individuals appear before him without counsel, Judge Henderson will try to ensure that they understand what is occurring and that they have a full opportunity to be heard. As one of his clerks, Sarah Ruby, said, "He knows when to take time and explain things to people."

Two examples of Judge Henderson's concern for unrepresented litigants occurred during settlement hearings in class action lawsuits. In both instances, the individuals appeared in Judge Henderson's court in response to notices that had been sent to all members of the class informing them of a proposed settlement. The first case involved a challenge to United Parcel Service's policy of not allowing hearing-impaired employees to be delivery truck drivers. The employee who appeared before Judge Henderson wanted to express his disgruntlement over how he had been treated, but he had no idea what a legally appropriate objection to the settlement might be. Because of the employee's hearing impairment, Judge Henderson arranged for the employee's mother to speak for him over the telephone. The mother, according to Judge Henderson, was "almost irrational." Nonetheless he heard her out and tried to explain to both her and her son what a valid objection might be.

The second case stemmed from the mortgage foreclosure crisis. The unrepresented plaintiffs, an Hispanic couple with limited English language ability, had lost their house to foreclosure. They incorrectly assumed that the settlement notice was a summons to appear in court because they were in trouble with the law. Realizing the plaintiffs' misunderstanding, Judge Henderson delayed the proceeding and had one of the attorneys, who was fluent in Spanish, explain the situation and assure the plaintiffs that nothing bad was going to happen to them. After relating this story, Shelley Cavalieri, Judge Henderson's clerk at the time, characterized him as "a deeply compassionate person to the folks who are in his courtroom." She continued, "In class actions, we think about big social change happening, and individual plaintiffs sort of disappear sometimes. When Judge Henderson is judge the individual doesn't disappear. That's the kind of judge he is."

For Judge Henderson, these incidents were not extraordinary: "I do that all the time. I want everyone who comes into my court to feel that they've had their day in court." According to Emily Galvin, another of Judge Henderson's clerks, "The most important thing for him is that people leave feeling they've been heard."

Problem Solving

Of all the accolades from attorneys and former clerks, the one Judge Henderson regards as least apt is "intellectual." Yet, his explanation for that self-assessment reveals much about why lawyers and colleagues extol his intellect and judgment:

I will go to the judges' lunch room and we'll start talking about a legal issue or a case. And you get into a discussion. . . . And they will say, "Well, you know, the *Jones* case, you know that footnote in there that—,". . . I don't think that way, I could not engage in that discussion. I don't carry knowledge around in that way. . . . I can only start dealing with those cases when I get it before me. They can talk abstractly. "Well, that case is — da, da, da — and this footnote, and what Justice Burger had in mind." I don't think that way. Those are intellects.

I can take a case and say, "Here's what it means right here in this brief, in this matter before me," and work with it that way. And that's a different process, and I don't see that as an intellectual process as much as I think I have good problem-solving abilities. I know how to apply things, I know how to resolve things that are brought to me. I think I'm good at that, but I don't see that as a real intellectual process. . . . I see myself more as . . . someone who has learned to come up with a good product . . . rather than that kind of intellectual, free-floating kind of knowing the subtleties abstractly of a case or doctrine. . . .

. . . [I]f I . . . were a fighter, I'd be a counterpuncher. You know, I think I can respond to things, I have ideas, I'm good at responding. But I don't think I'm good at sitting down, tossing out . . . the stimulating ideas.

Judge Henderson may not be an "intellectual" in the commonplace but narrow sense in which he used the term to denote purely or at least predominantly abstract, logical thinking. However, his legal problem solving, as he would surely admit, involves applying intellect and reason to concrete, everyday situations. And it involves more. Just as effective counterpunchers must have some understanding of — perhaps even empathy with — their opponents to anticipate when and how they will strike, wise judicial problem solvers, as Chapter Two discussed, must have empathy with those appearing before them. Perhaps the highest form of intellectualism is being able to combine, as Judge Henderson has in his problem solving, logic and reason with real-world understanding and empathy.

Interacting with Jurors

The physical features of the courtroom make the judge the center of attention, but Judge Henderson has taken a small but symbolically important step toward shifting the focus in his courtroom to juries, the representatives of common citizens. Instead of following the usual practice of having those present stand as he enters the room, Judge Henderson has instructed his deputy clerk to announce the commencement of a court session by saying, "Remain seated and come to order." The familiar "All rise" is reserved for the entrances and exits of juries. And when the order is given, Judge Henderson rises with everyone else to show respect for the jurors.

Like other judges, Judge Henderson repeatedly tells jurors to render their verdict solely on the basis of the evidence presented at trial and to avoid reading about or otherwise gaining information about the case outside the courtroom. There are two reasons for this order. First, the party who is hurt by the information will not have an opportunity to rebut it or put it in context. Second, jurors may hear evidence that the court has ruled is inadmissible — for example, evidence that a court has deemed more prejudicial than probative. Judge Henderson has no illusions about the substantial risk that jurors may not follow his admonition — sometimes intentionally because of an obsessive curiosity and more often inadvertently because of the ubiquity of the mass media, including blogs, Internet news sources, and social networking sites, such as Twitter and Facebook. Yet, Judge Henderson firmly believes that any de-emphasizing of the command would lead to even more breaches.

When Judge Henderson finds jurors shirking their responsibilities or not taking them seriously, he reacts quickly but always in a measured way because he knows that his bite will probably not have to be as big as his bark. And, if there is an opportunity, he blends his expression of disapproval with humor (which may be lost on the misbehaving juror).

One of Judge Henderson's early discoveries after becoming chief judge was that large numbers of people were simply ignoring their summonses to jury duty. He had the US Marshals serve as many of these individuals as they could find with orders to show cause why they should not be held in contempt. However, he never had to follow through with the contempt threats. The orders to show cause were sufficient to get most of the slackers' attention.

A problem that Judge Henderson sometimes encounters is the late juror. He regularly explains to jurors the importance of being punctual by pointing out that a single juror's tardiness will inconvenience everyone associated with the case by delaying the entire proceeding. If these words are not sufficient, and occasionally they are not, he threatens the late juror with the possibility of jail. One such juror, a young man in his twenties, was about fifteen minutes late for the start of trial in the morning and then late returning from the lunch break. On both occasions, Judge Henderson told him that his behavior was not acceptable. The juror was late again the next morning, and Judge Henderson said nothing. However, when the court adjourned for lunch, he called for the US Marshall to escort the juror to a holding cell where, Judge Henderson said, he would remain overnight as well as during the lunch break. Judge Henderson made sure the juror received a satisfactory lunch. Then, at the close of the afternoon session, Judge Henderson said to the juror, "Well, you've caught me in a good mood. You can go home tonight, but don't be late again." From the outset, Judge Henderson knew that he would not make the juror spend a night in jail—unless perhaps the juror were late again. That situation, though, never arose. The juror had learned his lesson.

On another occasion, a prospective juror was trying desperately to get herself disqualified in the hope that she could go home. In questioning her along with other prospective jurors, Judge Henderson asked the litany of usual questions to ensure that the chosen jurors would not be biased: Do you know any of the parties to this action? Are you or any of your family members engaged in the same occupations as the parties to the action? Do you have any reason to distrust people who share characteristics of the parties? Etc., etc. The woman who wanted to go home raised her hand with every question. Finally, Judge Henderson asked, "Do any of you scuba dive?"—a question that had absolutely no relevance to anything about the case. Once again, the woman's hand shot up.

Judge Henderson realized that at least one and probably both parties would not want her on the jury. She had effectively disqualified herself. But Judge Henderson was not about to let her ploy succeed. He dismissed her as a prospective juror in his case. However, instead of allowing her to go home (which would have been the normal thing to do) he ordered her back to the jury assembly room, where she would be called for another case.

Some Notable
(and One not so Notable) Decisions

In over thirty years on the bench, Judge Henderson has handled thousands of cases. The ensuing chapters include stories of some of his most notable decisions. This section contains brief descriptions of other important rulings.

All federal district court judges deal with numerous complaints alleging discrimination on the basis of race, gender, disability, and sexual orientation. Judge Henderson's two most significant discrimination cases are High Tech Gays v. Defense Ind. Sec. Clearance Office and Kraszewski v. State Farm General Ins. Co.[3] *High Tech Gays* (Chapter Twenty) involved discrimination against gays and lesbians by the Defense Department in the granting of security clearances. In *Kraszewski*, Judge Henderson found State Farm General Insurance Company liable for discriminating against women who sought to become sales agents, and he approved what was then the largest settlement ever in a discrimination case, $157 million — which by the time all remaining issues were settled rose to over $250 million.

Alan Goldstein, who was clerking for Judge Henderson at the time of the *Kraszewski* trial, has described the statistical evidence of gender discrimination as "overwhelming" and the testimony of female employees as "damning" to State Farm. But, according to Goldstein, one of the "most damning" things occurred

---

3. Other important discrimination cases include Barefield v. Chevron U.S.A., Inc. (class action lawsuit against Chevron Oil Co. for discriminating against blacks and Hispanics in the workplace; pursuant to a settlement agreement, Chevron established a damage fund for the plaintiff class), Arnold v. United Artists Theater Circuit, Inc. (improved access to movie theaters for individuals with disabilities), Bates v. United Parcel Service, Inc. (protection of hearing impaired employees from discrimination by U.P.S.; Judge Henderson's initial ruling on the merits was reversed in part by the Ninth Circuit, which overruled one of its own precedents upon which Judge Henderson had properly relied; eventually, plaintiffs and U.P.S. reached a settlement in which U.P.S. agreed to pay plaintiffs $5.8 million and to make substantial accommodations for the hearing impaired), Ramirez v. Greenpoint Mortgage Funding, Inc. (class action on behalf of Black and Hispanic consumers against mortgage lender for discriminatory pricing policies; $15 million settlement for benefit of the plaintiff class), and Curtis-Bauer v. Morgan Stanley & Co., Inc. ($16 million settlement of class action race and gender discrimination suit against Morgan Stanley).

when a white, middle-aged, male State Farm executive took the witness stand. The case was being tried without a jury; and Goldstein's co-clerk and one of Judge Henderson's externs, both of whom were female, were sitting in the jury box to observe the trial. Before the State Farm executive began his testimony, he turned and winked at the two women. "It just confirmed everything," Goldstein recalled.

On the environmental front, Judge Henderson — in addition to protecting dolphins from tuna fishers (Chapter Ten) — has issued rulings to enforce the Clean Water Act and the Clean Air Act. For example, in Golden Gate Audubon Soc. v. U.S. Army Corps of Engineers, he protected wetlands from development; in Citizens for a Better Environment v. Deukmejian, he authorized environmental groups to sue to enforce the Clean Air Act; in the same action, he held that the defendants were liable for failing to adopt and implement measures to ensure adequate clean air in the Bay Area; and in three separate cases, he found that oil companies (Exxon, Shell, and Union) were illegally dumping selenium into San Francisco Bay.

A case that began in 2000 and as of mid-2016 still had no end in sight is Allen v. City of Oakland. *Allen* is a federal civil rights suit against the city for the actions of the Oakland Police Department and several of its officers, known as the "Riders." Allegedly, the Riders, with the apparent tacit approval of the Department, engaged in extensive misconduct, including kidnapping, evidence planting, and beatings. In 2003, Judge Henderson approved a settlement that called for the payment of $10.9 million to 119 plaintiffs and numerous Police Department reforms. Much like the defendants in Judge Henderson's East Palo Alto special education case (Chapter Eighteen), the city — despite the appointment of a monitor, new court orders, a new settlement, and the appointment of a compliance office with powers substantially similar to those of a receiver — has consistently failed to meet its obligations under the settlement agreements.[4]

In other noteworthy cases, Judge Henderson:

- Prevented the Postal Service from firing an employee who refused on religious grounds to distribute draft registration forms (McGinnis v. U.S. Postal Service).
- Severely limited the extent to which a sexual harassment defendant could inquire during discovery into the plaintiff's past sexual history (Priest v. Rotary). The decision, which has been widely cited by both federal and state courts, predated by more the ten years the enactment of similar protections against the admission of such evidence in federal trials.

---

4. In a separate case, Coles v. City of Oakland, Judge Henderson presided over the settlement of claims that the Oakland police used excessive force during a 2003 anti-war demonstration. The settlement involved (1) injunctive relief and (2) damages and attorneys' fees totaling nearly one million dollars.

- Made Medicaid available to thousands by striking down state income eligibility requirements that were inconsistent with federal law (Sneede v. Kizer).
- Held that a sixth grader's charges of sexual harassment stated valid civil rights claims against school teachers and administrators (Oona R.-S. v. Santa Rosa City Schools).
- Protected the procedural rights of death row inmates (Ashmus v. Calderon).
- Rejected a high school salutatorian's claim that he had a constitutional right to use a public school commencement address as an occasion for religious proselytizing (Lassonde v. Pleasanton Unified School Dist.).

And like other judges, Judge Henderson has had to deal with his share of bizarre litigants. For example, here is Judge Henderson's description of the relevant facts in Barrier v. Johnson, a case in which the plaintiff claimed that the police illegally detained him:

> On March 19 and April 17, 1996, plaintiff Paul Barrier visited the San Rafael Police Department in order to report activities that he believed worthy of police investigation. On these two occasions, Barrier explained to defendant Officer Katie Benninger and other officers that his sperm had been stolen and had been used, without his knowledge, to sire children intended for satanic sacrifice. Barrier cited as evidence for this claim "biophysical" feelings he experienced when in the presence of certain children, feelings he had hitherto only experienced when in the company of his own children. These feelings, together with physical similarities Barrier perceived between himself and the children he had encountered, led Barrier to conclude that these children must, in fact, be his. During the course of his discussions with police, Barrier produced photographs of children in support of his claims, as well as certain videotapes and printed material regarding "biophysics." Barrier also admitted that he had followed at least one child that he suspected was his.
>
> During the course of the second interview at the police station, the officers present concluded that Barrier was "disoriented, paranoid, obsessive with conspiracy" [sic] and feared that Barrier might kidnap a child that he believed was his. As a result, Officer Benninger completed an Application for 72-Hour Detention for Evaluation and Treatment, and Barrier was detained for mental evaluation. . . .

The defendants moved to dismiss the complaint on the ground that they had qualified immunity. Judge Henderson granted the motion.

In Chambers

Although the courtroom and the proceedings that occur there symbolize the power and authority of the judiciary, most of the real work of judging occurs not on the bench but in chambers before and after hearings. Judges and their law clerks study briefs, research the law, and prepare memoranda, orders, and opinions. Whereas some judges maintain a strict division of labor and limit their clerks to basic research tasks, Judge Henderson works collaboratively with his clerks on all aspects of his cases. In addition to giving them specific research assignments, he will seek out their views and use his clerks as sounding boards for his own ideas. When decisions are to be embodied in written opinions, he will discuss the tone and substance of what he wants to say with his clerks and often ask them to prepare initial drafts. Typically, these drafts become the working bases for the final products.

The work is demanding; and primarily by his own example, Judge Henderson instills a work ethic in his clerks. Just as he regularly arrived at the East Bayshore Neighborhood Center well before 8 a.m. during his days as a legal services lawyer, he has often been the first person to arrive at his chambers. And while he no longer has to type his own letters, he nevertheless has sometimes been inundated with a backlog of cases. A backlog, however, never creates panic. As Jonathan Rowe observed:

> Thelton was truly GREAT AT DEALING WITH OVERLOAD. I recall one morning in his office, looking around at literally 20 huge piles of paper, each representing a separate thorny case he had to deal with. Gratuitously, I offered to help (knowing already that these piles were cases only Thelton could move forward, because either they were bench trials where we clerks had not been present, or they were motions where we'd already written our bench memos), because I was genuinely concerned he was overloaded (this was back in the bygone days when federal courts had too much work). When Thelton declined my gratuitous offer, I asked how he was EVER going to get through so much work. "You can't let the sight of the 19 other piles bog you down," Thelton said, "you just pick up one and get it done, and after that, you pick up another, and get it done, and soon enough, they'll all be gone." Of all the many lessons I learned from Thelton Henderson, this one was the most valuable to me.

One manifestation of Judge Henderson's work ethic was the close attention he paid to the monthly statistical reports of pending cases for each judge in the Northern District. As Karen Kramer, who served as one of his law clerks for many years, recalled:

> Since all judges start out with roughly the same number of cases as their colleagues, [Judge Henderson] would watch these statistics very closely

each month to see if his caseload number was going up (which meant he was being inefficient) or going down (which meant he was being efficient). We worked very hard on the backlog and his caseload steadily declined until one month [February, 1989] he was finally #1 (i.e., the judge with the lowest caseload). . . . I framed this report and it's in his office. He maintained his number 1 status for quite a while, and I think he stayed #1 or #2 until he was Chief Judge [at which point the reports were no longer relevant because he had only half a case load.]

Despite the hard work, the environment in Judge Henderson's chambers is casual and low-key. Unlike some judges, he has no dress code for his clerks; and his irrepressible sense of humor permeates the chambers. Jonathan Rowe recalls an incident from August, 1982:

Judge [Robert] Aguilar, whom I'd never met, stops by to chat with Thelton. I was just back from one of my many Michigan vacations, decked out as usual in my shorts, sandals and t-shirt, and sporting a ridiculously deep suntan for a white man (this was before the days of skin cancer awareness). Judge Aguilar interrupts himself, mid-sentence, to stare at me. Thelton doesn't miss a beat, and in a confidential-style tone, tells Aguilar: "I require all my clerks to approximate my skin color as closely as possible."

At some point, the chambers acquired a little red scooter and a small bicycle that clerks would ride up and down the hall to other chambers or to the copy machine. To celebrate clerks' birthdays, Judge Henderson would play a kazoo, and on special occasions he and his clerks would sometimes exchange light-hearted doggerels. For example, on Jonathan Rowe's 29th birthday, Judge Henderson composed a poem with these lines:

Like John Wayne to this job he strode.
On his shoulders he bore the clerk's load.
Though he follows all orders,
Sometimes he's on the borders.
And he's demolished the office dress code.

When Judge Henderson became chief judge, Karen Kramer presented him with a Superman cape.

One of the cases that Karen worked on involved the prosecution of an attorney/drug dealer. Judge Henderson, in what he realized was a close call, relied on Karen's research and draft opinion to deny the drug dealer bail on the ground that he was a flight risk. The defendant immediately appealed, and on Karen's 30th birthday she and Judge Henderson received an opinion bearing the Ninth Circuit's official stamp. The opinion not only reversed Judge Henderson's decision but also uncharacteristically provided a scathing critique of his and Karen's research and reasoning. Karen was devastated. Judge Henderson tried to mollify her by offering to call one of the Ninth Circuit judges to seek an explanation. Then, as Karen put it, "after letting me twist in the wind," Judge Henderson revealed that he and Karen's husband, Cliff Rechtschaffer, who had also clerked for Judge Henderson and who had friends at the Ninth Circuit, conspired to write the opinion. Cliff had gotten the official stamp from one of his friends.

A few weeks later, the Ninth Circuit did reverse Judge Henderson's decision, but he and Karen had the last laugh. The drug dealer fled the jurisdiction and was never seen again.

Karen got back at Judge Henderson in an incident, some details of which must remain vague in order to protect the guilty. When he was chief, Judge Henderson was particularly frustrated with one of his colleagues, Judge X. Over the course of several months, Judge X had tried Judge Henderson's patience with a series of indecisive and sometimes conflicting memos about a particular issue that was of no great importance to begin with. Judge Henderson had expressed his frustration to his clerks, and one morning when he read another memorandum of the same ilk, he reached his limit. Crumpling the memo and throwing it on the ground, he said, "[Expletive deleted] I'm going down to Judge X's chamber right now to take care of this!" At that point, much to Judge Henderson's relief and amusement, Karen revealed that she was the author of the crumpled memo.

Life beyond the Courthouse

Those who have known Judge Henderson for many years or appeared frequently in his courtroom have seen a gradual but persistent decline in his physical strength. Not long after becoming a judge, he gave up tennis. A few years later, he was walking with a slight but noticeable limp. In 2006, he began using a cane regularly. Since suffering a bad fall in 2010, he has alternated between a walker and a wheelchair. This is all the result of a degenerative muscular disease that continues to sap his strength.

Particularly for someone who has loved and excelled at sports, the gradual, irreversible loss of physical strength over the years has had to have been discouraging. Judge Henderson, however, has never complained or let his disability affect his relationship with others. He has continued to be the same humble, considerate person that he has always been. His sense of humor never flags, and he remains as active as his physical condition allows.

One recreational outlet for Judge Henderson has been poker, which he continues to play on a regular basis. He is a part of three different games, one of which is all judges; and periodically he and other poker playing friends spend a weekend in Las Vegas. Judge Henderson wins more often than he loses, at least when he is not in Vegas, but the stakes are not high. The real reward is the honing of tactical (i.e., bluffing) skills:

> I think — and this is a part of poker I like — I think poker really reflects a basic part of one's personality. There's a player in a game that we've been playing in for years and I'm convinced that he will blink in certain situations. You know, it's just part of his personality. . . .
>
> And I'm interested in that, and I'm always wondering what my basic personality is, that the other players get. I think it is that I love to bluff. I love to try something to see if I can pull it off. . . . I think in the rest of my life, I'm a pretty reserved guy. I think maybe this appeals to some part of me that wants to be wild and adventuresome, and I probably get it out in poker.

Another reason for Judge Henderson's love of poker may be simply that he is good at it. He has an uncanny ability to measure a person's character and to anticipate how people will function in various settings, to determine whether they are bluffing or not. The early success of the minority admissions program at Stanford depended very much upon his assessment of the applicants' skills and willingness to work hard, and that same ability has served him well as a judge. At least in areas of the law with which he is familiar, he has, as Jonathan Rowe observed in relating the story about the stuffed bird patent lawyers, "great common sense [that] would allow him [easily] to figure out which side was bullshitting."

A second major recreational outlet that Judge Henderson only recently had to severely curtail was fishing. For years, he was an avid, if not initially successful, fisherman. It began when he was growing up in South Central and his Uncle Fred would take him to fish at the San Pedro Pier. Then there was a long hiatus, except for a fruitless 1968 effort at Lake Tahoe and a very brief expedition to the San Francisco Bay. Recalling the good times he had had with his Uncle Fred, Judge Henderson bought a fancy new reel and headed for the Berkeley Pier with his son, Geoff. With the judge's first cast, the reel went sailing into the Bay. The trip was over.

In the mid-1970s, Judge Henderson began fishing with Mort Cohen, with whom he became friends while teaching at Golden Gate Law School. For one of their early trips, Judge Henderson organized a group of about twenty to go salmon fishing in the Pacific Ocean west of San Francisco Bay. Judge Henderson became seasick, according to his recollection, soon after crossing under the Golden Gate Bridge from the relative calm of the Bay to the rougher ocean waters. Mort Cohen placed the onset of Judge Henderson's illness at an earlier point — almost immediately after they left the dock. Indeed, Mort suggested that the judge might get seasick merely from wading. Both of them, however, agreed on one important fact. Despite Judge Henderson's incapacity below deck in the captain's quarters, it was his line that caught the first salmon.

For more than thirty years, Judge Henderson, usually accompanied by Mort Cohen and sometimes by others as well, took every opportunity to improve his fishing skills — from Alaska, to the rivers and streams of California and southern Oregon to Mexico. And often the fishing was mixed with poker.

When he was fishing with guides or strangers, Judge Henderson — never one to flaunt his credentials — would not identify himself as a member of the judiciary. If asked about his occupation, the most he would say is that he was a lawyer. On a return trip from fishing at Cabo San Lucas, a US customs agent — in what can only be explained as an act of blatant racism — forced him but not his companion, Mort Cohen, against the wall and frisked him. Even in this instance, Judge Henderson did not reveal his status.

Off the Bench on the Bench: True Believer

In the early 1980s, Judge Henderson's friend, Brenda Wong Aoki, was having dinner with the casting director for the film *True Believer* starring James Woods and Robert Downey Jr. When the casting director mentioned that there were three judges in the movie and that he hoped to find a black person to cast in one of the roles, Brenda said that she knew a real black judge. As a result, Judge Henderson got a screen test:

> "Okay," one of them said, "I understand you're a real judge, is that right? I said, "Yes." They said, "Oh. Okay, read for the part of Judge whatever." I read for it, and he said, "Okay, show more anger." And I tried to show more anger, and I realized as I was doing it that in my own court, probably the most severe thing I could say, in a very calm voice, [was], "Counsel. I don't want that to happen again." That's the way I control — [laughter]. So I was working from that and they wanted me to scream, and I don't scream in court. So finally they kept saying, "A little more anger," and it wasn't coming. So they said, "Okay, we'll try this other judge." [laughter] So I read for it, and that's the part I got.

In the movie, according to a nameplate on the bench, Judge Henderson is playing the role of Judge Bau. However, the credits at the end of film identify him as "Judge Baum." Baum was the original name for the character, but during the shooting someone decided that "Baum" did not seem to be sufficiently African American. The solution was to obliterate the "m" on the name plate, a change that never made it to the credits.

Judge Henderson's most memorable line — indeed one of his only three lines — was "Mr. Dodd, are you ready to give your closing argument?" But Judge Henderson made the most of it. He had a party to celebrate his movie debut, and rented a theater in Berkeley for a showing of the film. Guests received a flyer with Judge Henderson's photograph superimposed on an advertisement featuring a picture of James Woods and Robert Downey Jr. Below the picture were excerpts from what purported to be reviews by Pauline Kael, Gene Siskel, and Roger Ebert:

> This movie takes fire in the opening scene when Judge Bau (played by that exciting newcomer, Thelton Henderson) delivers the never-to-be forgotten line, "Thank you counsel" in a rich stentorian baritone. By the time Judge Bau says, "Mr Dodd, are you ready to give your closing argument?" the audience will be limp from emotion. Although the movie never quite reaches this dramatic level again (indeed, what movie could), it is well worth watching Henderson's co-star, James Woods, attempt to meet the enormous acting challenge posed by the judge. — Pauline Kael

> Don't miss the opening scene — it's a gem. — Siskel

> "Mr. Dodd, are you ready to give your closing argument?" is a line that can only be compared to one other in film history. Not since Clark Gable said, "Frankly, my dear, I don't give a damn," has a single line taken such hold of the imagination of the American public. — Ebert

Tributes to Judge Henderson and His Tribute to His Clerks

On April 16, 2010, Judge Henderson's alma mater, Boalt Hall, hosted a day-long symposium to honor his thirty years on the bench. Lawyers and academics, including former clerks, participated in panels that discussed Judge Henderson's landmark decisions in civil rights, environmental law, and prison reform. When the symposium was in its second hour, Judge Henderson asked for the microphone:

> I know this is out of order. I'm not supposed to participate, but this is going to go on all day, and I need to confess now. In my criminal trials when the attorney is giving a closing argument or in a sentencing he or she is waxing eloquently about the defendant, who has been charged with some vile thing. . . . And I often watch the defendant while it's going on, and there's this look like, "Who is he talking about?" And I know I must have that look now.

The most compelling comments during the symposium were not about particular cases but about how Judge Henderson has approached the task of judging.

After describing several of his very early civil rights decisions, LaDoris Cordell observed:

> In each case the judge spelled out the factual backgrounds and the bases for his rulings specifically and clearly. Now, penning decisions in this fashion — clearly and specifically — would seem to be a no-brainer. But sadly spelling out the specific reasons for one's rulings is not necessarily common practice for trial judges. The thinking among many on the bench is the fewer the words, the less likely one is to be reversed. So "granted" or "denied" or "affirmed" is preferable to opinions that put it all out there. But putting it all out there was clearly how this baby judge began.

It was a courageous approach that has served him well throughout his judicial career; and as LaDoris Cordell pointed out, "The benefits went far beyond the specific cases in which he ruled." A number of Judge Henderson's decisions, including some of his earliest opinions, have been cited and relied on by courts across the country.

Later in the day, Judge Myron Thompson, who sits on the federal district court in Alabama, asked, "Why does one judge have a particularly stellar legacy?... "What sets Judge Henderson apart?" His answer, as noted in Chapter Two, focused on Judge Henderson's empathy or, as Judge Thompson characterized it, "the ability not to discriminate,... the ability to transcend yourself."

Recently retired Magistrate Judge Wayne Brazil, who had served with Judge Henderson in the Northern District of California for twenty-five years, added:

> I wanted to just express my appreciation and admiration for what Judge Thompson has offered as ... a really profound insight into a very, very fundamental source of Judge Henderson's greatness, and that is the capacity to put himself in other people's places and to feel the world through other people's eyes.... Judge Thompson said as a federal district judge you don't represent anyone. That's correct, but Judge Henderson represents some *thing*. What he represents is the system of justice, and it's not the system as some institution or set of organizations. It's the system of justice in a spirit. It's the system of justice that is so deeply rooted in the capacity for respect and understanding that respect for everybody is the center of the definition of law. There's no one I've ever known that exemplified that more than Judge Henderson.

Judge Henderson's empathy with people of varied backgrounds and interests is strikingly evident in his selection of law clerks. Some have followed the traditional clerkship paths to academia and private practice. However, relatively few have gone to the large firms that often attract law clerks of other federal judges. Instead, Judge Henderson's former clerks who have decided to make a career of law practice have tended to join small firms or engage in public interest law. And then there are the many former clerks who have abandoned the law altogether to pursue other careers, including painting, fiction writing, and publishing. As a whole, they constitute as diverse and interesting a group of people as one could hope to meet; and Judge Henderson has not just met them, but has worked closely with them and remained friends with them over the years.

When the symposium honoring Judge Henderson concluded, he joined many of his former clerks for dinner, where he paid tribute to them in all of their diversity:

> . . . I can't even *begin* to imagine there being a symposium but for my clerks' energy, brightness, idealism, inspiration, and willingness to help provide me the backbone needed on those really tough decisions we've had to make over these past thirty years. . . .
>
> But, alas, there are also those hard times when my clerks embarrass me. I know some of you are probably thinking I'm going to point out that time you got me reversed, or tell some really terrible story that you've hidden away or maybe even forgotten since your clerkship, but don't worry. That's not what I mean.
>
> What I mean is that every time I go down to the judges' lunchroom and have lunch with my colleagues, I am always embarrassed when we start talking about our clerks.
>
> One of them might say, "I'm so proud. One of my clerks just got promoted to partner at the biggest firm in — fill in the blank: (city), (state), (country), (world)."
>
> And then another judge might respond with: "That's great. But did you know that one of my clerks is now managing partner at that firm?"
>
> Of course, I have a few clerks who have gone on to big firm careers that — in all seriousness — make me very proud. But the majority of you have reduced me to saying things such as:
>
> Lots of my clerks are tree huggers.
>
> Most work for public interest groups.
>
> I've sometimes had to hire a few of my clerks back year after year because no one else would hire them, and I thought it would reflect poorly on *me* if they couldn't find a job.
>
> And those are the ones who are still working as lawyers!
>
> Some are forming their own literary group; one writes books in England; one writes poetry in New York; one is publisher of a magazine in San Francisco.
>
> One now heads a cancer research organization, where her main job is to beg people for money.
>
> And, well, you know how the rest goes.

How utterly humiliating. I'm the Rodney Dangerfield of the Northern District. I don't get no respect. And the only way I can save face is to blurt out that, well, my very first law clerk [Joshua Bolten] was a big shot at Goldman Sachs and was George W.'s chief of staff. That shuts them up every time. They simply *cannot* wrap their head[s] around *that* one.

I've already hired my term clerk for next year, Sarah Ruby, and for the year after that, Emily Galvin — both of whom are here tonight. And I just want to beg the two of you — finally — let me walk tall into the judges' lunchroom without having to go back thirty years to my first law clerk, or having to make excuses for my low-achieving-mostly-do-gooder law clerks. When you leave me, I want you both to go out there and set the world's record for billable hours in one year.

I'm kidding, of course — unless that's what you decide you really want to do! I'm so proud of all of you. It is probably true that my clerks have gone on to be the most unconventional group of former federal law clerks around, but I wear that as a badge of honor. You have all gone on and followed your hearts and your dreams and done what you've wanted to in this world, and I could not be any happier.

I've said it before, and I'll say it again. I couldn't have done this without any of you. Thank you, again, so very much.

Dolphins, Vietnam Veterans, and Johnny Spain

Chapter Ten

Dolphin-Safe Tuna

Between 1989 and 2004, Judge Henderson issued a series of rulings protecting dolphins from needless slaughter by the tuna fishing industry. In each instance, he was responding to requests by environmental groups and concerned citizens to enforce existing federal law—namely the Marine Mammal Protection Act (1972), the International Dolphin Conservation Program Act (1997), and the Dolphin Protection Consumer Information Act (1990), the last of which established the "dolphin safe" label for canned tuna. The nominal defendants were various Secretaries of Commerce in three presidential administrations, two Republican and one Democratic.

Humans and Dolphins

From ancient times to the present, people have revered dolphins, sometimes imbuing them with human attributes. According to Greek mythology, the sea god, Poseidon, used a dolphin as a messenger to woo his beloved Amphitrite. Dionysus saved pirates from drowning by turning them into dolphins. As a result, they spent the rest of their lives helping rather than preying on humanity. In the modern era, the 1963 movie "Flipper" (and the television series by the same name that began the following year) portrayed dolphins as playful, highly intelligent animals. Flipper was as lovable as Lassie but considerably smarter. More recently, swimming with dolphins has become so popular that the Marine Mammal Protect Act places restrictions not only on commercial fishers but also on overexuberant dolphin enthusiasts.

The attraction to dolphins is not surprising. They are, indeed, playful and highly intelligent. They utilize rudimentary tools, have a sophisticated system of communication, and create social bonds among themselves. Moreover, some dolphins seem to crave interaction with humans. Therapists have used dolphins to treat individuals with autism and other disabilities, and there are stories of dolphins banding together to save humans from shark attacks.

Dolphins, Yellowfin Tuna, and Purse Seine Fishing

Human beings are not the only species attracted to dolphins. In the Eastern Tropical Pacific Ocean (ETP), a vast expanse of water from southern California to Chile that spreads west nearly three thousand miles, yellowfin tuna tend to congregate in the sea below dolphins frolicking near the surface. Noting this relationship, tuna fishers for years have sought out pods of dolphins in order to locate the tuna beneath them.

Pole and line fishing for tuna posed no significant threat to dolphins. However, in 1959, technological innovations permitted fishing for tuna with large purse seine nets — nets that hang vertically in the water with floats on top, weights on the bottom, and bottom rings that can be pulled together like those on a purse. In a practice known as "setting on dolphins," the fishers — with the aid of small motor boats, dynamite, and helicopters — would encircle a large area, herd the dolphins and the tuna beneath them into a smaller and smaller space, and deploy their nets in a circle around the dolphins. The bottom of the net would then be closed, preventing escape from below; and the net — containing tuna and dolphins — would be hoisted onto the ship. The fishers had no interest in the dolphins. Those that survived the ordeal were released. Many, however, died or were injured in the process. Between 1959 and 1972, when Congress passed the Marine Mammal Protection Act, millions of dolphins had been killed in purse seine nets. In the early 1970s, the US fleet alone was responsible for over 300,000 dolphin deaths per year.

The Marine Mammal Protection Act (MMPA)

The 1972 MMPA declared that eliminating the "the incidental kill or incidental serious injury of marine mammals . . . in the course of commercial fishing operations" was an "immediate goal." To help achieve this goal, the statute strictly limited the number of dolphins that could be trapped in purse seine nets; and subsequently, purse seine net fishers devised ways to limit dolphin mortality.

As a result, by the end of the 1970s the number of dolphins killed by the US fleet was reduced by over 90%. During this time, the US fleet was comprised of over 100 purse seine netters, but the size of the fleet diminished substantially in the 1980s — at least in part because of MMPA requirements, which led some ship owners to operate under foreign flags.

The MMPA also gave the Secretary of Commerce broad regulatory authority to protect dolphins. Administrative enforcement of the MMPA, however, was at best lax.

The MMPA and the US Tuna Fleet

In 1988, Earth Island Institute, "a national organization whose members share a commitment to the protection of marine mammals," was the lead plaintiff in a lawsuit filed in San Francisco Federal District Court to enforce provisions of the MMPA. The case was assigned to Judge Henderson. Relying on a recent amendment to the MMPA, Judge Henderson ordered the entire (by then only thirty-five boats) US tuna fleet to carry observers to ensure that the fishers did not exceed the congressionally mandated dolphin-kill limit.

Five years later, the National Marine Fisheries Service listed the northeastern offshore spotted dolphin as "depleted," a condition that had existed since 1988. According to the MMPA, this designation required the Secretary of Commerce to ban their killing in the course of commercial fishing for yellowfin tuna. The Secretary, however, refused to follow the clear mandate of the statute.

The 1988 Earth Island Institute lawsuit was still pending in January 1994, when the plaintiffs asked Judge Henderson to order the Secretary to comply with the law. The government's formal defense was based on an intricate and convoluted interpretation of the MMPA that defied both the statute's language and the clear legislative intent. The underlying rationale for the Secretary's recalcitrance, however, undoubtedly had more to do with promoting international trade and avoiding an embargo on foreign tuna than with parsing words of a statute. Although a ban on killing dolphins could be enforced directly only against the US fleet, MMPA requirements, as the next section discusses, had implications for the importation of foreign tuna.

Judge Henderson's opinion accompanying his order that the "[d]efendants are enjoined, effective immediately, from permitting the taking of any northeastern offshore spotted dolphins" is not light reading; but it is a detailed and compelling refutation of the government's statutory argument. There was no appeal from this order, as there had been no appeal from the 1989 order requiring observers on US tuna boats.

The MMPA and Imported Tuna

Regulating the US fleet was only a small step toward the goal of preventing the slaughter of dolphins. Even before the reduction in the fleet's size, the United States was the world's largest importer of tuna; and other governments did not regulate their tuna fishers to the same degree that the United States did. To address this problem, the MMPA provided from the outset for a ban on imported tuna that did not meet MMPA standards.

Despite this mandate, Republican and Democratic administrations in the 1970s and early 1980s — apparently because of concerns with trade and international relations — did virtually nothing to limit the importation of tuna caught by killing and endangering dolphins. In response, Congress strengthened the import provisions of the MMPA in 1984 and again in 1988. The 1984 amendment banned the importation of tuna caught with purse seine nets in the Eastern Tropical Pacific Ocean unless the foreign government established that its "average rate of . . . incidental taking . . . of marine mammals" was "comparable" to that of the United States. The 1988 legislation defined comparability as no more than twice that of the US fleet by the end of 1989 and no more than 1.25 that of the US fleet after 1989. The administration, however, remained reticent to follow the law.

Despite the 1988 amendments, the administration allowed countries that had not met the 2.0 comparability standard to import tuna after December 31, 1989. When Earth Island Institute sought a preliminary injunction to enforce the new comparability standard, the administration's excuse for its nonaction centered around "a long standing agency policy" that data from which to make comparability findings for any given year was not due until July 31 of the following year. Then, once the data was in, it would "take [additional] time" to analyze it to determine whether the comparability standard had been satisfied. However, as Judge Henderson pointed out, a comparability finding could be based on data for less than a full year. The statute required only that the comparison of US and foreign incidental takings be for "the same time period." More important, the defendants' position was patently inconsistent with Congress' objectives in amending the MMPA. As Judge Henderson explained:

> From the legislative history, it is clear that the Congress was frustrated with what it considered to be agency foot-dragging in implementing the import ban to address the "foreign fleet problem." It is therefore understandable that Congress implemented strict guidelines establishing standards which apply as of specific dates. . . .
>
> With the 1988 amendments, Congress explicitly stated that as of the end of 1989 the agency may not make the finding of "comparable" which is necessary to overcome the import ban unless the importing government

has made a showing that its average incidental taking rate does not exceed 2.0 times that of United States vessels. Congress explicitly stated that these comparability findings must have been made by the end of 1989 in order for tuna imports to have continued. There is no way to implement the will of the legislature when the requisite data regarding 1989 was not even collected from the foreign governments until July 31 of 1990.

On August 28, 1990, Judge Henderson enjoined the Secretary of Treasury from allowing the importation of yellowfin tuna until the Secretary of Commerce had made the requisite comparability findings. The defendants did not appeal, but their subterfuge continued:

> On September 6 the government ostensibly imposed the embargo ordered by the district court. The very next day, however, [it] made the required comparability findings and lifted the embargo for Mexico, despite the fact that Mexico had exceeded the [MMPA] limits. . . .

Judge Henderson granted Earth Island Institute's request for an injunction barring the importation of yellowfin tuna from Mexico, and the Ninth Circuit affirmed.

Mexico responded to the embargo by filing a complaint with the General Agreement on Tariffs and Trades (GATT). A GATT dispute settlement panel concluded that Mexico should prevail, as did a subsequent panel in response to a complaint about the US tuna embargoes from the European Union. Neither decision was adopted by the GATT Council, and thus neither became binding.

The government's final act of recalcitrance in this phase of the tuna–dolphin saga came only a few months after its effort to remove the embargo on Mexican tuna. In addition to Mexico, four other countries — Ecuador, Panama, Vanuatu, and Venezuela — were engaging in purse seine net fishing in the ETP and exporting tuna to the United States. On December 27, 1990, the National Marine Fisheries Service "purported to extend" the 1989 comparability standards for these five nations until May 31, 1991. However, beginning in 1990 the MMPA comparability standard became more strict (going from no more than twice the number of dolphins killed by the US fleet to no more than 1.25 times the number), and only the 1989 finding with respect to Panama satisfied the stricter standard.

In March 1991, Judge Henderson reinforced his August 28, 1990 order with a preliminary injunction prohibiting the importation of tuna from any country that did not satisfy the MMPA comparability requirements, including the 1.25 kill rate. The government did not appeal.

The Tuna Boycott and "Dolphin-Safe" Tuna

As part of its effort to protect sea mammals, Earth Island Institute in 1986 began promoting the boycott of tuna caught with purse seine nets. Undoubtedly, the most compelling support for the boycott came from Samuel LaBudde, a biologist who signed onto a Panamanian purse seine netter as a cook. Using a video camera, LaBudde surreptitiously recorded hundreds of dolphins dying in purse seine nets. With the distribution of his video, the boycott became international. By 1990, Starkist, Chicken-of-the-Sea, and Bumble Bee, the three major US tuna canning companies (and the three largest in the world), agreed to stop dealing in tuna intentionally caught by setting on dolphins with purse seine nets. That same year Congress passed the Dolphin Protection Consumer Information Act (DPCIA), which established the legal standard for the "dolphin safe" label on canned tuna. The label could legally be used only if the tuna were not "harvested using purse seine nets intentionally deployed on or to encircle dolphins."

The boycott, the DPCIA (with its strict requirement for the "dolphin safe" label), and Judge Henderson's rulings enforcing the MMPA all contributed to international awareness of the plight of dolphins and, in turn, to substantial reductions in their needless slaughter. At the same time, these developments inevitably affected and created tensions with countries that had substantial tuna fishing industries but less rigorous laws for protecting dolphins. Embargos and the requirements for obtaining the "dolphin safe" label adversely affected these nations' tuna fisheries.

International Cooperation and International Pressure to Relax the "Dolphin Safe" Standard

With globalization and the increased popularity of free trade in the late 1980s and the 1990s, some individuals and institutions — including the administrations of the first President Bush and President Clinton — focused on international cooperation as the primary vehicle for protecting dolphins. Indeed, even among environmentalists there was a division over the question whether it was preferable to protect dolphins primarily through international cooperation or primarily through strict congressional mandates.

In 1992, the United States and nine other countries became signatories to the La Jolla Agreement, a voluntary accord that established annual dolphin-kill limits for the next seven years (under 5,000 by the end of 1999) and a goal of eventually bringing the kill rate to zero. Three years later, the Declaration of Panama gave the terms of the La Jolla Agreement the status of formal international law.

As a result of lobbying by Mexico and other Latin American countries, the Panama Declaration called for the United States to adopt legislation that would relax the requirements for using the "dolphin safe" label. Tuna caught with purse seine nets set upon dolphins were to be considered "dolphin safe" as long as "no dolphins were observed to be killed or seriously injured during the set."

Congress enacted the International Dolphin conservation Program Act (IDCPA) in 1997 to implement the Panama Declaration. The IDCPA, however, did not immediately change the criteria for the "dolphin safe" label. Congress was concerned that even if there were no observable dolphin deaths or injuries, the psychological stress to dolphins from setting on them with purse seine nets might hinder the recovery of depleted species. To address this possibility, the IDCPA required the Secretary of Commerce to undertake research — including three specifically mandated stress studies — to determine whether the use of purse seine nets was having a "substantial adverse impact on any depleted dolphin stock in the eastern tropical Pacific Ocean." Additionally, Congress ordered the Secretary to make an "initial finding" on the "substantial adverse impact" question by March 31, 1999, and a "final finding" on that question by December 31, 2002. If the Secretary concluded in either finding that purse seine netting had no substantial adverse impact on depleted dolphin stock, the standard for "dolphin-safe" tuna would be that sought by the Panama Declaration: Tuna could receive the "dolphin safe" label as long as the purse seine netting caused no observable death or serious injury. In the meantime, the standard for the "dolphin-safe" tuna label would remain unchanged. Only tuna caught without setting on dolphins with purse seine nets could claim to be "dolphin safe."

The Secretary's Initial Finding

On April 29, 1999, the Secretary of Commerce published his initial finding, concluding that there was insufficient evidence to establish that purse seine fishing was having a substantial adverse impact on depleted dolphin stock. As a result of that finding, the more lax standard for "dolphin-safe" tuna would become effective the following year. However, in response to the Secretary's action, Earth Island Institute, its founder David Brower, and other individuals and environmental groups asked Judge Henderson to overturn the Secretary's initial finding and preserve the original, more strict criterion for the "dolphin safe" label.

Judge Henderson began his analysis of the case by noting that his authority was limited. He could overturn the Secretary's decision only if was "arbitrary, capricious, an abuse of discretion, or otherwise not in accordance with the law" or "without observance of procedure required by law" — a standard that demands giving deference to the Secretary's expertise. Nonetheless, Judge Henderson concluded that the plaintiffs should prevail. The Secretary had not even begun two of the required stress studies, and his finding did not take into account any preliminary data from the third study. Moreover, the available scientific evidence "all pointed in the direction of a significant adverse impact."

Judge Henderson acknowledged that "scientific findings in the area of marine mammal conservation must often of necessity be made on the basis of less than complete or perfect information." However, he continued:

> [T]he Secretary's actions cannot be reconciled with Congress' intent that the initial finding—and any resulting label change—would be informed by preliminary data from the mandated stress research projects. Indeed it would flout the statutory scheme to permit the Secretary to fail to conduct mandated research, and then invoke a lack of evidence as a justification for removing a form of protection for a depleted species, particularly given that the evidence presently available to the Secretary is all suggestive of a significant adverse impact.

The Secretary appealed to the Ninth Circuit, but the Ninth Circuit affirmed Judge Henderson's ruling:

> In urging this court to reverse the district court, the Secretary . . . stress[es] that this case involves international concerns and competing policies for protecting dolphins. That it does, but it is not our role to make policy decisions about . . . dolphin conservation. Such decisions are within Congress's bailiwick, and both the Secretary and this court must defer to congressional intent. . . .

The Secretary's Final Finding

On December 31, 2002, the Secretary made his "final finding." Undeterred by Judge Henderson and the Ninth Circuit, the Secretary—still without the benefit of completed stress tests mandated by congress—concluded that "the chase and intentional deployment on or encirclement of dolphins with purse seine nets is not having a significant adverse impact on depleted dolphin stocks in the [ETP]." Once again, Earth Island Institute asked Judge Henderson to set aside the finding. On April 10, 2003, Judge Henderson issued a preliminary injunction preventing the change in the standard for "dolphin-safe" tuna. A little over a year later, he made the injunction permanent; and in 2007 the Ninth Circuit affirmed that decision. The government decided not to pursue the matter further.

What follows are excerpts first from Judge Henderson's preliminary injunction ruling and then from his permanent injunction opinion. The chapter concludes with Judge Henderson's own tuna fishing story.

The Preliminary Injunction: Earth Island Institute v. Evans, 256 F. Supp. 2d 1064, 1069-1071, 1073-1075 (N.D. Cal. 2003)

As defendants concede, the IDCPA squarely requires the Secretary to make his findings regarding significant adverse impact based solely on the "best available scientific evidence." In [setting aside the initial finding], however, this Court expressed its concern that the Secretary was injecting international trade policy considerations into his decision-making process. The Ninth Circuit also noted that the Secretary . . . had "stress[ed]" "international concerns," but that such concerns were not properly before the Court. While the Secretary has wisely refrained in this case from expressly invoking trade policy concerns as grounds for affirming his final finding, there is little doubt that he has continued to face pressure to consider factors beyond the scientific evidence. Indeed, on December 3, 2002, Secretary of State Colin L. Powell personally wrote the Secretary that "[t]he Department of State has an ongoing interest in this matter because this finding will profoundly affect our role as the lead USG representative to the [International Dolphin Conservation Program]" and encouraged the Secretary to make a finding of no significant adverse impact. . . .

[T]he Secretary concedes that with respect to two of the three mandated research projects, so little was accomplished that they are effectively rendered meaningless. . . .

The Secretary's earlier failure to comply with his congressionally mandated research obligations, and subsequent reliance on a lack of evidence regarding these very research subjects to support his initial finding was troubling in 1999. The continuation of this pattern in 2002 raises a serious question as to whether the Secretary's actions have been influenced by competing factors beyond the scientific evidence, and thus beyond that which Congress intended the Secretary to consider. . . .

In addition, plaintiffs have presented declarations from two scientists who have attested under oath that defendants impeded their scientific research into the effects of the purse seine fishery on dolphins. Dr. Southern also states that her supervisor stated to her that "there's science and there's politics, and the politics dictates what sort of science can be used." While defendants strenuously contest the substance of these declarations, and there is clearly a dispute of fact, the court concludes that they are sufficient, in conjunction with all of the above, to raise a serious question as to the integrity of the decision-making process. . . .

. . . [Judge Henderson then reviewed the available scientific evidence.]

In sum, the *best available* scientific evidence before the Secretary showed that: (1) dolphin stocks were still severely depleted and not recovering as they should in light of low reported death rates, (2) some force was acting to suppress their recovery, (3) adverse indirect effects of the purse seine fishery are probable, and could plausibly account for the failure of the dolphin stocks to recover, and (4) it is *unlikely* that the competing theory — a large-scale change in the ETP ecosystem — explained the failure of the dolphins to recover. Moreover, while the evidence before the Secretary was inconclusive because insufficient research barred population-level inferences, the lack of definitive results is not, as the Ninth Circuit has emphasized, a proper basis for "defaulting" to a finding of "no significant adverse impact" since findings in the area of marine science must often be based on incomplete information. . . .

As the Secretary rightly emphasizes, this is an entirely separate proceeding from that which concerned his initial finding. Nonetheless, certain parallels are striking. As was the case in 1999, the best available evidence before the Secretary, while not conclusive, is "all suggestive of a significant adverse impact." And again, the Secretary's rationale for declining to find a significant adverse impact is largely based on the absence of more conclusive evidence regarding the stress and other effects of the purse seine fishery — although conclusive evidence is not required. Finally, there is again a serious question as to whether the Secretary can justify the lack of progress on the mandated research, and, in this instance, whether research was suppressed. The Secretary has yet to compile the Administrative Record underlying his final finding and thus the Court's conclusions at this point represent no more than a preliminary assessment. Based on this assessment, however, the Court concludes that plaintiffs have demonstrated a likelihood of proving that the Secretary's final finding is contrary to the best available evidence, and thus constitutes an abuse of discretion.

The Permanent Injunction:
Earth Island Institute v. Evans,
2004 W.L. 1774221, 6, 26, 31-32
(N.D. Cal. 2004)

On June 2, 2003, the Secretary filed the massive Administrative Record in this case, which consists of thousands of pages.

. . . [T]he Administrative Record provides compelling corroboration of this Court's preliminary observations in its ruling on Plaintiffs' Motion for Preliminary Injunction. It reflects an agency that (1) continued to drag its feet on conducting critical mandated research, (2) continued to ignore the fact that the best scientific evidence that *was* available, while not conclusive, pointed toward the fishery as the cause of the dolphins' failure to recover as expected, and (3) compromised the integrity of its finding by allowing trade policy considerations to infect the decision-making process. . . .

[Judge Henderson next spent five pages discussing the failure to complete the scientific research and 11 ½ pages reviewing the scientific evidence. Then, in language worthy of Rhett Butler ("Frankly, my dear, I don't give a damn") or Judge Bau ("Mr. Dodd, are you ready to give your closing argument?"), Judge Henderson continued:]

. . . [T]he record is replete with evidence that the Secretary was influenced by policy concerns unrelated to the best available scientific evidence. . . . [T]his Court has never, in its 24 years, reviewed a record of agency action that contained such a compelling portrait of political meddling. . . .

. . . Plaintiffs have amply met their burden of demonstrating that (1) the Secretary's offered explanation for its decision runs counter to the evidence before the agency and (2) the agency relied on facts which Congress did not intend it to consider. Accordingly, the Court finds that the Secretary's final finding is "arbitrary, capricious, an abuse of discretion, or otherwise not in accordance with the law.". . .

"[D]olphin safe" shall continue to mean that "no tuna were caught on the trip in which such tuna were harvested using a purse seine net intentionally deployed on or to encircle dolphins, and that no dolphins were killed or seriously injured during the sets in which the tuna were caught."

Judge Henderson Fishing for Tuna

Judge Henderson tells this story about himself in his *Oral History:*

> Shortly after [the order placing observers on the tuna boats] I went fishing in Cabo San Lucas, and Mort [Cohen] and I used to go down, and we would fish for dolphin, or — I mean [laughter], talk about a Freudian slip! — for marlin. We would catch marlin, and I've never wanted one stuffed on my ceiling, but this particular time it was tuna season. Without really thinking we set out and the guide said, "Well, let's try for some tuna." I said, "Okay, I love tuna," and the next thing I know I said, "Hey, a dolphin!" [laughter] And we sat on the dolphin! I mean, not sat and threw nets, but we followed the dolphin [laughs], and I thought, "Uh-oh, this is getting []eerily like this case!" And threw our lures, the big lure that we threw out there, right in the midst of the dolphin. I said, "I'm not going to do that. What if we catch a dolphin?" The guides, who had been doing . . . this for a

living assured me that dolphin are much too smart to go after this lure, that no dolphin has ever been caught. So we fished among the dolphin. But Mort and I thought, "Oh boy, if this ever gets back to the newspapers [laughter], I'm dead meat!"

The guides were correct. The expedition was dolphin-safe.

Chapter Eleven

Agent Orange

Just as the dolphin cases forced Judge Henderson to deal with the reluctance of the federal government to enforce environmental laws, Nehmer v. United States Department of Veterans Affairs has required Judge Henderson to address multiple failures of the Department of Veterans Affairs (VA) to meet its obligations to veterans of the Vietnam War. As Ninth Circuit Judge Stephen Reinhardt wrote in an opinion affirming one of Judge Henderson's orders in *Nehmer*, "It is a disturbing story, and the performance of the . . . VA has contributed substantially to our sense of national shame." But for Judge Henderson's persistence, the story would be even more disturbing.

Background

During its war effort in the 1960s and early 1970s, the US government sprayed Vietnam with nearly nineteen million gallons of the defoliant, Agent Orange. In addition to destroying crops and a lush jungle-like terrain, Agent Orange — which contains highly toxic dioxin — inflicted injuries on the people of Vietnam and on American military personnel. Those injuries and the concomitant suffering have extended far beyond the end of the war. Agent Orange has been associated with birth defects, various cancers, and immunological diseases.

As of October 1, 1983, over 9,000 Vietnam veterans with a diagnosed disability that they alleged was based on exposure to Agent Orange had filed claims with the VA. The VA, however, recognized only one disease — chloracne, a skin cancer — as arising from Agent Orange. As a result, the VA had rejected nearly 8,000 of the 9,170 claims on the ground that the established diseases were not "service connected."

In 1984, the manufacturers of Agent Orange reached a $180,000,000 settlement with service members and their families who claimed injuries from their exposure to Agent Orange. Although $180,000,000 may at first blush seem large, it resulted in maximum individual payments of only slightly more than $10,000. The vast majority of claimants received substantially less.

Causation had been an issue from the outset in all claims for compensation based on exposure to Agent Orange. For many veterans, it was difficult to establish the extent to which they came into contact with Agent Orange and its critical toxic agent, dioxin. This problem was exacerbated because various manufacturers used differing amounts of dioxin in their Agent Orange brews, and the government mixed batches from various manufacturers indiscriminately. Even if exposure in Vietnam could be established, there was the greater problem of showing that a particular veteran's disease was caused by that exposure rather than by exposure to dioxin at some other time or by some factor (e.g., genetic abnormality) unrelated to dioxin.

Mounting evidence demonstrated a statistical correlation between Agent Orange and various diseases, but it was virtually impossible *in a particular case* to rule out alternative causes or even to establish that dioxin exposure in Vietnam merely aggravated a disease. Indeed, the difficulty of proving causation was one of the important reasons given by Federal District Judge Jack Weinstein for approving the settlement in the suit against the manufacturers of Agent Orange: If the case had proceeded to trial and if the plaintiffs had prevailed, the defendants would have been liable for billions of dollars. However, according to Judge Weinstein, "the scientific data available to date make it highly unlikely that, except perhaps for those who have or have had chloracne, any plaintiff could legally prove any causal relationship between Agent Orange and any other injury, including birth defects."

The same year that Agent Orange manufacturers agreed to settle claims against them for $180,000,000, Congress enacted the Veterans' Dioxin and Radiation Exposure Compensation Standards Act (Dioxin Act). This statute "dramatically alter[ed]" the manner in which the VA was to deal with Agent Orange claims. The new law directed the VA to institute a rule-making process with a panel of experts for the purpose of identifying diseases sufficiently associated with Agent Orange to be regarded as service connected. Once such a disease was so identified, a veteran with that disease and exposure to Agent Orange in Vietnam could receive benefits without independent proof that the disease was service connected.

After completing its rule-making process, the VA issued a regulation in August 1984 that essentially reaffirmed its earlier position: Only one disease, chloracne, would be regarded as service connected for the purposes of the Dioxin Act. In theory, veterans were free to establish in individual cases that other diseases were caused by exposure to Agent Orange in Vietnam and were, therefore, service connected. However, by December 1987, the VA had relied on its August 1984 regulation to deny over 31,000 applications for veterans' benefits.

Causation and the Dioxin Act

In February 1987, veterans filed a class action challenging the VA's interpretation of the Dioxin Act. Twenty-seven months later, Judge Henderson, to whom the case was assigned, rejected most of the plaintiff's claims; however, he ruled in their favor on two critical issues relating to causation.

The first issue was whether the VA used the correct standard for determining whether a disease should be regarded as service connected. As Judge Henderson, quoting both plaintiffs' and defendant's expert witnesses, explained:

> Plaintiffs . . . argue that the VA erred by requiring proof of a "cause and effect" relationship between dioxin exposure and various diseases. Plaintiffs contend that Congress intended only that there be a significant "statistical association" between dioxin and a particular disease in order to grant service connection for that disease.
>
> . . . A statistical association "means that the observed coincidence in variations between exposure to the toxic substance and the adverse health effects is unlikely to be a chance occurrence or happenstance." The cause and effect relationship "describes a much stronger relationship between exposure to a particular toxic substance and the development of a particular disease than 'statistically significant association' does. . . . [I]t is often not possible, based on the sound scientific and medical evidence that currently exists, to demonstrate that there is a cause and effect relationship" between human exposure and disease, because of "society's aversions to experimentation on humans."

Judge Henderson made clear that there is nothing inherently arbitrary or unscientific about the VA's use of the "cause and effect" standard. Rather, the question before him was simply one of statutory interpretation: Did the Dioxin Act mandate the "cause and effect" standard, as the VA claimed; or did it mandate the more relaxed "statistical association" standard, as the plaintiffs claimed?

Judge Henderson acknowledged that the statutory language was "at best ambiguous"; however, he concluded that statements of senators and congressmen about their understanding of the legislation "overwhelmingly suggested" that Congress intended for the VA to apply the "statistical association" test. In addition, Judge Henderson pointed out that use of "statistical association" was consistent with prior VA practices; and he discerned no reason for Congress to have opted for a more rigorous standard in this case. Indeed, the defendants had admitted that "Congress intended the VA to act in accordance with prior principles and procedure."

The second causation issue involved application of the VA's "benefit of the doubt" policy. In individual adjudications, the VA would give the benefit of the doubt to claimants when "there is an approximate balance of positive and negative evidence regarding the merits of an issue." The VA, however, admittedly had not applied this policy in determining which diseases were service connected for the purposes of the Dioxin Act.

Relying once again on traditional tools of statutory construction, Judge Henderson held that the VA had erred in not applying the "benefit of a doubt" policy to its rule-making process for establishing service connected diseases.

He then concluded:

> These errors compounded one another, as they increased both the *type* and the *level* of proof needed for veterans to prevail during the rulemaking proceedings. We find that these errors . . . sharply tipped the scales against veteran claimants. . . . [T]here is a substantial possibility that the errors shaped the conclusions reached by the Advisory Committee and the Administrator. Accordingly, we hereby invalidate the portion of the Dioxin regulation which denies service connection for all other diseases but chloracne. We also void all benefit denials made under section 311(d) [the regulation finding only chloracne to be service related], and remand this matter to the Advisory Committee and the VA for further proceedings not inconsistent with this opinion.

Settlement and the Agent Orange Act

Within a week of Judge Henderson's decision, Edward Derwinski, the newly appointed Secretary of the VA, announced that the government would not appeal. Instead, in what the *Washington Post* characterized as a "sharp reversal in position," the VA committed itself to issuing new regulations and to reexamining previously denied claims.

In early 1991, Congress passed the Agent Orange Act, which called for new rule making to determine what diseases associated with Agent Orange are service connected. A few months later, Judge Henderson approved and incorporated into a "Stipulation and Order" an agreement reached between the parties in *Nehmer*. The agreement, consistent with the Agent Orange Act and Judge Henderson's 1989 order, required new rule making to determine what diseases are service connected, and it required the VA to reconsider claims voided by the 1989 order "if and when the VA issues new Agent Orange regulations service-connecting diseases other than chloracne." Payment of benefits was to be retroactive to the date on which the claim was filed

Between 1990 and 1996, the VA, pursuant to its rule making, found that a number of cancers were linked to Agent Orange and, therefore, entitled to service connected status.

Parsing the Settlement Agreement and Retroactivity Issues

The VA's apparent willingness to comply with Judge Henderson's order belied a bureaucratic intransigence that required ongoing judicial oversight. First, the VA took a narrow, unprecedented view of what prior claims it had to reopen. Second, the VA refused to pay retroactive benefits to some Vietnam veterans who suffered from lung cancer even though the VA had recognized lung cancer as service connected. Third, the VA attempted to limit the amount of retroactive benefits paid to the estates of deceased veterans. Fourth, after declaring chronic lymphocytic leukemia (CLL) to be service connected in 2003, the VA refused to readjudicate prior claims based on that disease and to pay retroactive benefits. Finally, the VA argued that by its own regulation it had divested Judge Henderson of the authority to interpret his 1991 Stipulation and Order.

In each of these instances, the VA based its position on a narrow parsing of language in the settlement agreement and various statutes. In each instance, Judge Henderson disagreed; and when the VA appealed, the Ninth Circuit affirmed Judge Henderson's rulings.

More Recalcitrance, a Threat of Contempt, and Improved Compliance

The VA's position with respect to chronic lymphocytic leukemia (CLL) was a continuing concern. In April 2006, after holding that veterans with CLL were entitled to retroactive benefits, Judge Henderson ordered the VA "to begin processing the CLL claims immediately, and to 'act in good faith to use all resources at their disposal to perform the tasks [identified in the order] as quickly as possible.'" Thereafter, Judge Henderson attempted to monitor the VA's progress through "telephonic and in-court status conferences and related status statements." As Judge Henderson elaborated:

> [T]he Court has attempted to work with the parties to establish an orderly and fair procedure to ensure reasonably prompt payment to *Nehmer* class

members with CLL claims. The Court has endeavored to do so within the existing resource and personnel capacities of the VA. Most recently, the Court issued an order on March 29, 2007, requiring that defendant provide certain detailed information about the pace and progress of its efforts to process *Nehmer*-related CLL claims. The Court expressed particular concern that the pace of defendant's efforts had slowed dramatically at the end of 2006 and early 2007. The Court notified defendant in that order that the disintegration of the VA's claims process was a blatant violation of the Court's past orders and the prior representations made by defendant.

Despite this admonition, the VA had no reasonable explanation for the decline in processing claims. Moreover, the VA actually misrepresented its progress to the court by double- and triple-counting claims. Judge Henderson explained:

> Throughout this process, the Court has periodically required defendant to produce data showing "the rate at which CLL claims are being processed to completion by the Philadelphia Resource Center [(PRC)]." Defendant has responded by submitting the number of draft decisions that have been completed per month, pending final review by the central office in Washington, D.C. The Court has always had the understanding, which it has expressed repeatedly without correction by defendant, that this data showed the rate of processing claims to completion at the PRC level, and that progress toward the goal of completing all CLL claims . . . could be accurately measured by the number of completed draft decisions. It was not until the most recent filings that the Court came to understand that the data actually counts some claims multiple times. It appears that every time the central office returns a file to the PRC for correction, it is counted as a new draft decision for the PRC to process. Thus, for example, when a single claim is completed at the PRC it is counted once as a completed draft decision; when it is returned and corrected, it is counted again as a completed draft decision; and it may be returned even further times, being counted again and again. This appears to have occurred for several hundred draft decisions. . . . Thus, defendant has made it appear for months that it has been making faster progress than in actuality.

Judge Henderson issued an order to show cause why the VA should not be held in contempt for violating the court's orders.

The threat of contempt shook the VA out of its bureaucratic malaise. The VA promised and then followed through on its promise to process CLL claims even more rapidly than it had prior to the 2006–2007 slowdown. Judge Henderson decided to forego a contempt citation and instead issued new orders reinforcing his previous rulings.

New Service Connected Diseases

In 2010, the VA listed Parkinson's disease, chronic B-cell leukemias, and ischemic heart disease as related to Agent Orange. At the same time, the VA initiated a fast-track system for processing new claims. Nonetheless, anecdotal evidence suggests that some veterans who apply for Agent Orange benefits still experience long delays. Judge Henderson, however, has received no new complaints. His Agent Orange saga has probably ended.

Chapter Twelve

Unshackled:
The Johnny Spain Case

On some occasions, resolving a case on technical, procedural grounds in order to avoid a ruling on the merits of a controversy may constitute the wise exercise of judicial discretion. Other times, however, searching for procedural reasons to avoid facing difficult or potentially unpopular substantive decisions can both distort procedural doctrine and work a substantial injustice to litigants.

Judge Henderson has always been sensitive to the value of procedural regularity; but when a case is ripe for a judgment on the merits, he has never backed away from making hard or controversial decisions. A good example of both of these aspects of Judge Henderson's approach to judicial decision making is the case of Johnny Spain, a former member of the Black Panther Party. Spain had been convicted of murder twice in California state courts — once as a teenager and a second time when he was in prison serving a life sentence for the first murder.

In 1981, Spain filed a petition for a writ of habeas corpus challenging his second conviction. The case was assigned to Judge Henderson, whose concern with procedural regularity led him initially to dismiss it. Federal law requires that state courts have a full opportunity to resolve the issues raised in a federal habeas corpus petition before a federal court rules on the merits of those claims; and Judge Henderson believed there was a question whether Spain had complied with this mandate. Spain's attorney initially wondered whether Judge Henderson was trying to duck a controversial case, but the judge was merely being cautious. Any potential decision in Spain's favor would be at risk of being reversed if the Ninth Circuit or the Supreme Court held that Spain had not "exhausted" his state remedies.

Once the state Supreme Court refused to give further consideration to the issues, Spain refiled his habeas petition, and Judge Henderson addressed its merits. As is typical with habeas petitions, Spain's claims did not directly raise the question of guilt or innocence. Rather, they challenged the fundamental fairness of the trial process that led to his conviction. Nonetheless, Judge Henderson's willingness to take Spain's petition seriously resulted in the undoing of a conviction that was not only procedurally flawed but factually suspect.[1] And as a consequence of that decision, Judge Henderson contributed to the possibility that Johnny Spain — who had never seen even one day of freedom as an adult — would, after over twenty years of self-education, introspection, and often inhumane treatment, be given an opportunity to lead a productive life.

For Judge Henderson, Johnny Spain's case was in the most important sense elegantly simple and straightforward:

> [It is the court's] duty to protect and vindicate individual rights and the constitutional guarantees that ensure our ultimate freedom.... [T]his court's only role is to examine whether the individual petitioner, Johnny L. Spain, received his constitutional rights . . . during the trial that resulted in his conviction on two counts of murder and on conspiracy to escape.

Thus, Judge Henderson expressed great umbrage when one of the state's lawyers suggested that a decision in Spain's favor would be fostering crime. Nonetheless, as Judge Henderson understood, the Johnny Spain case evoked strong feelings:

> [P]etitioner's pre-trial and trial proceedings [leading to the second conviction in 1976] took place during extremely trying times. They were times of great passion over politics and social conditions, sometimes leading to the use of unlawful violence in pursuit of political ends.

Much of that passion had to do with Johnny Spain's membership in the Black Panther Party and his close relationship with prison radical and fellow Black Panther inmate, George Jackson.

---

1. Judge Henderson might never have had this opportunity were it not for the persistence and self-sacrifice of Dennis Riordan. Now recognized as one of the leading appellate criminal lawyers in California, Riorden was a recent law school graduate when he helped Charles Garry defend Johnny Spain during his second murder trial. For the next fourteen years, Riordan was Spain's primary appellate attorney, pursuing the case in both state and federal courts and before California parole officials. He devoted hundreds of unpaid hours to Spain's cause; and when Judge Henderson set the bail for Spain's ultimate release, Riordan signed a personal security bond to help meet the bail requirements.

Becoming Johnny Spain

Johnny Spain was born Larry Armstrong in Jackson, Mississippi in 1949. His father was a black man, and his mother was a white married woman, whose white husband initially thought he was the father and accepted Larry into the Armstrong family. By the time that Larry was ready to begin school, his physical features suggested his mixed-race heritage. Although the Supreme Court had already decided Brown v. Board of Education, Larry's fitting in at the all white neighborhood school would have been difficult. Moreover, and of greater concern for Mrs. Armstrong, white students had begun to harass Larry; the family had received threatening messages from the Ku Klux Klan; and a cross had been burned on their front lawn. Emmett Till, a black fourteen-year-old from Chicago, had recently been kidnapped and murdered in nearby Money, Mississippi. Till's "crime" was allegedly whistling at a white woman.

To avoid the danger and difficulty of trying to raise Larry in Jackson, the Armstrongs — without ever talking to Larry about race — arranged for him to become Johnny Larry Spain, the foster son of Helen and John Spain, who were black and lived in Los Angeles. Despite his athletic prowess, his better than average grades in school, and his new family's efforts to demonstrate their love, Johnny Spain had a troubled youth in California. He felt abandoned by his Mississippi family; he ran away; he associated with gangs; he fought; he stole; and when he was only seventeen, he fatally shot a man during a street-corner robbery. He received a life sentence on May 5, 1967.

The Black Panthers, George Jackson, and Johnny Spain

The Black Panther Party was cofounded in Oakland, California, in1966 by Huey Newton and Bobby Seale. The Panthers had a ten-point plan that included calls for full employment, decent housing and education, and freedom from incarceration "for all black and oppressed people." They provided free medical clinics, and a free children's breakfast program that began in San Francisco and spread across the nation. More famously outside the black community, they openly carried loaded firearms and demanded the right to self-defense. Their peaceful but armed march through the California legislature in the spring of 1967 to protest proposed gun-control legislation brought them national publicity. Over the next several years a number of police officers and Panthers were injured, sometimes fatally, in violent interactions. FBI Director J. Edgar Hoover called the Black Panther Party the country's "greatest threat to internal security."

For Hoover, however, the threat seemed to stem less from openly bearing arms or proclaiming a right to self-defense than from the free children's breakfast program, which was a powerful community-organizing tool.

The Panthers' radical views and actions gained the attention of George Jackson, a charismatic prisoner, who was serving a one year to life sentence for a 1960 gas station robbery that netted $71. Through his protests and writing, Jackson sought to call attention to and improve the lot of black inmates. He joined the Black Panther Party and recruited Johnny Spain to become a member when the two of them met in Soledad State Prison in 1969.

In January 1970, three inmates, including Jackson's close friend and fellow radical, W. L. Nolen, were killed in the prison yard. Officials claimed that they were trying to quell a racial disturbance. Three days later, a guard was murdered in what appeared to be a retaliatory action. George Jackson, Fleeta Drumgo, and John Clutchette — who became known as the Soledad Brothers — were charged with the homicide. Their case gained national notoriety, as many questioned whether the charges were legitimate or whether Jackson and his codefendants had been selected for prosecution because of their prison activism.

Jackson was transferred to San Quentin to await his trial, and some months later Johnny Spain was transferred to the cell adjoining Jackson's. They spent many hours discussing radical political philosophy.

In August 1970, George Jackson's younger brother, Jonathan, made a daring but ill-fated effort to secure his sibling's release. With two accomplices, Jonathan broke into a Marin County courtroom during a trial and kidnapped the judge and several jurors at gunpoint. His plan was to exchange them for George's freedom; but Jonathan, the judge, and two others were killed in a shoot-out with the police during the escape attempt. Political activist and university professor Angela Davis, a supporter of the Soledad Brothers, was the owner of a shotgun used in the kidnapping attempt. As a result, she was charged with conspiracy, kidnapping, and murder. At her trial she was acquitted of all charges.

On August 21, 1971, only two days before George Jackson's trial was to begin, he, two other inmates, and three guards were killed in what appeared to be an escape attempt orchestrated by Jackson. Bob Dylan memorialized Jackson's death with a song that included these lyrics:

> I woke up this mornin',/There were tears on my bed./They killed a man I really loved/Shot him through the head./Lord, Lord,/They cut George Jackson down./Lord, Lord,/They laid him in the ground.

The events of that day — and particularly what instigated the violence — will always remain obscure. Was Jackson the victim of dissension within the Black Panther Party? Were prison guards or other state actors involved in a conspiracy to ensure that Jackson would not go to trial and possibly be acquitted on the charge of murdering the Soledad guard? (Fleeta Drumgo and John

Clutchette, the two remaining Soledad Brothers, were both subsequently acquitted in their murder trials.) Had Jackson in fact planned to escape? Did his lawyer, as the state claimed, smuggle into the prison a gun that Jackson tried to conceal in an Afro wig?

Stephen Bingham, the attorney who allegedly smuggled the gun to George Jackson, initially fled the jurisdiction. Later, he was tried and acquitted of all charges relating to the San Quentin incident.

Whatever happened on the day of George Jackson's death, Johnny Spain became one of the "San Quentin Six," charged with murder and conspiracy. Of the six, only Spain was a member of the Black Panther Party, and only Spain was convicted of murder. Three of Spain's codefendants were acquitted, and two others were convicted of assaults. The prosecutors conceded that Spain did not actually kill the guards of whose murders he was convicted. Rather, his convictions were based on his alleged involvement with George Jackson in a conspiracy.

Habeas Corpus

After failing to prevail on his state court appeals, Johnny Spain filed a habeas corpus petition in federal district court. His petition offered two grounds for overturning the San Quentin Six convictions. First, the trial judge had engaged in private discussions with a potentially biased juror without informing the defendant of either the potential bias or the communications. Second, Spain was heavily shackled throughout the proceedings. As a result, he alleged, he could not fully participate in his defense. Spain's attorney thought the first ground for relief was so compelling that he considered not even pursuing the second claim.

When Judge Henderson received the case, he initially made his decision — as most judges would have — on the basis of the briefs and the arguments of counsel. The juror communication issue seemed straightforward to him, as well. Indeed, the state appellate court had conceded that the trial judge had acted unconstitutionally; and there were ample facts and precedent for concluding, as Judge Henderson did, that the error was not harmless. Thus, Judge Henderson granted Spain's writ of habeas corpus because of the unconstitutional *ex parte* communication between the trial judge and the juror. At the conclusion of his opinion, Judge Henderson noted that his holding made it unnecessary to address the question whether Johnny Spain's shackling claim had merit.

The Ninth Circuit affirmed Judge Henderson's ruling. However, the Supreme Court, in a decision that both misrepresented the facts and took a newly expansive, albeit supportable, view of the harmless error doctrine, reversed. As a result, the case was returned to Judge Henderson for resolution of the shackling issue.

At that point, many judges would probably have done what Judge Henderson did the first time — rely on the record, the briefs, and the oral argument to render a decision. There was much in the record to draw upon: It contained photographs of the shackles, which included leg irons, a waist chain to which each arm was secured by individual chains, and chains that held Spain in his chair; proof that Spain had worn the chains almost daily for nearly six years — four years of pretrial proceedings and seventeen months of trial; Spain's repeated complaints about the pain from the chains and even his asking to be excused from the courtroom on several occasions because of the pain; and medical recommendations (which were ignored) that the chains be removed for trial. In short, there was compelling evidence of pain and seemingly inappropriate brutalization.

On the other hand, Spain had interrupted the pretrial proceedings on several occasions. However, most of the concerns about the risks that Spain posed to safety in the courtroom were a matter of guilt by association stemming from Spain's membership in the Black Panther Party. The Party's most popular slogan was "Off the pigs" (i.e., kill the police); various Panther members, including Party founder, Huey Newton, had been involved in shoot-outs with the police; and Jonathan Jackson's failed kidnapping attempt had occurred in the same courtroom where the San Quentin Six were tried.

On the face of the record Judge Henderson found that the shackling was unconstitutional. But was the shackling perhaps harmless error? What impact did it actually have on Spain's ability to assist with his defense? To what extent were his complaints perhaps exaggerated? Judge Henderson was not willing to speculate. Instead, he called for an evidentiary hearing, which was conducted by Magistrate Judge Joan Brennan, a former federal prosecutor.

Judge Brennan reviewed medical reports, including Spain's medical history; and she heard testimony from witnesses, including Spain, his attorney, and two psychological experts. Spain's testimony alone covered over 100 pages. The magistrate's findings contained a detailed analysis of the type, number, and weight (twenty-five pounds) of the chains and a careful assessment of the witnesses' credibility. Her findings included the following:

> There were seven to eight inches of chain between each of Spain's handcuffs and his waist chain. In order to write while chained, Spain had to reach out and up from his waist chain. Because his handcuff was connected to the waist chain, such movement would dig the waist chain into the side of his waist opposite the writing hand. The same dynamic occurred when Spain tried to scratch his nose or ear.
>
> The chains caused pain in Spain's wrists, around his ankles and waist. He resorted to wearing ace bandages under the handcuffs, but the bandages

in turn caused circulation problems. The waist chain rubbed his waist "almost raw." The padlocks used to connect the handcuffs and neck chain to the waist chain[, according to Spain,] "would bear into my back with every movement of the chain."

The evidence before us clearly establishes that the shackling preoccupied Spain during the trial. The record is replete with contemporaneous statements to this effect. [For example,] in a [1975] declaration [accompanying a] . . . petition to have the shackles removed, Spain stated, "I am in constant pain and discomfort. After sitting in the stationary manner for a period of twenty minutes, I am just beside myself. I get exasperated and cannot concentrate. . . . These shackles and chains must be removed. I cannot endure the pain. If I were permitted to stand up and move my body for a moment or two every fifteen or twenty minutes, then I could endure the trial."

. . .

Spain's preoccupation with shackling had a direct impact on his ability to cooperate with counsel in his defense since he occasionally directed his outrage at the chains toward his counsel . . . in the form of resentment that [Charles] Garry was not doing enough to secure Spain's release from the chains. This exasperated an already difficult situation. Spain's conferences with his attorney were limited to three locations: the courtroom, the holding cell behind the courtroom (where Spain was connected to the "elephant chain"), or the visiting room at San Quentin (where no personal contact was allowed, and the posting of a guard interfered with the confidentiality of the conference). In all these locations, Spain was chained. Garry never saw Spain out of chains.

. . . Garry's statement that "more than three-quarters of . . . [their time together] was [spent] talking about how he was being treated . . . how degraded he felt [when he walked into the courtroom]" is probably close to the truth. . . . [I]t is clear that the chains were a significant factor inhibiting Spain's ability to cooperate with his counsel. . . .

Since the chains had a significant impact on [Spain's] ability to cooperate with counsel, it follows that they inhibited his counsel's ability to prepare him to testify. . . . Spain had the right to make an intelligent and informed choice whether to take the stand in his own defense. By grossly interfering with his ability to cooperate with counsel in preparing to take the stand the shackling significantly affected Spain's choice not to testify.

Judge Henderson adopted Judge Brennan's findings and incorporated them into his opinion granting Spain's writ of habeas corpus. The Ninth Circuit affirmed, and the Supreme Court declined further review.

Eventual Release

As virtually every case discussed in this book illustrates, the wheels of justice typically move slowly. And so it was for Johnny Spain. Judge Henderson's second order overturning Spain's San Quentin Six murder conviction was issued in September, 1986. Spain, however, remained incarcerated for another eighteen months. The state had the right to appeal Judge Henderson's decision; and if it lost, as it did, the state had the option to retry Spain on the original charges. There was no automatic right to release pending these actions. Moreover, Judge Henderson's decision had no impact on the life sentence for Spain's first murder conviction. It is important to note, however, that a "life" sentence rarely lasts for life, and that was especially true in California before the state enacted tougher sentencing laws in the 1990s. By the time Johnny Spain was convicted the second time, he had already served more time than many murderers serve.

After rejecting Spain's request for parole twice in 1986, the parole board announced that one of its panels would consider a new request for parole in February 1988. Judge Henderson issued an order directing the panel to disregard the San Quentin Six conviction in making its decision.

Spain had become a model prisoner in the years following the San Quentin Six trial; and as a result, an unprecedented number of guards and other prison officials supported his 1988 request for parole, as they had in 1986. Nonetheless, only two of the three panel members voted in Spain's favor, and their decision was only that he should be released sometime within the next two years.

The following month a California state judge ruled that the parole authorities had miscalculated Spain's eligibility for parole and that he was entitled to immediate release from confinement for the initial murder conviction. The next day, after Spain posted bail to assure his presence at any retrial on the San Quentin Six charges, Judge Henderson ordered his release. Johnny Spain was finally a free man — a status that became permanent after the Ninth Circuit's affirmance of Judge Henderson's ruling, the state's decision not to pursue a reprosecution, and the parole board's eventual conclusion that Spain did not require further imprisonment.

Since his release, Johnny Spain — whom his attorney, Dennis Riorden, has described as "very smart," "charismatic," and while incarcerated "probably the best athlete in the California prison system" — has pursued a variety of interests that reflect those traits. For example, he helped to teach a popular course on prisons at Stanford University; and he has been a high school athletic director. Life has sometimes been difficult, but Johnny Spain has stayed out of prison — now for a longer time than his period of incarceration.

Doors

Unless there is an evidentiary hearing at which the prisoner testifies, judges deciding habeas corpus cases typically do not have an occasion to meet the petitioners. There was such a hearing in Johnny Spain's case; but because it took place before Magistrate Judge Brennan, Judge Henderson never had any contact with Spain during the time of his incarceration.

Once Johnny Spain was released from prison, Dennis Riordan, several times asked if his client could meet the judge. To avoid any appearance of bias or impropriety, Judge Henderson deferred Riordan's request until after the habeas corpus decision had been affirmed. At that point, the meeting occurred. Judge Henderson asked Johnny Spain what was the biggest change now that he was free. "Doors," Spain responded. Opening and closing doors — something he had not been permitted to do for himself for nearly twenty-one years.

Institutional Reform Litigation and the Limits of Judicial Power: California Prisons and an East Palo Alto School District

Chapter Thirteen

Institutional Reform Litigation

A traditional lawsuit typically pits a single plaintiff against a single defendant with the former seeking either money damages or an injunction against a particular practice. By contrast, institutional reform litigation involves a group or class of plaintiffs who may seek similar relief but whose primary focus is broad-ranging reform of an institution's day-to-day practices. For example, the school desegregation cases sought to bring a fundamental change in the manner in which school districts dealt with the educational needs of their students. Similarly, the goal of Judge Henderson's prisoners' rights cases (Chapters Fifteen–Seventeen) is to prevent future prisoner abuse and neglect by changing the underlying culture that led to the need for judicial intervention in the first place; and in his East Palo Alto special education case (Chapter Eighteen), the ultimate objective is for the school district to institutionalize changes that will lead to compliance with federal protections for children with disabilities. Because defendants in these types of cases have their own entrenched bureaucratic values and practices, the task is invariably difficult. This chapter first discusses the limited ability that courts have to enforce their mandates. The chapter then turns to a consideration of strategies and techniques that courts may use in trying to bring about institutional change.

The Least Equal Branch

The federal judiciary—along with the executive and congress—is one of the three supposedly coequal branches of the national government. In many respects, though, the judiciary is the weakest of the three. Unlike the executive, the judiciary has no armies or law enforcement agencies to compel litigants to comply with its decisions; and unlike congress, the judiciary has no power to tax and to spend revenues to ensure that its orders are obeyed.

To be sure, the judiciary is not completely impotent. Using the contempt power to punish disobedience or to coerce compliance with court orders, imposing sanctions against lawyers and litigants who abuse the judicial process, awarding attorneys' fees to a prevailing party, and appointing monitors to oversee or receivers to carry out court orders can be effective enforcement tools. Moreover, courts can typically rely on the cooperation of other branches of government for appropriating funds, executing warrants, and performing other routine tasks essential to the effective operation of the judiciary. Finally, the very power to declare a law unenforceable — or to validate its legitimacy by upholding it against, for example, claims of unconstitutionality — can have wide-ranging consequences.

Nonetheless, compliance with judicial mandates depends to a substantial extent upon the willingness of losing litigants and others to obey court decisions; and this, in turn, is part of the reason why it is important for courts to provide reasoned bases for their rulings: The primary power of the judiciary stems from the respect that it engenders in the rest of society, a respect that must be strong enough for people to submit to its authority even when they believe a case is wrongly decided.

Consider, for example, Bush v. Gore, the Supreme Court's decision awarding the 2000 presidential election to George Bush. Many individuals — lay people and legal experts alike — disagreed with the Court's reasoning, its decision to inject itself into the political process, and its ultimate result. However, the nation accepted the decision in large measure because the Supreme Court over the decades had established its fundamental legitimacy through its process of reasoned decision making. Had that not been the case, imagine the turmoil that might have followed the Court's ruling. Who would have intervened if Florida election officials had decided to ignore the Supreme Court and proceed with their recount? And if Al Gore won the recount and claimed the presidency, what should the Electoral College have done? If both Bush and Gore demanded to be sworn in as president of the United States, who would have mediated that dispute? Would our country have been on the verge of a second civil war?

In all likelihood, cooler heads would have prevailed at some point in the process; and the presidential election would have been resolved without resort to force. Moreover, the Supreme Court could have played a role, for example, by ordering the recount to stop and threatening voting officials with contempt. Ultimately, though, in the absence of voluntary compliance, the Court would have had to depend upon police agencies and other nonjudicial actors to carry out its wishes.

This is not to say, of course, that obedience to judicial authority, including Supreme Court mandates, has always been a reality — a matter to be discussed shortly. Nor is it to say that respect and voluntary compliance play no role in the ease with which other branches of government can carry out their missions.

Rather, the point is that because the judiciary's enforcement tools are so minimal compared to the powers that the other branches of government can exercise, the judiciary is necessarily more dependent upon good will and voluntary compliance than is either the executive or the legislature.

In some respects, the relative weakness of the judiciary may be an asset to the proper functioning of our federal system. Unlike presidents and legislators, federal judges are appointed, not elected; and federal judges' appointments are for "good behavior" — that is for life, in the absence of impeachment or retirement. In short, the federal judiciary is a profoundly nondemocratic institution. Furthermore, despite efforts to diversify the federal bench in terms of race and gender, there is a pervasive elitism among federal judges. For example, until very recently, they have been overwhelmingly white males; they are relatively wealthy, politically well connected, and professionally successful; and they are often graduates of the most prestigious schools. This elitism tends to give judges a shared vision of the world that on occasion may be quite narrow. Recall, for example, Judge Henderson's story about his fellow judge who found unbelievable the testimony about racial epithets scrawled on the walls in a workplace restroom. Finally, in times of sharp ideological tensions in the other branches of government, judicial appointments sometimes reflect the extreme positions of whichever political party happens to be in power. (This last factor, of course, may cut against the concern with sameness inherent in judges' elitism — but not in a very satisfactory way.) So, for all of these reasons — lack of political accountability, perhaps narrow-minded elitism, and sometimes extremist views, it is arguably desirable that judges derive their power almost exclusively from the good will and voluntary compliance that they engender with their reasoned decision making. And as a result of this need for acceptability, judicial decisions tend not to stray from the mainstream. In other words, the need for the judiciary to maintain credibility with the people acts as a check on judicial power just as electability is a check on the actions of presidents and legislators.

Limited ability to ensure obedience to judicial mandates, however, is not always a virtue. One obligation of federal courts is to enforce statutes and constitutional guarantees that protect the weak, the unpopular, the disadvantaged, and the politically powerless — for example, neo-Nazis wanting to express their First Amendment rights to free speech by marching though a predominantly Jewish community, women and minorities seeking equal rights in the workplace, or criminal defendants seeking to exclude from evidence an unconstitutionally obtained confession. When a court is cast in this role, its decisions upholding claims for relief are occasionally wildly unpopular and often decidedly nonmajoritarian in the sense that they are designed to benefit directly only a small portion of the population, sometimes in direct defiance of the majority's expressed desire. In these cases, courts' dependence upon the good will and voluntary compliance of the people is crucial but sometimes lacking.

There may be an outright refusal to obey a judicial command or, in some situations, efforts to undermine a holding by interpreting it narrowly and developing exceptions that tend to swallow the rule. A court may be able to alleviate the latter problem by issuing subsequent rulings that reinforce and broaden its initial decision, but it is virtually powerless in the face of widespread or persistent resistance to its commands.

A good example of both the value of reinforcing decisions and the futility of effectively overcoming committed resistance is Brown v. Board of Education and its progeny.

Brown's 1954 declaration that segregated schools are inherently unequal and the Court's 1955 order that desegregation must proceed "with all deliberate speed," met stiff resistance from all levels of government. Even federal judges in the South, with a few notable exceptions, initially used what power they had to thwart rather than further *Brown's* command. For example, in 1956, the Fourth Circuit rejected a constitutional challenge to a North Carolina pupil placement law, which gave school officials discretion to assign pupils to particular schools on the basis of facially nonracial criteria. The criteria for placement were vague, and there was a cumbersome administrative process for aggrieved black students and their parents who wanted to challenge placement decisions. As a result, the law (like other pupil placement laws throughout the South) was effective in maintaining a pattern of segregated schools. The previous year, Federal District Judge Joe Estes had rejected the claim that black students in Mansfield, Texas were entitled to attend the only high school in the district. According to the court, the school district's representation that it was carefully studying how to proceed with integration and its offer to provide transportation (which previously had been the responsibility of the students and their families) to an all black school twenty miles away in Fort Forth constituted sufficient compliance with *Brown.*[1]

In 1956, the vast majority of senators and house members from the eleven states of the Confederacy signed the Southern Manifesto, which "commend[ed] the motives of those states which have declared the intention to resist forced integration by any lawful means." The Manifesto characterized *Brown* as an "unwarranted" decision made by justices who, "with no legal basis . . . , . . . exercise[d] . . . naked judicial power and substituted their personal political and social ideas for the established law of the land." *Brown*, the Manifesto continued,

---

1. The Fifth Circuit reversed, and Judge Estes appropriately ordered that black students be allowed to attend the local high school. However, when Judge Estes issued his order, the 1956–1957 school year was about to begin. Abetted by a recently formed Citizens' Council, a local newspaper, and the implicit support of Texas Governor Allan Shivers, segregationists demonstrated, burned crosses, and burned black students in effigy. No black students enrolled in Mansfield High School that year.

was a "clear abuse of judicial power," whereby the Court was "undertaking to legislate, in derogation of the authority of Congress, and to encroach upon the reserved rights of the states and the people."

And as Richard Kluger observed in *Simple Justice*, his detailed account of the *Brown* litigation and its aftermath, resistance to *Brown* was not limited to the South:

> . . . Much of the nation remained in calculated disregard of *Brown* because neither the President nor the Congress came to the aid of the Court. Congress, of course, was still run by the very Dixiecrats who conceived the Southern Manifesto, so it was unlikely that the Court could look there for enforcement legislation to bolster the desegregation process. But President Eisenhower might reasonably have been expected to urge his country to accept the Court's decision. Yet this soldier of rectitude never did that, except in the most offhand way. . . .
>
> In 1956 federal court orders in the Autherine Lucy case involving the University of Alabama and in the desegregation of the high school in Mansfield, Texas, were defied, and the President did nothing about it. In 1957, Governor Orval Faubus of Arkansas posted National Guardsmen at the entrance of Little Rock Central High School to prevent the court-ordered admission of a handful of Negro students. Eisenhower finally had to act when talks with Governor Faubus led nowhere. He reluctantly dispatched crack paratroopers, who stood watch while a few anxious black youngsters came to school at the white man's fortress.

If the federal judiciary had simply acquiesced, as some judges had, in the opposition to *Brown*, that unanimous decision may well have become only a minor blip in the history of race relations in our country. For the most part, though, federal judges did not allow that to happen. The Supreme Court and eventually lower federal courts throughout the land issued rulings to implement *Brown* and (much more importantly, it turns out) to extend *Brown's* reach beyond education to declare segregation unconstitutional in various public facilities, including buses, beaches, golf courses, and jails. These reinforcing decisions helped to establish *Brown* as "our nation's single most authoritative statement that a system of racial caste is constitutionally and morally impermissible." Outside of the courtrooms, *Brown* and its progeny became both a catalyst and a symbol for civil rights struggles of the late 1950s and early 1960s, which in turn led to the Civil Rights Act of 1964 and the Voting Rights Act of 1965.

Despite these achievements (including some early successes with school desegregation), resistance to *Brown's* promise of equal educational opportunity for blacks and whites has remained strong. Whites, particularly in the North, often fled to the suburbs in an effort to preserve de facto segregation, and local governments did not have the will on their own to make implementing *Brown* a priority. By 1974, the Supreme Court itself seemed to give up on the venture when it severely restricted the availability of interdistrict transfers as a remedy for school segregation. As a result, the early twenty-first century finds many schools as segregated or more segregated than they were in 1954; and with few exceptions, predominantly minority schools continue to provide inferior educations to their students.

Strategies and Techniques for Institutional Reform

As the school desegregation cases demonstrate, a court order, or even a series of court orders, may do little to change institutional practices. Instead, after a period of time, the court initially issuing the order(s) — or an appellate court — will declare that there has been "substantial compliance"; the case will come to an end; and it will be back to business as usual.

So what is a court to do? The problem is extremely complex. Courts have neither the expertise nor the resources to run schools, prisons, or other institutions. Nor typically — and certainly in the case of Judge Henderson — do they have the desire to do so. Yet, when faced with constitutional or statutory violations, courts must act. What form should that action take? To what extent should judges defer to institutional administrators? If violations continue, at what point does deference become intolerable? And if deference does become intolerable, how can courts best use the limited capacity they have to enforce their commands?

Once a court finds a statutory or constitutional violation — for example, that the treatment of prisoners violates the Eighth Amendment prohibition against cruel and unusual punishment — a fairly typical approach to devising a remedy is to rely on the parties, perhaps aided by a panel of experts, to formulate an agreement for the court to approve and incorporate into a binding order. That, however, is often only the beginning. The order may require the development of policies and practices and the training of personnel with the hope that education and institutional change will make future violations less likely. To ensure that such steps are taken, the court may require a Special Master or monitor to oversee the defendants' compliance and to make periodic reports to the court. The reports may generate additional disputes about their accuracy or the meaning of the underlying order. In either case, the judge, at a minimum, will probably have to issue supplemental or clarifying orders.

If compliance remains elusive, a court's options are limited and potentially very time consuming. Holding individuals or institutions in contempt for violating the judge's orders provides a symbolic vindication of the court's authority; and in extreme situations, a judge has the authority to place an entire institution in receivership. These actions, however, require a substantial investment of judicial time to build an appropriate record; and in the long run, they may do little to alter an institution's underlying intransigence — especially if there is delay for an appeal. Often, less dramatic steps can be more effective — for example, holding regular hearings to explore the difficulties of compliance, being encouraging whenever possible, adjusting a specific order or timetable where appropriate, and limiting the use or threat of a contempt sanction to specific individuals who have discrete court-ordered tasks to perform. But, of course, these steps will not always work, and they may eventually become a greater drain on judicial resources than more dramatic action.

Whatever strategy the judge initially employs in a particular case will almost certainly require revision as circumstances of that case change. And what works in one case may not work in another case. Part of the difference from one case to another may inhere in the nature of the institution involved. For example, one might expect prison guards to be less sympathetic to inmates (and thus less amenable to change) than teachers are to children with disabilities. The type of institution involved, however, may be less significant than other factors: To what extent does the institution have a strong leader committed to bringing about the changes demanded by the court? What political or financial pressures make compliance difficult even if the institutional leaders are committed to complying with a court's demands? To what extent have the parties or the court been able to foster a spirit of cooperation? Are the plaintiffs and their attorneys in a position to oversee compliance with the court's orders, or will compliance depend upon the court's taking on that role, perhaps primarily through a Special Master or a monitor?

A critical issue that cuts across all of these variables is the question of the judge's personal investment in institutional change contemplated by the initial order. At one extreme, some judges take a largely "hands-off" attitude. For them, once an order issues, the case is finished. They are ready to move on and will return to the case only if required to do so by a motion for further action from one of the parties.

At the other extreme are judges who maintain an active commitment to bringing about the institutional change. They craft their orders from the outset to ensure regular feedback and, thus, continuing judicial involvement. They make their commitment clear to the parties; and when progress is not forthcoming, they initiate efforts to resolve the impasse. They try to work with and through the parties, but typically they do not — and should not — try to micromanage the institution in need of reform. As noted earlier, judges are not likely to have the expertise to assume such a role. In addition, any such efforts may cause resentment and, therefore, become counterproductive. Finally, the

Supreme Court has repeatedly emphasized the need for local autonomy and judicial deference to institutional authority. Even if, as a last resort, a judge takes the extreme step of appointing a receiver to oversee an institution, it is important for the receiver to work with, not simply dictate orders to, institutional personnel.

Judge Henderson unabashedly places himself among those judges who view an ongoing personal commitment to institutional change as essential. As he explained in the context of discussing his prison cases:

> I have repeatedly said in my cases — and not just my prison cases, I might add — that I am *not* just going to go away. I will be here for the long haul. . . .
>
> . . . It is my decided experience, as well as that of my colleagues around the country with whom I have talked and met, and of a growing body of academics, that [a] passive approach is ill-suited to curing unconstitutional conduct. The barriers and obstacles . . . are often simply too high to surmount without sustained, persistent, and perhaps aggressive judicial intervention. . . .
>
> . . . [W]hen I look back over all the things I have done right and done wrong in my years on the bench, I think there is one clear lesson to be learned: if a court is to have any hope of effecting meaningful and long-term institutional change, while at the same time providing our prison administrators the deference that is their legitimate due, the court must faithfully and consistently adhere to what Professor [Susan] Sturm has termed the "catalyst approach."
>
> In essence, the approach aims to prod defendants to take the primary role in both the development and implementation of constitutional remedies that the court orders — and, if necessary, to change the underlying culture in the institution that created the unconstitutional conditions in the first place. Achieving this is more difficult than I ever would have imagined until I actually started trying to do it.
>
> For this approach to be effective, the court must make it clear that it is ready and willing to use — and actually does use when necessary — all of its available powers. This includes using the leverage of credible deadlines and doable performance measures, accompanied by the threat and impositions of sanctions, including contempt, when necessary. It may also include appointing special masters and using independent experts. . . . The court must also sustain involvement in the case through, for example, frequent meetings with the parties, formal hearings in court, and site visitations, because the court behind the ruling must be a real person, not an abstraction. . . .

Of course, being an effective catalyst for change means one must not only use sticks but also hold out carrots. When defendants make progress, this must be recognized at hearings, in written orders, and during visits.

Judge Henderson might have added that an effective catalyst requires much more than trying to adhere to the strategies he describes. In addition, one must have a sense of the capabilities and good faith of the defendants, of how they are likely to react to judicial encouragement or threats, of when to be patient, and when and how to exhibit firmness. These are not skills learned from a book or a law review article. Rather, they are matters of intuition, common sense, and experience. They are the largely intangible factors that made Judge Henderson a successful liaison between the federal government and the civil rights community in Alabama and Mississippi, and that allowed him to identify minority students who would succeed at Stanford Law School. They include the qualities of patience and instinct (sometimes aided by experts/guides) that make one a good fisherman, and they include a good poker player's ability to size up others and anticipate their actions. Indeed, to the extent that one can hone the skills necessary to be an effective catalyst, Judge Henderson's favorite pastimes, fishing and poker, may be the ideal vehicles.

Professor Sturm, who first coined the phrase "catalyst approach," limited her detailed analysis to prison litigation, but the general principles of that approach are applicable in other contexts as well. Indeed, given the enormity of the problems and the limited powers of the judiciary, the catalyst approach may be, in Judge Henderson's words, "the only effective way for courts to make a positive contribution" in institutional reform litigation.

As the ensuing chapters will chronicle, Judge Henderson has enlisted the aid of experts, Special Masters, receivers, and monitors to give advice and oversee the execution of his orders; he has reinforced prior rulings with new rulings; he has called parties to court for regular progress reports; he has praised their progress when it exists; and he has, when necessary, resorted to using the contempt power. Nonetheless, when the parties are recalcitrant, progress can be painfully slow. In these situations other judges might have given up, as the Supreme Court did with the promise of desegregated education; but Judge Henderson has persevered, overseeing several cases for more than a decade. His persistence is a tribute to both his patience and his commitment to the rule of law.

Chapter Fourteen

Judge Henderson's Prison Trilogy: Introduction

Litigation involving prisons and prisoners' rights is part of the normal fare for any federal court, and Judge Henderson has had his share of such cases. He has ruled both for and against prisoners and has presided over the trial of a female guard's successful sex discrimination claim. Of all of his prison cases, though, three class action lawsuits are particularly noteworthy: Madrid v. Gomez, in which inmates established that their conditions of confinement at California's Pelican Bay State Prison constituted cruel and unusual punishment in violation of the Eighth Amendment to the US Constitution; Plata v. Schwarzenegger, in which Judge Henderson placed the entire California prison medical system in receivership; and Coleman/Plata v. Schwarzenegger, in which plaintiffs, claiming that overcrowding was the primary cause of underlying Eighth Amendment violations, sought and eventually obtained an order reducing the size of the California prison population.[1]

---

1. In the first case, the named defendant was the head of the Department of Corrections; and in the latter two cases, the named defendant was the governor of California. All three cases have spanned a number of years; and as the occupants of those offices changed, so have the named defendants in new rulings and orders. For the sake of simplicity, the text ignores these purely formal name changes. When the text refers to the cases by their full names, the defendants are identified as Gomez and Schwarzenegger. They were the named defendants when Judge Henderson made his most significant rulings.

Early Prison Litigation

Until the last third of the twentieth century, courts avoided involvement in issues relating to prison conditions and correctional decision making. As a result, prisoners had virtually no opportunity for judicial redress of their grievances — no right to challenge their overcrowded or unsanitary conditions or their brutalization by individual guards. Then, in the late 1960s and the 1970s, lawyers began to apply the lessons from victories in the civil rights struggle to litigation on behalf of prisoners. Courts — including the Supreme Court — came to recognize and enforce prisoners' rights to certain constitutional protections, including the guarantee of due process and, most important for present purposes, the Eighth Amendment right to be free from "cruel and unusual punishment."

Two of the early landmark Eighth Amendment decisions came from Alabama. In 1972, Federal District Judge Frank Johnson, after detailing gross inadequacies and abuses in the Alabama prison medical care system, concluded that the "failure . . . to provide sufficient medical facilities and staff to afford inmates basic elements of medical care" violated the inmates' Eighth Amendment rights. In another case four years later, following an "admission by defendants' lead counsel . . . that the evidence conclusively established aggravated and existing violations of plaintiffs' Eighth Amendment rights," Judge Johnson held that "[t]he living conditions in Alabama prisons constitute cruel and unusual punishment." The Fifth Circuit Court of Appeals affirmed both holdings. However, as Judge Johnson discovered, getting from finding a constitutional violation to fashioning an appropriate remedy is exceedingly difficult. Political rivalries, legislative and executive recalcitrance, and bureaucratic incompetence hindered Johnson's efforts. By 1986, the year after the cases were terminated, there had been some progress; and prison officials "were quick to volunteer that Judge Johnson's order had been essential as a catalyst for reform." Yet, as Larry Yackle reported in his extensive study of the Alabama prison litigation, "Something fundamental had not changed; men and women were still kept in cages, and long enough to ensure that they could never again function as ordinary citizens."

Prison Populations

During the last quarter of the twentieth century and the early twenty-first century, the prison and local jail populations in the United States soared from approximately 200,000 to over 2.25 million. The reasons for this dramatic increase are both numerous and complex. They include a trend toward harsher penalties, especially for multiple offenders; the incessant but failed war on drugs, which has led to the incarceration of an extraordinary number of individuals for minor crimes; the movement in the 1960s and 1970s to de-institutionalize the mentally ill, which led to their incarceration in increasing numbers for crimes; and a failure to invest in effective and more cost-efficient prevention, diversion, and mental health programs.

California, which incarcerated approximately 20,000 individuals in state prisons in the mid-1970s, kept pace with the national trend. By 2007, its thirty-three prisons and related facilities housed over 170,000 inmates, and its county jails contained thousands more offenders.

Incarceration practices, both nationally and in California, have not necessarily made the public safer. Evidence of a correlation between increased incarceration and reduced crime rates is, at best, mixed. Moreover, increased incarceration leads to overcrowding, which in turn makes it more difficult both to meet inmates' daily needs and to prepare them for eventual return to society — all of which inevitably exacerbate recidivism. For example, California's inmate population at the end of 2008 was almost twice the design capacity of its prisons; medical and mental health services were grossly inadequate; and California's most violent prisoners, after being kept in extreme isolation for months or sometimes years, were released directly from that isolation to the public at the end of their sentences. Even though the isolation often creates or contributes to their mental health problems, California made little effort to provide these newly free citizens with the means to function in a social environment.

California's Inability to Respond Effectively to Prison Overcrowding

The burgeoning population in the nation's prisons became a particularly acute and intractable problem in California. When the state's prisons were operating at over 200% of design capacity in 2006, Governor Arnold Schwarzenegger proposed a $6 billion plan that would have provided for two new prisons and space for 83,000 prisoners. Three months later, he proposed allowing the California Department of Corrections and Rehabilitation (CDCR) to contract for 8,500 beds in community correctional facilities. The legislature rejected the governor's recommendations, and he responded by calling for a special legislative session to consider CDCR proposals to alleviate overcrowding. Once again, the legislature refused to act. Governor Schwarzenegger then issued a "Prison Overcrowding State of Emergency" proclamation, the immediate objective of which was to authorize the transfer of prisoners to constitutionally adequate facilities in other states. The following year the legislature adopted and the governor signed Assembly Bill 900 (AB 900), which was to provide over $7 billion to alleviate overcrowding. The state, however, has been slow to implement AB 900.

Both before and after the Governor's 2006 proposals, various commissions had recommended comprehensive reform measures for dealing with California's prison overcrowding problem. The recommendations included

> diverting non-violent, non-serious offenders and technical parole violators from prison;. . . expanding rehabilitative programs; reforming California's determinate sentencing system; transferring low-risk prisoners in the later part of their sentences to community-based reintegration facilities;. . . [and] reforming parole. . . .

Despite these repeated calls for comprehensive reform, both the governor's original 2006 proposals and AB 900 made virtually no effort to address the core problems. Instead, they focused primarily on increasing the capacity of California's prisons as the solution for overcrowding. As Steve Fama, one of the lawyers for plaintiffs in Plata v. Schwarzenegger, said, "Trying to solve overcrowding by building more beds is like trying to cure obesity by buying a bigger pair of pants."

The state's more recent efforts to deal with overcrowding are discussed in Chapter Seventeen.

The California Correctional Peace Officers Association and the Code of Silence

As the California prison population increased, so did the power of the California Correctional Peace Officers Association (CCPOA), the prison guards' union. From a humble beginning in 1957, the CCPOA has become one of the most potent forces in California politics, contributing millions of dollars to state ballot initiatives and to candidates for public office from both major parties. The CCPOA strongly supported the 1994 adoption of California's three strike law, which fueled the increase in prison population and overcrowding; and in 2006, the CCPOA successfully opposed a plan that would have sent many parole violators to half-way houses, rather than return them to prison. In 1990, the CCPOA contributed over $1 million to the winning gubernatorial campaign of Republican Pete Wilson. Eight years later, it spent more than twice that amount to help elect a Democratic governor, Gray Davis. Davis responded by negotiating a new contract with the union. The contract provided for a 37% pay increase at a time when California was facing severe fiscal difficulties.

Gray Davis' immediate successor, Arnold Schwarzenegger, and the CCPOA had a rocky relationship, some of which is described in the next two chapters. When the contract that CCPOA had negotiated with Davis expired in 2006, Schwarzenegger and the union were unable to come to terms on a new agreement—a circumstance that persisted throughout Schwarzenegger's governorship.

During the 2010 election cycle, the CCPOA spent a total of $7 million dollars on 107 different candidates, 104 of whom were elected to office. One of the successful recipients of the CCPOA's support was Democratic gubernatorial nominee Jerry Brown, who received $2 million. Within six months of Brown's taking office, his administration negotiated and the legislature approved a new contract with the CCPOA.

In the eyes of many—including Judge Henderson and an independent commission appointed by Governor Arnold Schwarzenegger—the union has had too much control over corrections and correctional policy. Perhaps the most blatant example of this control has been the "code of silence," which over the years (until very recently) has insulated prison guards from disciplinary action for abusing prisoners and, as a result, has contributed to union members having substantial authority over day-to-day prison activities with little accountability or oversight.

Judge Henderson elaborated on this "code of silence" in Madrid v. Gomez:

[It is an] unwritten but widely understood code . . . designed to encourage prison employees to remain silent regarding improper behavior of fellow employees, particularly where excessive force has been alleged. Those who defy the code risk retaliation and harassment. . . .

Several prison staff admitted to a code of silence problem. For example, one Program Administrator agreed, in his deposition, that a code of silence "frequently" operates among officers of Pelican Bay, and that this fact can make it difficult, as a supervisor, to determine what really happened during an incident. Notably, in open court this same administrator was reluctant to testify about the code of silence; after agreeing that he knew "what the code of silence is at Pelican Bay," he was asked if it operates frequently, to which he would respond only that "I don't know how to answer that." The Chief Deputy Warden also acknowledged the code of silence, as did former Program Administrator Rippetoe. Captain Jenkins also acknowledged that the code of silence has hampered his investigations of excessive force at Pelican Bay. Defendant Gomez similarly agreed that lack of candor can impede some investigations at Pelican Bay: "There are people that . . . are not forthcoming . . . that are not as honest as they should be, and that makes an investigation more difficult to prove."

We also observed at trial that prison staff frequently could not recall the identity of other staff whom they testified did or said certain things, although other details were easily recalled. Prison staff also report to internal investigators, with notable frequency, that they had just looked the other way, been distracted by something else, or had their visibility impaired at the moment the alleged misuse of force was said to have occurred. [For example, one officer] "claimed that he was unable to observe what was happening . . . because the helmet he was wearing . . . blocked his view."

Those who violate the code of silence risk hostility from other prison staff. After Sergeant Cox testified that he witnessed an inmate being hit on the head with the butt of a 38 millimeter gas gun, he was recalled as a witness. He testified that, after his appearance at trial, he had been told by various senior staff (whom he would not name unless ordered by the Court) that he had been a snitch and that he should "watch his back" and that "the administration wasn't very happy with me." Similarly, Officer Powers made the following comments to an internal investigator: "what do I say; you know the position I'm in . . . about ratting off that, how am I going to work here anymore. . . . [I]f an officer 'rats' on a fellow officer, that officer becomes an outcast." Captain Jenkins also agreed that he has "seen evidence of the situation where an officer reports another officer and is not too long thereafter reported upon himself," and that this "has been an issue" at Pelican Bay.

Underlying Problems

In his prison cases, Judge Henderson has grappled with systemic problems of inmate abuse for over twenty years. Looking back in 2008 on the still ongoing litigation, he offered this description of the underlying problems:

> As Professor [Susan] Sturm explains, "Participants in the prison system have strong disincentives to pursue change, due to the political powerlessness of inmates, due to the structural isolation of corrections from the larger community, and due to the lack of political consensus and support for reform." In addition, she notes that guard unions and senior guards may view court ruling as "illegitimate" and "may exert substantial pressure upon the rank-and-file workers not to engage in reform activity," and that "those who support reform efforts . . . are often ostracized."
>
> Institutional change also frequently entails significant additional costs for the state, and perhaps political risks for politicians who might support institutional change — which makes it difficult to garner support from legislators and governors, even when the need for change is readily

acknowledged. I have been told more than once that it is okay for me — a judge with tenure — to "hug a thug," but that it is suicide in the world of electoral politics. Therein lies a very large part of the problem that litigators face, and that I face as a federal judge trying to enforce a consent decree.

. . . [A]nother significant contributing factor to the problem is [what Thorstein Veblen called] . . . trained incapacity. . . .

"Trained incapacity" refers to a situation in which erecting barriers to change becomes an ingrained means of self-preservation for bureaucrats, so that, when serious institutional problems threaten or challenge the bureaucracy — or require it to bend or flex — we find that those within the institution have actually trained themselves to be incapable of responding. In other words, they have trained themselves to say, "it can't be done," or "we don't do it that way," and devise almost ingenious ways and reasons to make that so.

Progress for Judge Henderson has been slow; but given the enormity of the problems, he has achieved remarkable success.

Chapter Fifteen

Judge Henderson's Prison Trilogy, Part I: Madrid v. Gomez

[D]ry words on paper cannot adequately capture the senseless suffering and sometimes wretched misery that defendants' unconstitutional practices leave in their wake. The anguish of descending into serious mental illness, the pain of physical abuse, or the torment of having serious medical needs that simply go unmet is profoundly difficult, if not impossible, to fully fathom, no matter how long or detailed the trial record may be.

That was Judge Henderson's conclusion after hearing weeks of testimony about the conditions of confinement at Pelican Bay State Prison. The case was Madrid v. Gomez, a class action lawsuit in which Pelican Bay inmates claimed that they were being subjected to cruel and unusual punishment in violation of the Eighth Amendment.

The Prison

Pelican Bay State Prison, situated in the far northwest corner of California, is a "supermax" facility for the state's most violent offenders. Although it was designed to hold under 2,500 inmates, the population in 1995, when Judge Henderson wrote his opinion, varied "between 3,500 and 3,900 prisoners ... on any given day." Over a decade later the prison population was roughly the same.

Almost immediately after Pelican Bay opened for business in December 1989, judges in the Northern District of California began receiving civil rights complaints from Pelican Bay prisoners. The inordinate number of complaints led to a court-requested investigation and eventually, in October 1991, to the filing and assignment of *Madrid* to Judge Henderson.

Prior to the trial, which included dozens of witnesses and thousands of exhibits, Judge Henderson visited Pelican Bay to tour the facilities. Prison authorities insisted that Judge Henderson wear a bulletproof vest; and as if that were not enough to emphasize the constant danger at Pelican Bay, they treated Judge Henderson to a minor "riot." Just as he was nearing the top of a guard tower, shots rang out; and for a few seconds chaos seemed to ensue in the yard below. The episode, Judge Henderson realized at the time, was staged for his benefit. The message was clear: Pelican Bay is a dangerous place; don't mess with it.

As Judge Henderson observed, Pelican Bay includes three separate facilities: a small minimum security unit; the maximum security prison, which houses the majority of inmates and which has a "daily routine . . . comparable to that of other maximum security prisons in California"; and the notorious Secure Housing Unit or SHU:

> Located in a completely separate complex inside the security perimeter, the SHU has gained a well-deserved reputation as a place which, by design, imposes conditions far harsher than those anywhere else in the California prison system. The roughly 1,000–1,500 inmates confined in the SHU remain isolated in windowless cells for 22 and 1/2 hours each day, and are denied access to prison work programs and group exercise yards. Assignment to the SHU is not based on the inmate's underlying offense; rather, SHU cells are reserved for those inmates in the California prison system who become affiliated with a prison gang or commit serious disciplinary infractions once in prison. They represent, according to a phrase coined by defendants, "the worst of the worst."
>
> . . . The cellblocks are marked throughout by a dull sameness in design and color. The cells are windowless; the walls are white concrete. When inside the cell, all one can see through the perforated metal door is another white wall.
>
> . . . Inmates in adjoining cells can hear but not see each other.

An exercise pen, to which SHU inmates are permitted five visits per week, has twenty-foot high cement walls, a skylight, and some access to fresh air. However, it is not much of a respite from isolation and monotony:

> As the Court observed during its tour of the SHU, some inmates spend the time simply pacing around the edges of the pen; the image created is hauntingly similar to that of caged felines pacing in a zoo.

Some prisoners are assigned to the SHU for fixed periods of days or weeks, but others can spend months or even years there "with no opportunity for normal social contact with other people."

Physical Abuse

Judge Henderson's factual findings in *Madrid* began with the physical abuse of prisoners. He then turned to the prisoners' medical and mental health treatment and to conditions in the SHU.

An incident involving inmate Arturo Castillo illustrates both Judge Henderson's attention to detail and his care in explaining how he resolved factual issues in the face of conflicting testimony:

> On January 31, 1991, Arturo Castillo refused to return his food tray in protest against a correctional officer . . . who had called him and other inmates derogatory names. After leaving the tray near the front of the cell, Castillo retreated to the back and covered himself with his mattress for protection, in anticipation of a cell extraction. It is undisputed that Castillo, who is small in stature, made no verbal threats or aggressive gestures. Nor did he possess, or pretend to possess, any kind of weapon. Shortly thereafter, Sergeant Avila warned Castillo that if he did not give up his food tray, it was going to be very painful. Castillo refused to hand Avila the tray, stating that if they wanted the tray, they would have to come and get it. The supervising lieutenant then authorized his sergeants to forcibly remove Castillo from the cell.

> To accomplish this removal, two rounds from a 38 millimeter gas gun were fired into the cell. A taser gun was also fired, striking Castillo in the chest and stomach. Then, without attempting to retrieve the tray (which remained near the front of the cell), some number of officers entered the cell, walked past the tray, and advanced toward Castillo. Castillo testified that one of the officers then hit him on the top of his head with the butt of the gas gun, knocking him unconscious. When he regained consciousness, he was on the floor with his face down. An officer was stepping on his hands and hitting him on his calves with a baton, at which point Castillo passed out a second time. When he regained consciousness again, he was dragged out of the cell face down; his head was bleeding, and a piece of his scalp had been detached or peeled back. At that point, it became clear that Castillo had been seriously injured, and he was taken to the infirmary and then to the hospital by ambulance.

> According to the incident report, Castillo sustained his head injury when he fell and accidentally hit his head on the toilet during the incident. Lieutenant Trujillo, who was present at the time, also testified that he saw

Castillo "falling forward" and heard a "loud bang" and "somebody saying that he hit the toilet."

We do not . . . find defendants' explanation of the injury credible. First, Trujillo's testimony loses much of its force since he never actually saw Castillo's head hit the toilet even though he was "looking into the cell during the entire cell extraction." Nor did he recall seeing any blood on the toilet. Second, Castillo's credible testimony was unequivocally corroborated by Sergeant Cox, who observed the entire episode. Cox, who Trujillo admits "had a clear view" of the extraction, testified that he witnessed another sergeant "hit [Castillo] in the head with a 38 millimeter gun, by the butt of the gun." Cox further testified that he was "basically . . . ordered to keep my mouth shut and leave the area." In addition, plaintiffs' medical expert, Dr. Armond Start, gave unrebutted testimony that Castillo's head laceration was more likely the result of a high-velocity accelerated blow to the head than of a collision with a blunt, stationary object, particularly given that the injury occurred on the top of the head.

Of the many incidents of abuse that Judge Henderson catalogued, the most dramatic involved Vaughn Dortch, a mentally ill inmate. After Dortch smeared himself and his cell with his own feces, guards gave him a bath in scalding water at the prison infirmary. As a result, Dortch suffered second-degree and third-degree burns over one-third of his body.

Although there was a shower near Dortch's cell, which would have provided a more efficient method of cleaning Dortch than a bath . . ., the officers instead forcibly escorted Dortch to a bathtub in the [SHU] infirmary, located some distance away in another complex. . . .

According to Barbara Kuroda, the nurse on duty at the infirmary,. . . Dortch was in the bathtub with his hands cuffed behind his back, with an officer pushing down on his shoulder and holding his arms in place. Subsequently, another officer came into the nurse's station and made a call. Kuroda's unrebutted testimony is that she overheard the officer say about Dortch, who is African-American, that it "looks like we're going to have a white boy before this is through, that his skin is so dirty and so rotten, it's all fallen off." Concerned by this remark, Kuroda walked over toward the tub, and saw Dortch standing with his back to her. She testified that, from just below the buttocks down, his skin had peeled off and was hanging in large clumps around his legs, which had turned white with some redness. Even then, in a shocking show of indifference, the officers made no effort to seek any medical assistance or advice. Instead, it appeared to Kuroda that the officers were simply dressing Dortch to return him to his cell. When Kuroda told them they could not return him in that condition, Officer

Williams responded, in a manner described by Kuroda as disparaging and challenging, that Dortch had been living in his own feces and urine for three months, and if he was going to get infected, he would have been already. Williams added, however, that if Kuroda wanted to admit him, she could do the paperwork. Dortch then either fell, or began falling, to the floor from weakness, at which point Kuroda had Dortch taken to the emergency room. Although Dortch was not evidencing any pain at this point, Kuroda testified that this did not surprise her. Because severe burns destroy the surrounding nerve endings, the victim does not experience any pain until the nerves began to mend. Dortch was ultimately transported to a hospital burn center for treatment. . . .

. . . Dortch had received second- and third-degree burns that eventually required skin grafts on his legs and buttocks, surgical excision of part of his scrotum, and extensive physical therapy.

Given the extreme cruelty and the racial overtones in Vaughn Dortch's treatment, it would have been reasonable to infer the worst about the officers' intentions. Judge Henderson, however, was circumspect in his conclusions:

Based on the record before us, we cannot say that any of the staff involved in the incident specifically intended the severity of the burns inflicted upon Dortch. It is unclear whether the officers knew the actual temperature of the water or the full extent of the burns that were being inflicted. Nor did Dortch yell out in pain to alert the officers. On the other hand, officers were observed holding Dortch down in the tub, and the burns he was experiencing must have been visible.

Although we assume, for purposes of this case, that those involved did not intend to inflict third-degree burns, it is nonetheless clear, from all of the surrounding circumstances, that Dortch was given the bath primarily as a punitive measure and for the purpose of inflicting some degree of pain, in retaliation for, and perhaps out of frustration with, his prior offensive conduct.

Here, as elsewhere, this even-handed assessment of the evidence contributed to the overall strength of Judge Henderson's conclusion that the defendants had violated the plaintiffs' constitutional right to be free from cruel and unusual punishment. For example, while Judge Henderson found that firearms had been used "unnecessarily and in some cases recklessly," he concluded that lethal force — unlike the nonlethal force to which Castillo, Dortch and many others had been subjected — "has not been applied maliciously for the purpose of causing harm." And Judge Henderson found plaintiffs' evidence insufficient to establish that there had been inadequate training in the use of force.

The stories of Arturo Castillo and Vaughn Dortch were only the tip of the iceberg. The use of excessive force in removing prisoners from cells was common. Other abusive practices included handcuffing and chaining inmates in a fetal position for hours and confining inmates nude or partially clothed during inclement weather in outdoor metal mesh holding cages the size of telephone booths.

Judge Henderson elaborated on the use of fetal restraints:

[N]o expert at trial defended the use of fetal restraints. Plaintiffs' expert described such restraints as a painful, repugnant, humiliating punishment, and termed their level of use at Pelican Bay "unprecedented" in modern corrections. Defendants' expert Daniel McCarthy testified that he had never previously used or seen anyone use a fetal restraint in his forty years in the California Department of Corrections, and did not believe that it would be an acceptable technique.

With respect to taking prisoners clothing and confining them in mesh booths, Judge Henderson acknowledged that "officials will [sometimes] need to take an inmate's clothes, [for example] as potential evidence after an incident. . . ." However, he continued:

[P]roviding substitute clothes is not only a matter of health and safety in inclement weather, but a matter of common dignity, given the public placement of the cages and the routine presence of female staff

One of the plaintiffs' experts, Vince Nathan, had served as a court-appointed expert or monitor in prison condition cases from Texas, Georgia, Michigan, and Puerto Rico and had been a consultant for the National Institute of Corrections and the Arkansas and New Mexico correctional systems. After visiting Pelican Bay, interviewing inmates and staff, and spending over 300 hours reviewing documents, Nathan testified:

I have simply never observed the level of violence . . . the overt reliance upon violence. I've just never seen anything like it. I don't think you'll find anything like it. I don't think you'll find it at Marion, Illinois. I know you won't find it at Georgia State Prison, which is the maximum security prison for the state of Georgia. I know you won't find it in the state of Texas. I know you won't find it in the state of Ohio. There just isn't any parallel. . . . It is a place in which officers exercise unfettered discretion to take whatever physical action they deem appropriate or necessary to control, to punish, to accomplish whatever objective it is they wish to accomplish.

Not surprisingly, Judge Henderson concluded:

Plaintiffs have convincingly documented a staggering number of instances in which prison personnel applied unjustifiably high levels of force, both pursuant to, and in contravention of, official prison policies. Simply put, the evidence before the Court is proof of the most powerful, unambiguous kind that a pattern of excessive force has become an undeniable reality at Pelican Bay.

He then added:

If anything, that pattern is, in reality, stronger than reflected in the findings here, given the operative code of silence and the fact that the testimony by prison staff often seemed calculated to reveal no more than necessary. Inadequacies in the supervision of the use of force and the investigatory process also obscure the full parameters of the pattern. Certainly, much has transpired at Pelican Bay of which the Court will never know.

Medical Needs

Turning to the prisoners' medical needs, Judge Henderson reviewed Pelican Bay's medical care system and cited numerous examples of nonexistent or inadequate treatment. Two of the many victims of poor medical care were Vaughn Dortch and Arturo Castillo, both of whom required treatment as a result of their brutalization by prison guards.

The doctors who initially attended to Dortch after his severe burns

attempted to minimize or deny the full extent of his injuries, saying that Dortch merely had "dead skin" or "exfoliation." His transfer to the hospital was delayed over an hour, until he went into shock and his blood pressure became dangerously low because medical staff had not started fluid resuscitation.

Relying on a detailed report of the incident by one of plaintiffs' expert witnesses, Judge Henderson characterized Dortch's initial medical care as "grossly inadequate."

Arturo Castillo was returned to his cell after spending a week in the infirmary recovering from his guard-inflicted head wound. He

subsequently told an MTA [a medical technical assistant, who is a licensed vocational nurse] that his wound had become painful, dirty, and itchy, and even filed a grievance, but the MTA merely told him he could see a doctor in two weeks. Castillo received no medical attention at all until weeks after he complained, when a piece of his scalp finally became so severely infected that it fell off.

Castillo's inadequate treatment was not atypical, at least in the early 1990s:

> Dr. [Armond] Start[, one of plaintiffs' experts,] conducted a survey of over 3000 sick call slips to determine the average number of days inmates waited for an appointment. . . .
>
> Each sick call slip was examined for symptoms that Pelican Bay doctors identified as requiring immediate or same-day referral to a physician: cardiac symptoms, significant abdominal pain, and unresolved bleeding. Dr. Start found that the average delay before a physician appointment for a cardiac symptoms was 11.27 days; for unresolved bleeding, 12.75 days; and for abdominal pain 16.8 days.

After characterizing this data as demonstrating "abysmal delays in patient treatment," Judge Henderson pointed out that by 1995, the year of his opinion, there had been some improvement in the access to medical care. Nonetheless, Judge Henderson concluded that overall

> the quality of medical care provided to inmates at Pelican Bay often falls dramatically below community standards, [and] medical staff and administrators have taken no effective steps to systematically review the care provided or to supervise the physicians providing it.
>
> . . . Pelican Bay has failed to produce a health care system in which even . . . basic needs are consistently met. As Dr. Start noted, "in addressing the known and foreseeable health care needs of the inmates, Pelican Bay ranks among the very worst, if not the worst, of the many prisons I have evaluated.". . . .
>
> Sheer callousness aside, defendants' behavior unambiguously evinces a conscious disregard for inmates' serious medical needs. Defendants knew that the plaintiffs had serious medical needs, knew that the medical system at Pelican Bay was inadequate to serve those needs, and nevertheless failed to remedy the gross and obvious deficiencies of the system

Mental Health Needs

Judge Henderson took a similar approach to describing Pelican Bay's mental health system. He began by pointing out that even one of the defendants' experts agreed that the mental health care delivery system did not meet constitutional standards, and that the warden had emphasized the need for mental health services in his 1991 budget request. Then, after listing a number of deficiencies in the system, Judge Henderson noted that at least three factors contributed to particularly severe mental health problems in the extreme isolation of the SHU:

[First,] the SHU . . . house[s] the most dangerous and disruptive inmates. Since . . . inmates suffering from mental illness are more likely to engage in disruptive conduct, significant numbers of mentally ill inmates within the California prison system are ultimately transferred to the Pelican Bay SHU.

Second, the severity of the environment and restrictions in the SHU often cause mentally ill inmates to seriously deteriorate; other inmates who are otherwise able to psychologically cope with normal prison routines may also begin decompensating in the SHU. Roughly two-thirds of the inmates are double celled; however, this does not compensate for the otherwise severe level of social isolation in the SHU. The combination of being in extremely close proximity with one other person, while other avenues for normal social interaction are virtually precluded, often makes any long-term, normal relationship with the cellmate impossible. Instead, two persons housed together in this type of forced, constant intimacy have an "enormously high risk of becoming paranoid, hostile, and potentially violent towards each other." The existence of a cellmate is thus unlikely to provide an opportunity for sustained positive or normal social contact.

Third, defendants chose to provide only limited psychiatric services to inmates in the SHU. Aside from the obvious limitations which ensue from lack of staffing,. . . defendants have made no effort to provide appropriate treatment for inmates suffering from major mental disorders. The prison is not equipped to provide *any* inpatient or intensive outpatient treatment or involuntary medication. At the same time, delays prevent urgently needed care from being provided off-site as well. While inpatient care can be provided elsewhere in 3 to 5 days, this does not help the inmate who needs immediate hospitalization or involuntary medication. Similarly, a one to three month delay effectively denies adequate treatment for the seriously ill inmate needing immediate intensive outpatient treatment. And in some cases, security concerns preclude any transfer at all.

Consider, for example, the plight of "Inmate 4":

Inmate 4 . . . was institutionalized for much of his childhood and adolescence in state psychiatric hospitals, suffering from developmental disability, a seizure disorder, and behavioral problems, but until his transfer to the SHU in May of 1992, he seemed to have had few behavioral disturbances since 1988. Given his psychiatric history, however, Dr. [Stuart] Grassian, [another of plaintiffs' experts,] noted that "it is not at all surprising that within just a few weeks of his incarceration at Pelican Bay [SHU], he became increasingly psychotic, increasingly agitated, and increasingly out of control."

Over the next several weeks, Inmate 4 made multiple suicide attempts and was "'in severe distress, suffering from auditory and visual hallucinations.'" By mid-August,

MTAs and correctional officers reported that at times they found him "out of control," screaming, or incoherent. The inmate repeatedly said that he was being attacked by demons and that he would try to kill himself to get away from them. . . . On September 9, he again tried to kill himself by swallowing a piece of the fire sprinkler.

When Dr. Grassian interviewed Inmate 4 less than a week after his last suicide attempt, the inmate was disheveled, despondent, and desperate. He explained that "my heart starts racing, I get dizzy spells, scared, nervous, shaking, crying. I hear voices telling me to tear up my mattress. Demons come out. I see them. . . . I never saw them before SHU." Inmate 4 was eventually recommended for transfer to the California Medical Facility at Vacaville by the Pelican Bay staff.

"Inmate 1" was another victim of the SHU. "By April 1992, he was suffering from a paranoid, hallucinatory psychosis." In late August, a staff psychiatrist recommended that Inmate 1 be transferred to Vacaville for observation and treatment, but he was still in the SHU when Dr. Grassian first interviewed him on September 17. According to Dr. Grassian, Inmate 1 was "actively psychotic and delusionally fearful of being killed." In November, the transfer to Vacaville finally occurred, and Inmate 1 improved "dramatically" — so much so that after four months he was returned to the Pelican Bay SHU. When Dr. Grassian again interviewed Inmate 1 two months later, Inmate 1 had "degenerated into a psychotic state; he was agitated, terrified, and hallucinatory."

In summarizing his finding with respect to the mental health system at Pelican Bay, Judge Henderson wrote:

[T]he evidence plainly shows that there have been, and continue to be, chronic and pervasive problems with the delivery of mental health care at Pelican Bay. It also reveals defendants' deliberate indifference to the serious mental health needs of inmates. . . .

In short, defendants created a prison which, given its mission, size, and nature, would necessarily and inevitably result in an extensive demand for mental health services — perhaps more so than any other California facility; yet, at the same time, they scarcely bothered to furnish mental health services at all, and then only at a level more appropriate to a facility much smaller in size and modest in mission.

Judicial Restraint and the SHU

Despite his stinging indictment of the prison conditions at Pelican Bay, Judge Henderson's conclusions were ultimately measured and restrained. He recognized that Pelican Bay in general and the SHU in particular housed "uncooperative and combative" inmates; that both the use of force and the isolation of inmates were sometimes necessary to maintain order; that the prison staff had a "demanding and often thankless" job; and that many of the staff deplored the excessive violence at Pelican Bay. In addition, Judge Henderson emphasized that the court's role was limited:

> Throughout these proceedings, we have been acutely sensitive to the fact that our role in Eighth Amendment litigation is a limited one. Federal courts are not instruments for prison reform, and federal judges are not prison administrators. We must be careful not to stray into matters that our system of federalism reserves for the discretion of state officials. At the same time, we have no duty more important than that of enforcing constitutional rights, no matter how unpopular the cause or powerless the plaintiff. The challenge, then, in prison condition cases, is to uphold the Constitution in such a manner that respects the state's unique interest in managing its prison population. It is a challenge that requires us to draw constitutional lines when necessary, yet minimize any intrusion into state affairs.

It is undeniably true that the judiciary's role — as a matter of doctrine, as well as power and expertise — is limited. Courts "are not instruments of prison reform" in the sense that it is not their job to make broad choices about prison policy. For example, as Judge Henderson noted with respect to the health care systems at Pelican Bay:

> The Eighth Amendment does not require that prison officials provide the most desirable medical and mental health care; nor should judges simply "constitutionalize" the standards set forth by professional associations such as the American Medical Association or the American Public Health Association.

On the other hand, enforcing constitutional rights, limited as they are, may require significant institutional changes; and to that extent judges have an obligation to be agents of reform.

Perhaps the best illustration in *Madrid* of both judicial restraint and potentially reformative judicial intervention to protect constitutional rights is Judge Henderson's approach to the SHU. Reviewing the evidence, he noted that "many if not most inmates in the SHU experience some degree of psychological trauma," but that for some "the adverse psychological impact . . . will be relatively moderate." Accordingly, in what the state hailed as a major victory, Judge Henderson refused to close down the SHU:

> The decision to segregate inmates who threaten the security of the general population falls well within defendants' far ranging discretion to manage California's prison population. Defendants' discretion to determine the specific conditions of segregation is similarly broad. Given the "limitations of federalism and the narrowness of the Eighth Amendment" it is not the Court's function to pass judgment on the policy choices of prison officials. . . . Defendants are thus entitled to design and operate the SHU consistent with the penal philosophy of their choosing, absent constitutional violations. They may impose conditions that are "'restrictive and even harsh'"; they may emphasize idleness, deterrence, and deprivation over rehabilitation. This is not a matter for judicial review or concern unless the evidence demonstrates that conditions are so extreme as to violate basic concepts of humanity and deprive inmates of a minimal level of life's basic necessities.

The conditions in the SHU were that extreme, Judge Henderson concluded, for two categories of inmates that were frequently assigned to the SHU: (1) "the already mentally ill" and (2) "persons with borderline personality disorders, brain damage or mental retardation, impulse-ridden personalities, or a history of prior psychiatric problems or chronic depression." Their continued incarceration in the SHU would constitute cruel and unusual punishment. In reaching this conclusion, Judge Henderson noted:

> [T]he [California Department of Corrections'] own Mental Health Services Branch recommended excluding from the Pelican Bay SHU "all inmates who have demonstrated evidence of serious mental illness or inmates who are assessed by mental health staff as likely to suffer a serious mental health problem if subjected to RES [reduced environmental stimulation] conditions."

The Initial Order

Like other judges in similar cases, Judge Henderson concluded his opinion by calling upon the parties themselves, in conjunction with a Special Master "experienced in prison administration," to craft a remedy for the constitutional violations." His order, dated January 10, 1995, was brief. The Special Master, Thomas Lonergan, was to report to Judge Henderson every thirty days, and the parties were urged to have an agreed-upon remedial plan within 120 days.

As Judge Henderson knew, the truly difficult work was about to begin.

The Early Responses

While members of the Department of Corrections lauded Judge Henderson's decision not to close the SHU, plaintiffs' lawyers were equally effusive in their praise of his conclusions that conditions at Pelican Bay violated the Eighth Amendment. The immediate positive reaction from both sides to the controversy suggested not only that Judge Henderson had reached a reasonable middle ground but also that he would have the parties' cooperation in fashioning a remedy.

California Department of Corrections (CDC) Director James Gomez seemed to further the hope of swift remedial action in a February 9 letter to the *Los Angeles Times*. Although Gomez's letter tended to understate the existing difficulties at Pelican Bay, he asserted that "[t]he incidents cited by Judge Henderson are not acceptable," that changes will be made "to ensure this behavior is not tolerated and is eliminated," and that he was "committed to operating Pelican Bay as a safe and humane institution for both inmates and staff."

One sign of that apparent commitment related to the use of lethal force against prisoners. Prior to Judge Henderson's decision, it had been common for guards to fire upon inmates to break up fistfights. Between 1989 and 1994, the practice had resulted in the deaths of over two dozen California inmates — more than three times the number of inmates killed during that same time period in all other federal and state prisons combined. Within days of Judge Henderson's order, the CDC issued emergency regulations that prohibited such shooting except in extreme situations. In addition, the defendants began almost immediately to develop policies regulating the use of both lethal and nonlethal force at Pelican Bay. In consultation with the Special Master, the defendants expanded and revised the policies throughout the year. Characterizing the effort as "highly commendable," Judge Henderson approved — with minor modifications — the use of force policy in June 1996.

In other areas, though, the hope for speedy progress faded rapidly. By the fall of 1995, Special Master Thomas Lonergan reported that the defendants had "not independently taken any significant steps" with respect to excluding inmates from the SHU, that there had been no improvement in medical and mental health treatment of inmates, that the defendants were not acting in good faith about these matters, and that the parties were too adversarial. In a December 15, 1995 order, Judge Henderson set forth strict time lines for the accomplishment of various tasks and concluded his order with a demand that specified defendants — including James Gomez, head of the CDC — appear at a hearing in two weeks. At that hearing, Judge Henderson concluded that the prisoners were "still receiving grossly inadequate care."

[T]he systems for delivering medical and mental health care at Pelican Bay were even more dysfunctional and ineffective than . . . I comprehended them at the time of the trial. . . . [I]n fact . . . it's clear that there was not even a semblance . . . of any functioning health care system at that time, let alone one which is constitutionally sufficient. And this, of course, has made development of and implementation of a remedy . . . especially difficult, and I recognize that. It's not unlike trying to put a roof on a house which we're trying to do to keep the rain out when there aren't [even] four walls up to put it on.

Director Gomez agreed: "[T]hat things may have been in worse repair than we had anticipated I don't think is an unfair characterization." Judge Henderson concluded the hearing by imposing new deadlines. They included ten days to form a five-member team of medical experts to work with the Special Master, thirty days to have five full-time psychiatrists at Pelican Bay, and ninety days to have a comprehensive plan to remedy the constitutional deficiencies set forth in Judge Henderson's original order, now more than a year old.

Progress on Medical and Mental Health Issues

In October 1996, defendants filed a thirteen-volume "remedial plan for medical and mental health care services at Pelican Bay"—its fourth such proposed plan. Although the previous plans contained serious deficiencies, this plan, with minor modifications recommended by the Special Master, was a substantial step forward. It was, Judge Henderson said, "an excellent overall plan":

There is no doubt that defendants have finally . . . "built the house." Most importantly, it has been built through a voluntary process. The plan submitted to the Court is defendants' plan, and it represents defendants' policy choices.

With the exception of two matters relating to the SHU, Judge Henderson approved the plan in the spring of 1997 and ordered continued monitoring by the Special Master.

John Hagar replaced Thomas Lonergan as Special Master, and progress continued, albeit sometimes haltingly. The Special Master—along with various court-appointed experts—worked closely with the defendants to rectify many of the constitutional violations Judge Henderson identified in his initial opinion. In a series of orders addressing various matters (including the two unresolved SHU issues and prison disciplinary policy regarding the use of force), Judge Henderson adopted the Special Master's recommendations without serious objection from any of the parties.

The process leading to these and other orders was often slow and tedious. The Special Master and court experts would meet with the defendants to discuss a particular problem. The defendants would develop a proposed solution and submit it to the Special Master, sometimes missing deadlines that they set for themselves. The Special Master would respond, and the defendants might revise their proposal in light of the response. Eventually, the Special Master would submit the proposal to all of the parties along with his tentative recommendations; the parties would have an opportunity to offer written objections; and the Special Master would then prepare his final recommendation for the court. At every critical step, the Special Master was in contact with the parties, and he was regularly communicating with and reporting to Judge Henderson.

There were ample opportunities for both Judge Henderson and John Hagar to become frustrated with the process. They both realized, however, that a long-term solution to the unconstitutional conditions at Pelican Bay required institutional change and that institutional change was most likely to come if the defendants themselves were major players in crafting the necessary remedies. Just as the remedial plan for medical and mental health care services represented, as Judge Henderson said, "the defendants' policy choices," so too did subsequent corrective actions. The defendants were successfully reforming their own institution. Yet, in retrospect, it seems clear that they never would have made these reforms in the first place were it not for Judge Henderson's continued vigilance and John Hagar's day-to-day work with the parties.

One critically important example relates to the quality of medical care available to inmates. As the next chapter demonstrates, the inability to hire and retain qualified physicians has plagued the entire California prison system. The problem, however, was particularly acute at Pelican Bay, at least in part because of its isolation in the remote northwest corner of the state. The defendants' early attempts to improve the situation had largely failed. Then, in the summer of 2001 after counsel for both parties and the Special Master met to discuss the matter, the defendants presented a six-part proposal that included increased responsibilities for registered nurses and an expanded "tele-medicine" program. The Special Master characterized the proposal as "a significant improvement over prior corrective actions." After additional meetings and modifications, he recommended its adoption to the court.

As progress continued on the medical and mental health fronts at Pelican Bay, two class action lawsuits were challenging the adequacy of medical health and mental health services throughout the entire state prison system: Coleman v. Schwarzenegger (mental health) and Plata v. Schwarzenegger (medical health), the latter of which was assigned to Judge Henderson and is the subject of the next chapter. In May 2008, the Special Master, without objection from the parties, recommended that the limited monitoring of medical and mental health that was still required at Pelican Bay be transferred to the two statewide suits. Judge Henderson agreed:

> The fact that Pelican Bay State Prison [PBSP] has progressed so far that its remaining problems are best resolved on a statewide basis speaks volumes about the hard work, good faith, diligence, creativity, and commitment of the clinicians, correctional staff and management of PBSP. Together with other CDCR[1] officials, Plaintiffs, and the Special Master and his staff, they have radically improved medical and mental health care services at PBPS over the past thirteen years. As the Special Master's report notes, because PBSP has become an institution "ahead of the curve" in many aspects of care delivery, it is likely to be a prime candidate for testing the efficacy of programs designed to solve the lingering problems with the CDCR's medical and mental health systems state wide.

The Failure to Discipline Prison Personnel

Despite the defendants' early successes in curtailing excessive violence, their efforts to discipline Pelican Bay guards and other prison personnel were inadequate. The problem erupted in 2003–2004, but it had been simmering for years. Indeed, it was as old as the well-established "code of silence" that Judge Henderson described in his 1995 *Madrid* opinion.

Within months of that initial 1995 ruling, the state established a team of investigators to look into the abuse of Pelican Bay inmates by guards. The team's efforts led to the criminal conviction in state court of one guard, Jose Garcia. The investigators themselves, however, became the subject of intense scrutiny by the Department of Corrections; and after a few months they were stripped of their powers. The investigators, the prosecutor responsible for trying Garcia, Special Master John Hagar, and an independent analysis by the *Los Angeles Times* all concluded that the California Correctional Peace Officers Association (CCPOA), the prison guards' union, was responsible for short-circuiting a legitimate, professionally conducted investigation. Not surprisingly, the union denied any wrongdoing.

According to John Hagar, the CCPOA's resistance continued during an FBI investigation of prisoner abuse that began in 1998. Nonetheless, as a result of that investigation, Garcia and another Pelican Bay guard, Michael Powers, were

---

1. The California Department of Corrections (CDC) became the California Department of Corrections and Rehabilitation (CDCR) in 2005. [Author's footnote]

convicted of federal conspiracy charges in 2002. According to the evidence, Garcia and Powers would target rapists, child molesters, and generally uncooperative inmates for beatings and stabbings. The guards would then enlist other inmates to carry out the assaults and reward them with liquor, money, and other gifts and privileges.

Following the Garcia/Powers convictions, Assistant US Attorney Melinda Haag provided the CDC with information suggesting that several guards may have testified untruthfully at the trial. The CDC began to investigate; but the investigation seemed doomed from the start. Thomas Moore, acting director of the CDC's Office of Investigative Services (OIS), delayed four months before signing the documents that were essential for the investigation to begin. That, in effect, reduced the statute of limitations from one year to eight months. Once prepared, the forms were "vague and repetitive." The investigators had inadequate assistance; they were unaware of a recently adopted CDC plan for the investigation and discipline of prison guards; and they had no guidance or supervision from the OIS. And these types of problems were not unique to cases involving Pelican Bay guards. At least in part because of the "code of silence" and pressures from the CCPOA, the state's system for disciplining guards was dysfunctional.

Edward Alameida, who had become head of the CDC in 2001, officially shut down the investigation during a March 27, 2003 meeting with the investigators and other CDC officials. A few days before the meeting, Alameida had had a telephone conversation with CCPOA Vice President Chuck Alexander, who had inquired about the investigation. At the March 27 meeting, Alameida instructed one of his associates to inform Alexander of the meeting's outcome.

Alameida's action led to a detailed inquiry by the Special Master that culminated in a federal court hearing the following November. The investigators' story was dramatically different from Director Alameida's. The investigators testified that they told Alameida the allegations of perjury were true and that Alameida said he wanted the investigations to "go away." Alameida, by contrast, claimed that the March 27 meeting was not for the purpose of shutting down the cases. Indeed, he said that he did not know who called the meeting or why and that certainly it had nothing to do with the CCPOA or the telephone call from Chuck Alexander. He was, he said, misinformed about the status of the cases.

Special Master John Hagar found the investigators' testimony to be "credible." With respect to Director Alameida, he concluded:

> It is difficult to believe Alameida's . . . version of what transpired at the meeting of March 27. Even the most gross incompetence by the Directorate does not excuse [the] collective failure to inquire whether the investigations were complete. . . .

Mr. Alameida's explanation about his conversation with CCPOA Vice President Chuck Alexander is not believable. Mr. Alexander is an aggressive and intelligent advocate for correctional officer interests. He has been at the forefront of the CCPOA resistance to both State and Federal criminal investigations of Powers [and] Garcia . . . for more than a decade. . . . It is not believable that Alexander would call the Director of Corrections, ask about the status of investigations directly related to the Powers and Garcia cases, and simply accept Mr. Alameida's statement that he had no knowledge of the matter. Alameida's claim that he suddenly remembered a brief telephone conversation with Alexander that had taken place weeks earlier, and based on this memory told [an associate] to . . . inform Alexander the investigations had been shut down, is also not believable.

State Senator Gloria Romero, after hearing testimony at the November hearing, put the matter more tersely: "You either have a whole lot of people not telling the truth or the director not telling the truth."

Less than three weeks after the November hearing, Alameida announced his resignation as head of the CDC. In a subsequent opinion, Judge Henderson agreed with John Hagar's assessment of Alameida and his credibility:

The Court has carefully reviewed the documents and transcripts upon which the Special Master's findings are based. . . . The Court is amply satisfied that a neutral appraisal of the full record demonstrates that the Special Master's credibility determinations and factual findings are fair, persuasive, and well-supported by the record. . . . Indeed, the Court is well satisfied, based on its careful and independent review, that, at all times relevant hereto, Alameida had neither the will nor the intent to effectively investigate and potentially discipline the three Pelican Bay officers accused of the most serious charges — suspected perjury in federal court to cover up excessive force by fellow officers — but instead chose to shut down the investigation in order to appease the CCPOA. . . . The Court has no doubt that . . . Alameida . . . engaged in gross abuses of the public trust.

Despite this rebuke, Judge Henderson rejected John Hagar's suggestion that Alameida be held in criminal contempt for violating the court's orders relating to the investigation and discipline of use of force complaints. Alameida might have a valid defense, Judge Henderson concluded, because the court orders were not directed specifically to him. Moreover, litigating that issue would inevitably detract from the more important business of reforming the defendants' disciplinary processes. There remained the possibility of imposing "sanctions" on Alameida for acting in bad faith; but because of Alameida's resignation and deteriorating health, Judge Henderson chose not to pursue this remedy.

John Hagar had also suggested that Douglas Moore, "the highest level investigator in the Department of Corrections," be held in criminal contempt and that the court consider referring Moore to the US Attorney for a possible perjury prosecution. Judge Henderson rejected both of these suggestions, but he did sanction Moore with a $1,500 fine.

A Return to Progress

In a June 24, 2004 report to Judge Henderson, John Hagar characterized the CDC as having "lost control of its investigative and discipline processes," a fact that he attributed to the code of silence, the CCPOA's interference with investigations, and CDC's extreme deference to the CCPOA. At the same time, though, he saw reason for hope. Arnold Schwarzenegger, who became governor of California in November 2003,[2] had made some significant appointments to key correctional positions. Matthew Cate became the Inspector General with independent oversight of the CDC's disciplinary process, and he began immediately to work with Hagar. Jeanne Woodford left her position as warden of San Quentin to become head of the CDC, and she promised "real reform." Roderick Hickman, a former prison guard and career correctional official, joined Schwarzenegger's cabinet as Secretary of the Youth and Adult Correctional Agency. Hickman announced that he would not tolerate the code of silence; and by the end of February 2004, he presented a plan for investigating and disciplining guard misconduct. In March 2004, Judge Henderson appointed Michael Gennaco as a court expert to assist with the development of independent review procedures and code of silence training. Gennaco was head of the Office of Independent Review for the Los Angeles Sheriff's Department.

John Hagar concluded that "the right people have been assembled to continue the remedial effort," and that the defendants' "effort to formulate an adequate remedial plan is better organized and staffed today than at any time in the past nine years." He recommended that he continue his monitoring and working with the defendants "concerning the development and implementation of an adequate remedial plan to address the problems with investigations, adverse action discipline and the code of silence." Judge Henderson agreed.

---

2. Schwarzenegger, a Republican, won a special election in October to replace Democratic Governor Gray Davis, who was recalled.

The Continuing Ramifications of the CCPOA's Political Power

Governor Schwarzenegger — unlike his predecessors Gray Davis and Pete Wilson — never accepted political contributions from the CCPOA; and the defendants, under the leadership of Secretary Hickman, developed policies and training programs that undermined the code of silence. Nonetheless, the CCPOA remained a threat to institutional reform at Pelican Bay. Indeed, looking back at the long history of *Madrid*, Judge Henderson has said that dealing with the consequences of the CCPOA's political power was the most difficult aspect of the case.

One manifestation of that difficulty arose almost simultaneously with the filing of the Special Master's June 2004 report. The state's severe budget crisis prompted Governor Schwarzenegger to seek wage concessions from the CCPOA, which had negotiated a sweetheart contract with Gray Davis in 2002. In return for deferring pay raises, the Governor was willing to cede supervisory control over some prison work assignments to the CCPOA. Judge Henderson, believing that such an agreement could undermine the ability of the CDC to carry out its reforms, sent a strongly worded letter to Secretary Hickman and Peter Siggins, the Governor's Legal Affairs Secretary,[3] on July 19. After setting forth his concerns, Judge Henderson concluded:

> I do not intend to intrude upon the Administration's discretion, but I am resolved to correct the serious problems found by the Special Master. . . . If the State of California is no longer willing to manage the necessary corrective actions, I must consider the appointment of a receiver over the CDC to bring California's correctional system into full compliance with the Court's orders.
>
> . . . I would like to meet with Governor Schwarzenegger to discuss the State's continued non-compliance with my remedial orders. I would appreciate your contacting my secretary . . . to arrange this meeting.

The following day Peter Siggins responded that he along with Secretary Hickman and the Governor share "a commitment with the Court not only to improve the quality of correctional officer investigations and the discipline process but to hold all employees to the highest ethical standards."

Not surprisingly, given the state's dire financial situation, Judge Henderson's letter did not affect the arrangement that Governor Schwarzenegger had made with the union. It did, however, result in a telephone conversation with

---

3. In 2005, Governor Schwarzenegger appointed Peter Siggins to the California Court of Appeal.

the Governor. More important, from Judge Henderson's perspective, it got the Governor's attention in a rather dramatic way. One of the five people who received copies of the letter shared it with the press. As a result, the letter received wide coverage in both news stories and editorials. The editorials were for the most part supportive of Judge Henderson and critical of the Governor's bargain with the CCPOA. Several editorials referred to Schwarzenegger as a "girlie man," a term that originated in a Saturday Night Live skit about body-builders. Schwarzenegger had used the term in speeches to characterize Democratic presidential candidates, and, most notably, California legislators beholden to union interests.

In the wake of the letter, the telephone conversation, and the publicity, the Governor seemed to become more aware of and involved with prison issues. In mid-August, he toured a state prison near the capitol to demonstrate his commitment to prison reform; and while he said it would be "no sweat off my back" if Judge Henderson took over the prison system, he also expressed a commitment to work with Judge Henderson. The Governor described his telephone conversation with the judge as "wonderful" and said that Judge Henderson "is 100% with us."

Governor Schwarzenegger's "no sweat off my back" statement may have been more serious than it appeared to be at the time. Judge Henderson heard from several sources that the Governor would welcome a receivership in order to rid himself of prison problems.

Even though the CCPOA had gained some formal control over prison administration in return for deferring raises, it still did not have the political clout over policy and discipline that it enjoyed during Gray Davis' tenure as governor. As John Hagar reported, "[T]he Davis administration required the Director of Corrections to meet directly with CCPOA officials whenever the CCPOA wanted to talk, and regardless of the topic for discussion." By contrast, "[d]uring the first two years of the Schwarzenegger administration, the Governor's Office did not allow the CCPOA to interfere with the management prerogatives of CDCR [formerly CDC] officials." There was, for example, no possibility that a union official could put an end to an investigation with a telephone call to Secretary Hickman or CDCR Director Jeanne Woodford.

The CCPOA's political influence appeared to have a resurgence in 2006. In January Susan Kennedy, who had served as Gray Davis' Chief of Staff, became Governor Schwarzenegger's Chief of Staff. She and Fred Aguiar, another member of the Governor's cabinet, began to meet with CCPOA officials without informing Secretary Hickman. John Hagar reported that "prison reform ground to a halt following Susan Kennedy's February 14, 2006 lunch with [CCPOA President] Mike Jimenez."

Hickman resigned at the end of February, and Jeanne Woodford became Acting Secretary. She resigned six weeks later after the Governor's office rejected two of her personnel recommendations. One recommendation had been for Tim Virga, a former CCPOA member, to take a position that would make him the state's chief negotiator in contract talks with the CCPOA. (The contract that CCPOA had negotiated with Gray Davis was set to expire in July.) After initially announcing the appointment, the Governor's office reneged. Perhaps there was genuine concern that Virga's prior union membership created a conflict of interest. The CCPOA, however, had publicly expressed its dissatisfaction with Virga. Moreover, according to John Hagar, Virga's appointment "was derailed by the Governor's Office the day after a meeting between the Chief of Staff [Susan Kennedy], Cabinet Secretary [Fred Aguiar], and CCPOA officials." Governor Schwarzenegger quickly replaced Jeanne Woodford with James Tilton, who promised, "One of the first things I'm going to do is reconnect with the union and verify that those relationships are still there and make sure we still have an open dialogue."

Precisely what transpired in the meetings with CCPOA officials and members of the Schwarzenegger administration remains — and may always remain — unclear. Nonetheless, the notion that the Governor was willing to condone, if not actively promote, CCPOA interference in prison policy makes political sense. 2006 was an election year, and the CCPOA was reportedly prepared to spend as much as $10 million on its preferred candidates. Governor Schwarzenegger was unlikely to gain the CCPOA's endorsement, but he could reasonably hope that the CCPOA might remain neutral in the governor's race or at least not spend lavishly on his opponent.

On August 22, John Hagar filed a report with the court that set forth what was known of CCPOA's apparent political influence with the Schwarzenegger administration and the resignations of Rodrick Hickman and Jeanne Woodford, two of the strongest and most effective voices for prison reform. The Governor's office, Susan Kennedy and Fred Aguiar individually, and the CCPOA leadership all denied any improprieties.

Hagar's report raised serious concerns for Judge Henderson. Two factors, however, counseled against any immediate response. First, despite — or perhaps because of — the interaction between the CCPOA and his office, Governor Schwarzenegger had refused to seek the union's backing for his reelection bid. The CCPOA endorsed his Democratic opponent, Phil Angelides. Thus, there was virtually no chance that the union would be in a position to influence correctional policy during the brief remainder of the Governor's term. Second, any action by Judge Henderson on the eve of the election could have been construed as an inappropriate attempt by the judiciary to interfere with the political process.

Governor Schwarzenegger prevailed in the November election with an overwhelming seventeen-point victory. As Judge Henderson realized, there was no longer any reason for the Governor to grant political favors to the CCPOA; and despite strong evidence of the administration's and CCPOA's collusion to block reform in the early months of 2006, Judge Henderson's priority was to continue the progress that had been made during the first two years of Governor Schwarzenegger's initial term. He saw no value in picking a fight with the CCPOA; and it would have been counterproductive, he thought, to embarrass the Governor. At the same time, however, he knew that he should not completely ignore John Hagar's damning August 22 report.

As he had so often during the Pelican Bay litigation, Judge Henderson took a restrained, prudent middle course. He scheduled a hearing for December 2006 in which both Rod Hickman and Jeanne Woodford testified that they felt their efforts were undermined by Susan Kennedy, Fred Aguiar, and the CCPOA. The defendants, of course, were free to challenge that evidence. However, they chose not to call Kennedy and Aguiar to testify, and Judge Henderson did not force the matter. The evidence of interference stood unrefuted. It was time to move on.

Negotiations over the terms of a new CCPOA contract continued into Governor Schwarzenegger's second term, but the parties were unable to reach an agreement. The administration was willing to give the union pay raises of up to nearly 16% over three years, but only in return for concessions on its control over prison management. The CCPOA refused to cede its authority and made an unsuccessful attempt to circumvent the negotiating process by going directly to the legislature. In the fall of 2008, the CCPOA mounted and then quickly abandoned an effort to recall the Governor.

Reform Continues

John Hagar continued to work with the parties to improve the defendants' investigatory and disciplinary policies — an effort that gained important support in the spring of 2008 when Governor Schwarzenegger named Matthew Cate to replace the retiring James Tilton as Corrections Secretary. Cate, who had been serving as Schwarzenegger's Inspector General from 2004, had consistently been one of the administration's advocates for disciplinary reform and an end to the code of silence.

In October 2007, John Hagar reported:

> Overall, the timeliness and quality of internal affairs investigations and the CDCR discipline process has improved dramatically. . . .
> . . . [W]hile the system is not yet perfect, . . . as of the date of this report, defendants are in compliance in achieving the bottom line . . ., an overall effective use of force/code of silence related investigation and discipline program.

He concluded his assessment with a recommendation that he continue his monitoring at least through the remainder of 2007. A year later, citing "very positive progress made by the defendants," John Hagar recommended that the monitoring cease and that all use of force orders be terminated. That, in effect, was a recommendation to terminate the case.

None of the parties asked Judge Henderson to implement the Special Master's recommendation; and initially he did nothing on his own. He preferred to keep the case — and thus his options — open. However, after two inconsequential years, Judge Henderson decided to act. In the spring of 2011, with the concurrence of the plaintiffs, he terminated all remaining force-related orders and closed the case. In the meantime, Jerry Brown was elected Governor in 2010. Ron Yank, Governor Brown's Director of the Department of Administration — and, incidentally, the former attorney for CCPOA — was in the process of successfully negotiating a new contract with CCPOA. The issues were mostly economic, but Yank insisted that the contract contain a provision for continuing code of silence training.

A Success Story

For over fifteen years, Judge Henderson, his Special Masters, and his experts worked closely with the plaintiffs' attorneys and the state to reform the medical, mental health, and disciplinary systems at Pelican Bay. And because efforts at disciplinary reform involved personnel and policy issues that extended beyond Pelican Bay, much of the disciplinary reform has been statewide. The entire effort has been enormously time consuming and, by any measure, should be regarded as a huge success.

Moreover, because Judge Henderson insisted from the outset that the defendants themselves make the policy choices that would cure the underlying constitutional violations, the success is likely to be long lasting. Despite statewide difficulties with the prison medical health system that are the focus of the next chapter, medical and mental health reforms peculiar to Pelican Bay appear to be firmly entrenched in the day-to-day operations. Similarly, as John Hagar's 2007 and 2008 reports and Ron Yank's negotiations with the CCPOA illustrate, the state seems committed to regulating the use of force and undermining the code of silence.

Chapter Sixteen

Judge Henderson's Prison Trilogy, Part II: Plata v. Schwarzenegger (Nee Plata v. Davis)

In her "Prison Trilogy," Joan Baez sings of an inmate named Luna who "died to no one's great alarm." Unfortunately, there have been hundreds of Lunas in the California prison system. As Judge Henderson wrote in October 2005:

> [O]n average, an inmate in one of California's prisons needlessly dies every six to seven days due to constitutional deficiencies in the . . . medical delivery system. This statistic, awful as it is, barely provides a window into the waste of human life occurring behind California's prison walls due to the gross failures of the medical delivery system.

Plata v. Schwarzenegger: An Early but Ineffective Settlement

In April 2001, Judge Henderson began to preside over a class action lawsuit, Plata v. Schwarzenegger, in which the plaintiffs claimed that the quality of medical care in the California correctional system violated the Eighth Amendment ban on cruel and unusual punishment. The suit initially included all prisons except Pelican Bay, whose medical system was already under court order in Madrid v. Gomez.

In less than a year — and prior to any trial or evidentiary hearings — the defendants entered into a consent decree, in which they agreed to make comprehensive reforms to the California prison medical system. The defendants would work with court-appointed medical and nursing experts to phase in the new program over a seven-year period, with seven prisons slated for reform in 2003. Once they were fully implemented, the reforms would cost the state an estimated $122 million per year.

The defendants' willingness to become bound by a consent decree so quickly was in part attributable to the obvious deficiencies in the prison medical system, but it was also a tribute to Judge Henderson. The defendants knew from their first-hand experience with Judge Henderson in Madrid v. Gomez that he was fair, restrained, and firm. They had every reason to expect the same in *Plata*. And at the outset, Judge Henderson had reason to be optimistic. While the problems facing the prison medical system were staggering, the defendants seemed willing to do their part; and there was no "code of silence" to hinder reform efforts.

During the next three years, Judge Henderson made substantial, but ultimately unsuccessful efforts to encourage the defendants to develop and implement their own policies for reforming the prison medical system:

> [T]he Court Experts, plaintiffs, and the Court itself have provided specific achievable measures and have made innumerable informal suggestions as to how defendants can move forward. The Court invited the parties during monthly status conferences to contribute ideas as to possible remedies, and the Court especially encouraged defendants to consider ways in which they could take the actions necessary to solve the medical care problems through measures within their own control, including use of the extraordinary powers of the Governor. [In April, 2005, t]he Court went to the length of requesting that defendants present it with a series of proposed orders so that the Court could help empower them to overcome some of their bureaucratic hurdles on their own. Defendants did not submit a single proposed order. Finally, the Court . . . stated that "with respect to the substantive remedy itself, the Court encourages all parties to think as creatively as possible, and the Court will remain open to all reasonable alternatives." Even [then],. . . defendants were able to enact only very limited and piece-meal measures, with no prospect for system-wide reform or restructuring.

Judge Henderson on the Shocking Prison Medical Conditions and the State's Admitted Failures: Plata v. Schwarzenegger, 2005 W.L. 2932243 (N.D. Cal.) 1–5[1]

In the four years since this case was filed, . . . two things have become ever increasingly clear: (1) the Governor has appointed, and the State has hired, a number of dedicated individuals to tackle the difficult task of addressing the crisis in the delivery of health care in the California Department of Corrections and Rehabilitation (CDCR), and (2) despite the best efforts of these individuals, little real progress is being made. The problem of a highly dysfunctional, largely decrepit, overly bureaucratic, and politically driven prison system, which these defendants have inherited from past administrations, is too far gone to be corrected by conventional methods.

. . . A prevailing lack of accountability within California's struggling correctional system has resulted in a failure to correct basic problems and an increase in tell-tale signs of dysfunction. The CDCR has functioned for years under a decentralized structure in which individual wardens wielded extensive independent authority in determining prison standards and operating procedures. These "operational silos" resulted in a lack of accountability and responsibility among the various institutions. . . . To make matters worse, many prison medical staff believe that the warden is their "real boss" even though organization charts indicate that medical staff report to [the Director of Health Care Service].

The prison medical delivery system is in such a blatant state of crisis that in recent days defendants have publicly conceded their inability to find and implement on their own solutions that will meet constitutional standards. The State's failure has created a vacuum of leadership, and utter disarray in the management, supervision, and delivery of care in the Department of Corrections' medical system.

. . . Indeed, Undersecretary of Corrections Kevin Carruth testified that medical care simply is not a priority within the CDCR, is not considered a "core competency" of the Department, and [it] is "not . . . and . . . never will be the business of the Department of Corrections to provide medical care."

. . . A major problem stemming from a lack of leadership and a prison culture that devalues the lives of its wards is that custody staff present a determined and persistent impediment to the delivery of even the most basic aspects of

---

1. The ensuing text includes, without designation, excerpts from a second opinion by Judge Henderson issued several month later. *See* the endnote to this footnote for citation details.

medical care. Too frequently medical care decisions are preempted by custodial staff who have been given improper managerial responsibility over medical decision-making. . . .

. . . All in all, there is a common lack of respect by custody staff for medical staff, and custody staff far too often actively interfere with the provision of medical care, often for reasons that appear to have little or nothing to do with legitimate custody concerns. This exacerbates the problem of physician retention, and the evidence reflects that a number of competent physicians have left CDCR specifically due to conflicts with custodial staff.

Defendants have devised a long-term strategy to contract out health care management and much of the delivery of care. However, full implementation of that plan is, by defendants' own estimates, years away. In the meantime, roughly 162,000 prisoners are being subjected to an unconstitutional system fraught with medical neglect and malfeasance. Defendants themselves have conceded that a significant number of prisoners have died as a direct result of this lack of care, and it is clear to the Court that more are sure to suffer and die if the system is not immediately overhauled. . . .

Since entry of the Stipulated Injunction [i.e., the consent decree] . . . , . . . not a single prison has successfully completed implementation [of the new policies and procedures]. . . .

. . . In February 2005, the Court requested that the court experts provide a verbal report as to their findings thus far. The report was shocking. The experts reported that they observed widespread evidence of medical malpractice and neglect. When they attempted to review a backlog of 193 death records, the experts encountered prisons where the inmates' medical records could not even be located. The medical records in most CDCR prisons are either in a shambles or non-existent. This makes even mediocre medical care impossible. Among the records they were able to review, the experts found 34 of the deaths highly problematic, with multiple instances of incompetence, indifference, neglect, and even cruelty by medical staff. As just one example among many, a prisoner was identified with extremely high blood pressure, was placed on medication in 2002, and was not seen again for a year and a half, at which point he was found unconscious and then died. The experts concluded that the widespread problems they observed resulted from a combination of physician error and "a totally broken system."

Following the experts' verbal report, the Court decided to visit one of the prisons to gain a first-hand understanding of the situation. The Court toured San Quentin prison on February 10, 2005. To provide some context, San Quentin was supposed to have been "rolled out" over a year earlier (i.e., it was in the first group of institutions scheduled to achieve compliance in 2003), and it has been the subject of a number of past federal and state court orders. Nonetheless, the result of the tour was horrifying. Even the most simple and basic elements of a minimally adequate medical system were obviously lacking. For example, the main medical examining room lacked any means of sanitation — there was no sink and no alcohol gel — where roughly one hundred men per day undergo medical screening, and the Court observed that the dentist neither washed his hands nor changed his gloves after treating patients into whose mouths he had placed his hands. There can be no excuse for such failures, especially given the risk of infection that is obvious even to a lay person. It does not take a budget change proposal, a strategic plan, or the hiring of new personnel to keep a medical room sanitary.

Further, the Outpatient Housing Unit (OHU) is far too small for San Quentin's population. San Quentin has a rated capacity of 3,317 individuals, but currently houses approximately 6,000 men. The OHU has 32 cells, but 22 are reserved for mental health patients, and of the 10 remaining for medical purposes some are permanently used for disabled inmates. . . . Moreover, the OHU was in deplorable condition. The cells were dirty, the nursing station is beyond sight or sound of the cells, and there is no examination room on the unit so that examinations are often performed on the cell floors or even through the food slots.

The pharmacy was in almost complete disarray (with unlabeled cardboard boxes piled in no particular order, antiquated and dirty computers, wiring suspended like a drunken spider's web, and extremely frustrated nurses and technicians). . . . There are serious, long-standing problems with dispensing medication, renewing prescriptions, and tracking expired prescriptions. [A]nd there was an obvious shortage of medical supervisory and line staff. Additionally,. . . overcrowding . . . has resulted in prisoners being housed en masse (over 350 prisoners in double-bunks from wall to wall) in what was once a gymnasium, and along the first-floor corridors of five-tier units where they are subjected to having feces and urine flung at them from above, and where water continually seeps from the walls and collects in pools on the floors. It is beyond the Court's understanding how the State of California could allow an institution to sink into such deplorable condition.

Subsequently, the court experts issued two reports detailing the problems at San Quentin based on their extensive reviews of the institution. . . . [T]he experts "found a facility so old, antiquated, dirty, poorly staffed, poorly maintained, with inadequate medical space and equipment and over-crowded that it is our opinion that it is dangerous to house people there with certain medical conditions and is also dangerous to use this facility as an intake facility." The reports include numerous detailed examples of medical neglect and malfeasance. As just one example, the experts found a stack of hundreds of health services request forms on a nurse's desk waiting to be logged, triaged, or prioritized; many of these were for medication refill. The triage nurse position had been vacant for over a month, during which time the forms simply accumulated.

The contract nurse assigned to the area commented, "Some of these guys are either dead or better, one of the two."

The experts thus concluded with respect to San Quentin that "overall compliance with the Stipulated Order and subsequent Court Orders was non-existent." In fact, the experts stated that "there has been indifference to beginning the process required in the Stipulated Order." Unfortunately, the court experts' recent informal report to the Court indicates that many of the issues identified in the February visits of the experts and the Court have yet to be adequately addressed. The experts further have advised the Court that while San Quentin may be the worst of the 32 state prisons in terms of the condition of the physical plant, it is paralleled by a number of other prisons in terms of physician and nurse vacancies, incompetent medical staff, lack of supervision, and all other aspects of medical care delivery.

. . . The [overall] vacancy rate for physician positions is over 15%, and this does not account for the additional significant percentage of incompetent doctors who need to be replaced. The rates differ from institution to institution, depending partly on the desirability of the location and the culture of the prison. At one institution, there are only two doctors responsible for approximately 7,000 prisoners. . . .

. . . Vacancy rates at some institutions are as high as 80% for Registered Nurses (RNs) and 70% for medical technical assistants (MTAs) (i.e. licensed vocational nurses who are also custody officers). . . .

. . . According to a CDCR commissioned study, compensation for CDCR staff registered nurses is 20–40% lower than for RNs in the private sector, and up to 57% lower for some supervising nurses. . . .

. . . The difficulty in recruiting qualified medical staff is compounded by the poor working conditions. . . .

. . . [Defendants' expert] Dr. [Ronald] Shansky testified that historically the CDCR would hire any doctor who had "a license, a pulse and a pair of shoes." According to [Court expert] Dr. [Michael] Puisis, 20–50% of physicians at the prisons provide poor quality of care. Many of the CDCR physicians have prior criminal charges, have had privileges revoked from hospitals, or have mental health related problems. An August 2004 survey by CDCR's Health Care Services Division showed that approximately 20 percent of the CDCR physicians had a record of an adverse report on the National Practitioner Databank, had a malpractice settlement, had their license restricted, or had been put on probation by the Medical Board of California. The Court Experts testified that the care provided by such doctors repeatedly harms prisoner patients. The Court finds that the incompetence and indifference of these CDCR physicians has directly resulted in an unacceptably high rate of patient death and morbidity.

. . . The evidence establishes beyond a doubt that the CDCR fails to provide competent nurses to fill the needs of the prison medical care system. According to the Court's nursing expert, Maddie LaMarre, CDCR nurses often fail to perform basic functions and refuse to carry out specific physician's orders. . . .

. . . At the institutional level, there are very few managers and supervisors that are competent. Thus, it is difficult to carry out central office directives. Just five or six prisons have an adequate chief physician and surgeon, and only one-third of the prisons have an adequate Health Care Manager.

. . . [C]entral office staff do not have the tools they need to handle the vast quantity of information necessary to handle a billion dollar, 164,000 inmate system. Data management, which is essential to managing a large health care system safely and efficiently, is practically non-existent. . . . As just one of innumerable examples, there are patients in the general prison population who need specialized housing, but the CDCR does not track them and headquarters staff is unaware of how many specialized beds are needed.

The Court has held two status conferences with the parties subsequent to the San Quentin tour. The Court has encouraged defendants to treat this situation as a state of emergency, to break out of the "business as usual" mind-set, and to take extreme measures to break through any bureaucratic or other barriers that are preventing implementation of the Stipulated Order. The Court also explained that it has a mandate to ensure that the Constitution is respected, and that on the strata of constitutional priorities, the preservation of life is the highest. At the March status conference, the Court instructed the parties to meet and confer, including the experts if necessary, to construct a plan for defendants to meet their deadlines and provide sufficient resources to meet their obligations under the Stipulated Injunction. The parties were unable to devise the requested plan, and defendants explained that doing so was an impossible task for them.

Nevertheless, defendants provided the Court with a document entitled "Strategies to Improve Program Compliance: Inmate Medical Service Program," dated April 2005. The document includes numerous damning admissions. Defendants state that the "current vacancy rate in upper management positions within the Health Care Services Division's Field Management Branch [is] now approximately 80 percent." Additionally, the Department lacks regional administrators who would provide clinical oversight to doctors and nurses in the field. Furthermore, "areas such as budget, personnel, contracts, procurement, information systems, physical plant, and space issues [] continue to pose fundamental barriers to compliance." The document also refers to CDC medical care as a "broken system."

Unfortunately, while recognizing the depth of the problem, defendants' strategies document fails to exhibit the force of will necessary to tackle the problem. Instead, it is fraught with the same kind of ineffective measures that have proven so inadequate over the past years. Most of the proposed actions in the document are followed by highlighted caveats such as: *"Implementation is contingent on Governor's approval, funding availability, and legislative approval."*

(emphasis in original) These kind of contingency statements are prime examples of the depth and breadth of the problem at hand.

Other elements of the strategies document are equally elusive. Defendants state that they will develop plans or proposals, with no indication of when the plans would be effectuated. The document also is vague and insufficiently detailed, has time periods that are excessively long, and fails to address how defendants will approach the critical task of removing incompetent medical staff from patient care.

Defendants have conceded at the recent status conferences that the most they are able to do at this point is to attempt to institute some "stop gap" measures, and even some of those appear beyond their capability. Moreover, defendants' representatives have publicly acknowledged that defendants are unable to correct the problem on their own, and that unconstitutional conditions will remain until an outside entity is hired to take over. Defendants have devised a plan to contract out health care management services, at headquarters and the institutions level, to a private entity. However, the process of identifying and selecting an appropriate entity or entities (assuming that such entities exist, are willing to take on the task, and will charge an amount the state is willing to pay) will, by defendants estimate, take at least eighteen months, and defendants have no estimate as to when the new entity will actually be able to make the changes necessary to show an improved standard of care in the prison system. Further, in this Court's experience, defendants' estimates for completing tasks have been consistently unreliable. In the meantime, prisoners continue to unnecessarily die, suffer, and go unattended.

The Need for a Receiver

After an evidentiary hearing in June 2005, Judge Henderson concluded that he had no alternative except to appoint a receiver to be in charge of the entire California prison medical delivery system. Taking over a medical system that was supposed to serve the needs of over 160,000 individuals was a monumental task, but the defendants had failed to provide the Court with alternative solutions. Moreover, the defendants did not oppose a receivership. Indeed, they appeared to welcome it.

Judge Henderson was both forceful and eloquent in elaborating on the need for a receivership:

> Looking at the full spectrum of powers typically exercised by the courts, there is no doubt that the imposition of a Receivership is a drastic measure. But it is not a measure that the Court has sought, nor is it one the Court relishes. Rather, the Court is simply at the end of the road with nowhere

else to turn. Indeed, it would be fair to say that the Receivership is being imposed on the Court, rather than on the State, for it is the State's abdication of responsibility that has led to the current crisis. Since the Court has jurisdiction over this matter, it has no choice but to step in and fill the void. But this is a disturbing result, not simply because it is a drastic measure for the Court, but because it exhibits a debilitation of the democratic process whereby the State executive branch has effectively turned over its obligations to the federal judicial branch. . . .

. . . To a significant extent, this case presents a textbook example of how majoritarian political institutions sometimes fail to muster the will to protect a disenfranchised, stigmatized, and unpopular subgroup of the population. This failure of political will, combined with a massive escalation in the rate of incarceration over the past few decades, has led to a serious and chronic abnegation of State responsibility for the basic medical needs of prisoners. The legal response to this political issue, however, is quite clear: When the state deprives individuals of their liberty, for whatever reason, it takes upon itself the obligation to provide those persons with certain services basic to their humanity, including medical care.

At the same time, Judge Henderson made it clear that he sought and expected the cooperation of state officials:

When appointing receivers, courts often remove the officials in charge of the entity responsible for the constitutional violations from power and place the receiver in their stead. As an expression of the Court's trust in the current State leadership, the Court will deviate from this practice and will not displace any State officials. This trust must continue to be earned. This Order shall serve as notice to the current leaders of the prison system and of the State that they must do everything in their power to work cooperatively with the Receiver, to create substantial reform in the executive branch (within CDCR and in all other relevant agencies), to seek legislative reform where necessary, and take all other necessary measures to eradicate the barriers that have led to the current crisis. . . .

Finally, he emphasized what he hoped would be the limited nature of his judicial intervention:

It bears emphasizing that establishment of the Receivership, while absolutely necessary, is intended as a temporary, not permanent, measure. The Court looks forward to the day, hopefully sooner rather than later, when responsible officials of the State will assume their legal obligations to run the CDCR in a manner that provides constitutionally adequate health care to all prisoners. As the Supreme Court has instructed, "[a] receivership is only a means to reach some legitimate end sought through the exercise of the power of a court of equity. It is not an end in itself." Once the Court is confident that defendants have the capacity and will to provide such care, the Court will relinquish control from the Receiver back to the State.

Finding a Receiver

The initial step of finding a receiver was no small task. Ideally, that person would have knowledge and experience both with prisons and the delivery of medical services, a commitment to providing quality medical care to prisoners, the creativity and patience to reform a largely dysfunctional system, and the administrative expertise to take charge of a statewide medical program that served over 160,000 persons.

Judge Henderson had hoped the parties could recommend a suitable receiver, but he soon realized the task was beyond them. In the fall of 2005, he hired a professional search firm; and after interviewing several finalists, he announced that Robert Sillen would begin to serve as receiver on April 17, 2006. The order creating the receivership gave Sillen extensive authority, including "all powers vested by law in the Secretary of the CDCR as they relate to the . . . California prison medical health care system"; the power to "hire, fire, suspend,. . . and take all other personnel actions" regarding CDCR or contract employees who perform medical health related services; "the power to establish personnel policies and . . . to negotiate . . . contracts . . . including contracts with labor unions"; and "the power to acquire, dispose of, modernize, repair, and lease property, equipment, and other tangible goods as necessary to carry out his duties." Once he began his duties as receiver, Sillen was to make bimonthly reports to the Court.

In the meantime, Judge Henderson continued to press the state to fix its broken prison medical system. In late November, he warned Governor Schwarzenegger to become involved with the problem and to find money for emergency reforms "the same way you find the money to build a tent to smoke cigars."[2] A few days later, Judge Henderson ordered an increase in salaries for doctors and nurses, and he ordered the Governor to appoint an individual with specific responsibility for carrying out the Court's orders. Less than three weeks before Sillen assumed his duties as receiver, Judge Henderson ordered the state to pay over $58 million that it owed to doctors who had treated inmates. Some of the

---

2. The reference is to an elaborate "smoking tent" that Governor Schwarzenegger had constructed on the capitol grounds for his cigar smoking, which was illegal inside the capitol building itself.

doctors had not been paid in over four years; some specialists were no longer responding when called to treat prisoners. The state complied with each of the orders, but little else changed.

The Receivership: Phase One

Robert Sillen seemed to be the perfect person for the receivership job. He began his career as a public health officer working to combat sexually transmitted diseases in Harlem. After receiving a master's degree in public health from Yale University, he became a hospital administrator first in New York and then at the University of California Medical Center before becoming the head of the Santa Clara Valley Medical Center. The Valley Medical Center was a struggling public hospital in Santa Clara County, California. Sillen received national attention and praise for making it a first-class operation. In 1993, he became head of the entire Santa Clara County public health system, which had 6,200 employees and a $1.4 billion annual budget. At the same time, he had joint responsibility for health care in Santa Clara County's jails and juvenile facilities. People who knew him described him as an outspoken, sometimes pushy individual who could get things done. And he was committed to making quality health care services available to the poor. The plaintiffs' lawyers praised Judge Henderson's choice, and the defendants expressed their eagerness to cooperate with Sillen. State Senator Gloria Romero, one of the legislature's most dedicated prison reform advocates, said, "I've heard nothing but accolades about his integrity and ability . . . to make things happen."

In early July 2006, Sillen filed the first of his bimonthly reports. His assessment was not encouraging:

> [T]he situation in California's prisons is, perhaps, worse than the descriptions [provided by Judge Henderson]. . . . Almost every necessary element of a working medical care system either does not exist, or functions in a state of abject disrepair.

Citing "systemic long term overcrowding," "instability of leadership," and "the poor reputation that CDCR has earned as an employer," Sillen suggested that "raising the medical care system to constitutional standards may require removing it from the umbrella of the CDCR."

The report focused on three particularly serious problems with which Sillen had begun to deal: the disarray in the prison pharmacy system, bureaucratic impediments to contracting with various providers of goods and specialty services, and (even after Judge Henderson's ordered pay raise) the low salaries for doctors and nurses. Ironically, the low salaries did not result in cost savings.

Rather, inadequate salaries hindered recruitment, which in turn forced the state to contract with private providers for basic services. As the report observed:

> These contractors are paid at an hourly rate which far exceeds the salaries of State employees; in fact, the salaries of the contractors often exceeds the salary of the CDCR managers who supervise them.

Despite this dire assessment, the receiver and his team of associates — with the aid of Judge Henderson's court orders — began to have some successes. Sillen's forceful, sometimes abrasive approach allowed him to cut through much of the CDCR bureaucracy and bring about reforms that the state could not achieve on its own. In September 2007, Sillen reported on a number of "first steps," including

> an overhaul of the pharmacy system, bringing medical staff salaries up to market levels, providing prisons with needed equipment and supplies . . ., revamping medical contracting and personnel practices,. . . constructing an adequate emergency room at San Quentin,. . . and launching a project to built up to 5,000 medical and 5,000 mental health beds statewide.

Sillen also reviewed a new CDCR study of inmate deaths in 2006:

> Of 426 deaths . . ., 66 of them — or 15 percent — were preventable (18) or possibly preventable (48). Among the non-preventable medical deaths (315), more than half reflected lapses in care that may have contributed to earlier death or more suffering among terminal patients.

Two months later, after prodding from Judge Henderson, the receiver filed a complex document setting forth specific goals and timetables for reforming the medical services delivery system.

At the same time that he was making progress, Sillen's self-assured, take-no-prisoners mentality increasingly was becoming a liability. The initial receivership order called for an advisory board; but despite Judge Henderson's urging, Sillen found excuses to ignore this requirement. Sillen's threat to "back up the Brink's truck" to raid the state treasury did not sit well with Judge Henderson (or, presumably, the defendants); and the plaintiffs' attorneys criticized Sillen for not responding to their advice about some of the most severe deficiencies in the prison medical system. At one point, the tension between the receiver and plaintiffs' attorneys became so great that Judge Henderson appointed Starr Babcock, a senior executive with the State Bar Association, to mediate their differences "so that the Court and all concerned can focus efficiently on the large task at hand."

Sillen's resistance to the advisory board bothered Judge Henderson more than the complaints from plaintiffs' lawyers. Both of these issues, however, paled in comparison to Sillen's intransigence on the question of salaries for receivership staff. In what Judge Henderson has acknowledged was not a wise decision, he followed his search firm's advice and gave Sillen a salary of $500,000 — twice what he had been making with Santa Clara County. Sillen, in turn, apparently used his own bloated salary as a basis for deciding the compensation for receivership employees. In any event, Sillen repeatedly ignored Judge Henderson's demands to rein in salaries. As a result, Judge Henderson began quietly looking for a new receiver in the fall of 2007. In a meeting with Sillen on January 23, 2008, Judge Henderson terminated Sillen's services and replaced him with McGeorge School of Law professor and former state government official Clark Kelso. Announcing the change, Judge Henderson had only praised for Sillen's past work:

> While the current Receiver has successfully used his unique skills and bold, creative leadership style to investigate, confront and break down many of the barriers that existed at the inception of the Receivership, the second phase of the Receivership demands a substantially different set of administrative skills and style of collaborative leadership.

The Receivership: Phase Two — Early Progress and Backsliding

Just as Robert Sillen seemed to be the ideal person for the receivership when it was created in 2006, Clark Kelso appeared to be — and has turned out to be — the ideal person to continue the receivership's work. He was the head of McGeorge's Capital Center for Government, Law, and Policy; he had worked in both the Davis and Schwarzenegger administrations, serving as Acting Insurance Commissioner in 2000; and he had close contacts with leaders in all three branches of state government. A 2007 profile described Kelso as "the state's handyman. When a department seems broken or plagued by scandal, he's the one brought in to fix it." Kelso immediately began to trim the receivership staff and prepare a less cumbersome, more user-friendly turnaround plan for the prison medical system.

By January 2010, Kelso was able to report substantial progress on a number of fronts, including inmate access to health care, staffing, and quality control. However, a major stumbling block remained — state funding to increase the number of beds available for medical care:

> [T]he initial planning efforts [began] in 2006 . . . with an agreement with the Administration to seek new funding in the amount of $6 billion to construct seven new facilities around the state which would have added approximately 10,000 beds for inmates [with medical and mental health

needs]. . . . The plan was intended to satisfy health care bed needs projected out to 2018. . . . The Administration also agreed to $1 billion in funding to improve facilities at existing prisons to support medical and mental health treatment. . . .

Beginning in 2008, the Administration withdrew its support for the investment. . . .

When the state reneged on its agreement, Judge Henderson, at Kelso's urging, ordered the defendants to show cause why they should not be held in contempt. After the show cause hearing, Judge Henderson deferred the contempt decision and ordered the defendants to release $250 million to the receiver within eleven days. The defendants received a stay of that order while they sought to appeal it. Several months later the Ninth Circuit held that the order was not appealable.

The ball was back in Judge Henderson's court. He was free to proceed with a contempt citation, but to what end? Any finding of contempt would have brought the inevitable delay of another stay and another appeal. And even if a contempt citation were affirmed, what remedy would actually further the objectives of the receivership? Monetary fines seemed unrealistic for an already financially strapped state, and committing the governor or other administration officials to jail — even if theoretically possible — was, as a practical matter, not going to happen.

Realizing his dilemma even before the Ninth Circuit ruling, Judge Henderson encouraged Clark Kelso to continue working with CDCR Secretary Matt Cate and to salvage as much as possible from the initial agreement. Kelso's January 2010 report described the result of those efforts:

> [W]ith the collapse of the national economy and California's budget, the Receiver began working collaboratively with Secretary Matt Cate and other CDCR staff to attempt to scale back construction plans to a level more consistent with available resources. These discussions ultimately resulted in the CDCR submitting a long-term bed plan . . . which provides approximately $2.34 billion in funding for healthcare-related construction to be financed by the sale of bonds previously authorized by AB 900.[3] Instead of 7 facilities and 10,000 new beds . . ., the new plan envisions only 1 new facility and approximately 1,600 beds for inmates with medical and mental health problems, the use of three juvenile justice facilities which would be converted to hold approximately 3,200 inmates with medical and mental health conditions, and allocation of $700 million for

---

3. AB 900, passed by the legislature and signed by the governor in the spring of 2007, called for 53,000 new prison beds, including 8,000 medical beds. [Author's footnote]

improvements to existing facilities. Although the current plan is likely to fall short of actual needs in some material respects, the Receiver believes it is the most that can be accomplished at this time given the state's serious financial problems and the amount of funding available under AB 900.

The outlook for the future, however, was not good. According to Kelso's January 2010 report:

> As of this date,... the state still has not provided access to any funding to implement this plan, [and] it remains uncertain whether funding will ever be made available for these purposes....

An Effort to End the Receivership and the Construction Plan for Medical Beds

In early 2009, while they were trying to appeal Judge Henderson's order to transfer $250 million to the receivership, the defendants for the first time questioned the very authority of the court to appoint a receiver. They filed a motion to replace the receiver with a Special Master and terminate the receiver's construction plan for medical beds. Judge Henderson denied that motion. A little over a year later the Ninth Circuit affirmed Judge Henderson's refusal to terminate the receivership and held that his ruling with respect to the construction plan was not appealable. The state made no further effort to pursue these matters.

Not surprisingly, the defendants have not offered an explanation for their shift from cooperating fully with the receiver to challenging the court's right to establish the receivership. At least three interrelated factors probably accounted for the state's change of position.

First, in large measure because of the state's dysfunctional revenue-raising rules and the political gridlock in the legislature, the national economic recession was particularly hard on California. Even though the receiver had been sensitive to the state's financial crisis, reforming the prison medical system after years of neglect would not be cheap. Spending money on prison reform is never politically popular, and that is especially true in difficult economic times.

Second, as the next chapter discusses in detail, the problem of overcrowding in California prisons — which is a large part of the reason for inadequate prison medical care — became the subject of litigation before a three-judge federal court panel that included Judge Henderson. Although it is possible to alleviate overcrowding with relatively innocuous remedies, the prospect of early release for some prisoners generated substantial political controversy. As a result, the three-judge court case took center stage. CDCR Secretary Cate and other members of the Schwarzenegger administration continued to cooperate quietly with the receiver on a day-to-day basis. Nonetheless, the three-judge court suit probably contributed to the state publicly taking a more adversarial position in *Plata*. (As noted later in the chapter, the defendants' renewed calls in 2012 and 2013 for terminating the receivership relate directly to overcrowding and the three-judge court litigation.)

Third, the gubernatorial aspirations of the then California Attorney General (and former governor and Democratic presidential candidate) Jerry Brown appear to have hindered the state's relationship with the receiver. Brown did not formally announce his candidacy until March 1, 2010. However, as far back as 2008, there was widespread speculation that Brown would run; and in apparent anticipation of his run, Brown had been positioning himself as a tough-on-crime, law-and-order public official. That stance is consistent with the state's resistance to the receivership and to Judge Henderson's $250 million transfer order; and as Attorney General, Brown was a significant decision maker on these issues.

A Brief Return to Significant Progress

Whatever the defendants' precise reasons for mounting the unsuccessful challenge to the receivership, the period from the Ninth Circuit's affirmation of the receivership in early 2010 until late 2012 was a time of progress and cooperation between the state and the receiver. Jerry Brown was elected governor of California in November 2010. He took office the following January, and he retained Matt Cate as the head of the CDCR. The good working relationship that Cate and Kelso developed during the Schwarzenegger administration continued. Kelso's Tri-Annual Reports to Judge Henderson regularly described progress in meeting the receiver's goals, including implementation of the scaled-down agreement for additional beds that Kelso had discussed in the January 2010 report. At the same time, though, the reports repeatedly pointed out that prison overcrowding and the state's severe budget problems hindered the receiver's work and required him to delay various projects.

In January 2012, Kelso reported that "we are now in a position to start contemplating the end of the Receivership." Judge Henderson then ordered the parties and the receiver to meet and confer about post-receivership planning and to file a joint response within four months. After receiving the response and Kelso's assessment that it was appropriate to begin the process of ending the receivership, Judge Henderson, on May 30, 2012, issued an order setting forth a proposed process to achieve that end. It included using court experts to evaluate the quality of care at each institution and having the receiver employ revocable delegations of authority to transfer power over medical care back to the state. He formalized those suggestions on September 5, and Kelso's September

15 Tri-Annual Report was by far the most positive to date. Yet, there were signs of potential difficulty.

Assertions of Constitutional Compliance

As Judge Henderson had pointed out in his May 30 order, the joint response regarding post-receivership planning indicated not only substantial progress but also serious disagreements — the most serious of which related to the continuing need for a receiver. As part of the joint response, the defendants had asserted:

> Any constitutional deficiencies in California's prison health care system have . . . been corrected, and the conditions which justified the Receiver's appointment no longer exist. . . .
>
> Based on the Receiver's progress on the Turnaround Plan, and Defendants' will and capacity to complete the Turnaround Plan, the Receivership should end and the Court should [appoint a special master]. . . . Defendants suggest that the Court enter such an order within thirty days. . . .

And in a response to the May 30 order, the defendants maintained that the receivership should end *immediately*.

The plaintiffs, the receiver, and Judge Henderson all disagreed. Indeed, in his September 5, 2012 order formalizing the process for terminating the receivership, Judge Henderson stated:

> The parties, the Receiver, and the Court must have sufficient time to evaluate whether the Defendants have successfully managed all . . . tasks [delegated to them pursuant to the Receiver's revocable delegations of authority]. Consequently, the Receivership will not end until after a reasonable period of time following the final revocable delegation of authority.

The defendants did not formally move to end the receivership. However, in early February 2013 they once again threatened to file a termination motion. This time their stated concerns were that the expert evaluations that Judge Henderson had called for as part of the process for ending the receivership might not be completed "in a reasonable period" and that the experts might "lose sight of the governing constitutional standards."

The defendants' threat was symptomatic of the deteriorating relationship between them and the receiver, which appears to have been exasperated by a change in the leadership of CDCR. In October 2012, Matt Cate left his position as Secretary to pursue other interests. Two months later, Governor Brown appointed Jeffrey Beard, a former Pennsylvania Corrections Secretary to replace him. Cate had recommended Beard, and Beard had been an expert witness for plaintiffs in the three-judge court case discussed in the next chapter. Thus, one might have expected the cooperation between the receiver and the CDCR to continue. That, however, was not to be. Whereas Matt Cate had maintained a low profile and worked closely with Clark Kelso, Jeffrey Beard made that kind of relationship virtually impossible by becoming an aggressive public advocate for the defendants' positions. For example, less than a month after being appointed Secretary in December 2012, Beard was widely cited in the press for his claim that California was providing constitutionally adequate medical care. Several months later, according to the Associated Press, Beard "scoffed" at a contrary assessment.

As Kelso noted in his May 22, 2013 Tri-Annual Report:

> Over the course of the last two reporting periods [September 1, 2012–April 30, 2013], the substance and tone of leadership set by State officials has changed from acquiescence bordering on support for the Receiver's work, to opposition bordering on contempt for the Receiver's work. . . .
>
> [T]he tone from the top of the Administration that improvements in prison healthcare have gone too far . . . interferes with our progress toward a final transition of prison medical care back to the State. We have lost at least six to nine months of time while the State essentially relitigates claims that it previously lost. . . .

Valley Fever

One example that Kelso cited in his May 22 report involved a problem that had been simmering since at least 2005: the state's inadequate response to the incidents of coccidioidomycosis (commonly referred to as Valley Fever or cocci) at eight prisons — most notably Pleasant Valley State Prison (PVSP) and, to a somewhat lesser extent, Avenol State Prison (ASP) — in the southern San Joaquin Valley. Valley Fever is a fungal disease caused by exposure to dust containing the coccidioides fungus, which inhabits the arid soils of the southwestern United States. The disease cannot spread from human to human, and most people with Valley Fever have flu-like symptoms that dissipate without antifungal treatment. However, in approximately 10% of the cases, individuals become seriously ill. For them, the disease can affect their lungs, soft tissues, joints, bones, or meninges (the membranes surrounding the spinal cord and brain). While anyone can develop a severe case of Valley Fever, those most at risk include African Americans, Filipinos, individuals with compromised immune systems (for example, from HIV or an organ transplant), and those with chronic illnesses (for example, diabetes or chronic lung disease). There is no vaccine to protect against the disease. In 2011, there were 640 reported cases of Valley Fever within the CDCR, nearly 85% of which occurred at PVSP and ASP.

After the defendants had reported an increased number of inmates, primarily at PVSP, with Valley Fever in 2005, the receiver asked the California Department of Public Health (CDPH) to investigate. CDPH confirmed that there had been an outbreak of Valley Fever at PVSP and made a number of recommendations. They included "inmate and staff education, environmental controls, and relocation of the highest risk groups to other prisons." PVSP only partially implemented the recommendations. Initially, the education efforts were minimal:

> PVSP "posted laminated signs in all medical clinics, inmate housing units and law libraries" regarding the "signs and symptoms" of cocci. . . . PVSP also alerted staff to "signs and symptoms" by providing information in two issues of the "In-Service Training Bulletin."

The relocation initiative did not include African Americans and Filipinos, groups that the CDPH identified as being at high risk. And PVSP did not follow the recommendation to increase prison ground cover, a proven method for reducing airborne cocci spores. The ground cover recommendation was deemed "not feasible" because the initial cost "could potentially exceed $750,000, in addition to significant ongoing maintenance costs."

Following the CDPH's final report in January 2007, the receiver convened his own committee of experts to study the problem. As a result of that committee's recommendations and continuing discussions between CDCR and the receiver, CDCR implemented additional mitigation efforts over the next several years not only at PVSP but at all eight prisons in the southern San Joaquin Valley. The efforts, however, were insufficient. An April 2012 report from the receiver's Public Health and Quality Management Units examined the cocci problem for the years between 2006 and 2010. According to the report:

- Despite mitigation efforts, including the "exclusion of inmates . . . most vulnerable to cocci," cocci rates failed to decline at all eight prisons.
- The rates of cocci infection as PVSP and ASP were much higher than the rates for the counties in which they are located.
- In comparison to the rate in California, the rate at PVSP was over 1,000 times higher, and the rate at ASP was 189 times higher.
- In the 2008/2009 and 2009/2010 fiscal years, 355 inmates required hospitalization for cocci.
- The cost for outside hospital care for inmates with cocci, for guarding them outside the institution, and for their antifungal treatment was approximately $23.4 million per year.

- Twenty-seven inmates died from cocci complications during the 2006–2010 period. "The rate of deaths due to cocci among African American inmates was eight times the death rate due to cocci among African Americans in California and twice the death rate due to cocci among non-African American inmates in California."

These findings led to further mitigation efforts and requests for assistance from both the CDPH and federal Centers for Disease Control and Prevention. The CDCR, however, refused, as it had before, to exclude African Americans, Filipinos, and diabetics from PVSP and ASP. According to Judge Henderson, this refusal continued

> even after CDPH provided its formal commentary on April 4, 2013, that "[a] factor that probably contributed to the high rates [in PVSP and ASP] is housing populations of inmates at risk for severe cocci disease, *such as African Americans and persons with diabetes or other chronic diseases.*" (emphasis in original)

In his May 22, 2013 Tri-Annual Report, Kelso characterized CDCR's response over the last few years to the "serious cocci problem at PVSP and ASP" as "anemic." He then suggested:

> Defendants' objections to the Receiver's updated cocci policy and their refusal even to take preliminary steps to implement the policy suggest that they may not yet possess the requisite concern for preventing unnecessary morbidity and death among inmates to justify further transition of the prison medical system back to Defendants' control.

On June 24, 2013, Judge Henderson ordered the defendants to exclude from PVSP and ASP any new high-risk inmates, including African Americans, Filipinos, and diabetics, within seven days. High-risk inmates currently incarcerated at PVSP and ASP were to be transferred out of those institutions within ninety days. Judge Henderson also ordered CDCR to provide its medical and nursing staff with additional cocci training. The order was a slightly modified version of the receiver's earlier recommendations that the CDCR had refused to implement.

The next day CDCR Secretary Jeffrey Beard announced to the press that Judge Henderson's order "could exacerbate violence between race-based prison gangs elsewhere in California." However, as Judge Henderson had noted in his order, "CDCR routinely transfers hundreds or thousands of inmates on a weekly basis." Moreover, by the time of Judge Henderson's June 24, 2013 order excluding African Americans and other high-risk inmates of PVSP and ASP, California's prisons contained 40,000 fewer inmates than in 2006, when CDCR first began its Valley Fever mitigation efforts.

A Bit of Optimism — and Continuing Problems

The state complied with Judge Henderson's June 24 order within the ninety-day time frame. Moreover, the receiver has continued to report some progress toward meeting the goal of providing constitutionally adequate medical care for California's prisoners, and he has not repeated his May 22, 2013 assessment that the "tone of leadership set by State officials" had become one of "opposition bordering on contempt for the receiver's work." Indeed, his second Tri-Annual Report for 2014 stated:

> The Receiver has been impressed at CDCR's renewed spirit of cooperation in achieving all of the goals. . . . That collaborative spirit makes our work so much easier to accomplish and helps ensure that we keep moving forward.

The path forward, however, has not been smooth. For example, the much bally-hooed rollout in July 2013 of a new health care facility in Stockton was extremely rocky; and upgrades to medical facilities in other institutions are years behind schedule.

Prison Overcrowding

The three-judge court order mandating a significant reduction in California's prison population is the subject of the next chapter. Without getting too far ahead of the story, it is important at this point to understand that both the state's inability to deal adequately with Valley Fever and the state's recent calls for terminating the receivership are inextricably related to the problem of overcrowding.

In addition to the fact that overcrowding, as the receiver's Tri-annual Reports have repeatedly stated, makes it difficult to provide adequate medical services to inmates, overcrowding is undoubtedly one of the reasons that the state was slow to exclude some inmates who are at high risk of contracting Valley Fever from PVSP and other southern San Joaquin Valley prisons. Making the eight southern San Joaquin Valley prisons unavailable to various categories of inmates could not help but put a strain on an overcrowded prison system and may well have been a significant reason — at least initially, when the prisons were at their most crowded — for CDRC's reluctance to exclude African Americans, who make up approximately 30% of the statewide prison population.

The defendants' claims that the receivership should end because the state is providing constitutionally adequate medical care to inmates is also, at its core, related to the overcrowding issue. The three-judge court discussed in the next chapter made a finding that overcrowding was the "primary cause" of the inmates' constitutionally deficient medical care. As a result of that and other findings, the court ordered a reduction in the state's prison population. The defendants met the court's early benchmarks, but sometime in 2012 it became apparent that the state would not meet the final two benchmarks with the population reduction plan that it was pursuing. Rather than voluntarily taking additional measures to reduce the prison population, the defendants began asserting that there was no need for further reductions because, the state claimed, inmate medical care had reached or surpassed the minimal standards required by the constitution. And since, in its view, the medical care was constitutionally adequate, there was no longer any need for the receiver. In short, it is likely that the state's position on overcrowding drove its calls in 2012 and 2013 to end the receivership.

The Conditions for Terminating the Receivership

In his order creating the receivership, Judge Henderson stated:

The Receivership shall remain in place no longer than the conditions which justify it make necessary, and shall cease as soon as the Court is satisfied, and so finds in consultation with the Receiver, that Defendants have the will, capacity, and leadership to maintain a system of providing constitutionally adequate health care. . . .

There are two important reasons why Judge Henderson focused on the defendants' will and capacity rather than on the actual achievement of constitutionally adequate medical care for prisoners. First, Judge Henderson's focus provides some assurance that improvements in the prison medical system developed during the receivership will be long lasting — that the reforms, in other words, will become institutionalized.

Second, Judge Henderson's focus on the defendants' "will, capacity, and leadership" is consistent with his goal of maintaining the receivership for "no longer than the conditions which justify it make necessary." The extreme step of appointing a receiver was necessary, recall, not merely because the state's prison medical health system was unconstitutional but also because the defendants, as they acknowledged, had been incapable of correcting the constitutional violations on their own. If and when the defendants demonstrate their will and capacity to operate a constitutionally adequate medical system for prisoners, the receivership, at least in theory, could end even as the lawsuit continues because some of the unconstitutional conditions have not yet been remedied. On the other hand, the achievement with the help of the receiver of a constitutionally adequate prison medical care system (assuming agreement on precisely what that means) would be no guarantee that the defendants, on their own, were prepared to maintain the same level of medical care. Thus, the receivership (and the underlying lawsuit) could continue beyond that point.

Evaluating the Quality of Medical Care

Assuming that progress in the delivery of medical care to prisoners continues, Judge Henderson eventually will have to decide when that care meets minimum constitutional standards. The task is inherently difficult because there is no bright-line test for determining what quality of health care is or is not constitutionally adequate. And the difficulty is compounded by disagreements over how to describe and measure the quality of health care actually being provided.

Between 2008 and early 2013, the state's Office of the Inspector General (OIG) conducted three rounds of evaluations of all thirty-three CDCR institutions. According to the receiver:

> When the OIG inspections began, more than 75 percent of the institutions earned low adherence scores. By the end of cycle three, no institution received low adherence scores, and over 75 percent of the 33 institutions earned high adherence scores. This seemed to indicate that the delivery of medical care to the patient-inmate population of California's correctional institutions had drastically improved.

This apparent conclusion, however, stands in sharp contrast to the findings of court-appointed experts. During 2013, acting pursuant to Judge Henderson's order, they evaluated ten prisons. According to the experts' reports, none was providing adequate medical care. Four had problems of varying seriousness that were relatively easily correctable. With respect to the other six, the experts concluded that "there are systemic issues that present an ongoing serious risk of harm to patients and result in preventable morbidity and mortality."

At Judge Henderson's suggestion, the parties, the OIG, the experts, and the receiver have been working to find a common set of standards for evaluating the quality of medical care at CDCR facilities. As of the end of 2014, they had not been successful. They had, however, narrowed their differences, and a new round of OIG evaluations began in January 2015. Clark Kelso has reported that the court experts believe the improved criteria for these new evaluations will probably be adequate to identify institutions where medical care is "clearly acceptable" or "clearly unacceptable"; however, the experts believe the new criteria "may not be sufficiently discerning with respect to those institutions in the middle."

The Work Remaining

In March 2015, Clark Kelso filed a sixty-five-page special report on the improvements in and current status of the prison medical health care system. Kelso described in detail the substantial improvements in health care since the appointment of a receiver in 2006. At the same time, though, he acknowledged that much remained to be done:

> At the system-wide level,. . . a number of improvements . . . must be completed. At the institution level, there is still wide variability in performance and, at some institutions, only partial implementation of system-level changes. Some institutions are much further ahead than others.
>
> . . . [T]he most significant and difficult work will undoubtedly have to take place at the institution level where statewide plans for change and change management confront the reality and inertia of decades of substandard care.

Moreover, Kelso pointed out, "[D]isagreements persist among the parties regarding the extent of the improvements and the appropriate timing of the next steps." These disagreements are particularly significant in light of the fact that OIG inspections are resuming without complete accord on the proper methodology for measuring the quality of each institution's medical care.

Kelso's report elaborated upon four areas of major concern: the failure to make information in health care records available on a timely basis; excessive rescheduling of appointments, which "creates backlogs and delays in seeing patients"; too high rates of hospital readmissions, which are probably the result of "shortcomings with chronic care, infection control, health information management and continuity of care, among other things"; and inadequate facilities:

> Most facilities are still grossly insufficient for providing appropriate medical care for patients. Treatment rooms are too small, poorly configured, lack basic equipment and fixtures, are not appropriately sanitized, and are disorderly.

Relying in part upon Kelso's special report, Judge Henderson, on March 10, 2015, issued an order that modified his May 5, 2012 order dealing with inspections and revocable delegations of authority as the means to transition away from the receivership. He noted, as had the receiver, that despite significant progress, much remained to be done; he observed that, at least for the present there was no need to resolve the remaining disagreements between the court experts and the OIG over the latter's methodology; and he reaffirmed that

> revocable delegations of authority continue to provide an appropriate mechanism for allowing Defendants an opportunity to demonstrate their will, capacity, and leadership to maintain a constitutional system of care, while, at the same time, ensuring that Receiver can step in expeditiously to address any issues if Defendants fail.

The order went on to set forth a blueprint for the eventual termination of the receivership and the closing of the case. It provides in part:

- After the OIG releases each medical inspection report, the Receiver shall determine whether that institution is suitable for return to CDRC control. . . . If the Receiver . . . [makes a positive determination], he will execute a revocable delegation of authority to the Secretary of the CDCR. . . .
- Prior to executing [or revoking] any delegation of authority, the Receiver shall meet and confer with the parties and consult with the court experts.
- The Receiver shall evaluate regularly, and no less frequently than monthly, whether any delegations should be revoked. . . .
- Any party who disagrees with the Receiver's decision to delegate or not delegate, or to revoke or not revoke a previous delegation, may challenge that decision by filing a motion before this Court. . . .
- While the Receiver will gradually take on more of a monitoring function as additional activities and institutions are delegated back to CDCR, transitioning from a Receivership to a special master or monitor would eliminate the revocability of the delegations. Accordingly, while the Receiver will ultimately become a monitor in function, he will remain a receiver and retain his powers over the inmate medical care system until this case terminates.
- Once all headquarters' functions and institutions have been revocably delegated to CDCR . . . [and left] in place without revocation for a one-year period, a rebuttable presumption of constitutional adequacy and sustainability will be created. Plaintiffs must file any motion challenging this presumption within 120 days of the expiration of the one-year period. If no such motion is filed, the parties shall promptly file a stipulation and proposed order terminating the Receivership and this case.

As of Judge Henderson's March 10 order, the receiver had made revocable delegations of authority to the CDCR in only two areas — (1) prison construction and activation and (2) the management of institutional health care access units, which are designed to facilitate the timely movement of prisoners to both on-site and off-site care. Between that date and June 2016, the receiver made revocable delegations of authority for medical operations to only three institutions: Folsom State Prison, Correctional Training Facility (Soledad), and Chuckawalla Valley State Prison. Unless there is a sudden, dramatic improvement — particularly at the institutional level — in the quality of medical care and agreement on how to measure the quality of that care, it seems likely that the receivership will remain in place and the case will remain open well beyond 2016.

Chapter Seventeen

Judge Henderson's Prison Trilogy, Part III: Coleman/Plata v. Schwarzenegger

In November 2006, one month after Governor Arnold Schwarzenegger declared a "Prison Overcrowding State of Emergency," the Plata v. Schwarzenegger plaintiffs filed a motion in Judge Henderson's court claiming that overcrowding was the primary cause of the unconstitutional state of the prison medical health system. Plaintiffs in Coleman v. Schwarzenegger, a lawsuit challenging the adequacy of the state prisons' mental health system, filed an identical motion in their case, which was being heard in the Eastern District of California by Judge Lawrence Karlton. Both motions sought a court-ordered reduction in the California prison population.

The *Coleman* Case

In 1990 — over a decade before the *Plata* litigation began — a group of mentally ill inmates filed a class action claiming that they were not receiving adequate mental health treatment. Following a trial, a magistrate judge found that the state's inadequate mental health services violated the plaintiffs' Eighth Amendment right to be free from cruel and unusual punishment. Judge Karlton adopted the magistrate judge's findings, granted injunctive relief, and appointed a Special Master to oversee compliance with the court's orders.

Just as the state has failed to provide beds for medical care, it has also failed to provide adequate accommodations for mentally ill prisoners. As Judge Karlton wrote in August 2009:

A significant amount of the remedial effort in *Coleman* has been spent on the as yet unsuccessful endeavor to develop a sufficient number of . . . care beds . . . and . . . adequate treatment space for all inmates with serious mental health disorders. The *Coleman* court has issued numerous orders addressing the need for mental health care beds and treatment space. . . .

. . . By the end of the first decade of remedial work in *Coleman*, the state had made some progress[,] but . . . two monitoring reports filed by the *Coleman* Special Master in 2006 reflected a troubling reversal in . . . progress. . . .

[According to the first report,] ". . . a growing number of the most seriously mentally ill inmates . . . were not receiving in a timely fashion the care they needed.". . .

[The second] report revealed that serious shortages in staffing and bed space, as well as substantial delays in transfers to necessary levels of care, continued unabated.

Among other findings, the Special Master reported that "the inexorably expanding demand for services resulting from the bulging population" had caused a "continuing deterioration of mental health staffing. . . . Twelve years after the determination that mental health treatment in CDCR was unconstitutional, the defendants still lacked the clinical resources to meet the needs of some 25 to 30 percent of inmates identified as seriously mentally disordered.". . .

. . . [T]he defendants did not object to any of the above findings, . . . including the Special Master's determination that the "escalating growth in the overall CDCR population" was a major cause of the CDCR's reversal in progress.

Judicial Responses to Overcrowding and the Prison Litigation Reform Act

Soon after federal courts began giving serious consideration to inmates' complaints about unconstitutional prison conditions, alleviation of overcrowding became a potential remedy. For example, in a 1977 case, the Fifth Circuit affirmed an order "forbidding new additions to the inmate population" in a Louisiana state prison; four years later, the Fifth Circuit recognized that "a district court may order a prison population reduced in order to alleviate unconstitutional conditions"; and in 1983 the Seventh Circuit upheld an order releasing inmates from the overcrowded Cook County, Illinois, jail. However, in 1996, as part of the Prison Litigation Reform Act (PLRA), Congress restricted the ability of federal courts to issue orders that cap prison populations or require the release of inmates. Any such order, according to the PLRA, must have been preceded by a less intrusive order for relief; that relief must have failed to remedy the right sought to be redressed; and the defendant must have had a reasonable time to comply with such a prior order.

Even if these conditions are satisfied, a single judge cannot release prisoners or impose a population cap. Instead, the PLRA provides that only a special three-judge federal court can issue such an order. Thus, a judge who makes the requisite findings regarding the ineffectiveness of less intrusive remedies must request the chief judge of the circuit court of appeals to empanel a three-judge court. And, according to the PLRA, the three-judge court can reduce or limit prison population only if it finds by "clear and convincing evidence" both that "crowding is the primary cause of the violation of the Federal right" and that "no other relief will remedy the violation of the Federal right."

The PLRA also codifies certain preexisting, common law limitations on judicial remedies for unconstitutional prison conditions: Orders granting prospective relief must (1) be "narrowly drawn," (2) extend "no further than necessary" to correct the underlying violation, and (3) be the "least intrusive means necessary" for achieving that purpose; and courts considering such orders (4) "must give substantial weight to any adverse impact on public safety or the operation of the criminal justice system caused by the relief."

In addition to these restrictions on the issuance of a prisoner release order, the PLRA creates what could become an administrative nightmare for any three-judge court considering such an order. It specifically grants the right of intervention in the action to

[a]ny State or local official including a legislator or unit of government whose jurisdiction or function includes the appropriation of funds for construction, operation, or maintenance of prison facilities, or the prosecution or custody of persons who may be released from, or not admitted to, a prison as a result of a prisoner release order.

That entitles potentially hundreds of individuals and entities to join the lawsuit, demand discovery, make various pretrial motions, and object to and offer evidence at trial.

Presumably the "legitimate" reason for such a provision is to ensure adequate representation to locales that could be adversely affected by a prisoner release order. A less charitable explanation is that the intervention rule is a procedural device designed to thwart prisoner release even if the requirements of the PLRA are satisfied. After all, one would think that the principal defendants would have a serious commitment to ensuring public safety; and as previously noted, the PLRA itself requires courts to give this factor "substantial weight." Moreover, generally applicable procedural rules require federal courts to permit intervention on an individualized basis when necessary to protect inadequately represented interests.

The Three-Judge Court in *Coleman/Plata*

In response to plaintiffs' overcrowding motions, Judge Henderson and Judge Karlton initially conducted separate hearings and received separate briefs. Then on June 27, 2007, they held a joint hearing. The question before them was straightforward and, in light of the record in both cases, fairly easy to answer: Had other less intrusive remedies failed, after a reasonable period of time, to cure the underlying Eighth Amendment violations? The defendants conceded that the constitutional violations were ongoing in both *Plata* and *Coleman*; and given the years of inaction and failed efforts, there was no serious claim that the defendants had not had a reasonable time to comply with the courts' mandates. Nonetheless, the *Plata* defendants argued that somehow their past failures were exempt from any "reasonable time" calculation because of the relatively recent appointment of a receiver. Judge Henderson responded:

> The Defendants' position would essentially have this Court wait years to see if the Receiver's Plan of Action is able to remedy the constitutional deficiencies in this case. . . . While the Court agrees that the Receiver has made much progress since his appointment, that fact does not render irrelevant the previous five years of complete and utter failure by Defendants to cure the constitutional deficiencies in the delivery of medical health care to prisoners. . . . Defendants have already been given ample opportunity to attempt to bring the delivery of medical care to prisoners up to constitutional standards. It is beyond reason that a willing and competent institution would not be able to show — over a period of several years and with this Court virtually screaming at every step of the way — significant progress in the hiring of medical personnel, the furnishing of adequate medical facilities, and the development of thoughtful and comprehensive plans for managing the delivery of medical health care. Yet, that is precisely what happened in this case, and it is why the appointment of a Receiver became necessary. To use the words of Defendants' counsel at the June 27, 2007 hearing, the appointment order was a "culminating order," and this Court finds it more reasonable to view such an order as the end of a series of less intrusive orders that failed to bring about any meaningful reform, rather than as a new beginning that requires this Court to wait more time, potentially years, to see whether the Receiver's plans will succeed or fail.

In separate orders the next month Judges Henderson and Karlton requested that Ninth Circuit Chief Judge Mary Schroeder convene a three-judge court. "For purposes of judicial economy and avoiding the risk of inconsistent judgments," they recommended — and Judge Schroeder agreed — that both cases should be assigned to the same three-judge panel.

The statute authorizing three-judge courts requires that the panel include the district court judge to whom the overcrowding motion was initially made and at least one court of appeals judge. There was no statutory language and no precedent for the situation where two district judges request the same three-judge court; but as Judges Henderson and Karlton expected, Judge Schroeder appointed both of them to the three-judge panel. The third judge, chosen from a randomly generated list of Ninth Circuit judges, was Stephen Reinhardt. Because the three-judge court would be an addition to the judge's normal case-load, the Ninth Circuit judges on the randomly generated list were permitted to opt out of the assignment. Judge Reinhardt was not the first name on the list, but he was the first to agree to hear the case.

Supporters of both sides in the litigation speculated that Judges Reinhardt, Henderson, and Karlton, all known for their liberal political views, would be favorably disposed to the plaintiffs. Indeed, Judges Henderson and Karlton had already articulated their concern that overcrowding was a serious problem that impeded the implementation of their orders. None of the judges, however, had addressed the specific questions that the PLRA required the court to answer. Moreover, without expressing any view about the ultimate outcome, Judge Henderson made it clear prior to the three-judge court trial that, in his view, the plaintiffs had a difficult task. The PLRA requires the plaintiffs to establish by a high standard of proof — "clear and convincing evidence" — not merely that overcrowding impeded the delivery of medical and mental health care but that overcrowding was "the *primary* cause" of the violation of plaintiffs' rights. In addition, the PLRA requires the plaintiffs to establish by the same high standard of proof that reducing prison populations is a "'remedy of last resort,'. . . that no other relief could remedy the constitutional violations. . . ." In any event, what seemed virtually certain to all of the parties, as well as the three-judge panel, was that the losing side, if there were no settlement, would exercise its right to appeal directly to the Supreme Court.

The Rhetoric, the Reality, and the Politics of Reducing Prison Populations

"Get tough on crime," "law and order" rhetoric has been the staple of many political campaigns including, for example, Richard Nixon's successful presidential bids and Rudolph Giuliani's mayoral triumphs in New York City. Perhaps most famously, the first President Bush ran a television advertisement linking his opponent, Democratic nominee Michael Dukakis, to Willie Horton, a convicted murderer. Horton had committed rape and armed robbery after being released on a weekend furlough program supported by Dukakis.

The typical fare offered by law and order candidates includes mandatory minimum sentences, less judicial discretion in sentencing, and longer sentences particularly for repeat offenders, all of which tend to increase prison populations. California, both through legislative action and popular initiatives, had embraced these policies with gusto; and despite severely overcrowded prisons, some law and order politicians — in response to the creation of the three-judge court — not surprisingly burnished their "tough on crime" reputations with claims that limiting California's prison population would endanger the public. Assemblyman Todd Spitzer characterized early release as "not an option because it will jeopardize public safety"; and Assemblyman Mike Villines proclaimed, "If we give in to a population cap, we are simply saying we are going to put criminals onto the street, we're going to make our citizens unsafe." San Diego County District Attorney Bonnie Dumanis added her voice to the chorus: "As an elected district attorney, my responsibility is to public safety, and I believe the safety of all Californians will be compromised if prisoners are released early." Governor Arnold Schwarzenegger declared, "[R]eleasing criminals back to our streets will be a public safety disaster."

Perhaps some of these politicians feared that the three-judge court might order a sudden, indiscriminate release of thousands of prisoners. Such an order could cause at least a temporary spike in crime — something that *might* have happened in Philadelphia after a 1990 court-ordered prisoner release, according to testimony elicited at Congressional hearing on the PLRA. However, there was apparently no effort systematically to verify the claims of increased crime and no attempt to design a strategy for release that took into account public safety concerns. In any event, the PLRA, as noted, requires any three-judge court to consider the effect of a prisoner release order on public safety; and neither the *Coleman/Plata* three-judge court nor any of the parties ever proposed a sudden, mass release of prisoners. Indeed, the three-judge court made it clear that it would not approve such an order.

Apart from the specter of a sudden, massive release of prisoners, the reality of early release is quite different from the law and order rhetoric of politicians. Empirical evidence supports the proposition that early release need not contribute to recidivism. More important, there is considerable agreement among experts that a significant, judiciously implemented reduction in the California prison population would actually contribute to, not detract from, public safety. Although this conclusion may initially seem counterintuitive, the reasons are not difficult to understand; and they were presented in elaborate detail to the three-judge court.

Most prisoners (including inmates serving "life" sentences) will eventually be released. With few exceptions, there is a close correlation between age and recidivism. Much criminal activity is strenuous work, and many inmates serving long sentences simply "age out" of the crime business. Thus, many older prisoners — who may be serving long sentences for serious crimes — will not present a recidivism threat regardless of whether they receive early release.

If prisoners are going to commit crimes after being released, they are likely to do so whether or not they happen to be released a few months early. Moreover, neither early release nor the prospect of a shorter sentence adversely affects the deterrence function of the criminal law. (The significant factors bearing on deterrence are the swiftness and certainty of punishment, not the length of sentence.) And there is no reason to believe the time it will take to apprehend and incarcerate repeat offenders depends on whether they were beneficiaries of early release.

At worst, as suggested, a large-scale early release might result in a temporary spike in criminal activity. That, however, should be an avoidable result. First, the releases can be spaced over a reasonable period of time. Second, and more important, early release can and should be based on an expanded system of credits awarded for good behavior and for the successful completion of rehabilitation and reentry programs. There is a growing body of empirical data about the efficacy of such programs and their ability to reduce recidivism.

Another safe way to reduce California's prison population is to divert low-risk individuals with short sentences. Many inmates enter the state prison system with sentences of only sixteen months. Between time spent in county jail prior to sentencing and good-time credits earned under the existing system, these inmates may end up serving no more than a few months in state prisons. Their incarcerations are likely to be too brief for them to benefit from prison rehabilitative efforts. If the state required them to serve the remaining time outside of prison and to participate in community-based rehabilitation programs, they would have a better chance of becoming reintegrated into society. Moreover, the benefits of the rehabilitation programs would not have to terminate at the end of the sentence. There is, of course, no guarantee against recidivism; but diversion, like early release based on an expanded good-time credit program, would at worst change only the timing of the recidivism. And because of the opportunities for rehabilitation, it is likely that recidivism would diminish.

At the time of the three-judge court hearing, California had one of the highest recidivism rates in the country. The reasons for this anomaly are complex, but two factors stand out. First, the state has tended to reincarcerate an inordinate number of individuals for technical parole violations that are not crimes.

The reincarceration is typically for only a few months, and there is no evidence that these brief periods of imprisonment contribute to rehabilitation or deterrence. On the contrary, they probably undermine rehabilitation because they inevitably interrupt any employment that the parolee may have as well as any participation in community-based support programs. At the same time, being reintroduced to prison for a short time may only exacerbate an individual's antisocial tendencies.[1]

A second significant reason for California's high recidivism rate is its failure, until very recently, to take even minimal steps to reintegrate individuals into society at the time of their release. It has not been uncommon, for example, for inmates to be released to society directly from the isolation of Pelican Bay's Secure Housing Unit.

To some extent, the failure to prepare inmates for life outside the prison walls is a direct result of overcrowding (which is due in part to the state's response to technical parole violations). New prisoners are classified according to their dangerousness, and the classifications are supposed to be used to determine the type of facility in which the inmates will be incarcerated. However, housing shortages due to overcrowding often require that inmates be assigned to more secure facilities than their classifications warrant. This type of placement has at least three adverse consequences. First, because placement in higher security facilities increases the cost of incarceration, the state is forced to use resources for incarceration that could be used more effectively for rehabilitation and reentry programs. Second, housing low-risk prisoners with higher risk prisoners inevitably creates the risk that the latter will adversely influence the former. Finally, and most important for present purposes, inmates who are not housed in accordance with their classifications are less likely to have access to the rehabilitation services that would be most beneficial to them.

The foregoing suggestions — judicious use of early release, diversion of low-risk offenders with short sentences, and reduction or elimination of incarceration for technical, noncriminal parole violations — are not the only ways to alleviate overcrowding in California's prisons. For example, Assembly Bill 900 (AB 900) contemplated a multibillion dollar program of new construction; Governor Schwarzenegger's state of emergency proclamation called for shipping prisoners to out-of-state facilities; there have been proposals for modifying the state's rigid sentencing laws; and more recently California has implemented its

---

1. Some parole violations are based on criminal conduct, and parole revocation is used as a substitute for criminal prosecution. If the crime is serious, the brief reincarceration may be inadequate from a public safety standpoint. If the crime is minor, reincarceration is likely to be undesirable for the reasons suggested in the text.

"Realignment" plan, which shifts responsibility (including custody) for certain offenses from the state to the counties. Nonetheless, the measures discussed in the preceding paragraphs would substantially reduce California's prison population without increasing recidivism or undermining deterrence. At the same time, the population reduction would make it easier for the state to provide rehabilitation and reentry services that would, in turn, reduce recidivism. Finally, the cost of providing these services at an enhanced level would be cheaper than to continue to pay well over $40,000 per inmate per year to maintain California's bloated prison population. In short, prisoner release makes sense both in terms of promoting public safety and utilizing scarce public resources wisely.

If prisoners in California receive early release, there is, of course, no guarantee that there will not be a Willie Horton among them. That specter accounts in large measure for both why politicians have been unwilling to solve California's prison crisis and why a federal court has been thrust into the position of considering whether to order a reduction in the state's prison population.

Politicians have told Judge Henderson that it is alright for him, as a judge, to "hug a thug," but that for them to do so would be political suicide. Regardless of the reality or the complexity of the facts, there will almost always be a George H. W. Bush trying to link an opponent to the likes of a Willie Horton. And the temptation to make that kind of association is understandable. Like "law and order" rhetoric generally, it makes a good sound bite that in all likelihood cannot be rebutted with the same economy of words. Consider, for example, Todd Spitzer's statement that releasing prisoners "is not an option because it would jeopardize public safety." Spitzer's pithy assertion, which could be easily captured in a short television spot, appears to demonstrate both his serious attitude about crime and his concern for the public. Now consider the relatively lengthy explanation of why Spitzer's statement is nonsense. It simply is not sound bite material.

State legislators (one hopes) are elected to do more than speak in sound bites. As the elected representatives of the people, it is their responsibility to grapple with and find solutions for society's pressing issues, including the difficult problems of crime and punishment: What antisocial conduct should be criminal? How long should a person be incarcerated for a particular crime? How much recidivism are we willing to tolerate? How much of our limited resources are we willing to devote to crime detection, prevention, and punishment? And how can we most effectively utilize those limited resources? These questions are much tougher to answer than the relatively simple question whether prisoner release in California will create a danger to public safety. They involve trade-offs and value choices — and ultimately compromise among competing views. Those are precisely the kinds of activities in which our elected legislators are supposed to engage. Yet, either because they believe the alluring simplicity of the sound bite or because they fear becoming the victims of sound bites (or both), they sometimes fall short.

The California legislature collectively abdicated its responsibility in the area of corrections and prison reform. As a result, successive governors and the leaders of the CDCR have been incapable of administering California's prisons in a manner that complies with constitutional mandates. That is why Judges Henderson and Karlton initially were forced to act in *Plata* and *Coleman*, and it is why the plaintiffs felt compelled to seek a population reduction order from a three-judge court.

Ideally, a court should not have to be in the position of appointing Special Masters or receivers for the prison system, much less having to consider a population reduction order. Yet, as even the PLRA with its strict requirements for prisoner release orders acknowledges, courts may sometimes have to grant such relief. When they do so, courts are not usurping the power of other branches of government. Rather, they are acting out of necessity to protect constitutional rights by filling a void created by the failure of the normal political process. As a result, they inevitably become political institutions themselves, and their success will depend at least in part on their political acuity.

From the outset, Judges Reinhardt, Henderson, and Karlton were conscious of the sensitive nature of their task. That consciousness manifested itself in their approach to managing the case, in settlement efforts, and in their ultimate opinion writing.

Case Management

The three-judge *Coleman/Plata* court found itself in the midst of a political thicket. Pursuant to the PLRA, 140 individuals and governmental entities took advantage of the opportunity to intervene in the case. Suddenly the defendants included counties, district attorneys, sheriffs, probation officers, thirty-one Republican members of the State Assembly, and thirteen Republican members of the State Senate (the statutory intervenors).

In addition to these statutory intervenors, the California Correctional Peace Officers Association (CCPOA) requested and was granted permission to intervene. Unlike the other intervenors, who, the PLRA assumes, may have interests similar to but not adequately protected by the principal defendants, the CCPOA based its claim to intervene on the ground that it had an interest similar to but not adequately represented by the *plaintiffs*: "[T]he relief under consideration by this Court . . . would directly affect working conditions for all CCPOA members."

The CCPOA's associating itself with the plaintiffs may seem strange, especially in light of its resistance to prison reform throughout the *Madrid* litigation. There are, however, at least two reasons why the CCPOA might have positioned itself in opposition to the defendants. First, as Governor Schwarzenegger's emergency declaration made clear, one of the state's methods for reducing overcrowding was to ship inmates out of state. The CCPOA had unsuccessfully challenged that action in court, presumably because removing prisoners to another state would threaten guard jobs. Second (and more generally), ever since Governor Schwarzenegger declined to seek the CCPOA' support during his 2006 run for the governorship, he and the CCPOA had been at odds. For example, as noted in the previous chapter, the CCPOA, in 2008, mounted a brief campaign to recall the governor. And the feuding continued. In what could only have been an effort to rankle the CCPOA, Governor Schwarzenegger in January 2010 floated the idea of spending state money to build prisons in Mexico to house California inmates.

Given the law and order rhetoric accompanying the announcement of the three-judge court, it was reasonable to expect that some of the intervenors would try to use the courtroom as a forum for their political agendas. At best, according to the conventional wisdom at the time, one could expect the statutory intervenors, like the principal defendants, to be interested in delaying a decision as long as possible. A ruling in the defendants' favor would maintain the status quo; a victory for the plaintiffs could bring about the prisoner release the defendants and some politicians had railed against.

To keep the case manageable, the court set strict time limits for various pretrial matters, combined groups of statutory intervenors, and made it clear that "the intervenors would not be permitted to extend these proceedings through duplicative or unnecessary discovery or arguments." As the trial neared, the court held that only one attorney (but not necessarily the same attorney) could question each witness on behalf of the statutory intervenors.

The court had initially decided that it would hear the case in two phases. Phase One would address the questions whether overcrowding was the primary cause of the continuing constitutional violations and whether no other remedy (except for prisoner release) would cure the violations. If the evidence demonstrated that the court must give an affirmative answer to both questions, Phase Two would consider the appropriate relief. The statutory intervenors, the court held, could participate only in Phase Two because the principal defendants adequately represented whatever interests the statutory interveners had in Phase One. Because of the relative smoothness of the pretrial proceedings, the court later rescinded this order and permitted all intervenors to participate in the entire trial.

Initial Settlement Efforts

In the meantime, Judges Reinhardt, Henderson, and Karlton initiated efforts to settle the case before any trial or possible court order reducing California's prison population. The judges appointed two prominent, moderate Republicans, Elwood Lui and Peter Siggins, to pursue negotiations with the parties and intervenors. Lui, a former state court of appeal justice and trial judge, had a long, distinguished record of public service. Siggins had been Governor Schwarzenegger's Legal Affairs Secretary and Interim Chief of Staff and was a current state court of appeal justice.

Lui's and Siggins' efforts appeared to bring the case close to settlement in the late spring of 2008. On the basis of their extensive talks with the various participants in the litigation, Lui and Siggins drafted a proposed agreement, the general framework of which had substantial support among the original parties and most of the intervenors. At a May 30 status conference, all the parties agreed that it would be desirable to continue the negotiations for another thirty days.

In a status report a month later, Lui and Siggins related that the original parties, the plaintiffs and the state, had "agreed in principle upon the approach to solving overcrowding." Moreover, the law enforcement intervenors (police chiefs, chief probation officers, and sheriffs) and all but one of the county intervenors "strongly supported the . . . Proposal in principle, but raised relatively minor objections" to some of the details. However, the district attorney and Republican legislator intervenors were not on board.

Even though the critical issue before the three-judge court was overcrowding, these latter intervenors criticized the Lui/Siggins proposal for focusing on a solution to overcrowding, rather than on the underlying constitutional violations. In addition, they objected to key aspects of the proposal, including any prison population cap and the diversion of low-risk offenders from the state prisons. Instead, they suggested, the underlying constitutional problems could be solved with implementation of the AB 900 construction programs, the continuing efforts of the *Plata* receiver, and rehabilitation programs.

Given the position of the district attorney and Republican legislator intervenors at the end of June, it is hard to imagine how they could ever have been serious about settlement. Judges Henderson and Karlton had previously documented the impact of overcrowding on the delivery of medical and mental health services; the completion of any construction pursuant to AB 900 was, at best, years away; because of the budget crisis, the state had reneged on its agreement with the *Plata* receiver; and the intervenors' rehabilitation programs were unspecified.

Lui and Siggins reported to the court that their efforts had been unsuccessful. They urged the parties to continue to explore settlement possibilities, and they expressed their willingness to offer continued assistance.

The Trial and a New Settlement
Overture from the Court

The trial occurred in November and December 2008. In addition to hearing three weeks of testimony, the court received hundreds of documents. After the closing arguments, all three judges were forceful and eloquent in expressing the view that they were dealing with a political problem that should be resolved in the political arena:

JUDGE REINHARDT:. . . Now is the time . . . for a different view of an issue that has been hard fought in the courtroom. Although we all believe in the adversary system, in the end the overwhelming problem of what to do about the crisis in our prison system is best resolved through the political process. . . .

. . . I hope that the next time we are together it will be so that you can tell us that California's leaders have not only recognized the seriousness of the crisis, but have finally agreed to take the necessary steps to resolve it, not over a period of five or ten years, but now.

If not, it will be for us . . . to tell you how it will be resolved.

I cannot possibly convey to you the depth of our reluctance to do it that way, but if you leave us no alternative, we will. . . .

JUDGE KARLTON:. . . It is so clear that the political situation has defined and created this crisis. And it is clear to me . . . that it is the political branches that have the responsibility to solve the problem that they created.

. . . We will do our duty. That's what we are sworn to do, but we do it reluctantly and only when you have demonstrated that there is nothing else and no other way to proceed. . . .

JUDGE HENDERSON: Judge Reinhardt, your remarks reflect . . . my thoughts. . . .

[N]othing in my 29 years on the bench has been more frustrating than feeling dragged . . . kicking and screaming into the political arena, into the political thicket in which we find ourselves.

I have thought many times about where we are now and where I am in my career, and I note that I started my legal career 47 years ago dealing with state — Southern state interposition to federal enforcement of civil rights. And all too often I feel I'm ending my career with that same problem.

On February 9, 2009, the court announced that it still needed time to review all of the evidence before issuing a final opinion but that it was making a "Tentative Ruling" "in order to give the parties notice of the likely nature of that opinion, and allow them to plan accordingly."

According to the court, the plaintiffs had presented "overwhelming evidence" that overcrowding was the primary cause of the underlying constitutional violations:

> There is . . . uncontroverted evidence that, because of overcrowding, there are not enough clinical facilities or resources to accommodate inmates with medical or mental health needs at the level of care they require. There is also uncontroverted evidence that, because of overcrowding, there are not enough clinical or custodial personnel to ensure that inmates with medical or mental health needs are receiving appropriate treatment, are taking the medications that they need to take, are being escorted to their medical appointments in a timely manner, and are having their medical information recorded and filed properly. . . .
>
> Almost every expert who testified in the first phase of the trial identified overcrowding as the main cause of the prison system's constitutionally inadequate medical and mental health care and as the problem that must be fixed before constitutionally adequate care can be delivered. Among the experts was Ms. Jeanne Woodford, the former acting Secretary of the California Department of Corrections and Rehabilitation, who testified that it is impossible to get inmates necessary mental health treatment and health care exams when operating in the overcrowded setting of California's prisons. Experts with correctional experience in states ranging from Texas and Pennsylvania to Maine and Washington testified to similar effect. Even defendants' expert, Dr. Ira Packer, agreed that the primary cause of the inadequacy in mental health care is that there are not enough mental health resources for the population.

The court then addressed the question whether relief other than a prisoner release order could remedy the constitutional violations:

> The two cases underlying [the] three-judge court proceedings have been in the federal courts for a very long time. . . . The respective district courts have issued a number of orders short of a prisoner release order aimed at remedying the constitutional violations. . . .
>
> The defendants argue that the Receivership and the Special Master's monitoring efforts constitute other "relief" short of a prisoner release order that could remedy the constitutional violations. But the defendants have opposed the Receiver's work in *Plata* and are seeking the dissolution of the Receivership. They have also been unable to bring their mental health care system into constitutional compliance at any point in the last fourteen years. Moreover, as [the defendants' acknowledge,] "California faces an unprecedented and potentially catastrophic $40 billion deficit." Even if it

were possible for . . . construction and renovation projects to proceed despite this deficit, they would take many years to complete. . . .

[W]e are at a loss to imagine what "other relief" short of a prisoner release order a court could grant.

Despite "compelling" evidence of the need for a prisoner release order, the court only "*tentatively* conclude[d] that there is no relief other than a prisoner release order that can remedy the constitutionally inadequate medical and mental health care in California's prisons." Similarly, after reviewing the evidence of various experts, the court only *tentatively* concluded that reducing the state's prison population to between 120% and 145% of design capacity — a reduction of approximately 40,000 to 60,000 inmates — was necessary and would not have an adverse impact on public safety. As the court explained:

We received evidence that the Independent Review Panel chaired by former Governor Deukmejian recommended 145% of design capacity as the outside limit for California prisons generally. . . . We received evidence that AB 900 Facility Strike Team leader Deborah Hysen recommended that the population in any new facilities constructed under AB 900 be limited to 130% of design capacity. Plaintiffs' experts generally agreed with that number as appropriate for California prisons in general. . . .

. . . Dr. James Austin,[2] . . . testified that such a population reduction could be implemented without adversely affecting public safety by adopting a combination of parole reform, diversion of low risk prisoners with short sentences, and good time credits. . . .

Many of these reform measures are also supported by the State and by state officials with a commitment to ensuring public safety. . . . We . . . infer from the universal official support for these measures that they are not likely to result in adverse public safety consequences.

Ironically, some of the more favorable evidence for the plaintiffs came from local government intervenors, who claimed that they had first-rate, but unfunded or underfunded rehabilitation programs. They urged the court to release prisoners and require the state to pay for the rehabilitation services. The court, however, was not convinced that it had the power to require such payments.

Except for uncertainty about the size of the prison population cap, nothing sounded very "tentative" about the court's conclusions: overcrowding was the primary cause of the underlying constitutional violations; only a prisoner release order would remedy the unconstitutional conditions; and the release

---

2. Dr. Austin, an expert witness for plaintiffs, had been a member of the CDCR's Expert Panel on Adult Recidivism Programs. [Author's footnote]

order would include a cap on the prison population. Yet, because there was no final decision, there was nothing to appeal.

Time for settlement remained; and there was much to discuss. The court had not yet addressed even tentatively some of most crucial, politically sensitive issues: What combination of means should the state use to reduce its prison population? How quickly would the reduction have to take place? Would there be interim benchmarks to satisfy? These were the types of issues with which Elwood Lui and Peter Siggins had been grappling the previous year; and they were the types of issues that the district attorney and Republican legislator intervenors had largely ignored as they focused on the underlying findings of constitutional violations.

The Tentative Ruling was an unambiguous signal that the court would somehow order a significant prison population reduction if there were no settlement. At the same time, the court made it clear once again that it would prefer to have the parties resolve the case on their own:

> The Court . . . will . . . ask the parties and intervenors to submit written proposals setting forth the specific percentages and dates that they believe should be incorporated into the order regarding the ultimate population cap and compliance date, as well as any interim percentages and dates they believe the Court should include in the order. The State will also be asked to specify . . . the measures it intends to adopt to ensure compliance in a manner that will best accomplish the objectives of the order, including ensuring public safety. . . .
>
> Prior to the issuance of a final order the State and the plaintiffs, as well as any intervenors who choose to participate, are encouraged to engage in discussions regarding joint recommendations with respect to all or any of the above matters as well as with respect to a settlement of all or any part of the dispute at issue in this proceeding. . . .

The court then concluded with an offer to appoint Lui and Siggins or some other referee to assist the parties with settlement negotiations.

The responses to the court's offer for settlement assistance were all positive with one exception. The principal defendants (the state and the governor) declined to participate in further negotiations. They requested a final appealable order as soon as possible.

Why the state backed away from pursuing a negotiated settlement is not clear. According to Judge Henderson, the three-judge court was surprised. Someday an insider from the Schwarzenegger administration may write about the case and shed some light on the matter. Until then, one can only speculate. The position of the district attorney and Republican legislator intervenors may have convinced the state that settlement was hopeless; or perhaps the state had never been willing to accept a prison cap of 120–145% of design capacity. In either case, given the ongoing prison and budget crises, the state may have believed that its least bad option was to seek as speedily as possible a resolution of the prison overcrowding issue from the Supreme Court — a resolution that could be more favorable to its perceived interests than even a negotiated settlement. In any event, the decision to forego further negotiations occurred at roughly the same time that the state challenged Judge Henderson's right to appoint the *Plata* receiver. Quite clearly, someone or something convinced the state to begin taking a harder line in its prison litigation.

An Almost Final Order

On August 4, 2009, the three-judge court issued a 120-page "Opinion and Order" that meticulously set forth its conclusions about the need for a prisoner release order. It began, however, not with its own assessment, but rather with the words and conclusions of the state's own independent agency, the Little Hoover Commission (LHC), and the state's Governor, Arnold Schwarzenegger (AS):

"California's correctional system is in a tailspin . . ." [quoting LHC] Tough-on-crime politics have increased the population of California's prisons dramatically while making necessary reforms impossible. [citing LHC] As a result, the state's prisons have become places "of extreme peril to the safety of persons" they house, [quoting AS] while contributing little to the safety of California's residents. [citing LHC] California "spends more on corrections than most countries in the world," but the state "reaps fewer public safety benefits." [quoting LHC]

The court continued:

Although California's existing prison system serves neither the public nor the inmates well, the state has for years been unable or unwilling to implement the reforms necessary to reverse its continuing deterioration.

 . . . [T]he medical and mental health care available to inmates in the California prison system is woefully and constitutionally inadequate, and has been for more than a decade. . . .

 . . . Since reaching an all-time population record of more than 160,000 in October 2006, the state's adult prison institutions have operated at almost double their intended capacity. . . . Thousands of prisoners are assigned to "bad beds," such as triple-bunked beds placed in gymnasiums or day rooms, and some institutions have populations approaching 300% of their intended capacity. In these overcrowded conditions, inmate-on-inmate violence is almost impossible to prevent, infectious diseases spread more easily, and lockdowns are sometimes the only means by which to maintain control. [And lockdowns, as the court later explained, severely limit inmates' access to medication and to medical and mental health services. Moreover, during lockdowns inmates cannot take advantage of rehabilitative services.] In short, California's prisons are bursting at the seams and are impossible to manage.

The court proceeded with a detailed summary of the *Plata* and *Coleman* litigation and then turned to the requirements of the PLRA.

On the question whether overcrowding was the primary cause of the constitutionally inadequate medical and mental health services, the court reiterated much of what it said in its Tentative Ruling but provided a richer, more detailed recitation of the evidence and an even more strongly worded conclusion:

> On the basis of the clear and convincing, indeed overwhelming and overwhelmingly persuasive, evidence . . ., we conclude that crowding is the primary cause of the state's unconstitutional failure to provide adequate medical and mental health care to California prisoners. Such is the opinion as well of some of the nation's foremost prison administrators, who testified that they have never previously witnessed such appalling prison conditions and that overcrowding is not only the primary cause of the constitutionally inadequate medical and mental health care in California's prisons, but also that until the problem of overcrowding is overcome it will be impossible to provide constitutionally compliant care to California's prison population. No credible evidence to the contrary was presented by defendants.

The court then considered possible alternatives to a prison population cap — creating new physical facilities, hiring additional personnel, continuing the work of the receiver and Special Master, and transferring inmates to other jurisdictions.[3] Although the court acknowledged that these options could contribute to easing the constitutional deficiencies, it determined that none of them, alone or combination with each other, could provide a feasible solution to the problem in a timely manner. That conclusion was supported by multiple experts,[4] and it left the court with no alternative but to consider a population cap.

To comply with the PLRA requirement that an order "be narrowly drawn, extend no further than necessary to correct the harm . . ., and be the least intrusive means necessary to correct that harm," the court considered three issues:

---

3. As the court pointed out, a judicial order to transfer prisoners would itself be a "prisoner release order" within the meaning of the PLRA.

4. Two defense experts had testified that it was possible to provide constitutionally adequate medical and mental health care in overcrowded facilities and that they had in fact done so. As the court observed, however, "the systems within which they worked had prison population controls in place."

whether a population cap should be institution specific, how to define the cap, and how to implement it.

The first question was easy to resolve. The constitutional violations existed throughout the system; none of the parties had argued for institution-specific caps; and, most important,

> an institution-by-institution approach to population reduction would interfere with the state's management of its prisons more than a single systemwide cap, which permits the state to continue determining the proper population of individual institutions.

The court left open the possibility of institution-specific caps in the future, but only if "it is demonstrated that a single system-wide cap provides inadequate relief."

The second question — defining the prison cap — was more difficult. In California, design capacity meant one inmate per cell and single beds in dormitories. At one extreme

> the evidence . . . demonstrated that even a prison system operating at or near only 100% design capacity faces serious difficulties in providing inmates with constitutionally sufficient medical and mental health care.

At the other extreme, as the court had noted in its Tentative Ruling, an Independent Review Panel had recommended a maximum cap of 145% of design capacity. That figure, however, seemed unrealistically high. The state had admittedly planned to some extent for prison populations well in excess of the original design capacity. For example, prisons built in the 1980s and 1990s had infrastructure components — water, wastewater, and electrical capacity — specifically created for populations of up to 190% of design capacity in cells and 140% of design capacity in dormitory areas. Incredibly, though, the state had failed to plan for any space or resources to meet medical and mental health needs of a prison population that might exceed 100% design capacity. Moreover, in making its 145% recommendation, the Independent Review Panel had not taken into account the space and staffing needs that would be required to provide medical and mental health services to an expanded prison population.

The court found that the 130% of design capacity limit urged by the plaintiffs was "reasonable" and "with considerable support in the record." However, there was some evidence, albeit "far less persuasive," suggesting that the constitutional violations could be cured with a somewhat higher cap — although not one as high as 145%. Noting that the defendants had not suggested an alternative to the plaintiffs' 130% figure, recognizing that choosing a particular percentage was not an exact science, and keeping in mind the PLRA's requirement that the cap extend no further than necessary to cure the constitutional violations, the court "out of caution" settled on a population cap of 137.5% of design capacity. The cap applied to the thirty-three adult state prisons. In effect, this meant a reduction in the prison population of approximately 46,000 inmates. The precise size of the reduction, of course, would depend upon the actual population at any given time and any new construction that might expand the available facilities.

The third question relating to the PLRA's narrowness requirement — how to implement the population cap — was potentially the thorniest but, at least for now, elegantly simple. The court directed the defendants to come up with their own plan to reduce within two years the prison population to 137.5% of design capacity. The defendants were to confer with the plaintiffs, the intervenors, the *Coleman* Special Master, and the *Plata* receiver, all of whom could file objections to aspects of the defendants' plan. The Supreme Court had given its blessing to "a nearly identical procedure," characterizing it as "'an exemplar of what should be done' in crafting statewide prospective relief." Such an approach, the Supreme Court said, "scrupulously respect[s] the limits on [the court's] role," and, at the same time, permits prison administrators to "exercise[] wide discretion within the bounds of constitutional requirements."

The court's final task was to consider the impact of its ruling on public safety and the criminal justice system. In a lengthy exploration of various prison population reduction methods available to the state — including, those discussed earlier in this chapter — the court reaffirmed its tentative conclusion and held that a 137.5% prison population cap would not endanger public safety or burden the criminal justice system. The court then offered a small caveat to its conclusion:

> [W]ere we in error and were there in fact some adverse effect, it would be small, given the number and types of individuals to be released early or diverted to non-prison settings, and given the number of counties, and the size of the state and its population [37 million]. Even considering the possibility of a minor adverse effect, we would, in view of the extremely serious injuries that continue to result from the long-standing constitutional violations at issue, be required to grant . . . the relief that [we order here].

As a legal matter, the court's caveat was sound. After all, the PLRA does not require that a prisoner release order have *no* adverse impact on public safety, but only that the court seriously consider any such possible impact. As a practical matter, though, the caveat was probably unnecessary. Each year under the existing system, the court noted, California releases well over 100,000 individuals from its prisons. Because of a lack of rehabilitative services (which is in large part a function of overcrowding), many of these individuals, according to the testimony of corrections and law enforcement officials, are more of a threat to the community than they were before going to prison. The court's population cap would create space and make available resources that could be used for rehabilitation services. Thus, a wisely implemented cap would almost certainly enhance, not detract from, public safety.

Finally, the three-judge court concluded its opinion as it had begun it — with the state's own analysis of the overcrowding problem:

> One of the most persuasive pieces of evidence before us is the report of the Expert Panel on Adult Offender Recidivism Reduction Programming, which was convened by the CDCR in 2007 to suggest strategies for reducing California's high recidivism rate. The panel consisted of CDCR's Chief Deputy Secretary for Adult Programs, academic researchers, consultants, and former and current secretaries of corrections in Pennsylvania, Arizona, Washington, Ohio, and Maine. The report recommended a comprehensive set of measures that would reduce California's prison population while also reducing recidivism.
>
> The CDCR Expert Panel concluded that, if the CDCR were to follow its recommendations to divert technical parole violators, implement parole reform, and expand good time credits, these changes alone would serve to reduce the prison population by between 38,500 and 43,500 inmates, and the parole population would be reduced by 6,500 to 11,500. The panel expected an additional reduction in the prison population of about 2,194 to 4,388 from evidence-based programming initiatives. After accounting for the costs of the additional programming recommended by the panel, full implementation of its recommendations would still save the state between $561 and $684 million a year. The proposed reduction resulting from the above measures alone would fall within the range necessary to comply with a 137.5% population cap. Other means suggested by the state and others, including the expert committees and the numerous other official committees, could reduce the prison population even further.

This conclusion, it seems, was part of a calculated effort to impress upon readers — particularly the justices of the Supreme Court, who would eventually be reviewing the case — two important points. First, the court was taking a moderate, thoughtful position widely supported among those most knowledgeable about the state's correctional crisis. Second, rather than foisting its own views on the defendants, the court was to a substantial extent adopting positions advocated by the governor and various state experts. This latter point, like the court's settlement efforts, was a response not just to the law but also to the political context within which the court found itself.

Characterizing the court's actions as partially political in no way detracts from the opinion's judicial craftsmanship or the legitimacy of the court's work. Indeed, as discussed in Chapter Two, all judicial decision making necessarily involves the consideration of personal views and values, including political values. Moreover, the court was filling a void created by the failures of other branches of government and, therefore, was necessarily acting—more than most courts—as a political institution.

Because of the case's inherently political nature and because there was no precedent (other than the language of the PLRA) for the court's action, it was reasonable to expect—despite possible disclaimers to the contrary—that the political views of individual Supreme Court justices would play a particularly strong role in their assessments of what the three-judge court had done. Judges Reinhardt, Henderson, and Karlton had to suspect that the Supreme Court's four most conservative justices (Alito, Roberts, Scalia, and Thomas) might not be sympathetic, at least initially, to any prisoner release order. On the other hand, Justice Anthony Kennedy, often the swing vote in close decisions, had spoken of the need for corrections reform in a 2003 keynote address to the American Bar Association:

> The subject of prisons and corrections . . . is the concern and responsibility of every . . . citizen. . . .
> . . . Our resources are misspent, our punishments too severe, our sentences too long.

And Justice Kennedy had reiterated his concern with correctional policy during a 2010 question and answer session at Pepperdine Law School:

> American sentences are 8 time longer than their equivalents in Europe. California's 3-strike law emanated from the electorate, and the sponsor of the initiative was the correctional officers association [CCPOA]—and that is sick. California has 185,000 people in prison, and the cost is astounding.

A carefully reasoned and documented opinion that relied on the state's own evaluations, that deferred to the state to establish the details of a prisoner release plan, and that came only after the court had done everything in its power to encourage settlement might well appeal to Justice Kennedy and at least four other members of the Court.

Supreme Court action, however, would have to wait. There was still no final, appealable decision. The three-judge court had not yet imposed a population cap on the state but had only mandated that the defendants submit a plan for implementing the cap. The defendants were given forty-five days to develop the plan.

The Final Order and a Stay

A little over a month later the defendants submitted their population reduction plan. It would have reduced the state's prison population in two years to only 166% of design capacity (or 151%, if proposed legislation were enacted).

This was far short of what the court had ordered or even what the state's own expert panel had advocated in 2007. The plaintiffs asked the court to hold Governor Schwarzenegger in civil and criminal contempt.

The defendants' obvious snub to the court was even more surprising than their earlier refusal to pursue a negotiated settlement. Given the Supreme Court's stated preference for remedial orders crafted by the parties, perhaps the defendants thought they would be in a stronger position before the Supreme Court if they could goad the three-judge court into imposing its own version of a prisoner release order on the state. The three-judge court, however, was not sidetracked from its primary goal. After some stern words, Judges Reinhardt, Henderson, and Karlton deferred the plaintiffs' contempt request and gave the state one more chance to comply with the court's earlier mandate.

Two months later the state submitted a revised plan that, the plaintiffs agreed, satisfied the court's 137.5% of design capacity prison cap. On January 12, 2010, the court issued a final order requiring the state to meet the 137.5% standard within two years and to meet designated interim goals as well. The court, however, did not endorse the specific components of the state's plan, some of which the court had not previously evaluated for their impact on public safety. Rather than having new evidentiary hearings for the purpose of making those evaluations or rejecting unevaluated items, the court chose to maximize the state's flexibility by forgoing judicial item-by-item oversight:

> Certain measures that we concluded would substantially reduce the prison population that we did evaluate positively from a public safety standpoint, such as changes with respect to the churning of technical parole violators, appear to be included only in part in the State's plan. We believe, as we did when we issued our prior Order, that it is appropriate for the State to exercise its discretion in choosing which specific population reduction measures to implement, and, in doing so, to bear in mind the necessity for ensuring the public safety. We are satisfied that, as we previously held, the reduction in prison population that we have ordered can be implemented safely and trust that the State will comply with its duty to ensure public safety as it implements the constitutionally required reduction. Should the State determine that any of the specific measures that it has included in its plan cannot be implemented without significantly affecting the public safety or the criminal justice system, we trust that it will substitute a different means of accomplishing the constitutionally required population reductions.

The court then stayed the effective date of its order pending Supreme Court review.

Another Settlement Failure and
a New State Initiative

In late 2009 or early 2010, the possibility of a settlement resurfaced. There is no public record, and many of the details of what happened and why are unknown (even to some of the participants). This much, however, seems clear: Despite the state's previous opposition to settlement discussions, the initiative for new talks came from the governor's office; talks resulted in a tentative agreement, which was presented to Governor Schwarzenegger in the spring of 2010; after sitting on the proposal for several weeks, the governor rejected it.

The following November the Supreme Court heard oral arguments in the appeal from the three-judge court ruling. That same month Jerry Brown was elected governor of California.

Brown began to push for what has become known as "Realignment" — a program encompassed in Assembly Bill 109 (AB 109), which was passed by the legislature and signed by the governor in the spring of 2011. Realignment gives more responsibility to the counties for dealing with parole violators and non-violent offenders, and it redefines certain felonies, making them punishable in county jails. Although the program does not actually transfer inmates from state prisons to county jails, the shifting to the counties of some responsibility for parole and for the incarceration of future nonviolent offenders would have a significant impact on crowding in the state prisons.

The Supreme Court Speaks

In a 5-4 decision on May 23, 2011, the Supreme Court affirmed every aspect of the three-judge court ruling. Justice Anthony Kennedy (joined by Justices Breyer, Ginsburg. Kagan, and Sotomayor) wrote the Court's opinion.[5]

The same facts that had so appalled first Judge Karlton and Judge Henderson and then the three-judge court also resonated with the Supreme Court majority:

> The degree of overcrowding in California's prisons is exceptional.... Prisoners are crammed into spaces neither designed nor intended to house inmates. As many as 200 prisoners may live in a gymnasium monitored by as few as two or three correctional officers.... As many as 54 prisoners may share a single toilet.

---

5. Justice Scalia (joined by Justice Thomas) and Justice Alito (joined by Chief Justice Roberts) filed dissenting opinions.

. . . Because of a shortage of treatment beds, suicidal inmates may be held for prolonged periods in telephone-booth sized cages without toilets.

In an appendix to its opinion, the Court took the unusual step of reproducing photographs of the crowded conditions and the telephone-booth sized cages.

As the Court acknowledged, existing medical and mental health services were woefully inadequate:

> At the time of trial, vacancy rates for medical and mental health staff ranged as high as 20% for surgeons, 25% for physicians, 39% for nurse practitioners, and 54.1% for psychiatrists. These percentages are based on the number of positions budgeted by the State. Dr. Ronald Shansky, former medical director of the Illinois prison system, [and Dr. Craig Haney, a psychiatrist] concluded that these numbers understate the severity of the crisis because the State has not budgeted sufficient staff to meet demand.

Moreover, the prospect of providing adequate medical and mental health care without reducing the size of the prison population had actually worsened in the months following the three-judge court decision:

> In October 2010, the State notified the *Coleman* district court that a substantial component of its construction plans had been delayed indefinitely by the legislature. And even if planned construction were to be completed, the *Plata* Receiver found that many so-called "expansion" plans called for cramming more prisoners into existing prisons without expanding administrative and support facilities.

In the Court's view, there simply was no viable alternative to ordering a reduction in the prison population:

> At one time, it may have been possible to hope that these violations would be cured without a reduction in overcrowding. A long history of failed remedial orders, together with substantial evidence of overcrowding's deleterious effects on the provision of care, compels a different conclusion today.
> . . . The Court cannot ignore the political and fiscal reality behind this case. California's Legislature has not been willing or able to allocate the resources necessary to meet this crisis absent a reduction in overcrowding. There is no reason to believe it will begin to do so now, when the State of California is facing an unprecedented budgetary shortfall.

The burden was now on the state to comply with the three-judge court's population reduction order. That order required an initial report by the state within fourteen days of the Supreme Court's decision. The three-judge court, however, did not simply wait for the state's report. In a conference call the day after the decision, the three judges decided to ask Peter Siggins if he would work with the parties to implement the court's mandate and hopefully reach a settlement. Judge Henderson contacted Siggins, who agreed to assist, but his role was limited. Don Spector, lead counsel for the plaintiffs, was temporarily out of the country; and Governor Brown had a more immediate interest than settlement with the plaintiffs. He hoped to use the Supreme Court's decision as leverage with the legislature to obtain funding for AB 109.

Population Reduction

During the pendency of the appeal, the state had transferred over 9,000 prisoners to out-of-state facilities; and on June 7, 2011, the state reported to the three-judge court:

> Today, the prison population for in-state adult institutions stands at approximately 143,500 inmates, a reduction of approximately 19,000 inmates since November 2006 when the Plaintiffs filed their motions to convene the three-judge court. Stated in terms of "design capacity," the State's prisons were operating at approximately 202% when the Plaintiffs filed their motions to convene the three-judge court, and they are now operating at approximately 179%. This is the lowest level of crowding, as defined by design capacity, since 1995.

The next month the state reported that the governor had been successful in obtaining funding for the AB 109 Realignment program and that it would become effective on October 1, 2011.

As a result of Realignment, the state was only a few weeks late in meeting the three-judge court's December 2011 benchmark of decreasing the prison population to 167% of design capacity, and the state met the June 2012 benchmark of 155% over two months early. In their June 2012 status report to the three-judge court, the defendants stated, "[T]here is no need at this time to modify the order or to undertake additional crowding-reduction measures to achieve compliance." Only the December 2012 benchmark of 147% and the final goal of 137.5% by June 27, 2013 remained.

The Agony of Judicial Restraint

Despite the enormity of the three-judge court's prison population reduction order, Judges Reinhardt, Henderson, and Karlton had acted with incredible restraint from the outset. The three judges adhered strictly to the requirements of the PLRA. They recognized that ideally the underlying problems should be resolved through the political rather the judicial process. They did everything in their power to encourage a settlement so they could avoid ruling on the merits. They detailed in a tentative ruling how the population reduction could occur without endangering public safety or burdening the state's strapped finances. They relied heavily on the state's own assessment of overcrowding. In setting a specific prison population cap, they gave the benefit of the doubt to the state. After holding that the state must reduce its prison population to 137.5% of design capacity, they refused to impose their policy preferences on the state. Rather, they insisted that the state come up with its own plan. And when the state finally came up with its plan that included elements not previously evaluated by the court, they nonetheless deferred, as they should have, to the state and its policy choices.

The state's choices, however, brought about mixed results. Reduction of the state's prison population is clearly a plus. So too are the Realignment plan's recognition that the state "must reinvest its criminal justice resources to support community-based corrections programs and evidence-based practices"[6] and the plan's key premise: "Criminal justice policies that rely on building and operating more prisons to address community safety are not sustainable, and will not result in improved public safety."

On the other hand, from the outset there were two significant problems with Realignment. First, no resources were devoted specifically to data collection and evaluation of programs that the counties adopt. Thus, it may be difficult to tell what has worked and what has not worked. Stanford Law Professor and criminologist Joan Petersilia, her colleagues, and students have been engaging in valuable research that at least to some extent should alleviate this concern.

Second, funds allocated to the counties to deal with their increased responsibility for nonserious crimes were virtually condition free. There was no requirement that counties develop "community-based corrections programs and evidence-based practices." Some counties opted to spend substantial portions of their Realignment money for increasing the capacity of their jails. Others used the funds for purposes that were only marginally related to dealing with the individuals being diverted to their care. As a result of these problems, either (or perhaps both) of two results could occur: (1) Overcrowding could simply be shifted from the state prisons to the county jails; (2) the danger to public safety that so consumed some critics of the three-judge court could become a

---

6. The Realignment plan defines evidence-based practices as "supervision policies, procedures, programs, and practices demonstrated by scientific research to reduce recidivism among individuals under probation, parole, or post-release supervision."

reality. There are some indications, albeit far from conclusive, that both of these phenomena may be occurring.

It is clear from their opinions that Judges Reinhardt, Henderson, and Karlton believed neither of these consequences was necessary. Yet, they did not have the ability to force the legislature to revise the Realignment program or to compel the counties to spend their money more wisely. If they had tried to do so, they would have been abandoning their appropriately limited role as jurists. They could only watch and hope. Having to watch and hope, however, was insignificant compared to the agony and frustration of trying to exercise appropriate judicial restraint when the defendants began to defy the three-judge court's orders.

Digging In

Despite the defendants' June 2012 claim that there was no need for additional overcrowding measures or for a modification of the three-judge court's order, they had previously taken a contrary position. In April 2012, the state produced a report, "The Future of California Corrections" ("the Blueprint"), which it characterized as a plan "to save billions of dollars, end federal court oversight and improve the prison system." The Blueprint stated that California wanted to bring home the over 9,500 inmates currently housed out of state. However, even without this addition to the prison population, the Blueprint acknowledged that the state would not meet the 137.5% goal by June 2013. According to the Blueprint, the state would seek a modification from the three-judge court "to raise the final benchmark to 145 percent of design capacity."

The defendants never formally requested a modification of the 137.5% goal, but whether such a request would have been appropriate was the subject of inquiries by the court and responses by the parties. After extensive briefing on the question, the three-judge court, in a September 7, 2012 opinion and order, stated:

> Defendants . . . suggested that the only question that they would seek to litigate on a motion to modify is whether Eighth Amendment compliance could be achieved with a prison population higher than 137.5% design capacity. That question has already been litigated and decided by this Court and affirmed by the Supreme Court, and this Court is not inclined to permit relitigation of the proper population cap at this time.

During the ensuing months, the defendants offered varying assessments of how they could meet the 137.5% goal; and in November 2012, they stated, contrary to their previous projections, that they would miss the December 147% benchmark.

The defendants' position hardened in 2013. On January 7, they filed a motion to vacate the prison population reduction order in its entirety. The defendants had initially based the motion on two grounds: First, the state was now providing constitutionally adequate medical and mental health care; second, as a result the substantial reductions in the prison population, overcrowding was no longer the primary cause of whatever constitutional violations may remain.

At the same time that they filed their motion to vacate, the defendants, consistently with their first claim, filed a motion in the *Coleman* mental health case to terminate all injunctive relief. However, they did not file a similar motion in the *Plata* medical health case. The *Coleman* court denied the motion, and the defendants voluntarily abandoned before the three-judge court their claim that the state was providing constitutionally adequate health care.

The second claim — that overcrowding was no longer the primary cause of whatever unconstitutionality may remain — was, standing alone, essentially the same argument that defendants made when they were contemplating a motion to raise the population reduction goal to 145%. The three-judge court rejected it for the same reason it had rejected it earlier: The defendants were merely seeking to relitigate an issue that had already been decided in a judgment affirmed by the Supreme Court.

Of course, it would be theoretically possible to show that the original prediction about the level of overcrowding at which constitutionally adequate health care could be provided was wrong and that the current level of crowding was not the primary cause of the constitutional violations. However, in a lengthy, detailed discussion, the three-judge court persuasively demonstrated that the defendants had no credible evidence to support these hypotheses.

On January 8, 2013, the day after the defendants had filed their motion to vacate, Governor Brown, declaring that "prison crowding no longer . . . inhibit[s] the delivery of timely and effective health care to inmates," terminated Governor Schwarzenegger's 2006 Overcrowding Emergency Proclamation. The three-judge court characterized the Governor's action as "arrogating unto himself the authority to declare, notwithstanding the orders of this Court, that the crisis in the prisons was resolved." In a January 13 status report, the defendants announced that they would take no further action to comply with the three-judge court population reduction order.

Two weeks later, the three-judge court extended the deadline for meeting the 137.5% goal for six months to the end of 2013.[7] At the same time, the court specifically ordered the defendants to continue to comply with its orders. Nonetheless, in their February and March status reports, the defendants repeated

---

7. The defendants had requested the extension the prior November. In December, the court denied the request as premature. The defendants had not yet responded to a previous order to submit by January 7, 2013 plans for how they would comply with the 137.5% goal in June, 2013, and how they would comply if the deadline were extended six months.

their assertion that they would no longer comply with the population reduction order.

In an April 11 opinion and order, the three-judge court denied the defendants' motion to vacate. With respect to the defendants' conduct, the court stated:

> Defendants have thus far engaged in openly contumacious conduct by repeatedly ignoring both this Court's Order and at least three admonitions to take all steps necessary to comply with that Order. . . . What further steps they will take to comply is . . . clear: None. . . .
>
> Being more interested in achieving compliance with our Order than in holding contempt hearings, this Court has exercised exceptional restraint. Reserving its right to take whatever action may be appropriate with respect to defendants' past conduct, this Court now orders defendants once more to take steps *beyond* that of Realignment and to do so forthwith.

The court then discussed several safe ways to reduce the prison population. First, noting that "Realignment diverts only a small sub-set of low-risk prisoners and parolees to county jails," the court observed that "[s]ignificant opportunity for further diversion thus remains." Second, the court pointed out that over 4,000 prisoners serving term-to-life sentences were over fifty-five years old. With a proper assessment program in place, the court suggested, many of these individuals could be released early without endangering public safety. Third, the court stated that the expansion of good time credits beyond it current limited scope to what other jurisdictions provide would in itself "reduce the prison population by far more than the amount necessary to comply with the 137.5% population cap." Fourth, the court mentioned the possibility of sending more prisoners out of state but made it clear that, in light of other options, such transfers would not be necessary.

Finally, the court ordered the defendants to list, *in their order of preference*, all possible population reduction measures that had been suggested by the court or identified by the parties (the "List") and to create a "Plan" for complying with the court's population reduction order by selecting measures that it would implement. The List was to include an assessment of the extent to which each measure could reduce the prison population. In addition, the court ordered the defendants "to begin without delay to develop a system to identify prisoners who are unlikely to reoffend or who might otherwise be candidates for early release" (the "Low Risk List").

The defendants appealed the April 11 orders to the Supreme Court; and when the three-judge court issued additional orders, discussed in the next two sections, the defendants included them as part of the appeal. On October 16, 2013, the Supreme Court dismissed the appeal for lack of jurisdiction.

The Three-Judge Court's June 20, 2013 Order

In May, the defendants "announced that they were making some progress" with the Low Risk List, and they submitted their List and Plan. The List, however, did not indicate any preferences among the various measures; and the Plan, as the defendants conceded, did not comply with the court's order to reach a prison population to 137.5% of design capacity. According to the three-judge court, the Plan would reduce the prison population to only 142.6% of design capacity by December 31, 2013. In terms of numbers of prisoners, the plan would fail to meet the court-ordered goal by over 4,000 inmates. Furthermore, the Plan relied on measures that would require legislative action, which, the leader of the state senate had made clear, would not be forthcoming.

On June 20, the three-judge court, after reciting in detail how it had consistently deferred to the defendants' discretion to decide how to meet the population reduction order, concluded that complete deference was no longer possible:

> As the Supreme Court stated [in affirming the 137.5% order], "[c]ourts may not allow constitutional violations to continue simply because a remedy would involve intrusion into the realm of prison administration." At this point, this Court's "intrusion" into state affairs is necessitated by defendants' own intransigence.... Because the defendants have expressed no preference at all among the measures on the List, they have forfeited any challenge to this Court's selection....

The court then ordered the defendants to implement an "Amended Plan," — their original Plan plus Item Four on their List, which dealt with good time credits. Item Four called for awarding good time credits to all prisoners and awarding the credits retroactively. It would result in the release of over 5,000 prisoners by December 31, 2013. By contrast, the good time credit measure in the defendants' Plan would have led to the release of only 247 inmates.

The defendants had argued that the immediate release of some prisoners as a result of retroactive good time credits and the early release of prisoners convicted of violent crimes would threaten public safety. The three-judge court, however, pointed out that it had addressed this concern in its original 2009 opinion and order. A CDCR expert panel had recommended making good time credits retroactive and extending them to all prisoners; and as the court explained in 2009, experts had testified that "there is no statistically significant relationship between an individual's length of stay in prison and his recidivism rate." Dr. James Austin had testified that "reducing the length of stay by a 'very moderate period' — four to six months — would have no effect on recidivism rates." Other leading experts in the country ... — including the now Secretary of CDCR, Jeffrey Beard — [all] testified that the expansion of good time credits could be implemented safely, both prospectively and retroactively.

In short, prisoners who are released early due to good time credits may recidivate, but early release affects only when the crimes are committed, not whether they are committed. Moreover, the three-judge court's Amended Plan required a *lower* average per month reduction in the prison population over the next six months (approximately 1,800 inmates per month) than the average monthly reduction required by the original order (approximately 1,900 inmates per month).

Nonetheless, if the defendants were seriously concerned about the possible adverse consequences of Item Four's retroactive good time credits, they could substitute three court-approved alternatives to Item Four. First, they could modify the court-ordered expanded good time credit measure as long as the modification resulted in the release of the same number of prisoners. For example, they could expand credits for nonviolent offenders and reduce or eliminate the credits for violent offenders. Second, the defendants could "at their discretion substitute for prisoners covered by any measure or measures in the Amended Plan an equivalent number of prisoners" from the Low Risk List. Third, as long as they did not reduce the number of prisoners released, they could substitute any measure(s) in the List for any measure(s) in the Plan. Thus, the three-judge court, in effect, ordered the defendants to fully implement an expanded good time credit program only if alternatives of their own choosing would not satisfy the 137.5% goal by December 31, 2013. The state still retained discretion over the means of reducing its prison population.

The June 20 opinion and order contained two other provisions to help ensure compliance with the December 31 deadline. First, pursuant to authority granted by the PLRA, the three-judge court waived all state and local laws and regulations that would otherwise prohibit the defendants from implementing the Amended Plan. Second, the court ordered the defendants to use the Low Risk List "to remedy any deficiency" that might occur in releasing prisoners pursuant to the Amended Plan:

> The Court wishes to make perfectly clear what this means: Defendants have no excuse for failing to meet the 137.5% requirement on December 31, 2013. No matter what implementation challenges defendants face, no matter what unexpected misfortunes arise, defendants shall reduce the prison population to 137.5% by December 31, 2013, even if it is achieved solely though the release of prisoners from the Low-Risk List. This Court acknowledges that requiring defendants to create such a list may prove unnecessary. ... However, in the past, defendants have repeatedly found

new and unexpected ways to frustrate this Court's orders. Accordingly, the Low-Risk List is intended to obviate any such action.

In an unsuccessful motion to stay the three-judge court's order, the defendants cited a recent study showing that

> even inmates that CDCR considered "low risk" recidivate such that 41% are returned to California prison within three years, and that 11% of such "low risk" offenders have been "rearrested for a violent felony within three years of release."

These figures suggest the need for more or better rehabilitation programs. They do not, however, show that early release increases crime.

In its June 20 opinion, the three-judge court also addressed the issue of ensuring that there would be a "durable remedy" for overcrowding. The court offered three reasons for anticipating a probable rise in the prison population, over the next several years. First, the state planned to return its out-of-state prisoners; second, the state's projections had consistently underestimated the prison population; and third, new construction projects, upon which the defendants were relying "to provide additional design capacity," may well be delayed, as they had been in the past. The court stated that it would have to retain jurisdiction beyond the December 31 deadline and perhaps issue new orders to ensure that the 137.5% cap became "durable."

Finally, the three-judge court responded to the plaintiffs' renewed request to begin contempt proceedings against the defendants. The request had "considerable merit," but once again the court, stating that its "first priority" was population reduction, deferred any contempt proceedings.

Squeezing the Three-Judge Court

The defendants continued to resist expanding good time credits and releasing low-risk offenders; and from June 20 until mid-September, the prison population grew by approximately 1,000 inmates. However, on September 12, 2013, Governor Brown signed Senate Bill 105 (SB 105), which offered hope for some relief— both short term and long term. It provided funds for the immediate transfer of inmates, both in state and out of state, and for rehabilitation services. In addition, SB 105 created a Recidivism Reduction Fund "to be available for appropriation by the legislature for activities aimed at reducing the state's prison population."

Four days later the defendants asked the three-judge court to extend the 137.5% deadline to December 31, 2016. They noted that pursuant to SB 105 they could immediately transfer 2,500 prisoners to in-state facilities, avoid bringing home the 9,000 out-of-state prisoners, and "achieve durable reforms," — but only if the court's deadline were extended:

> State prisons are just one part of the larger, interconnected criminal justice system. . . . When the state changes its policies to reduce prison popula-tion, the entire criminal justice system must absorb the changes. State and local officials must find ways to protect public safety while helping offenders, who would have otherwise been in prison, successfully reinte-grate into our communities. For a prison-crowding solution to last, it must be developed in consultation with the state and local officials who will place [sic] a decisive role its implementation.
>
> Recognizing the interconnected nature of criminal justice in Califor-nia, SB 105 mandates that additional solutions be developed in conjunc-tion with criminal justice stakeholders and the Legislature through California's democratic process, to ensure that the resulting reforms will be sustainable. But these further reforms will take time to develop. . . .

Yes, given the complexities of the criminal justice system, durable reforms require collaboration. But why, one might ask, did the state not act on this insight two or four or even ten years earlier? Neither overcrowding nor the interconnected nature of the criminal justice system was a new phenomenon. And why would it be reasonable at this point to grant a *three-year* extension when the original order, affirmed by the Supreme Court, called for the popula-tion reduction to take place over a two-year period (which had already been extended by six months)?

Most important for present purposes, how would the state — at least in the absence of a long-term expanded good time credit program or serious sentenc-ing reform — permanently reduce the prison population to 137.5% of design capacity even by December 31, 2016? The defendants' only answer was that a lasting solution to prison overcrowding "must be developed in consultation with the state and local officials. . . ." That, of course, was what the state should have been doing for at least the last two years.

Yet, the three-judge court was in a bind. The state, by its own estimate, would have to reduce the prison population by 8,500 inmates to meet the December 31 deadline.[8] Given the absence of adequate rehabilitation and reentry pro-grams (which the state's September 16 filing acknowledged were not yet in

---

8. The defendants' September 16 Status Report and Request for an Extension, where the 8,500 figure appears, does not indicate what the figure includes or how it was derived. The projection appears to be considerably higher than what the three-judge court had assumed in June would have been required to meet the 137.5% goal. For a comparison of the June and September figures, *see* the endnotes to this footnote.

place) and the previously noted high recidivism rate among released prisoners, requiring the state to release thousands of prisoners in a three-month period of time would do little, if anything, to contribute to a durable solution to over-crowding.[9] On the other hand, if the court would not require such release or extend its deadline, the defendants made clear what they would do to meet the December 31 goal of 137.5%: transfer inmates to out-of-state facilities — an expensive option that would not contribute to a durable solution, and that would "result in thousands [more] prisoners being incarcerated hundreds or thou-sands of miles from the support of their families." Moreover, to finance the out-of-state transfer of prisoners, SB 105 mandated a substantial reduction in funds that would otherwise be available to fight recidivism. In short, the court, it seemed, had little choice but to grant an extension.

There was one glimmer of hope. The three-judge court had heard a rumor that Governor Brown was amenable to the possibility of a negotiated settlement. With that in mind, the court once again secured the services of Peter Siggins and ordered the parties to meet and confer in a "confidential and informal" process that Siggins would facilitate. The court also extended the 137.5% dead-line for several months to allow for the negotiations and ordered the defendants not to make any arrangement for the out-of-state transfer of inmates "[d]uring the meet-and-confer process and until further order of the Court."

The order to refrain from arranging for out-of-state transfers was unfortu-nate for two reasons. First, it was almost certainly unnecessary. The defendants had made it clear that they would resort to out-of-state transfers only if they were required to meet the December 31, 2013 deadline of 137.5%. Since the court had extended that deadline, there was no pressure for the defendants to take such action during the time necessary for the court-ordered meet-and-confer sessions. If, at some point in the future, the defendants began to use their resources for out-of-state transfers at the expense of programs to rehabilitate prisoners and reduce recidivism, the court could then decide the propriety of prohibiting the transfers.

Second, the order was the first of the three-judge court's mandates specifi-cally to limit the state's discretion in deciding how to reduce its prison popula-tion. As such, it was a departure from the court's commitment to judicial restraint. Given the defendants' stated preferences and the court's extension of the deadline, the departure was more theoretical than real. Nonetheless, the day

---

9. Perhaps the same could be said of the three-judge court's June 20 order. As of that date, however, the state, as noted earlier in the text, had to reduce its prison population by only approximately 1,800 inmates per month to satisfy the Amended Plan. By contrast, even if the state began acting immediately, it would now have only three and a half months to reduce its prison population by 8,500 inmates — over 2,400 inmates per month.

after the three-judge court's order, the defendants, in their appeal to the Supreme Court (which had not yet been dismissed), submitted a supplemental brief complaining that the court had "imposed [on the state] its policy preferences for how to reduce prison overcrowding."

Getting Back on Track

The meet-and-confer sessions did not result in a settlement, and on January 13, 2014, the three-judge court ordered both plaintiffs and defendants to offer proposals designed "to achieve durable compliance with this Court's orders to maintain a prison population of no more than 137.5% design capacity." Plaintiffs responded by demanding immediate compliance with the 137.5% goal — a proposal that, in the three-judge court's words, was "neither durable nor desirable." By contrast, the defendants reduced their extension request from three to two years and offered a proposal that included:

- A commitment to meet the 137.5% goal by February 28, 2016, with interim benchmarks of 143% by June 30, 2014 and 141.5% by February 15, 2015.
- The three-judge court's appointment of a compliance officer, who would have the authority to release low-risk offenders in the event that the defendants missed a benchmark or the final goal.
- An agreement not to appeal "any order concerning compliance with the population cap or subsequent orders necessary to implement defendants' proposed order, including an order by a Compliance Officer directing the release of inmates."
- An agreement not to increase the current population level of approximately 8,900 out-of-state prisoners.
- The expenditure of millions of dollars to implement recidivism reduction measures pursuant to SB 105.
- Implementation of various other population reduction measures, including parole reform, increased use of prospective good time credits for nonviolent offenders, and transferring inmates to county jails and other in-state facilities.

On February 10, 2014, the three-judge court issued an order that incorporated the key elements of the defendants' proposal.[10] In addition, the court

---

10. In April 2014, the court appointed Elwood Lui to be the compliance officer. That same month, District Judge Kimberly Mueller was named as the three-judge court replacement for Judge Karlton when he retired later in the year. Judge Mueller also took over Judge Karlton's prisoner mental health class action.

noted that the defendants had agreed to "consider the establishment of a commission to recommend reforms of state penal and sentencing laws," and the court ordered the defendants to "explore ways to attempt to reduce the number of inmates housed in out-of-state facilities."

In an opinion accompanying its order, the three-judge court accurately summarized the defendants' prior efforts at prison population reduction:

> In the four and a half years between our 2009 order and the date of this opinion, defendants have instituted only one significant measure to relieve overcrowding in California prisons: "Realignment," a program that shifted responsibility for criminals who commit non-serious, non-violent, and non-registerable sex crimes from the state prison system to county jails. Apart from Realignment, defendants have taken no significant steps toward reducing the prison population and relieving overcrowding despite repeated orders by this Court requiring them to do so. Instead, defendants have continually failed to implement any of the measures approved by this Court and the Supreme Court that would have safely reduced the California prison population and alleviated the unconstitutional conditions of medical and mental health care in the prisons.

Moreover, as noted in the previous chapter, the defendants' obduracy spilled over into their dealings with the receiver in *Plata*.

The reasons for the defendants' dramatic change of position in early 2014 may never be fully known. However, at least four factors probably contributed to their decision to stop resisting the three-judge court. First, the defendants desperately needed an extension of the 137.5% goal. Neither the immediate release of thousands of prisoners nor sending them out of state was a desirable option. And to get an extension, the defendants must have realized that would have to make significant concessions. Second, the recent negotiations facilitated by Peter Siggins undoubtedly gave the defendants a good sense of what the three-judge court was likely to find acceptable. Indeed, in the introduction to their proposal, the defendants stated, "During the meet-and-confer process, it became clear that the Court was disinclined to approve a three-year extension, and that additional measures would be needed to secure an extension." Third, Governor Brown was almost certainly contemplating a run for a second term. Given his hard-line, law-and-order stance, he probably did not want to risk a massive prisoner release in 2014. Finally, and perhaps most important, the Supreme Court, as noted earlier, had dismissed the defendants' appeals in October 2013. The defendants' January 2014 proposal was their first substantive submission to the three-judge court after the dismissal. Prior to that time, the defendants, perhaps encouraged by their lawyers, may have held out hope that, after a substantial reduction in the prison population, the Supreme Court would save them. The Supreme Court, after all, had stressed that the original three-judge court order may be subject to modification as circumstances change. The dismissal of the defendants' appeals presumably put that hope to rest.

A Durable Solution?

The defendants met the summer 2014 benchmark of 143%; and in late January 2015, they announced that they had reduced the prison population to below the 137.5% goal over a year early. But is that population level sustainable for the long run?

Two positive signs are the implementation of population control measures that were incorporated into the three-judge court's February 10, 2014 order and the California voters' adoption of Measure 47 in November 2014. That measure calls for misdemeanor sentencing for some nonserious and nonviolent drug and property crimes that were previously punishable as felonies. Since misdemeanor jail time is served in county facilities, Proposition 47 will limit to some extent the number of new admissions to state prisons. In addition, Proposition 47 allows some state prisoners currently serving time for the affected crimes to petition for resentencing and, thus, potential release or transfer to county facilities.

On the other hand, in the fall of 2013, the CDCR projected that, primarily as a result of new admissions, the prison population would *increase* by 10,000 inmates over the next six years to 142,890 on June 30, 2019. Six months later, the CDCR revised the June 30, 2019 projection upward by nearly 4,000 inmates. Measure 47 had not yet been adopted when the state made these projections. Nonetheless, the numbers are staggering. In addition, at some point the state will have to accommodate the approximately 8,800 prisoners being housed out of state. Finally, there is growing concern that Realignment has created undesirable situations for some overcrowded county jails.

If the defendants' current efforts fall short of providing a durable solution to overcrowding, there are at least two additional, significant measures available to accomplish that end. First, as the three-judge court urged in its December 13, 2013 order, the defendants could adopt a more expansive good time credit program. Second, the state could further reduce the flow of new prisoners into the system and the length of time that prisoners remain incarcerated by reforming its sentencing laws.

Chapter Eighteen

Recording Atrocities Redux: Special Education in East Palo Alto

Several years after his stint with the Justice Department, Judge Henderson, expressing frustration with the role of Justice Department lawyers in the South as mere "observers," characterized his job as "recording atrocities." He has voiced similar frustration — and with good reason — about the difficulties he has faced for two decades in trying to get the Ravenswood Elementary School District in East Palo Alto, California, to comply with his orders. The case is Emma C. v. Eastin.

Judge Henderson's Description of the Factual Background: Emma C. v. Eastin, 2001 W.L. 1180636, 1–3 (N.D. Cal.)

The plaintiffs in this action are children with physical, mental, or learning disabilities who attend or have attended school in Ravenswood, a relatively small district serving roughly 5,000 elementary students in East Palo Alto, California. Plaintiffs' suit, filed in 1996, alleged that Ravenswood was in violation of the Individuals with Disabilities Education Act ("IDEA"), as well as other state and federal laws governing education of disabled children. Under the IDEA, qualified, disabled children are entitled to a "free appropriate public education" that includes an Individualized Education Plan ("IEP") tailored to each such child's unique needs. . . .

The plaintiff[s] ... challenged every aspect of Ravenswood's special education efforts, alleging *inter alia* that Ravenswood fails to (1) adequately identify children with disabilities, (2) adequately assess and evaluate children once they are identified, (3) follow proper procedures in developing Individual Educational Programs ("IEPs") for children with disabilities, (4) properly implement IEPs, (5) minimize the segregation of children of disabilities to that which is necessary, (6) hire and maintain adequately trained and credentialed special education staff, and (7) maintain adequate records. The complaint further alleged that the California Department of Education ("CDE") had failed in its obligations to effectively monitor special education services at Ravenswood and ensure that pupils are provided with a free and appropriate public education.

In response to the lawsuit, CDE initiated a comprehensive investigation into the allegations in the complaint. The resulting January 8, 1998 report, compiled by a team of six professional staff, substantiated the plaintiffs' allegations, finding widespread noncompliance with special education requirements. . . .

This sweeping critique was likely no surprise to either CDE or Ravenswood. CDE had previously reviewed Ravenswood's special education services in 1993, and found the District to be noncompliant in numerous areas. . . . Ravenswood's failure to take effective corrective action in the face of identified problems is a pattern that has been consistently repeated.

[To begin the process of remedying the deficiencies identified in the January 8, 1998 Compliance Report,] CDE contracted with outside consultants Dr. Alan Coulter and Dr. Kathleen Gee to perform a Needs Assessment of Ravenswood. With the assistance of a team of nationally known, experienced consultants, they investigated the delivery of special education services at Ravenswood and issued a comprehensive [Needs Assessment] Report on July 15, 1998 which confirmed the widespread failures in the area of special education. . . . .

Based upon the [Needs Assessment] and the Compliance Report, Drs. Gee and Coulter developed a draft Ravenswood Corrective Action Plan ("RCAP") which contains a "comprehensive, step-by-step blueprint for transforming the District into a model of IDEA compliance." Specifically, the RCAP divides the actions needed to bring Ravenswood into compliance with governing law into four broad categories: (1) the development of systems and structures required to ensure the provision of a free appropriate education ("FAPE") in the least restrictive environment ("LRE"); (2) the provision of qualified and trained personnel to serve children with disabilities, (3) the proper identification, referral, and assessment procedures for children with, or suspected of having, disabilities, and (4) the actual implementation of appropriate individual education programs ("IEPS") for each child with disabilities in the LRE. Within each category, the RCAP identifies specific corrective activities, expected results, a timeline for performing the activity, the individual responsible for performance, and measures to determine compliance.[1]

Ravenswood had an opportunity to review the draft RCAP in a series of meetings and negotiated various changes. [In the latter part of 1998,] CDE formally issued the RCAP as its corrective action plan . . . obliging Ravenswood to implement the plan by June 30, 2001.

Dr. Charlie Mae Knight, Her Allies, and Her Record

From 1985 until 2003 Ravenswood's superintendent was the colorful, enigmatic Dr. Charlie Mae Knight. During her tenure she raised substantial amounts of private money for the district; and in 1997, Governor Pete Wilson praised Knight "for doing a first class job for California's kids." Signs of potential difficulty, however, predated her arrival in East Palo Alto. Immediately before coming to Ravenswood, Knight had been superintendent of the Lynwood School District in Los Angeles. After serving in that capacity for two tumultuous years, during which there were concerns about financial improprieties, Knight was suspended by the Lynwood School Board. She resigned when the board bought out the remainder of her contract. A few months later she became head of the Ravenswood School District.

Once at Ravenswood, Knight hired a number of allies from Lynwood and elsewhere. They included her former special education supervisor, who became associate superintendent and later a loyal Ravenswood School Board member; a Lynwood financial administrator, who had been criticized by a grand jury for his spending at Lynwood and who became Ravenswood's controller; and a maintenance supervisor. Knight's secretary had worked for Knight before she was at Lynwood; and the secretary's daughter, who had a master's degree but no state certificate in special education, was one of Ravenswood's special education teachers. The managing partner of the law firm that Ravenswood first hired to defend the special education suit had worked with Knight when she was

---

1. CDE subsequently added a fifth section to the RCAP in response to findings concerning Ravenswood made by the United States Department of Education, Office of Civil Rights. This fifth section concerns the adoption of procedures to implement Section 504 of the Rehabilitation Act, and focuses on training interpreters, delivering appropriate special education instruction to students who have limited English proficiency, hiring staff with appropriate training and credentials, and providing parents with translated documents upon request. [Footnote by the court.]

at Lynwood. A former school principal whom Knight had recruited for Lynwood moved to East Palo Alto, opened a McDonald's franchise, and "for years" peddled his burgers and fries to Ravenswood for its lunch program — even though by 2001 the district had yet to meet "a 1977 state nutritional goal for fat reduction." Knight claimed the former principal's move to East Palo Alto was merely a coincidence. A 2003 San Jose Mercury News editorial characterized Knight as "a woman who ran Ravenswood as a personal fiefdom, embedding friends to fortify her power and punishing any who dared oppose her."

In 1992, Knight established an emergency loan fund for the district with an initial grant of $9,900. Recipients of loans from the fund included school board members and various Ravenswood employees, some of whom were renting property owned by Knight and who used the proceeds to pay their rent. Loans to renters and others who owed Knight money led to a 19-count felony conflict-of-interest indictment against Knight in 2000. Most of the prosecution witnesses — present and former employees of the district who had received loans — were sympathetic to the defense. Knight claimed that she was not personally responsible for approving any of the loans, and the jury found sufficient reasonable doubt to acquit her.

During Knight's tenure, the district spent lavishly on travel, including at least $600,000 in a period from 1998 to 2001. For the 1999 to 2000 school year, "[t]he district's travel spending . . . averaged out to $67 per pupil, more than twice as much as the $31 average for 20 similarly sized elementary districts." "[D]ozens of staff members, including many whose jobs have nothing to do with teaching, such as maintenance supervisors and district secretaries," attended education conferences at the district's expense; and both administrators and school board members made frequent international junkets to recruit teachers. Their destinations included Spain, Mexico, the Philippines, Pago Pago, and American Samoa.

Money spent on travel pales in comparison to the amount the District has spent on or approved for attorneys' fees — over $75,000 to represent the District in various grand jury investigations; over $100,000 for Knight's personal defense against the conflict-of-interest charge; and over $300,000 in 2000 alone to defend the special education lawsuit. That $300,000, though, turned out to be only a token. Between March and November of 2002, the district paid an Atlanta law firm $2 million. The charges included almost $100,000 for air fare (much of it first class), almost $15,000 for meals (including 49 meals of over $100), and hotel stays of as much as $349 per room per night.

A 2001 San Jose Mercury News investigation of the Ravenswood School District revealed, among other things, that the District could not account for millions of dollars in federal and state aid (including over a million dollars supposedly spent on special education between 1995 and 1997); that the district substantially overstated the number of children receiving subsidized lunches; that after a fire in 1997, District officials filed claims that inflated the losses by over $100,000; and "that Ravenswood has a higher percentage of teachers on emergency credentials, 57 percent, than any other district in California." One of the investigation's more troublesome findings related to improving standardized test scores for Ravenswood student:

> The students' performance plummets once they move on to high school. And two teacher aides have said they were told to help students cheat on [a] standardized test. . . . One student . . . confirmed . . . that an aide had filled in answers for him.

And throughout Charlie Mae Knight's tenure, progress on special education reform was close to nonexistent.

The First Efforts at Settlement

In May 1989, even before the Ravenswood Corrective Action Plan (RCAP) became final, the District agreed to comply with it as part of a proposed settlement. That agreement, however, turned out to be largely rhetorical. As Judge Henderson reported:

> [During 1998 and 1999,] Drs. Gee and Coulter [, who made the Needs Assessment that led to the RCAP,] each spent about two weeks a month . . . in the District attending meetings with principals, teachers, psychologists, general administration staff and parents. Through this intensive contact, they became very familiar with Ravenswood's [early] efforts to implement the RCAP. [According to Dr. Coulter]. . . . .:
>> [W]e were faced with fundamental and continual resistance to implementation of the RCAP from top administrative levels, resistance that permeated and trickled down to the lower levels of administration. It was my impression that Dr. Knight did not take the time to fully understand the RCAP . . . did not provide the oversight necessary to implement the RCAP, did not set up an accountability and management structure that would ensure implementation of the RCAP, and did not set a tone among her faculty and staff that would encourage RCAP implementation. It was as though Dr. Knight thought that the RCAP would 'just go away' if she herself ignored it.
> Dr. Gee's observations were similar. . . . Due to their frustration, and after "much deliberation," Dr. Coulter and Dr. Gee both resigned in May 1999 from their positions monitoring RCAP implementation for CDE.

In the meantime, other aspects of a settlement proved to be elusive. There were two groups of defendants — the Ravenswood defendants, which included the School District and Charlie Mae Knight, and the state defendants, which included the California Department of Education (CDE). At least initially, Ravenswood "apparently declined to participate in a comprehensive settlement with all the parties." As a result, by early 1999 the only "settlement" proposal that the parties could agree to was in fact two separate settlements — one between the plaintiffs and the Ravenswood defendants and another between the plaintiffs and the state defendants.

Judge Henderson gave preliminary approval to the terms of the RCAP as an appropriate remedy, but he rejected the parties' proposed dual agreements as "wholly inadequate to protect [plaintiffs'] . . . interests." As Judge Henderson explained:

> [T]he separate agreements . . . failed to resolve very serious disputes between defendants with respect to their respective legal and financial obligations. The settlement agreements also failed to adequately address the important issue of monitoring and court supervision of the remedial process. The Ravenswood agreement completely failed to address the issue. The CDE agreement, while it addressed monitoring and court supervision, was not binding on Ravenswood and was overly simplistic on this point. [In addition,] the proposed agreements were out of date, obsolete in certain respects, and poorly drafted, leaving many items vague and unclear.

At the hearing in March 1999, when he rejected the proposed settlement, Judge Henderson warned Ravenswood of his concerns:

> I'm gravely troubled. Let me repeat that. I'm gravely troubled by the apparent attitude of the Ravenswood school district in light of the record in this case. Nothing in Ravenswood's approach to this litigation — from the inception of this case up to and including its approach to this motion for preliminary approval — gives me reason to believe that the school district understands the implications of its conduct or is committed to moving forward and advancing the remedial process in a productive and constructive manner.

By September the parties signed a "much improved" consent decree, to which Judge Henderson gave final approval in January 2000. At the same time, however, Judge Henderson warned the parties of "the Court's growing concern about the District's ability to perform the functions mandated by the RCAP and the consent decree, and of the potential need for the CDE to perform an expanded role in ensuring the special education needs of the plaintiff[s] . . . are met."

The court order approving this settlement made it clear that the RCAP itself was part of and "shall be enforced as an order of the Court and that [it] may be modified or supplemented only upon Court approval." Pursuant to the agreement, Judge Henderson appointed a monitor, Mark Mlawer, to oversee and report on the defendants' compliance.

Judge Henderson on the Early Record of Noncompliance (January 2000 through April 2001): Emma C. v. Eastin, 2001 W.L. 1180636, 3–5 (N.D. Cal.)

[Even though Ravenswood had committed itself to implementing the RCAP in mid-1998,] it became apparent [soon after the January, 2000 approval of the consent decree] that Ravenswood had done virtually nothing to begin implementing the RCAP. . . . Accordingly, the Court Monitor was forced to recommend to the Court, in consultation with the parties, a revamping of many of the original RCAP deadlines. Under the new terms, agreed to by Ravenswood, it was still required to achieve final RCAP implementation by June 30, 2001, but the deadlines for completing key specific activities were substantially extended from the previous deadlines. The Court emphasized again that "the RCAP as modified . . . constitutes a final order of the Court and shall be enforced as an order of the Court. . . . In this respect, the Court notes that it expects that the person(s) identified as the "Person Responsible" for each corrective action in the RCAP *shall be accountable for the satisfactory completion of such action.*" (emphasis added).

As the number and difficulty of the required RCAP activities increased, the Monitor's monthly report cards began to show a disturbing trend of increasing non-compliance. While the early report cards in 2000 showed compliance rates ranging from 36% to 85.71%, they dropped dramatically to 27.27% in June, then 0% for July and August, 8.11% for September, and then 0% for October and November. In November 2000, plaintiffs wrote to the Court expressing their concerns regarding the lack of implementation of the RCAP. In response, and in order to help facilitate and encourage a more intensified effort by Ravenswood, the Court commenced monthly meetings at the Courthouse to address issues pertaining to RCAP implementation as they arose. These meetings were attended by the Court Monitor, counsel, one member of the Board of Trustees of Ravenswood, the Ravenswood Superintendent and Assistant Superintendent responsible for Special Education, the State

Superintendent of Public Instruction or a senior designee, and either [myself] or court staff.

Compliance rates nonetheless continued to hover at abysmal rates (0% for December 2000, 7.69% for February 2001, 0% for March 2001). . . .

At the same time, Ravenswood's approach to RCAP implementation was less than cooperative and sometimes outright recalcitrant. . . . [On January 24, 2001,] the Court again warned the parties "of the Court's growing concern about the District's apparent inability to perform the functions mandated by the RCAP and the Consent Decree and of the potential need for the CDE to perform an expanded role."

In early March 2001 — three months before the RCAP was to have been fully implemented — Ravenswood responded to the mounting record of non-compliance by proposing that the Court extend the already modified RCAP deadlines substantially, in some cases up to two years. Plaintiffs this time objected to any extensions of the RCAP deadlines, convinced that this approach would result only in further delay rather than genuine progress. On March 19, 2001, plaintiffs filed a Motion for an Order to Show Cause Why Defendants Should Not be Held in Contempt of Court and Be Sanctioned.

At the April 30, 2001 hearing on plaintiffs' motion, the Court agreed with CDE and plaintiffs' assessment that the "current state of RCAP implementation is intolerable." Specifically, the Court [stated] . . .:

> [T]he Monitor's last 11 monthly report cards present a stark pattern of consistent non-compliance with the RCAP. Of the 200 items that Ravenswood should have completed by now under the modified RCAP deadline, it has failed to fully and satisfactorily complete over two-thirds . . . of them. [These failures relate not to] collateral parts of the RCAP [but to] . . . the very core of the remedial plan. . . .

The Court was also disturbed that Ravenswood's actions continued to reflect a lack of commitment to implementing the remedy. . . . As the Court Monitor has reported, the Superintendent has, in his presence, and in the presence of staff, complained about the RCAP and suggested that it is unfair that Ravenswood has to implement a remedial plan while other districts do not. Such remarks appear more designed to denigrate the RCAP rather than motivate and energize staff to embrace and implement the remedy. . . . In yet another example, a memo from the Superintendent concerning an RCAP-required training for principals went largely unheeded when eight of the District's 13 principals failed to attend. [And of the five principals who did attend, "two . . . were more than an hour late for the two-hour session."]

. . . [A]t this same April 30th hearing, the Court again emphasized to Ravenswood that its negative attitude, and failure to embrace the remedy, was deeply disturbing . . .:

[I]t's alarming that the District nowhere in its papers even acknowledges that there's a problem with the rate of implementation of the remedy. . . . The District's answer to the current situation is simply to give itself a lengthy, up to two-year, extension for meeting many of the RCAP requirements. If the Court felt that Ravenswood was doing all it could possibly do, or reasonably do, and simply needed more time, this might be a well received suggestion. It is not, however, given the record before me. In my experience with this District over the years in this case . . . I see a District that's so far appeared disinterested, unmotivated and unwilling, or some combination thereof, to turn the RCAP into more than just a symbolic piece of paper. . . . [I]t's almost as if [Ravenswood] signed the papers, the consent decree, and then said, Why are you bothering us? Go away.

More Pressure, More Cronyism, and Continued Noncompliance

Judge Henderson deferred the plaintiffs' request for a contempt citation; however he

ordered that both the Ravenswood Superintendent, Dr. Knight, and CDE's Ravenswood liaison, Christine Pittman, appear personally in court every 30 days over the next three months to testify regarding the efforts being made to implement the RCAP. In addition, CDE was ordered to substantially increase its assistance to the District. Specifically, it was directed to prepare a work plan and schedule of activities for the District to follow that was designed to complete each RCAP requirement, provide the District with all necessary training and technical assistance resources to complete the work plan, and work closely with Ravenswood personnel to ensure they understood the actions needed to complete the work plan.

He then made it clear that in the absence of "a 'dramatic turnaround in both action and attitude,'" he would act to find Ravenswood in contempt of court.

The threat of contempt "clearly caught the attention" of Charlie Mae Knight. In May 2001, she testified that she was "spending 95% of her time on special education" and that she

has 'been in [the Court Monitor's] office more times in the last month than [she has] been in since he's been here [starting back in January, 2000].'. . . . [I]n June 2001, she testified that she now has ten people working on RCAP implementation in different capacities.

One of the individuals about whom Knight testified was a Texas educator, Gwen Morrison, whom Knight hired as a consultant. Another was Simona

Vezzoli, who was hired to develop a computer program to track special education students. Knight appeared to have difficulty pronouncing Vezzoli's name but was effusive in praising her: "'We begged and pleaded she would come. . . . She's a student at the University of California-Berkeley. We were able to persuade her to modify her courses so she could coordinate the system for us.'" Knight, however, was not completely forthcoming about either individual. She did not mention that Morrison was an old friend, who had been charged with double billing her home district for expenses; that she (Knight) had testified at Morrison's first criminal trial, which ended in a hung jury; and that Morrison had then acknowledged her double billing and pled no contest to misdemeanor charges. Knight also did not mention that Vezzoli was her son's girlfriend and that the couple lived in a condominium owned by Knight in East Palo Alto.

Despite Charlie Mae Knight's recently professed interest in special education, noncompliance continued to be the order of the day. According to Christine Pittman, the CDE's liaison to Ravenswood, "The district staff report that they do not know district policy or procedure in key areas." Monitor Mark Mlawer's August 3 report described Ravenswood's progress as "very meager." In some instances, the District was actually losing ground:

> For example, although the RCAP requires placing students in the least restrictive environment in which their individualized education program can be satisfactorily implemented, the trend in the District has been toward *increased* segregation of disabled students, with the number of disabled students in county self-contained programs rising almost 50 percent from 61 in 1995 to 90 in 2000.

Moreover, the District was not utilizing available resources. Mark Mlawer reported "that . . . '[t]he majority of special educators, special therapists, and psychologists interviewed were not made aware by the district . . . that consultants hired by the monitor were available to assist them'." Christine Pittman testified about a similar failure of the District to use resources provided by the CDE:

> One small example concerns an experienced consultant, Judy Hegenauer, referred to the District by CDE. Dr. Knight testified that Ms. Hegenauer "did not have adequate time to devote to this project." However, when CDE recruited her "she had two weeks available, but unfortunately, by the time the District contacted her, she only had five days left."

An ongoing problem was ineffective communication between the school district and its parents and students. In 2001, 67% of the Ravenswood students were Latino, and 9% were Pacific Islanders. Many of them and their parents were not proficient in English. Nonetheless,

> [a]lthough the RCAP requires the district to translate IEP and other special education documents in the primary languages of the students and parents, the district "initially failed to develop a plan for this activity, failed to include the district's multilingual office in the process, and later failed to implement the plan eventually developed per CDE instruction to contract with Stanford University for the services. There was no follow through by [the Assistant Superintendent of Special Education], no coordination between district administrators, and no oversight by the superintendent. The net result is that documents are not being translated on a timely basis by qualified staff and parents are therefore unable to understand the contents of IEPs."

The language problem was not limited to document translation. A 14-year-old student from Mexico who spoke no English was assigned to a special education class where neither the teacher nor the aides spoke Spanish or were certified to teach English as a second language. "The boy ... was left to spend his days drawing with a box of crayons." Another special education student who spoke only Spanish was given speech therapy in English. Some non-English speaking students were erroneously classified as having disabilities solely because of their lack of English proficiency. Others, who did have disabilities, were not properly diagnosed because of the district's lack of special education personnel with foreign language skills.

The "Full Extent" of the Court's Powers

Judge Henderson concluded his April 30, 2001 hearing with the following statement: "You can be assured that I'm prepared to use the full extent of [a federal court's] powers ... as is needed, to get this RCAP implemented and implemented fully."

But what is the "full extent" of the court's powers?

The most obvious — and frequently the most effective — power is to use the bench as a "bully pulpit." A court's ability to persuade, to threaten, to order parties to testify, and generally to oversee the carrying out of orders is limited only by the court's time and patience. As illustrated by his efforts in this case, Judge Henderson has devoted much more energy than many federal judges do to the task of monitoring and trying to ensure compliance with court orders. However, if a party is steadfastly recalcitrant, these efforts can be for naught.

The violation of a court order — and the RCAP, recall, was incorporated in a court order — can result in a contempt sanction, either criminal or civil. The purpose of "criminal" contempt is to impose punishment — a fixed fine or jail sentence — for violating a court order. "Civil" contempt, by contrast, is designed to coerce compliance with a court order. A civil contempt fine typically increases daily until the contemnor agrees to comply with the court order. Incarceration for civil contempt has a similar purpose. Thus, it can last until, but only until, the incarcerated individual agrees to obey the court order.

Incarceration of any kind, of course, is not a possibility for institutional entities, like a school district; and since the individual defendants had always expressed a willingness to comply with Judge Henderson's orders, incarceration for civil contempt would not have been an option. Removing individual administrators or teachers from the school system to serve criminal contempt jail sentences seems counterproductive — except perhaps for the possibility that a very brief time in jail (or even the threat of incarceration) may serve as a wake-up call. However, carrying out that threat, as surely the defendants would learn from their lawyers if they did not already know it, could be difficult. The court would have to convene a separate contempt trial, in which the parties could call witnesses. There could be disputes about such matters as whether or the extent to which a particular order was violated; whether circumstances made compliance impossible and, therefore, excusable; and whether the particular defendant or somebody higher or lower in the administrative chain of command was ultimately responsible for the violation. Judge Henderson anticipated and tried to meet this last possibility by ordering specific individuals to perform distinct tasks. The other problems, however, would remain. Moreover, a defendant's acquittal might intensify general recalcitrance; and a conviction might do nothing more than make the contemnor a martyr.

Monetary fines would be equally problematic. In addition to its own fines, the District almost certainly would take on the responsibility for any fines meted out against individual administrators or teachers; and large monetary fines would decrease the possibility of devoting more of the District's resources to special education.

The one remedy that, superficially at least, has some appeal would be for Judge Henderson to order a receivership or state takeover of Ravenswood. However, receiverships designed to address a school district's educational, as opposed to financial, problems have not fared well. For example, the Compton (California) Unified School District was in state receivership from 1993 until late 2001; and although the state substantially improved Compton's finances and physical facilities, the receivership did little for the quality of education. Student test scores remained low and drop-out rates high. The experience was not atypical.

What, then, is the "full extent" of a court's power? The short answer, at least in the context of *Emma C.*, was "almost nothing." The practical choices for Judge Henderson appeared to be to continue his efforts to threaten and cajole the parties into compliance with his orders or to impose a receivership on the Ravenswood School District. The prior performance of the defendants (including the CDE) and the record of receiverships elsewhere suggested reasons for pessimism about both alternatives.

Contempt, Fraud, and a Principal's "Dismissal"

Speaking from the bench in a July 26, 2001 hearing on Ravenswood's implementation of the RCAP, Judge Henderson said, "I've tried mightily to get this done with a carrot rather than stick." He then ordered Ravenswood to show cause why it should not be held in contempt. Both the plaintiffs and the CDE asked Judge Henderson to order a state takeover of the District as the remedy for a contempt finding. A hearing was set for August 22.

At that hearing, an attorney for Ravenswood submitted a petition with 394 signatures that expressed support for the school board and Charlie Mae Knight. The petition was addressed to "Judge Felton [*sic*] Henderson." The signers were identified as "parents and friends of the Ravenswood City School District." Despite this plea, Judge Henderson held that the district was in contempt and ordered the parties to file papers addressing the question of an appropriate remedy.

Three weeks later the San Jose Mercury News revealed that the petition, which had been sent to the Ravenswood attorneys from a fax machine in Knight's office only hours before the contempt hearing, was fraudulent. The signatures were cut and pasted from earlier petitions supporting Knight on different matters. Additionally, the Mercury News investigation "found signatures listing addresses that do not exist, signatures of people who insist they neither saw the petition nor support the district's leadership, and signatures from out-of-towners who say they have never heard of Knight and her district." According to the Mercury News, "No one interviewed remembered signing a petition this summer, in the weeks leading up to Aug. 22. . . ."

To her credit, the attorney who had submitted the petition disavowed the fraud as soon as she was made aware of it. She said that Gwen Morrison, Knight's consultant friend from Texas, had called and then faxed the petition. Both the attorney's inquiry and a later investigation by Magistrate Judge Elizabeth LaPorte revealed that Marthelia Hargrove, a Ravenswood principal and long-time Knight supporter, had brought the petition to the superintendent's office.

Hargrove claimed that she had merely found the petition on a counter at her school while she was sorting mail. There was never definitive proof to the contrary, but Magistrate Judge LaPorte, who wrote a detailed report on her investigation, was not convinced:

> The Court finds Ms. Hargrove's story of the sudden appearance of the doctored petitions out of the blue, with its amazingly coincidental timing for the hearing, utterly implausible and not worthy of credence. . . .
>
> . . . [T]he conclusion is inescapable that Ms. Hargrove knew that the petitions were doctored and played a role in doctoring them, either alone or more likely with help from others.

With respect to Gwen Morrison, LaPorte concluded:

> [I]nconsistencies in [her] various statements about what she knew about the petitions, when she knew it and her role in faxing them seriously compromise her credibility . . .
>
> . . . Her selective memory reflects, at the least, an attempt to minimize the role of Ms. Hargrove and herself.

Judge Henderson adopted Laporte's recommendations that those involved with the petition undergo ethics training and that the District be fined $10,000. In addition, he required Ravenswood to pay attorneys fees for the time spent by plaintiffs' lawyers on the petition issue:

> While the Superintendent may or may not have had her hand directly in the proverbial cookie jar, her reckless disregard for the integrity of the judicial process encouraged, permitted, and enabled this misconduct to occur. . . . [T]here was neither acceptance of responsibility nor appropriate corrective action. . . . [T]he Ravenswood defendants engaged in a pattern of obfuscation and denial in a clear effort to protect and excuse the culpable parties.

In early October 2001, Judge Henderson postponed for six months the decision whether to impose a receivership on Ravenswood:

> Ravenswood . . . asserts that it now stands ready and able to tackle the RCAP with renewed determination and additional resources, and that it is "poised to make substantial progress." [Judge Henderson then catalogued a number of steps that Ravenswood had taken, including greater involvement of the Board, an alliance with the University of San Francisco' Education Department, the hiring of key administrative personnel, and the hiring of a new consultant, Dr. Michael Norman].
>
> The Court remains skeptical that Ravenswood will be able to efficiently and effectively purge its contempt even with the assistance of

Dr. Norman. . . . If the fundamental problem lies with the District's top leadership, then the hiring of a part-time consultant who reports to the Board and Superintendent and has limited authority will not ultimately succeed. . . .

Notwithstanding these concerns, the Court very reluctantly concludes that it is constrained under case precedent to give Ravenswood one final opportunity to demonstrate that it is capable of effectively implementing the RCAP in a prompt and efficient manner. . . .

In reaching this conclusion, the Court has . . . taken into consideration that neither CDE nor plaintiffs have yet presented the Court with more than the abstract notion of a receivership. No specific administrator(s) have been proposed who can be evaluated; nor has any such administrator outlined any approach for bringing the District into compliance on an efficient timetable.

Judge Henderson then set forth a number of specific tasks for Ravenswood, the CDE, and the Court Monitor. One of the plaintiffs' attorneys, acknowledging the legal constraints on ordering a state takeover of the District, characterized Judge Henderson's ruling as "very, very thoughtful."

The six-month extension and the contract of Ravenswood's new consultant, Michael Norman, ended on March 31, 2002. However, Monitor Mark Mlawer's report for the final month of the extension would not be available until well into April, and fairness required that Ravenswood have an opportunity to review it. Then all of the parties needed to reassess their positions. A hearing on the takeover was scheduled for June 18.

In what may well have been a ruse designed only to obtain Judge Henderson's sympathy prior to the takeover hearing, the school board announced in court papers filed at the end of May that it was "'pursuing the dismissal'" of Marthelia Hargrove, the Ravenswood principal who was at least partially responsible for the fraudulent petition supporting Charlie Mae Knight. The board "rehired" Hargrove in July because it had not given her proper notice of her dismissal — even though the board was fully aware of the relevant facts well before the May 15 notice date. Judge Henderson has compared Hargrove's "dismissal" to the "riot" he observed at Pelican Bay.

A New Lawyer, a New School Board, and a New Settlement

As the June 18 hearing date neared, Judge Henderson was becoming increasingly concerned about the ability of plaintiffs' lawyers to handle the complexity of the litigation. In contrast to Ravenswood, which at this point had four law firms working on the case, the plaintiffs from the outset had been represented by only three attorneys: a San Francisco lawyer with a small private practice; an attorney from a disability rights organization who, because of an illness, had been working out of her home; and a lawyer with the Community Law Project, a legal clinic for Stanford law students. Not only had Judge Henderson rejected their first proposed settlement as inadequate to protect plaintiffs' interest, but he had observed a continuing lack of aggressive advocacy on plaintiffs' behalf. Although the plaintiffs' lawyers had urged that Ravenswood be held in contempt and had, along with the CDE's lawyers, argued for a state takeover of the district, neither plaintiffs nor the CDE had been helpful in providing details about how such a takeover would work; and the plaintiffs had offered nothing other than their contempt motion and vague takeover request to remedy the increasingly obvious fact that the current settlement agreement was a failure.

Judge Henderson expressed his concern about plaintiffs' legal resources to Harry Bremond, his long-time friend and a partner at Wilson Sonsini, a large Palo Alto based firm with a national and international practice. Bremond then mentioned the case to Robert Feldman, the head of Wilson Sonsini's litigation department and father of a child with special needs. Feldman volunteered to become part of the plaintiffs' legal team; and because he needed time to familiarize himself with the case, Judge Henderson postponed the hearing that had been set for June 18.

In the meantime, there was growing dissatisfaction in East Palo Alto with Charlie Mae Knight and the Ravenswood School Board. In March 2002, "92 percent of Ravenswood teachers passed a measure of no-confidence in the district's leadership;" and in April, the teachers' union sought Knight's dismissal or resignation. By early summer, a group calling itself the Coalition for Quality Education began seeking reform candidates to run for the school board in November.

During the late summer and fall, plaintiffs' lawyers, led by Robert Feldman, engaged in serious discussions with Ravenswood about settling the contempt charge. On October 31, 2002, the Ravenswood School Board approved a tentative settlement, the details of which were not made public. Plaintiffs' lawyers, however, expressed skepticism about the value of the board's action. In part because of its expenditures for attorneys' fees, Ravenswood did not have the financial resources to implement the settlement, and the state defendants had not agreed to provide the necessary funding.

Three of five seats on the Ravenswood School Board were at stake in the November 5 election. The candidates included two pro-Knight incumbents and a slate of three anti-Knight reformers. The reform slate won handily. The old board, though, was not finished with its business. Despite an order from Judge Henderson to keep the lawsuit in abeyance until the new board members were seated, the old board filed papers seeking the removal of Court Monitor Mark Mlawer. The three newly elected board members were quick to criticize the filing as an additional unwarranted legal expense; and Judge Henderson, who denied the request, characterized it as a "blatant disregard" of his prior order.

On December 9, at the first meeting after the new board members took their oaths, they and the one other member present voted unanimously to put Knight on administrative leave. The board named Floyd Gonella, outgoing head of the San Mateo County School District, as its interim superintendent. Knight formally resigned at the end of the school year.

Two months after the new members were seated, the board approved a settlement agreement with plaintiffs and the CDE. The new accord replaced the RCAP with the Ravenswood Self-Improvement Plan (RSIP), which contained streamlined criteria for meeting the needs of Ravenswood's special education students. Although there was still a dispute between Ravenswood and the CDE over funding, the board announced that it would begin immediately to implement those portions of the agreement that did not require additional money. In May Judge Henderson resolved the funding issue by allocating the costs between the CDE and Ravenswood on 3:1 basis. Despite the fact that Ravenswood had urged that the state be required to assume a larger portion of the cost, Interim Superintendent Floyd Gonella declared, "I'm totally elated with the confidence [Judge Henderson] demonstrated for this district to move forward and implement the plan."

An End in Sight?

That would have been a nice end to this chapter. The case, however, drags on. For the first four years under the new settlement agreement, Ravenswood made substantial, if sometimes halting, progress in implementing the RSIP. Then, during the 2007–2008 school year, there was "significant regression," particularly with respect to core provisions of the RSIP covering the actual delivery of services to students with disabilities. Mark Mlawer, who continues to monitor Ravenswood's compliance with the RSIP, attributed the 2007–2008 failures to an ineffective human resources administrator and staffing failures.

For the next year and a half, there was renewed progress. In January 2010, Judge Henderson ordered the parties to set final deadlines for meeting each RSIP requirement. Pursuant to that order, the parties — with the assistance of Mark Mlawer — met and agreed upon a July 2014 date for full compliance.

With occasional backsliding, Ravenswood has continued to make progress in achieving the RSIP goals. However, it did not meet the July 2014 deadline; and by mid-2016 Ravenswood was still substantially noncompliant. In the meantime, a dispute has arisen about the nature and quality of the state's monitoring of the school district's compliance with the RSIP.

The Individuals with Disabilities Education Act requires states to monitor school districts' compliance with the statute. The CDE's obligation to

Ravenswood, however, is not limited to its federally imposed monitoring obligation. The 2003 amended settlement agreement (like its 2001 predecessor) is incorporated into a court order, and that order obligates the CDE to provide monitoring and services that are specific to Ravenswood. The CDE has been objecting — unsuccessfully so far — to monitoring requirements mandated by Judge Henderson. The matter is critical. Given Ravenswood's record of non-compliance and missed deadlines for nearly two decades, it seem unlikely that over the long term the district will be able to sustain compliance with the RSIP without (or perhaps even with) effective monitoring.

In comparing *Emma C.* to Madrid v. Gomez, the long-running Pelican Bay prisoners' rights case, Judge Henderson noted that his efforts in *Madrid* led to substantial systemic change that is likely to be permanent. By contrast, he has yet to see that happen with *Emma C.* "I have a feeling we're just treading water."

Postscript

After an unsuccessful 2006 run for the East Palo Alto City Council, Charlie Mae Knight became one of seven candidates for two available seats on the Ravenswood School Board in the fall of 2008. Ravenswood student scores on statewide achievement tests had risen substantially since Knight was superintendent, but they were still well below the California goal. In her campaign, Knight blamed the current state of affairs on the special education consent decree, which, she claimed, diverted resources from the majority of students. Knight finished third, well behind the two winners. Knight fared better in 2014. At age 82, she finished second among five candidates for three positions on the Ravenswood School Board. Marcelino Lopez, one of the reform candidates whose 2002 election led to Knight's resignation, retained his seat with a third-place finish.

Post-Postscript: Receivership Reconsidered

By June 2005, when Judge Henderson decided to appoint a receiver for the California prison medical system, he had seen over two years of steady improvement under the RSIP in East Palo Alto. However, that progress came after nearly a decade of extreme intransigence by Charlie Mae Knight and the Ravenswood School Board. It had taken Judge Henderson only four years to conclude in *Plata* that the prison medical system was so dysfunctional that a receiver was necessary. Should he perhaps have made the same decision during the early years of the East Palo Alto litigation?

In some respects, the similarities between the two cases are striking. Both involve defendants that are public institutions lacking the political motivation and will to meet legal mandates in serving their constituencies. The defendants in both cases suffer from what Judge Henderson has characterized as "bureaucratic dysfunction" or (using Thorstein Veblin's terminology) "trained incapacity." And during the years of inaction, countless prisoners with medical problems and children with special needs were denied assistance, which they required and to which they were entitled.

Nonetheless, a takeover of the Ravenswood School District would have been fraught with both legal and practical difficulties. From a legal standpoint, a receivership is not merely "an 'extraordinary remedy' to be invoked only when the facts indicate that all other remedies will fail." In addition, a court must consider the "probable effectiveness" of such action; and there are a number of practical considerations that, at the very least, make appointing a receiver for Ravenswood much more problematic than appointing a receiver for the California prison medical system

Whereas in *Plata* Judge Henderson was able to focus on a relatively narrow, discrete aspect of the prison system, that option was not available in East Palo Alto. One of the goals of special education is to maximize the extent to which special education students can be integrated into the regular classroom experience. Thus, as all of the parties in *Emma C.* realized, it would have been counterproductive to limit a receivership to the special education program. Any takeover would have to have been complete. The receiver, at a minimum, would have to assume the responsibilities of the school board and presumably replace, at least temporarily, the superintendent and perhaps other administrative personnel, as well. If replaced personnel did not voluntarily relinquish their salaries, paid leaves of absence or litigation over firings would consume valuable district resources. In addition, any interim superintendent would have to deal with the fact that allies of Charlie Mae Knight were embedded throughout the system.

An additional problem in structuring the receivership would have been deciding what, if any, role the state should play. In *Plata*, the state seemed relieved to give Judge Henderson authority over its dysfunctional prison medical system, but in East Palo Alto both the plaintiffs and the CDE had asked Judge Henderson to turn over the operation of the school district to the State Superintendent of Public Instruction. If Judge Henderson had appointed an independent receiver, as he did in *Plata*, he undoubtedly would have incurred the wrath of not only Charlie Mae Knight's supporters in East Palo Alto[2] but

---

2. In June, 2000, the school board responded to Charlie Mae Knight's conflict-of-interest indictment by renewing her contract for two years. A year later when she was

the CDE as well. Yet putting the state in charge of the school district was not an attractive option. Despite the CDE's assistance to Ravenswood, its track record in dealing with special education was less than stellar. Indeed, in their original contempt motion, the plaintiffs had asked that the CDE, as well as Ravenswood, be held in contempt. And after the CDE added its voice to the call for a receiver, it did little to suggest that it was prepared for the task.

Finally and probably most important from a practical standpoint, schools and prisons are very different types of institutions. Prisons are relatively invisible, and their inmates tend to be isolated and not welcome outside the prison walls. By contrast, school children are a community's pride and joy; local property taxes are an important source of school funding; and citizens vote regularly on school bond measures and for school board members. In short, schools are an almost constant focus of community interest — unfortunately not always for the quality of the education they provide but inevitably for their symbolic role in the front lines of social movements and cultural battles. The school desegregation cases, the controversy over HIV-positive Ryan White's right to attend public school, the question of prayer in the classroom, and the conflict over what, if any, role creationism should have in a school's curriculum are only a few examples.

East Palo Alto was no exception when it came to the importance of its schools for the local citizens — as Judge Henderson well knew from his legal services experience and continuing ties with the area. For years East Palo Alto had been an economically depressed, often marginalized community with a constantly shifting population. In the 1950s, the area was well integrated; however, by the end of the next decade it was predominantly black,[3] and by the end of the 1990s

---

acquitted, the board publicly commended her. By that time, however, Knight was already the focal point of some dissension in the community. Her critics became more vocal and more numerous in 2002.

3. A significant factor in this demographic change was the decision of the Sequoia Union High School District in the mid-1950s to build a new school, Ravenswood High, in East Palo Alto. Opponents of the school correctly predicted that its construction would lead to white flight and segregation of the community. In the mid to late 1960s, when the Sequoia Board began considering busing plans to desegregate Ravenswood High, black community leaders who had initially opposed building Ravenswood once again took issue with the Sequoia Board — this time to argue against interference with their black community school. Efforts to integrate Ravenswood High in the early 1970s resulted in more students leaving the school than coming to it. The Sequoia District closed Ravenswood High School in 1976.

The story of Ravenswood High School is a classic example of what can go wrong when outsiders make educational policy decisions for a local community. Even though East Palo Alto is formally part of the Sequoia Union High School District, it is not

was predominantly Hispanic. Incorporation in 1983 brought some degree of political power to the residents of East Palo Alto; but without a solid economic base, there was little that the community could do to better itself. Crime rates remained high, and in 1992 East Palo Alto was dubbed "murder capital" of the nation. Since that nadir, crime has decreased, property values have risen, and economic development has taken hold. East Palo Alto, though, is still struggling. Throughout this entire period, there have been only two constants. First, from the late 1950s community activists led initially by people like Gertrude Wilks and Bob Hoover and later by people like Marcelino Lopez devoted themselves to trying to bring quality education to the children of East Palo Alto. Second, from well before incorporation and the election of city councils, the Ravenswood School Board had been and continued to be a democratically elected voice of the people. Despite the board's failures and political struggles that have sometimes undermined educational objectives, a decision to remove the community from educational decision making would have been a huge blow. One could reasonably expect hostility even from those who were not supporters of Charlie Mae Knight.

At the time of the greatest arguable need for a receiver in East Palo Alto, Judge Henderson had not yet appointed a receiver in *Plata*; and when he eventually made the decision in *Plata*, the situation was improving in East Palo Alto. Thus, Judge Henderson never had occasion to make the specific comparison between a potential receivership in *Emma C.* and the receivership in *Plata*. Nonetheless, in hindsight, it appears that his instincts served him well in both cases.

Yes, after 20 years the Ravenswood School District is still falling short in its duty to provide special education, and in the interim many special needs children have passed through the District without any help at all. However, Judge Henderson has probably done everything that a judge could reasonably do — and much more than most would do — to improve the situation. Ultimately, *Emma C. v. Eastin* is an unfortunate example of a basic truth: A court's traditional powers to enforce its mandates are extremely limited and likely to be ineffective in the face of entrenched recalcitrance. The judiciary is truly the least equal branch.

---

unreasonable to think of East Palo Alto as separate from the rest of the District. The District encompasses all of southern San Mateo County, which includes Menlo Park, Atherton, Woodside, Redwood City, Belmont, and San Carlos. All of those communities are and were considerably whiter and wealthier than East Palo Alto, an unincorporated area (until 1983) at the southern tip of the county.

Judge Henderson's Judicial Activism and His Judicial Restraint: Two Examples (with Two Ninth Circuit Reversals and Two Supreme Court Vindications)

Chapter Nineteen

The (Mostly) False Rhetoric of Judging

In 1987, when there was scant public support for gay rights and little law protecting gays and lesbians against discrimination, Judge Henderson issued a groundbreaking decision that protected gays and lesbians against discrimination by the Defense Department. The Ninth Circuit reversed. Nine years later in two separate opinions, Judge Henderson held that Proposition 209, California's recently adopted anti-affirmative action initiative, was probably unconstitutional. Once again, the Ninth Circuit reversed. Subsequent Supreme Court decisions, however, have vindicated Judge Henderson's rulings in both cases.

Perhaps surprisingly, the 1987 gay rights decision attracted virtually no public attention. By contrast, Judge Henderson's Proposition 209 opinions subjected him to scathing criticism as an arrogant, activist judge, who usurped power not properly belonging to the judiciary.

The rhetoric of Judge Henderson's critics was — and to some extent still is — popular, particularly among conservatives, for expressing disapproval of decisions with which they disagree. The rhetoric itself, however, often has little substantive content.

This chapter explains why the rhetoric is short on substance and why, at the same time, it has appeal. The next two chapters discuss Judge Henderson's gay rights and Proposition 209 rulings in detail. They suggest that Judge Henderson was "activist," although not inappropriately so, in the gay rights case. By contrast, to the extent that there is substance to the notion of overreaching judicial activism, which Judge Henderson's Proposition 209 critics claimed to deplore, the critics should have praised his decisions and rebuked the Ninth Circuit.[1]

---

1. Appendix C discusses the Ninth Circuit opinion.

Chief Justice Roberts' Baseball Analogy

Chapter Two discussed the analogy between judging and baseball umpiring that Chief Justice Roberts drew at his confirmation hearing. The analogy
was a form of pandering to the notion, popular primarily among political
conservatives, that good judges exercise "judicial restraint" by "applying,"
not "making" law. These paragons of judicial restraint are the so-called "strict
constructionists" lauded by conservative lawmakers and recent Republican
presidents. They stand in sharp contrast — so the rhetoric goes — to politically
liberal, "activist" judges who usurp the legislative function by "making law"
from the bench. However, the relationships between judicial activism and
judicial restraint, between law application and lawmaking, and between strict
and nonstrict construction, especially as those phrases are used in the media
and by politicians, have very little to do with the reasoned critique of judicial
decision making.

Applying Law versus Making Law

The "applying law" versus "making law" dichotomy is virtually devoid of
meaning in the judicial context. The core of the first-year curriculum at most
law schools — torts, contracts, and property — is almost entirely judge-made
law. More important for present purposes, whenever judges decide cases, they
are applying frequently ambiguous and sometimes inconsistent legal principles in a unique factual setting. Consider, for example, claims that a particular surveillance activity violates the Fourth Amendment prohibition against
unreasonable searches and seizures, that a public display of the Ten Commandments is an unconstitutional "establishment" of a religion in violation of
the First Amendment, or that taking race into account in university admissions violates the Equal Protection Clause of the Fourteenth Amendment. To
the extent that prior law has not definitively and satisfactorily settled the issue
(in which case one might reasonably wonder why there was litigation in the
first place), the judge's decision will be "making" new law. In other words,
judges — regardless of whether they are considered liberal or conservative,
restrained or activist — make law all of the time. Indeed, "making" law is an
integral part of the process of interpreting and applying law. As a result, the
terms "making" and "applying" are simply not helpful concepts in the context
of evaluating judicial conduct. Rather, they are almost always after-the-fact
labels used to demonstrate one's displeasure or agreement with a particular
result.

Judicial Restraint and Judicial Activism

"Judicial restraint" and "judicial activism" are concepts that can have some independent content. From a nonpolitical perspective, "restraint" in contrast to "activism" typically connotes characteristics such as deciding cases on narrow rather than broad grounds,[2] following existing precedent rather than overruling earlier decisions or abandoning them in anticipation of what a higher court may do in the future, and being deferential to rather than second-guessing other branches of government. The point about deference, however, requires some qualification. As Chapter Twenty (High Tech Gays) explains, well established federal constitutional law requires courts to scrutinize carefully legislation that infringes upon certain fundamental rights or that makes distinctions on the basis of certain classifications, including race and gender. Applying clear precedent to invalidate a racially discriminatory statute, for example, would be an act of judicial restraint from the standpoint of precedent, but activist — and appropriately so — in the sense that it overturned a statute.

Another example of appropriate judicial activism is Judge Henderson's appointment of a receiver in *Plata*. By any definition of the term, the decision to take over the state's prison medical system was activist. Yet, when other branches of the government fail to uphold the law, the only alternative to such activism may be an abdication of judicial responsibility.

To the extent that the concepts of judicial activism and restraint have substantive content, they bear no necessary relationship to political liberalism or conservatism. For example, the Supreme Court during the tenure of Chief Justice Rehnquist was considered politically conservative (at least in relation to the Warren Court), but the Rehnquist Court was relatively unrestrained and activist in dealing with federal statutes. During its first 200 years, the Supreme Court

---

2. An opinion that is "restrained" in the sense that one can glean a narrow basis for its holding may also be "activist" in the sense that the court provides sweeping statements about the law that go far beyond what is necessary to decide the case. Two recent examples from the Supreme Court are Hudson v. Michigan (majority opinion by Justice Scalia) and Herring v. United States (majority opinion by Chief Justice Roberts), both limiting the scope of the rule excluding evidence obtained in violation of the Fourth Amendment. Other cases had imposed limitations on the exclusionary rule, and those cases arguably provide some support for the results in *Hudson* (exclusionary rule not applicable when police violate Fourth Amendment requirement that they knock and announce their entry) and *Herring* (exclusionary rule not applicable when underlying Fourth Amendment violation is based on negligent police recordkeeping). The majority opinions in both cases, however, went far beyond the narrow holdings to offer broad-based criticisms of the exclusionary rule itself, a staple of American constitutional law for federal courts since 1914 and for state courts since 1961.

had invalidated only 127 federal statutes; the Rehnquist Court overturned twenty-six acts of congress between 1995 and 2001.

Or consider Kelo v. City of New London, a 2005 Supreme Court case upholding the right of a municipality to promote economic recovery by condemning several homes (not themselves blighted) and then transferring the property to private developers. The municipality's action was authorized by a state statute. Moreover, it was taken pursuant to a "'carefully considered' development plan," which, the Supreme Court stressed, was designed for the general public good and not "to benefit any particular class of identifiable individuals."

Perhaps the municipality's decision was unwise; perhaps the state's statutory eminent domain authority should have been more constrained than it was; perhaps the *Kelo* Court should have reached the opposite conclusion. (There were four dissenting justices, and the case received bipartisan criticism.) Whatever one thinks of these matters, one thing is clear: The *Kelo* majority decision was consistent with principles of judicial restraint. There was ample precedent to support the Court's result. More important, the Court's decision gave deference to state and local lawmaking processes. Citizens of New London and other cities throughout the country remained free to lobby their state legislatures and local governments — and even congress — for restrictions on the power of eminent domain. Nonetheless, conservative critics of the *Kelo* decision were quick to use the label "judicial activism." For example, Republican Representative Jeff Miller of Florida called *Kelo* "a frightening example of judicial activism"; Ned Rice in National Review Online cited *Kelo* as an example of "blatant judicial activism"; and Republican Representative Geoff Davis of Kentucy called *Kelo* a "nefarious" ruling that demonstrated "the inherent danger of judicial activism."

People may sometimes disagree over whether a particular decision — *Kelo*, for example — is politically liberal, politically conservative, or neither. There is no doubt, however, that in the popular culture "judicial activism" has become a catch phrase used by political conservatives to express contempt for judicial decisions with which they disagree; and not surprisingly, given the source of the contempt, it is most often directed at decisions that happen to be or are perceived as being politically liberal.

In short, according to the politically conservative rhetoric — which in recent years has carried the day in the popular culture (and to a lesser, but not insubstantial, extent in the legal culture), judicial activism is an anathema, and it is typically associated with political liberalism.

Strict Constructionism

"Strict constructionism," like "judicial restraint," can have some substantive content. It has been used to describe the view that federal powers — including congressional power — should be narrowly construed; and it has also been used to describe various theories of constitutional interpretation that try to discern the original meaning of the Constitution's words or the original intent of the framers. Most familiarly, though, "strict constructionism" is simply another code phrase for political conservatism. For example, during his 1968 presidential campaign, Richard Nixon promised to appoint to the Supreme Court "law and order" justices, who were "strict constructionists" and would "apply," not make law. Similarly, President George W. Bush committed himself to appointing "strict constructionists" like Justices Antonin Scalia and Clarence Thomas. Both Scalia and Thomas are politically conservative. As a matter of judicial philosophy, however, Scalia specifically eschewed the label "strict constructionist."

Dialing Down the Rhetoric (a Bit)

The recent conservative majority on the Supreme Court (Chief Justice Roberts, Justices Scalia, Thomas, Alito, and often Justice Kennedy) has led to more decisions with which conservatives agree. Correspondingly, the rhetoric from the right extolling the virtues of strict constructionism and judicial restraint has become somewhat — but by no means completely — muted. This phenomenon is simply a manifestation of the reality that results tend to be more important to politicians than judicial philosophy.

An Accounting for the False Rhetoric of Judging

Even in the federal system, where judges are appointed (as they are in some state systems), the selection process, as noted in Chapter Seven, is highly political. Politicians recommend individuals for judicial appointment and lobby on their behalf; and typically (Judge Henderson being a notable exception) potential judicial candidates come to the attention of their advocates because of their own political activities and party loyalty. Or if the potential candidates are already judges being considered for promotion to a higher court, they come to the President's attention because of political assessments of their performance on the bench. Thus, it is not surprising that politicians evaluate judges from a political perspective and that those political evaluations become part of the popular culture.

But why is the rhetoric of judicial selection and evaluation couched in nonpolitical terms? Why has "judicial activism" become a pejorative phrase that bears no necessary relationship to the extent to which judges adhere to precedent? Why do nonlawyers and lawyers alike persist in making the false dichotomy between making law and applying law? Indeed, why did Chief Justice Roberts perpetuate that falsehood with his baseball analogy? And why did Justice Sotomayor insist at her confirmation hearing that judges do not make but only apply law?

With respect to Chief Justice Roberts and Justice Sotomayor, the answer is undoubtedly in large measure political. As they certainly knew, rhetoric embracing "judicial restraint" and eschewing judicial lawmaking is popular in conservative political circles. The Senate, which would vote on their confirmations, contained enough conservatives to block the nominations; and Roberts and Sotomayor, understandably, wanted to be confirmed.

Ultimately, though, the answer goes well beyond politics. It has to do with a perceived need for legitimacy. Because federal judges have lifetime tenure and because they—or least Supreme Court justices—have the final word on the legality or constitutionality of a party's actions, there is a strong sense that judicial decisions should be guided by principle, not the whims of particular judges or justices. Indeed, that is why judges offer reasons for their decisions and why, even in overruling precedent, they try to explain that in some fundamental way they are adhering to tradition. It is why legislators couch their political preferences for judges in neutral sounding terms: they do not want to acknowledge (perhaps even to themselves) that the judges they appoint inevitably will be making law and—as Chapter Two discussed—that judges' political views will affect their lawmaking. Finally, it is why the formalistic notion that judges merely apply law has so much appeal—and why in popular parlance judicial restraint is good and judicial activism is bad. As Professor Erwin Chemerinsky put it:

> There is enormous appeal to formalism, as there is to many myths. The idea that we are a nation of laws, not of men and women, was articulated long ago in Marbury v. Madison. If judges just applied the law in a formalistic way, then results would be the product not of the human beings in robes, but of the laws themselves. The identity of the judges would have little effect, so long as individuals on the bench had the intelligence and honesty to carry out their duties.

The myth of formalism has particular appeal in a milieu that lauds democratic, majoritarian politics. In that context, an appointed judiciary is the outlier and must gain legitimacy from its restraint—that is, from its mere "application" of rules established by others. By contrast, if one focuses on (1) our form of government as being primarily about checks and balances, (2) the founders being wary of the tyranny of the majority, and (3) the judiciary as an institution charged with protecting minority interests enshrined in the Constitution, one can more comfortably embrace the notion of inevitable judicial lawmaking and engage in candid, open debate about the underlying values at stake.

Chapter Twenty

High Tech Gays: Suspect Classifications and Fundamental Rights

High Tech Gays, based in San Jose, California, was a social and advocacy group for gays and lesbians from 1983 through 1997. Many of its members worked in the computer, aerospace, and related industries in Silicon Valley, where the nature of the work often required security clearances in order to have access to classified information. Gays and lesbians, however, were at a distinct disadvantage in obtaining timely clearances. Defense Department regulations automatically subjected them to more detailed security checks that were not regularly required for nonhomosexuals.

In 1984, High Tech Gays and three individually named plaintiffs filed a lawsuit challenging the Defense Department's security clearance procedures for gays and lesbians. They claimed that the Department's treatment of gays and lesbians violated the equal protection[1] and due process mandates of the

---

1. The Fourteenth Amendment to the Constitution contains guarantees of both "due process" and "equal protection." The Fourteenth Amendment, however, applies only to actions by states, not the federal government or it agencies; and the defendant in *High Tech Gays* was a federal entity. Nonetheless, since 1954 — the year in which the Supreme Court decided Brown v. Board of Education, it has been clear that the same equal protection principles that limit state governmental action also limit federal action. The Bill of Rights, the first ten Amendments to the Constitution, are constraints on the federal government, and the Fifth Amendment — like the Fourteenth — contains the right to "due process of law." In Bolling v. Sharpe, a challenge to Washington, DC's segregated schools and a companion case to *Brown*, the Supreme Court held that the Due Process Clause in the Fifth Amendment encompasses the rights established by the Equal Protection Clause

Constitution. The case, High Tech Gays v. Defense Indus. Sec. Clearance Office, was assigned to Judge Henderson.

In the mid-1980s a number of large companies — especially in Silicon Valley, often as a result of efforts by High Tech Gays and other gay advocacy groups — were extending family health benefits to gay couples. However, unlike the situation with racial minorities and women, there was relatively little law, either legislative or judicial, protecting gays and lesbians from discrimination. To a substantial extent Judge Henderson, whose instincts and experience made him sensitive to the discrimination against gays, would be making new law, regardless of which way he ruled.

Judge Henderson wrote a bold opinion upholding the plaintiffs' claims and declaring the Defense Department practices unconstitutional. A Ninth Circuit panel reversed Judge Henderson, and the full court, over a vigorous dissent, refused to reconsider the issue. Judge Henderson and the Ninth Circuit dissenters, however, have been vindicated. The Ninth Circuit panel's reasoning, such as it was, was based primarily on a case that the Supreme Court subsequently repudiated.

The Facts and the Issue

Unlike many of Judge Henderson's cases, the relevant facts were straightforward and not in dispute. The security clearance process could involve three stages of investigation: (1) an initial records check; (2) an expanded investigation, which included interviews; and (3) a review and — if the decision was unfavorable — an adjudication, at which the applicant was entitled to appear with counsel and cross-examine witnesses.

Straight (i.e., nongay and nonlesbian) individuals would receive a Secret clearance after the initial records check unless the check revealed adverse information, in which case there would be an expanded investigation. Straights seeking a Top Secret clearance were required at the outset to undergo an expanded investigation. The Defense Department would then grant the Top Secret clearance unless there was unresolved adverse information. Straights seeking both Secret and Top Secret security clearances would get to the third stage of the process — review and adjudication — only if an expanded investigation did not resolve any adverse information. Normally, the government did not investigate allegations of consensual sexual conduct between heterosexuals unless the behavior suggested that the person may be susceptible to

---

in the Fourteenth Amendment. In short, equal protection principles apply fully to both state and federal actors.

coercion or blackmail, had committed a criminal act, or was "reckless and irresponsible."

By contrast, gays and lesbians seeking both types of security clearances automatically had to undergo expanded investigations, and their cases were automatically subjected to the review and adjudication process. The initial records check—the only screening required for straights seeking a Secret clearance—usually took approximately two months. The expanded investigation would typically add another two to two-and-a-half months to the process, and the review/adjudication stage could add months more. In short, for Secret and Top Secret security clearances, the Defense Department required all gays and lesbians—because of and only because of their sexual orientation—to undergo extensive and time-consuming reviews that it required of straights only on an individualized, case-by-case basis.

The government justified its intense scrutiny of gays and lesbians seeking security clearances in part on the manual governing the policies for expanded investigations. The manual characterized homosexual activity as "sexual misconduct," "aberrant sexual behavior," and "deviant sexual conduct," and it

use[d] homosexuality as a general term that encompasses all types of homosexual experience and would include a long-term affectional, emotional, and sexual relationship between two openly gay people or a simple, casual dating relationship between two openly gay people.

According to the manual, homosexuality—like bestiality, fetishism, exhibitionism, necrophilia, nymphomania or satyriasis, masochism, sadism, pedophilia, transvestism, and voyeurism—may "cast doubt on the individual's morality, emotional or mental stability, and may raise questions as to his or her susceptibility to coercion or blackmail."

Ultimately, most gays and lesbians received security clearances. The lawsuit was not about discrimination in the granting of clearances. Rather, the lawsuit challenged the process by which security clearances were granted. That process—with its automatic delays for gays and lesbians—was both demeaning and often costly in terms of lost job opportunities and promotions.

The Constitutional Framework

A critical part of equal protection and due process analysis is the level of scrutiny with which a court assesses the claimed unconstitutionality. Will a court examine closely the purported reasons for the discrimination or classification and require a strong justification to uphold the law? Or will the court give substantial deference to the decision makers who created the challenged rule? Over the years, the Supreme Court has tended to divide equal protection and due process claims into three categories and, while maintaining some flexibility, has utilized a different level of scrutiny for each category.

At one extreme, a court's scrutiny is most rigorous if the rule in question burdens a "suspect class" (e.g., by discriminating against a racial minority) or a "fundamental right (e.g., by conditioning the right to vote on property ownership). In such a case, the court will apply "strict scrutiny" in evaluating the purported justification for the government's action. Under this test, the discrimination or classification will survive only if it is "precisely tailored to serve a compelling governmental interest," a test that is difficult to satisfy.

Some classifications (most notably, those based on gender) are regarded as "quasi-suspect." In dealing with these classifications, courts apply "heightened" — or, as it is sometimes called, "intermediate" — scrutiny. To be constitutional, the rule must be "substantially related to a legitimate state interest."

At the other extreme courts apply a "rational basis" test in evaluating equal protection and due process challenges to (1) economic regulations, (2) age discrimination, and (3) other classifications that are neither (a) "suspect" or "quasi-suspect" nor (b) infringements on fundamental rights. If there is a rational basis for the distinction — regardless of whether the judge agrees with it — the constitutional challenge will fail. Just as it is difficult for the government to meet the "strict scrutiny" test, it is difficult — but by no means impossible — for equal protection and due process claims to prevail under the "rational basis" test.

Quite obviously, the application of any of these three tests involves making important, sensitive value judgments about which reasonable people may sometimes disagree. In addition, some constitutional law scholars maintain that there is "a spectrum of standards . . . [rather] than three fixed tiers." Whether it is a matter of different value judgments, a spectrum of standards, or both, it is clear that there is some flexibility in the application of each level of scrutiny. For example, all racial classifications are subject to strict scrutiny; and while it is virtually impossible to find a "compelling state interest" for discrimination against racial minorities, courts have held that some affirmative action programs (despite claims of discrimination against whites) serve a "compelling state interest."[2]

Toward the lax end of the spectrum, at least rhetorically, is Cleburne v. Cleburne Living Center, Inc., where the Supreme Court considered an equal protection challenge to a city ordinance that required a special use permit to operate homes for people with mental retardation but did not require similar

---

2. Some have claimed that, at least in the past, the level of scrutiny was sometimes more lax when affirmative action programs were at issue.

permits for "other care and multiple dwelling facilities." The Court refused to hold that mental retardation was a suspect or quasi-suspect classification. Nonetheless, the Court, purporting to apply rational basis analysis, held the ordinance unconstitutional. The fears of elderly residents in the neighborhood, negative views of the majority of nearby property owners, and concern that children at nearby school may harass occupants of the home were not, in the Court's view, a sufficient rational basis for upholding the ordinance. In his concurring opinion, Justice Marshall observed that the "ordinance is invalidated only after being subjected to precisely the sort of probing inquiry associated with heightened scrutiny."

An initial question for Judge Henderson — for which there was no clear answer — was what level of scrutiny to apply in evaluating the plaintiffs' equal protection claim.

Quasi-Suspect Class and Heightened Scrutiny

Drawing on Supreme Court cases describing the characteristics of suspect and quasi-suspect classifications, Judge Henderson concluded that gays and lesbians should be considered a quasi-suspect class, which required "intermediate" or "heightened" scrutiny of the government's practices. He noted that the Court had justified treating race as a suspect class because "laws disfavoring racial groups likely reflected 'prejudice and antipathy'." With respect to gender, the Court had "observed that heightened scrutiny is proper because 'the sex characteristic frequently bears no relation to the ability to perform or contribute to society,' and that classifications based on gender likely reflected 'outmoded notions of the relative capabilities of men and women,' rather than 'meaningful considerations' about the sexes."

These criteria, Judge Henderson explained, apply to gays and lesbians:

Lesbians and gay men have been the object of some of the deepest prejudice and hatred in American society. Some people's hatred for gay people is so deep that many gay people face the threat of physical violence on American streets today. . . .

Wholly unfounded, degrading stereotypes about lesbians and gay men abound in American society. Examples of such stereotypes include that gay people desire and attempt to molest young children, that gay people attempt to recruit and convert other people, and that gay people inevitably engage in promiscuous sexual activity. Many people erroneously believe that the sexual experience of lesbians and gay men represents the gratification of purely prurient interests, not the expression of mutual affection and love. They fail to recognize that gay people seek and engage in stable, monogamous relationships. Instead, to many, the very existence of lesbians and gay men is inimical to the family. For years, many people have branded gay people as abominations to nature and considered lesbians and gay men mentally ill and psychologically unstable.

As with attitudes about racial groups . . ., these attitudes about gay people reflect "prejudice and antipathy" against gay people, because they do not conform to the mainstream. The stereotypes have no basis in reality and represent outmoded notions about homosexuality, analogous to the "outmoded notions" of the relative capabilities of the sexes that require heightened scrutiny of classifications based on gender. The fact that a person is lesbian or gay bears no relation to the person's ability to contribute to society. Rather than somehow being enemies of American culture and values, lesbians and gay men occupy positions in all walks of American life, participate in diverse aspects of family life, and contribute enormously to many elements of American culture.

In addition, the pervasive discrimination against gay people has seriously impaired their ability to gain a politically viable voice for their views in state and local legislatures and in Congress. . . . "Homosexuals attempting to form associations to represent their political and social beliefs, free from the fatal reprisals for their sexual orientation they anticipate in jobs or other social activities" are the type of "discrete and insular minority" that meets the . . . test for suspect classification.

Given this description, one might wonder why Judge Henderson found homosexuality to be only a "quasi-suspect" class and not a suspect class. There are several reasons. First, equal protection principles derive from the Fourteenth Amendment, which was directed primarily at discrimination on the basis of race, the prototype suspect class. In terms of the present-day reality of discrimination, it may be appropriate to draw analogies between race and homosexuality, but the history of equal protection is more limited. Second, despite substantial, continuing discrimination against women, the Supreme Court has treated gender as only a "quasi-suspect" class. Third, as noted in the preceding section, Cleburne v. Cleburne Living Center, Inc., one of the Supreme Court's most recent cases dealing with suspect and quasi-suspect classification, had refused to extend even "quasi-suspect" class status to the people with mental retardation. Fourth, discrimination against gays and lesbians, which continues to be politically acceptable in some quarters today, was considerably more pervasive 1987, when Judge Henderson issued his decision. Indeed, despite Judge Henderson's civil rights and civil liberties background, John Lewis, the law clerk who assisted Judge Henderson with *High Tech Gays*, took care in revealing his own sexual orientation to the judge at the beginning of his clerkship. Lewis came out to the judge only after consulting with a prior law clerk about how she thought the judge would respond. Under these circumstances, there is little doubt that holding gays and lesbians to constitute a suspect class would have meant sure reversal on appeal. Reflecting back on the case, Judge Henderson has said, "I was trying to take a baby step instead of a giant step [so that] the Ninth Circuit would more likely accept it."

Fundamental Rights and Strict Scrutiny

In a series of decisions the Supreme Court has recognized a fundamental due process constitutional right to privacy. Griswold v. Connecticut, emphasizing the importance of marital privacy, struck down a ban on the use of contraceptives. Subsequent decisions dealing with intimate aspects of a person's life have made it clear that the privacy right is not limited to marital relationships. Carey v. Population Services, International invalidated a ban on the sale of contraceptives to minors; Eisenstadt v. Baird overturned a conviction for distributing contraceptives to an unmarried individual;[3] and, of course, Roe v. Wade and its progeny have upheld (but allowed restrictions upon) a woman's right to have an abortion.

Relying primarily upon *Griswold* and *Carey*, Judge Henderson held that the Defense Department regulations at issue in *High Tech Gays* interfered with the fundamental right of gays and lesbians to engage in homosexual activity. As a result, he held, the regulations were subject to strict scrutiny. To justify this ruling, Judge Henderson had to deal with and distinguish, Bowers v. Hardwick, a 1986 5-4 Supreme Court decision holding that homosexuals do not have a fundamental right to engage in sodomy.

---

3. Because the statute in *Eisenstadt* restricted the distribution of contraceptives only to unmarried individuals, the Court based its holding on the Equal Protection Clause. The Court's reasoning, however, made it clear that the *Griswold* privacy notion was not limited to marital privacy:

> If under *Griswold* the distribution of contraceptives to married persons cannot be prohibited, a ban on distribution to unmarried persons would be equally impermissible. It is true that in *Griswold* the right of privacy in question inhered in the marital relationship. Yet the marital couple is not an independent entity with a mind and heart of its own, but an association of two individuals each with a separate intellectual and emotional makeup. If the right of privacy means anything, it is the right of the *individual*, married or single, to be free from unwarranted governmental intrusion into matters so fundamentally affecting a person as the decision whether to bear or beget a child.

Bowers v. Hardwick

On the morning of July 5, 1985, Michael Hardwick, an openly gay man, was walking home from his all night job at a gay club in Atlanta, Georgia. A police officer observed him throw a beer bottle onto the street and issued a ticket. When Hardwick failed to show up at his scheduled court appearance, the officer secured a warrant and went to Hardwick's house. Hardwick was not at home, but he learned of the officer's visit and paid his fine the next day. The officer, however, had not received word that the matter had been resolved when he paid a second visit to Hardwick's home three weeks later. A houseguest answered the door, said he did not know if Hardwick was home, and invited the officer to look around. The officer discovered Hardwick and another man in the back bedroom engaging in oral sex. He arrested them for sodomy, which a Georgia criminal statute defined as "any sexual act involving the sex organs of one person and the mouth or anus of another."

The prosecutor did not pursue the sodomy case, so there was no occasion to raise the questions whether the statute was unequally enforced against homosexuals or whether such unequal enforcement would be a violation of the equal protection guarantee. However, Hardwick, along with a married couple — designated John and Mary Doe — filed a lawsuit challenging the constitutionality of the Georgia sodomy statute as a violation of the *Due Process* Clause.

Because the Does, unlike Hardwick, had not been threatened with a sodomy prosecution, the lower courts held that they did not have "standing" — that is, they did not have a sufficient personal interest in the matter to pursue the claim. The Does did not seek review of that ruling before the Supreme Court, which observed at the outset of its opinion:

> The only claim properly before the Court, therefore, is Hardwick's challenge to the Georgia statute as applied to consensual homosexual sodomy. We express no opinion on the constitutionality of the Georgia statute as applied to other acts of sodomy.

The Court then went on to hold that there was no "fundamental [due process] right to engage in homosexual sodomy." Thus, the statute would survive constitutional challenge if it had a rational basis. Noting that twenty-five states had sodomy statutes, the Court found such a rational basis in the "majority sentiments about the morality of homosexuality."

Judge Henderson's Response to *Hardwick*

Judge Henderson acknowledged *Hardwick's* holding was the law of the land, but he maintained that *Hardwick* did not control the case before him, which dealt with a classification "that disadvantages lesbians and gay men because of *any* homosexual activity or sexual preference."

> *Hardwick* does not hold, for example, that two gay people have no right to touch each other in a way that expresses their affection and love for each other. Nor does *Hardwick* address such issues as whether lesbians and gay men have a fundamental right to engage in homosexual activity such as kissing, holding hands, caressing, or any number of other sexual acts that do not constitute sodomy under the Georgia statute. *Hardwick* simply did not address the issue of discrimination based on sexual orientation or sexual preference itself.
>
>   . . .
>
> Furthermore, a central rationale for the *Hardwick* Court's finding that lesbians and gay men have no fundamental right to engage in sodomy was the fact that many states continue to outlaw sodomy. However, the same cannot be said about other types of homosexual activity. None of the fifty states outlaws the act of two people of the same sex kissing one another, holding hands together, or caressing each other. . . . Missouri is the only state in the union that specifically outlaws sexual acts involving the hand. Only three other state statutes could conceivably be construed to outlaw such behavior. . . .
>
> The rationale of previous Supreme Court cases . . . that establish a right to privacy mandates that this Court find that lesbians and gay men, as well as all people, have a fundamental right to engage in affectional and sexual activity that has not been traditionally proscribed as sodomy. . . .

It is hard to know what to make of Judge Henderson's effort to distinguish *Hardwick* because it is difficult to know what to make of *Hardwick* in the first place. The Court's previous privacy cases, as well as *Hardwick* itself (by focusing only on "homosexual sodomy"), strongly suggest that the fundamental constitutional right to privacy extends to at least some intimate behavior. But what, then, is the rationale for *Hardwick*? Is *Hardwick* primarily about a particular sexual practice — sodomy — that just happened to arise in a lawsuit by a homosexual? Or is *Hardwick* primarily about *homosexual* sodomy?

Judge Henderson based his conclusion on the premise that *Hardwick* was primarily about sodomy in general:

> [I]t appears to this Court that the proper interpretation of *Hardwick* is that under the Constitution no person has a fundamental right to engage in sodomy, not that lesbians and gay men have no fundamental right to engage in other types of affectional or sexual activity.

It is important to note that, at present, it has not been established that anyone, heterosexual or homosexual, has a fundamental right to engage in sodomy. The United States Supreme Court has never held that heterosexuals have a fundamental right to engage in sodomy. Significantly, eighteen of the twenty-four states and the District of Columbia that continue to proscribe sodomy proscribe it for heterosexuals as well as homosexuals. Justice Stevens' dissent in *Hardwick* observed that "[t]he history of the statutes cited by the majority . . . reveals a prohibition on heterosexual, as well as homosexual, sodomy." Justice Stevens further stated that "the homosexual and the heterosexual have the same interest in deciding how he will live his own life, and, more narrowly, how he will conduct himself in his personal and voluntary associations with his companions. State intrusion into the private conduct of either is equally burdensome."

From this premise (i.e., that *Hardwick* applies to sodomy in general, not just to homosexual sodomy), Judge Henderson's effort to distinguish *Hardwick* has substantial merit. As he elaborated:

> Affectional and sexual intimacy plays an extremely important role in the lives of all people, both gay and straight alike. "Highly personal relationships" and "certain kinds of personal bonds" lie at the heart of a person's "ability independently to define one's identity." Affectional and sexual relationships form a "central . . . part of an individual's life." Sexual intimacy for gay people and straight people is a "sensitive, key relationship of human existence, central to family life, community welfare, and the development of human personality."
>
> Protecting people's right to engage in such intimate sexual relationships of their choosing is an essential element of American liberty because this aspect of life occupies such an important part of all human beings' lives. The freedom to express physically such basic human emotions and feelings is "implicit in the concept of ordered liberty." People's liberty to engage in such physical expressions of affection is "deeply rooted in this Nation's history and tradition." The Supreme Court has long recognized that a primary purpose of the Bill of Rights is to secure "individual liberty."

On the other hand, if one reads *Hardwick* as focusing on *homosexual* sodomy, Judge Henderson's fundamental rights argument loses much of its force. If *homosexuals* do not have the fundamental right to commit sodomy but others do, it is a stretch to maintain that homosexuals have the fundamental right to engage in other, less intimate activity.

Judge Henderson's interpretation of *Hardwick* leaves open the question why it might be appropriate to confer fundamental rights status on intimate sexual behavior but to make an exception for sodomy. The alternative interpretation, though, — that is, the interpretation of *Hardwick* as a case about *homosexual* sodomy — leaves open an even bigger question: What is it about sodomy that is more troublesome when it is practiced by homosexuals rather than heterosexuals? Neither that question nor the question of unequal enforcement of the sodomy laws was specifically before the Court in *Hardwick*. The inequality inherent in this latter view of *Hardwick*, however, is palpable.[4]

Although Judge Henderson's interpretation of *Hardwick* as a case about sodomy in general poses a less troublesome question than the alternate interpretation, his goal was not to minimize *Hardwick's* anomalies. Rather, his primary concern was trying to square *Hardwick* with his empathetic vision of fairness for gays and lesbians that was perhaps different from — but not necessarily inconsistent with — the result in *Hardwick*. That sense of fairness, as Judge Henderson explained, included but went far beyond, sexual intimacy. By contrast, at least overtly, *Hardwick* expressed neither empathy with nor disdain for gays and lesbians. Instead, the Court framed the issue as being about a particular type of sexual conduct. Emphasizing the "ancient roots" of the prohibitions against sodomy, the Court held that homosexuals, and perhaps others, had no fundamental right to engage in such conduct.

Nonetheless, the *Hardwick* Court did nothing to allay the implication that homosexual sodomy may be worse than heterosexual sodomy. Indeed, although the Court expressed "no opinion" on whether prohibiting nonhomosexuals from engaging in sodomy would be constitutional, its rationale for holding that at least homosexuals have no fundamental right to commit sodomy — "majority sentiments about the morality of homosexuality" — tends to support the implication that homosexual sodomy may be worse than heterosexual sodomy. That unrebutted implication, in turn, demonstrates, as Judge Henderson had documented, that homosexuals are subject to irrational discrimination. Thus, either Judge Henderson was correct in his analysis of *Hardwick*; or if he was wrong, *Hardwick* is itself strong evidence that gays and lesbians should be treated as a quasi-suspect class for equal protection purposes. Either way, then, *Hardwick* supports the proposition that a court should apply some form of heightened scrutiny to the Defense Department's treatment of homosexuals.

---

4. In theory, an intermediate position could be that married couples, but only married couples, have the right to commit sodomy. This would be consistent with the focus on marital privacy in Griswold v. Connecticut. However, as noted earlier in the text, the constitutional right to privacy extends well beyond the marriage relationship; and while the status of marriage confers a number of benefits, it is hard to imagine why sodomy should be singled out as a practice permissible only by married couples. Traditionally, criminal prohibitions against sodomy and other expressions of disapproval have not carved out an exception for marriage. Rather, they have condemned either sodomy in general or homosexual sodomy.

Rational Basis?

Judge Henderson did not discuss how the Defense Department practices fared under a "strict scrutiny" or "heightened scrutiny" test. Instead, he held that the practices could not be justified even under the minimal "rational basis" standard. *A fortiori* the government could not meet a higher standard.

Initially, it is important to note that the rational basis the Supreme Court found for the sodomy statute in *Hardwick* has no relevance to the rational basis analysis in *High Tech Gays*. Whatever one may think of the Supreme Court's assertion that the "majority sentiments about the morality of homosexuality" provides a rational basis for sodomy statutes, the government made no claim that its security clearance rules and practices were based on "majority sentiments of morality." Instead, the government offered four justifications, each of which Judge Henderson dealt with in detail.

First, the government claimed that "homosexual conduct may constitute a criminal violation and call into question an individual's willingness to uphold public law." Judge Henderson noted a variety of problems with this purported rational basis for the government's discrimination: (1) sodomy is not a crime in the majority of states; (2) in most states where it is criminal, it is not limited to homosexual conduct; (3) prosecutions for sodomy are virtually nonexistent; (4) the government regulations encompass all homosexual activity, not merely sodomy; and (5) disrespect for one law does not imply disrespect for law in general.

Second, Judge Henderson addressed the argument that "a 'homosexual may face emotional tension, instability or other difficulties since society has not recognized his sexual practice as mainstream'." The government's effort to defend this supposed rational basis seemed both desperate and bizarre. As Judge Henderson observed:

> [D]efendants provide what can only be regarded as a submission of questionable impact, an excerpt from a book by John Barron entitled *KGB The Secret Work of Soviet Secret Agents*, subtitled "with photographs of agents, assassins, seductresses and victims,".... Defendants provide absolutely no evidence that suggests that Mr. Barron has any professional expertise regarding the psychological well-being of lesbians and gay men. In the book, Barron baldly claims without support that the KGB believes that "homosexuality often is accompanied by personality disorders that make the victim potentially unstable and vulnerable to adroit manipulation." According to Barron, the KGB believes that the fact that homosexuals are aware that they are different makes them want to seek revenge against society.

In rejecting this supposed rational basis, Judge Henderson, citing the positions of the American Psychiatric Association, the American Psychological

Association, the American Public Health Association, the American Nurses Association, and the Council of Advanced Practitioners in Psychiatric and Mental Health Nursing of the American Nurses Association, pointed out that "[f]or years the uncontroverted consensus of the American professional psychological community has been that homosexual orientation itself is not a psychological problem."

The defendant's third purported rational basis was that gays and lesbians who are secretive about their activity could be subject to blackmail. However, Judge Henderson noted, the government presented no proof that gays and lesbians were particularly susceptible to blackmail; and it could offer no cases to support its theory. Moreover, this government claim ignored the fact that *openly* gay and lesbian individuals are subjected to expanded investigations and adjudications. Finally, the breadth of the government's purported concern was astounding. As Judge Henderson wrote:

> Defendants' policy represents a simplistic approach to complex issues regarding national security and potential blackmail and is not founded on any rational basis. The fact that people have aspects of their lives that they do not on their own initiative tell supervisors, associates, or even close family members does not imply that those people are security risks. All people have aspects of their lives, often private consensual sexual activities, that they prefer to keep private. This fact does not mean that those people would be susceptible to blackmail if someone were to learn of the private information. . . . Defendants' policy is founded upon deep-seated prejudice, not a rational basis.

Fourth, the government claimed it was appropriate to subject all gays and lesbians to expanded investigations because it also conducts expanded investigations of heterosexual conduct that "may involve 'extramarital relations, sex with minors, prostitution, sex through force and other circumstances that may be indicative of poor judgment or may subject an individual to blackmail or undue coercion'." This proffered justification, Judge Henderson maintained,

> lies at the heart of much of the prejudice and discrimination that lesbians and gay men face. The fact that [the government] conducts expanded investigations of people who are involved with bestiality, sado-masochism, pedophilia and other such sexual practices does not justify expanded investigations into lesbians and gay men. The argument that engaging in affectional, emotional, and sexual relationships with people of the same sex is comparable to engaging in sex through force and sex with minors betrays the dignity that lesbians and gay men, as well as all citizens, deserve. The mere fact that gay people engage in consensual sexual relationships

with people of their own sex in no way affects their trustworthiness to hold a security clearance, just as the fact that straight people engage in consensual sexual relationships with people of the opposite sex does not affect their trustworthiness.

In a strongly worded conclusion, Judge Henderson captured the core of the problem:

The Defense Department's unequal treatment of gay people perpetuates the very types of archaic stereotypes that the [government] manual implies and that the equal protection clause attempts to extinguish, e.g., that all lesbians and gay men are emotionally unstable, sexually perverted, and particularly prone to blackmail and that homosexuality is deviant sexual behavior parallel to necrophilia, masochism, and pedophilia. Branding all lesbians and gay men as people who require more extensive investigation than straight people casts gay people as innately inferior.

The Ninth Circuit

Despite the force of Judge Henderson's arguments, a Ninth Circuit panel disagreed with all three of his major conclusions. The panel held that gays and lesbians did not constitute a quasi-suspect class, that *Hardwick* stood for the proposition that there is no fundamental right to homosexual activity, and that there was a rational basis for subjecting all gays and lesbians to expanded investigations and adjudications. Appendix B discusses the Ninth Circuit decision. For now, it is worth noting that both Judge Henderson and the Ninth Circuit panel were "making" new law — (1) by reaching opposing views on the quasi-suspect class issue, for which there was no controlling precedent, (2) by drawing conflicting conclusions about the scope and meaning of *Hardwick*, and (3) by providing original analyses of what does or does not constitute a rational basis for the government's security clearance policies.

When a majority of the full Ninth Circuit voted not to rehear the matter, Judge William Canby, joined by Judge William Norris, wrote a stinging dissent. Thirteen years later, the Supreme Court went far in vindicating Judge Henderson.

Lawrence v. Texas

Lawrence v. Texas arose from facts strikingly similar to those in *Hardwick*: Responding to a weapons disturbance, the police entered Lawrence's apartment (apparently legally), where they discovered him engaged in sex with another man. Both men were prosecuted and convicted[5] under a statute similar to the Georgia sodomy statute at issue in *Hardwick*—except that the Texas law applied only to activities by members of the same sex. The state courts rejected their due process and equal protection challenges to the statute. In 2003, the Supreme Court overturned the convictions.

Because the Texas statute applied only to homosexual conduct, the Court could easily have rested its decision on Equal Protection grounds. If *Lawrence* had relied on the Equal Protection Clause, however, it would have stood only for the proposition that the state cannot single out homosexual sodomy for criminal punishment. Such a holding would have left *Hardwick* intact; and like *Hardwick*, it would have said nothing about the impropriety of regulating private sexual conduct on a nondiscriminatory basis. Moreover, recall that *Hardwick* based its holding in part on the "majority sentiments about the morality of homosexuality." The *Hardwick* implications that homosexual sodomy and even homosexuality itself were somehow disreputable—even if no longer criminal—would have remained unaffected and perhaps even been strengthened by the failure to confront them directly.

For the Supreme Court majority those implications were unacceptable. Relying on the Due Process Clause, the Court specifically overruled Bowers v. Hardwick. According to the Court, *Hardwick's* "continuance as precedent demeans the lives of homosexual persons. . . . [I]t was not correct when it was decided, and it is not correct today."

During the course of its analysis, the Court made no specific reference to a "fundamental rights" or "heightened" or "strict" scrutiny. Nonetheless, three things are clear. First, in language echoing Judge Henderson's discussion of "affectional and sexual intimacy," the Court held that private, consensual sexual activity (including homosexual sodomy) is part of the liberty that is protected by the Due Process Clause:

> Liberty presumes an autonomy of self that includes freedom of thought, belief, expression, and certain intimate conduct. The instant case involves liberty of the person both in its spatial and in its more transcendent dimensions. . . .

---

5. The "facts" recited here are from the Supreme Court's opinion. However, as Dale Carpenter points out in his book, *Flagrant Conduct: The Story of Lawrence v. Texas*, the claim that Lawrence was involved in a sex act with another man may be false. There is substantial evidence—including subsequent statements by both Lawrence and his co-defendant—that the allegation of sex was a fabrication. That allegation came from the police report; and because Lawrence and his co-defendant pled no context, there was never an occasion to challenge the content of the report in court.

When sexuality finds overt expression in intimate conduct with another person, the conduct can be but one element in a personal bond that is more enduring. The liberty protected by the Constitution allows homosexual persons the right to make this choice. . . .

The petitioners are entitled to respect for their private lives. The State cannot demean their existence or control their destiny by making their private sexual conduct a crime. Their right to liberty under the Due Process Clause gives them the full right to engage in their conduct without intervention of the government.

Second, the Court's detailed discussion and rejection of much of the underlying reasoning in *Hardwick* demonstrates that the Court was applying a form of heightened scrutiny to its evaluation of the Texas statute.

Third, the Court regarded its due process holding as encompassing a holding based on the Equal Protection Clause:

Equality of treatment and the due process right to demand respect for conduct protected by the substantive [due process] guarantee of liberty are linked in important respects, and a decision on the latter point advances both interests.

Thus, although *Lawrence* is a due process case, it supports Judge Henderson's equal protection analysis, as well as his due process analysis. If *Lawrence* had been the law of the land in 1987, it would have provided important support for Judge Henderson's conclusions.

A Work in Progress

California has a strong domestic partner law, which gives registered domestic partners virtually the same legal rights as married people. Nonetheless, in May 2008, the California Supreme Court joined the Supreme Judicial Court of Massachusetts in upholding *on state constitutional grounds* the right of gays and lesbians to marry:

[D]rawing a distinction between the name assigned to the family relationship available to opposite-sex couples and the name assigned to the family relationship to same-sex couples, and . . . reserving the historic and highly respected designation of "marriage" exclusively to opposite-sex couples while offering same-sex couples the new and unfamiliar designation of domestic partnership . . . pose[s] a serious risk of denying the official family relationship of same-sex couples the equal dignity and respect that is a core element of the constitutional right to marry.

John Lewis, Judge Henderson's former law clerk, and John's long-time partner, Stuart Gaffney, were two of the named plaintiffs in the California case.

John and Stuart asked Judge Henderson to preside at their marriage ceremony at San Francisco's City Hall on June 17, 2008. Judge Henderson, who at the time used a cane and walked with difficulty, could not find a parking place near an accessible entrance to City Hall. As a result, he had to climb very slowly the ten steps to the Polk Street entrance — and then, once inside the door, another five steps to get to the main floor. "It was a struggle but very worthwhile," he said afterward. "It was a joyous event, where hundreds of gay and lesbian couples had come to exchange marriage vows."

On November 4, 2008, California voters — despite the efforts of John Lewis, Stuart Gaffney, and thousands of others, both gay and straight — approved Proposition 8, a state constitutional amendment, which provided, "Only marriage between a man and a woman is valid or recognized in California." On the same day, Florida and Arizona voters approved similar state constitutional amendments. Those states, however, had not previously recognized gay marriages. California was the first state to take away from gays and lesbians a previously recognized right.

Proposition 8 nullified the decision that gave John and Stuart the right to marry, but the California Supreme Court held that Proposition 8 applied only prospectively. Thus, California continued to recognize the legitimacy of marriages, like John's and Stuart's, that occurred prior to the adoption of Proposition 8.

Just as Bowers v. Hardwick implicitly suggested that discrimination against gays and lesbians was acceptable, Proposition 8, both by denying same-sex couples the right to marry and by officially taking away a previously recognized right, inevitably marked gays and lesbians as second-class citizens. The adoption of Proposition 8 was an example of the irrational antipathy toward gays and lesbians that Judge Henderson so eloquently decried in *High Tech Gays*.

Proposition 8, however, was not the last word on gay marriage in California. On August 4, 2010, Federal District Judge Vaughn Walker, in Perry v. Schwarzenegger, struck down Proposition 8 as a violation of both the Due Process and the Equal Protection Clauses of the Fourteenth Amendment. Although the defendants (the governor, the attorney general, and various state officials) continued to enforce Proposition 8 throughout the litigation, they had refused to defend it at trial, and they refused to appeal Judge Walker's decision. The defense — and an appeal — came from Proposition 8's original proponents, who were allowed to intervene at trial. The Ninth Circuit affirmed Judge Walker's decision, but on June 26, 2013, the Supreme Court held that the intervenors lacked standing to appeal. According to the Court, the intervenors' "only interest . . . was to vindicate the constitutional validity of a generally applicable law," and that interest was insufficient to meet the standing requirement of a "concrete and particularized injury." The Supreme Court remanded the case to the Ninth Circuit, which dismissed the appeal. Judge Walker's decision striking down Proposition 8 became the law of the case.

On the same day that it decided *Perry*, the Supreme Court, in United States v. Windsor, invalidated Section 3 of the federal Defense of Marriage Act (DOMA). For the purpose of interpreting and applying all federal laws, Section 3 had defined the terms "marriage" and "spouse" to mean only opposite-sex marriages and spouses. The plaintiff in *Windsor* was the surviving partner of a same-sex marriage. She lived in New York, a state that recognized same-sex marriages; and she was the beneficiary of her deceased partner's estate. However, because of DOMA, the Internal Revenue Service had refused to grant her an estate tax exemption available to surviving spouses.[6] According to the Supreme Court:

> DOMA singles out a class of persons deemed by a State entitled to recognition and protection to enhance their own liberty. It imposes a disability on the class by refusing to acknowledge a status the State finds to be dignified and proper. DOMA instructs all federal officials, and indeed all persons with whom same-sex couples interact, including their own children, that their marriage is less worthy than the marriages of others. The federal statute is invalid for no legitimate purpose overcomes the purpose and effect to disparage and to injure those whom the State, by its marriage laws, sought to protect in personhood and dignity. By seeking to displace this protection and treating those persons living in marriages less respected than others, the federal statute is in violation of the Fifth Amendment.

With Section 3 invalidated, there was now no general federal definition of "marriage" or "spouse" that addressed the same-sex marriage issue. The Court left for another day the question whether it would be unconstitutional to deny federal benefits to married same-sex couples in states that do not recognize same-sex marriages.

New York was only one of a growing number of states that had recognized same-sex marriages in the years after John and Stuart were married; and polls

---

6. This was only one of many consequences of Section 3. For example, as the Supreme Court pointed out, Section 3

prevents same-sex married couples from obtaining government healthcare benefits they would otherwise receive. It deprives them of the Bankruptcy Code's special protections for domestic-support obligations. It forces them to follow a complicated procedure to file their state and federal taxes jointly. It prohibits them from being buried together in veterans' cemeteries.

have continued to show increasing support for same-sex marriage, especially among younger people. Moreover, in the wake of the DOMA decision, a number of lower courts struck down state bans on same-sex marriage. Then on June 26, 2015, in Obergefell v. Hodges, the Supreme Court held that all same-sex couples have the same right to marry that opposite-sex couples enjoy. There was widespread celebration, and President Obama, as well as all of the declared Democratic presidential candidates for the 2016 election, praised the result. There were, however, four dissenters in *Obergefell*; Republican 2016 presidential hopefuls criticized the decision; and discrimination against gays and lesbians, often in the name of religious liberty, continues.

At some point, Proposition 8, DOMA, criticism of same-sex marriage, and discrimination against gays and lesbians are bound to seem as anachronistic as the bans on interracial marriage and homosexual sodomy struck down by the Supreme Court in Loving v. Virginia and Lawrence v. Texas. In the meantime, it is clear that Judge Henderson, despite the Ninth Circuit's reversal of his *High Tech Gays* decision, was on the right side of history.

Chapter Twenty-One

Proposition 209: Inequality in the Political Process

Although Lawrence v. Texas went far in vindicating Judge Henderson's *High Tech Gays* decision, the state of the law in 1987 when Judge Henderson issued his opinion was, as Chapter Twenty noted, far from clear. The precedent that Judge Henderson cited seemed at odds with the antigay implications of Bowers v. Hardwick, and precisely what *Hardwick* stood for was itself uncertain. In the face of this ambiguity, Judge Henderson, without any direct Supreme Court authority, found homosexuality to be a quasi-suspect classification; and he ruled that gays and lesbians have a fundamental right to engage in intimate behavior other than sodomy. As a result, he became one of the first federal judges to extend constitutional protections to homosexuals. By any accounting, *High Tech Gays* was an activist decision.[1] Yet, as Judge Henderson carefully explained, it was within the parameters of the existing law.

In contrast to *High Tech Gays*, Coalition for Economic Equity v. Wilson, which involved a challenge to Proposition 209 — California's anti-affirmative action law — is one of Judge Henderson's most constrained, judicially conservative decisions. In concluding that Proposition 209 was probably unconstitutional, Judge Henderson remained unmoved by political turmoil surrounding the lawsuit and focused exclusively on the specific issue before him. He developed a strong factual record, and he adhered faithfully to Supreme Court precedent that was much less ambiguous than the precedent applicable to *High Tech Gays*.

---

1. One could characterize Judge Henderson's narrow interpretation of *Hardwick* as an act of judicial restraint or strict constructionism. However, that narrow reading allowed Judge Henderson to be activist in expanding constitutional protections for gays and lesbians.

Admittedly, *Coalition for Economic Equity* was activist in the sense that Judge Henderson found a state constitutional amendment to be probably unconstitutional. However, as noted in the Chapter Nineteen discussion of judicial activism and judicial restraint and as elaborated on in the preceding chapter, well-established Supreme Court precedent requires courts to subject to close scrutiny laws that infringe upon certain classifications and fundamental rights. And as the ensuing analysis demonstrates, Judge Henderson was exercising judicial restraint by relying on two closely analogous Supreme Court cases, both of which had invalidated initiative provisions adopted by popular vote.

Ironically, though, *Coalition for Economic Equity* is the one case for which Judge Henderson has received the most notoriety and vilification as an "activist" judge. Former Representative Tom DeLay of Texas (then the House majority whip) called for Judge Henderson's impeachment; and in an appeal from Judge Henderson's ruling, a panel of the Ninth Circuit added its own rebuke. Judge Henderson himself has appropriately declined to become involved in the political fray or to criticize his fellow jurists.

Having some sense of both (1) the depth of feelings generated by *Coalition for Economic Equity* and (2) the vehemence and irrationality of the response to Judge Henderson's ruling is an important part of understanding Judge Henderson's strength of character and commitment to principle.

Proposition 209 and the Assignment of the Case to Judge Henderson

On November 5, 1996, the voters of California passed Proposition 209 by a margin of 54–46%. The Proposition added the following language to the California Constitution:

> The state [including any political subdivision or governmental instrumentality of or within the state] shall not discriminate against, or grant preferential treatment to, any individual on the basis of race, sex, color, ethnicity, or national origin in the operation of public employment, public education, or public contracting.

At first blush the language may seem innocuous, but its purpose — as the drafters and proponents acknowledged — was dramatic: to bring an end to government-sponsored affirmative action programs that provide preferences to minorities and women in public employment, education, and contracting.

The following day a group of plaintiffs filed a lawsuit in federal court in San Francisco claiming that Proposition 209 violated the Equal Protection Clause of the US Constitution. The plaintiffs included the NAACP, the California Labor

Federation, the AFL-CIO, and a number of minority and women business organizations and individuals. The defendants included Governor Pete Wilson,
California Attorney General Dan Lungren, and various other state and local
officials.

The case was initially assigned randomly to Judge Vaughn Walker; however,
the plaintiffs, with the concurrence of two defendants, requested that the case
be assigned to Judge Henderson because he was handling a related matter in
which the Coalition for Economic Equity was involved as a defendant-intervenor.
The related case was W.F. Spencer & Sons, Inc. v. City and County of San Francisco, a challenge to the constitutionality of San Francisco's preferential treatment program for minority and women contractors.

California Attorney General Dan Lungren charged that "the plaintiffs
were . . . shopping their case around to find a judge of their choosing." The
charge, however, was unfounded. The plaintiffs were merely following Civil
Local Rule 3–12, which required parties to notify the court of related cases, so that
the judge assigned to the earlier case — in this instance Judge Henderson —
could decide whether the cases should be tried before the same judge.

According to the rule, cases were related

> when both concern (1) some of the same parties and . . . the same or simi-
> lar claims, or . . . (3) the same facts and the same questions of law, or (4)
> when both actions appear likely to involve duplication of labor if heard by
> different judges, or might create conflicts and unnecessary expenses if con-
> ducted before different judges.

Because Proposition 209, if valid, was "inevitably implicated in the *Spencer*
action" and because the Coalition was a party to both lawsuits, Judge Henderson found that the cases were related and assigned *Coalition for Economic Equity*
to himself.

To the extent that there was legal maneuvering to control which judge would
hear the case, the culprits appear to have been the proponents of Proposition
209. Several days *after* the Coalition for Economic Equity had filed its related
case motion, W.F. Spencer, for the first time, expressed its intent to seek a dismissal of some of its claims. As Judge Henderson observed, "Spencer's proposed
dismissal raises the specter that it may be advanced in part by a desire to impact
this Court's resolution of the pending related case notice."

Because of the importance of proceeding expeditiously with the Proposition
209 case and because "any changes to Spencer's current action remain unresolved and may remain so for some time in the future," Judge Henderson made
the related case finding on the basis of *Spencer* "in its current posture."

One of the defendants then moved to disqualify Judge Henderson because
of his prior association with civil rights groups, including the ACLU, which represented some of the plaintiffs. The motion was referred to a randomly selected

colleague, Judge Fern Smith, who concluded that Judge Henderson should proceed with the case.

The Equal Protection Issue

Even before the adoption of Proposition 209, it was clear that racial and gender discrimination were unlawful. Moreover, the Supreme Court had restricted the extent to which public entities could consider race and gender in affirmative action programs by requiring that they pass the rigorous "strict scrutiny" test: "[O]nly programs that are 'narrowly tailored' and 'necessary to break down patterns of deliberate exclusion' perpetrated by the enacting agency are permitted." In short, Proposition 209 was simply a reaffirmation of preexisting law — with one "narrow but significant" exception: It was designed to prohibit the limited "government race- and gender-conscious affirmative action programs . . . that are still permissible under the United States Constitution." As Judge Henderson emphasized:

> [P]laintiffs' constitutional challenge . . . is not . . . a facial challenge to the entire initiative. Rather, . . . it is a challenge only to that slice of the initiative that now prohibits governmental entities at every level from taking voluntary action to remediate past and present discrimination through the use of constitutionally permissible race- and gender-conscious affirmative action programs.

The US Constitution, of course, takes precedence over state constitutions. Yet how, one might ask, can putting an end to preferential treatment be unconstitutional? Isn't preferential treatment, as Proposition 209 suggests, the equivalent of discrimination? And isn't the Constitution supposed to be color (and gender) blind?

In a perfect world the answer to the latter questions would be clearly "yes," but our world is far from perfect. None of us is in fact blind to race and gender. Race and gender traditionally have been and continue to be bases for unwarranted discrimination; and affirmative action programs, despite their problems, have provided important opportunities for unfairly disadvantaged individuals. A truly color and gender blind constitution would not only prohibit affirmative action, but it would also fail to recognize racial and sexual discrimination in the first place![2]

---

2. Stephen Colbert, the Bill-O'Reilly-like political pundit character on Comedy Central's television program, "The Colbert Report," claimed to be racially color blind and

Nonetheless, shouldn't we strive for color and gender blindness in education, employment, and contracting, as Proposition 209 mandates? Shouldn't
the law express and promote our most noble ideals? And isn't equal — not
preferential — treatment one of those ideals?

Again, the answers, at least in the abstract, may be yes. The issue, however, is
not as simple as it may appear. First, while equal opportunity may be a desirable goal, the reality is that people today do not have equal opportunities. A
well-nourished child living in an intellectually stimulating home environment
and attending a resource-rich school has a much better opportunity to succeed
educationally than an undernourished child living with a poorly educated
parent and attending an overcrowded school. Suddenly declaring things to
be equal does not change reality; instead, it inevitably locks into place existing
inequalities.

Second — and more to the point with respect to Proposition 209 — except in
relatively severe cases of racial or sexual discrimination, reasonable people are
likely to disagree about what striving for the ideal of equality means in practice. Debates over various types of affirmative action are a perfect example.
Typically, we use the political process to mediate these disagreements. Much
day-to-day institutional policy making and political decision making involves
addressing claims of individuals and groups for better or equal or preferential
treatment. Should university admissions policies consider race, poverty, geography, or the fact that an applicant's parents graduated from the institution?
Should union apprenticeship programs give preferences on the basis of race or
gender, or family membership? Should municipalities give preference to locally
owned construction companies or companies owned by or employing large
numbers of minorities and women?

On these and myriad other matters, groups and individuals band together —
through political campaigns, campaign contributions, lobbying, and voting —
to promote their interests and preferences. Sometimes the interests are altruistic,
and other times they are decidedly selfish. In either case, people have substantial latitude in pursuing their goals for preferential treatment — unless, after
Proposition 209, they happen to be promoting interests of minorities or women.
For example, veterans and children of alumni may seek preferential admissions
policies from colleges and universities, and colleges and universities may choose
to adopt such policies. Local construction companies are free to seek preferential treatment from municipalities, and municipalities are free to accommodate
them. After Proposition 209, however, women and minorities cannot seek or
receive similar treatment from any state agency. Their only recourse, if they

---

unable to visually identify race. He believed he was white because people tell him so, he
belonged to an all-white country club, and he owned Jimmy Buffett records.

wish to seek the same opportunities that others can enjoy, is to obtain a state constitutional amendment that would repeal or limit the scope of Proposition 209.

Until the adoption of the Nineteenth Amendment in 1920, women did not have the constitutional right to vote; and more recently, some states relied on poll taxes and literacy tests to restrict the participation of minorities in the political process.[3] In a similar, more subtle (but no less real) manner, Proposition 209 burdens the ability of women and minorities to participate fully in the political process. Indeed, Proposition 209 creates two distinct political processes for those who wish to establish rules and policies that permit preferential treatment in public education, employment, or contracting. Anyone seeking a preference not based on gender or race is free to lobby the legislature or appropriate decision maker — for example, the university board of regents or a local city council — in an effort to achieve that end. By contrast, women, minorities, and their supporters who seek preferences for women and minorities protected by the federal constitution cannot utilize those paths. Instead, they must resort to the onerous, expensive task of trying to amend the California constitution. And that is the nub of the issue:

> Is Proposition 209 unconstitutionally discriminatory because it severely restricts the extent to which minorities and women — and only minorities and women — can pursue their interests through the political process, or is it simply a legitimate example of a political process working to express the preference of California voters?

Individuals may have gut instincts about what the answer to this question should be, but the legal answer — the answer that a judge must provide — requires more: an interpretation of the US Constitution, which in turn requires applying relevant precedents of the Supreme Court. As Judge Henderson put it:

> It . . . cannot be overemphasized that this case does not call upon this Court to adjudicate whether affirmative action is right or wrong, or whether it is no longer an appropriate policy for addressing the continuing effects of past and present discrimination against racial minorities and women. Such questions, while they are most certainly of vital public policy interest, lie beyond the purview of this Court. . . . .

---

3. The Twenty-Fourth Amendment, adopted in 1964, abolished poll taxes in federal elections. Two years later, in Harper v. Virginia State Board of Elections, the Supreme Court relied on the Equal Protection Clause to extend the poll tax prohibition to state elections. The Civil Rights Act of 1964 and the Voting Rights Act of 1965 substantially restricted the extent to which governments could rely on literacy tests to prohibit voting.

Rather, the substantive issues raised by this action are considerably more narrow, albeit no less important: whether the particular *method* chosen by Proposition 209 to curtail affirmative action is unlawful. . . .

In short, the critical issue in *Coalition for Economic Equity* was equal access to the political process, not the desirability of racial and gender (or any other type of) preferences.

A Temporary Restraining Order, a Preliminary Injunction, and Ninth Circuit Intervention

The first step in the lawsuit was to determine whether the plaintiffs were entitled to a temporary restraining order (TRO) — a ruling that would prevent state officials from acting immediately to dismantle affirmative action programs during the time necessary for the parties and the court fully to address the issues. Judge Henderson granted the plaintiffs' request for a TRO on November 27. In doing so, he made what turned out to be a massive understatement: "[W]henever issues affecting race and gender enter into the electoral process, some degree of controversy is inevitable."

Two days before Christmas, Judge Henderson in effect extended the TRO by granting a preliminary injunction against enforcement of Proposition 209 until a further hearing by the district court. In both of these decisions, he concluded that Proposition 209 was likely to be declared unconstitutional, but neither was a final decision on that issue. Rather, they simply maintained the status quo while the ultimate decision was pending.

On January 3, 1997, the defendants filed a notice of appeal. A few days later, Californians Against Discrimination and Preferences, Inc. (CADAP) a sponsor of Proposition 209 and a defendant-intervenor in the case, filed an application with the Ninth Circuit to stay — that is, put on temporary hold — Judge Henderson's preliminary injunction pending resolution of the appeal. CADAP's stay application was assigned to a "motions panel" that comprised three of the most conservative judges in the circuit. Diarmuid O'Scannlain and Edward Leavy were appointed to the Ninth Circuit by President Ronald Reagan. O'Scannlain had been chairman of the Oregon Republican Party and a member of President Reagan's transition team in 1980. Andrew Kleinfeld, the third member of the panel, was appointed to the Federal District Court of Alaska by President Reagan and to the Ninth Circuit by the first President Bush. "Kleinfeld had been active in anti-abortion groups — and in 1984, led an unsuccessful effort to ban a book about homosexuality [from school libraries]. . . ."

According to Kleinfeld, "the book 'raised interesting possibilities' of wrongful death litigation, if someone read the book, decided to become homosexual and contracted AIDS."

If the case had proceeded according to customary practice, the motions panel would have first ruled on the stay application. Then, sometime later, a three-judge "merits panel" would have decided whether to reverse or affirm Judge Henderson's granting of the preliminary injunction. Since Judge Henderson had not ruled definitively on the constitutionality of Proposition 209, the merits panel would not have had to reach that question. Instead, it could — and normally would — have played a more limited role by upholding or vacating the preliminary injunction and, in either event, returning the case to Judge Henderson. Judge Henderson would then have conducted a full trial on the merits and decided whether to issue a permanent injunction. That decision, in turn, would have been appealable.

But that is not what happened.

First, on February 10, 1997, after hearing arguments on the question whether to stay the preliminary injunction, the motions panel "deferred submission of the stay application," and chose to retain jurisdiction over the preliminary injunction appeal. Second, and more important, the panel used the preliminary injunction appeal as the occasion for deciding the ultimate merits of the case. On April 8, 1997, the panel issued an opinion upholding the constitutionality of Proposition 209.

Judge Henderson — regardless of whether his preliminary injunction was affirmed or reversed — had anticipated conducting a full trial in which he would hear more evidence to support or undermine his initial conclusion that Proposition 209 was probably unconstitutional. For example, the plaintiffs presumably would have presented not only additional evidence of how women and minorities were adversely affected by Proposition 209 but also evidence of how other groups — veterans, relatives, locally owned companies — benefitted or could benefit from preferences. The point would have been to show how Proposition 209 disadvantaged women and minorities and only women and minorities. But the motions panel's preemptive decision that Proposition 209 was constitutional made additional evidence irrelevant. The plaintiffs' only recourses were to ask the entire Ninth Circuit to review the panel's decision (*en banc* review) and to ask the Supreme Court to review the final Ninth Circuit decision. The full Ninth Circuit and Supreme Court both declined.

The next section consists of excerpts from Judge Henderson's findings. In considering the findings with respect Proposition 209's adverse impact on affirmative action, it is important to keep in mind Judge Henderson's statement about the narrowness of the issue before the court. The case was *not* about the merits of affirmative action; and Judge Henderson's findings were not intended to demonstrate that racial and gender preferences are desirable. Rather, the only question before Judge Henderson was whether the method employed by Proposition 209 — prohibiting women and minorities, and only women and minorities, from seeking preferential treatment — was unconstitutional. As part of the demonstration that Proposition 209 might be unconstitutional, the plaintiffs had to establish and Judge Henderson had to find that Proposition 209 had a racial and gender focus and that it would adversely affect women and minorities. Without the first finding, there would be no constitutional violation; and without the second, there would be no cognizable injury.

Judge Henderson's Factual Findings: Coalition for Economic Equity v. Wilson, 946 F. Supp. 1480, 1493–1499 (N.D. Cal. 1996)

A. Characterization of Proposition 209

[Relying primarily on the official California Ballot Pamphlet, Judge Henderson demonstrated the obvious, but legally critical, fact that Proposition 209 was intended to and would eliminate preferential treatment programs for minorities and women and for only minorities and women.]

[B]. Effect of Proposition 209 on Affirmative Action Programs

Any California public entity that implements Proposition 209 is required to end voluntary race- and gender-conscious affirmative action programs in three areas: contracting, employment, and education. We thus briefly review each of these areas in turn.

1. Contracting

Race- and gender-conscious affirmative action programs in California in the area of public contracting have taken various forms, from requiring that prime contractors to make good-faith efforts to utilize women- or minority-owned subcontractors to providing an advantage in evaluating bids. These programs are designed to address the continuing effects of past or present bias against the use of women- and minority-owned contractors on public sector projects. According to the evidence before the Court, their effect has been to provide such contractors with substantial opportunities not previously available.

The experience of Antonio Ruiz provides one such example. Mr. Ruiz owns Ruiz Construction Company & Associates which engages in general engineering and construction work. It is Mr. Ruiz' experience that "contractors accept the bids of those contractors with whom they have established ties." In 1985, Ruiz qualified to participate in the city of San Francisco's voluntary affirmative action program, which was adopted to remedy past discriminatory practices by the city in its letting of contracts. Prior to this time, Ruiz was unable to "get many large contractors to even accept [his] bids for subcontract work," and he in fact had obtained "only one contracting job with the City." By participating in the City's affirmative action program, he was able to break through the old patterns of doing business and obtain subcontracts. The exposure he gained led to additional business with prime contractors, and allowed him to build his business substantially and "form joint ventures to bid as a prime contractor on City contracts." [Here Judge Henderson cited the declarations of five additional individuals who provided similar accounts of how affirmative action has affected women and minority contractors.]

The record further demonstrates that implementation of Proposition 209 would substantially reduce opportunities in public contracting for women and minorities. [Here Judge Henderson cited evidence that weak or race/gender-neutral affirmative action programs tend to be ineffective or counterproductive. He also cited the declaration of one minority contractor who estimated that without affirmative action "his firm would lose up to 50 to 75%" of its public contracting work.]

2. Employment

Race- and gender-conscious affirmative action programs in California in the area of public employment generally allow an employer to consider the ethnicity or gender of an otherwise qualified applicant as one of many factors. Some programs may also utilize hiring goals. Such programs are typically designed to address the continuing effects of past or present bias against the hiring and/or promotion of women and minority employees. According to the evidence before the Court, their effect has been to provide such employees with substantial opportunities not previously available.

The use of voluntary affirmative action in California's civil service provides one such example. In 1971, then-Governor Ronald Reagan issued an Executive Order establishing voluntary affirmative action in the California civil service. Subsequently, state agencies and departments began using hiring goals and timetables in an effort to correct the existing underutilization of women and minorities. As a consequence, the "index of gender and race segregation in state agencies" declined by 11 and 16 percent respectively between 1979 and 1986. [Here Judge Henderson cited the declarations of three individuals who provided corroborating evidence.]

The record also indicates that implementation of Proposition 209 would substantially reduce opportunities for women and minorities in public employment.

3. Education

Race- and gender-conscious affirmative action programs in California in the area of public education range from voluntary desegregation and "magnet school" programs at the elementary school level to financial aid and admissions programs at the college and graduate school level. The evidence before the Court demonstrates that, overall, these programs have benefitted minorities and women.

The University of California provides one example. Where the number of eligible applicants exceeds the spaces available, the University of California campuses select between 40 and 60% of students based upon their grades, test scores and course work. The remaining selections are made using a combination of criteria including California residence, physical and learning disabilities, educational disadvantage, family income, ethnicity, leadership ability, public service, special athletic, artistic or musical ability, composition of a student's family (whether student comes from a single- or two-parent family) and a student's family's college history (whether student is first-generation college bound). . . .

The record indicates that, without the present race- and gender-conscious affirmative action efforts, the number of African American enrollments "could be reduced across the system by as much as 40 to 50 percent while Chicano/Latino enrollments could be reduced by 5 to 15 percent. . . . American Indian enrollments could be reduced by 40 to 50 percent. Filipino enrollments could increase by 5 percent or decline by 5 percent." On the other hand, Asian American enrollments would increase by 15 to 25 percent. White enrollments would likely remain roughly the same.

The above estimates may well understate the actual decreases that would occur over time. As acceptance rates fall for African American, Latino and American Indian students, the applicant pool from these groups may fall as well, since high school students consider the probability of admission when deciding where to apply for college.[4]

---

4. In the fall of 1997, the first year of Proposition 209's implementation, the entering law school class at Boalt Hall, the University of California's Berkeley Law School, had only one African American student. That is a 50% drop from the two African American students who were in Judge Henderson's Boalt Hall entering class of 1962.

During the next ten years minority admissions throughout the University of California system rose to levels slightly higher than they were immediately before the passage of Proposition 209. However, at the University's prestige schools, Berkeley and UCLA,

The record also suggests that, absent race-and gender-conscious admission programs, the admissions of African American, Latino, and American Indian students at California's public medical schools will significantly decrease. This in turn is likely to have a negative effect on the delivery of health care services in those communities. "On average, black physicians care for nearly six times as many black patients and Hispanics physicians care for nearly three times as many Hispanic patients as other physicians."

[C]. Impact of Proposition 209 on the Political Process

Prior to the passage of Proposition 209, anyone seeking to petition his or her government representatives to adopt, amend, or retain race- or gender-conscious affirmative action programs faced the same burdens as those faced by any constituent seeking preferential treatment for any group in the area of contracting, employment or education.[5] Typically, this burden involves directly petitioning and lobbying the specific representatives or policymakers with authority to adopt such programs. Such programs can generally be approved by

---

minority enrollment continued to be significantly below pre-Proposition 209 levels. According to a January, 2007 article in the Education Life supplement of the New York Times:

> This year, in a class of 4809, there are only 100 black freshmen at the University of California at Los Angeles — the lowest number in 33 years. At Berkeley, 3.6 percent of freshmen are black, barely half the statewide proportion. (In 1997, just before the full force of Proposition 209 went into effect, the proportion of black freshmen matched the state population, 7 percent.) The percentage of Hispanic freshmen at Berkeley (11 percent) is not even a third of the state proportion (35 percent). White freshmen (29 percent) are also below the state average (44 percent). . . .
>
> Chancellor [Robert] Birgeneau says he finds the low proportion of blacks and Hispanics appalling, and two years into his tenure, he has not found a remedy. . . . His university, Dr. Birgeneau says, loses talented black applicants to private universities like Stanford, where African-American enrollment was 10 percent last year — nearly three times that of Berkeley.
>
> "I just don't believe that in a state with three million African-Americans there is not a single engineering student for the state's premier public university," says the chancellor, who has called for reinstating racial preferences. [Author's footnote]

5. This would include, for example, constituents seeking preferential treatment for veterans or the disabled in employment, for local businesses in contracting, or for athletes, artists or California residents in admissions to public schools. [Footnote by the court]

simple majority vote or by executive decision. In other cases, a local initiative process may be required.

After the passage of Proposition 209, women and minorities who wish to petition their government for race- or gender-conscious remedial programs face a considerably more daunting burden.[6] Before such persons can approach their school district, city council, county government, or any other subdivision of government with such a proposal, they must first obtain an amendment to the California Constitution that would either (a) repeal Proposition 209, or (b) permit the specific government entity at issue to adopt a particular race- or gender-conscious affirmative action program.

The California Constitution can be amended through either an initiative constitutional amendment or a legislative constitutional amendment. Either method places a heavy burden on those seeking to advocate the use of constitutionally-permissible affirmative action programs in their local communities. [As Judge Henderson explained in detail, a campaign to amend the state constitution costs millions of dollars.]. . . .

As a result of the new political-process hurdles erected by Proposition 209, members of the plaintiff class are effectively precluded from petitioning local and state policymakers and representatives to adopt, maintain, or expand race- or gender-conscious affirmative action programs. For example, the Coalition for Economic Equity (Coalition), a named plaintiff in this action, has proposed fifteen amendments to the City of San Francisco's affirmative action policy. Members of the Coalition have met with City Supervisors in preparation for a vote on the proposed legislation by the entire San Francisco Board of Supervisors. The Coalition is now precluded from further pursuing this legislation through the normal political channels that were available prior to the adoption of Proposition 209.

The Supreme Court Precedents

Three Supreme Court cases spoke to the question whether Proposition 209 violated the Equal Protection Clause by burdening women's and minorities' access to the political process. The two most relevant cases were Hunter v. Erickson, decided in 1969, and Washington v. Seattle School Dist. No. 1, decided in 1982.

---

6. Defendants have not questioned the substantial evidence before the Court showing that women and minorities continue to face the effects of past and present discrimination and thus will continue to have an interest in using the political process to seek remedial action through affirmative action programs. [Footnote by the court]

In *Hunter*, the Akron, Ohio, city council had adopted a fair housing ordinance that banned discrimination in the rental and sale of housing. Then, in a popular referendum, the people of Akron repealed the ordinance and, at the same time, required that any future ordinance regulating property with respect to "race, color, religion, national origin or ancestry" must be approved by a majority of the people in a general election. The repeal alone was not troublesome, because all ordinances were subject to repeal by the referendum process; however, the Court held, it was a violation of the Equal Protection Clause to subject only certain ordinances — essentially fair housing ordinances — to the general election requirement.

Admittedly, the election requirement was facially neutral. It "treats Negro and white, Jew and gentile in an identical manner." Nonetheless, "the reality is that the law's impact falls on the minority," and "it places [a] special burden on racial minorities within the governmental process" — the burden of having to win an election in order to receive protection against discrimination, whereas other groups can receive protections or benefits merely by persuading a majority of the city council of the merits of their positions. For example,

[t]he automatic referendum system does not reach housing discrimination on sexual or political grounds, or against those with children or dogs, nor does it affect tenants seeking more heat or better maintenance from landlords, nor those seeking rent control, urban renewal, public housing, or new building codes.

In short, the Court held, the popularly enacted charter amendment "discriminates against minorities, and constitutes a real, substantial, and invidious denial of the equal protection of the laws."

Washington v. Seattle School Dist. No. 1 reaffirmed the *Hunter* principle:

[T]he political majority may generally restructure the political process to place obstacles in the path of everyone seeking to secure the benefits of governmental action. But a different analysis is required when the State allocates governmental power nonneutrally, by explicitly using the *racial* nature of a decision to determine the decisionmaking process. State action of this kind, the Court said [in *Hunter*], places *special* burdens on racial minorities within the governmental process," thereby "making it *more* difficult for certain racial and religious minorities [than for other members of the community] to achieve legislation that is in their interest." Such a structuring of the political process . . . [is] "no more permissible than [is] denying [members of a racial minority] the vote, on an equal basis with others."

The issue in *Seattle* was similar to the issue in *Hunter*. After the local school board voluntarily adopted a mandatory busing program to ease segregation,

opponents of the busing plan sponsored a statewide initiative that would virtually prohibit busing for desegregation purposes but allow busing for all other
purposes. The initiative was adopted by a large margin, and the Seattle School
District sued to have it declared unconstitutional.

Like Proposition 209 and the referendum provision in *Hunter*, the ban on
busing for desegregation was facially neutral. The Supreme Court, however, had
"little doubt that the initiative was effectively drawn for racial purposes."
Indeed, as the district court had found, "[p]roponents of the initiative candidly
'represented that there would be no loss of school district flexibility other than
in busing for desegregation purposes'." This "racial focus," in the Court's view
"suffice[d] to trigger application of the *Hunter* doctrine."

The Court then explained why the initiative "work[s] a reallocation of power
of the kind condemned in *Hunter*":

> The initiative removes the authority to address a racial problem — and
> only a racial problem — from the existing decisionmaking body, in such a
> way as to burden minority interests. Those favoring the elimination of *de
> facto* school segregation now must seek relief from the state legislature, or
> from the statewide electorate. Yet authority over all other student assign-
> ment decisions, as well as over most other areas of educational policy,
> remains vested in the local school board. Indeed, by specifically exempt-
> ing from Initiative 350's proscriptions most nonracial reasons for assign-
> ing students away from their neighborhood schools, the initiative
> expressly requires those championing school integration to surmount a
> considerably higher hurdle than persons seeking comparable legislative
> action. As in *Hunter*, then, the community's political mechanisms are
> modified to place effective decisionmaking authority over a racial issue at
> a different level of government. In a very obvious sense, the initiative thus
> "disadvantages those who would benefit from laws barring" *de facto*
> desegregation "as against those who . . . would otherwise regulate" stu-
> dent assignment decisions; "the reality is that the law's impact falls on the
> minority."

Neither *Hunter* nor *Seattle* discussed what has become a common feature of
equal protection analysis — the level of judicial scrutiny to which racial and
gender classifications are subjected. Judge Henderson, however, did address the
issue. The state, he said, had offered only one reason for reordering the political
process to the detriment of women and minorities: to guard against possible
liability for adopting affirmative action programs that turn out to be unconstitutional because they themselves do not survive heightened scrutiny analysis. Even if this were a legitimate state interest, Judge Henderson concluded,
Proposition 209 was "a hopelessly overbroad means to that end." For example, Proposition 209 outlawed even affirmative actions programs that had

already received judicial approval. Thus, the state had not supplied a sufficiently strong basis for satisfying the intermediate scrutiny test applicable to
gender classifications, much less the strict scrutiny test applicable to racial
classifications. Nothing in the Ninth Circuit panel's opinion or in the cases on
which it relied questions this aspect of Judge Henderson's decision.

Since the Equal Protection Clause applies to both gender and racial classifications, *Hunter* and *Seattle* would seem to be dispositive of the constitutionality of Proposition 209: Although facially neutral, Proposition 209, as Judge
Henderson documented, clearly had a racial and gender focus, and it substantially impaired the ability to advance the interests of women and minorities in
the political process. The defendants and the Ninth Circuit, however, believed
that a third Supreme Court case, Crawford v. Board of Education of the City
of Los Angeles, should be controlling. *Crawford* had upheld an antibusing
initiative.

California courts had interpreted the *state* constitution as requiring more
extensive desegregation efforts than those mandated by the federal constitution. In response, California voters adopted Proposition 1, which prohibited
the use of court-ordered busing to achieve *state* constitutional objectives. In
Crawford, the Supreme Court characterized Proposition 1 as merely a "repeal"
of a state constitutional right. The change, according to the Court, did not "distort[] the political process for racial reasons or . . . allocate[] governmental or
judicial power on the basis of a discriminatory principle."

The *Crawford* Court also held that "Proposition 1 does not embody a racial
classification. . . . The benefit it seeks to confer — neighborhood schooling — is
made available to all regardless of race. . . ." At the same time, however, the
Court acknowledged that Proposition 1 did not bar court-ordered busing to
enforce state *statutory* law. Thus, neighborhood schooling is protected only
from busing ordered to enforce the state *constitution*. It seems unlikely that a
state constitution would require busing for any purpose except to promote
desegregation. If so, Proposition 1, despite its facial neutrality, would appear to
have a racial focus. Moreover, the Court conceded that "court ordered busing
[to promote desegregation] . . . prompted the initiation and probably the adoption of Proposition 1."

Whatever one thinks of the Court's effort to distinguish *Crawford* from
Hunter and *Seattle* on the ground that Proposition 1 did not have a racial focus
or classification, this aspect of *Crawford* should not be significant in resolving
the question of Proposition 209's constitutionality. In *Crawford*, no lower court
had made factual findings on the racial focus question. By contrast, Judge Henderson's findings made it clear that Proposition 209 had at least as much of a
racial (and gender) focus as the provisions held unconstitutional in *Hunter* and
Seattle.

In a dissenting opinion, Justice Marshall argued that *Crawford* was no different from *Hunter* and *Seattle*:

I fail to see how a fundamental redefinition of the governmental decision-making structure with respect to the same racial issue can be unconstitutional when the State seeks to remove the authority from local school boards, yet constitutional when the State attempts to achieve the same result by limiting the power of its courts. . . .

. . . California's Proposition 1 works an unconstitutional reallocation of state power by depriving California courts of the ability to grant meaningful relief to those seeking to vindicate the State's guarantee against *de facto* segregation in the public schools.

. . . Indeed, Proposition 1, by denying full access to the only branch of government that has been willing to address this issue meaningfully, is far worse for those seeking to vindicate the plainly unpopular cause of racial integration in the public schools than a simple reallocation of an often unavailable and unresponsive legislative process. . . . "It surely is an excessively formal exercise . . . to argue that the procedural revisions at issue in *Hunter* [and *Seattle*] imposed special burdens on minorities, but that the selective allocation of decisionmaking authority worked by [Proposition 1] does not erect comparable political obstacles."

To the extent that Justice Marshall's comparison is correct, there is an inconsistency between *Hunter* and *Seattle*, on the one hand, and *Crawford*, on the other. Nonetheless, *Seattle* clearly reaffirmed the *Hunter* principle; and since *Seattle* and *Crawford* were decided on the same day, one does not overrule the other. Thus, the task for Judge Henderson (and later the Ninth Circuit panel) was to find some reasoned basis for distinguishing *Seattle* and *Crawford*.

Reconciling *Crawford* with *Hunter* and *Seattle*

According to Judge Henderson, two factors made Proposition 209 more like the laws struck down in *Hunter* and *Seattle* than Proposition 1, which the Supreme Court upheld in *Crawford*. First, he noted that *Crawford*, according to the Supreme Court, involved a "mere repeal," which did not "distort[] the political process for racial reasons." By contrast, Judge Henderson's extensive factual findings made it clear that Proposition 209 was not a "mere repeal." Rather, like the laws at issue in *Hunter* and *Seattle*, it had a racial focus and restructured the political process to the detriment of minorities and women.

Second, Judge Henderson pointed out that Proposition 209's restructuring of the political process, like the restructuring in *Hunter* and *Seattle*, was substantial. It "not only repeals all existing state and local affirmative action programs, but also prohibits the adoption of such programs in the future." Proposition 1, by contrast, had a more limited impact on the political process. While it prohibited court-ordered busing to achieve state-mandated desegregation, local school boards remained free to adopt their own busing or other desegregation programs.

Given the tension that exists between *Hunter/Seattle* and *Crawford*, Judge Henderson's largely factual basis for distinguishing the cases is not only reasonable but probably the ideal way to approach the cases. In the absence of some clear *a priori* legal principle to distinguish a "mere repeal" from a reordering of the political process, it makes good sense to assess the constitutionality of laws like Proposition 1 and Proposition 209 by looking at the extent to which they adversely affect the ability of women or minorities to participate in the political process. Indeed, the Court's emphasis on the burdens in *Hunter* and *Seattle* and the limited impact of Proposition 1 in *Crawford* seemed to invite such an approach.

The Political Reaction to Judge Henderson's Decision

To borrow a phrase from the Ninth Circuit panel, "the ink [on Judge Henderson's November 27, 1996, restraining order] was barely dry" when the critics went public. The panel had written, "The ink on Proposition 209 was barely dry when plaintiffs filed this law suit." Despite this gratuitous, pejorative remark, the panel conceded that the plaintiffs' alacrity had no adverse legal consequences. Moreover, the plaintiffs had had months to prepare the lawsuit. By contrast, it is highly unlikely that many, if any, of Judge Henderson's early critics had tried to read and understand his opinion.

The day after Judge Henderson issued his temporary restraining order, Governor Pete Wilson called the ruling "an affront to common sense." Two days later on national television Wilson characterized the restraining order as "an utter perversion of the equal protection clause." Ward Connerly, one of Proposition 209's sponsors, said, "Time for another Boston Tea Party. The four and a half million people who voted for 209 have just been given a thumbing of the nose by one man in a robe." California Assemblyman Bernie Richter chimed in, "It is well known that this guy [Judge Henderson] is probably the most leftist, wacko, liberal judge sitting on the bench in the United States. It would be an understatement to say he is to the left of Lenin." Representative Ed Royce (CA) issued a press release referring to Judge Henderson as "an unapologetic proponent of 'judicial activism'." California Attorney General Dan Lungren suggested that "Henderson should have quoted Alice in Wonderland, because Alice in Wonderland told us that words don't matter. It's the master who matters. . . ."

Columnists and editorial writers across the country were similarly disparaging in their reactions to the restraining order. Debra Saunders, claiming that Judge Henderson "snatch[ed] the case away from another judge," referred to him as a "king." Bob Wiemer wrote in Newsday that Judge Henderson, after giving "lip service to judicial restraint," "blithely" issued a temporary restraining order. Paul Craig Roberts called Judge Henderson "a prime candidate for impeachment," a theme picked up later by Representative Tom DeLay (TX). An editorial about the restraining order in the Augusta (Georgia) Chronicle was entitled "Judicial Tyranny," and an editorial in the Chattanooga Free Press began, "Here we have the latest, and a most flagrant, example of sheer judicial arrogance — with no small degree of stupidity."

The negative publicity continued for months, and Judge Henderson received hundreds of pieces of hate mail, some of them threatening death. Missouri Senator (later Attorney General) John Ashcroft said, "[T]his case epitomizes the problem of judicial activism," and Senator Orrin Hatch (UT) accused Judge Henderson of the "willful imposition of his own personal agenda." Anita Blair, Executive Vice President and General Counsel of the conservative Independent Women's Forum, characterized Judge Henderson's decisions "scandalously biased, illogical and legally insupportable." Following the Ninth Circuit's reversal of Judge Henderson's decision, Tony Snow declared that Judge Henderson's "opinion [was] so weak that an appellate panel berated him and refused to let him touch the case again." There were only rare references in the popular media to Judge Henderson's reasoning. At the same time, however, innumerable editorials and even some news stories described Judge Henderson as a black, liberal, former ACLU board member, and Carter appointee, as if these characteristics, and these characteristics alone, accounted for his decision.

Sound Bites and the Public Framing of the Issue

Despite Judge Henderson's carefully reasoned analysis, the political reaction to his rulings (although perhaps not its vehemence) was understandable. From a public relations standpoint, the argument for the unconstitutionality of Proposition 209 was a nightmare. The discriminatory impact of Proposition 209 is not as readily apparent as are many other forms of discrimination. For example, being denied the right to vote is a much more visible injury than the unequal access to the political process created by Proposition 209; and it is not immediately obvious that a neutrally phrased rule — particularly one purporting to ban discrimination and preferences — can itself be discriminatory. Moreover, *Hunter* and *Seattle*, the cases that provided the basis for the argument of unconstitutionality, were not well known even in many legal circles. A media outlet dedicated to an in-depth discussion of contemporary issues would probably have difficulty keeping the public's attention during a detailed discussion of the constitutionality of Proposition 209. By contrast, Proposition 209 contained simple, straightforward language; it expressed an American ideal; it was adopted by a majority of the California voters; and it was easy to defend in the press with pithy sound bites.

In reversing Judge Henderson, the Ninth Circuit panel utilized its rhetorical advantage. Indeed, Judge William Norris, dissenting from the decision not to rehear the case, characterized the panel's opinion as a "political manifesto." Notable lines that caught the attention of the press included:

> As a matter of "conventional" equal protection analysis, there is simply no doubt that Proposition 209 is constitutional.
>
> If merely stating this alleged equal protection violation does not suffice to refute it, the central tenet of the Equal Protection Clause teeters on the brink of incoherence. [As Judge Norris pointed out, this sentence is a paraphrase of an uncited line from one of Justice Scalia's dissents: "If merely stating this alleged 'equal protection' violation does not suffice to refute it, our constitutional jurisprudence has achieved terminal illness."]
>
> While the Constitution protects against obstructions to equal treatment, it erects obstructions to preferential treatment by its own terms.

And in its most memorable and most quoted statement, the panel said:

> A system which permits one judge to block with the stroke of a pen what 4,736,180 state residents voted to enact as law tests the integrity of our constitutional democracy.

Judge Henderson had addressed the same matter with these equally quotable but largely ignored words:

> [O]ur system of democracy teaches us that the will of the people, important as it is, does not reign absolute but must be kept in harmony with our Constitution. . . .
>
> [T]he issue is not whether one judge can thwart the will of the people; rather, the issue is whether the challenged enactment complies with our Constitution and Bill of Rights.

Technically, the statements are not inconsistent. Indeed, in the same paragraph containing its "stroke of the pen" sentence, the Ninth Circuit panel acknowledged that courts have an obligation to interpret and apply the constitution — which, by the way, is exactly what the Supreme Court had done in both *Hunter* and *Seattle*, where it had invalidated provisions adopted in general elections. Nonetheless, the "stroke of the pen" statement is what catches readers' attention. Standing alone it contains a strong innuendo that Judge Henderson acted improperly, and it was so understood by much of the media. For example, Joe Gelman, quoting the "stroke of a pen" statement, said that Judge Henderson "received what amounted to an unprecedented stinging rebuke from 9th Circuit Court of Appeals Judge Diarmuid O'Scannlain." According to Mark Rosenbaum, lead counsel for the plaintiffs, the panel's opinion treated Judge Henderson "with utter contempt and disrespect."

There are two versions of the paragraph with the "stroke of pen" statement. In the first version, which prompted the media reaction and which was subsequently withdrawn, the panel's rebuke was less qualified and more personal. In the second, now official version, the panel (1) removed a clearly pejorative phrase from the first sentence, (2) made its criticism somewhat less personal by substituting "court" for "district judge," (3) and added a final sentence acknowledging Supreme Court case law that authorizes "one judge . . . with the stroke a pen" to invalidate popularly enacted initiatives.[7]

---

7. The two versions of the paragraph are set forth here with the differences highlighted in bold type.

The original, withdrawn paragraph:

No doubt the district court is correct, **at least in theory**. Judges apply the law; they do not sua sponte thwart wills. If Proposition 209 affronts the federal Constitution — the Constitution which the people of the United States themselves ordained and established — the **district judge** merely reminds the people that they must govern themselves in accordance with principles of their own choosing. If, however, the **district judge** relies on an erroneous legal premise, the decision operates to thwart the will of the people in the most literal sense: What the people of California willed to do is frustrated on the basis of principles that the people of the United States neither ordained nor established. A system which permits one judge to block with the stroke of a pen what 4,736,180 state residents voted to enact as law tests the integrity of our constitutional democracy.

And the revised paragraph:

No doubt the district court is correct. Judges apply the law; they do not sua sponte thwart wills. If Proposition 209 affronts the federal Constitution — the Constitution which the people of the United States themselves ordained and established — the **court** merely reminds the people that they must govern themselves in accordance with principles of their own choosing. If, however, the **court** relies on an erroneous legal premise, the decision operates to thwart the will of the people in the most literal sense: What the people of California willed to do is frustrated on the basis of principles that the people of the United States neither ordained nor established. A system which permits one judge to block with the stroke of a pen what

The panel may have come to its own conclusion that its original paragraph was too much of a personal attack on Judge Henderson. However, the panel made no significant corrections to its rambling, often irrelevant analysis (*see* Appendix C *infra*), and its changes to the "stroke of a pen" paragraph were relatively minor. Thus, it may be more likely that the panel grudgingly modified its original language in response to pressure from other judges — perhaps in order to avoid the prospect of *en banc* review.

The Ninth Circuit Panel's Legal Analysis

The Ninth Circuit panel clearly won the battle in the media; but from the standpoint of judicial craftsmanship it was Pyrrhic victory. The panel's effort to deal with the tension between *Hunter/Seattle* and *Crawford* is virtually nonexistent. After setting forth the facts of *Crawford* and suggesting that the critical issue was whether it or *Hunter/Seattle* should govern the case before it, the panel made only two passing references to *Crawford*. First, the panel cited *Crawford* for the proposition that "the Equal Protection Clause is not violated by the mere repeal of race-related legislation or policies that were not required by the Federal Constitution in the first place." The panel, however, made no effort to refute Judge Henderson's factual findings and conclusion that Proposition 209 involved much more than a "mere repeal."

Second, without any elaboration or attempt to provide context, the panel quoted the following sentence from *Crawford*: "It would be paradoxical to conclude that by adopting the Equal Protection Clause of the Fourteenth Amendment, the voters of the state thereby had violated it." That indeed would be paradoxical. The *Crawford* Court's rhetorical flourish, however, did nothing to advance a reasoned resolution of the issue before it or the issue before the panel. *Crawford* involved not a mere "adopt[ion] of the Fourteenth Amendment"; rather, *Crawford*, like *Hunter* and *Seattle*, limited the ability of individuals to pursue certain permissible but not constitutionally required remedies. The question, thus, was how to distinguish *Crawford* from *Hunter* and *Seattle*. Judge Henderson had specifically addressed that issue. The panel did not.

Instead of providing reasoned bases for distinguishing the cases and justifying its view that Proposition 209 is similar to *Crawford* and that Judge Henderson misapplied the law, the panel simply offered conclusory, sometimes

---

4,736,180 state residents voted to enact as law tests the integrity of our constitutional democracy. **These principles of judicial review are no less true today than in the days of** *Marbury v. Madison,* 5 U.S. (1 Cranch) 137, 2 L.Ed. 60 (1803); *see, e.g., Pierce v. Society of Sisters,* 268 U.S. 510, 45 S.Ct. 571, 69 L.Ed. 1070 (1925) (*upholding* **district court injunction against state-wide initiative measure**).

inconsistent rhetoric. For example, the panel accepted all of Judge Henderson's findings as true, and, at the same time, claimed that Proposition 209, in contrast to *Hunter* and *Seattle*, "addresse[d] in neutral-fashion race-related and gender-related matters."

Appendix C provides a more complete discussion of the Ninth Circuit panel's opinion.

Anticipatory Overruling?

Although the Ninth Circuit panel made it clear that in its view Judge Henderson had applied an incorrect legal principle, the panel never identified that principle. Nor did the panel suggest an alternative legal principle — except for its conclusory statements about the self-evident meaning of equality or its assertions that the constitutional ideal was color blindness. Those conclusory declarations, however, were not merely the panel's own sentiments. They were quotations from — or based on quotations from — Supreme Court cases, some of which were decided more recently than *Seattle*. Perhaps, the panel believed that these more recent Supreme Court pronouncements indicated that *Hunter* and *Seattle* were anachronisms. In other words, perhaps the panel believed that at the next opportunity the Supreme Court would overrule those cases or at least strictly limit them to their facts. The panel's opinion contains only implicit support for this supposition, but it is a plausible inference to draw from the panel's failure to provide a coherent basis for distinguishing Proposition 209 from the laws invalidated in *Hunter* and *Seattle*.

One difficulty with this explanation for the panel's decision is that less than a year earlier the Supreme Court decided Romer v. Evans. *Romer* held unconstitutional on equal protection grounds a Colorado referendum prohibiting any level of government from taking action to protect gays and lesbians from discrimination. Since the Court found no rational basis for the referendum, there was no need to invoke *Hunter* or *Seattle*. The Court's holding, however, reaffirmed the basic notion that burdening the political process for select groups can be a denial of equal protection.

Nonetheless, if the supposition about anticipatory overruling is correct, it raises the question whether a court should base a ruling on existing precedent or whether it is appropriate to try to anticipate what the Supreme Court may do in the future. As Judge Henderson pointed out, the Supreme Court had addressed this issue and given an unambiguous answer: Lower courts must follow Supreme Court precedent until it is overruled. Thus, to the extent that the Ninth Circuit panel may have been relying on the implications it saw in more recent decisions to disregard *Seattle's* holding, the panel would have been violating the clear mandate of the Supreme Court.

In some instances, a more recent case may so clearly anticipate the overruling of an older case that the older case, even if it is more directly on point, could reasonably be regarded as implicitly overruled. For example, Brown v. Board of Education, read narrowly, dealt only with segregated schools, but quite clearly its rationale undermined Plessy v. Ferguson, a case upholding the separate-but-equal doctrine in the context of public transportation. In Browder v. Gayle, a case challenging the segregated bus system in Montgomery, Alabama, a three-judge district court panel relied on *Brown* to strike down the segregation requirement, even though *Plessy* had not been formally overruled. The decision, however, was not unanimous. A dissenting judge argued that the court should have followed *Plessy*, which was "precisely in point."

Whatever one thinks of a case like *Browder*, it should offer no solace to the Ninth Circuit panel. *Hunter* and *Seattle*, as Judge Henderson demonstrated and as the panel made no serious effort to refute, were the cases most directly on point. The panel did not and could not cite any post-*Seattle* decision that was as inconsistent with those cases as *Brown* was with *Plessy*.

Competing Visions of Equal Protection

Ultimately, what was at stake in *Coalition for Economic Equity* was more basic than judicial activism or restraint, judicial craftsmanship, or even the uses of precedent. The key to the disagreement between Judge Henderson and the Ninth Circuit panel was a fundamental divergence of views about the meaning of "equal protection" in the context of racial and gender issues.

The Ninth Circuit panel regarded the first and foremost objective of the Equal Protection Clause as embodying the ideal of a color-blind and gender-blind society. From this perspective, there is simply no place for gender or racial preferences, which are themselves a form of discrimination. That the Supreme Court had left a narrow opening for some race- and gender-specific programs was something with which the panel had to live but not promote.

Judge Henderson had a very different perspective on the matter. He regarded the Equal Protection Clause as a vehicle for helping to ensure equal opportunities for traditionally disadvantaged individuals and groups. From this perspective, anything that may hinder those individuals and groups in achieving equal opportunities is potentially suspect. That the Supreme Court had left *only* a narrow opening for some race- and gender-specific programs was something with which he had to live; but because the opening was so narrow, it was particularly important to be sensitive to and to subject to serious scrutiny all state-sponsored discrimination against minorities and women.

The Ninth Circuit panel's perspective is idealized and seems to assume a status of substantial existing equality (or perhaps indifference to the question of existing equality). By contrast, Judge Henderson's perspective is realist. It recognizes and tries to deal with existing factional tensions and inequalities; and it is consistent with the historic purpose of the Equal Protection Clause. As a result, while the Ninth Circuit panel saw only discrimination in racial and gender preferences, Judge Henderson saw discrimination in the singling out of race and gender for special adverse treatment in the political process.

Neither Judge Henderson nor the Ninth Circuit panel could decide the case before it without making some at least implicit assumption about the proper perspective from which to view the Equal Protection Clause. And as both Judge Henderson's and the panel's opinions indicate, the Supreme Court had made statements that supported both of their perspectives. Not surprisingly, in the absence of clear guidance from the Supreme Court, neither Judge Henderson nor the panel dealt explicitly with why one perspective was preferable to the other. Judge Henderson, however, did the next best — or perhaps even the better — thing. He made detailed findings that Proposition 209 would have a very real and substantial negative impact on minorities and women, and only on minorities and women. That is a classic equal protection concern. By contrast, nothing in the Ninth Circuit panel's opinion even attempts to address the question why an equal protection perspective that ignores documented discrimination might be acceptable, much less consistent with precedent.

The Supreme Court Six Years and Ten Years Later

Nearly six years after the Supreme Court refused to hear the plaintiffs' appeal from the Ninth Circuit's ruling; the Court breathed new life into the notion that racial preferences can indeed be constitutional. The case was Grutter v. Bollinger, which involved a rejected white applicant's equal protection challenge to the University of Michigan Law School's avowedly race-conscious admissions policy. In upholding the University's policy, the Court acknowledged that the University's compelling interest in promoting diversity in its student body justified "the narrowly tailored use of race in selecting applicants for admission."

Grutter has important implications for the Proposition 209 debate. First, *Grutter* demonstrated that race-conscious programs were not anomalous remnants from the past. Strict scrutiny was not a death knell for such programs. Rather,

strict scrutiny [and, by analogy, heightened scrutiny with respect to gender] is designed to provide a framework for carefully examining the importance and the sincerity of the reasons advanced by the governmental decisionmakers for the use of race [and gender] in that particular context.

Second, *Grutter* made it clear that a realist perspective on equal protection had carried the day:

> *Context matters when reviewing race-based governmental programs under the Equal Protection Clause. . . .*
>
> . . . Just as growing up in a particular region or having particular professional experiences is likely to affect an individual's views, so too is one's own, unique experience of being a racial minority *in a society, like our own, in which race unfortunately still matters.*

Finally, some of *Grutter's* reasoning suggested that the approval of race-conscious affirmative action may not be limited to educational institutions. For example, in her opinion for the Court, Justice O'Connor wrote, "Effective participation by members of all racial and ethnic groups in the civil life of our Nation is essential if the dream of one Nation, indivisible, is to be realized." And citing briefs from General Motors, 3M Company, and others, Justice O'Connor observed, "[M]ajor American businesses have made clear that the skills needed in today's increasingly global marketplace can only be developed through exposure to widely diverse people, cultures, ideas, and viewpoints."

The potentially broad implications of *Grutter*, however, were short lived. In Parents Involved in Community Schools v. Seattle School Dist. No. 1, decided in 2007, the Court struck down as unconstitutional two locally adopted race-conscious desegregation programs. Four of the five justices in the majority interpreted the "strict scrutiny" test so narrowly that Justice Breyer, in dissent, claimed that the test had been transformed into a rule that "in practical application . . . is fatal . . . across the board." Justice Kennedy, the fifth member of the majority, did not join in the most extreme portions of the plurality opinion.[8] Nonetheless, the fact remains that the Seattle program condemned by all five members of the *Parents Involved* majority placed "even *less* emphasis on race" than the Seattle program the Court had previously saved from the state's antibusing initiative — thereby weakening but not explicitly overruling, one of the two cases that set forth the controlling law when Judge Henderson preliminarily enjoined the implementation of Proposition 209.

---

8. Despite Justice Kennedy's reservations, *Parents Involved*, like *Grutter*, was essentially a 5-4 decision. Justices Breyer, Ginsburg, Souter, Stevens had been part of the majority in *Grutter*, and they dissented in *Parents Involved*. Justice O'Connor, the fifth member of the *Grutter* majority, had been replaced by Justice Alito, who voted with the majority in *Parents Involved*. There had been one other change in the make-up of the Court. Chief Justice Roberts, author of the *Parents Involved* majority opinion, had replaced Chief Justice Rehnquist, one of the *Grutter* dissenters.

A Rejection of the *Hunter/Seattle* Doctrine but Vindication for Judge Henderson

Three years after *Grutter* upheld the University of Michigan Law School's race-conscious admissions policy, Michigan voters approved a state constitutional amendment, Proposal 2, that was the equivalent of Proposition 209. When a case challenging the constitutionality of Proposal 2 eventually reached the Supreme Court, Justice Sotomayor offered this description of its impact on college and university admissions policies:

> Prior to the enactment of the constitutional initiative . . ., all of the admissions policies of Michigan's public colleges and universities — including race-sensitive admissions policies — were in the hands of each institution's governing board. The members of those boards are nominated by political parties and elected by the citizenry in statewide elections. . . .
>
> As a result of [Proposal 2], there are now two very different processes through which a Michigan citizen is permitted to influence the admissions policies of the State's universities: one for persons interested in race-sensitive admissions policies and one for everyone else. A citizen who is a University of Michigan alumnus, for instance, can advocate for an admissions policy that considers an applicant's legacy status by meeting individually with members of the Board of Regents to convince them of her views, by joining with other legacy parents to lobby the Board, or by voting for and supporting Board candidates who share her position. The same options are available to a citizen who wants the Board to adopt admissions policies that consider athleticism, geography, area of study, and so on. The one and only policy a Michigan citizen may not seek through this long-established process is a race-sensitive admissions policy that considers race in an individualized manner when it is clear that race-neutral alternatives are not adequate to achieve diversity. For that policy alone, the citizens of Michigan must undertake the daunting task of amending the State Constitution.

The District Court had rejected the challenges to Proposal 2. However, relying on *Hunter* and *Seattle*, a panel of the Sixth Circuit and then a majority of Sixth Circuit *en banc* had held — as Judge Henderson had held with respect to Proposition 209 — that the amendment violated the Equal Protection Clause. On April 22, 2014, the Supreme Court reversed in a 6-2 decision.[9] The case, Schuette v. Coalition to Defend Affirmative Action, Integregration and Immigration Rights

---

9. Justice Kagan recused herself.

and Fight for Equality by Any Means Necessary (BAMN) effectively put an end to the *Hunter/Seattle* doctrine.

The result in *Schuette* was not surprising. Four of the six justices voting to uphold the constitutionality of Proposal 2 had previously articulated color-blind views of the Equal Protection Clause that were similar to those set forth by the Ninth Circuit panel in reversing Judge Henderson. For example, in *Parents Involved*, the 2007 case striking down race-conscious desegregation programs in the state of Washington, Chief Justice Roberts — in a portion of his opinion joined by Justices Alito, Scalia, and Thomas — maintained that using race in assigning pupils to schools was fundamentally inconsistent with Brown v. Board of Education. He then declared in a widely quoted passage, "The way to stop discrimination on the basis of race is to stop discriminating on the basis race."

In a forceful *Schutte* dissent, Justice Sotomayor challenged this color-blind view of the Constitution and gave voice to the realist vision of the Equal Protection Clause that underlay Judge Henderson's Proposition 209 decisions:

> My colleagues are of the view that we should leave race out of the picture entirely. . . . We have seen this reasoning before. [citing Chief Justice Roberts' "The way to stop discrimination on the basis of race" statement] It is a sentiment out of touch with reality, one not required by our Constitution, and one that has properly been rejected as "not sufficient" to resolve cases of this nature. . . .
>
> Race matters. Race matters in part because of the long history of racial minorities being denied access to the political process. [Earlier in her opinion, Justice Sotomayor elaborated on that history, from denial of the right to vote, to literacy tests and other impediments to voting, to making it more difficult for minorities to participate equally in the political process.] And although we have made great strides, "voting discrimination still exists; no one doubts that." [citing Chief Justice Roberts' opinion for the Court in Shelby County, Ala. v. Holder]
>
> Race also matters because of persistent racial inequality in society — inequality that cannot be ignored and that has produced stark socioeconomic disparities. [multiple citations with examples]
>
> And race matters for reasons that really are only skin deep, that cannot be discussed any other way, and that cannot be wished away. Race matters to a young man's view of society when he spends his teenage years watching others tense up as he passes, no matter the neighborhood where he grew up. Race matters to a young woman's sense of self when she states her hometown, and then is pressed, "No, where are you really from?", regardless of how many generations her family has been in the country. Race matters to a young person addressed by a stranger in a foreign language,

which he does not understand because only English was spoken at home. Race matters because of the slights, the snickers, the silent judgments that reinforce that most crippling of thoughts: "I do not belong here."

In my colleagues' view, examining the racial impact of legislation only perpetuates racial discrimination. This refusal to accept the stark reality that race matters is regrettable. The way to stop discrimination on the basis of race is to speak openly and candidly on the subject of race, and to apply the Constitution with eyes open to the unfortunate effects of centuries of racial discrimination. As members of the judiciary tasked with intervening to carry out the guarantee of equal protection, we ought not sit back and wish away, rather than confront, the racial inequality that exists in our society. It is this view that works harm, by perpetuating the facile notion that what makes race matter is acknowledging the simple truth that race does matter.

Only Justice Ginsburg joined Justice Sotomayor's dissent, which relied on *Hunter* and *Seattle* to argue that Proposal 2 violated the Equal Protection Clause. However, even the Justices voting to uphold the constitutionality of Proposal 2 demonstrated the correctness of Judge Henderson's Proposition 209 decisions and fallacy of the Ninth Circuit's reasoning in reversing him seventeen years earlier.

Justices Scalia and Thomas (in an opinion by Justice Scalia) agreed with the dissenters that the continued validity of *Hunter* and *Seattle* would require a ruling that Proposal 2 (and, thus, Proposition 209 as well) was *unconstitutional*. They wanted to overrule *Hunter* and *Seattle*.

Justice Kennedy (in an opinion joined by Chief Justice Roberts and Justice Alito) offered a new rationale for *Hunter* and *Seattle* that made them irrelevant to the question of Proposal 2's (and Proposition 209's) constitutionality. He claimed that *Hunter* and *Seattle* stood only for the proposition that a state's action (e.g., the referendum in *Hunter*; the initiative in *Seattle*) violates the Equal Protection Clause when it aggravates or risks or has the purpose of aggravating an established racial injury (e.g., housing discrimination in *Hunter*; school-segregation in *Seattle*). Justice Kennedy then concluded:

> This case . . . is about who may resolve [the debate about racial preferences]. There is no authority in the Constitution of the United States or in this Court's precedents for the Judiciary to set aside Michigan laws that commit this policy determination to the voters.

Justice Kennedy's statement about "this Court's precedents" is true, of course, only if one ignores, as he did, the reasoning of *Hunter* and *Seattle*. Justices Scalia and Thomas characterized Justice Kennedy's opinion as having "reinterpret[ed]" *Hunter* and *Seattle* "beyond recognition." Justices Sotomayor and Ginsburg had a similar reaction: "We ordinarily understand our precedents to mean what they actually say, not what we later think they could or should have said."

The remaining justice, Breyer, acknowledged in a separate concurring opinion that *Hunter* and *Seattle*

> reflect an important principle, namely, that an individual's ability to participate meaningfully in the political process should be independent of his race. . . . [R]acial minorities, like other minorities, must have the same opportunity as others to secure through the ballot box policies that reflect their preferences.

He believed, however, that *Hunter* and *Seattle* should not apply to the University's race-conscious admission policy for two reasons. First, the policy was designed to promote diversity rather than to compensate for past discrimination. Second, although the elected boards of trustees had formal authority over university admissions policies, Justice Breyer viewed the effective decision makers as unelected university administrators, to whom the boards had delegated authority. He was unwilling to apply *Hunter* and *Seattle* to a situation in which decision-making power moved from "an administrative process to an electoral process."

Neither of these limitations on the *Hunter/Seattle* doctrine had been a focus of the litigation in *Coalition for Economic Equity*, and neither was mentioned by the Ninth Circuit in reversing Judge Henderson. Moreover, even if Judge Henderson or the Ninth Circuit had accepted these limitations, they, at most, would have provided a basis for validating only *some* applications of Proposition 209.

To summarize, Justice Breyer appears to have acknowledged the at least partial correctness of Judge Henderson's Proposition 209 ruling. More important, whatever one thinks of the reinterpretation versus overruling debate, the seven other justices — Sotomayor joined by Ginsburg; Scalia joined by Thomas; Kennedy joined by Roberts and Alito — confirmed Judge Henderson's conclusion that the Court's reasoning in *Hunter* and *Seattle* demanded a finding that Proposition 209 was unconstitutional. In short, despite the result in *Scheutte*, the Supreme Court had vindicated Judge Henderson.

Reflections

In March of 2007, nearly ten years after the Ninth Circuit's decision, I asked Judge Henderson to reflect upon his experiences with Proposition 209. Here is what he said: "At the time it was a very painful experience for me. I was surprised

at the reaction. . . . I thought we'd put together a class A opinion. . . . analyti-
cally sound. . . . I felt good about it." He explained that he assumed the Ninth
Circuit would affirm his decision, but that the Supreme Court might reverse
him and in the process overrule *Hunter* and *Seattle*.

> I was shocked at the vitriol. They actually had a rally here at the federal
> building on the steps. A conservative talk show host got a rally up here, set
> up a radio booth, vilified me. People would come into the courtroom, sit
> in the back and glare [as if to say], "Who is this villain judge?". . . . I started
> having a U.S. Marshal sit in my courtroom in case these people got out of
> hand. So it was a . . . traumatic period for me. I felt misunderstood. I felt
> bruised, it was a very difficult period for me. I withdrew somewhat.

Some of the hate mail Judge Henderson received contained threats to his
safety. Those were turned over to the F.B.I. for investigation; and for a time,
Judge Henderson had two US Marshals stationed outside his house from dusk
until he left for work.

> It wasn't a good period, but all wounds heal. Ten years later I look on it
> as an unpleasant memory, but I've recovered from it.
> I think I'm more savvy in these areas now. . . . Proposition 209 broad-
> sided me. . . . I'll do a better job of knowing when I'm making a contro-
> versial ruling. . . . But if it's the ruling I think is proper,. . . I'll still make it.

Coda

Chapter Twenty-Two

The Ninth Circuit?

Judge Henderson's judicial career has been devoted to finding solutions rather than creating conflict. However, he has never compromised principle to avoid conflict; and as a result, he has sometimes been a lightning rod for unfair criticism by those who disagreed with his rulings, most notably his decisions in the Proposition 209 case. As LaDoris Cordell wrote in the Introduction to Judge Henderson's Oral History,

> [H]e is a man of enormous courage. Thelton has never equivocated in his rulings, nor pandered to those in power. He has made his decisions based exclusively upon what is right. And he has done so at great cost, both to him — on occasion inviting hatred from the far right rabble, and to us — guaranteeing that he would never be elevated to his rightful spot on the appellate court.

Elevating Judge Henderson to the Ninth Circuit would have been a well-deserved recognition of his achievements; and at one point that appeared to be a serious possibility. He was one of five individuals recommended by Senator Barbara Boxer for a vacancy on the Ninth Circuit in August 1993. However, shortly after that time — if not before — Judge Henderson, as LaDoris Cordell correctly observed, doomed any chance that he might otherwise have had to serve on the appellate court. Perhaps surprisingly, his fate appears to have been sealed not by his most politically controversial decisions, the rulings on Proposition 209 in November and December 1996, but by his earlier decision in Madrid v. Gomez:

> I won't mention the attorney's name — but a very well-connected attorney who's a friend of mine, very high up and big in Democratic politics —. One day, not long ago, we were talking and we had talked about the time when I was being considered and being asked by senators to move up to the Ninth Circuit. . . .

. . . He said, "Well, you know, as matter of fact as an insider, your chances for the Ninth Circuit were over when you ruled on Pelican Bay [in January, 1995]." Absolutely shocked me. . . . [I]t wasn't a controversial ruling. . . . It was a controversial issue, how you treat prisoners. . . . It was in the papers. . . . But the attorney general didn't even appeal my ruling, that's how right it was. So I was startled that some people in the political process saw that as disqualifying me from going to the Ninth Circuit.

In some respects, the fact that Judge Henderson was not appointed to the Ninth Circuit is a significant loss for us all. With a still predominantly white federal judiciary, Judge Henderson's appointment to what is generally considered a higher and, therefore more prestigious, court would have made him a role model — both for minorities striving for advancement in our legal system and for the nation as a whole as we continue to struggle with racism. Moreover, the very independence of the judicial system is at risk when politics so clearly trumps merit. As Judge Henderson observed,

[W]hat you have to worry about . . . and I worry about it for ambitious people who want to make that move, I would hope we don't have a system where someone is hesitant to rule. . . . I can't imagine ruling any other way on Pelican Bay. I would hate to see someone say, "Well, gee, that's the right ruling, but gee, I want to go up to the Ninth Circuit. I'm going to modify so that I don't disqualify." That would be tragic in our system if things like that happen. I have no reason to think they do, but certainly that's the message that the politicians send. . . .

He might have added that the message has only grown louder in recent years.

There may be additional losses. On the Ninth Circuit, Judge Henderson would have been ruling on principles of law that have binding effect on all district courts in the circuit. And because the only binding precedents for the Ninth Circuit are those of the Supreme Court, he would have had relatively more discretion to further his sense of fairness and justice. Thus, it is possible that as an appellate judge, he could have had a greater impact on the development of the law than he has had as a district court judge.

On the other hand, both Judge Henderson's ability to influence the law and his value as a role model may well be paramount at the district court level. Very few of the hundreds of cases that any district judge hears each year are appealed. Thus, even though Judge Henderson has relatively less discretion as a district judge, he has had many more opportunities to issue rulings that have an immediate impact on people's lives. By contrast, on the Ninth Circuit he would almost always have been hearing appeals as part of a panel of three judges. A single appellate judge's efforts to sway the other panel members may be less significant than a well-reasoned, factually documented district court opinion.

In addition, much of the positive impact that Judge Henderson has had would be lost if he had been appointed to the Ninth Circuit. His problem-solving skills are ideally suited for the trial court and would have been largely wasted in the more abstract consideration of broad legal principles at the Ninth Circuit level. There is no guarantee — in fact it is improbable — that a district judge taking over Judge Henderson's cases would have had the patience and commitment to stick with them the way he has. Finally, and most important, on the Ninth Circuit Judge Henderson would have been dealing almost exclusively with lawyers. He would not have had the opportunity that he has taken advantage of on a daily basis as a district court judge to demonstrate his empathy with and respect for the parties and jurors who find themselves involved in the judicial process.

The words of Tony Amsterdam at Judge Henderson's investiture bear repeating.

> The court to which Thelton goes, the court of first impression, is also a court on the front line. It is a court that stands, to all of us, for what the legal system means to the people. If anybody deserves to be on a court like that, and will grace it, it is Thelton Henderson.

And he has.

Appendices

Appendix A

The Legal Framework

Familiar television courtroom dramas almost always portray trial courts. The cast includes a single judge, lawyers for each party who examine witnesses and make legal arguments to the judge, and perhaps a jury to resolve factual disputes. If the losing party appeals the trial court's decision, the setting will be quite different. There will be no jurors and no witnesses to testify. Instead, the attorneys will present arguments about whether the lower court properly applied to the law to a panel of judges. If the judges hearing the appeal are not unanimous in their view of the law, the majority will prevail.

The Federal Court Structure

The federal judiciary, like most state judicial systems, is divided into three levels of courts. In the federal system, there are (1) the trial courts, the most numerous and prestigious of which are the district courts, (2) twelve regional circuit courts of appeals, and (3) the Supreme Court of the United States.

Most federal law suits begin and end in the district courts, where typically a single judge presides over the trial. Occasionally, however, a federal statute will call for a three-judge trial court.

The losing party in the district court can appeal to the circuit court of appeals for the circuit within which the district court sits. A three-judge panel will then hear the appeal. After the panel's decision, a majority of the entire court of appeals may but seldom does vote to rehear the case *en banc*. In an *en banc* appeal, all of the court of appeals judges in the circuit (or, in the case of the Ninth Circuit, eleven judges) will review the panel's decision.

Further review by the Supreme Court is unlikely because each year the Supreme Court hears fewer than 100 cases — most of which are appeals from the circuit courts of appeals that the Court has chosen to consider. Except in situations where their number is reduced by a recusal or a vacancy on the Court, all nine justices — the Chief Justice and the eight Associate Justices — sit together to rule on the cases before them.

Jury Trials and Bench Trials

The Sixth Amendment guarantees the right to a jury trial for all criminal defendants. Litigants in other cases — plaintiffs and defendants in "civil" cases — may or may not be entitled to a jury trial. The right typically exists in suits for money damages; but there is no right to a jury trial, for example, in suits to have a statute or practice declared unconstitutional and in actions seeking to enjoin a particular practice or to enforce a statute.

In a jury trial, the jury will find the facts and the judge will interpret and apply the law. Usually this means that the judge will give the jury instruction explaining what the law requires, and then the jury will return a "general verdict" — for example, not guilty or guilty in a criminal case; not liable or liable for a specified sum in a civil case. Occasionally in civil cases, the judge will ask the jury to return a "special verdict" — that is, the judge will ask the jury answer specific factual questions. Then, on the basis of the answers, the judge will decide whether the defendant is or is not liable.

If there is no right to a jury trial or if the parties have waived that right, the judge will conduct a "bench trial." In a bench trail, the judge is both fact finder and law applier.

Burdens of Proof

Fact finders, be they juries or judges, can never be absolutely certain about what happened. They are necessarily dependent upon witnesses, some of whom may lie and each of whom will have somewhat unique memories and perceptions about what happened. Even if there are films, recordings, other mechanical devices, or laboratory analyses, the fact finder will be dependent upon the human frailty of individuals who calibrated the devices or tried to follow the laboratory protocol.

The law accommodates this uncertainty by standard of proof rules, which are expressed in terms of probabilities. In civil cases, the typical standard of proof by which the law asks fact finders to reach their conclusions is a preponderance of evidence — that is, more likely than not. In criminal cases, because of the severe consequences of a conviction, the law requires proof of beyond a reasonable doubt of facts necessary to establish a defendant's guilt.

The Fact–Law Distinction and Appellate Review

As suggested previously, the terms "fact" and "law" are typically used to describe the dichotomy between the jury's (or the judge's in a bench trial) role in finding facts and the judge's role in resolving legal controversies: Jurors decide facts; judges interpret and apply the law. The distinction between fact and law is critical (regardless of whether the judge or jury is fact finder) for appellate review. Losing parties — except for a prosecutor in a criminal case because of the double jeopardy prohibition — may always appeal a trial judge's interpretation of the law. For the most part, however, facts are not likely to be subject to review on appeal.

If a jury or judge has made specific factual findings and if there is sufficient evidence to support those findings, an appellate court in most types of cases must accept the findings as true. Similarly, if the fact finder has reached a general verdict without articulating specific facts, an appellate court in most types of proceedings must accept as true facts that are consistent with the verdict — as long as there is sufficient evidence in the record to support those facts.

Three factors support the distinction between the nonappealability of facts and the appealability of law. First, juries — and trial judges in bench trials — are in a better position than are appellate courts to evaluate witnesses' credibility. Particularly when witnesses give conflicting testimony, a proper assessment of their credibility may depend in part upon their tone of voice or general demeanor. A trial judge or a jury will be able to observe these matters, but an appellate judge is likely to have nothing but a cold transcript with the words of witnesses (and whatever supporting or impeaching documentation the parties may have presented at trial).

Second, factual disputes tend to be idiosyncratic to a particular case, whereas legal disputes tend to be about broad principles that will apply to a number of specific fact situations. Although it is important to try to get facts right, getting them wrong in one case will not have an adverse impact on unrelated cases. On the other hand, an incorrect legal rule, because of its breadth, may have an impact on a number of cases.

Third, and perhaps most important, permitting trial judges to articulate and rely on differing interpretations of the law would undermine the principle that the law should treat similar situations similarly. Appellate review of questions of law helps to ensure uniformity in the application of the law.

An Elaboration on the Fact–Law Distinction

The dichotomy between fact-finding and law interpretation is more nuanced than the terms "fact" and "law" suggest. Consider the following situation, which raises both questions of fact and law:

> A plaintiff brings a federal sex discrimination claim based on the theory that her employer subjected her to a hostile work environment. The plaintiff must establish that sexual harassment occurred, and witnesses may have different versions of whether or how often harassing acts actually occurred. These conflicts about what actually happened are factual disputes for the jury (or judge in bench trial) to resolve.

> Even if there is complete agreement about what actually happened, the plaintiff can prevail only if the harassing activity was sufficiently severe or pervasive to meet the legal definition of "abusive work environment." In interpreting the sex discrimination provisions of the 1964 Civil Rights Act (Title VII), the Supreme Court has made it clear that a few isolated instances of harassment are not sufficient. But where is the line between isolated instances and serious harassment that has an impact on the work environment? What, in other words, are the legal contours of "abusive work environment"?

If the judge determines that no reasonable person could consider the harassment sufficiently severe or pervasive to constitute an abusive work environment, the judge will terminate the case in the defendant's favor. However, if reasonable people could disagree and if there is a jury, the jurors will decide whether the work environment was abusive. Thus, the jury's fact-finding will include giving content to the legal norm "abusive work environment."

Another nuance to the fact/law distinction is that judges — both trial and appellate — are inevitably fact finders when they interpret and apply law. For example, the constitutionality of an affirmative action program is clearly a matter of law for the judge to decide. The judge must determine whether the program satisfies a "compelling governmental interest," and is "narrowly tailored to further that interest," a test required by the Supreme Court. And in making that determination, the judge will be a fact finder in at least one, and possibly two, ways. First, the judge may have to resolve specific factual disputes between the parties. For example, if the proponents of the affirmative action program are trying to justify it as a needed remedy for past discrimination, how pervasive was that discrimination? The parties may disagree. Second, in making the ultimate decision whether the affirmative action program is constitutional or in resolving any other legal issue, judges are making decisions about how the law will affect people in their daily lives; and in order to do this, judges have to make factual assumptions about the real world. Thus, in considering the constitutionality of an affirmative action program, a judge's factual assumptions about existing racism, existing equality of opportunity, their social significance, and the likely impact of the affirmative action program on racism and equal opportunity, while rarely fully articulated, will be important to the decision. This is not to say that a judge's idiosyncratic view of the world will or should trump established precedent; it is only to recognize that the law does not exist in a vacuum. Factual premises about people's character, how they live, and how institutions operate are an inevitable part of the law interpretation process. In short, interpreting law involves fact-finding.

As these illustrations demonstrate, one cannot rely on *a priori* definitions of law and fact to satisfactorily distinguish between judge functions and jury functions (or what is appealable and not likely to be appealable). Rather, "law" and "fact" are after-the-fact labels applied to matters that we have concluded should be decided, respectively, by judges or by juries (or judges in bench trials). The labels, however, are a common, convenient shorthand. Moreover, with the benefit of statutes, precedent, and tradition, there is rarely a dispute about what constitutes law interpretation and what constitutes fact-finding.

Binding Precedent and Stare Decisis

In our system of trial and appellate courts, each court is bound by the precedents established by its superior courts. For example, all courts must adhere to the decisions of the US Supreme Court, and each federal district court must follow the decisions of its circuit court of appeals. Thus, Judge Henderson's Northern District of California court must follow the ruling of both the Supreme Court and the Ninth Circuit Court of Appeals. His court, however, would not be bound by the decision of another district court or even a court of appeals decision from another circuit.

An important consequence of this structure is that district court judges have relatively less discretion in shaping legal principles than do appellate courts, especially the Supreme Court. Even the Supreme Court, however, does not have a completely free hand in giving content to federal statutes and constitutional principles. The doctrine of stare decisis — that is, the notion that courts should follow their earlier decisions — acts as a constraint on, but not an absolute bar to, reconsideration of earlier decisions.

Two values underlie the notion of stare decisis. First, it is sometimes more important that a legal principle be settled than that it be right. There may not be a consensus on what the "right" answer is; however, if the law is clear and not likely to change, individuals can adjust their expectations and behaviors to conform to the law. For example, people may disagree over whether housing inspectors should be required to obtain search warrants, but once that issue is settled, both inspectors and homeowners will know what the law demands.

Second, stare decisis is an important check on the ability of judges to promote their personal political agendas. To facilitate fair, unbiased decisions, judges tend to be somewhat insulated from the day-to-day political process. For example, federal judges do not face elections, and they can be removed from office only by impeachment. A concomitant of this political insulation is that judges — including Supreme Court justices — have an obligation to subjugate their personal preferences to the established law.[1] If they did not do so — if, in other words, they acted (or if they were perceived as acting) solely on the basis of their personal policy preferences, there would inevitably be calls for greater political accountability. Greater political accountability, of course, would lead to greater pressure to make politically popular decisions, which, in turn, would result in a less independent — and potentially less fair and more biased — judiciary.

To be sure, the highest court that has ruled on an issue can and sometimes does change its mind. Brown v. Board of Education and its progeny overruled the separate-but-equal doctrine of Plessy v. Furguson; Gideon v. Wainwright, holding that indigents charged with serious crimes are entitled to the appointment of counsel, overruled Betts v. Brady; and when Lawrence v. Texas struck down a sodomy statute as unconstitutional, it overruled Bowers v. Hardwick, which had upheld a similar statute.

Whenever a court overrules a prior decision, it is likely to offer an explanation for its action that purports to transcend politics or mere personal preference. For example, a court may say that it is returning to sounder, preexisting precedent. Or perhaps a court will say that the old decision was right for its time, but new technology, the lessons of experience, or a better understanding of history has called into question the wisdom of that decision. One may sometimes doubt the soundness of a court's explanation or even question its sincerity. Nonetheless, in offering these types of reasons for overruling an earlier decision, a court — at least at a rhetorical level — honors an important underlying rationale for stare decisis: Even as the court departs from specific precedent, it claims to be holding true to broader, enduring principles.

---

1. When there is uncertainty about how the law should apply to a particular case, judges' preferences and values will inevitably influence their decisions. This is neither good nor bad. Rather, as Chapter Two explains, it is an unavoidable part of the decision-making process.

Appendix B

High Tech Gays in the Ninth Circuit

As noted in Chapter Twenty, the Ninth Circuit panel hearing the appeal from Judge Henderson's *High Tech Gays* decision disagreed with him on all critical points. According to the panel, the Defense Department's security clearance rules did not interfere with a fundamental right, and gays and lesbians did not constitute a suspect or quasi-suspect class. Thus, the Department's rules were constitutional as long as they had a rational basis, which, according to the panel, they did.

The panel began its fundamental rights analysis by misstating the holding of Bowers v. Hardwick: "The Supreme Court has ruled that homosexual activity is not a fundamental right protected by substantive due process. . . ." As Judge Henderson pointed out, *Hardwick* dealt only with homosexual *sodomy*, not all homosexual *activity*. Nonetheless, as explained in Chapter Twenty, *Hardwick* itself was unclear about whether the holding was premised on a concern with sodomy in general or with *homosexual* sodomy. Although Judge Henderson took the former view, the latter view — despite its implicit and glaring endorsement of irrational discrimination — is not inconsistent with anything in the *Hardwick* opinion. Indeed, the fact that *Hardwick* found a rational basis in the "majority sentiments about the morality of homosexuality" is some evidence, albeit far from conclusive, that *Hardwick* is about *homosexual* sodomy. And, as Chapter Twenty suggested, if homosexuals have no fundamental right to commit sodomy but others do, it is hard to see how homosexuals would have a fundamental right to less intimate activity. Thus, the panel's conclusion, while based on a misstatement of *Hardwick's* holding, is not an implausible expansion of *Hardwick's* due process analysis.

The panel's rationale for holding that gays and lesbians do not constitute a quasi-suspect class for equal protection purposes is much more troublesome.

Initially, the panel identified from Supreme Court cases two criteria for quasi-suspect classification that, in its view, gays and lesbians lacked:

> [First,] homosexuality is not an immutable characteristic; it is behavioral and hence is fundamentally different from traits such as race, gender, or alienage, which define already existing suspect and quasi-suspect classes. The behavior or conduct of such already recognized classes is irrelevant to their identification.
>
> [Second,] . . . legislatures have addressed and continue to address the discrimination suffered by homosexuals on account of their sexual orientation through the passage of anti-discrimination legislation. Thus, homosexuals are not without political power; they have the ability to and do "attract the attention of the lawmakers," as evidenced by such legislation.

The notion that homosexuality is different from race or gender in that it is "behavioral" incorrectly suggests that homosexuality, unlike race or gender, is somehow volitional. As Judge William Canby observed in his dissent from the decision not to rehear the case *en banc*:

> There is every reason to regard homosexuality as an immutable characteristic for equal protection purposes. . . .
>
> . . . [B]y the overwhelming weight of respectable authority,. . . [s]exual identity is established at a very early age; it is not a matter of conscious or controllable choice.

The panel's claim that gays and lesbians do not lack the political power necessary to be a suspect class is equally fatuous. Once again, Judge Canby has a more realistic perspective:

> [The panel's] support for this proposition is that one state broadly bars employment discrimination against homosexuals, two other states more narrowly bar discrimination against homosexuals, and a few cities bar some types of discrimination. That showing is clearly insufficient to deprive homosexuals of the status of a suspect classification. Compare the situation with that of blacks, who clearly constitute a suspect category for equal protection purposes. Blacks are protected by three federal constitutional amendments, major federal Civil Rights Acts of 1866, 1870, 1871, 1875 (ill-fated though it was), 1957, 1960, 1964, 1965, and 1968, as well as by antidiscrimination laws in 48 of the states. By that comparison, and by absolute standards as well, homosexuals are politically powerless. They are so because of their numbers, which most estimates put at around 10 per cent of the population, and by the fact that many of them keep their status secret to avoid discrimination. That secrecy inhibits organization of homosexuals as a pressure group. Certainly homosexuals as a class wield less

political power than blacks, a suspect classification, or women, a quasi-suspect one. One can easily find examples of major political parties openly tailoring their positions to appeal to black voters, and to female voters. One cannot find comparable examples of appeals to homosexual voters; homosexuals are regarded by the national parties as political pariahs.

In addition to maintaining that gays and lesbians did not satisfy the criteria for a suspect classification, the panel claimed that Bowers v. Hardwick, although it was decided on due process grounds, somehow precluded the panel from finding that gays and lesbians constitute a suspect class for equal protection purposes: Since "the Constitution confers no fundamental [due process] right upon homosexuals to engage in sodomy,... homosexuals cannot constitute a suspect or quasi-suspect class ... for equal protection purposes."[2]

At an abstract level this notion of due process/equal protection equivalence has some appeal. The content of both due process and equal protection reflects important societal values, and it is possible (although not necessarily persuasive) to state traditional equal protection claims in due process terms and vice versa. For example, instead of saying that the exclusion of blacks from public accommodations is a violation of equal protection, one could claim that it is fundamentally unfair (i.e., a violation of due process) to deny blacks access to public accommodations. Similarly, one can characterize a woman's due process right to an abortion as her equal protection right to control her own body. Nonetheless, the panel's equivalency argument is fundamentally flawed. In deciding whether an interest is "fundamental" for the purposes of the Due Process Clause, a court has no specific guidance from the constitutional language. As a result, many judges—including Supreme Court Justices and the three judges of the Ninth Circuit panel—have concluded that there should be "'great resistance to expand the substantive reach of [due process principles]....'" By contrast, the equal protection guarantee, while not specific about details, invites with both its words and its history an examination of government

---

2. Because the guarantee of equal protection against federal action emanates from the Due Process Clause of the Fifth Amendment, *see* footnote 1 in Chapter Twenty *supra*, the panel at one point suggested that its perceived requirement for due process/equal protection equivalence may be limited to *Fifth Amendment* equal protection claims and not necessarily applicable to Fourteenth Amendment equal protection claims against state governments. Only a few sentences earlier, though, the panel acknowledged that "[t]his Court's approach to Fifth Amendment equal protection claims has always been precisely the same as to equal protection claims under the Fourteenth Amendment."

The panel's "precisely the same" observation was a correct statement of the law. There is no basis for treating equal protection claims differently because they arise under the Fifth rather than the Fourteenth Amendment.

discrimination. The unwillingness to read the Due Process Clause expansively should not be a basis for avoiding an examination of overt discrimination to determine whether more than rational basis scrutiny is warranted. Rather, when the underlying concern is whether to apply heightened or strict scrutiny, courts should look to see whether the challenged law affects an important interest *or* a questionable classification (or both).

Perhaps not surprisingly, the panel avoided the best argument it could have made for the proposition that homosexuals do not constitute a suspect class. As noted in Chapter Twenty, the Supreme Court in Cleburne v. Cleburne Living Center, Inc. refused to grant quasi-suspect class status to people with mental retardation. If — for whatever reason — people with mental retardation are not a quasi-suspect class, a lower court arguably should be reluctant to grant that status to others, including homosexuals. Had the Ninth Circuit panel taken this route, it would have had to grapple (as it should have in any event) with the fact that *Cleburne* — despite its holding with respect to quasi-suspect classification — examined quite rigorously and rejected the supposed rational bases for requiring a special use permit for homes that serve people with mental retardation. The Ninth Circuit panel cited *Cleburne* several times but never mentioned its facts or its rigorous rational basis analysis. Instead, the Ninth Circuit, after relying of *Cleburne* for the general proposition that rational basis analysis was appropriate, required very little to satisfy itself that there was a rational basis for the Defense Department's discrimination against gays and lesbians.

The Ninth Circuit panel did not directly dispute any of Judge Henderson's rational basis analysis. Instead, the panel found a rational basis for the government's discriminatory conduct in a claim that the government cobbled together only after Judge Henderson had issued his opinion: Counterintelligence agencies target homosexuals; therefore, the Defense Department needs to investigate all homosexuals to determine whether they may be "susceptible to coercion or blackmail or otherwise vulnerable to counterintelligence efforts." The government had made this claim for the first time in a motion asking Judge Henderson to reconsider his decision. Judge Henderson had denied the motion.

As the panel pointed out, there was some evidence in the record to support the proposition that the KGB, the Russian secret service agency, sought to exploit individuals with vulnerabilities, including matters relating to sexuality. However, there was no evidence suggesting that gays and lesbians were in fact particularly susceptible to such efforts.

Judge Canby argued in his dissent that the KGB's alleged targeting of homosexuals was itself irrational. To enshrine that irrationality as a rational basis for the Defense Department policies, he said, "helps to perpetuate the wrongful discrimination." The panel, however, was willing to accept irrationality as part of its rational basis: "[T]he counterintelligence agencies' reasons for

targeting homosexuals — *even if based on continuing ignorance or prejudice —
are irrelevant.*"

If the Ninth Circuit panel had relied on *Cleburne* to deny quasi-suspect class status to homosexuals and then engaged in a more rigorous examination of the government's claimed justification for its discriminatory policy, perhaps the panel would have reached the same conclusion. After all, there is no precision even in *Cleburne* about how rigorous the rational basis inquiry should be; and at least at the margins, reasonable people can disagree about what constitutes a rational basis. That would have been a respectable effort. Instead, the panel misstated the due process holding of *Hardwick*, engaged in a shallow and logically indefensible analysis of the suspect class issue, ignored the facts and reasoning of *Cleburne*, and was exceedingly solicitous of the government's claimed rational basis.

Appendix C

Rush to Judgment: The Ninth Circuit's Proposition 209 Opinion

Unlike most federal cases, Coalition for Economic Equity v. Wilson, the Proposition 209 case, was resolved with incredible alacrity. Typically, one can measure the time from the filing a complaint to the final ruling by the trial court in months and sometimes years. An appellate court decision affirming or reversing the trial judge may not be forthcoming for another year or two or even more. By contrast, the entire time from the commencement of the action to the Ninth Circuit's upholding the constitutionality of Proposition 209 was less than five months!

Because the state planned to begin implementing Proposition 209 immediately after its passage, it was important for Judge Henderson to consider as quickly as possible plaintiffs' requests for a temporary restraining order and a preliminary injunction. Thus, it is not surprising that — after holding expedited evidentiary hearings — he ruled on the temporary restraining order request only three weeks after the filing of the suit and on the preliminary injunction request four weeks later. Furthermore, given his preliminary assessment that Proposition 209 was probably unconstitutional, it is not surprising that he enjoined its enforcement. If Proposition 209 were ultimately found unconstitutional, the precipitous dismantling of affirmative action programs as the litigation proceeded would cause irreparable harm to minorities and women. And to the extent there was a possibility that Judge Henderson might, after a full trial, change his mind or be reversed on appeal, he concluded that:

the balance of hardships . . . tips decidedly in plaintiffs' favor. . . . [A] preliminary injunction would impose little hardship on members of the defendant class, who would merely be required to suspend their Proposition 209 implementation plans pending trial.

The public interest also favors the entry of a preliminary injunction. As an initial matter, a number of named defendants have urged this Court to act swiftly and give clear guidance with respect to Proposition 209. This request, of course, is neutral with respect to the granting or denial of the present motion. Nonetheless, the Court believes the preservation of the pre-election status quo not only serves the public need for plain guidance, but also harmonizes that interest with the compelling interest in remedying discrimination that underlies existing constitutionally-permissible state-sponsored affirmative action programs threatened by Proposition 209.

The speed with which the case was decided was a function of the Ninth Circuit motions panel's decision to short-circuit the normal trial and appellate process by deferring the stay application, assuming jurisdiction over the preliminary injunction appeal (rather than referring the appeal to a merits panel), and then using that appeal as a vehicle for deciding the ultimate merits of the case.

The Motions Panel's Decision to Consider the Preliminary Injunction Appeal

The O'Scannlain, Leavy, Kleinfeld motions panel's decision to retain jurisdiction over the preliminary injunction appeal in *Coalition for Economic Equity* was not unique. The panel made the same decision in another affirmative action related case, Monterey Mechanical Co. v. Wilson.

In *Monterey Mechanical*, the trial court had refused to preliminarily enjoin the enforcement of a statutory requirement that contractors receiving state contracts make good faith efforts to meet goals for subcontracting work to minorities, women, and disabled veterans. The motions panel, having decided to retain jurisdiction over the preliminary injunction appeal, held that the statutory requirement violated the Equal Protection Clause. If the panel had merely reversed (or affirmed) the refusal to grant preliminary injunction and remanded the case, the trial court presumably would have heard evidence about the actual impact of the good faith requirement (was it substantial or de minimus?) and the need for such a good faith requirement to compensate for past discrimination. Both of these factual matters are relevant to the question of the requirement's constitutionality. However, just as the motions panel took it upon itself to decide that Proposition 209 was constitutional, it decided on its own that the statutory good faith requirement was unconstitutional.

Ninth Circuit Judge Stephen Reinhardt, who had unsuccessfully sought *en banc* review of *Monterey Mechanical*, criticized the motions panel's failure to refer both that case and *Coalition for Economic Equity* to merits panels:

> I . . . believe the motions panel that decided this case and the [Proposition 209] case . . . improperly assumed jurisdiction over these two cases in contravention of our internal court rules. I have been persuaded, however, not to discuss that matter in this opinion, but rather to do so within the confines of the court. I omit the discussion reluctantly. . . .

Judge Kleinfeld, author of the *Monterey Mechanical* decision, responded by citing a court statistic showing that motions panels had retained jurisdiction over 46 of 50 preliminary injunction appeals during the first eleven months of 1997. For him, that statistic was sufficient to justify the panel's deciding the merits of the preliminary injunction appeal in *Monterey Mechanical* — and presumably in *Coalition for Economic Equity*, as well.

Despite the numbers, there is good reason for Judge Reinhardt's concern. Typically, the work of a motions panel consists of routine matters about which there is relatively little controversy. Many — probably the vast majority — of the 46 preliminary injunction appeals cited by Judge Kleinfeld fit this description. As explained in the next section, appellate courts are supposed to apply a deferential standard of review in evaluating appeals from the grant or denial of a preliminary injunction. Thus, there is often no need for an extended discussion or for final resolution of the underlying substantive issues. However, the O'Scannlain, Leavy, Kleinfeld motions panel's final opinions in both *Coalition for Economic Equity* and *Monterey Mechanical* demonstrate that the preliminary injunction appeals were not run-of-the-mill but rather implicated serious, complex constitutional issues. And at least in *Coalition for Economic Equity*, the panel obviously realized this *before* it announced that it would decide the merits of the preliminary injunction appeal. The panel had just heard oral arguments on the application for a stay; and as the panel acknowledged, the arguments "focused primarily on the merits underlying the preliminary injunction itself." Indeed, in its very next sentence, the motions panel offered the focus of the argument as its reason for assuming jurisdiction over the merits of the preliminary injunction appeal: "We *thus* deferred submission of the stay and expedited submission on the merits. . . ." In short, the motions panel knowingly assumed jurisdiction over a preliminary injunction appeal that, from its perspective, was likely to be far from routine.

Since the oral arguments on the stay application in *Coalition for Economic Equity* had familiarized the motions panel with the issues in the case, one might think that an interest in efficiency would warrant the decision to retain jurisdiction over the merits of the preliminary injunction. There is, however, a substantial countervailing concern. Stay arguments will inevitably address the underlying issues. If filing a stay application were to become the occasion on a regular basis for motions panels to assume jurisdiction over the merits of an appeal, that practice would encourage judge shopping. Whenever a trial court granted a preliminary injunction and the appellant thought that a particular motions panel might be favorable to the appellant's positions, the appellant would file a stay application in the hope that motions panel would consider the merits of the appeal. Indeed, that appears to be precisely what happened in *Coalition for Economic Equity*. CADAP filed its application for a stay within days after the announcement of the names of the O'Scannlain, Leavy, Kleinfeld motions panel, even though Judge Henderson had not yet ruled on the request for a stay that CADAP had presented to him only days earlier.

The Motions Panel's Decision to Consider the Merits of Proposition 209

The usual role of a panel hearing an appeal from the granting or denying of a preliminary injunction is quite limited in comparison to its role in considering an appeal from the final judgment of a trial court. In considering whether the final decision of a trial court — for example, the issuance of *permanent* injunction — should be reversed, an appellate court's conclusion that the trial judge misapplied the law would be grounds for reversal. By contrast, the case law makes it clear that misapplication of the law is not a sufficient basis reversing a preliminary injunction. Rather, the appellate court must find that the trial judge's ruling was based on an incorrect legal premise or was an abuse of discretion. Although the distinction between the former standard and the preliminary injunction standard may sometimes be elusive, the latter supposedly gives an appellate court less leeway to reverse a district court than the former. Consider, for example, Gregorio T. v. Wilson, the case upon which the O'Scannlain, Leavy, Kleinfeld motions panel relied for the proposition that it could assume jurisdiction over the merits of the preliminary injunction. In *Gregorio T.*, the court refused to reverse the preliminary injunction because it held that while the trial court *may* have misapplied the law, the trial court had not abused its discretion.

The primary reason for this deferential approach to preliminary injunction rulings is that there has not yet been a full opportunity to develop the case at trial. For example, as suggested in Chapter Twenty-One, if the motions panel had returned *Coalition for Economic Equity* to Judge Henderson, the plaintiffs presumably would have presented more evidence of how Proposition 209 adversely affected minorities and women and how other groups benefitted or could benefit from the preferences that were denied to minorities and women. A more complete record on this point would — or at least should — have made it more difficult for an appellate court to declare, as the motions panel did, that Proposition 209 was race and gender neutral.

Ironically, Judge O'Scannlain, author of the Ninth Circuit motions panel's Proposition 209 opinion, had acknowledged the limited scope of review normally accorded to appeals from the grant or denial of a preliminary injunction in an appeal from another of Judge Henderson's preliminary injunction rulings:

> Detailed consideration of the merits of the constitutional claim is neither necessary nor appropriate. . . . [T]he district court did not abuse its discretion in refusing to grant a preliminary injunction. This court need not say more. Our decision on this narrow issue today should not be regarded as determinative of the ultimate resolution of the dispute.

Nonetheless, it will sometimes be possible for a panel hearing the appeal from a preliminary injunction to issue a ruling that terminates the litigation. Assume, for example, that in reviewing Judge Henderson's preliminary injunction, the motions panel (1) accepted as true "all facts alleged in the complaint or found by the district court," (2) drew all reasonable inferences from those facts in plaintiffs' favor, and (3) concluded (a) that Judge Henderson relied on an incorrect legal premise and (b) that Proposition 209 was race and gender neutral. Given these assumptions, there would have been no justification for maintaining the preliminary injunction. Moreover, regardless of the extent to which these assumed findings and conclusions were or were not grounded in reality, they would have been binding, authoritative statements about the case; and they would have left no room for any further action by Judge Henderson.

But these were not merely hypothetical findings and conclusions. They were the motions panel's actual findings and conclusions; and as the ensuing sections demonstrate, they are deeply flawed. Before turning to that analysis, however, there is one further matter to consider: Was the panel's claim of jurisdiction over the preliminary injunction simply a crass political act of three conservative jurists who wanted to highjack the case away from Judge Henderson and promote their own agenda? In other words, did the panel intend from the outset to reach the ultimate merits of the case and hold that Proposition 209 was constitutional?

Several factors support this hypothesis. First, the panel, in contrast to what motions panels typically do, assumed jurisdiction over what it had to know was, from its perspective, far from a run-of-the-mill preliminary injunction appeal. Second, with probably the same insight, the motions panel chose to exercise jurisdiction over a preliminary injunction appeal in another affirmative action related case, *Monterey Mechanical*. Third, in both cases, the motions panel used the preliminary injunction appeals as occasions to ban affirmative action.

The panel's opinion itself provides further evidence of the highjacking hypothesis. The panel began by paying lip service to the supposedly limited scope of review in preliminary injunction cases. It claimed that it would reverse Judge Henderson only if he applied "an erroneous legal premise" or had "abuse[d his] discretion." Mere disagreement about how to apply the law to the facts would not warrant reversal. However, except for the panel's conclusory statements about the supposedly obvious meaning of the Equal Protection Clause, it made no attempt to identify the incorrect legal premise upon which Judge Henderson supposedly relied. It made no attempt to explain how, if Judge Henderson was wrong, his effort to apply relevant Supreme Court precedent to tentatively resolve the case could be an abuse of discretion. And the panel incongruously maintained both that it accepted as true all facts alleged by the plaintiffs and found by Judge Henderson and that Proposition 209 was race and gender neutral. Why would the panel issue such an opinion unless its overarching goal was to reach a particular result regardless of the actual law and facts?

For those who believe that law is nothing but politics, the possibility that the panel highjacked the case to promote its own policy preferences may not be surprising. However, for those who believe that law can and should act as a restraint on individual judges' personal beliefs and values, this suggestion should be deeply disturbing. To the extent that it resonates as a plausible basis for the panel's action, it is only because the panel failed to provide more persuasive rationales for its actions and conclusions.

A somewhat more charitable (but considerably less likely) hypothesis is that the motions panel, without prejudging the case, wanted to honor California voters by resolving the constitutionality of Proposition 209 as quickly as possible. However, if this were a factor in its decision making, the panel did not mention it; and for good reason. There simply is no precedent for fast-tracking challenges to voter-approved initiatives or referenda in a way that avoids the normal trial and appellate processes, and it is hard to imagine why one would want to do so. If a different motions panel had gotten the case, decided to reach the merits, and held Proposition 209 unconstitutional, proponents of the Proposition would undoubtedly have cried foul. In the absence of some particularized need in an individual case, both promotion of respect for the judiciary and a concern with careful, thorough consideration of the issues should caution against deviating from the norm.

Whatever the reason or combination of reasons for the panel's decision to reach the ultimate merits of the case, its end product demonstrates the peril of abandoning procedural regularity.

"Conventional" Equal Protection Analysis

Before turning what it characterized as the "political structure" equal protection analysis mandated by "the so-called *'Hunter'* doctrine," the panel discussed the applicability of "'conventional' equal protection analysis" to Proposition 209. The panel offered no explanation for its decision to bifurcate the equal protection analysis into "conventional" and "political structure" categories. Perhaps the panel chose to talk about conventional equal protection initially as a way of exploiting its rhetorical advantage. The notion that a rule barring specific preferences cannot itself be discriminatory seems much less evident once one understands the facts and holdings of *Hunter* and *Seattle*. Another possibility is that the panel wanted to imply that *Hunter* and *Seattle* were doctrinal outliers that should be strictly limited to their facts. However, *Hunter* and *Seattle*, despite their relative obscurity, were well within the mainstream of conventional equal protection doctrine. Courts have regularly invoked the Equal Protection Clause to protect minorities and women against exclusion and discrimination both within and without the political process. Indeed, as the panel itself acknowledged, the political structure cases "do not create some paradoxical exception" to traditional equal protection analysis.

Whatever the reasons for its bifurcated equal protection analysis, the panel's first sentence was unambiguous: "As a matter of 'conventional' equal protection analysis, there simply is no doubt that Proposition 209 is constitutional." This assertion, though, is seemingly at odds with the panel's correct elaboration on the core of conventional equal protection doctrine:

> ". . . [A]ny individual suffers an injury when he or she is disadvantaged by the government because of his or her race.". . .
>
> The Equal Protection Clause guarantees that the government will not classify individuals on the basis of impermissible criteria. Most laws, of course — perhaps all — classify individuals one way or another. Individuals receive, or are correspondingly denied, government benefits on the basis of income, disability, veteran status, age, occupation and countless other grounds. Legislative classifications as a general rule are presumptively valid under the Equal Protection Clause. . . .
>
> The general rule does not apply, however, when a law classifies individuals by race or gender. Any government action that classifies persons by race is presumptively unconstitutional and subject to the most exacting judicial scrutiny. To be constitutional, a racial classification, regardless of its purported motivation, must be narrowly tailored to serve a compelling governmental interest, an extraordinary justification. When the government classifies by gender, it must demonstrate that the classification is

substantially related to an important governmental interest, requiring "an exceedingly persuasive" justification.

Given this elaboration of conventional equal protection doctrine and the panel's acceptance of Judge Henderson's findings, one might reasonably have expected the panel to conclude that the racial and gender classifications created by Proposition 209 should be subject to serious scrutiny. The panel, however, ignored Judge Henderson's findings and reached a conclusion consistent with its opening sentence:

> Proposition 209 *prohibits* the State from classifying individuals by race or gender. A law that prohibits the State from classifying individuals by race or gender *a fortiori* does not classify individuals by race or gender. Proposition 209's ban on race and gender preferences, as a matter of law and logic, does not violate the Equal Protection Clause in any conventional sense.

The "*a fortiori*," of course, ignores both (1) the fact that Proposition 209, by forbidding race and gender preferences and only race and gender preferences, does create racial and gender classifications with respect to the ability to utilize the political process and (2) the holding of *Seattle*, which struck down state statute that prohibited classifying students by race for the purpose of school busing.

A Bizarre Detour

The panel then turned to its "political structure" analysis. However, before discussing the applicability of *Hunter* and *Seattle* to Proposition 209, the panel engaged in a bizarre discourse that turned the notions of "majority" and "minority" on their heads. Noting that "women and minorities . . . constitute a majority of the California electorate," the panel considered whether Proposition 209 could "deny equal protection to members of a group that constitutes a majority of the electorate that enacted it." "Is it possible," the court asked, "for a majority of voters impermissibly to stack the political deck against itself?" In other words, can the majority — that is, in the panel's view, the combination of women and minorities — enact a law that disadvantages them in the political process and then cry foul?

Perhaps, given the panel's assumptions, the answer to its question should be "no," but it is not clear why the question is relevant. Nothing in *Hunter* or *Seattle* indicates that the make-up of the electorate was critical to the decisions.[3]

---

3. Admittedly, as the Ninth Circuit panel noted, *Hunter* had declared, "The majority needs no protection against discrimination. . . ." This statement, however, was made in the context of explaining that the anti-fair-housing referendum requirement, despite its

Moreover, in other cases, some of which the Ninth Circuit panel cited with approval, the court had invalidated or subjected to heightened scrutiny preference programs without mentioning the make-up of the promulgating body.[4]

In any event, *minorities* did not make up a majority of the California electorate; a majority of the women voting on Proposition 209 voted *against* the initiative; and as the Ninth Circuit panel acknowledged, "Proposition 209 burdens members of insular minorities within the majority that enacted it." As Judge William Norris correctly observed in his dissent from the denial of a rehearing *en banc*:

> [T]he panel would have us believe that *Hunter* and *Seattle* are inapposite because Proposition 209 burdens *majority*, not minority interests. In putting forward this remarkable argument, the panel seizes upon a statement in *Hunter* that "[t]he majority needs no protection against discrimination." It then puts its own spin on the word "majority" by turning women and racial minorities into one undifferentiated "group." In other words, the panel transforms racial minorities into a numerical majority by lumping them together with women. Presto! Proposition 209 burdens the interests of the majority, not the minority. To borrow the panel's (uncited) paraphrase of Justice Scalia, "if merely stating this alleged 'equal protection' [argument] does not suffice to refute it, our constitutional jurisprudence" has gone very far astray.

The panel itself must have been troubled by both the scope and the relevance of its question, for after raising the issue the court chose to ignore it with respect to minorities. With respect to women, the court said, it would have decided that Proposition 209 did not violate the equal protection rights of women if only Judge Henderson had made a finding that women constituted a majority of the electorate. Judge Henderson, of course, had no reason to make such a finding. The information, however, was readily available and not subject to dispute. The panel, had it been serious about the issue, could have taken judicial notice of the fact that women comprised a majority of the electorate.

---

facial neutrality, disadvantaged minorities. It was not a limitation on the holding, and *Seattle* makes no reference at all to the make-up of the electorate.

4. In City of Richmond v. J.A. Croson Co., the Court subjected to strict scrutiny and found a preference program unconstitutional for minority contractors. In explaining why a program benefitting minorities should be subject to strict scrutiny, the Court noted that five of the nine members of the city council adopting the program were black. It is clear from other parts of the opinion, however, that this fact was not critical to the decision.

The Effort to Distinguish *Hunter* and *Seattle*

Just as the panel had accurately stated the core of "conventional" equal protection doctrine, it accurately set forth the holdings of *Hunter* and *Seattle*. The panel, however, found that *Hunter* and *Seattle* were distinguishable for two reasons. First, Proposition 209 "does not isolate race and gender antidiscrimination laws from any specific area over which the state has delegated authority to a local entity." Second, in contrast to *Seattle*, which disadvantaged minorities at only one level of government (local school districts), Proposition 209 does not "treat race and gender antidiscrimination laws in one area differently from race and gender antidiscrimination laws in another. Rather, it prohibits all race and gender preferences by state entities."

If "antidiscrimination laws" in the first explanation includes preferences prohibited by Proposition 209, the explanation is simply untrue. As Judge Henderson's opinions demonstrate, Proposition 209 does "isolate" race and gender preferences — and only race and gender preferences — in areas where local entities otherwise have substantial authority with respect to preferences. If "antidiscrimination laws" does not include such prohibited preferences, the explanation is irrelevant, for the only constitutional issue before the court was whether Proposition 209 can legally prohibit those preferences.

The second explanation is also irrelevant. Even if gender and race preferences are treated equally at all levels of government, the fact remains that they are treated differently from other preferences, thereby restructuring the political process to the detriment of women and minorities. As Judge Norris wrote in his dissent from the denial of a rehearing, "Neither *Hunter* nor *Seattle* — nor common sense, for that matter — supports the proposition that *expanding* the levels at which the State disadvantages minorities will render that action any less constitutionally suspect."

The *"Au Contraire!"* Argument

Following its effort to distinguish *Hunter* and *Seattle*, the panel observed:

When people enact a law that says race somehow matters, they must come forward with a compelling state interest to back it up. Plaintiffs would have us also require the people to come forward with a compelling state interest to justify a state law that says that race cannot matter in public contracting, employment, or education. Plaintiffs' counsel went even one step further at oral argument. He urged that "the people of the State of California are not entitled to make a judgment as to whether compelling state interests have been vindicated. That is for the courts." *Au Contraire!* That most certainly *is* for the people of California to decide, *not* the courts. Our authority in this area is limited to deciding whether the interests proferred by the people are sufficient to justify a law that classifies among individuals. If Federal courts were to decide what interests of the people are in the first place, judicial power would trump self-government as the general rule of our constitutional democracy.

Despite the court's *"au contraire!,"* plaintiffs' counsel had it exactly right, as — ironically — the court acknowledged in the first sentence of this quotation. Whenever a law implicates race, the Constitution requires that courts subject the law to strict scrutiny, and the law can pass constitutional muster only if the *courts* conclude that it vindicates compelling state interests. There may, of course, be a question about whether a particular law implicates race or gender and, therefore, requires strict or heightened scrutiny. The Ninth Circuit panel obviously believed Proposition 209 was not such a law, but nothing that it said here — or elsewhere in its opinion — satisfactorily explains why. Somehow the inequality in access to the political process created by Proposition 209 and documented by Judge Henderson eluded the panel, notwithstanding its purported acceptance of all of Judge Henderson's findings.

But Elderly Women and Disabled Minorities Can Seek Preferences

After asserting — without citation to any authority — that "[i]mpediments to preferential treatment do not deny equal protection," the panel elaborated on its declaration in a footnote:

> Proposition 209 only prohibits preferential treatment based on race or gender. "Those seeking preferences based on any ground other than race or gender, such as age, disability, or veteran status," who "continue to enjoy access to the political process at all levels of government," include, we must remember, everyone — members of all races and both genders. If the state ever prohibited women and minorities from seeking preferences on a basis available to everyone else, such as age, disability, or veteran status, the state would violate Proposition 209's prohibition against race or gender discrimination.

The panel's statement is accurate, but it is irrelevant to the question before the court. The fact that some types of discrimination are unconstitutional does not mean that other forms are not. For example, if it is unconstitutional to preclude black women with disabilities from seeking preferential admissions treatment from universities, or if it is unconstitutional to prohibit black women with disabilities from living in public housing, it does not follow that it is constitutional to preclude all black women or all women from seeking preferential admissions policies or access to public housing.

The Supposed Inapplicability of *Hunter* and *Seattle* to Protect Affirmative Action Interests

The Ninth Circuit panel maintained that somehow *Hunter* and *Seattle* should not be interpreted to condone preference programs, because preference programs, in the panel's view, are themselves discriminatory:

> When the government prefers individuals on account of their race or gender, it correspondingly disadvantages individuals who fortuitously belong to another race or to another gender. . . .
> . . . We have recognized . . . that "'stacked deck' programs [such as race-based 'affirmative action'] trench on Fourteenth Amendment values in ways that 'reshuffle' programs [such as school desegregation] do not." Unlike racial preference programs, school desegregation programs are not inherently invidious, do not work wholly to the benefit of members of one group and correspondingly to the harm of certain members of another group, and do not deprive citizens of rights. . . .
> . . . It is one thing to say that individuals have equal protection rights against political obstructions to equal treatment; it is quite another to say that individuals have equal protection rights against political obstructions to preferential treatment. While the Constitution protects against obstructions to equal treatment, it erects obstructions to preferential treatment.

The difficulty with this line of reasoning is twofold: First, the panel's analysis ignores here, as it does elsewhere, the gender and racial discrimination in access to the political process created by Proposition 209: Race and gender preferential programs can and do pass constitutional muster under the Equal Protection Clause; but unlike all other preference programs, their adoption at any level of government in California will require a state constitutional amendment. Second, the only constitutional "obstruction" placed on preferential treatment programs based on race or gender is that they, like other race and gender classifications, be subjected close scrutiny under the Equal Protection Clause — a reality that the panel acknowledged in an otherwise mystifying portion of its opinion:

> To hold that a democratically enacted affirmative action program is constitutionally permissible because the people have demonstrated a compelling

state interest is hardly to hold that the program is constitutionally required. The Fourteenth Amendment, lest we lose sight of the forest for the trees, does not require what it barely permits.

Nobody, of course, was claiming that any affirmative action program was constitutionally required. As Judge Norris noted in his dissent:

> [T]he district court did not hold that any particular legislation, including race-based preference programs, was required. . . . All that is constitutionally required is that minorities have opportunity, on equal terms, to seek "legislation in [their] behalf" within existing channels of government.

Judge Henderson was careful to point out that the issue posed by Proposition 209 was not the desirability of preference programs but "whether the particular *method* chosen by Proposition 209 to curtail affirmative action is unlawful." The Ninth Circuit panel, by ignoring Proposition 209's discrimination and expressing its disdain for even constitutionally permissible affirmative action programs, substituted personal preference for constitution principle. As Judge Norris wrote:

> The panel justifies its result by drawing a distinction between affirmative action programs and antidiscrimination laws. . . . It rationalizes this by characterizing all affirmative action programs as inherently discriminatory — even those that pass constitutional muster. . . . The Equal Protection Clause is aimed at securing equality, the panel complains, and so affirmative action programs are not worthy of protection under the *Hunter-Seattle* doctrine because — in the panel's opinion — they do not secure "equal treatment.". . .
>
> In resting its decision on the view that affirmative action programs do not secure "equality," the panel injects into the *Hunter-Seattle* analysis a test that looks to the personal views of individual judges about the relative merits of affirmative action programs and antidiscrimination laws. There is absolutely no reason to believe that the Supreme Court intended any such result. . . . Nowhere has the Court suggested that the *Hunter-Seattle* doctrine permits judges to rely upon their own subjective impressions as to whether a particular measure aimed at benefitting minorities is also an effective means of securing equality, or whether the social costs associated with that measure are worth the potential benefits. . . .
>
> The panel's distinction . . . has the effect of transforming constitutional analysis into an arena for political debate over the "desirability and efficacy" of affirmative action. . . .
>
> The question of the constitutionality of Proposition 209 has nothing to do with the wisdom of affirmative action programs. The *Hunter–Seattle* doctrine does not call for judges to determine whether constitutionally

permissible, beneficial programs are also wise and just means of securing equality.

Judicial Activism Run Amok

So, we have (1) the ignoring of factual findings that the panel purported to accept, (2) broad, unsupported assertions of supposed constitutional principles, (3) non-sequiturs, (4) irrelevancies, and (5) ultimately a decision divorced from precedent and based almost entirely on the judges' personal beliefs. It is hard to imagine an opinion more sloppy and less true to the ideals of judicial restraint that conservatives regularly praise. Indeed, regardless of what one thinks of judicial restraint, it is hard to imagine an opinion that goes further in ignoring both facts and existing legal precedent.

Endnotes

Throughout the book (1) statements about Judge Henderson, his court, and his parents, and (2) quotations or views attributed to him or his mother, Wanzie, or others speaking to him, for which there is no specific citation, are based on the author's extensive personal interviews and telephone conversations with the judge.

Some of that same information also exists in the following sources:

Thelton Henderson, "The Honorable Thelton E. Henderson: Making a Difference, the Federal Judiciary and Civil Rights in the United States, 1933–2002," an interview conducted by Leah McGarrigle in 2001 and 2002, Regional Oral History Office, The Bancroft Library, University of California, Berkeley, 2005 [**hereinafter Oral History**].

Abby Ginzberg's documentary film, "Soul of Justice: Thelton Henderson's American Journey" (2005) [**hereinafter Soul of Justice**].

Transcript (in the author's possession) of an August 24, 1968 interview that Judge Henderson gave in Berkeley, California to Larry Sager [**hereinafter 1968 Interview**]. (In quotations from the 1968 Interview, spelling and punctuation have been corrected without indication.)

Because the first two of these sources are readily available and because the third source is much closer in time to the actual events, I have tended to rely on them rather than my interviews and conversations for specific quotations.

Information in Chapter Six about the East Palo Alto Legal Service Program and Stanford Law School for which there is no citation is based on the author's personal knowledge.

Portions of *Stanford Law School* and *"Dean Henderson is Here Now"* (Chapter Six), the introduction and *"I Made Every Mistake I Could Possibly Make"* (Chapter Seven), and *Strategies and Techniques for Institutional Reform* (Chapter Thirteen) previously appeared in slightly different form in Richard Kuhns, Three Stories and a Brief Comment about Institutional Reform Litigation, 13 Berkeley J. Afr.-Am. L. & Pol'y 218 (2011).

Unless otherwise noted, sources for newspaper articles and web-based news stories have been one or more of the following: (1) Westlaw, (2) Lexis/Nexis, or (3) the news outlet's web page. Specific web citations are omitted for the sake of brevity.

In quoted material throughout the text, internal citations and footnotes have been deleted without indication. Footnote numbers that remain in quoted material have been changed so that the footnote numbering in each chapter is consecutive.

Chapter One
Introducing Thelton Henderson

"Fn. 1.": For a brief outline of the history of South Central, *see* Public Broadcasting System, Timeline: South Central Los Angeles, Crips and Bloods: Made in America, available at http://www.pbs.org/independentlens/cripsandbloods/timeline.html (last visited December 1, 2014).

"Fn. 1. . . . (officially South Los Angeles since 1993)": *See* Calvin Sims, In Los Angeles, It's South-Central No More, N.Y. Times, April 10, 2003.

On Judge Henderson's South Africa trip, *see* Oral History at 233–51.

"The San Francisco program. . . .": The description of the San Francisco program is based on my conversations with Judge Henderson and my observations while accompanying him to drug court.

"Fn. 2. . . . popularity throughout the country.": *See* Peggy Fulton Hora & Theodore Stalcup, Drug Treatment Courts in the Twenty-First Century: The Evolution of the Revolution in Problem-Solving Courts, 42 Ga. L. Rev. 717 (2008); William H. Simon, Community Courts and Community Justice: Commentary: Criminal Defendants and Community Justice: The Drug Court Example, 40 Am. Crim. L. Rev. 1595 (2003).

"Fn. 2. . . . However . . . protect defendants' rights. . . .": *See* Mae C. Quinn, Whose Team Am I on Anyway? Musings of a Public Defender about Drug Treatment Court Practice, 26 N.Y.U. Rev. L. & Soc. Change 37 (2000).

"Fn. 2. . . . Indeed, there is a growing literature. . . .": *See, e.g.,* Morris B. Hoffman, Problem-Solving Courts and the Psycholegal Error, 160 U. Pa. L. Rev. PENNumber 129, available at http://www.pennumbra.com/essays/122011/Hoffman.pdf; Mae C. Quinn, The Modern Problem-Solving Court Movement: Domination of Discourse and Untold Stories of Criminal Justice Reform, 31 Wash. U. J.L. & Pol'y 57 (2009).

On the drug court recidivism rates, *see* National Institute of Justice, Do Drug Courts Work? Findings from Drug Court Research, available at http://www.nij.gov/topics/courts/drug-courts/work.htm (last visited June 7, 2102).

"The last hearing was a young kid. . . .": Oral History at 323–24.

"a man who has made a difference": Leah McGarigle, who conducted the interviews for Judge Henderson's Oral History, aptly used the phrase "Making a Difference" in the book's title. *See* Oral History.

Chapter Two
Judge Henderson and the Art of Judging
The Nature of Judging: Politics or Principle — or Both?

"A conception . . . popular in the nineteenth century. . . .": *See* Douglas Lind, Logic, Intuition, and the Positivist Legacy of H.L.A. Hart, 52 S.M.U. L. Rev. 135, 135–38 (1999).

"still given voice today. . . .": *See* Erwin Chemerinsky, Symposium: The Role of the Judge in the Twenty-First Century: Seeing the Emperor's Clothes: Recognizing the Reality of Constitutional Decision Making, 86 B.U. L. Rev. 1069, 1069 (2006). [hereinafter Seeing the Emperor's Clothes]

"'Judges are like umpires. . . .'": Confirmation Hearing on the Nomination of John G. Roberts, Jr. to be Chief Justice of the United States, Hearing before the S. Comm. on the Judiciary, 109th Cong. 55 (2005) [**hereinafter Roberts Confirmation Hearing**].

For a critique of Roberts' baseball analogy, *see* Seeing the Emperor's Clothes at 1069–70.

"Fn. 2. . . . '[t]he task of a judge. . . .'": Confirmation Hearing on the Nomination of Hon. Sonia Sotomayor to be an Associate Justice of the Supreme Court of the United States, Hearing before the S. Comm. on the Judiciary, 111th Cong. 59 (2009); *see also, e.g., id.* at 64, 70, 79.

On the legal realists' movement, *see, e.g.*, William Twining, Karl Llewellyn and the Realist Movement (1933); Douglas Lind, Logic, Intuition, and the Positivist Legacy of H.L.A. Hart, 52 S.M.U. L. Rev. 135, 135–38, 148–48 (1999).

On acknowledgments prior to the legal realist movement that judges make law, *see* Brian Z. Tamanaha, The Realism of Judges Past: A Challenge to the Assumptions and Orientation of the "Judicial Politics" Field, 56 Clev. St. L. Rev. 77 (2008); Brian Z. Tamanaha, Understanding Legal Realism (April, 2008). St. John's Legal Research Paper No. 08-0133, available at SSRN: http://ssrn.com/abstract=1127178 (last visited May 1, 2008); *but cf.* Brian Leiter, Tamanaha on "the Bogus Tale about Legal Formalists" (April 30, 2008), available at Brian Leiter's Legal Philosophy Blog: http://leiterlegalphilosophy.typepad.com/leiter/2008/04/tamanaha-on-the.html (last visited May 1, 2008) (questioning Tamanaha's thesis about formalism).

On the studies demonstrating a relationship between politics and ideology, on the one hand, and judicial selection or judging, on the other, *see, e.g.*, Lee Epstein et al., The Increasing Importance of Ideology in the Nomination and Confirmation of Supreme Court Justices, 56 Drake L. Rev. 609 (2008); Lee Epstein & Jeffrey A. Segal, Advice and Consent, The Politics of Judicial Appointments (2005) [**hereinafter Advise and Consent**]; Jeffrey A. Segal & Harold J. Spaeth, The Supreme Court and the Attitudinal Model (1993). For a particularly interesting study in which a mathematical model with an ideological focus outperformed legal experts in predicting the results in Supreme Court cases, *see* Theodore W. Ruger et al., Essay: The Supreme Court Forecasting Project: Legal and Political Science Approaches to Predicting Supreme Court Decisionmaking, 104 Colum. L. Rev. 1050 (2004).

"'[I]t's my job to call balls and strikes'": Roberts Confirmation Hearing at 56.

"The strike zone that matters. . . .": David James Duncan, The Brothers K 126 (1992).

"Supreme Justice Antonin Scalia has repeatedly stated. . . .": *See, e.g.*, Seeing the Emperor's Clothes at 1070; 60-Minute Interview with Justice Scalia, available at http://www.cbsnews.com/stories/2008/04/24/60minutes/main4040290.shtml (last visited April 24, 2008).

"'rolled her eyes and said. . . .'": Seeing the Emperor's Clothes at 1070.

"[T]he statements are indeed nonsense. . . .": *Id.*

"Is he simply afraid to be candid. . . .?": Justice Scalia's lack of candor (and/or self-delusion) is on full display in his book Reading Law: The Interpretation of Legal Texts (2012) co-authored with Bryan Garner. *See* Richard A. Posner, Reflections on Judging 179–219 (2013).

"a speech to Berkeley law students. . . .": *See* Sonia Sotomayor, Raising the Bar: Latino and Latina Presence in the Judiciary and the Struggle for Representation: Judge Mario G. Olmos Memorial Lecture, 13 La Raza L.J. 87, 91–92 (2002) [**hereinafter Raising the Bar**].

"Gingrich labeled Sotomayor a racist": *See* Gingrich Calls Sotomayor a Racist, United Press Int'l, May 27, 2009.

"Andrew McCarthy in the National Review maintained, 'Judge Sotomayor. . . .'": *See* Andrew C. McCarthy, Rule of Law or Rule of Lawyers? National Review, May 27, 2009.

"While recognizing the potential effect. . . .": Raising the Bar at 91–92.

On the voting records of Democratic and Republican appointees to the Supreme Court, *see* Advise and Consent at 121–29.

"judging is not all about politics": *See* Pauline T. Kim, Lower Court Discretion, 82 N.Y.U. L. Rev. 383, 386 (2007) ("[W]hile many empirical studies have shown that political preferences influence lower court decision making, they also suggest that the effect of ideology is modest.").

On constraints that may inhibit judges from voting consistently with their ideologies, *see id.* at 406–08.

The Exercise of Discretion in Determining and Applying the Law

On the reality and importance of discretion in judicial decision making, *see generally id.*

Judge Henderson and the Exercise of Discretion

"'acknowledged that his sympathies. . . .'": Jack Bass, Unlikely Heroes 115 (1981).

"[My sympathies weren't what] made me. . . .": *Id.* at 115–16 (reporting 1979 interview with Judge Skelly Wright).

"Such candor about deciding cases. . . .": *Id.* at 116 (emphasis added).

On the sentencing reform movement, *see, e.g.*, Kate Stith & Steve Y. Koh, The Politics of Sentencing Reform: The Legislative History of the Federal Sentencing Guidelines, 28 Wake Forest L. Rev. 223 (1993); Michael M. O'Hear, Legal and Sociological Consequences of the Federal Sentencing Guidelines: National Uniformity/Local Uniformity: Reconsidering the Use of Departures to Reduce Federal-State Sentencing Disparities, 87 Iowa L. Rev. 721 (2002).

On the Federal Sentencing Guidelines, *see* An Overview of the United States Sentencing Commission, available at http://www.ussc.gov/general/USSCoverview.pdf (last visited April 27, 2008).

"Fn. 5. . . . United States v. Booker": 543 U.S. 220 (2005).

On Judge Henderson's willing to be harsh in sentencing, *see* Dean Calbreath, Judge Notes Lawyer Bashing in Sentencing Errant Attorney, Daily Journal, June 7, 1988, page 1 (sentencing of attorney who misappropriated $200,000); The State, Los Angeles Times, May 14, 1986, page 2 (sentencing of reputed leader of drug gang) (Judge Henderson is erroneously identified as "Thomas" Henderson).

"criminal defense lawyers. . . .": Interview with Judge Henderson, September 4, 2011.

The Agony of Discretion: Judge Henderson's Epiphany

"[A] typical argument would be. . . .": Recorded statements presented by LaDoris Cordell at Boalt Hall symposium honoring Judge Henderson's thirty years on the bench, Friday, April 16, 2010 (video of proceedings provided to author by Thelton E. Henderson Center for Social Justice, University of California at Berkeley School of Law).

"Criminal sentencing day. . . .": Memorandum from Jonathan Rowe to author, September 17, 2011.

"Fn. 6.": On the history of Watts and South Central Los Angeles, *see* South Central History, available at www.southcentralhistory.com (last visited September 25, 2014).

"I have taken my name. . . .": Jack B. Weinstein, No More Drug Cases, N.Y. L.J., April 15, 1993, at 2, quoted in Martha Minnow, Judge for the Situation: Judge Jack Weinstein, Creator of Temporary Administrative Agencies, 97 Colum. L. Rev. 2010, 2032 (1997).

Procedural and Remedial Discretion

"Kraszewski v. State Farm General Ins. Co.": 38 Fair. Empl. Prac. Cas. 197, 1985 W.L. 1616 (N.D. Cal.)

"Trial judges also have substantial discretion. . . .": *See* Pauline T. Kim, Lower Court Discretion, 82 N.Y.U. L. Rev. 383, 417–19, 435–36 (2007) (discussing procedural discretion and citing other examples).

Fact-Finding

"Madrid v. Gomez": 889 F. Supp. 1146 (N.D. Cal. 1995).

"Spain v. Rushen": Spain v. Rushen, unpublished 1986 opinion. *See* Spain v. Rushen, 883 F.2d 712, 715 (9th Cir. 1989).

"The detailed findings. . . .": *See id.*

"Crawford v. Marion County Election Bd.": 553 U.S. 181 (2008).

"Justice Souter . . . detailed the burdens. . . .": *See id.* at 211–23 (Souter, J., dissenting).

"'Supposition based on extensive internet research. . . .'": *Id.* at 202 n.20 (opinion of Stevens, J.)

"[O]ur task. . . .": Indiana Democratic Party v. Rokita, 458 F. Supp. 2d 775, 784 n.6 (S.D. Ind. 2006).

"[T]here is something remarkable. . . .": Crawford v. Marion County Election Bd. 472 F.3d 949, 951–52 (7th Cir. 2007).

The Malleability of "Facts": Discretion in Fact-Finding

On the O.J. Simpson verdict, *see, e.g.*, Deborah Hellman, The Expressive Dimension of Equal Protection, 85 Minn. L. Rev. 1, 19–22 (2000); Christo Lassiter, The O.J. Simpson Verdict: A Lesson in Black and White, 1 Mich. J. Race & L. 69 (1996); Glenn Harlan Reynolds, Book Review: Of Dissent and Discretion, 9 Corn. J. L. & Pub. Pol'y 685, 694 n.40 (2000).

On the acquittals in the Rodney King beating case, *see, e.g.*, James Joseph Duane, What Message Are We Sending to Criminal Jurors When We Ask Them to "Send a Message" with Their Verdict, 22 Am. J. Crim. L. 565, 592–94 nn.83–87 (1995); Nancy S. Marder, The Interplay of Race and False Claims of Jury Nullification, 32 U. Mich. J. L. Ref. 285, 294–301 (1999); Paul H. Robinson et al., Making Criminal Codes Functional: A Code of Conduct and a Code of Adjudication, 86 J. Crim. L. & Criminology 304, 328 (1996); Richard K. Sherwin, A Manifesto for Visual Legal Realism, 40 Loy. L.A. L. Rev. 719, 734–36 (2007).

On Clarence Thomas and Anita Hill, *see* Jane Mayer & Jill Abramson, Strange Justice: The Selling of Clarence Thomas (1994); Mark V. Tushnet, Book Review: Clarence Thomas: The Constitutional Problems, 63 Geo. Wash. L. Rev. 466 (1995).

"When I was a very new judge. . . .": Judge Henderson recounts this incident in Oral History at 134. The version in the text is from a March 29, 2008 interview with Judge Henderson.

The Art of Great Judging

"it also requires empathy": There is a growing legal literature on empathy and judging. *See, e.g.*, Rebecca K. Lee, Judging Judges: Empathy as the Litmus Test for Impartiality, 82 U. Cinn. L. Rev. 145 (2013); Thomas B. Colby, In Defense of Judicial Empathy, 96 Minn. L. Rev. 1944 (2012) [hereinafter **Judicial Empathy**]; Kathryn Abrams, Empathy and Experience in the Sotomayor Hearings, 36 Ohio N.U. L. Rev. 263 (2010); Susan A. Bandes, Empathetic Judging and the Rule of Law, 2009 Cardozo L. Rev. de novo 133 [hereinafter **Empathetic Judging**].

"the ability not to discriminate. . . .": Remarks of Judge Myron Thompson at Boalt Hall symposium honoring Judge Henderson's thirty years on the bench, Friday, April 16, 2010 (video of proceedings provided to author by Thelton E. Henderson Center for Social Justice, University of California at Berkeley School of Law). [hereinafter **Remarks of Judge Myron Thompson**]

"I am reminded each day. . . .": Raising the Bar at 93.

" 'three elements of a just decision' ": Jack B. Weinstein, The Role of Judges in a Government of, by, and for the People: Notes for the Fifty-Eighth Cardozo Lecture, 30 Cardozo L. Rev. 1, 21 (2008).

"Some judges and lawyers. . . .": *Id.* at 26–28.

Empathy, Compassion, and the Rule of Law

"Psychologists and other scholars debate. . . .": *See, e.g.,* Forum, against Empathy, Boston Review, August 28, 2014 (commentary by Paul Bloom with responses from Nomy Arpaly, Simon Baron-Cohen, Jack W. Berry & Lynn E. O'Connor, Elizabeth Stoker Bruenig, Leanardo Christov-Moore & Marco Iacoboni, Barbara H. Fried, Sam Harris, Leslie Jamison, Marianne La France, Christine Montross, Jesse Prinz, and Peter Singer). *See also* Simon Baron-Cohen, The Science of Evil: On Empathy and the Origins of Cruelty (2011).

"empathy is not, or at least should not be, a one-way street. . . .": *See* Judicial Empathy at 1961–64.

The Unwarranted Attack on Empathy

"undeserved bad press. . . .": *See, e.g.,* Charles Krauthammer, Sotomayor: Rebut, Then Confirm, The Washington Post, May 29, 2009, page A17; Karl Rove, "Empathy" Is Code for Judicial Activism, Wall Street Journal Abstracts, May 28, 2009, sec. A, page 13. *See generally* George Lakoff, Empathy, Sotomayor, and Democracy: The Conservative Stealth Strategy, The Huffington Post, May 30, 2009 (quoting and discussing some of the conservative critics).

"and even academics": *See, e.g.,* Lino A. Graglia, Birthright Citizenship for Children of Illegal Aliens: An Irrational Public Policy, 14 Tex. R. L. & Pol. 1, 11 (2009); Stephen G. Calabrese, Obama's "Redistribution" Constitution: The Courts Are Poised for a Takeover by the Judicial Left, Wall Street Journal, October 28, 2008 [hereinafter **"Redistribution" Constitution**].

"These attacks on empathy did not surface. . . .": *See* Empathetic Judging at 137–38 (quoting Justice Alito and, on behalf of Justice Thomas, Senator John Danforth and Judge Guido Calabrisi).

"they appeared to begin. . . .": *See, e.g.,* Ed Whelan, Obama's Empathy Standard, Nat. Rev. Online, May 12, 2009; "Redistribution Constitution."

"We need somebody who's got the heart. . . .": *See* Carrie Dann, Obama on Judges, Supreme Court, First Read on msnbc.com, July 17, 2007 (quoting Barack Obama).

"the 'empathy' nominee": The "Empathy" Nominee, Wall Street Journal, May 27, 2009.

"In making Sonia Sotomayor. . . .": *Id.*

"to approach decisions without any particular ideology. . . .": Remarks of President Barack Obama, The Nomination of Judge Sonia Sotomayor to be an Associate Justice on the Supreme Court, Federal News Service, May 26, 2009 [**hereinafter Remarks of President Barack Obama**].

" 'because [empathy] is invisible. . . .' ": Jack B. Weinstein, The Role of Judges in a Government of, by, and for the People: Notes for the Fifty-Eighth Cardozo Lecture, 30 Cardozo L. Rev. 1, 28 (2008).

"he invoked . . . Holmes' . . .": *See* Remarks of Barak Obama (citing Oliver Wendell Holmes, The Common Law 1 (1881)).

"It is something to show. . . .": Oliver Wendell Holmes, The Common Law 1 (1881).

"[It is] experience being tested. . . .": Remarks of President Barack Obama.

Judge Henderson's Empathy and the Limits of Discretion

"As Judge Thompson explained. . . .": *See* Remarks of Judge Myron Thompson.

"a hearing impaired U.P.S. driver": *See Looking Out for the Unrepresented* in Chapter Nine.

" 'self-effacing [and] humble. . . .' ": Interview with Judge Martin Jenkins, April 3, 2008.

"recent, renewed criticism of the SHU": *See, e.g.,* James Ridgeway & Jean Cansella, America's Ten Worst Prisions: Pelican Bay: Where a Christmas Card Might Land You in the Hole, Mother Jones, May 8, 2013; Scott Detrow, A Look Inside Pelican Bay Prison's Notorious Isolation Unit, KQED News, October 4, 2013, available at http://ww2.kqed.org/news/2013/10/03/pelican-bay-security-housing-unit-shu (last visited November 12, 2014).

Chapter Three The Early Years

Wanzie

On the education of blacks in the South, *see* James D. Anderson, The Education of Blacks in the South, 1860–1935, 110–11, 148–52 (1988).

Reading

"[Jefferson High School] was the hippest school. . . .": Oral History at 17.

Speedball

" 'terrific breakaway artist[]' ": John de la Vega, Spectacular Show, Los Angeles Times, November 23, 1950, page 39 (using the phrase to describe Thelton and his teammate and fellow half-back, Jerry Drew).

"a member of the All-League. . . .": *See* John de la Vega, Fremont, Canoga Dominate All-League Prep Choices, Los Angeles Times, December 20, 1950, page C3.

"It was exciting to be on a good football team. . . .": Oral History at 17–18.

Chapter Four
College, the Army, and Law School
Undergraduate Days

"Fn. 1. The University housing office. . . .": *See* Oral History at 41.

"'determined to succeed'": *Id.* at 27.

"I remember to this day. . . .": *Id.*

"all of a sudden. . . .": *Id.* (emphasis in original).

"[T]here's room in football. . . .": *Id.* at 34–35.

"somewhat 'alienating'": *Id.* at 36.

"I remember — this was my second season. . . .": *Id.*

The "Dozens Cousins"

On Thelton's meeting Russ and Troy, *see* Oral History at 48–49.

Boalt Hall (1959–1962)

On Rosa Parks and the Montgomery bus boycott, *see* Taylor Branch, Parting the Waters: America in the King Years 1954–63 at 124–36, 143–207 (1988).

On the CORE freedom rides, *see id.* at 412–58.

On the CORE picketing in Berkeley, *see* University of California, Berkeley, Media Resource Center, available at http://www.lib.berkeley.edu/MRC/pacificaviet/html#1960 (last visited June 19, 2007).

"'Thelton wasn't going to jump up. . . .'": Henry Ramsey in Soul of Justice.

The decision affirming James Meredith's right to attend the University of Mississippi was an order by Justice Black, who reported that all of the other justices concurred in his judgment. Meredith v. Fair, 83 S.Ct. 10 (1962).

Chapter Five
The Justice Department

On the Justice Department's voter registration activity, *see* Taylor Branch, Parting the Waters: America in the King Years 1954–63 at 332–34, 409–11 (1988) [**hereinafter Parting the Waters**].

On James Meredith's efforts to enroll at the University of Mississippi, *see* Parting the Waters at 647–72.

On President Kennedy's political base, *see* Parting the Waters at 414. *See also* Taylor Branch's commentary in Soul of Justice; Howard Zinn, Kennedy: The Reluctant Emancipator, The Nation, December 1, 1962 reproduced in Reporting Civil Rights, Part I: American Journalism 1941–1963, 702 (2003).

On President Kennedy's inaugural address, *see* Parting the Waters at 383–84.

"To protect the racial sensibilities. . . .": *Id.* at 671 (emphasis in original).

On not rocking the boat, *see, e.g., id.* at 399–400, 472–73, 477–79; Richard Kluger, Simple Justice 756 (2004).

On only observers, *see* John Doar's description in Soul of Justice.

"For example, at an October 7, 1963. . . .": Telephone interview with Richard Wasserstrom, January 14, 2008.

On the beating, trial, and conviction of the SNCC workers, *see* Taylor Branch, Pillar of Fire: America in the King Years 1963–65 at 151–52 (1998) [**hereinafter Pillar of Fire**].

"'I found myself too often in the role of a note taker. . . .'": 1968 Interview at 3.

"I was naive. . . .": *Id.* at 3–5.

"Even the picture taking. . . .": On the FBI filming in Selma on October 7, 1963, *see* 1968 Interview at 5–6.

"'neglect of logical . . . despair'": Parting the Waters at 520. *See id.* at 520–21 (FBI report, after multiple requests by John Doar, on the murder of Herbert Lee), 508–09 (FBI report on the beating of Bob Moses).

"Richard Wasserstrom maintained. . . . 'obstructive force.'": Telephone interview with Richard Wasserstrom, January 14, 2008.

"In 1964. . . .": Peter Franck, one of the editors of the New University Thought conducted the interview, which appeared in vol. 3, no. 4 at 36. Judge Henderson obtained copies of the FBI memoranda in a Freedom of Information Act request (copies of the article and the memoranda in author's possession).

Preparation

"One morning they had a staff meeting. . . .": Oral History at 71.

"I use [the Kennedy story]. . . .": *Id.*

The Evolution from Voter Registration Lawyer to Valued Resource

"'You really shouldn't tell me. . . .'": Thelton Henderson in Soul of Justice.

For an elaboration on Thelton's role as a liaison between the civil rights community and the Justice Department, *see* Oral History at 69–70.

"Looking back on it. . . .": 1968 Interview at 10.

Three Realities: Segregation, Danger, and Role Conflict

"Brown v. Board of Education": 347 U.S. 483 (1954).

"On one occasion Thelton rented. . . .": For a brief statement about the limited housing available to Thelton (including reference to the Jackson funeral home), *see* Gordon A. Martin, Jr., Count Them One by One: Black Mississippians Fighting for the Right to Vote 47–48 (2010).

"'[T]o give you an idea. . . .'": Oral History at 61.

On A.G. Gaston and his motel, *see* Diane McWhorter, Carry Me Home at 262–63 (2001).

On bombings in Birmingham, *see, e.g.*, Parting the Waters at 570–71 (three church bombings in January 2002), 683 (December 2002, bombing of church that had been bombed twice before), and 888–92 (September 2003, church bombing in which four young girls were killed).

"That same night. . . .": *See id.* at 793–95; Claude Sitton, 50 Hurt in Negro Rioting after Birmingham Blasts, N.Y. Times, May 13, 1963, available at http://partners.nytimes.com/library/national/race/051363race-ra.html (last visited July 12, 2007).

"The bombings were. . . .": *See* Martin Luther King, Jr., Why We Can't Wait 103–06 (1963) (quotations from page 105).

"in an alley immediately outside. . . .": *See* Oral History at 74–75.

"Fn. 1. The bomb was very close. . . .": *See* Martin Luther King, Jr., Why We Can't Wait at 106.

"Thelton returned. . . .": *See* Jeff Prugh, American Whitewash at 281–86, 357–61 (2011).

"[A]fter I more or less accepted. . . .": Letter from Thelton Henderson to Russ Ellis, April, 1962 (emphasis in original) (copy in author's possession).

Arrests (Segregation, Danger, and Role Conflict)

On the lunch counter sit-in and ensuing demonstrations in Jackson, Mississippi, *see* Pillar of Fire at 101–02; Anne Moody, Coming of Age in Mississippi (1968), reproduced in Reporting Civil Rights, Part I: American Journalism 1941–1963 at 857–81 (2003) [**hereinafter Coming of Age**].

On the Justice Department sending Judge Henderson and John Doar to Jackson, *see* Pillar of Fire at 101.

On the June 1 arrest of Medgar Evers and Roy Wilkins, *see* Coming of Age at 872.

On the arrest of Judge Henderson on his way to Woolworth's, *see* Oral History at 62.

On the arresting officer's trembling, *see* Coming of Age at 872.

" 'about how much danger. . . .' ": Pillar of Fire at 144 n.*.

"To the best of my knowledge. . . .": 1968 Interview at 31–32.

" 'O.K., take him off.' ": *Id.* at 32.

"[W]e drove an awfully long way. . . .": *Id.* at 33.

"Well, I was never happier. . . .": *Id.* at 33–34.

The Jackson, Mississippi Concert (Role Conflict)

On spending the evening of June 11 with Medgar Evers, *see* Oral History at 73.

On the Kennedy address and the Evers assassination, *see* Parting the Waters at 823–25.

"I Got My Hat in Forest, Mississippi" (Segregation and Danger)

Jim Thomas provided some details of this story and corroborated others. Telephone interview with Jim Thomas, January 29, 2008. The story also appears in Oral History at 67.

On the town and history of Forest, Mississippi, *see* Welcome to Forest, Mississippi available at www.forest-ms.com (last visited February 14, 2012).

"Finally, this '56 Clevy. . . .": 1968 Interview at 35–36.

"I get in the car. . . .": *Id.* at 36–37.

"The Flight to Birmingham" (Segregation and Danger)

On SNCC's voter registration efforts in Selma, *see* Howard Zinn, SNCC: The New Abolitionists 147–66 (1965); Pillar of Fire at 82–85; Encyclopedia of Alabama, Student Nonviolent Coordinating Committee in Alabama (SNCC), available at http://encyclopediaofalabama.org/face/Article.jsp?id=h-1847 (last visited January 10, 2009).

On Freedom Day in Selma, *see* Parting the Waters at 900; John Herbers, Alabama Police Rough Up 4 As Selma Negroes Seek Vote, N.Y. Times, October 8, 1963, available at http://query.nytimes.com/mem/archive/pdf?res=FB0710F7345A177B93CAA9178BD95F478685F9 (last visited September 26, 2011) [**hereinafter Selma Negroes Seek Vote**]; Transcript, Bridge to Freedom (1965), Eyes on the Prize: America's Civil Rights Movement 1954–58, available at http://www.pbs.org/wgbh/amex/eyesontheprize/about/pt_106.html (last visited July 19, 2007).

"'By the end of the day. . . .'": Selma Negroes Seek Vote.
On the Baldwins' red Ford, *see* Oral History at 79.
"'I have to stop for something.'": 1968 Interview at 7.
On "The Flight to Birmingham," *see* Oral History at 80.

Martin Luther King and the Car
(Segregation, Danger, and Role Conflict)

On the request for the car, *see* Pillar of Fire at 155–56.
On Governor Wallace's charge that Judge Henderson had driven Dr. King to Selma, *see* 1968 Interview at 25.
On the national publicity generated by the Selma demonstrations, *see, e.g.,* Selma Negroes Seek Vote
On the church bombing in which four girls were killed, *see* Parting the Waters at 888–92.
On Thelton's resignation, the reaction to it, and Burke Marshall's apology, *see* Pillar of Fire at 166.

Looking Back

"'eyes and ears . . . under constant and steady pressure. . . .'": John Doar in Soul of Justice.
"'In a time when the world. . . .'": Taylor Branch in Soul of Justice.

Chapter Six
Law Practice, Legal Services, and Academia

"'We were . . . poster children. . . .'": Interview with Troy Duster, August 24, 2011.
"'think you're there for the wrong reason.'": *Id.*

Private Practice

On Judge Henderson's practice, first with Donald Warden and then with Fitzsimmons & Petris, *see* Oral History at 97–100.
"Fn. 1. Warden later changed. . . .": *See* Hamillian Actor, Anatomy of a Smear: Who Paid for Obama's Education, The Daily Kos, September 27, 2008 (including internal citations), available at http://www.dailykos.com/story/2008/09/27/612878/-Anatomy-of-a-Smear-Who-Paid-For-Obama-s-Harvard-Education# (last visited October 6, 2014).
"Because he felt bad. . . .": *See* Oral History at 98.
"[H]e was accused of killing. . . .": *Id.* at 99.
"'could have had a . . . rather successful criminal defense practice'"; "'just a mouthpiece'"; and "'real criminals'": *Id.* at 100.
"So that affected me. . . .": *Id.*

The East Bayshore Neighborhood Legal Center

On Gideon v. Wainwright, *see* Anthony Lewis' excellent book, Gideon's Trumpet (1964).
For background on the Office of Economic Opportunity Legal Services Program and its successor, the Legal Services Corporation, *see* John Dooley & Alan V. Houseman, Legal Services History; Earl Johnson, Jr., Justice and Reform: The Formative Years of the American Legal

Services Program (1974); Alan W. Houseman, Civil Legal Assistance in the Twenty-First Century: Achieving Equal Justice for All, 17 Yale L. & Pol'y Rev. 369 (1998).

"Thelton insisted on escorting. . . .": Telephone interview with Roy Schmidt, January 9, 2008.

" 'What's happening here . . .' ": 1968 Interview at 48.

On the concern with black women relating their domestic problems to white Stanford students and a white Stanford lawyer, see 1968 Interview at 49–50.

On the relationship between East Palo Alto and Stanford, see Matt Turnbull, Helping without Hurting: The Ethical Issues in the Service Relationship between East Palo Alto and Stanford University (B.A. Honor's Thesis, 2006) 37–46, 72–73, available at haas.stanford.edu/files/Turnbull%20tHESIS.pdf (last visited February 1, 2008).

Turnbull and two community leaders, whom he quotes, are critical of the Stanford Community Law Clinic in East Palo Alto for being concerned more with its own needs rather than the needs of the community. Id. at 40–41. The Law Clinic is an outgrowth of the Stanford involvement in the East Bayshore Neighborhood Legal Center. However, to the extent that the criticism is valid, it is not applicable to at least the early years of Stanford's involvement in the Neighborhood Legal Center. Judge Henderson was in charge of the Neighborhood Legal Center, and the Stanford lawyer and the volunteer students were there to assist him. By contrast, Stanford operates the Law Clinic, and students receive academic credit for their work at the Clinic. Thus, Stanford has an independent interest in the operation of the Law Clinic.

From an academic perspective, the experience for students at the Law Clinic may be superior to the experience students received at the Neighborhood Legal Center. However, it should be possible to provide first-rate educational experience without sacrificing the interests of the East Palo Alto community. See id. at 50–51.

Stanford Law School

"That was seventy-five years. . . .": See History, Stanford Law School, available at https://law.stanford.edu/about/history (last visited August 24, 2016). An earlier version of the website, available at http://www.law.stanford.edu/school/history (last visited January 22, 2008), touted the fact that the law department graduated its first minority student, a Chinese American, in 1896. That student, however, was an undergraduate, who had only a minor in law. See https://web.archive.org/web/20080123224347/http://www.law.stanford.edu/school/history (last visited August 24, 2016).

The story of the circumstances leading to Stanford's minority admissions program is based in part on telephone interviews in January 1968 with former Assistant Dean Robert Keller and Stanford Law School graduates Leroy Bobbitt, class of 1969, Owen O'Donnell, class of 1968, and Ed Steinman, class of 1968.

On Stanford's hiring Thelton, see Oral History at 100–01.

"According to Bob Keller. . . .": Telephone interview with Robert Keller, January 25, 2008. LaDoris Cordell, whom Thelton recruited to the law school, confirmed that when she arrived in 1971, the two-year first-year program, which had been very stigmatizing to minority students, no longer existed. Telephone interview with LaDoris Cordell, February 6, 2008.

"My personal belief. . . .": E-mail from Leonade Jones, January 28, 2008.

"She describes Thelton as being 'very instrumental'. . . .": Telephone interview with Leonade Jones, January 28, 2008.

"LaDoris Cordell . . . credits Thelton. . . .": Telephone interview with LaDoris Cordell, February 6, 2008. On LaDoris initial contacts with Judge Henderson, *see* Oral History at iii.

"'one of my heroes.'": Interview with Judge James Ware, August 22, 2011.

"'Thelton provided a feeling. . . .'": *Id.*

"Dean Henderson Is Here Now"

"Thelton peered slowly. . . .": Oral History at v.

"While it is undeniably true. . . .": *Id.*

"When he arrived at Stanford. . . .": On the difficulties Thelton faced and his success with the minority admissions program, *see id.* at 109–12

"I have remained friends. . . .": *Id.* at 112–13.

Rosen, Remcho, & Henderson

"'I thought I just don't want. . . .'": *Id.* at 118.

On establishing Rosen, Remcho, & Henderson, *see id.* at 118–21.

On the form letter inquiring about Thelton's interest in a federal judgeship, *see id.* at 125.

Chapter Seven
Appointment to the Bench

"an application form, which he received in early January 1979": Letter from Mary G. Wailes, Secretary, State Bar of California, to Thelton Henderson dated January 5, 1979 (copy in author's possession).

"form letter from Sam Williams": Letter from Samuel L. Williams to Thelton Henderson dated January 12, 1979 (copy in author's possession).

"Judicial Nominating Commission": There were actually two Commissions—the United States Circuit Judge Nominating Commission for the Ninth Circuit Court of Appeals and the Federal Judicial Selection Committee for the federal District Courts in California. Sam Williams was the chairman of both committees.

"When President Carter took office. . . .": Elliot E. Slotnick, Symposium: Federal Judicial Selection in the New Millennium, 36 U.C. Davis L. Rev. 587, 592 (2003).

The Federal Judiciary and the Appointment Process

On the federal judiciary and the appointment process generally, *see* Sheldon Goldman, Picking Federal Judges: Lower Court Selection from Roosevelt through Reagan (1997) [**hereinafter Picking Federal Judges**]; David S. Law, Appointing Federal Judges: The President, the Senate, and the Prisoner's Dilemma, 26 Cardozo L. Rev. 479 (1995) [**hereinafter Prisoner's Dilemma**].

On the conflicts in the appointment process for lower court federal judges, *see* Michael J. Gerhardt, Symposium: Federal Judicial Selection in the New Millennium, Judicial Selection as War, 36 U.C. Davis L. Rev. 667 (2003)

On President George W. Bush's nominees and the "nuclear option," *see* David S. Law & Lawrence Solum, Positive Political Theory and Law: Judicial Selection, Appointments Gridlock, and the Nuclear Option, 15 J. Contemp. Legal Issues, 51, 52–53, 58–63 (2006). On the nuclear option generally, *see* Nuclear Option, available at http://en-wikipedia.org/wiki/Nuclear_option (last visited June 12, 2012).

On the Senate's eventual adoption of the nuclear option, *see* Jeremy W. Peters, In Landmark Vote Senate Limits Use of the Filibuster, N.Y. Times, November 21, 2013.

On the power of senators in the appointment process for District Court judges, *see* Prisoner's Dilemma at 487–88.

"One of the office boys. . . .": United States District Court, Northern District of California, Induction Ceremony: Honorable Thelton E. Henderson, San Francisco, California, July 30, 1980, at 23–24 (copy in author's possession).

The Selection Committee for California District Court Judges

On President Carter's nominating committee for Courts of Appeals judges, *see* Picking Federal Judges at 236–84.

Information in the text about the Federal Judicial Selection Committee in California is based on Alan Neff, Breaking with Tradition: A Study of the U.S. District Judge Nominating Commissions, 64 Judicature 257 (1981) [**hereinafter Breaking with Tradition**] and a telephone interview with Robert Gnaizda, March 14, 2008 [**hereinafter Gnaizda interview**].

"The Committee consisted of. . . .": *See* Fed. Court Panel Seeks Nominations, The Recorder, March 8, 1978.

"Initially Cranston . . . for every fourth District Court judgeship.": *See* Breaking with Tradition at 262.

"Usually, though,. . . recommendations to President Carter.": *See* Gnaizda interview.

"Hayakawa was known. . . .": *See* J.Y. Smith, Outspoken U.S. Senator S. I. Hayawaka Dies at 85, The Washington Post, February 22, 1992, page D4.

On Thelton's long relationship with Sam Williams, *see* Oral History at 123.

"I Made Every Mistake I Could Possibly Make"

On individuals seeking advice from Thelton about judgeships, *see* Oral History at 125.

"I filled out my application. . . .": *Id.* at 125–26.

"'much more politically prominent. . . .'": *Id.* at 126.

"He said, . . . 'Well I see from your resume. . . .'": *Id.*

"believed he was out of the running": *See id.*

"'clear standards and limits and a sense of moral outrage.'": Troy Duster in Soul of Justice.

On Judge Henderson's reaction to his interview with the Selection Committee and his learning that he, along with Robert Aguilar and Marilyn Patel, had been recommended to Senator Cranston by the Committee, *see* Oral History at 126.

Enlisting Support

On Senator Cranston's moving quickly to recommend Robert Aguilar to President Clinton, Thelton's efforts to enlist support for his candidacy, the opposition to Thelton from some of the black political establishment, the reopening of the selection process, and the telephone call that Judge Henderson received from LaDoris Cordell, *see id.* at 127–28. Senator Cranston recommended Robert Aguilar on May 23, 1979. *See* Nominees for New Federal Judgeships, The Recorder, May 24, 1979, page 1.

"Years later Sam Williams. . . .": *See* Oral History at 131.

"debunked the notion that Thelton was 'insufficiently devoted. . . .' ": Letter from Morris J. Baller to Senator Alan Cranston, July 16, 1979 (copy in author's possession).

"He possesses, as you must already know. . . .": Letter from Colleen Haas to Senator Alan Cranston, July 5, 1979 (copy in author's possession).

On Judge Henderson's call from LaDoris Cordell, *see* Oral History at 128.

The Last Hurdle

On Judge Henderson's call from Marilyn Patel and his call to John Doar, *see id.* at 128.

"Then [Senator Cranston] said. . . .": Oral History at 129.

Wanzie

". . . I just met with Senator Cranston. . . .": *Id.*

The Final Steps

On President Carter's nomination and the confirmation by the Senate, *see* Alice J. Porter, Washington Update; People: On the Federal Bench, 12 The National Journal (#21), May 24, 1980, page 873; letter from Judge Henderson to Duke Short, Chief Minority Investigator, U.S. Senate Judiciary Committee, June 13, 1980 (copy in author's possession); Letter from Senator Edward Kennedy to Judge Henderson, June 27, 1980 (copy in author's possession); United States Senate, Ninety-Sixth Congress, Second Session, Executive Calendar, June 26, 1980 (copy in author's possession).

"The ideal role. . . .": United States District Court, Northern District of California, Induction Ceremony: Honorable Thelton E. Henderson, San Francisco, California, July 30, 1980, at 12–13 (copy in author's possession).

" 'commensurate skills . . . .' ": *Id.* at 17.

"All of us in our office. . . .": *Id.* at 19.

"He is the outstanding demonstration. . . .": *Id.* at 21–23.

"The court to which Thelton goes. . . .": *Id.* at 24–25

Chapter Eight
Rashomon

"At a personal level. . . .": Oral History at v–vi.

On John Doar's accolades, *see* Oral History at 129.

" 'very forceful. . . .' . . . 'an incredible model. . . .' ": Telephone interview with Sam Miller, August 22, 2007.

" 'The surest sign. . . .' ": Memorandum from Jonathan Rowe to author, September 17, 2011.

"[T]he first year is almost like a train wreck. . . .": Interview with Judge Martin Jenkins, April 3, 2008.

" 'highly intelligent,' 'well versed . . . ,' . . . 'the courage. . . .' ": Telephone interview with Bob Gnaizda, March 14, 2008.

" 'He will be immune. . . .' ": *See* Maura Dolan, Prison Takeover Threat Called Real; Though Such a Move Would Be Highly Unusual, Those Who Know the Judge Who Issued the Warning Say He Means It, Los Angeles Times, July 22, 2004, part B, page 1.

" 'The governor will find. . . .' ": *See id.*

Chapter Nine
On and Off the Bench

" 'Sometimes when people go on the bench. . . .' ": Justice Anthony Kennedy in Soul of Justice.

The Beginning

"('absolutely none') . . . They have. . . .": Remarks of LaDoris Cordell (with prerecorded answers from Judge Henderson) at Boalt Hall symposium honoring Judge Henderson's thirty years on the bench, Friday, April 16, 2010 (video of proceedings provided to author by Thelton E. Henderson Center for Social Justice, University of California at Berkeley School of Law).

Latent Racism

"On another occasion. . . .": *See* Soul of Justice (Judge Henderson recounting the incident).

"A similar situation arose. . . .": Telephone interview with David Oppenheimer, August 9, 2011.

Chief Judge and Senior Status

On Judge Henderson becoming Chief Judge, *see* Pamela A. MacLean, First Black Chief Federal Judge in West, United Press International, October 2, 1990. [**hereinafter First Black Chief Federal Judge**]

" 'like herding cats' ": Oral History at 154; Rex Bossert, San Francisco Daily Journal, The Reluctant Jurist, San Francisco Daily Journal, June 22, 1994.

On Judge Henderson's reluctance to become Chief Judge and the encouragement for him to do so, *see* First Black Chief Federal Judge.

On Judge Peckham as Chief Judge and Kumi Okamoto, *see* Oral History at 153–55.

" 'comes with the job'. . . 'invaluable,' ": *Id.* at 154, 155.

"I made a dreadful mistake. . . .": *Id.* at 155.

"I felt like a captain. . . .": *Id.* at 154.

On senior status generally, *see* Frederic Block, Senior Status: An "Active" Senior Judge Corrects Some Common Misunderstandings, 92 Cornell L. Rev. 533 (2007).

Being Prepared

"Lawyers who have appeared. . . .": Various interviews. *See* Oral History at 170.

"Like any judge, Thelton worried. . . .": Memorandum from Jonathan Rowe to author, September 17, 2011.

Being Firm but Compassionate

"Judge Henderson would say to Barbara Slenkin-Slater. . . .": Telephone interview with Barbara Slenkin-Slater, November 24, 2008.

"'no middle gears'": According to the lore in Judge Henderson's chambers, Jonathan Rowe is the source of the "no middle gears" characterization. However, Rowe, while admitting that it sounds like something he might have said, has no recollection of the words for which he is most remembered. E-mail from Jonathan Rowe to author, September 19, 2011.

"'The Lawyer without a Dime'. . . . [to end of section]": Memorandum from Jonathan Rowe to author, September 17, 2011.

"'Manic Monday'": *Id.* ("As the bouncy girl-band ('The Bangles') once sang, it's another Manic Monday. . . .")

Looking Out for the Unrepresented

"'He knows when to take time . . .'": Interview with Sarah Ruby, June 2, 2011.

"After relating this story,. . . .": Remarks of Shelley Cavalieri at Boalt Hall symposium honoring Judge Henderson's thirty years on the bench, Friday, April 16, 2010 (video of proceedings provided to author by Thelton E. Henderson Center for Social Justice, University of California at Berkeley School of Law).

"'The most important thing. . . .'": Interview with Emily Galvin, August 23, 2011.

Problem Solving

"I will go to the judges' lunch room. . . .": Oral History at 170–71.

Interacting with Jurors

For an elaboration on Judge Henderson's view of juries, *see* Oral History at 263–64.

Some Notable (and One Not so Notable) Decisions

"Kraszewski v. State Farm General Ins. Co.": 38 Fair Empl. Prac. Cas. 197, 1985 W.L. 1616 (N.D. Cal.).

"Fn. 3. . . . Barefield v. Chevron U.S.A., Inc.": 1988 W.L. 188433 (N.D. Cal.).

"Fn. 3. . . . Arnold v. United Artists Theater Circuit, Inc.": 158 F.R.D. 439 (N,D. Cal. 1994). *See* Felicia H. Ellsworth, Comment: The Worst Seats in the House: Stadium-Style Movie Theaters and the Americans with Disabilities Act 1109, 1113 n. 24 (2004) ("Joint Stipulation for Amendment of Settlement Order and Granting Injunctive Relief Dated August 14, 1996, Arnold v. United Artists Theater Circuit, Inc, No C 93 0079 TEH (ND Cal filed January 17, 2001), available at http://www.usdoj.gov/crt/ada/uaamend.htm").

"Fn. 3. . . . Bates v. United Parcel Service, Inc.": 2004 W.L. 2370633 (2004).

"Fn. 3. . . . reversed in part. . . .": *See* Bates v. United Parcel Service, Inc., 511 F.3d 974 (9th Cir. 2007) (en banc).

"Fn. 3. . . . reached a settlement": *See* Bates v. United Parcel Service, Inc., 2009 W.L. 3359018.

"Fn. 3. . . . Ramirez v. Greenpoint Mortgage Funding, Inc.": 633 F. Supp. 2d 922 (N.D. Cal. 2008) (terms of settlement provided to author by Judge Henderson).

"Fn. 3. . . . Curtis-Bauer v. Morgan Stanley & Co., Inc.": 2008 W.L. 4667090 (N.D. Cal.).

"approved what was then the largest. . . .": *See* Harriet Chang, State Farm Settles Sex Bias Law Suit for $157 Million; Biggest Ever Discrimination Case Award, San Francisco Chronicle, April 29, 1992, page A1.

"over $250 million.": *See* Brad Seligman, Judge Henderson's Class Actions: Innovation to Ensure Effective Systemic Remedies, 13 Berkeley J. Afr.-Am. L. & Pol'y 257, 259 (2011).

"Alan Goldstein . . . recalled.": Remarks of Alan Goldstein at symposium honoring Judge Henderson's thirty years on the bench, Friday, April 16, 2010 (video of proceedings provided to author by Thelton E. Henderson Center for Social Justice, University of California at Berkeley School of Law).

"Golden Gate Audubon Soc. v. U.S. Army Corps of Engineers": 717 F. Supp. 1417 (N.D. Cal. 1988). *See also* Golden Gate Audubon Soc. v. U.S. Army Corps of Engineers, 796 F. Supp. 1306 (N.D. Cal. 1992).

"Citizens for a Better Environment v. Deukmejian": 731 F. Supp. 1448 (N.D. Cal. 1990); 746 F. Supp. 976 (N.D. Cal. 1990); 775 F. Supp. 1291 (N.D. Cal. 1991).

"three separate cases. . . .": *See* California Public Interest Research Group v. Shell Oil Co., 840 F. Supp. 712 (N.D. Cal. 1993); Citizens for a Better Environment — California v. Union Oil Co. of California, 861 F. Supp. 889 (N.D. Cal. 1994) (Union & Exxon).

"Allen v. City of Oakland": No. C00-4599-TEH (N.D. Cal.). *See* University of Michigan Law School, The Civil Rights Litigation Clearing House, Case Profile: Allen v. City of Oakland, available at http://www.clearinghouse.net/detail.php?id=5541 (last visited October 31, 2014); Janine DeFao, "Riders" Victims Unmollified; Huge Payout Won't Heal Wounds from Oakland Cop Scandal, San Francisco Chronicle, February 20, 2003, page A 17.

"Fn. 4. . . . Coles v. City of Oakland": 2007 W.L. 39304 (N.D. Cal.)

"McGinnis v. U.S. Postal Service": 517 F. Supp. 517 (N.D. Cal. 1980).

"Priest v. Rotary": 98 F.R.D. 755 (N.D. Cal. 1983).

"widely cited by both federal and state courts ": *See, e.g.,* EEOC v. Bryan C. Donahue, 746 F. Supp. 662, 665 (W.D. Pa. 2010); Longmire v. Alabama State Univ., 151 F.R.D. 414, 418 (M.D. Ala. 1992); Williams v. District Court, 866 P.2d 908, 915 (Colo. 1993) (concurring opinion); Westmoreland Coal Co. v. West Virginia Human Rights Comm., 181 W. Va. 368, 373, 382 S.E. 2d 562, 567 (1989).

"protections against the admission. . . .": *See* Fed. R. Evid. 412 (as amended in 1994).

"Sneede v. Kizer": 728 F. Supp. 607 (N.D. Cal. 1990). *See also* Sneede v. Kizer, 1990 W.L. 155532 (N.D. Cal.).

"Oona R.-S. v. Santa Rosa City Schools": 890 F. Supp. 1452 (N.D. Cal. 1995).

"Ashmus v. Calderon": 31 F. Supp. 2d 1175 (N.D. Cal. 1998), *aff'd.* 202 F.3d 1160 (9th Cir. 2000).

"Lassonde v. Pleasanton Unified School Dist.": 167 F. Supp. 2d 1108 (N.D. Cal. 2001).

"Barrier v. Johnson": 1996 W.L. 721838 (N.D. Cal.).

"On March 19 and April 17. . . .": *Id.* at 1.

In Chambers

"Thelton was truly GREAT. . . .": Memorandum from Jonathan Rowe to author, September 17, 2011.

"Since all judges start out. . . .": E-mail from Karen Kramer to author, April 20, 2012.

"Judge [Robert] Aguilar. . . .": Memorandum from Jonathan Rowe to author, September 17, 2011.

"on Jonathan Rowe's 29th birthday. . . .": E-mail from Jonathan Rowe to author, September 19, 2011.

"When Judge Henderson became chief . . . [to end of section]": Conversation with Judge Henderson, Karen Kramer, Jonathan Rowe, and Susan Kessler, October 21, 2011.

Life beyond the Courthouse

"I think—and this is a part of poker I like. . . .": Oral History at 306.

On Judge Henderson and fishing, *see id.* at 291–93.

"Mort Cohen placed the onset. . . .": Telephone interview with Mort Cohen, June 1, 2012.

"When he was fishing. . . .": *See id.*

Off the Bench on the Bench: *True Believer*

" 'Okay,' one of them said. . . .": Oral History at 300.

"Guests received a flyer. . . .": Copy of the flyer in author's possession.

Tributes to Judge Henderson and His Tribute to His Clerks

"I know this is out of order. . . .": This and all other quotations in this section, except the last one, are from the symposium honoring Judge Henderson's thirty years on the bench, Friday, April 16, 2010 (video of proceedings provided to author by Thelton E. Henderson Center for Social Justice, University of California at Berkeley School of Law).

"A number of Judge Henderson's decisions. . . .": *See, e.g.,* Madrid v. Gomez, 889 F. Supp. 1148 (N.D. Cal. 1995); Priest v. Rotary, 98 F.R.D. 755 (N.D. Cal.1983).

"I can't even *begin*. . . .": Thelton Henderson, speech to law clerks following dinner at Boalt Hall, April 16, 2010 (copy in author's possession).

Chapter Ten
Dolphin-Safe Tuna

Humans and Dolphins

"From ancient times. . . .": *See* The POD, Out of the Depths: Dolphins and Whales in World Mythology, available at http://www.people-oceans-dolphins.com/Mythology/index .html (last visited January 9, 2010); Bullfinch's Mythology 162–65 (1978) (Dionysus/Bacchus turning sailors to dolphins); Ancientspiral.com, Whales and Dolphins, available at http:// www.ancientspiral.com/dolphin1.htm (last visited January 9, 2010) (Dionysus; Arctic myths); Allcreatures.org, Dolphins: From Mythology to Public Policy, available at http://www.all-crea tures.org/articles/ar-dolphinsfrom.html (last visited January 9, 2010) (Greek and Indian mythology) [hereinafter **Mythology to Public Policy**].

" 'Flipper,' . . . .": On "Flipper," the movie, *see* Wikipedia, Flipper (1963 Film), available at http://en.wikipedia.org/wiki/Flipper_(1963_film) (last visited January 2, 2009); on "Flipper," the television series, *see* Wikipedia, Flipper (1964 TV Series), available at http://en.wikipedia .org/wiki/Flipper_(1964_TV_series) (last visited January 2, 2009).

"swimming with dolphins has become so popular. . . .": A variety of organizations offer opportunities to swim with dolphins. *See, e.g.,* Water Planet, Human/Dolphin Interactions, available at http://www.waterplanetusa.com/interactions.php (last visited January 9, 2010).

"Marine Mammal Protection Act places restrictions . . . on over-exuberant. . . .": *See* Strong v. United States, 5 F.3d 905 (5th Cir. 1993); Amy Samuels et al., A Review of the Literature Pertaining to Swimming with Dolphins (2000), available at http://mmc.gov/reports/work-shop/pdf/samuelsreport.pdf (last visited January 9, 2010).

"The attraction to dolphins. . . .": *See* Mythology to Public Policy; Psychophysiological Mechanisms of Theraputic-Dolphin Interactions, available at http://www.littletree.com.au/dolphin2.htm (last visited January 9, 2010); Mike Celizic, Dolphins Save Surfer from Becoming Shark Bait: A Pod of Bottlenose Dolphins Helped Protect the Severely Injured Boarder, TODAY Show.com., November 8, 2007; International Institute of Dolphin Therapy, Dolphin Therapy for Children and Parents, available at http://www.dolphintherapy.ru/en (last visited September 4, 2009); The Henry Spink Foundation, Dolphin Therapy, available at http://www.henryspink.org/dolphin_therapy.htm (last visited September 4, 2009). *But see* Christopher Wanjek, Dolphin Therapy Smells Fishy, Live Science, March 11, 2008, available at http://www.livescience.com/health/080311-bad-dolphin-therapy.html (last visited September 4, 2009).

Dolphins, Yellowfin Tuna, and Purse Seine Fishing

"yellowfin tuna tend to congregate. . . .": *See* Earth Island Institute v. Mosbacher, 746 F. Supp. 964, 966–67 (N.D. Cal. 1990).

"tuna fishers for years. . . .": *See* Journal of Biology, A Brief History of Tuna and Dolphins, May 4, 2004, available at http://jbiol.com/content/3/2/6 (last visited January 9, 2010).

"the fishers . . . would encircle. . . .": *See* Brower v. Evans, 257 F.3d 1058, 1060 (9th Cir. 2001).

"Between 1959 and 1979 . . .": *See id. See also* Earth Island Institute v. Hogarth, 484 F.3d 1123, 1127 (9th Cir. 2007).

"Marine Mammal Protection Act": 16 U.S.C. sec. 1361 et seq.

"responsible for over 300,000 deaths. . . .": *See* Earth Island Institute v. Mosbacher, 929 F.2d 1449, 1450 (9th Cir. 1991); Dorothy J. Black, International Trade v. Environmental Protection: The Case of the U.S. Embargo on Mexican Tuna, 24 L. & Policy in Int'l Bus. 123, 123 (1992); Eugene H. Buck, Dolphin Protection and Tuna Seining, CRS Report to Congress (updated August 29, 2007) [**hereinafter Dolphin Protection**], available at http://www.ncseonline.org/NLE/CRSreports/Marine/mar-14.cfm (last visited December 15, 2008) [**hereinafter Dolphin Protection**].

The Marine Mammal Protection Act (MMPA)

"The 1972 MMPA . . . 'immediate goal.' ": 16 U.S.C. sec, 1371(a)(2).

"To help achieve. . . .": *See* Earth Island Institute v. Mosbacher, 746 F. Supp. at 967.

"reduced by over 90%. . . .": *See* Dolphin Protection. On the reduction in dolphin kill internationally, *see* Earth Island Institute v. Evans, 256 F. Supp. 2d 1064, 1066 (N.D. Cal. 2003) ("[W]hile the number of reported dolphin deaths was 423,678 in 1972, that number dropped to a little over 120,000 in 1986, to 15,550 per year in 1992, and is estimated to be under 2,000 per year at present.")

"the size of the fleet. . . .": *See* Mark Schoell, The Marine Mammal Protection Act and its Role in the Decline of San Diego's Tuna Fishing Industry, 45 J. San Diego History, No. 1 (1999), available at www.sandiegohistory.org/journal/99winter/tuna.htm (last visited December 7, 2008). Other reasons for the decline were the 1982–83 El Nino, which forced tuna to Western Tropical Pacific, where they do not associate with dolphins; the movement of canneries to other countries with lower wages; more vigilant enforcement of the 200 mile territorial limit by Latin American countries; and the development of larger, more efficient seine netters. *See id.*; Dolphin Protection.

"The MMPA also gave. . . .": *See* Earth Island Institute v. Mosbacher, 746 F. Supp. at 967.

The MMPA and the US Tuna Fleet

"'a national organization. . . .'": Earth Island Institute v. Mosbacher, 746 F. at 966.

"Relying on a recent amendment. . . .": *See id.* at 967; Judge Extends Order that U.S. Protect Dolphins, N.Y. Times, June 19, 1989, sec. A, p. 17.

"Five years later. . . .": *See* Earth Island Institute v. Brown, 865 F. Supp. 1364, 1367, 1373 n.11 (N.D. Cal. 1994).

"According to the MMPA. . . .": 16 U.S.C. sec 1371.

"plaintiffs asked Judge Henderson. . . .": *See* Earth Island Institute v. Brown, 865 F. Supp. at 1367.

"intricate and convoluted interpretation. . . .": *See id.* at 1368–75.

"undoubtedly had more to do. . . .": *See* Brower v. Evans, 257 F.3d at 1061; *see also* Earth Island Institute v. Evans, 2004 W.L. 1774221, and Earth Island Institute v. Evans, 256 F. Supp. 2d 1064 (N.D. Cal. 2003), both of which are excerpted later in the chapter.

"had implications for the importation. . . .": *See* Earth Island Institute v. Brown, 865 F. Supp. at 1367 n.4.

"Judge Henderson's opinion": *See* Earth Island Institute v. Brown, 865 F. Supp. 1364.

"'[d]efendants are enjoined. . . .'" *Id.* at 1377.

The MMPA and Imported Tuna

"world's largest importer. . . .": *See* Dorothy J. Black, International Trade v. Environmental Protection: The Case of the U.S. Embargo on Mexican Tuna, 24 L. & Policy in Int'l Bus. 123, 128 & n.54 (1992).

"other governments did not regulate. . . .": *See* Earth Island Institute v. Mosbacher, 929 F.2d at 1450 ("Although the [MMPA] brought about a material reduction in the number of dolphins killed the United States fleet, dolphin slaughter by foreign nations remained a growing problem.")

"provided from the outset. . . .": *See* 16 U.S.C. sec. 1371(a)(2).

"Despite this mandate. . . .": *See* Earth Island Institute v. Mosbacher, 746 F. Supp. at 967–68; Joshua Floum, Defending Dolphins and Sea Turtles: In the Front Lines in an "Us-Them" Dialectic, 10 Geo. Int'l Envtl. L. Rev. 943–46 (1998).

"The 1984 amendment. . . .": *See* Pub. Law. 98-364, 98 Stat. 440 (1984); Earth Island Institute v. Mosbacher, 747 F. Supp. at 968.

"The 1988 legislation. . . .": *See* Pub. Law 100-711, 102 Stat. 4755 (1988); Earth Island Institute v. Mosbacher, 746 F. Supp. at 970; Earth Island Institute v. Mosbacher, 929 F.2d at 1451-52.

"When Earth Island Institute sought a preliminary injunction. . . .": *See* Earth Island Institute v. Mosbacher, 746 F. Supp. at 966.

"the administration's excuse . . . 'long standing . . .' . . . 'take [additional] time'. . . .": *Id.* at 971.

"for 'the same time period.'": *Id.* at 970–71 (interpreting 16 U.S.C. sec. 1371(a)(2)(B)(ii)(II) (1988)).

"From the legislative history. . . .": Earth Island Institute v. Mosbacher, 746 F. Supp. at 971, 972.

"On August 28, 1990, Judge Henderson enjoined the Secretary. . . .": *See id.* at 976.

"On September 6. . . .": Earth Island Institute v. Mosbacher, 929 F.2d at 1451.

"Judge Henderson granted. . . . Ninth Circuit affirmed": *See* Earth Island Institute v. Mosbacher, 929 F.2d at 1451–53.

"Mexico responded. . . . neither became binding.": *See* Defenders of Wildlife v. Hogarth, 177 F. Supp. 2d 1336, 1339 (C.I.T. 2001).

"On December 27. . . . 'purported to extend'. . . .": *See* Earth Island Institute v. Mosbacher, 1991 W.L. 163753, 3 (N.D. Cal).

"only the 1989 finding. . . .": *See id.*

"Judge Henderson reinforced. . . .": *Id.* at 6–7.

The Tuna Boycott and "Dolphin-Safe" Tuna

"As part of its effort. . . .": *See* Earth Island Institute, Questions and Answers about Earth Island Institute's Dolphin Safe Tuna Program, January 2007, available at http://www.earthis land.org/immp/QandAdolphinSafe.html (last visited January 2, 2009).

"Samuel LaBudde, a biologist. . . .": *See* Jim Okerblom, Tuna Boat Tapes Reignite Dolphin-Killing Debate, San Diego Union-Tribune, April 8, 1988, page A-1; The Dolphin Institute, Resource Guide: Conservation: Threats to the Bottlenose Dolphin and Other Marine Mammals, available at http://www.dolphin-institute.org/resource_guide/conservation.htm (last visited January 2, 2009) [**hereinafter Dolphin Institute Research Guide**].

"By 1990, Starkist. . . .": *See* European Cetacean Bycatch Campaign, The Tuna Boycott Which Led to the "Dolphin Safe" Tuna Label, available at http://www.eurocbc.org/page322 .html (last visited January 2, 2009).

"The Dolphin Protection Consumer Information Act": 16 U.S.C. sec. 1385 (1990).

"'harvested using purse seine nets. . . .'": 16 U.S.C. sec. 1385(d) (1990). *See* Brower v. Daley, 93 F. Supp. 2d 1271, 1074 (N.D. Cal. 2000).

"created tensions with. . . .": A number of articles in international law and business journals discuss these tensions. One of the most thoughtful is Dorothy J. Black, International Trade v. Environmental Protection: The Case of the U.S. Embargo on Mexican Tuna, 24 L. & Policy in Int'l Bus. 123 (1992).

International Cooperation and International Pressure to Relax the "Dolphin Safe" Standard

"International cooperation. . . .": *See generally* Michael Scott, the Tuna-Dolphin Controversy (1998), available at http://www.maninnature.com/Fisheries/tuna1a.html (last visited December 24, 2008).

"Indeed, even among environmentalists. . . .": *See generally* Joshua Floum, Defending Dolphins and Sea Turtles: In the Front Lines in an "Us-Them" Dialectic, 10 Geo. Int'l Envtl. L. Rev. 943–46 (1998).

"In 1992. . . .": *See generally* Dolphin Institute Research Guide; Brower v. Daley, 93 F. Supp. 2d at 1074. For the terms of the La Jolla agreement, *see* Inter-American Tropical Tuna Commission, La Jolla Agreement for the Reduction of Dolphin Mortality in the Eastern Pacific Ocean, available at http://www.temple.edu/lawschool/drwiltext/docs/The%20La%20Jolla%20 Agreement.pdf (last visited December 24, 2008). The nine other countries joining in the La Jolla Agreement were Columbia, Costa Rica, Ecuador, Mexico, Nicaragua, Panama, Spain, Vanuatu, and Venezuela.

"Three years later. . . .": *See* Dolphin Institute Research Guide; Brower v. Daley 93 F. Supp. 2d at 1074.

"'no dolphins were observed. . . .'": *See* Brower v. Daley, 93 F. Supp. 2d at 1075.

"International Dolphin Conservation Program Act": Pub. L. No. 105–42, 111 Stat. 1122.

"Congress was concerned. . . .": *See* Brower v. Daley, 93 F. Supp. 2d at 1075–76.

"'a substantial adverse impact. . . .'": 16 U. S. C. sec. 1414(a). *See* Brower v. Daley, 93 F. Supp. 2d at 1075.

"Additionally, congress ordered. . . .": *See id.* at 1075–76.

The Secretary's Initial Finding

"On April 29, 1999. . . .": *See id.* at 1070.

"'arbitrary, capricious. . . .'": 5 U.S.C. sec. 706(2)(A),(D), set forth at Brower v. Daley, 93 F. Supp. 2d at 1082.

"Nonetheless, Judge Henderson concluded. . . .": *See* Brower v. Daley, 93 F. Supp. 2d 1071.

"'all pointed in the direction. . . .'": *Id.* at 1087.

"'scientific findings. . . .'": *Id.* at 1088.

"[T]he Secretary's actions. . . .": *Id.* at 1089

"In urging this court. . . .": Brower v. Evans, 257 F.3d at 1065–66 (9th Cir. 2001).

The Secretary's Final Finding

"On December 31, 2002. . . .": *See* Earth Island Institute v. Evens, 256 F. Supp. 2d at 1067.

"'the chase and intentional deployment. . . .'": *Id.*

"On April 10, 2003. . . .": *See* Earth Island Institute v. Evans, 256 F. Supp. 2d at 1064.

"made the injunction permanent.": *See* Earth Island Institute v. Evans, 2004 L.W. 1774221.

"the Ninth Circuit affirmed. . . .": *See* Earth Island Institute v. Hogarth, 494 F.3d 757 (9th Cir. 2007).

Judge Henderson Fishing for Tuna

"Shortly after [the order. . . .": Oral History at 223–24.

"The expedition was dolphin-safe.": *See id.* at 224.

Chapter Eleven
Agent Orange

"Nehmer v. United States Department of Veterans Affairs": When the lawsuit was filed, the Department of Veterans Affairs was called the Veterans' Administration. The name change occurred in 1988. The Department of Veterans Affairs Act of 1988, Pub. L. No. 100–527, secs. 2 & 10, 102 Stat. 2635 (1988). *See* Nehmer v. United States Department of Veterans Affairs, 494 F.3d 846, 849 n.1 (9th Cir. 2007). Judge Henderson's first substantive ruling in the case is Nehmer v. United States Veterans' Administration, 712 F. Supp. 1404 (N.D. Cal. 1989).

"'It is a disturbing story. . . .'": Nehmer v. United States Department of Veterans Affairs, 494 F.3d at 849.

Background

"nearly nineteen million gallons": *See* Institute of Medicine of the National Academies, Health of Veterans and Deployed Sources, available at http://veterans.iom.edu/agent.asp ?id=6162 (last visited July 21, 2009).

On the use of herbicides in Vietnam, *see* Jeanne Mager Stellman et al., The Extent and Patterns of Usage of Agent Orange and Other Herbicides in Vietnam, 422 Nature 681 (April 17, 2003), available at http://www.stellman.com/jms/Stellman1537.pdf and at http://www.nature.com/ index.html?file=/nature/journal/v422/n6933/full/nature01537_fs.html (last visited July 21, 2009).

On dioxin, *see* National Institute of Environmental Health Sciences — National Institute of Health, Dioxins, available at http://www.niehs.nih.gov/health/topics/agents/dioxins (last visited July 21, 2009).

"Agent Orange has been associated. . . .": *See* Thomas Boivin, A Brief Summary of Hatfield/10–80 Division Work on the Agent Orange Dioxin Issue in Vietnam, available at http:// www.ffrd.org/Lawsuit/VAVA/Hatfield.pdf (last visited July 21, 2009); Nguyen Thi Gnoc Phuong, testimony before House Committee of Foreign Affairs, Subcommittee on Asia, the Pacific, and the Global Environment, May 15, 2008, available at http://foreignaffairs.house .gov/110/phu051508.pdf (last visited July 21, 2009).

"As of October 1. . . .": *See* House Report 98–592, U.S. Code Cong. & Adm. News, 98th Cong., 2d Sess., 1984, at 4452.

"a $180,000,000 settlement. . . .": *See* In re Agent Orange, 597 F. Supp. 239 (E.D.N.Y. 1984), *aff'd*, 818 F.2d 145 (1987).

"it resulted in maximum individual payments. . . .": *See* In re Agent Orange, 611 F. Supp. 1396, 1422–23 (E.D.N.Y. 1985).

"Causation had been an issue from the outset. . . .": *See generally* In re Agent Orange, 818 F.2d at 148–50.

"merely aggravated": Federal law defines a "service-connected" disability as one that "was incurred or aggravated . . . in the line of duty." 38 U.S.C. sec. 101(16).

"'the scientific data available. . . .'": In re Agent Orange, 597 F. Supp. at 749

"Veterans' Dioxin and Radiation Exposure Compensation Standards Act": Pub. L. No. 98–542, 98 Stat. 2725 (1984).

"'dramatically alter[ed]'": Nehmer v. United States Veterans' Administration, 712 F. Supp. at 1407.

"could receive benefits. . . .": The Dioxin Act did not specify the precise significance of having a disease that the rule-making process found to be service connected. Rather, it instructed the VA to adopt regulations on this matter. *See* sec. 5(b)(2)(A)(ii)&(iii).

"the VA issued a regulation in August 1984. . . .": 38 C.F.R. 3.311(a)(d). *See* Nehmer v. United States Veterans' Administration, 712 F. Supp. at 1408.

"the VA had relied on its August 1984 regulation. . . .": *See* Nehmer v. United States Veterans' Administration, 118 F.R.D. 112, 120 (N.D. Cal. 1987).

Causation and the Dioxin Act

"In February 1987, veterans challenged. . . .": *See* Nehmer v. United States Veterans' Administration, 712 F. Supp. at 1408.

"Plaintiffs . . . argue. . . .": *Id.* at 1416.

"Judge Henderson made clear. . . .": *See id.* at 1416–17.

"'at best ambiguous'": *Id.* at 1417.

"'overwhelmingly suggest'": *Id.* at 1418.

"In addition, Judge Henderson pointed out. . . .": *See id.* at 1418–20.

"Indeed, the defendants had admitted that 'Congress. . . .'": *Id.* at 1419.

"'There is an approximate balance. . . .'": *Id.* at 1420.

"Relying once again. . . .": *See id.* at 1420–22.

"These errors compounded one another. . . .": *Id.* at 1423.

Settlement and the Agent Orange Act

"announced that the government would not appeal.": *See* Bill McAllister, Veterans Dept. To Restudy Agent Orange; Action Could Open Way to More Payments, The Washington Post, May 12, 1989, page A1.

"'sharp reversal in position'": *Id.*

"committed itself. . . .": *See id;* Associated Press, VA Accepts Ruling; Will Review Agent Orange Claims It Denied, Los Angeles Times, May 12, 1989, part 1, page 22; Charles Mohr, U.S. Won't Appeal Agent Orange Case, N.Y. Times, May 12, 1989, page 12A.

"the Agent Orange Act": Pub. L. No. 102–4, 105 Stat. 11 (1991), 38 U.S.C. sec. 1116. The statute also created two presumptions favorable to veterans: that military personnel serving in Vietnam were exposed to Agent Orange and that a disease identified as service connected was in fact service connected in individual cases. 38 U.S.C. sec. 1116(a)&(f).

"A few months later. . . . '. . . diseases other than chloracne.'": *See* Nehmer v. United States Department of Veterans Affairs, 32 F. Supp. 1175, 1177 (N.D. Cal. 1999).

"Between 1990 and 1996. . . .": *See id.* at 1177 & n.2.

Parsing the Settlement Agreement and Retroactivity Issues

"First, the VA. . . .": *See* Nehmer v. United States Veterans' Administration, 32 F. Supp. 2d 1175. The VA claimed that pursuant to the 1991 Stipulation and Order, it had to reopen prior claims only if (1) the claim initially alleged Agent Orange as a factor responsible for the disease or (2) the VA's denial of benefits specifically mentioned the regulation voided by Judge Henderson in 1989. Such rigor in pleading, however, was inconsistent with both VA practices and the remedial purpose of Judge Henderson's Stipulation and Order. *See id.*

"Second,. . . . Third,. . . .": *See* Nehmer v. Veterans' Admin. of Government of United States, 284 F.3d 1158 (9th Cir. 2002)

"Fourth,. . . . Finally,. . . .": *See* Nehmer v. United States Department of Veterans Affairs, 494 F.3d 846.

More Recalcitrance, a Threat of Contempt, and Improved Compliance

"In April 2006,. . . '. . . as quickly as possible.'": Nehmer v. United States Department of Veterans Affairs, 2007 WL 1795707 (N.D. Cal.) at 1.

"'telephonic and in-court status conferences. . . .'": *Id.*

"[T]he Court has attempted. . . .": *Id.*

"the VA had no reasonable explanation. . . .": *See id.* at 2.

"Throughout this process. . . .": *Id.* at 1.

"Judge Henderson issued. . . .": *See id.* at 2.

New Service Connected Diseases

"In 2010,....": *See* Unites States Department of Veterans Affairs, Public Health, Agent Orange: Diseases Related to Agent Orange Exposure, available at http://www.publichealth.va.gov/exposures/agentorange/diseases.asp (last visited January 25, 2012) (listing diseases).

"At the same time....": *See* United States Department of Veterans Affairs, Agent Orange Fast Track Claims Processing System, available at https://www.fasttrack.va.gov/AOFastTrack (last visited February 4, 2012).

"Anecdotal evidence suggests....": *See* Kristina Derro, New Agent Orange Regulations and Nehmer's Implications on Pending Claims, Legal Help for Veterans, November 17, 2010, available at http://www.legalhelpforveterans.com/2010/11/new-agent-orange-regulations-and-nehmer%E2%80%99s-implications-on-pending-claims (last visited February 3, 2012) (longer delay for normal claims because of priority given to old claims for newly recognized diseases); Comments following Lauren Bailey, A Faster Track for Agent Orange Claims, Vantage Point: Dispatches from the United States Department of Veterans Affairs, November 11, 2010, available at http://www.blogs.va.gov/VAntage/477/a-faster-track-for-agent-orange-claims (last visited February 3, 2012).

Chapter Twelve
Unshackled: The Johnny Spain Case

"On some occasions . . . may be a wise exercise of judicial discretion.": *See* Alexander Bickel, The Supreme Court, 1960 Term — Forward: The Passive Virtues, 75 Harv. L. Rev. 40 (1961).

"Other times, however,....": *See* Gerald Gunther, The Subtle Vices of the "Passive Virtues" — A Comment on Principle and Expediency in Judicial Review, 64 Colum. L. Rev. 1 (1964).

"led him initially to dismiss it.": *See* Spain v. Rushen 543 F. Supp. 757, 764 (N.D. Cal. 1982).

"Spain's attorney wondered....": Telephone interview with Dennis Riorden, November 27, 2009 [hereinafter **Riorden Interview**].

"Once the state supreme court....": *See id.*

"Fn. 1": On Dennis Riordan, *see* NYU Law, Alumnus/Alumna of the Month: Dennis Riordan, 2005–06, available at http://www.law.nyu.edu/alumni/almo/pastalmos/20052006almos/dennisriordanapril/index.htm (last visited October 8, 2009); Marianne Costantinou, Meet the Top Ten Lawyers, SF Gate — San Francisco Chronicle, May 4, 2003.

"Fn. 1 . . . Riorden signed a personal security bond....": Riorden Interview.

"[It is the court's] duty....": Order and Opinion, Spain v. Rushen, No. C 81–4858 TEH (N.D. Cal. filed September 22, 1986) at 2 [hereinafter **Spain v. Rushen, unpublished 1986 opinion**].

"Thus, Judge Henderson....": Riorden Interview.

"[P]etitioner's pre-trial and trial....": Spain v Rushen, unpublished 1986 opinion at 1.

Becoming Johnny Spain

On Johnny Spain's life story *see*, Lori Andrews, Black Power, White Blood: The Life and Times of Johnny Spain (2000) [hereinafter **Black Power, White Blood**]; Chip Brown, The Transformation of Johnny Spain, Esquire, January 1988, available at http://www.chipbrown.net/articles/spain.htm (last visited September 12, 2009).

On the Emmett Till murder, *see* http://www.emmetttillmurder.com (last visited October 11, 2009).

For accounts of the incident that led to Johnny Spain's murder conviction, *see* People v. Gray, 263 Cal. App. 2d (2d Dist) 692, 693–95, 69 Cal. Rptr. 751, 751–53 (1968); Black Power, White Blood at 69–72.

The Black Panthers, George Jackson, and Johnny Spain

On the Black Panther Party, its founding, and its ten-point program, *see* http://www.black-panther.org (last visited September 9, 2009); *see also* Black Power, White Blood at 88–91.

"Their peaceful but armed march. . . .": *See* Beth Schelle, The History of the Black Panthers, available at http://www.qualityinformationpublishers.com/thehistoryoftheblackpanthers .aspx (last visited September 9, 2009); Jessica Lindsey, "All Power to the People" — Visions of the Black Panther Party, available at http://class.csueastbay.edu/ethnicstudies/jes2/Lindsey -BPParty.htm (last visited September 9, 2009).

"FBI Director . . . community-organizing tool.": *See* Public Broadcasting System, A Huey Newton Story: People: Hoover and the F.B.I., available at http://www.pbs.org/hueypnewton/ people/people_hoover.html (last visited December 26, 2014).

"Over the next several years. . . .": For example, in 1967, Huey Newton was wounded and a police officer was killed in a shoot-out following a traffic stop. *See* People v. Newton 8 Cal. App. 3d 359, 887 Cal. Rptr. 394 (1st App. Dist. 1970). In 1969, Chicago Black Panther leader Fred Hampton and Mark Clark were fatally shot by a police officer during an early morning raid. Hampton's and Clark's families sued the City of Chicago and eventually accepted a nearly $2 million settlement. *See* Nathaniel Sheppard, Jr., Plaintiffs in Panther Suit "Knew We Were Right," N.Y. Times, November 14, 1982, sec., 1, part 2, page 82. *See also* Black Power, White Blood at 113–14.

"George Jackson, a charismatic prisoner. . . .": *See* Black Power, White Blood at 88–92, 109–11; Norman O. Richmond, Jackson, George, Encyclopedia of African American History, 1896 to the Present: From the Age of Segregation to the Twenty-first Century, reproduced at Oxford African America Studies Center, available at http://www.oxfordaasc.com/article/opr/t0005/ e0620 (last visited October 9, 2009).

"his . . . writing": George Jackson, Blood in My Eye (1972); George Jackson, Soledad Brother: The Prison Letters of George Jackson (1970).

"In January 1970. . . .": *See* Black Power, White Blood at 115–19; Paul Liberatore, The Road to Hell: The True Story of George Jackson, Stephen Bingham, and the San Quentin Massacre 44–46 (1996) [hereinafter The Road to Hell]; Tony Hill, If We Must Die: Part V of It Makes a Long Time Man Feel Bad, Harvard Crimson, October 27, 1971; African American Registry, September 23, available at http://www.aaregistry.com/african_american_history/1169/George_ Jackson_Soledad_Brother (last visited October 9, 2009); Wikipedia, Soledad Brothers, available at http://en.wikipedia.org/wiki/Soledad_Brothers (last visited October 9, 2009). On George Jackson's friendship with W.L. Nolen, *see* Black Power, White Blood at 95–98, 108; The Road to Hell 19, 43–44.

"Jackson was transferred. . . .": *See* Black Power, White Blood at 120, 125, 145–53.

"In August 1970, George Jackson's younger brother. . . .": *See* Spain v. Rushen, 883 F.2d 712, 731 (9th Cir. 1989) (Noonan, J., dissenting).

"Political activist . . . Angela Davis . . . was acquitted. . . .": *See* Paula C. Johnson, At the Experience of Injustice: Experiences of African American Women in Crime and Sentencing, 4 Am. U. J. Gender & L. 1, 2 & n. 3 (1995).

"On August 21, 1971. . . .": For accounts of and some theories about what happened, *see* Black Power, White Blood at 156–67; Craig Moore, Exit the Dragon, San Francisco Chronicle Magazine, August 19, 2001, page 6; Reynolds Holding, An Insider's Account of a Prison Break, San Francisco Chronicle, August 25, 1996, page 5/Z1.

"I woke up this mornin'. . . .": The full lyrics are available at http://www.bobdylan.com/us/songs/george-jackson (last visited August 15, 2016).

"(Fleeta Drumgo and John Clutchette. . . .)": *See* Crain Marine, Exit the Dragon: It's Been 30 Years since George Jackson Died in a Pool of Blood in San Quentin. His Death Still Reverberates in America, San Francisco Chronicle Magazine, August 19, 2001, page 6.

"Stephen Bingham. . . .": *See* James S. Kunen, The Life of a Fugitive: False Murder Charge Sent Attorney Stephen Bingham into Exile. Last Month He Cleared His Name, People, July 29, 1986, page 24; Mariann Hansen & Mark A. Stein, Jury Acquits Bingham in Prison Deaths: Rejects Charges He Smuggled Gun in '71 San Quentin Riot, Los Angeles Times, June 28, 1986, part 1, page 1.

"Of the six. . . . involvement with George Jackson in the conspiracy": *See* Spain v. Rushen, 543 F. Supp. at 760; Henry Weinstein, Abstracts, N.Y. Times, August 13, 1976, sec. 1, page 1; Dan Morain, Parole Panel Denies Release of San Quentin Six Murder Figure Spain, Los Angeles Times, July 31, 1986, part I, page 27; Ex-Black Panther Free Pending Trial, The Washington Post, March 11, 1988, page A18. On Spain being the only one of the six who was a member of the Black Panther Party, *see* Spain v. Rushen, 543 F. Supp. at 760.

Habeas Corpus

"Spain's attorney thought the first ground. . . .": Riorden Interview.

"Indeed, the state appellate court. . . .": *See* Rushen v. Spain, 464 U.S. 114, 117 (1983); *cf. id.* at 137 n.115 (suggesting some ambiguity in the state court opinion).

"Thus, Judge Henderson granted. . . .": *See* Spain v. Rushen, 543 F. Supp. 757 (N.D. Cal. (1982).

"The Ninth Circuit affirmed. . . .": *See* Spain v. Rushen, 701 F.2d 186 (9th Cir. 1983).

"However, the Supreme Court. . . .": *See* Rushen v. Spain, 464 U.S. 114 (1983).

"misrepresents the facts": *See id.* at 136 n.13 (Marshall, J., dissenting).

"There was much in the record. . . .": *See* Spain v. Rushen, 543 F. Supp. at 762–63.

"Spain had interrupted. . . .": *See* Spain v. Rushen, 883 F.2d at 719 n.10.

"The Party's most popular slogan. . . .": *See id.* at 730 (Noonan, J., dissenting).

"various Panther members. . . .": *See id.*; People v. Newton 8 Cal. App. 3d 359, 887 Cal. Rptr. 394.

"Jonathan Jackson's failed kidnapping attempt. . . .": *See* Spain v. Rushen, 883 F.2d at 731 (Noonan, J., dissenting).

"Judge Henderson found. . . .": Spain v. Rushen, unpublished 1986 opinion at 15–21.

"Instead, he called for an evidentiary hearing. . . .": Judge Henderson's order was directed to Chief Magistrate Frederick J. Woelflen, who assigned the case to Magistrate Joan Brennan. Order, Spain v. Rushen, No. C 81-4858 TEH, (N.D. Cal. filed January 28, 1985).

"Judge Brennan reviewed. . . .": *See* Evidentiary Report, Spain v Rushen, No. C 81-4858 TEH (JSB) (N.D. Cal. filed October 9, 1985).

"There were seven. . . .": *Id.* at 4, 8–10, 12.

"Judge Henderson adopted. . . .": *See* Spain v. Rushen, unpublished 1986 opinion; Spain v. Rushen, 883 F.2d at 715.

"The Ninth Circuit affirmed,. . . .": *See* Spain v. Rushen, 883 F.2d at 712, *cert. denied*, 495 U.S. 910 (1990).

Eventual Release

"By the time Johnny Spain was convicted. . . .": *See* Peter W. Greenwood et al., RAND Corp., Three Strikes and You're Out: Estimated Benefits and Costs of California's New Mandatory Sentencing Law 58 (1994) (Table D-7, citing 1990 data); Associated Press, Figure in Bloody Prison Break Will Be Freed if Parole Board Agrees, Los Angeles Times, November 1, 1986, part I, page 38.

"After rejecting Spain's request. . . .": *See* Pamela A. MacLean, Parole Denied Former Black Panther Johnny Spain, United Press International, December 5, 1986; Dan Morain, Parole Panel Denies Release of San Quentin Six Murder Figure Spain, Los Angeles Times, July 31, 1986, part I, page 27 [**hereinafter Parole Panel Denies Release**].

"Judge Henderson issued an order. . . .": Order, Spain v. Rushen, No. C 81-4858 TEH (N.D. Cal. filed March 24, 1987). *See* Dan Morain, Parole Voted for Ex-Black Panther Johnny Spain, Los Angeles Times, February 12, 1988, part 1, page 19 [**hereinafter Parole Voted for Johnny Spain**].

"Spain had become a model prisoner. . . .": *See* Associated Press, Figure in Bloody Prison Break Will Be Freed If Parole Board Agrees, Los Angeles Times, November 1, 1986, part 1, page 38; Parole Panel Denies Release.

"Nonetheless, only two of the three panel members. . . .": *See* Parole Voted for Johnny Spain.

"The following month a California state judge ruled. . . .": Riorden Interview. *See* Terry Pristin, Judge Clears Way for Parole of Ex-Black Panther Spain, Los Angeles Times, March 9, 1988, part 1, page 3.

"The next day,. . . .": Riorden Interview. *See* Dan Morain, Spain Granted Bail after 21 Years in Jail, Los Angeles Times, March 10, 1988, part 1, page 1.

"the Ninth Circuit's affirmance. . . .": *See* Spain v. Rushen, 883 F.2d 712 (9th Cir. 1989), *cert. denied*, 495 U.S. 910 (1990).

"the state's decision not to pursue. . . .": *See* Erik Ingram, Ex-Panther Spain Won't Be Retried, DA Says, San Francisco Chronicle, April 28, 1990, page A3.

"the parole board's eventual conclusion. . . .": The state trial judge's decision granting Spain immediately release was eventually vacated, and the case was returned to the parole board. Spain had in fact been free for two years when the board finally ruled that he was suitable for parole! Riorden Interview. *See* Mercury News Wire Service, Ex-Panther Spain Ruled OK for Parole, San Jose Mercury News, September 12, 1990, page 4B.

"Since his release. . . .": Riorden Interview. *See* Dwight Garner, The 9-Year-Old Poet with the Big Advance, N.Y. Times Magazine, February 4, 2001, page 36; Dan Morain, Killer Lectured at Stanford; Johnny Spain Getting by with Help from Friends, Los Angeles Times, December 4, 1988, part 1, page 1.

Doors

Both Judge Henderson and Dennis Riorden have related the "doors" story to the author. The story also appears in Oral History at 200.

Chapter Thirteen
Institutional Reform Litigation

"institutional reform litigation": There is a vast literature on institutional reform litigation, On the legitimacy of such litigation, *compare, e.g.*, Malcolm M. Feeley & Edward Rubin, Judicial Policy Making and the Modern State: How the Courts Reformed American Prisons (1998) [**hereinafter Judicial Policy Making**] *with* John Choon Yoo, Who Measures the Chancellor's Foot? The Inherent Remedial Authority of Federal Courts, 84 Cal. L. Rev. 1121 (1996); *see* William A. Fletcher, The Discretionary Constitution: Institutional Remedies and Judicial Legitimacy, 91 Yale L.J. 635 (1982). On the role of various actors in institutional reform litigation, *see, e.g.*, Judicial Policy Making, *supra*; Margo Schlanger, Beyond the Hero Judge: Institutional Reform Litigation as Litigation, 97 Mich. L. Rev. 1994 (1999); Susan Sturm, Resolving the Remedial Dilemma: Strategies of Judicial Intervention in Prisons, 138 U. Pa. L. Rev. 805 (1990) [**hereinafter Strategies**]. The seminal article on the subject is Abram Chayes, The Role of the Judge in Public Law Litigation, 89 Harv. L. Rev. 1281 (1976). *See also* Owen M. Fiss, Forward: The Forms of Justice, 93 Harv. L. Rev. 1 (1979); Robert E. Buckholz, Jr. et al., Special Project: The Remedial Process in Institutional Reform Litigation, 78 Colum. L. Rev. 784 (1978); Note, Institutional Reform Litigation: Representation in the Remedial Process, 91 Yale L.J. 1474 (1982); Note, Complex Enforcement: Unconstitutional Prison Conditions, 94 Harv. L. Rev. 626 (1981); Note, "Mastering" Intervention in Prisons, 88 Yale L.J. 1062 (1979).

The Least Equal Branch

"Unlike the executive. . . .": *Cf.* Alexander Hamilton, Federalist Paper #78 ("The judiciary . . . has no influence over either the sword or the purse; no direction either of the strength or of the wealth of society; and it can take no active resolution whatever. It may truly be said to have neither *force* nor *will*, but merely judgment; and must ultimately depend upon the aid of the executive arm even for the efficacy of its judgments.").

"Bush v. Gore": 531 U.S. 98 (2000).

"lay people": *See, e.g.*, Harold Meyerson, The Purloined Presidency, The American Prospect, December 19, 2001; Jack Rakove, Election-ending Decision Is Unlikely to Shape Society, San Jose Mercury News, December 21, 2000.

"legal experts": *See, e.g.*, Jack M. Balkin, Essay: Bush v. Gore and the Boundary between Law and Politics, 110 Yale L.J. 1047 (2001); David A. Strauss, Symposium: Bush v. Gore: Bush v. Gore: What Were They Thinking? 68 U. Chi. L. Rev. 737 (2001).

"neo-Nazis wanting to express. . . .": *See* Nat. Socialist Party of America v. Village of Skokie, 432 U.S. 43 (1977).

"Brown v. Board of Education": 347 U.S. 483 (1954).

"the Court's 1955 order. . . .": *See* Brown v. Board of Education, 349 U.S. 294 (1955).

"the Fourth Circuit rejected. . . .": *See* Carson v. Warlick, 238 F.2d 724 (4th Cir. 1946), *cert. denied*, 353 U.S. 910 (1957).

"The criteria for placement. . . .": *See* Note, The Federal Courts and Integration of Southern Schools: Troubled Status of the Pupil Placement Acts, 62 Colum. L. Rev. 1448 (1962).

"Federal District Judge Joe Estes had rejected. . . .": *See* Jackson v. Rawdon, 135 F. Supp. 936 (N.D. Tex. 1955), *rev'd*, 235 F.2d 93 (5th Cir.), *cert. denied*, 352 U.S. 925 (1956).

"Fn. 1. The Fifth Circuit reversed": *See* Jackson v. Rawdon, 235 F.3d 93 (5th Cir.), *cert. denied,* 352 U.S. 925 (1956).

"Fn. 1. . . . . Judge Estes appropriately ordered . . . that year.": *See* Jack Bass, Unlikely Heroes (1981) 120–22; Gayle W. Hanson, Mansfield (Texas) School Desegregation Incident (1955–65), An Online Reference Guide to African American History, available at http://www.blackpast.org/aaw/mansfield-texas-school-desegregation-incident-1955-1965 (last visited August 18, 2016).

"Southern Manifesto . . . '. . . states and the people.' ": 102 Cong. Rec. 3948, 4004 (1956); *id.* at 4459–61 (statement of Sen. Walter George (Ga.) Reading the Manifesto on the Senate floor). *See* Justin Driver, Supremacies and the Southern Manifesto, 92 Tex. L. Rev. 1053 (2014).

"Much of the nation. . . .": Richard Kluger, Simple Justice 752–54 (1975).

"The Supreme Court and eventually lower federal courts. . . .": *See* Kathleen Sullivan & Gerald Gunther, Constitutional Law 494 (16th ed. 2007) (citing Supreme Court cases); Jack Bass, Unlikely Heroes (1981) (examination of the implementation of Brown throughout the South).

"establish *Brown* as 'our nation's single most. . . .' ": Kenneth L. Karst, Belonging to America: Equal Citizenship and the Constitution 146 (1989). *See* Michael R. Belknap, The Real Significance of Brown v. Board of Education: The Genesis of the Warren Court's Quest for Equality 863, 50 Wayne L. Rev. 863 (2004) (citing Karst at 882).

"*Brown* and its progeny became. . . .": *See* Richard Thompson Ford, Symposium: Brown at Fifty: Brown's Ghost, 117 Harv. L. Rev. 1305, 1305 (2004).

"(including some early successes . . .)": *See* Jack Bass, Unlikely Heroes (1981).

"resistance remained strong.": *See* Richard Kluger, Simple Justice 755–77 (1975); Joe R. Feagin & Bernica McNair Barnett, Symposium: Promises to Keep? Brown v. Board and Equal Educational Opportunity: Success and Failure: How Systemic Racism Trumped the Brown Board of Education Decision, 2004 U. Ill. L. Rev. Online 1099; Tony A. Freyer, Symposium: 50 Years Later: Brown in the Appellate Courts: Enforcing Brown in the Little Rock Crisis, 6 J. App. Prac. & Process 67 (2004); Leland B. Ware, Brown @ 50 Symposium: Educational Equality and Brown v. Board of Education: Fifty Years of School Desegregation in Delaware, 47 How. L. J. 299 (2004).

"Whites . . . often fled. . . .": *See* Richard Thompson Ford, Symposium: Brown at Fifty: Brown's Ghost, 117 Harv. L. Rev. 1305.

"By 1974, the Supreme Court itself. . . .": *See* Milliken v. Bradley, 418 U.S. 717 (1974). (severely limiting judicial interdistrict transfer orders); Richard Thompson Ford, Symposium: Brown at Fifty: Brown's Ghost, 117 Harv. L. Rev. 1305, 1313–18. *Cf.* Gary Orfield, Judicial Action Center Symposium: Brown Is Dead? Long Live Brown! I. Keynote Address: Why Segregation Is Inherently Unequal: The Abandonment of Brown and the Continuing Failure of Plessy, 49 N. Y. L. Sch. L. Rev. 1041, 1045–46 (Supreme Court began dismantling Brown in 1991).

"the early twenty-first century. . . .": *See* Gary Orfield, Reviving the Goal of an Integrated Society: A 21st Century Challenge, The Civil Rights Project, University of California at Los Angeles, January 2009, available at http://civilrightsproject.ucla.edu/research/k-12-education/integration-and-diversity/reviving-the-goal-of-an-integrated-society-a-21st-century-challenge/orfield-reviving-the-goal-mlk-2009.pdf (last visited July 31, 2011).

Strategies and Techniques for Institutional Reform

"back to business as usual.": *See, e.g.,* Bradley W. Joondeph, Note, Killing Brown Softly: The Subtle Undermining of Effective Desegregation in Freeman v. Pitts, 46 Stan. L. Rev. 147, 159–67

(1993); Neal Devins, Review Essay: The Hollow Hope: Can Courts Bring about Social Change, 80 Cal. L. Rev. 1027, 1045 (1992).

"At one extreme. . . .": *See* Thelton Henderson, Keynote Address: Confronting the Crisis of California Prisons, 43 U.S.F. L. Rev. 1, 6 (2008) [**hereinafter Keynote Address**]:

> I was at a workshop last fall in New York, attended by some of my judicial heroes—Wayne Justice, Jack Weinstein foremost among them. We were discussing how hands-on a judge needs to be, and I was hugely surprised to hear some judges say that they close the case after they find the constitutional violation and do not revisit it unless plaintiffs file a motion.

"At the other extreme. . . .": *See generally* Strategies.

"Finally, the Supreme Court has repeatedly emphasized. . . .": *See, e.g.*, Missouri v Jenkins, 515 U.S. 70, 98 (1995); Jones v. N.C. Prisoners' Labor Union, Inc., 433 U.S. 119, 1126 (1977).

"I have repeatedly said. . . .": Keynote Address, *supra* at 6, 8–9, 11.

"Professor Sturm, who first coined. . . .": *See* Strategies.

" 'the only effective way. . . .' ": Keynote Address at 9.

Chapter Fourteen
Judge Henderson's Prison Trilogy: Introduction

"He has ruled. . . .": *See, e.g.*, San Nicolas v. Alameida, 216 Fed. Appx. 627, 2006 W.L. 3836598 (9th Cir.) (affirming summary judgment for defendants in plaintiff's suit alleging deliberate indifference to his medical needs); Hollis v. Lee 2007 W.L. 963319 (N.D. Cal.), *aff'd sub nom.* Hollis v. Barrie, 2009 W.L. 965826 (9th Cir.) (alleged denial of medical treatment; summary judgment for defendant); Madrid v. Gomez, 889 F. Supp. 1146 (N.D. Cal. 1995) (conditions at Pelican Bay State Prison violated inmates' right to be free from cruel and unusual punishment).

"a female guard's. . . .": *See* Freitag v. California Department of Corrections, 2007 W.L. 1670307 (N.D. Cal.).

"Madrid v. Gomez": 889 F. Supp. 1146 (N.D. Cal. 1995).

"Plata v. Schwarzenegger": *Plata* has resulted in a number of opinions. Judge Henderson's opinion setting forth his decision to appoint a receiver is Plata v. Schwarzenegger, 2005 W.L. 2932253 (N.D. Cal.).

"Coleman/Plata v. Schwarzenegger": *Coleman/Plata*, too, has resulted in a number of opinions. For the court's conclusion that overcrowding was the primary cause of the Eight Amendment violations, *see* Coleman/Plata v. Schwarzenegger, 2009 W.L. 2430820 (E.D./N.D. Cal.).

Early Prison Litigation

"Then, in the late. . . .": *See, e.g.*, Holt v Sarver, 307 F. Supp. 362 (E.D. Ark. 1970), *aff'd*, 442 F.2d 304 (8th Cir. 1971); Newman v. Alabama, 349 F. Supp. 278 (M.D. Ala. 19972), *aff'd*, 503, F.2d 1320 (5th Cir. 1974).

"including the Supreme Court. . . .": *See, e.g.*, Wilwording v. Swensen, 404 U.S. 249 (1971); Estelle v. Gamble, 429 U.S. 97 (1976).

"Two of the early landmark Eighth Amendment decisions. . . .": *See* Pugh v. Locke, 406 F. Supp. 318 (M.D. Ala. 1976), *aff'd* 559 F.2d 283 (5th Cir. 1977); Newman v. Alabama, 349 F. Supp. 278, *aff'd* 503 F.2d 1320 (5th Cir. 1974).

"Federal District Judge Frank Johnson. . . .": *See generally* Jack Bass, Taming the Storm: The Life and Times of Judge Frank M. Johnson, Jr., and the South's Fight over Civil Rights (1993); Frank Sikora, The Judge: The Life and Opinions of Alabama's Frank M. Johnson, Jr. (2007)

"'failure . . . to provide. . . .'": Newman v. Alabama, 349 F. Supp. at 285.

"'admission by defendants' lead counsel. . . .'": Pugh v Locke, 406 F. Supp. at 322.

"'[t]he living conditions in Alabama prisons. . . .'": *Id*. at 329.

"However, as Judge Johnson discovered. . . .": *See* Larry Yackle, Reform and Regret: The Story of Federal Judicial Involvement in the Alabama Prison System (1989).

"'were quick to volunteer. . . .'": *Id*. at 259.

"'Something fundamental. . . .'": *Id*. at 260.

Prison Populations

"During the last quarter. . . .": *See* United States Department of Justice, Bureau of Justice, Prison Statistics (2009), available at http://www.ojp.usdoj.gov/bjs/prisons.htm (last visited June 6, 2009); John Pfaff, Reform School, Five Myths about Prison Growth Dispelled, Slate, February 19, 2009; Stephen Raphael & Michael A. Stoll, Why Are So Many People in Prison, Institute for Research on Poverty, Discussion Paper 1328-07 (2007), available at http://www .policypointers.org/Page/View/5906 (last visited June 6, 2009); Antonia, Moras, The Mentally Ill in U.S. Prisons — A Review, Human Rights Watch (2004), available at http://justice.uaa .alaska.edu/forum/21/1spring2004/b1_mentallyill.html (last visited June 6, 2009); Franklin E. Zimring et al., Punishment and Democracy: Three Strikes and You're Out in California (2001).

"The reasons for this dramatic increase. . . .": *See, e.g.*, Expert Report of David M. Bennet (submitted by Sonoma County Intervenors), Coleman/Plata v. Schwarzenegger, No. C01-1351-TEH (E.D./N.D. Cal. filed October 30, 2008) 8, 20–21.

"incarcerated approximately 20,000 individuals": *See* Health & Welfare Agency, Department of Corrections, California Prisoners 1974–75 (1975) 1, available at http://www.cdcr.ca.gov/Reports _Research/Offender_Information_Services_Branch/Annual/CalPris/CALPRISd1974_75.pdf (last visited March 26, 2014); Health & Welfare Agency, Department of Corrections, California Prisoners 1976 (1976) 1, available at http://www.cdcr.ca.gov/Reports_Research/Offender_Infor mation_Services_Branch/Annual/CalPris/CALPRISd1976.pdf (last visited March 26, 2014); Coleman/Plata v. Schwarzenegger, 922 F. Supp. 2d 882, 908 (E.D./N.D. Cal. 2009).

"By 2007. . . .": *See* California Department of Corrections & Rehabilitation, Spring 2008 Adult Population Projections 2008–13 (2008) 10, available at http://www.cdcr.ca.gov/Reports_ Research/Offender_Information_Services_Branch/Projections/S08Pub.pdf (last visited March 26, 2014). *See* Coleman/Plata v. Schwarzenegger, 922 F. Supp. 2d at 908.

For the names of the California prisons and when they began operation, *see* California Department of Corrections & Rehabilitation, Adult Facilities and Locations, available at http:// web.archive.org/web/20080222032638/http://www.cdcr.ca.gov/Visitors/Facilities/index.html (with links to individual prisons) (last visited March 26, 2014).

"and its county jails. . . .": *See, e.g.*, John Johnson, Jail Suicides Reach Record Pace in State: Incarceration: Last Year 38 Inmates Killed Themselves. Some Experts Blame the Recent Surge on Forcing More of the Mentally Ill behind Bars, Los Angeles Times, June 16, 2002, Metro, part 2, page 1.

"Evidence of a correlation. . . ." *See* Jenni Gainsborough & Marc Mauer, Diminishing Returns: Crime and Incarceration in the 1990s, The Sentencing Project (2000), available at

http://www.sentencingproject.org/Admin/Documents/publications/inc_diminishingreturns
.pdf (last visited June 6, 2009); Justice Policy Institute, Fact Sheet: Effective Investment in Public Safety: Mass Incarceration and Longer Sentences Fail to Make Us Safer (2007), available at http://www.justicepolicy.org/content-hmID=1811&smID=1588&ssmID=54.htm (last visited June 6, 2009); Pew Center on the States, The Impact of Incarceration on Crime: Two National Experts Weigh In (April, 2008), available at http://www.pewcenteronthestates.org/uploaded Files/Crime%20Incarceration%20QA.pdf (last visited June 6, 2009).

"For example, California's inmate population. . . .": *See* James Sterngold & Mark Martin, California's Prison Crisis; High Price of Broken Prisons; Tough Sentencing Creates Overcrowding that Endangers Inmates, Haunts Taxpayers, San Francisco Chronicle, July 3, 2005, page A1.

"Even though the isolation. . . .": *See* Vince Beiser, A Necessary Evil? Pelican Bay State Prison Houses "the Worst of the Worst" in the Starkest Isolation Imaginable. But these Supermax Units Are Turning Inmates into Mental Cases, and the Asylum Gate Opens Right Back onto Our Streets, Los Angeles Times, October 3, 2003, part I, page 12.

California's Inability to Respond Effectively to Prison Overcrowding

"over 200% of design capacity": *See* Coleman/Plata v. Schwarzenegger, 2009 W.L. 2430820 at 23.

"Governor Schwarzenegger then issued. . . .": *See* Office of the Governor, Proclamation, Prison Overcrowding State of Emergency, October 4, 2006, available at http://gov.ca.gov/index .php?/proclamation/4278 (last visited April 10, 2010).

"the legislature adopted and the governor signed. . . .": *See* Office of the Governor, Press Release: Gov. Schwarzenegger Signs Historic Bipartisan Agreement, Takes Important Step toward Solving California's Overcrowding Crisis, May 3, 2007 [**hereinafter Historic Agreement**], available at http://gov.ca.gov/index.php?/press-release/6119 (last visited April 21, 2010).

"The state, however, has been slow. . . .": *See* Plata/Coleman v. Schwarzenegger, 2009 W.L. 2430820 at 64–76; Legislative Analyst's Office, Policy Brief: A Status Report: Implementing AB 900's Prison Construction and Rehabilitation Efforts, May 14, 200, available at http://www.lao .ca.gov/2009/crim/AB900/ab900_051409.aspx (last visited April 21, 2010).

"diverting non-violent. . . .": *Id.* at 20.

"AB 900 made virtually no effort. . . .": AB 900 included some provisions for rehabilitation programs. The primary focus, however, was on new construction. *See* Historic Agreement.

"'Trying to solve overcrowding. . . .'": *See* Steven Harmon, Deal Struck on California Prison Crowding, San Jose Mercury News, April 26, 2007. *See also* Sonoma County, The Corrections Master Plan, Executive Summary, Coleman/Plata v. Schwarzenegger, No. C01-1351-TEH (E.D./N.D. Cal. filed October 30, 2008) 1 ("Available beds in any correctional facility have a tendency to become filled. *'Build it and they will come.'*") (emphasis in original).

The California Correctional Peace Officers' Association and the Code of Silence

"From a humble beginning. . . .": *See* Ben Carrasco & Joan Petersilia, Assessing the CCPOA's Political Influence and Its Impact on Efforts to Reform the California Correctional System, Sanford Criminal Justice Center Working Papers: California Sentencing and Corrections Policy Series, January 27, 2006, available at http://www.law.stanford.edu/program/

centers/scjc/workingpapers/BCarassco-wp4_06.pdf (last visited June 8, 2009); Institute of Governmental Studies, California Correctional Peace Officers Association, January 31, 2008, available at http://igs.berkeley.edu/library/htCaliforniaPrisonUnion.htm (last visited June 6, 2009); Public Eye, Defending Justice: Activist Resource Kit: Conservative Agendas & Campaigns 215–23, available at http://www.publiceye.org/defendingjustice/pdfs/chapters/incar ceration.pdf (last visited June 8, 2009).

"During the 2010 election cycle. . . .": *See* Steve Lopez, Donations Create "Winners"; Prison Guards' Union Backs 107, 104 Elected, Los Angeles Times, May 22, 2011, part A, page 2.

"Within six months. . . .": *See id;* California Correctional Peace Officers Association, On the Issues, 5150 Hot Line, May 20, 2011, available at http://www.ccpoa.org/issues/legislative/5150_ hotline/may_20_2011 (last visited July 8, 2011).

"In the eyes of many. . . .": *See* Thomas Peele, Judge to Rule on Contempt Charges; Corrections Director and Internal Affairs Chief Both May Be Charged in Handling of Perjury Case, Contra Costa Times, October 24, 2004, page A03 (quoting Judge Henderson as saying from the bench "The Union runs the prison system. I'm going to change that."); Corrections Independent Review Panel, Reforming California's Youth and Adult Correctional System (2004), available at http://cpr.ca.gov/Review_Panel (last visited June 8, 2009). *See also, e.g.,* Mark Martin, Governor Accused of Retreat on Prisons; Report Says Schwarzenegger Abandoned Reform Efforts and Caved in to Guards Union, San Francisco Chronicle, June 22, 2006, page A1 (quoting former Corrections Secretary Roderick Hickman as saying "The union has established a much more influential presence than they had before."); Jenifer Warren, Ex-Prison Chiefs Tell of Frustrations; Top Aides to the Governor Stymied Reform by Giving Guards Union Veto Power over Hiring, Two Former Corrections Leaders Say, Los Angeles Times, December 21, 2006, part B, page 1 ("Testifying in federal court, two corrections secretaries[, Roderick Hickman and Jeanne Woodford,] singled out the prison guards union and a pair of Schwarzenegger's top aides for most of the blame, saying the aides had given the union veto power of candidates for top jobs and a say in other key decisions.").

"[It is an] unwritten but widely understood code. . . .": Madrid v. Gomez, 889 F. Supp. at 1157–58.

Underlying Problems

"As Professor [Susan] Sturm explains. . . .": Thelton Henderson, Keynote Address: Confronting the Crisis of California Prisons, 43 U.S.F. L. Rev. 1, 40–43 (2008) (quoting Susan Sturm, Resolving the Remedial Dilemma: Strategies of Judicial Intervention in Prisons, 138 U. Pa. L. Rev. 805 (1990)).

Chapter Fifteen
Judge Henderson's Prison Trilogy, Part I:
Madrid v. Gomez

"[D]ry words on paper. . . .": Madrid v. Gomez, 889 F. Supp. 1146, 1280 (N.D. Cal. 1995).

[The named defendant, James Gomez, was the head of the California Department of Corrections (CDC), later renamed the California Department of Corrections and Rehabilitation (CDCR). In filings over the years, the named defendant has changed as director of the CDC/

CDCR has changed. The named plaintiff, Madrid, and the case number, C90-3094 TEH, have remained the same. For the sake of simplicity, all subsequent citations to the case in this chapter, including citations to specific documents, omit the name of the defendant, the case number, and the court (N.D. Cal.).]

The Prison

"Pelican Bay State Prison, situated. . . .": *See id.* at 1155.

"'between 3,500. . . .'": *Id.*

"Over a decade later. . . .": *See* California Department of Corrections and Rehabilitation website, available at http://www.cdcr.ca.gov/Visitors/Facilities/PBSP-Institution_Stats.html (last visited June 16, 2009) (3,461 inmates as of 2006–07 fiscal year).

"Almost immediately after Pelican Bay opened. . . .": *See* Court Decides Landmark Class Action Case in Favor of Pelican Bay State Prison Inmates; "Supermax" Prison Practices Rules Unconstitutional, Business Wire, January 11, 1995.

"Judge Henderson visited. . . .": *See* Soul of Justice for a brief account of Judge Henderson's visit and the "riot."

"The episode . . . was staged. . . .": *See* Former Prison Guards to Become Inmates, Tri-Valley Herald (Pleasanton, CA), February 7, 2003.

"Pelican Bay includes three. . . .": *See Madrid,* 889 F. Supp. at 1155.

"a 'daily routine. . . .'": *Id.*

"Located in a completely separate. . . . not see each other.": *Id.* at 1155, 1228, 1229.

"An exercise pen. . . .": *See id.* at 1228–29, 1230.

"As the Court observed. . . .": *Id.* at 1229.

"'with no opportunity. . . .'": *Id.*

Physical Abuse

"On January 31, 1991, Arturo Castillo. . . .": *Id.* at 1162–63.

"After Dortch smeared himself. . . .": *See id.* at 1166.

"Although there was a shower. . . .": *Id.* at 1166–67.

"Based on the record before us. . . .": *Id.* at 1167.

"'unnecessarily and some cases recklessly'": *Id.* at 1179.

"'has [not] been applied. . . .'": *Id.* at 1180.

"And Judge Henderson found. . . .": *See id.* at 1186.

"excessive force in removing prisoners. . . .": *See id.* at 1173–79,

"Other abusive practices. . . .": *See id.* at 1168–69 (fetal binding), 1171–72 (caging).

"[N]o expert at trial. . . .": *Id.* at 1168.

"Judge Henderson acknowledged that 'officials will [sometimes] need. . . .'": *Id.* at 1171.

"[P]roviding substitute clothes. . . .": *Id.*

"Vince Nathan. . . .": *See id.* at 1157 n. 8, 1161 n.16.

"over 300 hours": *See id.* ("Nathan . . . review[ed] all available written policies concerning the use of force at Pelican Bay, all Pelican Bay training materials, all control restraint memoranda, all shooting review reports, half of the files of internal investigations on excessive force, more than one hundred incident reports, and hundreds of pages of deposition testimony.")

"I have simply never observed. . . .": *Id.* at 1180.

"Plaintiffs have convincingly. . . .": *Id.* at 1181.

"If anything, that pattern. . . .": *Id.* at 1181 n.57.

Medical Needs

"reviewed Pelican Bay's medical care system. . . .": *See id.* at 1200–12.

"attempted to minimize. . . .": *Id.* at 1212.

"characterized Dortch's care as 'grossly inadequate.'": *See id.* at 1212 n.136.

"subsequently told an MTA. . . .": *Id.* at 1207.

"Dr. [Armond] Start. . . .": *Id.* at 1207 n.123. Dr. Start was an Associate Professor Medicine at the University of Wisconsin and former Director of Health Care for the Texas Department of Corrections. *See id.* at 1158 n.11.

"After characterizing this data. . . .": *See id.*

"the quality of medical care. . . .": *Id.* at 1208, 1210, 1213.

Mental Health Needs

"Judge Henderson took a similar approach. . . .": *See id.* at 1214–26 (reference to defendants' experts appears at pages 1214–15; reference to Warden's budget request appears at page 1215).

"[First,] the SHU. . . .": *Id.* at 1223, 1229–30 (emphasis in original) [The material in the second paragraph after the first sentence is inserted from pages 1229–30. Except for that insert, the quotation is from page 1223, where it appears as part of a single paragraph.].

"Inmate 4 . . . was institutionalized. . . .": *Id.* at 1233–34.

"Dr. [Stuart] Grassian": Dr. Grassian, was psychiatrist on the Harvard Medical School faculty *See id.* at 1158 n. 12 (setting forth Dr. Grassian's qualifications).

"'in severe distress. . . .'": *Id. at* 1234 (quoting a Dr. Fulton).

"MTAs and correctional officers. . . .": *Id.*

"'Inmate 1' was another victim. . . .": *See id.* at 1232 (entire paragraph, including quotations).

"[T]he evidence plainly shows. . . .": *Id.* at 1215, 1223.

Judicial Restraint and the SHU

"He recognized that. . . .": *See id.* at 1254 ("uncooperative and combative;" use of force), 1228 & 1261 (isolation), 1160 ("demanding and often thankless"), and 1161 n.17 (staff deplored excessive violence).

"Throughout these proceedings. . . .": *Id.* at 1279; *see also id.* at 1262, 1282.

"The Eighth Amendment does not require. . . .": *Id.* at 1256.

"Reviewing the evidence. . . .": *Id.* at 1235 (including quotations)

"state hailed as a major victory": *See* Bill Wallace, Conditions at Pelican Bay Prison Ruled Unconstitutional but Judge Says Isolation Unit Can Remain, San Francisco Chronicle, January 12, 1995, page A17.

"The decision to segregate. . . .": *Madrid,* 889 F. Supp. at 1261–62.

"that were frequently assigned to the SHU": *See id.* at 1223, 1232–34.

"'the already mentally ill' and (2) 'persons. . . .'": *Id.* at 1266, 1267.

"[T]he [California Department of Corrections'] own manual. . . .": *Id.* at 1236.

The Initial Order

"Like other judges . . . 120 days.": *See id.* at 1280–83. "Thomas Lonegran": Lonegran had had extensive experience as a Special Master in prison and other cases. *See id.* at 1282 n.231.

The Early Responses

"While members of the Department of Corrections. . . .": *See* Bill Wallace, Conditions at Pelican Bay Prison Ruled Unconstitutional But Judge Says Isolation Unit Can Remain, San Francisco Chronicle, January 12, 1995, page A17.

"James Gomez seemed to further the hope. . . .": Gomez's letter is available at Letters, Los Angeles Times, February 9, 1995, part B, page 6.

"Prior to Judge Henderson's decision. . . .": *See* Dan Morain, State Issues Tighter Use-of-Deadly-Force Policy at Prisons, Los Angeles Times, January 22, 1995, part A, page 20; Associated Press, California Acts to Stop Guards from Shooting Brawling Inmates, N.Y. Times, January 21, 1995, sec. 1, page 11.

"In addition, the defendants began. . . .": *See* Remedial Order Re: Use of Force and Investigatory Policy, *Madrid* (filed June 17, 1996).

" 'highly commendable' ": *Id.* at 2.

"By the fall of 1995 . . . Lonergan reported . . . inmates from the SHU. . . .": *See* October 25, 1005 [Special Master's] Recommendation Re: Exclusion from the Security Housing Unit and Enforcement of Court's Order of January 10, 1995, *Madrid* (filed November 1, 1995) at 8. [hereinafter October 25, 1995 Report]

"no improvement. . . .": *See* November 6, 1995, [Special Master's] Recommendations Re: Defendant's Revised Remedial Plan for Pelican Bay State Prison Health Care Delivery System — August 25, 1995, *Madrid* (filed November 11,1995) [hereinafter November 6, 1995 Report].

"not acting in good faith": *See* October 25, 1995 Report at 6–7, 19; November 6, 1995 Report at 4–6, 20.

"too adversarial": *See* October 25, 1995 Report at 19.

"In a December 15. . . .": *See* Order Re: Medical/Mental Health Care Delivery System, *Madrid* (filed February 5, 1996).

"At that hearing . . . '. . . inadequate care.' ": *See* Susan Sward, Judge Again Faults Pelican Bay for Poor Care: A Year after Order, Treatment "Grossly Inadequate," San Francisco Chronicle, February 5, 1996, page A16.

"[T]he systems for delivering. . . .": Remedial Order Re: Medical and Mental Health Care Services, *Madrid* (filed March 10, 1997) at 3 (quoting February 5, 1996 Tr. at 19).

" '[T]hat things may have been in worse repair. . . .' ": *Id.* (quoting February 5, 1996 Tr. at 27).

"new deadlines.": *See* Order Re: Medical/Mental Health Care Delivery System, *Madrid* (filed February 5, 1996) at 2–3, 5.

Progress on Medical and Mental Health Issues

"thirteen-volume 'remedial plan. . . .' ": *Id.* at 1.

" 'an excellent overall plan' ": *Id.* at 7.

"There is no doubt. . . .": *Id.* at 3–4.

"With the exception of two matters. . . .": *See id.* at 2 n.2, 13–17.

"a series of orders. . . .": *See, e.g.,* Order Re: Disciplinary Policy, *Madrid* (filed April 21, 1998); Order Re: Procedures for Mental Health Monitoring of SHU Inmates, *Madrid* (filed April 21,

1998); Order Re: History of Mental Illness, *Madrid* (filed September 1, 1998); Order Re: Phase-out of Monitoring of Use of Force Remedial Plan, *Madrid* (filed September 10, 1998; Stipulation and Order Vacating and Terminating the Court's September 29, 1997); Order Re: Cell Extractions of Mentally Ill Inmates at Pelican Bay State Prison, *Madrid* (filed March 29, 2000); Order Re: Defendants Revised Use of Force Policies, Phase-out of Use of Force Monitoring, and Partial Termination of Force Related Orders, *Madrid* (filed June 12, 2000); Order Re: Use of Force Audit Instrument, *Madrid* (filed May 10, 2001)

"One critically important example. . . .": *See* Special Master's Final Report Re Defendants' Case Management, Enhanced Tele-Medicine, QMAT and Inerim [*sic*] Physician Coverage Corrective Action Plans; Recommendations, *Madrid* (filed September 28, 2001) (quotation from page 3).

"Coleman v. Schwarzenegger": 2007 W.L. 30577 (originally filed in 1990 as Coleman v. Deukmejian).

"Plata v. Schwarzenegger": 2005 W.L. 2932243 (originally filed in 2001 as Plata v. Davis).

"In May 2008, the Special Master. . . .": *See* Special Master's Final Report and Recommendation to Cease Health Services Monitoring at Pelican Bay State Prison, *Madrid* (filed May 6, 2008).

"The fact that Pelican Bay. . . .": Order Re: Special Master's Report and Recommendation to Cease Health Services Monitoring at Pelican Bay State Prison, *Madrid* (filed May 23, 2008) at 2.

"Fn. 1. The California Department of Corrections. . . .": *See* James Sterngold & Mark Martin, Hard Times; California's Prisons in Crisis; High Price of Broken Prisons; Tough Sentencing Creates Overcrowding that Endangers Inmates, Haunts Taxpayers, San Francisco Chronicle, July 3, 2005, page A1.

The Failure to Discipline Prison Personnel

"the well-established 'code of silence'. . . .": The description from Judge Henderson's opinion is set forth in the preceding chapter.

"Within months. . . .": *See* Mark Arax & Mark Gladstone, Keeping Justice at Bay: A Team of State Investigators Looking into Allegations of Brutality by Pelican Bay Prison Guards Were [*sic*] Blocked after Union Complaints to Union Officials, Los Angeles Times, December 16, 1998 [**hereinafter Justice at Bay**].

"one guard, Jose Garcia": The conviction was eventually reversed. *See* Special Master's Final Report Re Department of Corrections "Post Powers" Investigations and Employee Discipline, *Madrid* (filed June 24, 2004) at 39 [**hereinafter June 24, 2004 Report**].

"The investigators, the prosecutor. . . .": *See* Justice at Bay.

". . . Special Master John Hagar. . . .": *See* June 24, 2004 Report at 38–41.

". . . independent analysis. . . .": *See* Justice at Bay.

"According to John Hagar. . . .": *See* June 24, 2004 Report at 41.

"Garcia and another Pelican Bay Guard. . . .": *See id.* at 41–42 (also describing the federal prosecution of another guard, David Lewis); Bob Egelko, Former Pelican Bay Guards Convicted; Pair Had Inmates Beaten, Stabbed, San Francisco Chronicle, May 16, 2002.

"reward them with. . . .": *See id. See also* Justice at Bay.

"Assistant US Attorney Melinda Haag. . . .": *See* June 24, 2004 Report at 44.

"Thomas Moore. . . . to eight months": *See id.* at 50.

"'vague and repetitive'": *Id.* at 51.

"unaware of a recently adopted CDC plan. . . .": *See id.* at 43, 51.

"no guidance or supervision. . . .": *See id.* at 52–53.

"At least in part because of. . . .": *See* Thomas Peele, Guards Shackle System Reforms; One-Year Statute of Limitations, Code of Silence Often Makes Wayward Corrections Officers Impervious to Discipline; Critics Say the Agency Can't Police Itself, Contra Costa Times, December 22, 2003, page A01 [**hereinafter Guards Shackle Reforms**]; *see also* June 24, 2004 Report at 87–102.

"Edward Alameida . . . in 2001": *See* CDCR Today, Edward S. Alameida, Jr. Appointed Director of the California Department of Corrections, September 20, 2001, available at http://cdcrtoday.blogspot.com/2001/09/edward-s-alameida-jr-appointed-director.html (last visited June 3, 2016).

"shut down the investigation. . . .": *See* June 24, 2004 Report at 62–64.

"Alameida had had a telephone conversation. . . .": *See id.* at 62.

"Alameida instructed one of his associates. . . .": *See id.* at 62, 64, 66.

"testified that . . . the allegations of perjury were true": *See id.* at 59; Thomas Peele, Prison Chief Says Decision Was Staff's; Edward Alameida's Account of Ending a Perjury Inquiry Conflicts with Others, Contra Costa Times, November 22, 2003 [**hereinafter Prison Chief Says**].

"The investigators testified that they told Alameida. . . .": *See* June 24, 2004 Report at 59; Prison Chief Says.

"that Alameida said he wanted the investigation to 'go away.' ": *See* June 24, 2004 Report at 59, 60.

"Alameida, by contrast,. . . .": *See id.* at 62–65; Prison Chief Says; Bob Egelko, State Prisons Chief Tells a Different Story; Contradicts Employees' Prior Testimony, Denies Interference from Guards' Union, San Francisco Chronicle, November 23, 2003, page A17.

"investigators' testimony to be 'credible.' ": *See* June 24, 2004 Report at 69.

"It is difficult to believe. . . .": *Id.* at 70–71.

"You either have a whole lot of people. . . .": *See* Prison Chief Says.

"Alameida announced his resignation. . . .": *See* Jenifer Warren & Dan Morain, State Corrections Director Resigns for "Personal Reasons;" The Prison Department Veteran Led the System for Two Years. Critics Content He Was too Close to the Guards Union, Los Angeles Times, December 12, 2003, part B, page 1.

"The Court has carefully reviewed. . . .": Order Re: (1) Special Master's Report Re "Post Powers" Investigations and Employee Discipline and (2) CCPOA's Motion to Intervene, *Madrid* (filed November 17, 2004) at 10–11 [**hereinafter November 17, 2004 Order**].

"John Hagar's suggestion. . . .": *See* June 24, 2004 Report at 119–21.

"Alameida might have a valid defense. . . .": *See* November 17, 2004 Order at 11.

"because of Alameida's resignation. . . .": *See id.* at 14.

" 'the highest level investigator' ": June 24, 2004 Report at 5.

"be held in criminal contempt": *See id.* at 119–21.

"consider referring Moore. . . .": *See id.* at 121.

"did sanction Moore. . . .": *See* Order Re: Sanctions Pursuant to Court's Inherent Power, *Madrid* (filed March 16, 2005) at 7.

A Return to Progress

" 'lost control. . . .' ": June 24, 2004 Report at 103.

"a fact that he attributed to. . . .": *See id.* at 98–104.

"reason for hope.": *See id.* at 107–09.

"Fn. 2. Schwarzenegger, a Republican, won. . . .": *See* John Broder, The California Recall: An Overview; Davis is Out; Schwarzenegger Is In by Big Margins in California Recall, N.Y. Times, October 8, 2003, sec. A, page 1.

"Matthew Cate. . . .": *See id.* at 107.

"Jeanne Woodford . . . 'real reform.'": Office of the Governor, Press Release: Governor Schwarzenegger Appoints Jeanne Woodford Director of the California Department of Corrections, February 19, 2004, available at http://gov.ca.gov/press-release/3213 (last visited February 1, 2010).

"Roderick Hickman . . . joined Schwarzenegger's cabinet. . . .": *See* Joe Matthews, Schwarzenegger Names Ex-Guard to Oversee Prisons; The Governor-Elect's Choice to Join His Cabinet as Head of the State's Youth and Adult Correctional Agency Is a Democrat, Los Angeles Times, November 16, 2003, part A, page 36.

"Hickman announced. . . .": *See* June 24, 2004 Report at 107; Thomas Peele, Prisons Secretary under Fire; Roderick Hickman Bristles at Criticism, Says He's Ready to Make Reforms, Contra Costa Times, January 22, 2004, page A01.

"In March 2004, Judge Henderson appointed. . . .": *See* Tim Reiterman & Jenifer Warren, State Will Oversee Probes of Guards; Judge Drops Harsher Measures after New Prison Officials Vow to Make Changes, Los Angeles Times, March 10, 2004, part B, page 1; Thomas Peele, Corrections Given One Last Chance; A Judge Warns that He May Put the Department under Federal Control for Its Failure to Discipline Employees, Contra Costa Times, March 4, 2004, page A01.

"'the right people have been assembled. . . .'": June 24, 2004 Report at 109.

"'effort to formulate an adequate remedial plan. . . .'": *Id.* at 107.

"'concerning the development and implementation. . . .'": *Id.* at 121–22.

"Judge Henderson agreed.": *See, e.g.,* Order, *Madrid* (filed July 29, 2004); Order Re: Special Master's Recommendations Re Defendants' Employee Disciplinary Matrix, *Madrid* (filed October 19, 2004); Order Re: (1) Special Master's Report Re "Post Powers" Investigations and Employee Discipline, and (2) CCPOA's Motion to Intervene, *Madrid* (filed November 17, 2004).

The Continuing Ramifications of the CCPOA's Political Power

"Governor Schwarzenegger . . . never accepted. . . .": *See* Special Master's Final Report Re Status of State of California Corrective Action Plans for Administrative Investigations and Discipline; Recommendations, *Madrid* (filed August 22, 2006) at 6 [hereinafter August 22, 2006 Report]. Within a month of this report, the CCPOA endorsed Schwarzenegger's challenger, Phil Angelides, for governor in the upcoming November election.

"the defendants, under the leadership of Secretary Hickman. . . .": *See id.* at 5, 8–16, 21–22.

"sweetheart contract with Gray Davis. . . .": *See* Andrew LaMar, Davis Oks Pay Raises after Gifts; Prison Guards' Union Has Given Governor More Than Half a Million Dollars since He Took Office, Contra Costa Times, July 31, 2002, sec. A, page 1; Michelle Guido, Davis Under Fire for Guards Contract; Big Financial Backer Gets Heafty Pay Raise, San Jose Mercury News, May 16, 2002, sec. A, page 1.

"In return for deferring pay raises. . . .": *See* Dan Morain, Deal Gives Guards Millions in Benefits; Schwarzenegger Cedes Power to Union, Agreed to New Perks in Winning a Delay in Pay Raise, Los Angeles Times, July 13, 2004, part A, page 1.

"Fn. 3. In 2005, Governor Schwarzenegger. . . .": *See* California Courts, Court of Appeal, 1st District, San Francisco, Peter Siggins, Associate Justice, available at http://www.courtinfo.ca.gov/courts/courtsofappeal/1stDistrict/justices/siggins.htm (last visited February 2, 2010).

"I do not intend to intrude. . . .": Letter from Judge Henderson to Peter Siggins & Roderick Hickman, July 19, 2004 (copy in author's possession).

"'a commitment with the Court. . . .'": Letter from Peter Siggins to Judge Henderson, July 20, 2004 (copy in author's possession).

"Judge Henderson's letter did not affect the arrangement. . . .": *See* Peter Nicholas & Jenifer Warren, Judge "Can Take" Prisons, Governor Says; But Schwarzenegger Adds that He Prefers to Avoid Receivership and Fix the Troubled System, Los Angeles Times, August 17, 2004 [here-inafter Judge "Can Take" Prisons]; Mark Gladstone, Judge Warns of Prison Takeover; He Says Reform Blocked by Guard Concessions, San Jose Mercury News, July 21, 2004, page 1A.

"a telephone conversation with the Governor.": *See* Judge "Can Take" Prisons.

"news stories": *See, e.g.*, Thomas Peele, Judge Losing Patience with Pace of Prison Reform, Contra Costa Times, July 21, 2004, page A15; Jenifer Warren, The State; Takeover of State Prisons Is Threatened; A Federal Judge Assails the Schwarzenegger Administration on Lack of Reform, Its Deal with Guards. He May Name Receiver to Run System, Los Angeles Times, July 21, 2004, part A, page 1.

"editorials": *See, e.g.*, Editorial, Schwarzenegger Cuts a Bad Deal, San Francisco Chronicle, July 22, 2004, page B8; Editorial, Prison Guards Prevail; Governor's Negotiations Result in a Worse Deal, San Jose Mercury News, July 21, 2004.

"referred to Schwarzenegger as a 'girlie man. . . .'": *See, e.g.*, Sue Hutchison, Girly-Man? Governor Should Look in the Mirror, San Jose Mercury News, July 24, 2004, page 1E; Editorial, Governor Acts Like Girlie Man, Oakland Tribune, July 26, 2004.

"originated in a Saturday Night Live skit . . .": *See, e.g.*, Saturday Night Live Transcript, available at http://snltranscripts.jt.org/88/88ghansfranz.phtml (last visited June 17, 2012).

"to characterize Democratic presidential candidates": *See* Hal Hinson, "Feed:" Before the Sound Bites, The Washington Post, October 14, 1992, page C1.

"to characterize . . . legislators beholden to union interests.": *See* Peter Nicholas, Gov. Criticizes Legislators as "Girlie Men"; In Speech in Ontario He Urges Voters to "Terminate" at the Polls Those Lawmakers Who Refuse to Approve His State Budget Plan, Los Angeles Times, July 18, 2004, part B, page 1.

"the Governor seemed to become more aware of. . . .": Telephone Interview with Judge Henderson, January 28, 2010.

"In mid-August. . . . 'is 100% with us.'": *See* Judge "Can Take" Prisons; Mark Gladstone, Judge Can Take Away Prison Control, Schwarzenegger Says, Contra Costa Times, August 17, 2004, page A08.

"'[T]he Davis Administration required. . . .'": August 22, 2006 Report at 6.

"'[d]uring the first two years. . . .'": *Id.*

"In January Susan Kennedy, . . .": *See id.* at 4.

"She and Fred Aguiar. . . .": *See id.* at 35.

"'prison reform ground to a halt. . . .'": *Id.* at 36.

"Hickman resigned. . . .": *See id.* at 29; Editorial, San Francisco Chronicle, February 28, 2006, page B6.

"Jeanne Woodford became Acting Secretary": *See* August 22, 2006 Report at 29.

"resigned six weeks later": *See id*; Mark Martin & Greg Lucas, Sacramento; Temporary Prisons Chief Bows Out after 2 Months; Resignation Adds to Governor's Stresses with Troubled System, San Francisco Chronicle, April 20, 2006, page B1.

"rejected two of her personnel recommendations.": *See* Jenifer Warren, Ex-prison Chiefs Tell of Frustrations; Top Aides to the Governor Stymied Reform by Giving the Guards Veto Power over Hiring, Two Former Corrections Leaders Say, Los Angeles Times, December 21, 2006, part B, page 1 [**hereinafter Ex-Prison Chiefs**].

"After initially announcing the appointment. . . .": *See* Steve Schmidt, Governor's Prison Negotiator a Tough Sell; Ethical Dilemma Seen in Selection of Former Guard, San Diego Union-Tribune, March 10, 2006, page A-3.

"Perhaps there was genuine concern. . . .": *See id.*

"The CCPOA, however,. . .": *See id*; Ex-Prison Chiefs.

"'was derailed by the Governor's office. . . .'": August 22, 2006 Report at 35.

"James Tilton, who promised, 'One of the first things. . . .' ": *See id.*; Jenifer Warren & Peter Nicholas, Gov. Acts Quickly to Name Chief of Prisons; a Day after Jeanne Woodford's Resignation, the Third Corrections Secretary in Two Months is Appointed. Guards Union Praises the Choice, Los Angeles Times, April 21, 2006, part A, page 1 [**hereinafter Gov. Acts Quickly**]

"the CCPOA was reportedly prepared. . . .": *See* Mark Martin, Governor Accused of Retreat on Prisons; Report Says Schwarzenegger Abandoned Reform Efforts and Caved in to Guards Union, San Francisco Chronicle, June 22, 2006.

"but he could reasonably hope. . . .": *See id.*; Gov. Acts Quickly.

"John Hagar filed a report. . . .": *See* August 22, 2006 Report.

"The Governor's office. . . .": *See id.* at 32–42; Memorandum of Governor Schwarzenegger in Response to Special Master's Final Report Re Status of State of California Corrective Action Plans for Administrative Investigations and Discipline; Recommendations, *Madrid* (filed September 12, 2006).

"Governor Schwarzenegger had refused. . . .": *See* Andy Furillo, Chances at Prison Guards' Support Spurned: Governor Skips His Interview with Union, Sacramento Bee, August 22, 2006, state & regional news section.

"the CCPOA endorsed. . . .": *See* Kate Folmar, Prison Guards' Endorsement Could Revive Angelides Campaign, San Jose Mercury News, September 7, 2006.

"seventeen-point victory.": *See* Election 2006: California Results, Los Angeles Times, November 9, 2006, part B, page 5.

"a hearing for December. . . .": *See* Ex-Prison Chiefs.

"Negotiations . . . continued. . . .": *See* Editorial: Looting Season: Guards Union, Trial Lawyers Line Up for Favors, San Diego Union-Tribune, September 12, 2007, page B-8.

"made an unsuccessful attempt. . . .": *See* Guards Union Gets "Punked," Inside Bay Area, November 17, 2007.

"CCPOA mounted and then quickly abandoned. . . .": *See* Jim Boren, Now that the Prison Guards Union Has Abandoned Schwarzenegger Recall, It's Time to Ask Whether this Powerful Union Has Lost Its Clout in Sacramento, Fresno Bee Editorial Opinion Blog, October 17, 2008; Matthew Yi, Prison Guard Union Takes Steps to Recall the Governor; Issues Are Similar to 2003, When California Voters Threw Out Davis over Fiscal Mess, San Francisco Chronicle, September 9, 2008, page A1.

Reform Continues

"Governor Schwarzenegger named Matthew Cate. . . .": *See* Michael Rothfeld, State Prisons Get Yet Another Leader; Matthew Cate, Fourth Corrections Secretary in Less than Five Years, Will Replace Retiring James Tilton, Los Angeles Times, April 16, 2008, part B, page 1.

"Overall, the timeliness and quality of internal affairs. . . .": Special Master's Final Report Re Status of Post Powers Remedial Plan Monitoring, *Madrid* (filed October 16, 2007) at 4–5.

"He concluded his assessment. . . .": *See id.* at 10.

"'very positive progress. . . .'": Special Master's Report Re Cessation of Force Related Remedial Plan Monitoring; Recommendation Re Termination of Force Related Orders, *Madrid* (filed October 18, 2008) at 2.

"John Hagar recommended. . . .": *See id.* at 9–12.

"In the meantime,. . . Ron Yank. . . .": Interview with Ron Yank, June 4, 2011.

Chapter Sixteen
Judge Henderson's Prison Trilogy, Part II:
Plata v. Schwarzenegger (Nee Plata v. Davis)

"inmate named Luna who 'died to no one's great alarm.'": *See* http://www.joanbaez.com/Lyrics/pristrilogy.html (last visited June 23, 2012).

"[O]n average, an inmate. . . .": Plata v. Schwarzenegger, 2005 W.L. 2932253 (N.D. Cal.) at 1.

[All subsequent citations to *Plata* in this chapter, including citations to specific documents filed in the case, omit the name of the defendant (originally Governor Gray Davis, then Governor Arnold Schwarzenegger, then Governor Jerry Brown), and the case number (C01-1351 TEH).]

Plata v. Schwarzenegger: An Early but Ineffective Settlement

"In April 2001, Judge Henderson. . . .": *See id.* at 1 & n.1.

"In less than a year. . . .": *See id.* at 1–2.

"the reforms would cost. . . .": *See* Jenifer Warren, State to Spend Millions on Better Inmate Care; Corrections: The Action is Part of a Class-Action Lawsuit Filed after Deaths of Eight Female Prisoners. The Plan Still Requires a Judge's Approval, Los Angeles Times, January 30, 2002, part 2, page 2.

"no 'code of silence'. . .": For an apparently isolated instance of an effort by San Quentin Warden Jill Brown to impose a code of silence on medical personnel, *see* Mark Gladstone, Probe Sought in Allegation of Prison Censure; Rights Group, in Letter, Complains of Warden's Threat against Physician, San Jose Mercury News, May 20, 2005, page 15A (describing apparent effort by San Quentin Warden Jill Brown to silence physicians and immediate action to investigate incident by CDC Director Jeanne Woodford). Following an investigation, Brown was removed from her position. *See* Mark Gladstone, San Quentin Warden Loses Post Amid Prison Troubles; She's Accused of Trying to Silence Health Staff, San Jose Mercury News, July 8, 2005, sec. A, page 8.

"[T]he Court Experts, plaintiffs, and the Court. . . .": *Plata*, 2005 W.L. 2932253 at 26.

Judge Henderson on the Shocking Prison Medical Conditions and the State's Admitted Failures: Plata v. Schwarzenegger, 2005 W.L. 2932243 (N.D. Cal.) 1–5

"Fn. 1. The ensuing text. . . .": The date of the opinion cited in the heading of this section, 2005 W.L. 2932243 (N.D. Cal.) is May 10. As this footnote indicates, the text — most of which is from the May 10 opinion — includes without designation, excerpts from an October 3 opinion, 2005 W.L. 2932253 (N.D. Cal.). Endnotes in this section identify and provide citations for those excerpts.

"In the four years . . . California Department of Corrections. . . .": In July 2005 — between the dates of the two opinions excerpted in this section, *see* previous endnote, the California Department of Corrections (CDC) was reorganized and renamed the California Department of Corrections and Rehabilitation (CDCR). In this paragraph from Judge Henderson's May 10 opinion, I have changed the reference from CDC to CDCR. On the CDC's change of name to CDCD, *see* Correction Agency Reorganizes, Becomes California Department of Corrections and Rehabilitation; Commitment to Public and Employee Safety Remains Paramount, PR Newswire, July 1, 2005.

". . . A prevailing lack of accountability . . . report to [the Director of Health Care Services].": *Plata*, 2005 W.L. 2932253 at 3–4.

". . . Indeed, Undersecretary of Corrections . . . '. . . to provide medical care.' ": *Id.* at 4.

". . . A major problem . . . conflicts with custodial staff.": *Id.* at 15.

"The medical records . . . makes even mediocre medical care impossible.": *Id.* at 14.

"There are serious, long-standing problems . . . expired prescriptions.": *Id.* at 16.

". . . The [overall] vacancy rate . . . poor working conditions. . . .": *Id.* at 11.

". . . [*Defendants'* expert] . . . high rate of patient death and morbidity.": *Id.* at 5. (emphasis added).

". . . The evidence establishes. . . . Health Care Manager.": *Id.* at 9.

". . . [C]entral office staff . . . beds are needed.": *Id.* at 4.

The Need for a Receiver

"over 160,000 individuals": *See* California Department of Corrections & Rehabilitation, Monthly Total Population Report Archive, available at http://www.cdcr.ca.gov/Reports_Research/Offender_Information_Services_Branch/Monthly/Monthly_Tpop1a_Archive.asp (last visited February 21, 2010).

"the defendants had failed to provide. . . .": *See Plata*, 2005 W.L. 2932253 at 28.

"Moreover, the defendants did not oppose. . . .": *See id.*

"Indeed, they appeared to welcome it.": *See id.* at 30.

"Looking at the full spectrum. . . .": *Id.* at 31–32.

"When appointing receivers. . . .": *Id.* at 30.

"It bears emphasizing. . . .": *Id.* at 33.

Finding a Receiver

"Judge Henderson had hoped . . . professional search firm": *See* James Sterngold, Overhaul of Prison Health System Delayed; Court Hires Search Firm after Original Effort Can't Find Manager for Struggling System, San Francisco Chronicle, November 3, 2005, page B1.

"he announced that Robert Sillen. . . .": *See* Order Appointing Receiver, *Plata* (N.D. Cal. filed February 14, 2006) at 2, available at http://www.cphcs.ca.gov/docs/court/PlataOrder AppointingReceiver0206.pdf (last visited October 7, 2013) [**hereinafter February 14, 2006 Order**]. *See* Barbara Feder Ostrov, County Health Czar Plans to Overhaul State Prison Health System, San Jose Mercury News, February 14, 2006.

"extensive authority, including 'all powers . . . his duties'": February 14, 2006 Order at 4.

"Sillen was to make bimonthly reports. . . .": *See id.* at 3.

"for emergency reforms 'the same way. . . .'": *See* Jenifer Warren, Gov's Youth Prison Plan is Criticized; the Proposal Would Put More Emphasis on Rehabilitation. Critics Back Principles but Worry about Lack of Details, Cost Estimates, Los Angeles Times, December 1, 2005, part B, page 1.

"Fn. 2. The reference is. . . .": *See* Johnny Mixx, Gov. Arnold Schwarzenegger's Smoking Tent, Blue Note Cigars, December 22, 2008, available at http://bluenotecigars.com/71/gov -arnold-schwarzeneggers-smoking-tent (last visited February 20, 2010) (picture included).

"A few days later. . . .": *See* Jenifer Warren, Gov. Is Ordered to Name Prison Healthcare Czar; In Sharp Words, a Judge Calls for the New Official to Make Immediate Fixes in the Ailing System, Including Raising Pay for Doctors and Nurses, Los Angeles Times, December 2, 2005, part B, page 1.

"Judge Henderson ordered the state to pay. . . .": *See* Order Re: State Contracts and Contract Payments Relating to Service Providers for CDCR Inmate/Patients, *Plata* (N.D. Cal. filed March 30, 2006) at 5. See Jenifer Warren, Prisons Ordered to Pay Doctors, Los Angeles Times, March 31, 2006, part B, page 1.

"Some of the doctors. . . .": *See id.*

The Receivership: Phase One

"He began his career. . . . available to the poor.": *See* Jenifer Warren, Outspoken, Abrupt but Effective: Colleagues Say that Bob Sillen, Named to Fix the State's Prison Medical System, Can Get Job Done, Los Angeles Times, February 21, 2006, part B, page 1; Barbara Feder Ostrov, County Health Czar Plans to Overhaul State Prison Health System, San Jose Mercury News, February 14, 2006; Jenifer Warren, Prison Health Chief Set; A U.S. Judge Picks a Santa Clara County Official to Take over Inmate Care in a Move Shifting Power from the State to the Federal Level, Los Angeles Times, February 12, 2006, part B, page 1.

"The plaintiffs' lawyers. . . . cooperate with Sillen.": *See* Jenifer Warren, Judge Names Receiver to Fix Prison Health System; Bob Sillen, 63, Will Have Unprecedented Powers to Revive the $1.2 Billion Medical Care Program, Los Angeles Times, February 15, 2006, part B, page 1 [**herein-after Judge Names Receiver**]; James Sterngold, Outsider to Run Health Care; Federal Judge Gives Extraordinary Powers to Receiver, San Francisco Chronicle, February 15, 2006, page B3.

"State Senator Gloria Romero. . . .": *See* Judge Names Receiver.

"The situation in California's prisons. . . .": Receiver's First Bi-Monthly Report, *Plata* (N.D. Cal. filed July 5, 2006) at 1–3.

[**The Bi-Monthly Reports eventually became Quarterly Reports and then Tri-Annual Reports. They, as well as other reports from the receiver, are all filed with the Plata court, and they are all available at the receiver's website: http://www.cphcs.ca.gov/receiver.aspx (last visited July 4, 2016). References to these reports will not include court filing information or the receiver's website.**]

"Citing 'systemic long term overcrowding'. . . .": *See id.* at 3.

"three particularly serious problems. . . .": *See id.* at 8–12, 22–26.

"These contractors are paid. . . .": *Id.* at 24.

"with the aid of Judge Henderson's court orders. . . .": *E.g., Plata,* 2007 W.L. 1624495 (N.D. Cal.); Order Granting Receiver's Motion for One Time Limited Waiver of California Government Code sec. 19080.3, *Plata* (N.D. Cal. filed April 25, 2007); Order Re: Receiver's Motion for a Waiver of State Law, *Plata* (N.D. Cal. filed October 17, 2006).

"'first steps'": Robert Sillen, Letter from Receiver, Vol. 2, number 4, September 19, 2006, available at http://www.clearinghouse.net/chDocs/public/PC-CA-0018-0044.pdf (last visited February 23, 2010).

"an overhaul of the pharmacy system. . . .": *Id.*

"Of 426 deaths. . . .": *Id.*

"prodding from Judge Henderson": *See* Order Appointing New Receiver, *Plata* (N.D. Cal. filed January 23, 2008) at 3 **[hereinafter January 23, 2008 Order]**; *Plata,* 2007 W.L. 2601391 (N.D. Cal.) at 1–3 **[hereinafter September 6, 2007 Order]**.

"a complex document setting forth. . . .": California Prison Health Care Receivership Corporation (CPR, Inc.), Prison Medical Care System Reform: Plan of Action, November 15, 2007. This document is a revision and elaboration of an earlier draft filed in May 2007. Both documents are available on the Governor's California Prison Health Care Services website, http://www.cprinc.org/receiver_tpa.aspx (last visited February 28, 2010). For Judge Henderson's comments on the document, *see* January 23, 2008 Order at 4.

"The initial receivership order. . . .": *See* February 14, 2006 Order at 9.

"despite Judge Henderson's urging. . . .": Judge Henderson eventually asked Starr Babcock, an executive with the state bar association, to put together the advisory group. *See* January 23, 2008 Order at 3.

"'back up the Brink's truck'. . . .": *See* Solomon Moore, Using Muscle to Improve Health Care for Prisoners, N.Y. Times, August 27, 2007, sec. A, page 12.

"plaintiffs' attorneys criticized Sillen. . . .": *See* Edwin Garcia, One Man Changing Prison Medical Care, Inside Bay Area, May 2, 2007; Mark Martin, Health Care Firm Accuses State Prisons' Medical Czar, San Francisco Chronicle, April 5, 2007, page B1.

"Judge Henderson appointed . . . '. . . task at hand.'": *See* September 6, 2007 Order at 5.

"While the current receiver. . . .": January 23, 2008 Order at 4–5.

The Receivership: Phase Two — Early Progress and Backsliding

"He was the head. . . .": *See* University of Pacific McGeorge School of Law Faculty Profiles, available at http://www.mcgeorge.edu/x509.xml (last visited February 27, 2010); January 23, 2008 Order (J. Clark Kelso: Biographical Information).

"'the state's handyman. . . .'": Harrison Sheppard, Clark Kelso: California's CIO; When Crisis Looms and Bureaucracy Blooms, Call this Guy, Prosper Magazine, October 2007, available at http://www.prospermag.com/article/142-71 (last visited February 27, 2010).

"trim the receivership staff": *See* Receiver's Seventh Quarterly Report at 51–52; Tom Chorneau, Prison Care Overseer's Spending Is Faulted; Inspector General Says Fired Official Misused State Funds, San Jose Mercury News, February 28, 2008, page A1.

"a less cumbersome, more user-friendly turnaround plan": Kelso released a draft plan in March 2008. Following public comment, he filed the plan with the Court in June. *See Plata*, 560 F.3d 976, 979–80 (9th Cir. 2009). The plan, Achieving a Constitutional Level of Medical Care in California's Prisons: The Federal Receiver's Turnaround Plan of Action, June 6, 2008, *Plata* (N.D. Cal. filed June 17, 2008), is available at http://www.clearinghouse.net/chDocs/public /PC-CA-0018-0076.pdf (last visited March 1, 2010) and at http://www.cphcs.ca.gov/receiver_ tpa.aspx (last visited October 2, 2011) [**hereinafter Turnaround Plan**].

"By January 2010, Kelso was able to report. . . .": *See* Achieving a Constitutional Level of Medical Care in California Prisons: Thirteenth Tri-Annual Report of the Federal Receiver's Turnaround Plan of Action, January 15, 2010, at 5–6 [**hereinafter Thirteenth Tri-Annual Report**].

"[T]he initial planning efforts. . . .": *Id.* at 58. For a more detailed account of the construction fiasco, *see* Receiver's Report on Options for Long-Term Care Bed Construction, February 6, 2009.

"When the state reneged. . . .": *See Plata*, 560 F.3d 976 (9th Cir. 2009) (recounting background of the order show cause and holding that Judge Henderson's order was not appealable); *Plata*, 2008 W.L. 4847080 (N.D. Cal.) (recounting background of the order to show cause and holding that defendants must transfer the $250 million by the end of the day, November 7, 2008).

"[W]ith the collapse. . . .": Thirteenth Tri-Annual Report at 58.

"Fn. 3. AB 900. . . .": *See* California Department of Corrections and Rehabilitation, Prison Reform: A Path toward Rehabilitation, Reform & Inform 1 & 3, available at http://www.cdcr .ca.gov/News/docs/Reform_and_InformNewsletter.pdf (last visited June 22, 2012).

"As of this date. . . .": Thirteenth Tri-Annual Report at 58.

An Effort to End the Receivership and the Construction Plan for Medical Beds

"In early 2009, while they were trying to appeal. . . .": *See Plata*, 2009 W.L. 500813 (N.D. Cal.).

"Judge Henderson denied that motion.": *Plata*, 2009 W.L. 799392 (N.D. Cal.).

"A little over a year later. . . .": *See Plata*, 603 F.3d 1088 (9th Cir. 2010).

"the state's dysfunctional revenue-raising rules. . . .": *See* Kevin O'Leary, The Legacy of Proposition 13, Time, June 27, 2009; Tax and Expenditure Limitation in California: Proposition 13 and Proposition 4, Institute of Government Studies, University of California (Berkeley), February 2005, available at http://igs.berkeley.edu/library/htTaxSpendLimits2003.html (last visited March 8, 2010) (describing property tax limitations and requirement that legislature pass all tax increases by 2/3 vote); Nordlinger v. Hahn, 500 U.S. 1 (1992) (describing and upholding the property tax provisions of Proposition 13).

"political gridlock. . . .": *See, e.g.*, Reinventing California Government for a New Century, The William & Flora Hewlett Foundation Newsletter, June 2009, available at http://www.hewlett .org/news/reinventing-california-government-for-a-new-century (last visited March 8, 2010); Go East or North, Young Man; Emigration from California, The Economist, August 29, 2009.

"substantial political controversy.": *See, e.g.*, Editorial, Locked Up; It's Some Assembly Democrats Who Are Blocking Much-Needed Prison Reform in California, Los Angeles Times, August 22, 2009, part A, page 26; (Assemblyman) Curt Hagman (D-Chino), Early Release Should Not Be Part of Overhaul, San Gabriel Valley Tribune, August 22, 2009; Lily Burk, Liberal Love Affair with Criminals, U.S. States News, August 20, 2009.

"CDCR Secretary Cate and other members. . . .": Interview with Judge Henderson, March 9, 2010.

"announce his candidacy until March 1. . . .": *See* Michael B. Farrell, Jerry Brown Says He's Ready to Lead California Again; Jerry Brown, California Attorney General and former Two-Term Governor, Made It Official Tuesday; He'd Like a Third Crack at the Governor's Job, Christian Science Monitor, March 2, 2010.

"speculation that Brown would run": *See, e.g.,* Dan Walters, Growth Fueling More Battles over Development, San Jose Mercury News, April 9, 2008; Carla Marinucci, McCain's Bay Area Titans; Ebay's Meg Whitman Is Latest Silicon Valley Powerhouse to Sign Up, San Francisco Chronicle, March 15, 2008.

"a tough-on-crime, law-and-order public official.": *See, e.g.,* Robert Faturechi, State to Seek High Court Review of Body-Armor Ruling; Judges Had Overturned the Law Barring Felons from Wearing the Gear, Los Angeles Times, December 30, 2009, part A, page 5; Phillip Matier & Andrew Ross, Brown NRA Brief Has Some Up in Arms, San Francisco Chronicle, November 23, 2009, page C1; Howard Mintz, Federal Judges Refuse to Delay California Prison-Overcrowding Order, San Jose Mercury News, September 3, 2009; Editorial, Attorney General Picks Odd Fight, Chico Enterprise-Record, March 6, 2009; Tim Herdt, Brown Wants to End Receivership; Attorney General Says Progress Made in State Prison Health Care, Ventura County Star, January 29, 2009 ("Some see Brown's decision to play a high profile role in an issue portrays as a case of coddling to criminals as an effort to exploit the issue for political gain.")

A Brief Return to Significant Progress

"Kelso's Tri-Annual Reports . . . regularly described progress. . . .": *See, e.g.,* Achieving a Constitutional Level of Medical Care in California's Prisons: Twenty-First Tri-Annual Report of the Federal Receiver's Turnaround Plan of Action for May 1 - August 31, 2012, September 15, 2012 [**hereinafter Twenty-First Tri-Annual Report**]; Achieving a Constitutional Level of Medical Care in California's Prisons: Eighteenth Tri-Annual Report of the Federal Receiver's Turnaround Plan of Action for May 1 - August 31, 2011, September 15, 2011 [**hereinafter Eighteenth Tri-Annual Report**]; Achieving a Constitutional Level of Medical Care in California's Prisons: Sixteenth Tri-Annual Report of the Receiver's Turnaround Plan of Action, for September 1 - December 31, 2010, January 15, 2011 [**hereinafter Sixteenth Tri-Annual Report**]; Achieving a Constitutional Level of Medical Care in California's Prisons: Amended Fifteenth Annual Report of the Federal Receiver's Turnaround Plan of Action, October 4, 2010 [**hereinafter Fifteenth Tri-Annual Report**].

"including implementation. . . .": *See* Eighteenth Tri-Annual Report at 43–44; Sixteenth Tri-Annual Report at 39–40.

"prison overcrowding and the state's severe budget problems. . . .": *See, e.g.,* Eighteenth Tri-Annual Report at 1; Sixteenth Tri-Annual Report at 2; Fifteenth Tri-Annual Report at 5.

"we are now in a position. . . .": Achieving a Constitutional Level of Medical Care in California's Prisons, Nineteenth Tri-Annual Report of the Federal Receiver's Turnaround Plan of Action for September 1, 2011 - December 31, 2011, January 13, 2012, *Plata* at 25.

"Judge Henderson then ordered the parties. . . .": *See* Order to Meet and Confer Re: Post-Receivership Planning, *Plata* (N.D. Cal. filed January 17, 2012), available at http://www.cphcs.ca.gov/docs/court/plata/2012-01-17_Order_to_Meet_and_Confer_Re_Post_Receivership_Planning.pdf (last visited October 9, 2013).

"Kelso's assessment that it was appropriate. . . .": *See* Achieving a Constitutional Level of Medical Care in California's Prisons: Twentieth Tri-Annual Report of the Federal Receiver's Turnaround Plan of Action for January l, 2012 - April 30, 2012, May 15, 2012, at 26.

"Judge Henderson, on May 30, 2012,. . . .": *See* Order Proposing Receivership Transition Plan, *Plata* (N.D. Cal. filed May 30, 2012), available at http://www.cphcs.ca.gov/docs/court/plata/2012-05-30_Order_Proposing_Receivership_Transition_Plan.pdf (last visited October 9, 2012) [**hereinafter June 30, 2012 Order**].

"using court experts . . . having the receiver employ. . . .": *See id.* at 1, 2.

"He formalized those suggestions. . . .": *See* Order Re: Receivership Transition Plan and Expert Evaluations, *Plata* (N.D. Cal. filed September 5, 2012) available at http://www.cphcs .ca.gov/docs/court/plata/2012-09-05_Order_Re_Receivership_Transition_Plan_and_Expert_Evaluations.pdf (last visited June 18, 2014) [**hereinafter September 5, 2012 Order**]

"Kelso's September 15 Tri-Annual Report. . . .": *See* Twenty-First Tri-Annual Report.

Assertions of Constitutional Compliance

"As Judge Henderson had pointed out. . . .": *See* June 30, 2012 Order at 1.

"Any constitutional deficiencies. . . .": Receiver's and Parties' Joint Report and Responses to Court's January 17, 2012 Order to Meet and Confer Re: Post-Receivership Planning, *Plata* (N.D. Cal. filed May 7, 2012) at 34–35, available at http://www.cdcr.ca.gov/news/docs/plata-joint-report-file-endorsed.pdf (last visited October 9, 2013) [**hereinafter Joint Report**].

"And in a response. . . .": *See* Order Re: Receivership Transition Plan and Expert Evaluations, *Plata* (N.D. Cal. filed September 5, 2012) at 2, available at http://www.cphcs.ca.gov/docs/court/plata/2012-09-05_Order_Re_Receivership_Transition_Plan_and_Expert_Evaluations.pdf (last visited October 9, 2012).

"The plaintiffs, the receiver . . . disagreed.": *See* June 30, 2012 Order at 1–2 (Judge Henderson: "Although Defendants assert . . . that they will be ready to take over control of the system within the next thirty days . . ., the record does not contain sufficient evidence to support that assertion."): Joint Report at 37 (plaintiffs and receiver).

"The parties, the Receiver, and the Court. . . .": September 5, 2012 Order at 7.

"This time their stated concerns. . . .'": *See Plata,* 2013 W.L. 654996 (N.D. Cal.) at 1.

"Two months later. . . .": *See* California Department of Corrections and Rehabilitation, about CDCR: Secretary Dr. Jeffrey Beard, available at http://www.cdcr.ca.gov/About_CDCR/Secretary.html (last visited December 26, 2014).

"Cate had recommended Beard": Conversation with Judge Henderson, August 8, 2013.

"Beard was widely cited in the press. . . .": *See, e.g.,* Don Thompson, California Challenges Feds' Inmate Population Cap, Associated Press, January 8, 2013; Howard Mintz, Governor: Drop California Prisons from Court Order to Shed Inmates, San Jose Mercury News, January 8, 2013.

"according to the Associated Press, Beard . . . 'scoffed'. . . .": *See* Don Thompson, $839M Inmate Complex Dedicated in Calif., Associated Press, June 25, 2013.

"Over the course of the last two reporting periods. . . .": Achieving a Constitutional Level of Medical Care in California's Prisons: Twenty-Third Tri-Annual Report of the Federal Receiver's Turnaround Plan of Action for January 1 to April 30, 2013, May 22, 2013, at 34–35 [**hereinafter Twenty-Third Tri-Annual Report**].

Valley Fever

"One example that Kelso cited. . . .": *See* Twenty-Third Tri-Annual Report at 28.

For background on Valley Fever in the California prison system, *see* Order Granting Plaintiffs' Motion for Relief Re: Valley Fever at Pleasant Valley and Avenal State Prisons, *Plata* (N.D. Cal. filed June 24, 2013) at 3–13, available at http://www.cphcs.ca.gov/docs/court/plata/2013-06-24_Doc-2661-Order-Re-Valley-Fever.pdf (last visited October 7, 2013) [**hereinafter June 24, 2013 Order**]; California Correctional Health Care Services Public Health and Quality Management Units, Coccidioidomycosis in California's Adult Prisons 2006–10, *Plata* (N.D. Cal. filed April 25, 1013) [**hereinafter Cocci Report**].

"In 2011, there were 640 reported cases. . . .": *See* June 24, 2013 Order at 4.

" 'inmate and staff education. . . .' ": *Id.*

"PVSP 'posted. . . . Bulletin.' ": *Id.* at 5.

"did not include African Americans and Filipinos. . . . '. . . ongoing maintenance costs.' ": *Id.*

"Following the CDPH's final report. . . .": *See id.* at 5–8.

"An April 2012 report": *See* Cocci Report.

"Despite mitigation efforts . . . non-African American inmates in California.": *Id.* at 1, 3, 4. *See* June 24, 2013 Order at 8.

"further mitigation efforts. . . .": *See* June 24, 2013 Order at 8–10.

"refused . . . to exclude African Americans. . . .": *See id.* at 11.

"even after CDPH provided its formal commentary. . . .": *Id.* (emphasis in original).

"Kelso characterized CDCR's response . . . as 'anemic.' ": Twenty-Third Tri-Annual Report at 28. Kelso had first used the adjective "anemic" to describe the defendants' response to cocci in a March 27, 2013 report. J. Clark Kelso, Report and Response of Receiver Regarding Plaintiffs' Motion re Valley Fever at 4. *See* Notice of Filing of Report and Response of Receiver Regarding Plaintiffs' Motion re Valley Fever, *Plata* (N.D. Cal. filed May 1, 2013).

"Defendants' objections. . . .": Twenty-Third Tri-Annual Report at 28.

"On June 24, 2013, Judge Henderson ordered. . . .": *See* June 24, 2013 Order at 25.

"The order was a slightly modified version. . . .": *See id.* at 24.

"Beard . . . 'could exacerbate violence. . . .' ": *See* Don Thompson, Calif. Prison Chief: Order Could Lead to Conflicts, Associated Press, June 25, 2013; Jennie Rodriguez-Moore, Final Prep for Prisoners, The Record (Stockton, California), June 26, 2013.

" 'CDCR routinely transfers. . . .' ": June 24, 2013 Order at 5 n.3.

"contained 40,000 fewer inmates. . . .": *See* Defendants' Response to April 11, 2013 Order Requiring List of Proposed Population Reduction Measures; Court-Ordered Plan, Coleman/Plata v. Brown, Nos. 2:90-cv-00520 LKK JFM P & C01-1351 TEH (N.D. Cal. filed May 2, 2013) at 1; California Department of Corrections and Rehabilitation, Fact Sheet, April 15, 2013 at 2 available at http://www.cdcr.ca.gov/News/docs/3JP-April-2013/3JP-Fact-Sheet-April-15-2013.pdf (last visited September 24, 2013).

A Bit of Optimism — and Continuing Problems

"The State complied . . .": *See* Achieving a Constitutional Level of Medical Care in California's Prisons: Twenty-Fifth Tri-Annual Report of the Federal Receiver's Turnaround Plan of Action for September 1 - December 13, 2013, February 1, 2014 at 36–38 [**hereinafter Twenty-Fifth Tri-Annual Report**]; Achieving a Constitutional Level of Medical Care in California's

Prisons: Twenty-Fourth Tri-Annual Report of the Federal Receiver's Turnaround Plan of Action for May 1 - August 31, 2013, October 1, 2013 at 35–36 [hereinafter **Twenty-Fourth Tri-Annual Report**].

"some progress . . .": *See, e.g.,* Achieving a Constitutional Level of Medical Care in California's Prisons: Twenty-Sixth Tri-Annual Report of the Federal Receiver's Turnaround Plan of Action for January 1 - April 13, 2014, June 2, 2014 at 1–2 [hereinafter **Twenty-Sixth Tri-Annual Report**]; Twenty-Fifth Tri-Annual Report at 1; Twenty-Fourth Tri-Annual Report at 1.

"The Receiver has been impressed. . . .": Twenty-Sixth Tri-Annual Report at 55.

"much ballyhooed rollout. . . .": *See* CDCR Dedicates New California Health Facility, States News Service, June 25, 2014; Facility Bustling as It Prepares for First Inmates, The Record (Stockton California), distributed by McClatchy-Tribune News, June 9, 2013; Vendor Fare Set for California Health Care Facility in Stockton; Facility Will Spend Millions of Dollars per Year on Supplies, States News Service, March 6, 2013.

"extremely rocky.": *See* Twenty-Fifth Tri-Annual Report at 1.

"upgrades . . . years behind schedule.": *See* Twenty-Fourth Tri-Annual Report at 31–32, 47.

Prison Overcrowding

"at least initially, when the prisons were at their most crowded": *See* Defendants' Report in Response to January 12, 2010 Order, *Coleman/Plata* (filed in N.D. June 7, 2011) at 5, available at http://www.cdcr.ca.gov/News/docs/6.7.11-Response-to-1.12.10-Order.pdf (last visited October 8, 2013).

"approximately 30% of the statewide prison population.": *See* California Department of Corrections & Rehabilitation, California Prisoners and Parolees 2010 at 21, available at http://www.cdcr.ca.gov/Reports_Research/Offender_Information_Services_Branch/Annual/Cal Pris/CALPRISd2010.pdf (last visited October 7, 2013).

The Conditions for Terminating the Receivership

"The Receivership shall remain in place. . . .": February 14, 2006 Order at 7.

Evaluating the Quality of Medical Care

"Between 2008 and early 2013. . . .": *See* Twenty-Fourth Tri-Annual Report at 33.

"When the OIG inspections began. . . .": *Id.*

"Judge Henderson's order": *See* September 5, 2012 Order.

"According to the experts' reports. . . .": *See* The reports are available at the receivers website: http://www.cphcs.ca.gov/experteval.aspx (last visited March 30, 2014). The reports for California State Prison (Sacramento), California Institution for Men, Central California Women's Facility, Salinas Valley State Prison, Corcoran State Prison, and Richard J. Donovan Correctional Facility each contain the quoted language at page 5 of the reports.

"At Judge Henderson's suggestion. . . .": *See* Twenty-Fourth Tri-Annual Report at 34.

"As of the end of 2014. . . .": Conversation with Judge Henderson, December 28, 2014; *see,* Achieving a Constitutional Level of Medical Care in California's Prisons: Twenty-Seventh Tri-Annual Report of the Federal Receiver's Turnaround Plan of Action for May 1 - August 31, 2014 at 1, 46–47.

"They had, however, narrowed. . . .": *See* Achieving a Constitutional Level of Medical Care in California Prisons: Twenty-Eighth Tri-Annual Report of the Federal Receiver's Turnaround Plan of Action for September 1 to December 31, 2014 at 44–45.

"a new round . . .": *See id.*

"Clark Kelso has reported . . . '. . . institutions in the middle.' ": *See* J. Clark Kelso, Special Report: Improvements in the Quality of California's Prison Medical Care System, March 10, 2015 at 13 [hereinafter **March 10, 2015 Special Report**].

The Work Remaining

"sixty-five-page special report": *See* March 10, 2015 Special Report.

"At the system-wide level. . . .": *Id.* at 1, 4.

" '[D]isagreements persist. . . .,' ": *Id.* at 1.

"failure to make . . . inadequate facilities (including internal quotations).": *See id.* at 3–4.

"Most facilities. . . .": *Id.* at 4.

"Judge Henderson, on March 10, 2015, issued an order. . . .": *See* Order Modifying Receivership Transition Plan, *Plata* (N.D. Cal. filed March 10, 2015), available at http://www.cphcs .ca.gov/docs/court/plata/2015-03-10-Doc%202841%20-%20Order%20Modifying%20Receivership%20Transition%20Plan-c1.PDF (last visited May 14, 2015). (Judge Henderson had seen a draft of Kelso's Special Report, which was filed on the same day as Judge Henderson's order.)

"despite significant progress, much remained. . . .": *Id.* at 3–4.

"at least for the present there was no need to resolve. . . .": *Id.* at 2–3

"revocable delegations of authority continue to provide. . . .": *Id.* at 4.

"After the OIG releases. . . .": *Id.* at 5–7.

"receiver had made . . . in only two areas. . . .": *See id.* at 4.

"which are designed to facilitate. . . .": *See* Turnaround Plan at 5.

"Between that date . . ., the receiver made. . . .": *See* Achieving a Constitutional Level of Medical Care in California's Prisons: Thirty-Second Tri-Annual Report of the Federal Receiver for January 1 - April 30, 2016 at 22.

Chapter Seventeen
Judge Henderson's Prison Trilogy, Part III: Coleman/Plata v. Schwarzenegger

"Governor Arnold Schwarzenegger declared. . . .": *See* Office of the Governor, Proclamation, Prison Overcrowding State of Emergency, October 4, 2006, available at http://gov.ca.gov/ news.php?id=4278 (last visited June 22, 2012).

"the *Plata* plaintiffs filed a motion. . . .": *See* Plata v. Schwarzenegger, 2007 W.L. 2122657 (N.D. Cal.) 1–2 (granting motion filed on November 13, 2006).

"Plaintiffs in Coleman. . . .": *See* Coleman v. Schwarzenegger, 2007 W.L. 2122636 (E.D. Cal.) 8 (granting motion filed on November 13, 2006).

[The motions led to the establishment of a three-judge court, which included both Judge Henderson and Judge Lawrence Karlton, who was hearing the *Coleman* case. Proceedings in the three-judge court were in fact proceedings in both *Plata* and *Coleman*. In citations to the three-judge court in this chapter, including citations to specific documents filed in the three-judge court proceeding, the case is referred to simply as *Coleman/Plata*. The named defendant (first Governor Arnold Schwarzenegger, then Governor Jerry Brown), the case numbers

(CIV S-90-0520 LKK JFM P for *Coleman* and C01-1351 TEH for *Plata*), and the courts (E.D. Cal. for *Coleman* and N.D. Cal. for *Plata*) are omitted.]

The Coleman *Case*

"In 1990. . . .": *See Coleman/Plata*, 922 F. Supp. 2d 882, 898 (E.D./N.D. Cal. 2009). [Two opinions in *Coleman/Plata* appear in volume 922 of F. Supp. 2d — the opinion cited here and a June 20, 2013 opinion that begins at page 1004. To avoid confusion, all references to the two opinions will include the beginning page number and year of decision.]

"Judge Karlton adopted. . . .": *See* Coleman v. Wilson, 912 F. Supp. 1282 (E.D. Cal. 1995). *See Coleman/Plata*, 922 F. Supp. 2d 882, 900 (2009) (Special Master appointed in separate order several months later).

"[A] significant amount. . . .": *Id.* at 903–09. The opinion is the joint effort of and is signed by three judges — Lawrence Karlton, Thelton Henderson, and Stephen Reinhardt of the Ninth Circuit Court of Appeals. The portion of the opinion describing the early *Coleman* litigation was drafted by Judge Karlton. Interview with Judge Thelton Henderson, May 14, 2010.

Judicial Responses to Overcrowding and the Prison Litigation Reform Act

"federal courts began giving serious consideration. . . .": *See* Chapter Seventeen *supra*.

"in a 1977 case,. . . '. . . inmate population'. . . .": *See* Williams v. Edwards, 547 F.2d 1206, 1215 (5th Cir. 1977).

"four years later . . . '. . . unconstitutional conditions.'": *See* Ruiz v. Estelle, 650 F.2d 555, 570 (5th Cir. 1981).

"the Seventh Circuit upheld. . . .": *See* Duran v. Elrod, 713 F.2d 292, 297 (7th Cir. 1983).

"as part of the Prison Litigation Reform Act. . . .": *See* 18 U.S.C. sec. 1326(a).

"cap prison populations": *See* 18 U.S.C. sec. 3262(g)(4) (defining prisoner release order as "any order . . . that has the purpose or effect of reducing or limiting the prison population or that directs the release from or nonadmission of prisoners to a prison"). *See* Tyler v. Murphy, 135 F.3d 594, 596–97 (8th Cir. 1998) (order capping prison population is "prisoner release order" within the meaning of the PLRA).

"Instead, the PLRA provides. . . .": *See* 18 U.S.C. sec. 3626(a)(3)(B).

"Thus, a judge . . . must request. . . .": *See* 28 U.S.C. sec. 2284.

"And, according to the PLRA. . . .": *See* 18 U.S.C. sec. 3626(a)(3)(E).

"certain preexisting common law limitations": *See Coleman/Plata*, 922 F. Supp. 2d 882, 919 (2009).

"Orders granting prospective relief . . . '. . . by the relief.'": *See* 18 U.S.C. sec 3626(a)(1)(A).

"[a]ny State or local official. . . .": 18 U.S.C. sec. 3626(a)(3)(F).

"Moreover, generally applicable. . . .": *See* Fed. R. Civ. Proc. 24; *Coleman/Plata*, 2007 W.L. 2765757.

The Three-Judge Court in Coleman/Plata

"Judge Henderson and Judge Karlton initially conducted separate hearings. . . . Then on June 27. . . .": *See* Plata v. Schwarzenegger, 2007 W.L. 2122657; Coleman v. Schwarzenegger, 2007 W.L. 2122636.

"The defendants conceded. . . .": *See Coleman/Plata*, 922 F. Supp. 2d 882, 919 (2009) (citing Coleman v. Schwarzenegger, 2007 W.L. 2122636 at 4 and Plata v. Schwarzenegger, 2007 W.L. 2122657 at 3).

"The Defendants' position. . . .' ": Plata v. Schwarzenegger, 2007 W.L. 2122657 at 3.

"In separate orders the next month. . . .": *See* Plata v. Schwarzenegger, 2007 W.L. 2122657; Coleman v. Schwarzenegger, 2007 W.L. 2122636.

" 'For purposes of judicial economy. . . .' . . . .": Plata v. Schwarzenegger, 2007 W.L. 21227657 at 6; Coleman v Schwarzenegger, 2007 W.L. 2122636 at 8.

"The statute authorizing three-judge courts. . . .": *See* 28 U.S.C. sec. 2284(b)(A)(1).

"As Judges Henderson and Karlton expected. . . .": Interview with Judge Thelton Henderson, April 17, 2010.

"Because the three-judge court. . . .": Interview with Judge Thelton Henderson, April 17, 2010.

"Supporters of both sides. . . .": *See* Schwarzenegger to Fight Prison Panel Decision, The Monterey County Herald, July 28, 2007 (quoting Democratic State Senator Gloria Romero); Todd Spitzer (on behalf of the California State Assembly Republican Caucus), Taking a Stand to Prevent Early Release of Dangerous Criminals, U.S. States News, August 15, 2007.

"Indeed, Judges Henderson and Karlton. . . .": *See* Plata v. Schwarzenneger, 2007 W.L. 2122657); Coleman v. Schwarzenegger, 2007 W.L. 2122636.

" 'the *primary* cause' ": 18 U.S.C. sec. 3626(a)(3)(E). *See Coleman/Plata*, 922 F. Supp. 2d 882, 917 (2009).

"a 'remedy of last resort'. . . .": *Id*. at 889, 918, 951.

"would exercise its right to appeal. . . .": *See* 28 U.S.C. sec 1253.

The Rhetoric, the Reality, and the Politics of Reducing Prison Populations

"Richard Nixon's successful presidential bids. . . .": *See, e.g.*, Stephen Smith & Kate Ellis, Campaign '68, American Radio Works, American Public Media, available at http://ameri canradioworks.publicradio.org/features/campaign68/b1.html (last visited May 24, 2010); Nixon Presidential Library and Museum, The President: 1968 Campaign, available at http:// nixon.archives.gov/thelife/apolitician/thepresident/index.php (last visited May 24, 2010); The Fear Campaign, Time, October 4, 1968; *see generally* Rick Perlstein, Nixonland: The Rise of a President and the Fracturing of America (2008).

"Rudolph Giuliani's mayoral triumphs. . . .": *See, e.g.*, Janet Crawley, Law and Order Image Fuels Giuliani's Climb, Chicago Tribune, November 3, 1993, page 19; Ron Scherer, Triumph of Pugnacious Politics, Christian Science Monitor, November 6, 2007, page 1.

"Perhaps most famously. . . .": *See* You Tube, Willie Horton 1988 Attack Ad, available at http://www.youtube.com/watch?v=Io9KMSSEZ0Y&NR=1 (last visited May 24, 2010). Although some have claimed that the advertisement was simply about crime, others have seen strong elements of racism in the advertisement. *Compare, e.g.*, Cahnman, On the Political Dark Side, The Next Right: Politics, Strategy, Action, January 1, 2009, available at http://www.thenex tright.com/category/blog-tags/willie-horton (last visited May 24, 2010) *with* David Love, The Willie Horton Ad Revisited 25 Years Later, The Grio, October 21, 2013 *and* Paul Farhi, Two Political Ads Share More than Fame and Controversy, The Washington Post, September 7,

2004, page A02. As Republican National Committee Chairman Michael Steele acknowledged in 2010, the Republican Party has pursued a "Southern Strategy" of appealing to white voters for over forty years. *See* Greg Sargent, Michael Steele Acknowledges GOP Had "Southern Strategy" for Decades, The Plum Line, April 22, 2010.

"California, both through legislative action. . . .": *See, e.g.,* A Primer: Three Strikes—The Impact after More Than a Decade, California Legislative Analyst's Office, October 2005, available at http://www.lao.ca.gov/2005/3_Strikes/3_strikes_102005.htm (last visited May 25, 2010); Michael Vitiello & Clark Kelso, A Proposal for Wholesale Reform of California's Sentencing Practice and Police, 38 Loy. L.A. L. Rev. 903 (2004); Jenifer Warren, Jerry Brown Calls Sentence Law a Failure; The Former Governor, Who Signed the Measure Creating Fixed Terms in 1977, Now Regrets It, Saying It Has Saddled the State with Recidivism, Los Angeles Times, February 28, 2003, part 2, page 1.

"Assemblyman Todd Spitzer characterized. . . .": *See* Nancy Vogel, Judges to Study Cap on Prisons; Impatient with State Efforts to Deal with Crowding, Jurists Call for a Panel that Could Limit Inmate Numbers, Los Angeles Times, July 24, 2007, part A, page 1.

"Assemblyman Mike Villines . . . a public relations disaster.'": *See* Schwarzenegger Joins with State Republicans, Law Enforcement Officials to Warn of Danger if Felons Are Release into Communities, States News Service, September 6, 2007.

"'As an elected district attorney. . . .'": *See id.*

"[R]eleasing criminals back to our streets. . . .": *See id.*

"Perhaps some of these politicians feared. . . .": *See Coleman/Plata,* 922 F. Supp. 2d 882, 987 (2009). ("[M]any witnesses [who opposed a prisoner release order] assumed that this court would require a sudden mass release of one-third of California's prisoners or a ban on accepting new or returned prisoners.")

"something that *might* have happened. . . .": *See* Hearings on Prison Reform before the Senate Committee on the Judiciary, 104th Cong., 1st Sess. 49 (1995) (statement of Lynne Abraham, District Attorney of Philadelphia); Hearings before the Subcommittee on Crime of the House Committee on the Judiciary, 104th Cong., 1st Sess. 259 (1995) (statement of Lynne Abraham), cited in Brown v. Plata, 563 U.S. 493, 577 n.9 (2011) (Alito, J., dissenting). *See also* Robert W. Milburn, Comment: Congress Attempts to Remove Federal Court Supervision over State Prisons: Is 3626(b)(2) of the Prison Litigation Reform Act Constitutional, 6 Temp. Pol. & Civ. Rts. L. Rev. 75, 76 (1997).

"no effort systematically to verify. . . .": *See* Hearings on S.3 before the Senate Committee on the Judiciary, 104th Cong., 1st Sess., 212 (statement of David Richman, lead counsel for the plaintiff class), cited in Brown v. Plata, 563 U.S. 493, 536 n.11 (2011).

"no attempt to design a strategy. . . .": *See* John S. Goldkamp & Michael D. White, Restoring Accountability in Pretrial Release: The Philadelphia Pretrial Release Supervision Experiments, 2 J. Experimental Criminology 143 (2006), available at http://www.pretrial.org/Docs/Documents/gldkmpwht06.pdf (last visited June 12, 1011).

"neither the *Coleman/Plata* three-judge court . . . not approve such an order.": *See Coleman/Plata,* 922 F. Supp. 2d 882, 987 (2009).

"Empirical evidence supports. . . .": *See Coleman/Plata,* 922 F. Supp. 2d 882, 976–79, 982–85 (2009); Brief of Center on the Administration of Criminal Law and 30 Criminologists as *Amici Curiae* in Support of Appellees, November 1, 2010, Brown v. Plata, 563 U.S. ___ (2011) (citing and discussing studies) [**hereinafter CACL Brief**].

"there is considerable agreement among experts. . . .": *See Coleman/Plata*, 922 F. Supp. 2d 882, 970 (2009) (noting that "there are a number of population reduction measures that will not have an adverse impact on public safety and that in fact may improve public safety, all of which have been recommended by the state, in various reports, by experts it retained to examine ways to reduce California's high recidivism rate"); *id.* at 971 ("[T]he current combination of overcrowding and inadequate rehabilitation or re-entry programming in California's prison system itself has a substantial adverse impact on public safety and the operation of the criminal justice system. A reduction in the crowding of California's prisons will have a significant positive effect on public safety by reducing the criminogenic aspects of California's prisons."); *id.* at 974 ("There was overwhelming agreement among experts for plaintiffs, defendants, and defendant-intervenors that is 'absolutely' possible to reduce the prison population in California safely and effectively."); *id.* at 997 (citing report by Washington State Institute for Public Policy — offered in evidence by defendants — for the proposition that the "decrease in recidivism resulting from an expansion of evidence-based programming would outweigh any potential adverse impact on crime rates resulting from decreased incarceration rates."); *id.* at 996–1003 (citing expert witnesses, empirical studies, and the CDCR's own expert panel for the proposition that a significant reduction in the prison population would not have an adverse impact on public safety).

"Most prisoners (including. . . .": *See, id.* at 908; Sentencing, Incarceration, & Parole of Offenders, Office of Victim & Survivor Rights & Services, California Department of Corrections and Rehabilitation, available at http://www.cdcr.ca.gov/Victim_Services/sentencing.html (last visited May 25, 2010).

"With few exceptions. . . .": *See* Joan Petersilia, Understanding California Corrections, California Policy Research Center, University of California (2006) 46–48, available at http://ucicorrections.seweb.uci.edu/pdf/rpt_Petersilia_CPRC_blulin.pdf (last visited May 26, 2010) [**hereinafter Petersilia**]; Michael Vitiello, Criminal Law: Three Strikes: Can We Return to Rationality, 87 J. Crim. L. & Criminology 395, 437–41 (1997); John H. Laub & Robert J. Sampson, Understanding Desistance from Crime, 28 Crime & Just. 1, 5 (2001).

"If prisoners are going to commit crimes. . . .": *See Coleman/Plata*, 922 F. Supp. 2d 882, 976–77 (2009).

"Moreover, neither early release. . . .": *See id.* at 976.

"At worst. . . .": *See id.* at 978, 988.

"(The significant factors. . . .)": *See* CACL Brief at 2, 10 & n.7 (citing and discussing studies).

"That, however, should be an avoidable result.": *See Coleman/Plata*, 922 F. Supp. 2d 882, 974–75, 978–79 (2009).

"There is a growing body. . . .": *See id.* at 978, 984; CACL Brief (citing and discussing studies).

"Another safe way to reduce. . . .": *See Coleman/Plata*, 922 F. Supp. 2d 882, 982–85 (2009).

"California had one of the highest. . . .": *See id.* at 908, 970 n.65; Expert Report of David M. Bennett (Submitted by Sonoma County Intervenors), *Coleman/Plata* (filed in N.D. October 30, 2008) 21 [**hereinafter Bennett Report**]; Little Hoover Commission, Solving California's Correctional Crisis: Time is Running Out, (2007) ii, 22, available at http://www.lhc.ca.gov/studies/185/Report185.pdf (last visited May 16, 2008) [**hereinafter Little Hoover Commission**].

"First, the state has tended to reincarcerate. . . .": *See Coleman/Plata*, 922 F. Supp. 2d 882, 979–80 (2009); Petersilia at 4, 71, 72, 75.

"On the contrary. . . .": *See* Petersilia at 71, 72, 75; Little Hoover Commission at 27.

"A second significant reason. . . .": *See Coleman/Plata*, 922 F. Supp. 2d 882, 977 (2009); Petersilia at 2, 39–44; Little Hoover Commission at 2, 24–26.

"It has not been uncommon, for example,. . . .": *See* Little Hoover Commission at 37.

"To some extent, the failure to prepare. . . .": *See Coleman/Plata*, 922 F. Supp. 2d 882, 971–74 (2009); Little Hoover Commission at 17, 25; Petersilia at x–xi, 11–15, 44.

"However, housing shortages. . . .": *See Coleman/Plata*, 922 F. Supp. 2d 882, 928 (2009); Petersilia at x, 14.

"First, because placement in higher security. . . .": *See* Petersilia at 14.

"Second, housing low-risk prisoners. . . .": *See Coleman/Plata*, 922 F. Supp. 2d 882, 971 (2009); Petersilia at 75.

"Finally, and most important. . . .": *See id.* at 972; Petersilia at 14–15, 44.

"proposals for modifying. . . .": *See, e.g., Coleman/Plata*, 922 F. Supp. 2d 882, 985–86 (2009); Little Hoover Commission at iii, 33–35.

"and more recently California. . . .": *See* CalRealignment.org., available at http://california realignment.org (last visited March 21, 2012); *see also* Susan Meeker, Prison Bill Could Cause Problems for County Jails, Colusa County Sun Herald, April 5, 2011; Steven Harmon, State Budget Plan: Five Years of Higher Taxes, $12.5 Billion in Spending Cuts, Contra Costa Times, January 10, 2011.

"Finally, the cost. . . .": *See Coleman/Plata*, 922 F. Supp. 2d 882, 994 (2009).

"Politicians have told Judge Henderson. . . .": *See* Thelton Henderson, Keynote Address: Confronting the Crisis of California Prisions, 42 U.S.F. L. Rev. 1, 7 (2008).

"The California legislature collectively. . . .": *See generally* Little Hoover Commission.

Case Management

"140 individual and governmental entities. . . .": *See Coleman/Plata*, 2007 W.L. 3020078 at 2.

"Suddenly the defendants included. . . .": *See id.; Coleman/Plata*, 2007 W.L. 2765757; *Coleman/Plata*, 2007 W.L. 2362653.

"In addition,. . . '. . . for all CCPOA members.'": *See Coleman/Plata*, 2007 W.L. 2765757 at 3.

"The CCPOA had unsuccessfully challenged. . . .": *See* California Correctional Peace Officers Association v. Schwarzenegger, 163 Cal. App. 4th 802, 77 Cal. Rptr. 3d 844 (2008).

"Governor Schwarzenegger in January 2010. . . .": *See* U.S. State News, Gov. Schwarzenegger Participates in Q&A at Sacramento Press Club Luncheon, January 27, 2010:

"set strict time limits. . . .": *See Coleman/Plata*, 2007 W.L. 3020078 at 3.

"combined groups of statutory intervenors": *See Coleman/Plata*, 2007 W.L. 3355071 at 3.

"made it clear that 'the intervenors. . . .'": *Id.* at 1.

"As the trial neared. . . .": *See Coleman/Plata*, 2008 W.L. 397295 at 1.

"The court had initially decided. . . .": *See Coleman/Plata*, 2007 W.L. 3020078.

"Because of the relative smoothness. . . .": Interview with Judge Thelton Henderson, May 3, 2010.

"the court later rescinded. . . .": *See Coleman/Plata*, 2008 W.L. 397295 at 2.

Initial Settlement Efforts

"The judges appointed. . . .": *See Coleman/Plata*, 922 F. Supp. 2d 882, 916 (2009).

"Lui, a former . . . justice and trial judge": After leaving the bench Elwood Lui joined the law firm of Jones, Day. His profile is available at jonesday.com/elui (last visited May 8, 2010).

"Siggins . . . current state court of appeals justice": Justice Peter Siggins' profile is available on the California Courts of Appeal website: http://www.courtinfo.ca.gov/courts/courtso fappeal/1stDistrict/justices/siggins.htm (last visited May 8, 2010).

"appeared to bring the case close to settlement": *See* Confidential Supplemental Status Report, *Coleman/Plata* (filed in N.D. June 30, 2008) at 5 [**hereinafter June 30, 2008 Status Report**]. *See also* Transcript of Proceedings, May 30, 2008, *Coleman/Plata* (filed in N.D. September 23, 2008) [**hereinafter May 30, 2008 Transcript**].

"On the basis of their extensive talks. . . .": *See* Status Report, May 27, 2008, *Coleman/Plata* (filed in N.D. June 2, 2008) at 3–10 [**hereinafter May 27, 2008 Status Report**].

"substantial support among. . . .": *See* May 30, 2008 Transcript; June 30, 2008 Status Report at 3.

"In a status report . . . not on board.": *See* June 30, 2008 Status Report at 3–4.

"these latter intervenors": *See* June 30, 2008 Status Report at 7–16 (statements of the district attorney intervenors and the Republican legislator intervenors attached as appendices to the Status Report).

"Lui and Siggins reported to the court. . . .": *See id.* at 2, 4–5.

The Trial and a New Settlement Overture from the Court

"three weeks of testimony . . . hundreds of documents.": *See Coleman/Plata*, 922 F. Supp. 2d 882, 916 (2009).

"JUDGE REINHARDT:. . . .": Transcript of Proceedings, February 4, 2009, *Coleman/Plata* (filed in N.D. February 12, 2009) at 44, 47–49.

"On February 9, 2009 . . . '. . . plan accordingly.' ": *See Coleman/Plata*, 2009 W.L. 330960 at 1.

" 'overwhelming evidence' ": *Id.*

"There is . . . uncontroverted evidence. . . .": *Id.* at 1–2.

"The two cases underlying. . . .": *Id.* at 3.

"Despite 'compelling' evidence. . . .": *See id.* at 2.

" '*tentatively* conclude[d]. . . .' ": *Id.* at 3 (emphasis added).

"*tentatively* concluded that reducing. . . .": *See id.* at 4. The 40,000 to 60,000 figure is extrapolated from data about prison population in *Coleman/Plata*, 922 F. Supp. 2d 882, 910–11 (2009).

"We received evidence. . . .": *Coleman/Plata*, 2009 W.L. 330960 at 4–5.

"Fn. 2. Dr. Austin. . . .": *See Coleman/Plata*, 922 F. Supp. 2d 882, 913 & n.39 (2009).

"Ironically. . . .": Interview with Judge Thelton Henderson, May 3, 2010. *See, e.g.,* Declaration of San Diego County Deputy District Attorney Lisa Rodriguez Submitted in Lieu of Direct Testimony by District Attorney Defendant Intervenors, *Coleman/Plata* (filed in N.D. October 30, 2008); *Coleman/Plata*, 2009 W.L. 2430820 at 114; Transcript of Proceedings, Thursday, December 11, 2008, *Coleman/Plata* (filed in N.D. December 12, 2008) (testimony of David Bennett on behalf of Sonoma County).

"The Court . . . will. . . .": *Coleman/Plata*, 2009 W.L. 330960 at 6.

"The court then concluded. . . .": *See id.*

"The responses. . . .": *See Coleman/Plata*, 922 F. Supp. 2d 882, 916 (2009).

"They requested a final appealable order. . . .": *See* Defendants' Response to Tentative Ruling, *Coleman/Plata* (filed in N.D. February 25, 2009) at 2.

An Almost Final Order

"a 120-page 'Opinion and Order'": *See Coleman/Plata*, 922 F. Supp. 2d 882 (2009) (117 pages of text plus a three-page table of contents according to F. Supp. 2d pagination).

"words and conclusions of . . . state's own independent agency . . .": *See* Little Hoover Commission, Solving California's Correctional Crisis: Time is Running Out, Executive Summary (2007) ii, available at http://www.lhc.ca.gov/studies/185/Report185.pdf (last visited May 16, 2008).

"words and conclusions of . . . Arnold Schwarzenegger": *See* Office of the Governor, Proclamation, Prison Overcrowding State of Emergency, October 4, 2006, available at http://gov.ca.gov/index.php?/proclamation/4278 (last visited April 10, 2010).

"'California's correctional system . . .'. . .": *Coleman/Plata*, 922 F. Supp. 2d. 882, 887 (2009).

"Although California's existing prison system. . . .": *Id.* at 887–88.

"[And lockdowns. . . .]": *See id.* at 937–38.

"a richer, more detailed recitation. . . .": *See id.* at 920–50.

"On the basis. . . .": *Id.* at 949.

"The court then considered possible alternatives. . . .": *See id.* at 950–59.

"Fn. 3. As the court pointed out. . . .": *See id.* at 958–59 & n.58.

"Fn. 4. Two defense experts. . . .": *See id.* at 961.

"'be narrowly drawn. . . .'": 18 U.S.C. sec. 2626(a)(2).

"none of the parties had argued for. . . .": *See Coleman/Plata*, 922 F. Supp. 2d 882, 963 (2009).

"an institution-by-institution approach. . . .": *Id.* at 963–64.

"but only if 'it is demonstrated. . . .'": *Id.* at 964.

"In California, design capacity meant. . . .": *See id.* at 910.

"the evidence . . . demonstrated. . . .": *Id.* at 966.

"as the court had noted in its Tentative Ruling. . . .": *See Coleman/Plata*, 2009 W.L. 330960 at 4–5.

"The state had admittedly planned . . . 100% design capacity.": *See Coleman/Plata*, 922 F. Supp. 2d 882, 910–11 (2009).

"Moreover, in making its 145% recommendation. . . .": *See id.* at 910, 968–69.

"The court found that the 130%. . . . '. . . support in the record.'": *See id.* at 962.

"some evidence, albeit 'far less persuasive'. . . .": *See id.* at 969.

"Noting that the defendants. . . .": *See id.* at 966.

"recognizing . . . not an exact science": *See id.* at 965.

"keeping in mind the PLRA's requirement. . . .": *See id.* at 962, 969.

"the court 'out of caution' settled. . . .": *See id.* at 969.

"In effect, this meant. . . .": *See* Brown v. Plata, 563 U.S. 493, 501 (2011).

"the court directed the defendants. . . .": *See Coleman/Plata*, 922 F. Supp. 2d 882, 1003 (2009).

"The defendants were to confer. . . .": *See id.* at 1004.

"to a 'nearly identical procedure'": *Id.* at 964 (citing Bounds v. Smith, 430 U.S. 827 (1977)).

"'an exemplar of what should be done'. . . .": *Id.* (citing Lewis v. Casey, 518 U.S. 343, 363 (1996)).

"'scrupulously respect[s] the limits . . .' . . . 'exercise[]wide discretion. . . .'": *Id.* at 833 (quoted in *Coleman/Plata*, 2009 W.L. 2430820 at 78).

"In a lengthy exploration. . . .": *See Coleman/Plata*, 922 F. Supp. 2d 882, 974–88 (2009).

"[W]ere we in error. . . .": *Id.* at 993–94.

"[37 million]": *See* United States Census Bureau, Table 1. Annual Estimates of the Population of the United States, Regions, States, and Puerto Rico, available at http://www.census.gov/popest/data/state/totals/2012/tables/NST-EST2012-01.csv (last visited October 23, 2013).

"Each year under the existing system. . . .": *See Coleman/Plata,* 922 F. Supp. 2d 882, 973 (2009).

"One of the most persuasive. . . .": *Id.* at 1001–02.

"The subject of prisons and corrections. . . .": Anthony M. Kennedy, Speech at the American Bar Association Annual Meeting, August 9, 2003, available at http://www.supremecourt.gov/publicinfo/speeches/viewspeeches.aspx?Filename=sp_08-09-03.html (last visited May 22, 2010).

"American sentences. . . .": *See* Justice Anthony Kennedy at Pepperdine, En Banc, The Los Angeles County Bar Association Blog, February 9, 1010, available at http://lacbablog.typepad.com/enbanc/2010/02/justice-anthony-kennedy-at-pepperdine.html (last visited October 9, 2013) (As set forth in the blog, there are quotation marks around the words "and that is sick." Since it appears that the entire passage is Justice Kennedy's statement, it is not clear why the quotation marks are there. They are eliminated in the footnote.)

"The defendants were given. . . .": *See Coleman/Plata,* 922 F. Supp. 882, 1003 (2009).

The Final Order and a Stay

"A little over a month later. . . .": *See Coleman/Plata,* 2010 W.L. 99000 at 1.

"The plaintiffs asked the court. . . .": *See* Donald Specter, Everything Revolves around Overcrowding: The State of California's Prisons, 22 Fed. Sent. Rptr. 194, 197 (2010) [**hereinafter California's Prisons**].

"was even more surprising": Interview with Judge Thelton Henderson, May 23, 2010.

"After some stern words. . . ." *See id;* California Prisons at 197; Order Rejecting Defendants' Population Reduction Plan and Directing the Submission of a Plan that Complies with the August 4, 2009 Opinion and Order, *Coleman/Plata* (filed in N.D. October 21, 2009).

"Two months later. . . .": *See Coleman/Plata,* 2010 W.L. 99000 at 1–2.

"Certain measures that we concluded. . . .": *Id.* at 2.

"The court then stayed. . . .": *See id.* at 4.

Another Settlement Failure and a New State Initiative

"Despite the state's. . . .": Interview with Donald Specter, May 28, 2010; Interview with Judge Thelton Henderson, May 23, 2010.

"Brown began to push . . . significant impact on crowding in the state prisons.": *See* California Department of Corrections and Rehabilitation, Overview. . . . AB 109: Public Safety Realignmnet (2011); Susan Meeker, Prison Bill Could Cause Problems for County Jails, Colusa County Sun Herald, April 5, 2011; Steven Harmon, State Budget Plan: Five Years of Higher Taxes, $12.5 Billion in Spending Cuts, Contra Costa Times, January 10, 2011.

The Supreme Court Speaks

"the Supreme Court affirmed. . . .": *See* Brown v. Plata, 563 U.S. 493 (2011).

"The degree of overcrowding. . . .": *Id.* at 1923–24.

"At the time of trial. . . .": *Id.* at 1932.

"In October 2010,. . . .": *Id.* at 1038.

"At one time. . . .": *Id.* at 1939.

"That order required. . . .": *See Coleman/Plata*, 2010 L.W. 99000 at 4.

"In a conference call . . . funding for AB 109.": Interview with Judge Thelton Henderson, June 4, 2011.

Population Reduction

"the state had transferred over 9,000 prisoners. . . .": *See* Brown v. Plata, 563 U.S. 493, 501 (2011); Defendants' Report in Response to January 12, 2010 Order, *Coleman/Plata* (filed in N.D. June 7, 2011) at 5, available at http://www.cdcr.ca.gov/News/docs/6.7.11-Response-to-1.12.10-Order.pdf (last visited October 8, 2013). *See* California Department of Corrections and Rehabilitation, Fact Sheet: Actions CDCR Has Taken to Reduce Overcrowding, May 23, 2011 (10,088 transferred out of state), available at http://www.cdcr.ca.gov/News/docs/FS-Actions-Reduce InmatePop.pdf (last visited June 12, 2011).

"Today, the prison population. . . .": *See* Defendants' Report in Response to January 12, 2010 Order, *Coleman/Plata* (filed in N.D. June 7, 2011) at 2, available at http://www.cdcr.ca.gov/News/docs/6.7.11-Response-to-1.12.10-Order.pdf (last visited June 12, 2011).

"The next month the state reported. . . .": *See* Defendants' Report in Response to January 12, 2010 Order, *Coleman/Plata* (filed in N.D. July 20, 2011) at 2, available at http://www.cdcr.ca.gov/News/docs/Defendants_Response_to_June_30_2011_Order.pdf (last visited March 23, 2012).

"the state was only a few weeks late. . . .": *See* Defendants' January 2012 Status Report in Response to June 30, 2011 Order, *Coleman/Plata* (filed in N.D. January 16, 2012) at 2, available at http://www.cdcr.ca.gov/News/docs/Jan-2012-Pop-Status-Update.pdf (last visited October 24, 2013); Defendants' December 2011 Status Report in Response to June 30, 2011 Order, *Coleman/Plata* (filed in N.D. December 15, 2011) at 2, available at http://www.cdcr.ca.gov/News/docs/December-3JC-Status-Report.pdf (last visited October 24, 2013).

"the state met the June 2012 benchmark. . . .": *See* Defendants' June 2012 Status Report in Response to June 30, 2011 Order, *Coleman/Plata* (filed in N.D. June 15, 2012) at 2, available at http://www.cdcr.ca.gov/News/docs/3JP-docs-06-26-12/June-2012-Filed-Population-Status-Report-Plata.pdf (last visited October 24, 2013).

"'[T]here is no need at this time. . . .'": *Id.*

The Agony of Judicial Restraint

"'must reinvest its criminal justice resources. . . .'": Cal. Penal Code sec. 17.5(4).

"Fn. 6. . . . 'supervision policies, procedures. . . .'": Cal. Penal Code sec. 17.5(9).

"'Criminal justice policies that rely. . . .'": Cal. Penal Code sec. 17.5(3).

"two significant problems. . . .": For an elaboration of these and other problems, *see* ACLU of California, Public Safety Realignment: California at a Crossroads (2012), available at http://aclusandiego.org/article_downloads/001251/Public%20Safety%20Realignment%20FINAL%20.pdf (last visited March 23, 2012).

"Stanford Law Professor. . . .": *See, e.g.,* Joan Petersilia, Voices from the Field: How California Stakeholders View Public Safety Realignment, Stanford Criminal Justice Center, January 2014, available at http://www.law.stanford.edu/publications/voices-from-the-field-how-california-stakeholders-view-public-safety-realignment (last visited September 2, 2014); Jeffrey Lin & Joan Petersilia, Follow the Money: How California Counties Are Spending Their Public Safety Realignment Funds, January 2014, available at http://www.law.stanford.edu/publications/

follow-the-money-how-california-counties-are-spending-their-public-safety-realignment-funds (last visited September 2, 2014).

"There are some indications. . . .": *See, e.g.,* Joan Petersilia, California Prison Downsizing and Its Impact on Local Criminal Justice Systems, 8 Harv. L. & Policy Rev. 327, 346 (2014); Paige St. John, Early Jail Releases Have Surged since California's Prison Realignment, Los Angeles Time, August 16, 2014.

Digging In

" 'The Future of California Corrections' ": California Department of Corrections and Rehabilitation, The Future of California Corrections, April 2012, available at http://www.cdcr.ca .gov/2012plan (last visited October 21, 2013) [**hereinafter Blueprint**].

" 'to save billions . . . system.' ": *Id.*

"The Blueprint stated. . . . to 145 percent of design capacity.' ": Blueprint, Executive Summary at 5, 8, available at http://www.cdcr.ca.gov/2012plan/docs/plan/exec-summary.pdf (last visited October 21, 2013). *See Coleman/Plata*, 922 F. Supp. 2d 1004, 1015–16 & n. 11 (2013).

"After extensive briefing. . . .": *See id.* at 2016.

"Defendants . . . suggested that the only question. . . .": *Coleman/Plata*, 2012 W.L. 3930635 at 1.

"varying assessments . . . 137.5% goal": *See Coleman/Plata*, 922 F. Supp. 2d 1004, 1020 & n. 19 (2013).

"in November . . . 147% benchmark.": *See id.* at 2016 n.12, 2019.

"On January 7. . . .": *See id.* at 1021.

"The defendants. . . . First,. . . second. . . .": *See id.* at 1023–24, 1028.

"At the same time that they filed their motion to vacate, the defendants. . . . However, they did not. . . .": *See id.* at 1023.

"The *Coleman* court denied. . . .": *See* 2013 W.L. 1397335.

"voluntarily abandoned. . . .": *See Plata/Coleman*, 922 F. Supp. 2d 1004, 1023–24, 1027–28 (2013).

"rejected it for the same reason. . . .": *See id.* at 1030–33.

"However, in a lengthy, detailed discussion. . . .": *See id.* at 1032–42.

"On January 8, 2013,. . . terminated . . . Emergency Proclamation.": *See* A Proclamation by the Governor of the State of California, January 8, 2013, available at http://www.cdcr.ca.gov/ News/docs/3JP-docs-01-07-13/Terminating-Prison-Overcrowding-Emergency-Proclama tion-10-4-06.pdf (last visited October 22, 2013).

" 'arrogating unto himself. . . .' ": Coleman/Plata, 922 F. Supp. 2d 1004, 1020 (2013).

"In a January 13 status report. . . .": *See id.* at 1021.

"Two weeks later. . . .": *See id.*

"Fn. 7. The defendants had requested . . . were extended six months.": *See id.* at 1018–19.

"At the same time. . . . Nonetheless. . . .": *See id.* at 1021.

"In an April 11th opinion and order. . . .": *See Coleman/Plata*, 922 F. Supp. 1004 (2013).

"Defendants have thus far. . . .": *Id.* at 1049–50.

"First . . . would not be necessary.": *See id.* at 1051–53.

"list *in their order of preference*' . . . '. . . candidates for early release.')": *See id.* at 1053–56.

"(the 'Low Risk List')": *See Coleman/Plata*, 952 F.2d 901, 904 (2013).

"The defendants appealed. . . .": *See* Notice of Appeal to the Supreme Court of the United States, *Plata/Coleman* (filed May 13, 2013), available at http://www.cdcr.ca.gov/News/docs/3JP -May-2013/3JP-05-13-13-Notice-of-Appeal.pdf (last visited October 22, 2013).

"included them as part of the appeal.": Appeals from the United States District Courts for the Eastern District of California and the Northern District of California: Appellants' Supplemental Brief Regarding Three-Judge Court's Order Prohibiting Appellants from Contracting for Capacity, Brown v. Plata/Coleman (filed September 25, 2013), available at http://www.cdcr .ca.gov/News/docs/3JP-Sept-2013/Supplemental-filing-Sept-24.pdf (last visited October 22, 2013); Appeals from the United States District Courts for the Eastern District of California and the Northern District of California: Jurisdictional Statement, Brown v. Plata/Coleman (filed August 9, 2013) at 2, available at http://www.cdcr.ca.gov/News/docs/3JP-August-2013/Plata2013JS& App.pdf (last visited October 22, 2013); Application for a Stay of Injunctive Relief Pending this Court's Final Disposition of Appeals Pursuant to 28 U.S.C. sec. 1253, Brown v. Plata/Coleman (filed July 10, 2013) at 6, available at http://www.cdcr.ca.gov/News/docs/3JP-July-2013/Appli cation-for-a-stay-of-the-Three-Judge-Courts-order-to-release-prisoners.pdf (last visited October 22, 2013).

"the Supreme Court dismissed the case. . . .": *See* Brown v. Plata, 2013 W.L. 4101821.

The Three-Judge Court's June 20, 2013 Order

"In May, the defendants 'announced. . . .'": *See Coleman/Plata*, 952 F. Supp. 2d at 920, 930.

"The List, however, did not indicate any preference. . . .": *See id.* at 926.

"the Plan, as the defendants conceded. . . .": *See id.* at 920.

"According to the three-judge court. . . .": *See id.* at 922.

"relied on measures that would require legislative action. . . .": *See id.*

"would not be forthcoming.": *See id.*; Howard Mintz, California Prisons: Gov. Jerry Brown Offers Plan for Overcrowding Crisis "Under Protest," San Jose Mercury News, May 3, 2013.

"after reciting in detail. . . .": *See Coleman/Plata*, 952 F. Supp. 2d at 923–25.

"As the Supreme Court stated. . . .": *Id.* at 925–26 (quoting Brown v. Plata, 563 U.S. 493, 511 (2011)).

"The court then ordered . . . more than enough to meet the 137.5% goal.": *See Coleman/ Plata*, 952 F. Supp. 2d at 927, 934–45.

"By contrast, the good time credit measure. . . .": *See id.* at 921.

"The defendants had argued. . . . The three-judge court, however, pointed out. . . .": *See id.* at 927–28.

"A CDCR expert panel. . . .": *See id.* at 928–29.

" 'there is no statistically significant. . . .' ": *Coleman/Plata*, 922 F. Supp. 2d 882, 976 (2009).

"Dr. James Austin . . . "reducing . . . no effect. . . .": *See id.*

"leading experts in the country. . . .": *Coleman/Plata*, 952 F. Supp. 2d at 927.

"Moreover, the three-judge court's Amended Plan. . . .": The original order, according to the three-judge court, called for a population reduction of approximately 46,000 prisoners, *see* Brown v. Plata, 563 U.S. 493, 511 (2011); *Coleman/Plata*, 922 F. Supp. 2d 882, 208, 270 (2009), over a 24-month period or an average of slightly more than 1,900 prisoners per month. As of June 2013, according to the defendants' projections, the state needed to reduce the prison population by 9,636 inmates to meet the 137.5% goal by the end of the year. *Coleman/Plata,* 952 F. Supp. 2d at 920–22 & n. 19. The Plan submitted by the defendants would, according to the three-judge court, reduce the prison population by 5,466 prisoners by the end of the year, *id.* at 921, and the three-judge court's expanded good time credit requirement would reduce the population by "as many as 5,385 prisoners by December 31, 2013." *See id.* at 927. Thus, the Amended

Plan would more than meet the 137.5% goal by reducing the prison population by "as many as" 10,851 over a six-month period or an average of slightly more than 1,800 prisoners per month.

"First, they could modify. . . .": *See id.* at 904, 929–30, 935.

"Second, the defendants could 'at their discretion . . .'. . . List.": *See id.* at 904, 935.

"Third, as long as they. . . .": *See id.*

"First,. . . the three-judge court waived. . . .": *See id.* at 931–34, 935.

"Second, the court ordered the defendants to use. . . .": *See id.* at 930, 935.

"The Court wishes to make perfectly clear. . . .": *Id.* at 930.

"unsuccessful motion to stay": *See Coleman/Plata*, 960 F. Supp. 2d 1057 (2013).

"even inmates that CDCR considered 'low risk'. . . .": Defendants' Motion to Stay Three-Judge Court's June 20, 2013 Order Requiring Defendants to Implement Amended Plan Pending Appeal; Memorandum of Points and Authorities, *Plata/Coleman* (filed June 28, 2013) at 7 (citing J. Petersilia & J. Greenlick Snyder, Looking Past the Hype: 10 Questions Everyone Should Ask about California's Realignment 5(2) Cal. J. Pol. Pol'y 266, 295 (2013)), available at http://www.cdcr.ca.gov/News/docs/3JP-June-2013/Plata-Coleman-Motion-to-Stay.pdf (last visited October 23, 2013) [**hereinafter Motion to Stay June 20, 2013 Order**].

"ensuring that there would be a 'durable remedy'. . . .": *See Coleman/Plata*, 952 F. Supp. 2d at 933–34.

"Finally, the three-judge court . . . deferred any contempt proceedings.": *See id.* at 936.

Squeezing the Three-Judge Court

"The defendants continued to resist. . . .": *See* Defendants' Request for an Extension of the December 31, 2013 Deadline and Status Report in Response to June 30, 2011, April 11, 2013, June 20, 2013, and August 9, 2013 Orders, *Coleman/Plata* (filed September 16, 2013) at 111–12, available at http://www.cdcr.ca.gov/News/docs/3JP-Sept-2013/File-Endorsed-3JC-Sept-16-Report.pdf (last visited October 23, 2013) [**hereinafter September 16, 2013 Request**].

"the prison population grew. . . .": *See* California Department of Corrections and Rehabilitation, Office of Research, Weekly Total Population Report Archive, available at http://www .cdcr.ca.gov/Reports_Research/Offender_Information_Services_Branch/WeeklyWed/Weekly _Wednesday_Tpop1a_Archive.html (last visited October 23, 2013).

"on September 12, 2013, Governor Brown . . . '. . . reducing the state's prison population.'": *See* September 16, 2013 Request at 2–5.

"Four days later the defendants asked. . . .": *See id.*

"State prisons are just one part. . . .": *Id.* at 3.

"The state, by its own estimate . . . 8,500 inmates. . . .": *See id.* at 11.

"Fn. 8. . . . "what the figure includes. . . .": In the same Status Report, the defendants stated that they "*will* . . . [i]mmediately reduce the prison population by transferring approximately 2,500 inmates to available in-state capacity. . . ." *Id.* at 2 (emphasis added). The verb "will" suggests that the 2,500 are part of the 8,500. On the other hand, in setting forth the 8,500 figure, the Status Report equated it with the shortfall that the three-judge court had discussed in its June 20 opinion:

> Defendants acknowledge that, in the Court's view, compliance with the population cap could be quickly and safely achieved through releasing the requisite number of inmates (8,500 based on current estimates) either through awarding early credits or using an early release system.

Id. at 11. This language suggests that the 2,500 transferees, who are *not* awarded early credits or given early release, may not be part of the 8,500 figure.

"Fn. 8. . . . appears to be considerably higher. . . .": In June, the court, using the defendants' presumably then current projections, assumed that the state would need to reduce its prison population by 9,363 inmates to meet the 137.5% goal at the end of December. According to the defendants' original Plan, slowing the return of out-of-state prisoners would reduce that number by 3,569 inmates, and transferring inmates to fire camps would reduce the number by another 1,250 inmates. Good time credits and expanded parole would reduce the population by another 647 inmates. That would leave a shortfall of 4,170 inmates. *See Coleman/Plata,* 952 F. Supp. 2d at 921–22. Thus, assuming the defendants had implemented or were implementing the reduction measures it presented to the court the previous summer, in less than three months the projected overpopulation increased by approximately 4,000 inmates. (If the 2,500 in-state transferees were not included in the 8,500 figure, *see* previous endnote, the increase would be more than 6,500 inmates.)

Perhaps the 8,500 figure — like the 9,396 figure — included the 3,569 out-of-state inmates originally slated for return in 2013. If so and if it also included the 2,500 transferees, then it is only slightly higher or perhaps even lower (depending on how many inmates were transferred to fire camps) than the June 20 estimate. Several factors, however, make this possibility unlikely. First, the CDCR's fall, 2013 population projections (although not yet public on September 16) predicted a significant and continuing rise in the prison population for the next six years. *See* California Department of Corrections and Rehabilitation, Fall 2013 Adult Population Projections Fiscal Years 2013/14–2018/19 (2013) at 2, available at http://www.cdcr.ca.gov/Reports_ Research/Offender_Information_Services_Branch/Projections/F13pub.pdf (last visited April 4, 2014). Second, the defendants represented in their September 16 Status Report that they already "had implemented the following measures . . . expanded fire camp capacity and slowing the return of out of state inmates." September 16, 2013 Request at 10–11. Thus, there would have been no reason to include the out-of-state prisoners or fire camp transferees in the 8,500 figure. Third, the out-of-state prisoner population remained relatively constant during the period from June through September, *see* California Department of Corrections and Rehabilitation, Office of Research Monthly Total Population Report Archive, available at http://www .cdcr.ca.gov/Reports_Research/Offender_Information_Services_Branch/Monthly/Monthly_ Tpop1a_Archive.html (last visited December 30, 2014), which suggests that the defendants had indeed implemented the slowdown and that the 3,569 inmates slated for return had not been returned and were not part of the 8,500 figure.

Apparently some combination of (1) inaccurate population projection estimates, (2) the State's failure to implement fully Plan items to which it had agreed, and (3) an increase in the number of new prisoners accounts for the 8,500 figure.

"absence of adequate rehabilitation and reentry programs. . . .": *See* September 16, 2013 Request at 2 (SB 105 would "[p]ermanently increase funding *beginning next fiscal year* by an estimated $100 million to bolster rehabilitation programs") (emphasis added); *id.* at 4 ("*With additional time,* SB 105 will allow the state to develop longer-term solutions to reduce recidivism.") (emphasis added). *See also id.* at 10, 12.

"previously noted high recidivism rate": *See* Motion to Stay June 20, 2013 Order at 7; *Coleman/Plata,* 922 F. Supp. 2d 882, 908, 970 n.65 (2009); Bennett Report at 21; Little Hoover Commission at ii, 22.

"defendants made it clear what they would do. . . .": *See* September 16, 2013 Request at 10–13.

"'result in thousands . . . families.'": Opinion Re: Order Granting Part and Denying in Part Defendants' Request for an Extension of December 31, 2013 Deadline, *Coleman/Plata* (filed in N.D. February 10, 2014) at 2.

"Moreover, to finance. . . .": *See* September 16, 2013 Request at 10–13.

"ordered the parties to meet and confer . . . also extended the 137.5% deadline. . . .": *See* Order Further Extending Meet-and-Confer Process, *Coleman/Plata* (filed in N.D. December 11, 2013); Order Extending Meet-and-Confer Process, *Coleman/Plata* (filed in N.D. October 21, 2013); Order to Meet and Confer, *Coleman/Plata* (filed in N.D. September 24, 2013).

"not to make any arrangements . . . '[d]uring the meet-and-confer process. . . .'": Order to Meet and Confer, *Coleman/Plata* (filed in N.D. September 24, 2013) at 3.

"complaining that the court had 'imposed. . . .'": Appeals from the United States District Courts for the Eastern District of California and the Northern District of California: Appellants' Supplemental Brief Regarding Three-Judge Court's Order Prohibiting Appellants from Contracting for Capacity, Brown v. Plata/Coleman (filed September 25, 2013) at 1, available at http://www.cdcr.ca.gov/News/docs/3JP-Sept-2013/Supplemental-filing-Sept-24.pdf (last visited October 22, 2013).

Getting Back on Track

"The meet-and-confer sessions . . . 'to achieve . . . capacity.'": *See* Order to File Proposed Orders Re: Defendants' Request to Extend Population Reduction Deadline, *Coleman/Plata* (filed January 13, 2014), available at http://www.cdcr.ca.gov/News/docs/3JP-Jan-2014/3JC-Jan-13-Req-for-Proposed-Orders.pdf (last visited April 17, 2014).

"Plaintiffs responded . . . 'neither durable nor desirable.'": *See* Opinion Re: Order Granting in Part and Denying in Part Defendants' Request for Extension of December 31, 2013 Deadline, *Coleman/Plata* (filed in N.D. February 10, 2014) at 2, available at http://www.cdcr.ca.gov/News/docs/3jp-Feb-2014/Three-Judge-Court-opinion-2-20-2014.pdf (last visited April 17, 2014) [hereinafter February 10, 2014 Opinion].

"By contrast, the defendants . . . and other in-state facilities.": *See* Defendants' Amended Application and [Proposed] Order Granting Defendants' Request for an Extension of April 18, 2014 Deadline, *Coleman/Plata* (filed in N.D. January 23, 2014) at 4–7, available at http://www.cdcr.ca.gov/News/docs/3JP-Jan-2014/Plata-FiledEndorsedAmendedApplicationforExtensionandProposed.pdf (last visited April 17, 2014) [hereinafter Defendants' Amended Application].

"On February 10, 2014, the three-judge court. . . .": *See* Order Granting in Part and Denying in Part Defendants' Request for Extension of December 31, 2013 Deadline, *Coleman/Plata* (filed in N.D. February 10, 2014), available at http://www.cdcr.ca.gov/News/docs/3jp-Feb-2014/Three-Judge-Court-order-2-20-2014.pdf (last visited April 17, 2014) [hereinafter February 10, 2014 Order].

"Fn. 10. In April 2014, the court appointed Elwood Lui. . . .": *See*, Order Appointing Compliance Officer, *Coleman/Plata* (filed in N.D. April 9, 2014), available at http://www.cdcr.ca.gov/News/docs/3JP-April-2014/04_9_4-Compliance_Officer_Order.pdf (last visited April 17, 2014).

"Fn. 10. . . . That same month . . . mental health class action.": *See* John Balazs, Eastern District of California Blog, September 15, 2015 (posting item from San Francisco Daily Journal), available at http://edca.typepad.com/eastern_district_of_calif/judge-kimberly-mueller (last visited January 30, 2015).

"'consider the establishment of a commission. . . .'": February 10, 2014 Order at 1.

"'explore ways to attempt to reduce. . . .'": *Id.* at 2.

"In the four and a half years. . . .": February 10, 2014 Opinion at 2.

"During the meet-and-confer process. . . .": *See* Defendants' Amended Application at 2.

A Durable Solution?

"The defendants met the summer, 2014 benchmark": *See* Twenty-Seventh Tri-Annual Report at 1, 29 (noting the defendants had received a two-month extension of the original June 30 deadline because of a misunderstanding about how to count the increased capacity at the new Stockton prison medical facility) [**hereinafter Twenty-Seventh Tri-Annual Report**].

"had reduced the prison population to below 137.5%. . . .": *See* California Department of Corrections and Rehabilitation, Weekly Population Report as of Midnight January 28, 2015, available at http://www.cdcr.ca.gov/Reports_Research/Offender_Information_Services_Branch /WeeklyWed/TPOP1A/TPOP1Ad150128.pdf (last visited January 30, 2015) [**hereinafter January 28, 2015 Population Report**]; Don Thompson, California Meets Judges' Prison Crowding Goal 1 Year Early, ABC News, January 29, 2015.

"the implementation of population control measures. . . .": The CDCR reports monthly on its progress. *See, e.g.,* Appendix B, Defendants' January 15 Status Report in Response to February 10, 2014 Order, *Coleman/Plata* (filed in N.D. January 15, 2015), available at http://www .cdcr.ca.gov/News/docs/3JP-Jan-2015/January-2015-Status-Report.pdf (last visited January 30, 2015).

"Proposition 47": *See* California Department of Corrections and Rehabilitation, Public and Employee Communications: Proposition 47 — What You Need to Know, available at http:// www.cdcr.ca.gov/news/Proposition_47.html (last visited January 3, 2015); Legislative Analyst's Office (The California Legislature's Nonpartisan Fiscal and Policy Advisor), Proposition 47: Criminal Sentences. Misdemeanor Sentences. Initiative Statute, November 4, 2014, available at http://www.lao.ca.gov/ballot/2014/prop-47-110414.aspx (last visited January 3, 2015).

"in the fall of 2013, the CDCR projected. . . .": *See* California Department of Corrections and Rehabilitation, Fall 2013 Adult Population Projections Fiscal Years 2013/14–2018/19 (2013) at 2, available at http://www.cdcr.ca.gov/Reports_Research/Offender_Information_Services_ Branch/Projections/F13pub.pdf (last visited April 4, 2014).

"Six months later. . . .": *See* California Department of Corrections and Rehabilitation, Spring 2014 Population Projections at iv, available at http://www.cdcr.ca.gov/Reports_Research/ Offender_Information_Services_Branch/Projections/S14Pub.pdf (last visited January 3, 2015). *See* Twenty-Seventh Tri-Annual Report at 29.

"the approximately 8,800 prisoners. . . .": *See* January 28, 2015 Population Report.

"there is growing concern. . . .": *See, e.g.,* Don Thompson, Brown Says Prison Realignment Works; Counties Say It Won't without Money, Orange County Register, April 19, 2014; Eric Granof, Jail Overcrowding Solutions in California Require Public-Private Partnerships, Half Way to Concord, December 2, 2013, available at http://halfwaytoconcord.com/jail-overcrowding-california (last visited April 21, 2014). *But cf.* Joan Petersilia, Voices from the Field: How California Stakeholders View Public Safety Realignment, January 2014, available at http:// www.law.stanford.edu/sites/default/files/child-page/443444/doc/slspublic/Petersilia%20

VOICES%20no%20es%20Final%20022814.pdf (last visited April 21, 2014) (various perspectives on realignment).

Chapter Eighteen
Recording Atrocities Redux:
Special Education in East Palo Alto

Judge Henderson's Description of the Factual Background:
Emma C. v. Eastin, 2001 W.L. 1180636, 1–3 (N.D. Cal.)

"the Individuals with Disabilities Education Act (IDEA)": 20 U.S.C. sec.1400 et seq.

Dr. Charlie Mae Knight, Her Allies, and Her Record

Most of the information in this section is based on Sara Neufeld & Fredric Tulsky, School Chief Benefits While Students Lag, San Jose Mercury News, June 28, 2001, page 1A [hereinafter School Chief Benefits]. The ensuing endnotes in this section cite School Chief Benefits only for direct quotations.

Ms. Neufeld wrote extensively about Ravenswood and the special education lawsuit for the San Jose Mercury News from 2000 to 2003. Her articles, many of which are cited in the endnotes to this chapter, are essential reading for anyone interested in an in-depth understanding of the Ravenswood Elementary School District under the leadership of Charlie Mae Knight.

For an extremely positive — but one-sided and conspiracy-theory-laden — view of Charlie Mae Knight and her contributions to the Ravenswood School District and the East Palo Alto community, *see* Barbara Morrow Williams, In the Silence of Her Friends: A Case Study of the Intersection of Gender, Race, Age, and Leadership in the Dismissal of a Public School Superintendent (Ph.D. thesis, University of Missouri-Columbia), available at https://mospace.umsystem.edu/xmlui/bitstream/handle/10355/4108/research.pdf?sequence=3 (last visited January 20, 2015).

"'for doing a first class job. . . .'": *See* School Chief Benefits; Vauhini Vara, Focus on East Palo Alto: A Hard Lesson to Learn, The Stanford Daily, January 23, 2002. S.L. Wykes, Governor Wilson Heaps Praise on Ravenswood's Knight, San Jose Mercury News, January 9, 1997, Peninsula ed, page 1B.

"After serving in that capacity. . . .": *See* Lee Harris, Knight Resigns, Lynwood Buys Out Contract, Los Angeles Times, August 1, 1985, part 9, page 1; Lee Harris, Board Majority Reopens Mismanagement Investigation; Lynwood School Chief Suspended, Los Angeles Times, June 6, 1985, part 10, page 1.

"Knight's secretary . . . at Lynwood": *See* Sara Neufeld & Fredric Tulsky, Despite Court Order, School District Fails Its Neediest Students; Friends of Superintendent Get Teaching, Consulting Jobs, San Jose Mercury News, June 29, 2001, page A1 [hereinafter Despite Court Order].

"'for years'": School Chief Benefits.

"'a 1977 . . . fat reduction.'": *Id.*

"'a woman who ran Ravenswood. . . .'": Editorial, What a Terrible Difference Charlie Mae Knight Made, San Jose Mercury News, April 1, 2003, page 8B.

On the emergency loan fund, the indictment, and the trial of Charlie Mae Knight, *see* Thaai Walker, Knight's Credibility Faces Test of Jurors; Final Arguments End in Conflicts Case, San Jose Mercury News, July 17, 2001, page 1A; Thaai Walker, School Chief Denies Wrongdoing; Knight Defends Role in Emergency Fund, San Jose Mercury News, July 14, 2001, page 1B; Thaai Walker & Sara Neufeld, Witness Denies Paying Rent to Schools Chief; Relative Testifies that Money Was a "Donation" for His Living, San Jose Mercury News, July 11, 2001, page 1B; Thaai Walker & Sara Neufeld, Testimony Begins in School Chief's Trial; In Opening Statements on Monday, Prosecutors Said They Would Use Loan Records and Other Documents to Discredit Their Own Witnesses, Who Are Expected to Support the Actions of Superintendent Charlie Mae Knight, San Jose Mercury News, July 10, 2001, page 1B.

"sufficient reasonable doubt": *See* Thaai Walker & Putsata Reang, East P.A. School Chief Cleared; Knight Is Acquitted on 19 Felony Conflict Counts Involving Loans; She Was Accused of Passing District Funds to Employees Who Owed Her Money, San Jose Mercury News, July 20, 2001, page 1A ("[Jury foreman Richard] King said he and most other jurors felt too much reasonable doubt existed").

"'[t]he district's travel spending. . . .'": Sara Neufeld & Fredric N. Tulsky, Traveling Far and Wide and District's Expense; Trustees, Staffers Take Lengthy Recruiting Trips, San Jose Mercury News, June 28, 2001, page 1A.

"'[D]ozens of staff members . . . secretaries'": *Id.*

"international junkets . . . American Samoa.": *See id.*

"Between March and November of 2002. . . .": The district managed to rack up over $1,500,000 in attorneys' fees in only three months. *See* Sara Neufeld, Ravenswood Paid Lawyers' First-Class Travel, Food; Atlanta Firm Billed District $2.1 Million, San Jose Mercury News, March 9, 2003, page 1A; Sara Neufeld, Legal Fees Drain School District Cash, Contra Costa Times, November 3, 2002, page A41.

"A 2001, San Jose Mercury News investigation. . . .": The investigation resulted in a number of articles, including School Chief Benefits are others cited in this section.

For more on the test score issue, *see* Sara Neufeld, School's Test Scores Helped by Cheating, Investigation Finds; Ex-East P.A. Students Say They Were Coached, San Jose Mercury News, June 14, 2002, page 1A.

For more on the test score issue and overbilling for school lunches, *see* Sara Neufeld, District Puts Aide on Leave, Appeals Loss of Meal Funds, San Jose Mercury News, August 29, 2001, page 1B.

"'that Ravenswood has . . . district in California.'": School Chief Benefits.

"The students' performance. . . .": *Id.*

The First Efforts at Settlement

The material in this section, including the quotations, comes from Emma C. v. Eastin, 2001 W.L. 1180636 (N.D. Cal.) at 3 & n.7, 4, 10. For more on the settlement, *see* Thaai Walker, Ravenswood Must Fix Special Ed Lawsuit: Settlement Forces School District to Overhaul Programs, Puts Statewide Institutions on Alert, San Jose Mercury News, January 10, 2000, page 1B; Carolyne Zinko, East Palo Alto District Ordered to Fix Program; Special Ed Classes Found Lacking, San Francisco Chronicle, January 5, 2000, page A11.

Judge Henderson on the Early Record of Noncompliance (January 2000 through April 2001): Emma C. v. Eastin, 2001 W.L. 1180636, 3–5 (N.D. Cal.)

"As the Court Monitor has reported . . . principals failed to attend.": These examples are inserted here from Emma C. v. Eastin, 2001 L.W. 1180636 at 11, 12.

"'two . . . were more than an hour late. . . .' ": Despite Court Order.

More Pressure, More Cronyism, and Continued Noncompliance

"ordered that both. . . .": Emma C. v. Eastin, 2001 W.L. 1180636 at 6.

"a 'dramatic turnaround. . . .' ": Id.

"'clearly caught the attention'. . . .": Id.

"'spending 95% of her time. . . .' ": Despite Court Order.

"has 'been in [the Court Monitor's] office. . . .": Emma C. v. Eastin, 2001 W.L. 1180636 at 13.

"One of the individuals . . . owned by Knight in East Palo Alto." [including quotations]: See Despite Court Order.

"'The district staff. . . .' ": Emma C. v. Eastin 2001 W.L. 1180636 at 12 (quoting Christine Pittman's August 13, 2001, declaration).

"'very meager' ": Id. at 8 (quoting August 3, 2001 Monitor's Report).

"For example, although the RCAP. . . .": Id. at 9.

"'that . . . "[t]he majority. . . ."' ": Id. at 12 (quoting June 2001, Timelines Report).

"Christine Pittman testified. . . .": See id.

"One small example. . . .": Id. at 12 n.15.

"In 2001, 67%. . . .": See School Chief Benefits (noting that "two-thirds of the district's children are still learning English").

"[a]lthough the RCAP. . . .": Emma C. v. Eastin, 2001 W.L. 1180636 at 12 n.16.

"A 14-year-old. . . . '. . . box of crayons.' ": See School Chief Benefits.

"Another special education student. . . .": See Despite Court Order.

"Some non-English speaking. . . .": Telephone interview with Mark Mlawler, March 24, 2009.

The "Full Extent" of the Court's Powers

"'You can be assured. . . .' ": Emma C. v. Eastin, 2001 W.L. 1180636 at 5 (quoting April 30, 2001, Tr. at 12).

On the contempt power generally, See Ronald Goldfarb, The Contempt Power (1963); Richard B. Kuhns, Limiting the Criminal Contempt Power: New Roles for the Prosecutor and the Grand Jury, 74 Mich. L. Rev. 484 (1975).

"However, receiverships designed to address. . . .": See Vanessa Allen et al., School District Governance Reform: The Devil Is in the Details, Public Policy Forum (2009), available at http://www.publicpolicyforum.org/pdfs/SchoolDistrictGovernance.pdf (last visited February 27, 2009); Jessica Portner, East P.A. District Could Become Fifth Taken over by State, San Jose Mercury News, November 24, 2001(discussing successes and failures of state's takeover of Compton School District).

Contempt, Fraud, and a Principal's "Dismissal"

"'I've tried mightily. . . .'": *See* Sara Neufeld, School District Scolded; Judge Suggests Ravenswood Could Face Contempt Charge; A Federal Judge Could Hold the Ravenswood District in Contempt for Not Meeting a Timetable for Special Education Improvements, San Jose Mercury News, July 27, 2001, page 1B.

"He then ordered. . . .": *See* Emma C. v. Eastin, 2001 W.L. 1180636, at 7.

"Both the plaintiffs and CDE . . . August 22.": *See id.* at 16; Sara Neufeld, School District Takeover Urged; East Palo Alto, Menlo Park Students not Getting Education, San Jose Mercury News, August 10, 2001, page 1A [hereinafter **Takeover Urged**].

"a petition with 394 signatures. . . .": *See* Sara Neufeld & Pete Carey, District Lawyer Disavows Petitions; Some Signatures Were from Fake Addresses, Non-Residents, and Those Opposed to Leaders; A Ravenswood School District Lawyer Wrote in a Letter to the Judge Hearing the District's Special-Education that the Signatures Were Collected in 1997 and 2000 for Other Matters; The Petitions Had Been Used to Argue against a State Takeover, San Jose Mercury News, September 15, 2001, page 1B [hereinafter **Lawyer Disavows Petitions**].

"addressed to 'Judge Felton [*sic*] Henderson.'": *See* Magistrate Judge's Report & Recommendation re Sanctions Emma C. v. Eastin, No. C96-4179 TEH (EDL) (N.D. Cal. filed February 12, 2002) at 1 [hereinafter **Magistrate Judge's Report**].

"'parents and friends. . . .'": *See* Lawyer Disavows Petitions.

"Three weeks later . . . different matters.": *See id.*

"'found signatures . . . her district.' . . . 'No one . . . Aug. 22. . . .'": *See id.*

"To her credit. . . .": *See* Magistrate Judge's Report at 1, 5–7, 10, 21 (describing attorney's role in dealing with the fraudulent signatures and concluding that she "acted promptly to investigate and withdraw the falsified petitions," and, therefore, should not be subject to sanctions).

"She said . . . sorting mail.": *Id.* at 4–9. *See* Sara Neufeld, Sanctions on District Urged; A Magistrate Recommended that Ravenswood City School District Be Fined $10,000 and Its Officials Be Required to Attend Ethics Training for Submitting False Petitions to the Court, San Jose Mercury News, February 13, 2002, page 1B; Sara Neufeld, Lawyer Says Principal Altered Documents; East Palo Alto Educator Denies Fraud in Court Statement Filed Wednesday; The Costano School Principal Says She Found the Fraudulent Petitions, Which Were Submitted to a Judge, While Sorting Mail at the School, San Jose Mercury News, November 22, 2001, page 1B.

"The Court finds. . . .": Magistrate Judge's Report at 14–15.

"[I]nconsistencies in [her] various statements. . . .": *Id.* at 16–17.

"LaPorte's recommendations.": *See id.* at 20–21

"Judge Henderson adopted. . . . In addition, he required. . . .": *See* Sara Neufeld, U.S. Judge Sets Higher Price for East P.A. District Penalty, San Jose Mercury News, April 20, 2002, page 1A.

"While the Superintendent. . . .": *See id.*

"Ravenswood . . . asserts. . . .": Emma C. v. Eastin, 2001 W.L. 1180636 at 18–19.

"Judge Henderson then set forth. . . .": *See id.* at 19–21.

"One of the plaintiffs'. . . 'very, very thoughtful.'": *See* Sara Neufeld, Court Gives Ravenswood Schools Another 6 Months to Solve Problems: District Gets Reprieve; a Federal Judge Gives District "One Last Opportunity" to Fix Special Education Program or Face Takeover by the State, San Jose Mercury News, October 5, 2001, page 1B.

"announced in court papers. . . .": *See* Sara Neufeld, Principal May Lose Job, San Jose Mercury News, June 1, 2002, page 1B. *See also* T.S. Mills-Faraudo, Ravenswood Officials Attend

Court-Ordered Ethics Class; Communication with Public, Each Other Cited as Important, San Mateo Times, June 4, 2002, front page (noting that Ravenswood board recently voted to dismiss Marthelia Hargrove).

"The board 'rehired' Hargrove. . . .": *See* Sara Neufeld, Board Rehires East P.A. Principal, San Jose Mercury News, July 27, 2002, page 1B. The Board said it would continue to pursue Hargrove's dismissal. *Id.* However, in mid-September the Board reached a settlement with Hargrove that allowed her to keep her position. *See* Sara Neufeld, Case against Principal Settled, San Jose Mercury News, September 13, 2002, page 6B. The following spring Hargrove was demoted from principal to teacher. *See* Thaai Walker, Ravenswood Board Demotes Principal, San Jose Mercury News, May 21, 2009, page 1B.

A New Lawyer, a New School Board, and a New Settlement

"Judge Henderson was becoming increasingly concerned. . . .": *See* Sara Neufeld, Judge Postpones Takeover Decision on School District, San Jose Mercury News, June 11, 2002, page 3B.

"In contrast to Ravenswood. . . .": *See id.*; Sara Neufeld, Diane Lipton, a Champion of the Disabled, Is Dead at 57, San Jose Mercury News, August 11, 2002, page 6B.

"because he needed time. . . .": *See* Sara Neufeld, District Hearing Delayed Again, San Jose Mercury News, June 20, 2002, page 1B.

"there was growing dissatisfaction. . . .": *See* Sara Neufeld, Community Speaks Out on Ravenswood Troubles; Emotions Ran High When about 200 People Gathered at a Forum to Tell Officials What They Think about the School District and the Way It's Being Run, San Jose Mercury News, February 8, 2002, page 1B.

"'92 percent . . . leadership'": Sara Neufeld, Teachers Seek School Chief's Ouster, San Jose Mercury News, April 4, 2002, page 3B.

"and in April. . . .": *See id.* Some of the teacher dissatisfaction related to a contract dispute and to a proposed reorganization. *See* Sara Neufeld, Teachers Keep Up Heat at Ravenswood Board Meeting, San Jose Mercury News, May 11, 2002, page 1B; Nicole C. Wong, Ravenswood Board Will Close Middle School in Reorganization; Plan Also Requires Teachers to Reapply for Jobs, San Jose Mercury News, April 27, 2002, page 1B.

"By early summer. . . .": *See* Sara Neufeld, 2 Seek School Board Seats; Power Struggle Looms in Ravenswood District, San Jose Mercury News, July 12, 2002, page 1B.

"serious discussions with Ravenswood. . . .": *See* Sara Neufeld, Ravenswood Takeover Looms Again; Special Education Lacking, District in Contempt, Lawyers Say, San Jose Mercury News, September 24, 2002, page 3B; Sara Neufeld, Settlement Sought in School Talks; Judge Gives East P.A. District, Students' Lawyers a Deadline, San Jose Mercury News, August 8, 2002, page 3B. *See also* East Palo Alto, San Jose Mercury News, September 18, 2009, page 3B.

"On October 31, 2002. . . .": *See* T.S. Mills-Faraudo, Ravenswood OK's Settlement, San Mateo Times, November 1, 2002, front page.

"Plaintiffs' lawyers, however, expressed. . . .": *See id*; Sara Neufeld, District OK's Deal over Disabled Kids, San Jose Mercury News, November 3, 2002, page 42A.

"In part because of its expenditures. . . .": *See* Sara Neufeld, Legal Fees Drain School District's Cash, San Jose Mercury News, November 3, 2009.

"The reform slate won handily.": *See* T.S. Mills-Faraudo, Anti-Superintendent Slate Takes Majority on Board, San Mateo Times, November 6, 2002, more headline news section.

"Despite an order from Judge Henderson. . . .": *See* Sara Neufeld, U.S. Judge Lashes Out at Ravenswood Board; "Plainly at Odds": Filing of Papers in Special Education Suit Sparks Judicial Anger, San Jose Mercury News, December 6, 2002, page 1B [**hereinafter Judge Lashes Out**].

"The three . . . were quick to criticize. . . .": *See* Sara Neufeld, District Seeks to Replace Monitor; New Board Protests Ravenswood Move, San Jose Mercury News, December 5, 2002, page 1B.

"and Judge Henderson. . . . prior order.": *See* Judge Lashes Out.

"On December 9, at the first meeting. . . .": *See* T.S. Mills-Faraudo, New School Board Puts Knight on Leave; After Taking Oath, New Majority Names County Chief Gonella as Temporary Replacement, San Mateo Times, December 10, 2002, front page.

"Knight formally resigned. . . .": *See* Sara Neufeld & Thaai Walker, School Chief Knight to Quit; The Embattled Ravenswood Superintendent Will Resign June 30, a Year before Her Contract Expires, Saving the District about $180,000, San Jose Mercury News, March 28, 2003, page 1C. *See also* Editorial, What a Terrible Difference Charlie Mae Knight Made, San Jose Mercury News, April 1, 2003, page 8B.

"Two months after . . . that did not require additional money.": *See* Sara Neufeld, Ravenswood to Press Forward; School District to Carry Out Reforms Despite Funding Issues, San Jose Mercury News, February 8, 2003, page 1B.

"Despite the fact . . . '. . . implement the plan.'": *See* T.S. Mills-Faraudo, Judge Orders State to Pay for Special Ed Plan; Program Includes Teacher Training, Integration, San Mateo Times, May 16, 2003, Headline News Section.

An End in Sight?

"For the first four years. . . .": *See* Mark A. Mlawer, RSIP Compliance Trends Report 2003–08, Emma C. v. Eastin, No. C96-4179 TEH (N.D. Cal. filed October, 2008) (copy on file with author) [**hereinafter Compliance Trends**].

"'significant regression'. . . .": *See* Mark A. Mlawer, Memo to Judge Thelton E. Henderson et al. Re RSIP Compliance Trends Report, 2003–08, October 28, 2008, Emma C. v. Eastin, No. C96-4179 TEH (N.D. Cal. filed October, 2008) at 5–6 (copy on file with author). *See* Mark A. Mlawer, RSIP Compliance Trends.

"Mark Mlawer, who continues to monitor. . . .": Telephone interview with Mark Mlawer, March 24, 2009.

"For the next year and a half. . . .": *See, e.g.,* Mark A. Mlawer, Memo to Judge Thelton E. Henderson et al. Re RSIP Quaterly Review Report (March 14, 2011), Emma C. v. Eastin, No. C96-4179 TEH (N.D. Cal. filed March, 2011) (copy on file with author); Mark A. Mlawer, Memo to Judge Thelton E. Henderson et al. Re RSIP Compliance Trends Report, 2002–10, October 29, 2010, Emma C. v. Eastin, No. C96-4179 T EH (N.D. Cal. filed October, 2010) (copy on file with author).

"In January 2010 . . . full compliance.": *See* Mark A. Mlawer, Memo to The Honorable Thelton E. Henderson Re RSIP Interim Benchmarks and Final Deadlines, June 23, 2010, Emma C. v. Eastin, No. C96-4179 TEH (N.D. Cal. filed June, 2010) (copy on file with author). Mlawler's memo notes that the July 2014 deadline does not apply to one RSIP requirement "due to its maintenance period."

"occasional backsliding": *See* Order Requiring Defendant Superintendent Gloria Hernandez-Goff's Attendance at Monitor's June 3 and 18, 2014 Meetings; and Further Directing Monitor to Meet with Board of Trustees (June 2, 2014), Emma C. v. Eastin, No. C96-4179 TEH (N.D. Cal. filed June 2, 2014).

"Ravenswood has continued to make progress. . . .": *See* Plaintiffs' Opposition to State Defendants' Motion Objecting to, and Seeking to Set Aside, Monitor's January 9, 2014 Report re State-Level Monitoring System (May 14, 2014), Emma C. v. Eastin, No. C96-4179 TEH (N.D. Cal. filed May 14, 2014) at 9 (copy on file with author) [**hereinafter Plaintiffs' May 14, 2014 Opposition**]; State Defendants' Notice of Motion and Motion Objecting to, and Seeking to Set Aside, Monitor's January 9, 2014 Report re State-Level Monitoring System, with Memorandum of Points and Authorities. . . . (April 16, 2014), Emma C. v. Eastin, No. C96-4179 TEH (N.D. Cal. filed April 16, 2014) at 8 (copy on file with author) [**hereinafter State Defendants' April 16, 2014 Motion**].

"did not meet the July 2014 deadline.": Conversation with Judge Henderson, September 7, 2014.

"still substantially noncompliant.": Telephone interview with Judge Henderson, May 29, 2016.

"In the meantime, a dispute has arisen. . . .": *See* Emma C. v. Eastin, 2014 W.L. 4220919 (denying state defendants' motion for a stay pending appeal of July 2, 2014 order); Emma C. v. Eastin, 2014 W.L. 2989946 (order denying state defendants' motion to set aside monitor's January 9, 2014 Report); Plaintiffs' May 14, 2014 Opposition; State Defendants' April 16, 2014 Motion.

"The Individuals with Disabilities Education Act requires. . . .": *See* 20 U.S.C. 1412.

"The 2003 amended settlement agreement. . . .": *See* Plaintiffs' May 14, 2014 Opposition at 8–9.

Postscript

"an unsuccessful 2006 run. . . .": *See* Joshua Molina & Sharon Noguchi, Knight Comeback Fails, but Ex-school Board Rival Voted Out, San Jose Mercury News, November 9, 2006, page 1B.

"one of seven candidates. . . .": *See* Banks Albach, Seven Candidates Compete for Two Ravenswood School District Seats, Contra Costa Times, August 19, 2008, News Section. One of the seven became inactive; Sharon Noguchi, Ex-Superintendent, Five Others Run for Board of Ravenswood School District, San Jose Mercury News, October 12, 2008, politics section.

"Ravenswood student scores. . . . diverted resources from the majority of students": *See* Sharon Noguchi, Ex-superintendent, Five Others Run for Board of Ravenswood School District, San Jose Mercury News, October 12, 2008, politics section.

"Knight finished third. . . .": *See* Neil Gonzales, Former E. Palo Alto Mayor Wins Seat on Ravenswood Board, Contra Costa Times, November 5, 2008, news section.

"At age 82, she finished second. . . .": *See* Sharon Noguchi, They're Ba-aa-aa-ack, Internal Affairs, San Jose Mercury News, November 6, 2014; Bonnie Eslinger, Former Superintendent Charlie Mae Knight Elected to School Board, San Jose Mercury News, November 5, 2014.

Post-Postscript: Receivership Reconsidered

"or (using Thorstein Veblin's terminology). . . .": *See* Thelton Henderson, Symposium: Confronting the Crisis: Current State Initiatives and Lasting Solutions for California's Prison Conditions: Keynote Address: Confronting the Crisis in California's Prisons, 43 U.S.F. L. Rev. 1, 7 (2008) (citing Thorstein Veblin, The Instinct of Workmanship and the State of the Industrial Arts 215, (1914)); *Underlying Problems* in Chapter Fourteen *supra*.

"From a legal standpoint. . . .": *See* Emma C. v. Eastin 2001 W.L. 1180636 at 17 (quoting CDE response to Order to Show Cause).

"'probable effectiveness'": United Mine Workers of America v. United States, 330 U.S. 258, 304 (1947), quoted in Emma C. v. Eastin, 2001 W.L. 1180636 at 17.

"Thus, as all of the parties. . . .": *See id.* at 19 n.25.

"In addition, any interim superintendent. . . .": *See* Takeover Urged.

"but in East Palo Alto both the plaintiffs and the CDE had asked. . . .": *See* Emma C. v. Eastin, 2001 W.L. 1180636 at 16.

"Fn. 2. In June 2000, the school board responded. . . .": *See* Thaai Walker & Lisa Fernandez, Superintendent Defended; Supporters Riled by Indictments over E. Palo Alto District Loans, San Jose Mercury News, June 10, 2000.

"Fn. 2. . . . A year later . . . publicly commended her.": *See* Sara Neufeld, Board Approves Funds to Respond to Series by MN, July 20, 2001, page 1A.

"Fn. 2. . . . By that time, however,. . . .": *See* Sara Neufeld, Parents Urge State Takeover of District, San Jose Mercury News, August 3, 2001, page 1B; Marshall Wilson & Alan Gathright, Acquitted School Boss Exasperated; East Palo Alto District Remains Under Cloud, San Francisco Chronicle, July 21, 2001, page A13.

"Fn. 2. . . . Her critics became more vocal. . . .": *See, e.g.,* Sara Neufeld, Teachers Seek School Chief's Ouster, San Jose Mercury News, April 19, 2002, page B3; Sara Neufeld, Community Speaks Out on Ravenswood Troubles; Emotions Ran High When about 200 People Gathered at a Forum to Tell Officials What They Think about the School District and the Way It's Being Run, San Jose Mercury News, February 8, 2002, page 1B.

"its track record. . . .": Telephone interview with Mark Mlawer, March 24, 2009. Mlawer notes that the problem was not unique to the CDE. Federal oversight of IDEA was lax; and as a result, state oversight of individual districts tended to be lax. Nonetheless, as Judge Henderson's description of Ravenswood's early noncompliance with the RCAP points out, CDE was actively involved in the litigation early on.

"the plaintiffs had asked that the CDE. . . .": *See* Emma C. v. Eastin, 2001 W.L. 1180636 at 4.

"it did little to suggest. . . .": *See* Emma C. V. Eastin, 2001 W.L. 1180636 at 19 ("neither CDE nor plaintiffs have yet presented the Court with more than an abstract notion of a receivership"); Sara Neufeld, State Outlines Intent in Proposed Takeover; Official May Hire Temporary Leader, San Jose Mercury News, June 1, 2002, page 1B (state receivership plan "did not include the names of potential administrators, as ordered by U.S. District Judge Thelton Henderson"); Sara Neufeld, Settlement Sought in School Talks; Judge Gives East P.A. District, Students' Lawyers a Deadline, San Jose Mercury News, August 8, 2002, page B3 (Judge Henderson admonishes CDE for not presenting written testimony that he had ordered; CDE asks to put case on hold for sixty days while it looks for new lawyer).

"school desegregation cases": *See, e.g.,* Richard Kluger, Simple Justice (2004).

"the controversy over HIV-positive. . . .": *See* U.S. Department of Human Services, HRSA HIV/AIDS Programs, Ryan White HIV/AIDS Program: About Ryan White, available at http://www.hab.hrsa.gov (last visited July 6, 2011).

"prayer in the classroom": *See* Kathleen Sullivan & Gerald Gunther, Constitutional Law (16 ed. 2007) 1293–305.

"role creationism should have. . . .": *See id.* at 1306–11.

"For years East Palo Alto. . . .": *See generally* The History of East Palo Alto, available at http://www.epa.net/info/epa_history.html (last visited March 25, 2009); Veronique de Turenne, California and the West; East Palo Alto Looks to Its Past for a New Name, Los Angeles Times,

November 8, 1998, part A, page 28; Mark A. Stein, East Palo Alto; Minority Cityhood: A Case-book, Los Angeles Times, January 21, 1987, part 1, page 1.

"Fn. 3. . . .": The material in the footnote is based primarily on the author's conversations with East Palo Alto residents (including Judge Henderson) when he worked at the East Bay-shore Neighborhood Center in the late 1960s. Much of the same information appears in Tracy Jan, Ravenswood revisited, reunited, September 11, 1996, available at http://www.paloaltoon-line.com/weekly/morgue/cover/1996_Sep_11.COVER11.html (last visited July 6, 2011).

"in 1992 East Palo Alto. . . .": See Vicky Anning, Reversal of Misfortune, Stanford Maga-zine, January-February 1998; Jenifer Warren, E. Palo Alto Murder Rate Worst in U.S.; Drug Wars Blamed, Los Angeles Times, January 5, 1993, part B, page 8.

"people like Gertrude Wilks and Bob Hoover": Gertrude Wilks founded Mothers for Equal Education. See Mothers for Equal Education, available at http://mothers4equaleducation. org/5001/5022.html (last visited July 6, 2011). On Bob Hoover, see, e.g., Banks Albach, Raising a City: What Began in the 1960s for Bob Hoover Became His Passion: Helping the Youth of East Palo Alto Thrive, Palo Alto Daily News, April 6, 2008; Kim Vo, "Mr. Bob" to Move out of East P.A.; Tireless Resident Guided Kids for Decades, San Jose Mercury News, March 16, 2006, sec. B, page 2.

"Marcelino Lopez": Lopez, Adam Mitchell, and Todd Gaviglio, were the reform slate elected to the Ravenswood School Board in 2002. See Sara Neufeld, Ravenswood Reform Slate Topples Incumbents, San Jose Mercury News, November 6, 2002, sec. B, page 1.

Chapter Nineteen
The (Mostly) False Rhetoric of Judging

Applying Law versus Making Law

On the question whether a particular type of surveillance may constitute an unreasonable search or seizure, compare, e.g., California v. Ciraolo, 476 U.S. 207 (1986) and Florida v. Riley, 488 U.S. 445 (upholding airplane and helicopter surveillance) with Kyllo v. United States, 533 U.S. 27 (2001) (striking down warrantless thermal imaging); or compare Katz v. United States 389 U.S. 347 (1967) (obtaining information via electronic device in public telephone booth is search and seizure) with United States v. White, 401 U.S. 745 (obtaining information via elec-tronic device concealed on government informer not a search or seizure).

On the question whether a public display of the Ten Commandments violates the First Amendment, compare Van Orden v. Perry, 545 U.S. 677 (2005) (display of Ten Commandments on Texas capitol grounds not a violation of First Amendment Establishment Clause) with McCreary County v. A.C.L.U., 545 U.S. 844 (2005) (display of Ten Commandments in county courthouses violates First Amendment Establishment Clause because display did not have a secular purpose).

On the constitutionality of considering race in university admissions policies, compare Gratz v. Bollinger, 539 U.S. 244 (2003) (holding unconstitutional the University of Michigan's use of race in its undergraduate admissions program) with Grutter v. Bollinger, 539 U.S. 306 (2003) (upholding the use of race in University of Michigan Law School's admission program).

Judicial Restraint and Judicial Activism

"Fn. 2. . . . Hudson v. Michigan": 547 U.S. 586 (2006).

"Fn. 2. . . . Herring v. United States": 555 U.S. 135 (2009).

"Fn. 2. . . . The majority opinions in both cases. . . .": *See* David A. Moran, The End of the Exclusionary Rule, Among Other Things: The Roberts Court Takes on the Fourth Amendment, 2006 Cato Sup. Ct. Rev. 283, 283 (commenting on *Hudson*); Adam Liptak, Justices Step Closer to Repeal of Evidence Ruling, N.Y. Times, January 30, 2009 (commenting on *Herring*).

"During its first 200 years. . . .": *See* Seth P. Waxman, Defending Congress, 79 N.C.L. Rev. 1073, 1074 (2001).

"overturned twenty-six acts. . . .": *See id.* The Burger Court, despite its relative conservatism was also quite "activist." *See* Vincent Blasi, The Rootless Activism of the Burger Court, in The Burger Court: The Counterrevolution that Wasn't (Vincent Blasi, ed. 1983) 211 ("in the hands of the Burger Court judicial activism has become a centrist philosophy"); Gene R. Nichol, Book Review: An Activism of Ambivalence, 98 Harv. L. Rev. 315 (1984) (reviewing The Burger Court: The Revolution that Wasn't).

"Kelo v. City of New London": 545 U.S. 469 (2005).

" ' "carefully considered" development plan' ": *Id.* at 478.

"not 'to benefit any particular class. . . .' ": *Id.* at 477.

"the case received bipartisan criticism": *See, e.g.,* Bill Salisbury, Groups Attack Eminent Domain: Bipartisan Coalition Aims to Block Seizing of Homeowners' Land, St. Paul Pioneer Press, December 30, 2005, page 1B; Matthew Vadum, DC Strip Mall in Eminent Domain Flap, The Bond Buyer, Financial Times Information, December 12, 2005; William Yardley, After Eminent Domain Victory, Disputed Project Goes Nowhere, N.Y. Times, November 21, 2005, page A1.

" 'a frightening example of judicial activism' ": Jeff Miller, Weekly Report from Washington, U.S. Fed. News, HT Media, June 24, 2005.

" 'blatant judicial activism' ": Ned Rice, The Man Who Couldn't Be Borked, National Review Online, October 13, 2005.

" 'nefarious'. . . 'the inherent danger. . . .' ": Geoff Davis, House Passes Bill to Protect Private Property Rights, U.S. Fed. News, HT Media, November 3, 2005.

Strict Constructionism

"federal powers — including congressional power. . . .": *See* Newberry v. United States, 256 U.S. 232, 281 (Pitney, J., concurring). This view of strict constructionism can lead to judicial activism, as it did in *Newberry*, where the Court struck down a federal statute. *See* Arthur D. Hellman, Judicial Activism: The Good, the Bad, and the Ugly, 21 Miss. C. L. Rev. 253, 254 n.10 (2002).

On President Nixon's promise to appoint "strict constructionists" to the Supreme Court, *see* James F. Simon, In His Own Image: The Supreme Court in Richard Nixon's America (1973); Donald Greer Stephenson, Jr., Campaigns and the Court: The U.S. Supreme Court in Presidential Elections 180–81 (1999); Ronald Dworkin, Special Supplement: The Jurisprudence of Richard Nixon, 18 N.Y. Rev. of Books, May 4, 1972; E.W. Kenworthy, Nixon, in Texas, Sharpens His Attack, N.Y. Times, November 3 1968, page 1, 79.

On Bush's commitment to appoint "strict constructionists" like Scalia and Thomas, *see, e.g.,* Neil A. Lewis, Hurdles to Agenda, N.Y. Times, January 2, 2001, sec. A, page 10; Bill Rankin, Move to the Right Seems Certain; Expect Backlash if any Bush Nominees Are Seen as Too

Conservative; The President-Elect: The Supreme Court, The Atlanta Journal & Constitution, December 17, 2000, page 6G.

On Scalia's rejection of the label "strict constructionist," *see* Antonin Scalia, A Matter of Interpretation 23 (1998).

Dialing Down the Rhetoric (a Bit)

"more decisions with which conservatives agree": *See, e.g.,* Schuette v. Coalition to Defend Affirmative Action, Integration and Immigration Rights and Fight for Equality by Any Means Necessary (BAMN), 134 S.Ct. 1623, 1629 (2014), *discussed in* Chapter Twenty-One; District of Columbia v. Heller, 554 U.S. 570 (2008), *discussed in* Erwin Chemerinsky, Judicial Activism by Conservatives, Los Angeles Times, June 27, 2008.

"but by no means completely": *See, e.g.,* Brian Tashman, Rod Parsley: It's not Judicial Activism if Judges Are Conservatives, Right Wing Watch, March 1, 2011, available at http://www .rightwingwatch.org/content/rod-parsley-its-not-judicial-activism-if-judges-are-conservatives (last visited May 14, 2015); Judicial Activism for Dummies, Red State, February 2, 2011, available at http://www.redstate.com/diary/scipio62/2011/02/02/judicial-activism-for-liberal-dummies (last visited May 13, 2015).

An Accounting for the False Rhetoric of Judging

"Justice Sotomayor insist at her confirmation hearing. . . .": *See* Confirmation Hearing on the Nomination of Hon. Sonia Sotomayor to be an Associate Justice of the Supreme Court of the United States, Hearing before the S. Comm. on the Judiciary, 111th Cong. 59 (2009); *see also, e.g., id.* at 64, 70, 79.

"There is enormous appeal. . . .": Erwin Chemerinsky, Symposium: The Role of the Judge in the Twenty-First Century: Seeing the Emperor's Clothes: Recognizing the Reality of Constitutional Decision Making, 86 B.U. L. Rev. 1069, 1071 (2006).

On the relationship between majoritarianism and the judiciary, *see, e.g., id.* at 1074–77.

Chapter Twenty
High Tech Gays: Suspect Classifications and Fundamental Rights

"Fn. 1. . . . Brown v. Board of Education": 347 U.S. 483 (1954).

"Fn. 1. . . . Bolling v. Sharpe": 347 U.S. 497 (1954).

"Judge Henderson wrote a bold opinion. . . .": *See* High Tech Gays v. Defense Indus. Sec. Clearance Office, 668 F. Supp. 1361 (N.D. Cal. 1987).

"A Ninth Circuit panel reversed. . . .": *See* High Tech Gays v. Defense Indus. Sec. Clearance Office, 895 F.2d 563 (9th Cir. 1990).

"over a vigorous dissent. . . .": *See* High Tech Gays v. Defense Indus. Sec. Clearance Office, 909 F.2d 375, 376 (9th Cir. 1990) (Canby, J., dissenting).

The Facts and the Issue

"the relevant facts. . . .": *See* High Tech Gays v. Defense Indus. Sec. Clearance Office, 668 F. Supp. at 1363–66.

"The Manual characterized. . . .": *See id.* at 1364

"use[d] homosexuality as a general term. . . .": *Id.*

"According to the manual . . . 'cast doubt on. . . .' ": *See id.*

"Ultimately, most gays. . . .": *See* High Tech Gays v. Defense Indus. Sec. Clearance Office, 909 F.2d at 376 (Canby, J. dissenting).

The Constitutional Framework

"tended to divide equal protection and due process claims into three categories. . . .": For Judge Henderson's description of the three categories, *see* High Tech Gays v. Defense Indus. Sec. Clearance Office, 668 F. Supp. at 1368.

"most notably, gender. . . .": Gender may have moved closer to the "suspect classification" category. *See* United States v. Virginia, 518 U.S. 515, 531 (1996) (state must show "exceedingly persuasive justification" for its discrimination); *id.* at 570–76 (Scalia, J., dissenting).

"but by no means impossible": *See* Romer v. Evans 517 U.S. 620 (1996).

"a spectrum of standards. . . .": *See* Kathleen M. Sullivan & Gerald Gunther, Constitutional Law 486 (16 ed. 2007).

"*all* racial classifications. . . .": *See* Adarand Constructors, Inc. v. Pena, 515 U.S. 200 (1995).

"some affirmative action programs. . . .": *See, e.g.,* Grutter v. Bollinger, 539 U.S. 306 (2003).

"Fn. 2. Some have claimed . . .": *See, e.g.,* Kathleen M. Sullivan & Gerald Gunther, Constitutional Law (16th ed. 2007) 486.

"Cleburne v. Cleburne Living Center, Inc.": 473 U.S. 432 (1985).

" 'other care and multiple dwelling facilities.' ": *See id.* at 448.

" 'ordinance is invalidated only after. . . .' ": *Id.* at 458 (Marshall, J., dissenting).

Quasi-Suspect Class and Heightened Scrutiny

" 'laws disfavoring racial groups. . . .' ": High Tech Gays v. Defense Indus. Sec. Clearance Office, 668 F. Supp. at 1369

"With respect to gender. . . .": *Id.*

"Lesbians and gay men. . . .": *Id.* at 1369–70.

"Fourth, discrimination against gays. . . .": *See generally* Mark Plotkin, Gay/Lesbian Law Pathfinder, LLRX.com, July 27, 2007, available at http://www.llrx.com/features/gaylesbianlaw .htm (last visited November 1, 2008); The Columbia Reader on Lesbians and Gay Men in Media, Society, and Politics, Larry P. Gross & James D. Woods (eds.) 1999.

"John Lewis, the law clerk who assisted. . . .": E-mail from John Lewis to author, May 22, 2012.

Fundamental Rights and Strict Scrutiny

"Griswold v. Connecticut": 381 U.S. 479 (1965).

"Carey v. Population Services, International": 431 U.S. 678 (1977).

"Eisenstadt v. Baird": 405 U.S. 438 (1972).

"Fn. 3. . . . If under *Griswold*. . . .": *Id.* at 453 (emphasis in original).

"Roe v. Wade": 410 U.S. 113 (1979).

"Relying primarily upon *Griswold* and *Carey*. . . .": *See* High Tech Gays v. Defense Indus. Sec. Clearance Office, 668 F. Supp. at 1372.

"Bowers v. Hardwick": 478 U.S. 186 (1986).

Bowers v. Hardwick

"On the morning of July 5. . . .": The Supreme Court opinion states without elaboration that Hardwick was arrested in his home. For an account of the events leading to the arrest, *see, e.g.,* Art Harris, The Unintended Battle of Michael Hardwick; After His Georgia Sodomy Case, a Public Right-to-Privacy Crusade, The Washington Post, August 21, 1986, sec. C, page 1; Aric Press et al., A Government in the Bedroom, Newsweek, July 14, 1986, page 36.

" 'any sexual act involving. . . .' ": Ga. Code Ann. sec. 16-6-2, quoted in Bowers v. Harwick, 478 U.S. at 188.

"The only claim. . . .": Bowers v. Hardwick, 478 U.S. at 188 n.2.

"no 'fundamental [due process] right to engage in homosexual sodomy.' ": *Id.* at 191.

" 'majority sentiments about the morality. . . .' ": *Id.* at 196.

Judge Henderson's Response to Hardwick

" 'that disadvantages lesbians and gay men. . . .' ": High Tech Gays v. Defense Indus. Sec. Clearance Office, 668 F. Supp. at 1370 (emphasis in original).

"*Hardwick* does not hold. . . .": *Id.* at 1370–72.

"The Court's previous privacy cases. . . .": *See, e.g.,* Carey v. Population Services, International": 431 U.S. 678 (1977); Griswold v. Connecticut, 381 U.S. 479 (1965).

"focusing only on 'homosexual sodomy. . . .' ": *See* Bowers v. Hardwick, 478 U.S. at 188 n.2, 190, 191, 192, 195, 196.

"[I]t appears to this Court. . . .": High Tech Gays v. Defense Indus. Sec. Clearance Office, 668 F. Supp. at 1371.

"Affectional and sexual intimacy. . . .": *Id.* at 1372.

"Fn. 4. . . . Traditionally, criminal prohibitions. . . .": *See* Survey on the Constitutional Right to Privacy in the Context of Homosexual Activity, 40 U. Miami L. Rev. 521 (1986).

"ancient roots": *See* Bowers v. Hardwick, 478 U.S. at 192.

Rational Basis?

"could not be justified. . . .": *See* High Tech Gays v. Defense Indus. Sec. Clearance Office, 668 F. Supp. at 1373

" 'homosexual conduct may constitute. . . .' ": *See id.*

"a variety of problems. . . .": *See id.* at 1373–74.

"Second Judge Henderson. . . . [D]efendants provide. . . .": *Id.* at 1374.

"Judge Henderson, citing the positions. . . .": *See id.* at 1374–1375.

" '[f]or years the uncontroverted consensus. . . .' ": *Id.* at 1374.

"gays and lesbians who are secretive. . . .": *See id.* at 1375. The government did present evidence that Timothy Dooling, one of the named plaintiffs, "was approached regarding blackmail." However, Dooling "unequivocally rejected the blackmail attempt." *See id.*

"Judge Henderson noted. . . .": *See id.* at 1375–76.

"Defendants' policy represents. . . .": *Id.* at 1376.

"heterosexual conduct that 'may involve. . . .' ": *See id.*

"lies at the heart of. . . .": *Id.* at 1376–77.

"The Defense Department's unequal treatment. . . .": *Id.* at 1377.

The Ninth Circuit

"The panel held. . . .": *See* High Tech Gays v. Defense Indus. Sec. Clearance Office, 895 F.2d 563 (9th Cir.1990).

"When a majority of the full Ninth Circuit. . . .": *See* High Tech Gays v. Defense Indus. Sec. Clearance Office, 909 F.2d 375 (9th Cir. 1990).

Lawrence v. Texas

"Lawrence v. Texas": 539 U.S. 558 (2003).

"Fn. 5. . . . There is substantial evidence. . . .": *See* Dale Carpenter, Flagrant Conduct: The Story of Lawrence v. Texas (2012).

"The Court could easily have rested. . . .": Justice O'Connor based her concurring opinion exclusively on the Equal Protection Clause. *Id.* at 579–85 (O'Connor, J., concurring)

" 'continuance as precedent. . . .' ": *Id.* at 575.

"Liberty presumes an autonomy. . . .": *Id.* at 562, 567, 578.

"Second, the Court's detailed discussion and rejection. . . .": *See* Cook v. Gates, 528 F.3d 42, 52–57 (1st Cir. 2008); Witt v. Department of the Air Force, 527 F.3d 806, 816–17 (9th Cir. 2008) (both concluding that *Lawrence* used some type of heightened scrutiny). *But see* Lofton v. Secretary of the Department of Children & Family Services, 358 F.3d 804, 817 (2004) (concluding that *Lawrence* applied rational basis standard). *See generally* Lawrence Tribe, Lawrence v. Texas: The "Fundamental Right" that Dare not Speak Its Name, 117 Harv. L. Rev. 1893 (2004).

"Equality of treatment. . . .": Lawrence v. Texas, 539 U.S. at 575.

"supports Judge Henderson's equal protection analysis": The *Lawrence* Court might have been able to overturn the convictions on equal protection grounds without considering whether homosexuality should be a quasi-suspect class or whether the Texas statute should be subject to heightened scrutiny. *See* Lawrence v. Texas, 539 U.S. 558, 581–83 (2003) (O'Connor, J., concurring) (approving Bowers v. Hardwick but arguing that in equal protection terms moral disapproval is not a sufficient rational basis for a statute proscribing only homosexual sodomy); *See also* Romer v Evans, 517 U.S. 615 (1996) (no rational basis to support state constitutional provision that prohibited extending protection of nondiscrimination laws to homosexuals).

A Work in Progress

"strong domestic partner law": *See* Cal. Fam. Code, sec. 297.5.

"in May 2008, the California Supreme Court . . .": *See* In re Marriage Cases, 43 Cal. 4th 757, 183 P.3d 384, 76 Cal. Rptr. 3d 683 (2008).

"the Supreme Judicial Court of Massachusetts": *See* Goodridge v. Department of Public Health, 440 Mass. 309, 798 N.E.2d 941 (2003).

"[D]rawing a distinction. . . .": In re Marriage Cases, 43 Cal. 4th at 434–35.

" 'Only marriage between a man and a woman. . . .' ": Cal. Const., Art I, sec. 7.5.

"applied only prospectively.": *See* Straus v. Horton, 46 Cal. 4th 364, 470, 207 P.3d 48, 93 Ca. Rptr. 3d 591 (2009). The primary issue in *Straus* dealt with the process by which Proposition 8 was adopted. The California Constitution distinguishes between "amendments" and "revisions." Although the former can be adopted through the initiative process, the latter must be approved by the legislature before being submitted to the people for a vote. Cal Const. Art XVIII. *See* Amador Valley Joint Union High Sch. Dist. v. State Bd. of Equalization, 22 Cal.3d 208,

221–22, 583 P.3d 1281, 1284–85, 149 Cal. Rptr. 239, 242–43 (1978). The opponents of Proposition 8 claim that it works such a substantial change in existing constitutional rights that it is a revision, not a mere amendment. The California Supreme Court disagreed and upheld Proposition 8.

"... Walker ... struck down Proposition 8. ...": *See* Perry v. Schwarzenegger, 704 F. Supp. 2d 921 (2010).

"Although the defendants ... intervene at trial.": *See id.* at 2660.

"The Ninth Circuit affirmed. ...": *See* Perry v. Schwarzenegger, 671 F.3d 1052 (1012).

"intervenors lacked standing. ...": *See* Perry v. Brown, 725 F.3d 1140 (2013).

"'only interest ... was to vindicate. ...'": *Id.* at 2266.

"'concrete and particularized injury.'": *Id.* at 2659.

"the Ninth Circuit dismissed. ...": *See* Perry v. Brown, 725 F.3d 1140 (9th Cir. 2013).

"United States v. Windsor": 133 S.Ct. 2675 (2013).

"Section 3 had defined. ...": *See id.* at 2683.

"The plaintiff in *Windsor.* ...": *See id.*

"Fn. 6. ... prevents same-sex married couples. ...": *Id.* at 2694.

"DOMA singles out. ...": *Id.* at 2695–96.

"The Court left for another day. ...": *See id.* at 2696.

"only one of a growing number of states. ...": *See, e.g., id.* at 2689 ("New York in common with, as of this writing, 11 other states and the District of Columbia, decided that same-sex couples should have the right to marry. ...").

"polls have continued to show increasing support. ...": *See* Emily Swanson, Gay Marriage Polls Find Personal Relationships Have Major Impact on Support, The Huffington Post, March 21, 2013.

"Moreover, in the wake of the DOMA. ...": *See, e.g.,* Bostic v. Rainey, 2014 W.L. 561978 (E.D. Va.); Bishop v. United States, 2014 W.L. 116013 (N.D. Okla.); Kitchen v. Herbert, 2013 W.L. 6697874 (D. Utah).

"Obergefell v. Hodges": 135 S.Ct. 2584 (2015).

"widespread celebration": *See* Hailey Branson, Jerome Campbell, & Lee Romney, In California, Jubilation over Same-Sex Marriage Rights Nationwide, Los Angeles Times, June 26, 2015; Carla Marinucci, Supreme Court Gay-Marriage Decision Doesn't Deter Conservatives, San Francisco Chronicle, June 26, 2015.

"President Obama, as well as all of the declared Democratic. ...": *See* David Nakamura, Obama on Same-Sex Marriage Ruling: "We Have Made Our Union a Little More Perfect," The Washington Post, June 26, 2015; Matthew Speiser, Here's How the 2016 Presidential Candidates Are Reacting to the Supreme Court's Ruling on Gay Marriage, Business Insider, June 26, 2015 [hereinafter The 2016 Candidates].

"four dissenters": *See* Obergefell v. Hodges, 135 S.Ct. at 2611–43 (Roberts, Scalia, Thomas, and Alito).

"Republican 2016 Presidential hopefuls. ...": *See* Amanda Marcotte, Rand Paul Would Rather End Marriage Than Share It with Gay People, Slate, June 29, 2015; The 2016 Candidates, *supra.*

"discrimination against gays and lesbians. ...": *See* Erik Eckholm, Next Fight for Gay Rights: Bias in Jobs and Housing, N.Y. Times, June 27, 2015; Curtis M. Wong, Sweet Cakes by Melissa's Owner Says Fine for Rejecting Lesbian Couple Will Leave Them Bankrupt, The Huffington Post, October 17, 2014.

"Loving v. Virginia": 388 U.S. 1 (1967).
"Lawrence v. Texas": 539 U.S. 558 (2003).

Chapter Twenty-One
Proposition 209: Inequality in the Political Process

"Coalition for Economic Equity v. Wilson": 946 F. Supp. 1480 (N.D. Cal. 1996), *rev'd*, 122 F.3d 692 (9th Cir. 1997).

"Former Representative Tom Delay. . . .": *See* Katharine Q. Seelye, House G.O.P. Begins Listing a Few Judges to Impeach, N.Y. Times, March 14, 1997, sec. A, page 24.

Proposition 209 and the Assignment of the Case to Judge Henderson

"On November 5, 1996. . . .": *See* Coalition for Economic Equity v. Wilson, 122 F.3d at 696, 697.

"The state [including any political subdivision. . . .": Calif. Const. art 1, sec. 31(a)&(f).

"government-sponsored affirmative action. . . .": Some activities undertaken in the name of "affirmative action" may not have racial and gender preferences. These activities would not be affected by Proposition 209. *See* Coalition for Economic Equity v. Wilson, 946 F. Supp. at 1489 n.4; Eugene Volokh, The California Civil Rights Initiative: An Interpretative Guide, 44 U.C.L.A. L. Rev. 1335 (1997).

"initially assigned. . . .": *See* Order, Coalition for Economic Equity v. Wilson, No. C96-4024 VRW (N.D. Cal. filed November 13, 1996) [**hereinafter November 13, 1996 Order**].

"with the concurrence of two. . . .": *See id.* at 2.

"F.W. Spencer & Sons, Inc. v. City and County of San Francisco": No. C-95 4242 THE (N.D. Cal.).

"California Attorney General Dan Lungren charged. . . .": *See* November 13, 1996 Order at 2; Harriet Chiang, How CCRI Is Being Enforced — and How It Isn't: S.F. Judge to Rule on Two Lawsuits, San Francisco Chronicle, November 14, 1996, page A15.

"Civil Local Rule 3–12, which required. . . .": *See* United States District Court, Northern District of California, Civil Local Rule 3–12 (b).

"when both concern (1) some of the same. . . .": *See* November 13, 1996 Order at 2. The current version of the rule is slightly different. See United States District Court, Northern District of California, Civil Local Rule 3–12(a).

" 'inevitably implicated. . . .'. . . and because. . . .": *See* November 13, 1996 Order at 3. *See also* Order, Office of the Clerk (N.D. Cal. filed November 20, 1996) (order signed by D.R. Gilman on behalf of the Assignment Committee affirming that *Spencer* and *Coalition for Economic Equity* are related and changing the initials in the case number of *Coalition for Economic Equity* from VRW to TEH).

"To the extent . . . 'in its current posture.' ": *See* November 13, 1996 Order at 3–5.

"One of the defendants then moved. . . .": The motion came from defendant-intervenor Californians against Discrimination and Preferences (CADAP). *See* Order Re: Recusal, Coalition for Economic Equity v. Wilson, No. C96-4024 TEH (N.D. Cal. filed December 20, 1996) (noting that CADAP's recusal motion based on two statutory provisions; denying motion under one statute and referring motion on other statutory ground to clerk for random assignment to another judge).

"Judge Fern Smith . . . concluded. . . .": *See* Order Denying Defendant-Intervenor's Motion for Recusal Pursuant to 28 U.S.C. sec. 144, Coalition for Economic Equity v. Wilson, No. C96-4024 TEH (FMS) (N.D. Cal. filed January 13, 1997).

The Equal Protection Issue

"'[O]nly programs that are. . . .'": Coalition for Economic Equity v. Wilson, 946 F. Supp. at 1489.

"'narrow but significant'": *Id.*

"[P]laintiffs' constitutional challenge. . . .": *Id.*

"Fn. 2. Stephen Colbert. . . .": *See* Wikipedia, Stephen_Colbert_(character), available at http://en.wikipedia.org/wiki/Stephen_Colbert_(character) (last visited June 23, 2010).

"Fn. 3. . . . Harper v. Virginia State Board of Elections": 383 U.S. 663 (1966).

"Fn. 3. . . . The Civil Rights Act. . . .": *See* South Carolina v. Katzenbach, 383 U.S. 301 (1966).

"It . . . cannot be overemphasized. . . .": Coalition for Economic Equity v. Wilson, 946 F. Supp. at 1490.

A Temporary Restraining Order, a Preliminary Injunction, and Ninth Circuit Intervention

"Judge Henderson granted the plaintiffs' request. . . .": *See* Coalition for Economic Equity v. Wilson, 1996 W.L. 691962 (N.D. Cal.).

"'[W]henever issues affecting race. . . .'": *Id.* at 1.

"Judge Henderson in effect extended the TRO by granting. . . .": *See* Coalition for Economic Equity v. Wilson, 946 F. Supp. 1480 (N.D. Cal. 1996).

"On January 3. . . . A few days later. . . .": *See* Coalition for Economic Equity v. Wilson, 122 F.3d at 698; Petition for Rehearing and Suggestion for Rehearing en Banc, Coalition for Economic Equity v. Wilson (9th Cir. filed May 19, 1997) at 3–4, available at http:/www.cir-usa.org/legal_docs/ccri/aclureb.htm (last visited November 1, 2013) [**hereinafter Petition for Rehearing**] (after CADAP filed it stay application with the Ninth Circuit, plaintiffs objected that CADAP lacked standing; state, *at the motions panel's request*, joined in the stay application, thereby mooting the standing question).

"Diarmuid O'Scannlain and. . . .": *See* United States Court of Appeals for the Ninth Circuit, Biographical Directory of Federal Judges, available at http://www.fjc.gov/public/home.nsf/hisj (last visited June 23, 2010).

"'Kleinfeld had been active. . . .'": Reynolds Holding, Prop. 209 Adversaries Play Shuttlecock, San Francisco Chronicle, March 2, 1997, page 5/Z5. *See* Brigid Schulte, Kleinfeld's Nomination Clears Senate Judiciary, States News Service, September 11, 1991.

"According to Kleinfeld, 'the book. . . .'": *See id.*

"normally would . . . have played a more limited role. . . .": *See, e.g.*, Gregorio T. v. Wilson, 54 F.3d 599 (9th Cir. 1995); Zepeda v. U.S.I.N.S., 753 F.2d 719, 724 (9th Cir. 1984); Sports Form, Inc. v. United Press Int'l, 686 F.2d 750, 752 (9th Cir. 1982).

"'deferred submission of the stay application'. . . .": *See* Coalition for Economic Equity v. Wilson, 122 F.3d at 699. *See* Coalition for Economic Equity v. Wilson, 107 F.3d 704 (9th Cir. 1997).

"On April 8 . . . an opinion. . . .": *See* Coalition for Economic Equity v. Wilson, 122 F.3d. 692 (9th Cir. 1997).

"The full Ninth Circuit and the Supreme Court. . . .": *See* Coalition for Economic Equity v. Wilson, 122 F.3d at 711, *cert. denied*, 522 U.S. 963 (1977).

Judge Henderson's Factual Findings: Coalition for Economic Equity v. Wilson, 946 F. Supp. 1480, 1493–1499 (N.D. Cal. 1996)

"[Here Judge Henderson cited evidence. . . .]": For verification of this hypothesis, *see* Ellis Cose, Going Down the Drain: "This Isn't Good for America," The Seattle Post-Intelligencer, November 26, 2006, page D1 [**hereinafter Going Down the Drain**].

"Fn. 4. In the fall of 1997. . . .": *See* John C. Jeffries, Jr., Bakke Revisited, 2003 Sup. Ct. Rev. 1, 15–16. Minority enrollment numbers for both Boalt Hall and U.C.L.A. Law School have improved in recent years. It has been suggested, however, that the admissions policies may not be truly race-neutral. *See id.* at 15–17 & nn. 63, 65.

"Fn. 4. . . . the two African American students. . . .": *See* Soul of Justice (Judge Henderson describing his first-year class).

"Fn. 4. . . . During the next ten years. . . .": *See* "Going Down the Drain;" Bob Egelko, Affirmative Action Upheld but High Court Sets Limits; 5–4 vote: Minority Status to Remain a Factor in Admissions, San Francisco Chronicle, June 24, 2003, page A1; Mitchell Lansberg et al., Race Neutral University Admissions in Spotlight; UC, Florida and Texas Systems Still Have Diversity after Dumping Affirmative Action, Los Angeles Times, January 17, 2003, part 1, page 1.

"Fn. 4 . . . This year, in a class of 4809. . . .": *See* Timothy Egan, Little Asia on the Hill, N.Y. Times, January 7, 2007, Education Life Supplement, page 24.

The Supreme Court Precedents

"Hunter v. Erickson": 393 U.S. 385 (1969).

"Washington v. Seattle School Dist. No. 1": 458 U.S. 457 (1982).

" 'race, color, religion. . . .' ": Hunter v. Erickson, 393 U.S. at 387

" 'treats Negro and white. . . .' ": *Id.* at 391.

" 'the reality is . . . it places [a] special burden. . . .' ": *Id.*

"[t]he automatic referendum system. . . .": *Id.*

" 'discriminates against minorities. . . .' ": *Id.* at 392.

"[T]he political majority. . . .": Washington v. Seattle School Dist. No. 1, 458 U.S. at 470 (emphasis in original).

" 'little doubt that the initiative. . . .' ": *Id.* at 471.

" '[p]roponents of the initiative. . . .' ": *Id.*

" 'racial focus'. . . 'suffice[d] to trigger. . . .' ": *Id.* at 474.

" 'work[s] a reallocation. . . .' ": *Id.*

"The initiative removes the authority. . . .": *Id.* at 474–75.

"Judge Henderson, however, did address. . . .": *See* Coalition for Economic Equity v. Wilson, 946 F. Supp. at 1508–09

"Crawford v. Board of Education of the City of Los Angeles": 458 U.S. 527 (1982).

"merely a 'repeal'. . . .": *Id.* at 539, 540.

"did not 'distort[]. . . .' ": *Id.* at 541.

"'Proposition 1 does not embody. . . .'": *Id.* at 537.

"At the same time, however,. . . .": *See id.* at 536 n.12.

"'court ordered busing [to promote desegregation]. . . .'": *Id.* at 539 n.18.

"focus or classification": *See id.* at 537 n.14 (acknowledging that *Hunter* involved a racial classification).

"In *Crawford*, no lower court. . . .": *See id.* at 562 & n.7 (Marshall, J., dissenting).

"I fail to see how a fundamental redefinition. . . .": Crawford v. Board of Education of the City of Los Angeles": 458 U.S. at 548, 545, 561 (Marshall, J., dissenting).

"To the extent that Justice Marshall's comparison is correct. . . .": There is a similar tension within *Seattle* itself. Why is not appropriate to view the state, through its initiative process, as having merely repealed a portion of the authority previously granted to local school boards? In his *Seattle* dissent, Justice Powell characterized the majority's holding in the following manner:

> Under today's decision th[e] heretofore undoubted supreme authority of a State's electorate is to be curtailed whenever a school board — or indeed any other state board or local instrumentality — adopts a race-specific program that arguably benefits racial minorities. Once such a program is adopted, *only* the local or subordinate entity that approved it will have authority to change it. The Court offers no authority or relevant explanation for this extraordinary subordination of the ultimate sovereign power of a State to act with respect to racial matters by subordinate bodies. It is a strange notion — alien to our system — that local governmental bodies can forever pre-empt the ability of a State — the sovereign power — to address a matter of compelling concern to the State. The Constitution of the United States does not require such a bizarre result.

Washington v. Seattle School Dist. No. 1, 458 U.S. at 495 (Powell, J., dissenting).

The Court responded, "Justice Powell's . . . observations on a State's right to repeal programs designed to eliminate *de facto* segregation . . . [are] largely beside the point. The State's *power* has not been questioned at any point." *Id.* 477 n.18 (emphasis in original). Yet, as the Ninth Circuit panel pointed out in reversing Judge Henderson, "Every statewide policy has the "procedural" effect of denying someone an inconsistent outcome at the local level." Coalition for Economic Equity v. Wilson, 122 F.3d at 706. In other words, any state law limiting the availability of preexisting opportunities necessarily burdens those individuals who can no longer take advantage of the opportunities. Thus, *Hunter* and *Seattle*, carried to their logical extreme, would indeed "limit the State's power," in the sense that any such legislation having a racial or gender focus (unless, perhaps it were a "mere repeal" by the same body that created the initial rule) would be, if not automatically unconstitutional, at least subject to heightened scrutiny under traditional Equal Protection Clause analysis. Perhaps this result would be desirable. As both *Crawford* and the Court's analysis in *Seattle* make clear, however, the Court was unwilling to embrace fully the implications of its analysis.

Reconciling Crawford *with* Hunter *and* Seattle

"First, he noted that *Crawford*. . . .": *See* Coalition for Economic Equity v. Wilson, 946 F. Supp. at 1508.

"Second, Judge Henderson pointed out. . . .": *See id.*

"Given the tension. . . .": The alternatives — available only to the Supreme, not lower courts, which must follow existing precedent — would be to repudiate *Crawford* and carry the *Hunter/*

Seattle doctrine to its logical extreme, or repudiate the *Hunter/Seattle* doctrine and leave these matters entirely to the political process. *See* Girardeau A. Spann, Proposition 209, 47 Duke L.J. 187 (1997). The first option has the disadvantage giving the judiciary perhaps too active a role in regulating the political process. The latter has the disadvantage of permitting substantial discrimination against minority interests. *See* final endnote to "*The Supreme Court Precedent*," *supra* (discussing similar tension within *Seattle* itself).

The Political Reaction to Judge Henderson's Decision

" 'The ink on Proposition 209. . . .' ": Coalition for Economic Equity v. Wilson, 122 F.3d at 700.

" 'an affront to common sense.' ": *See* Reynolds Holding, Judge Blocks Proposition 209; He Cites Immediate Threat to Women and Minorities, San Francisco Chronicle, November 28, 1996, page A1.

" 'an utter perversion. . . .' ": *See* ABC News, This Week with David Brinkley, December 1, 1996, Transcript # 788-1.

" 'Time for another Boston Tea Party. . . .' ": *See* California: Judge Temporarily Blocks Prop 209, The Hotline, American Political Network, Inc., December 2, 1996.

" 'It is well known that this guy. . . .' ": *See id.*

" 'an unapologetic proponent. . . .' ": Ed Royce, Press Release: Prop. 209 — The People's Will Overridden, 1996 FDCHe Media, December 5, 1996.

" 'Henderson should have quoted. . . .' ": *See* George Skelton, Capitol Journal: Making a Case that the People Have Spoken, Los Angeles Times, December 16, 1996, part A, page 3.

" 'snatch[ed] the case. . . .' ": Debra J. Saunders, Judge, Restrain Thyself, San Francisco Chronicle, December 13, 1996, page A33.

" 'lip service to judicial restraint,' 'blithely' ": Bob Wiemer, Affirmative Action Gets Orwellian Face, Newsday, December 2, 1996, page A30.

" 'a prime candidate. . . .' ": Paul Craig Roberts, Mocking the Civil Rights Act, The Washington Times, December 3, 1996, page A12.

"a theme later picked up. . . .": *See* Katharine Q. Seelye, House G.O.P. Begins Listing a Few Judges to Impeach, N.Y. Times, March 14, 1997, sec. A, page 24.

" 'Judicial Tyranny' ": The Augusta (Ga.) Chronicle, December 2, 1996, page A4.

" 'Here we have. . . .' ": Lee Anderson, Arrogant Judicial Dictatorship, Chattanooga Free Press, November 29, 1996, page A6.

"The negative publicity. . . .": There were a few refreshing exceptions. *See, e.g.,* Harriet Chiang, The Man behind Infamous Ruling; Fury Met Judge's Decision, San Francisco Chronicle, August 28, 1997, page A1; Reynolds Holding, The Judge Who Blocked Prop. 209, San Francisco Chronicle, December 15, 2006, page 8/Z5; Jenifer Warren, Judge Is No Stranger to Controversy, Los Angeles Times, December 16, 1996, part A, page 3.

"Judge Henderson received hundreds. . . .": Interviews with Judge Henderson and his assistant, Erma Smith, in Judge Henderson's chambers, March 28, 2007.

" '[T]his case epitomizes. . . .' ": John Ashcroft, Press Release: Activism, FDCHe Media, July 15, 1997.

" 'willful imposition. . . .' ": Orrin Hatch, Press Release: Webwire — Statement on CA Prop. 209, April 9, 1997.

" 'scandalously biased. . . .' ": *See* Independent Women's Forum Praises Court's Decision Upholding California's Proposition 209, PR Newswire, April 8, 1997.

"'opinion [was] so weak. . . .'": Tony Snow (Detroit News), Impeachment? Rep. Delay Proposes Way to Remove Power-mad Judges, The Dallas Morning News, March 17, 1997, page 13A.

"There were only rare references. . . .": *See, e.g.,* Reynolds Holding, The Judge Who Blocked Prop. 209, San Francisco Chronicle, December 15, 2006, page 8/Z5; Reynolds Holding, Prop. 209 Adversaries Play Shuttlecock, San Francisco Chronicle, March 2, 1997, page 5/Z5.

"innumerable editorials": *See, e.g.,* Jack Kilpatrick, "Equal Protection" At the Heart of Court Battle over California Law, Deseret News (Salt Lake City, UT), January 13, 1997, page A8; Landmark Ruling, The (Manchester, NH) Union Leader, April 11, 1997 (ignoring the fact that the Ninth Circuit panel was comprised of three conservatives and stating, "The Ninth Circuit Court of Appeals, one of the most liberal federal courts in the country, slapped down this judicial autocrat.").

"even some news stories. . . .": *See, e.g.,* Tim Golden, Federal Appeals Court Upholds California's Ban on Preferences, N.Y. Times, April 9, 1997, sec. A, page 1 (also noting that the three judges on the Ninth Circuit panel were appointed by Republican presidents); Nancy E. Roman, Calif. Bias Ban Survives Appeal; Only O'Connor Can Block Law Now, The Washington Times, August 22, 1997, page A1.

Sound Bites and the Public Framing of the Issue

"From a public relations standpoint. . . .": *Cf.* John Kaplan, The Limits of the Exclusionary Rule, 26 Stan. L. Rev. 1027 (1974) (making the same point about the Fourth Amendment exclusionary rule, which sometimes permits guilty individuals to go free because the police have violated the Fourth Amendment's ban on unreasonable searches and seizures).

"Indeed, Judge William Norris, dissenting from the decision. . . .": *See* Coalition for Economic Equity v. Wilson 122 F.3d at 714 (opinion of Norris, J., dissenting from denial of rehearing en banc).

"As a matter of 'conventional equal protection analysis. . . .": *Id.* at 701. *See, e.g.,* Ann Donnelly, We Can Do Better than Racial Quotas, The Columbian (Vancouver, WA), June 1, 1997, sec. B, page, 11; Tim Golden, Federal Appeals Court Upholds California's Ban on Preferences, N.Y. Times, April 9, 1997, sec. A, page 1.

"If merely stating this alleged equal protection violation. . . .": Coalition for Economic Equity v. Wilson, 122 F.3d at 702.

"[As Judge Norris pointed out . . .].": *See id.* at 716 (Norris, J., dissenting from denial of rehearing en banc) (citing Romer v. Evans, 517 U.S. 620, 639 (1996) (Scalia, J. dissenting)). *See also* Editorial, While Prop. 209 May Be Legal, It Is Still Divisive, San Jose Mercury News, April 10, 1997, page B8; Editorial, No Quotas, No Way, The Washington Times, April 10, 1997, page A16.

"While the Constitution protects against obstruction. . . .": Coalition for Economic Equity v. Wilson, 122 F.3d at 708. *See* Maura Dolan, U.S. Panel Upholds Prop. 209; Affirmative Action: Three 9th Circuit Justices Rule that Measure to Eliminate Preferences for Women and Minorities in College Admissions and Government Employment Is Constitutional. Opponents Will Appeal, but Some Analysts Believe They Face an Unhill Battle, Los Angeles Times, April 9, 1997, part A, page 1.

"its most memorable and most quoted. . . .": *See, e.g.,* Joan Beck, A Giant Step toward Ending Affirmative Action, Chicago Tribune, April 13, 1997, page C21; Michael Kelly, Repairing the Breach, The Baltimore Sun, April 11, 1997, page 23A. Even academic legal journals singled out this sentence. *See, e.,g.,* Kristofor J. Hammond, Note: Judicial Intervention in a Twenty-First

Century Republic: Shuffling Deck Chairs on the Titanic? 74 Ind. L.J. 653, 677 n.125 (1999); Note, The Constitutionality of Proposition 209 as Applied, 111 Harv. L. Rev. 2081, 2087 (1998).

"A system which permits. . . .": Coalition for Economic Equity v. Wilson, 122 F.3d at 699.

"equally quotable but largely ignored": But see Soul of Justice.

"[O]ur system of democracy teaches. . . .": Coalition for Economic Equity v. Wilson, 946 F. Supp. at 1490.

"so understood by much of the media.": See, e.g., Michael Kelly, Breach of Promise, The New Republic, April 28, 1997, page 4; Joe Gelman, The People's Will Prevails on Civil Rights Initiative, Times-Picayune, April 17, 1997, page B7.

" 'received what amounted to. . . .' ": Id.

"According to Mark Rosenbaum. . . .": Telephone interview with Mark Rosenbaum, August, 18, 2010. Mark Rosenbaum was himself subjected to an unwarranted rebuke by the Ninth Circuit panel. He is the attorney referred to in the panel's "au contraire!" statement discussed in Appendix C.

"Fn. 7. . . . No doubt the district court . . . at least in theory. . . .": Coalition for Economic Equity v. Wilson, 110 F.3d 1431, 1437 (9th Cir. 1997), withdrawn & superceded by, 122 F.3d 692 (9th Cir. 1997) (emphasis added).

"Fn. 7. . . . No doubt the district court is correct. . . .": Coalition for Economic Equity v. Wilson, 122 F.3d at 699 (emphasis added).

The Ninth Circuit Panel's Legal Analysis

"After setting forth the facts. . . .": See Coalition for Economic Equity v. Wilson, 122 F.3d at 705–06.

" 'the Equal Protection Clause is not violated. . . .' ": Id. at 705.

" 'It would be paradoxical. . . .' ": See Crawford v. Board of Education of the City of Los Angeles, 458 U.S. at 535 (quoted in Coalition for Economic Equity v. Wilson, 122 F.3d at 709).

"the panel accepted. . . .": See Coalition for Economic Equity v. Wilson, 122 F.3d at 705 ("We accept without questioning the district court's findings that Proposition 209 burdens members of insular minorities within the majority that enacted it who otherwise would seek to obtain race-based and gender-based preferential treatment from local entities."); id. at 710–11 ("Assuming all facts alleged in the complaint and found by the district court to be true, and drawing all reasonable inferences in plaintiffs' favor, we must conclude that, as a matter of law, Proposition 209 does not violate the United States Constitution.")

" 'addresse[d] in neutral–fashion. . . .' ": Id. at 707.

Anticipatory Overruling?

"constitutional ideal was color blindness.": See id. at 701 ("The ultimate goal of the Equal Protection Clause is 'to do away with all governmentally imposed discrimination based on race.' ") (quoting Palmore v. Sidoti, 466 U.S. 429, 439 (1984)).

"They were quotations from. . . .": See, e.g., Coalition for Economic Equity v. Wilson, 122 F.3d at 701 (quoting Shaw v. Reno, 509 U.S. 630, 643 (1993) for the proposition that "[r]acial distinctions 'threaten to stigmatize individuals by reason of their membership in a racial group and to incite racial hostility;' " Coalition for Economic Equity v. Wilson, 122 F.3d at 708 (quoting Shaw, 509 U.S. at 657 for the proposition that "[a]fter all, the 'goal' of the Fourteenth

Amendment, 'to which the Nation continues to aspire,' is 'a political system in which race no longer matters.'" *See also* Coalition for Economic Equity v. Wilson, 122 F.3d at 708–09 (quoting Adarand Constructors Inc. v. Pena, 515 U.S. 200 (1995) and City of Richmond v. J.A. Croson Co., 488 U.S. 469 (1989)).

"Romer v. Evans": 517 U.S. 620 (1996).

"As Judge Henderson pointed out. . . .": *See* Coalition for Economic Equity v. Wilson, 946 F. Supp. at 1504 n.25 (citing Rodriguez de Quijas v. Shearson/American Express, Inc., 490 U.S. 477, 484 (1989))

"Lower courts must follow. . . .": Other panels of the Ninth Circuit have specifically recognized this principle. *E.g.*, Smith v. University of Washington Law School, 233 F.3d 1188 (9th Cir. 2000); Ackerley Communications of the Northwest v. Krochalis, 108 F.3d 1095, 1099 (9th Cir. 1997); Carlo v. City of Chine, 105 F.3d 493, 499 (9th Cir. 1997). *See also* Coalition for Economic Equity v. Wilson, 122 F.3d at 716–17 (Norris, J., dissenting from rehearing en banc); *id.* at 117–18 (Hawkins, J., commenting on denial of rehearing en banc). *But cf.* Hopwood v. Texas, 78 F.3d 932 (5th Cir. 1996), *criticized in* Smith v. Washington, *supra* at 1200.

"Brown v. Board of Education": 347 U.S. 483 (1954).

"dealt only with segregated schools,": *See id.* at 495 ("*[I]n the field of public education* the doctrine of 'separate but equal' has no place.") (emphasis added).

"its rationale undermined. . . .": *See id.* at 494, quoting with approval the finding of a lower court ("Segregation of white and colored children in public schools has a detrimental effect upon the colored children. The impact is greater when it has the sanction of law; *for the policy of separating the races in usually interpreted as denoting the inferiority of the negro group.*") (emphasis added).

"Plessy v. Ferguson": 163 U.S. 537 (1896).

"Browder v. Gayle": 142 F. Supp. 707 (M.D. Ala. 1956).

"relied on *Brown* to strike down. . . .": *See id.* at 717 ("We cannot in good conscious follow our duty as judges by blindly following the precedent of Plessy v. Ferguson. . . . [W]e think that Plessy v. Ferguson has been impliedly, though not explicitly, overruled and that, under later decisions there is now no rational basis upon which the separate but equal doctrine can be validly applied to public carrier transportation."). The Supreme Court affirmed the district court's decision. Gayle v. Browder, 352 U.S. 903 (1956). For an account of this and other cases in which judges of Fifth Circuit acted to uphold the letter and spirit of *Brown*, *see* Jack Bass, Unlikely Heroes (1981).

"should have followed *Plessy* . . . 'precisely in point.'": *See* Browder v. Gayle, 142 F. Supp. at 718 (Lynne, J., dissenting). Judge Lynne noted that in an earlier opinion Judge Rives, author of the majority opinion, had said, "This Circuit follows the law as stated by the Supreme Court and leaves any need for modification thereof to that Court." *Id.* at 718. In Lynne's view, for lower court judges to "arrogate to themselves [the] prerogative ["of putting off the old and putting on the new"] would be the first, fatal step in making hollow the proud boast that ours is a 'government of laws and not of men.'" *Id.*

Competing Visions of Equal Protection

"Judge Henderson's perspective is realist.": *See generally* Kathleen Sullivan & Gerald Gunther, Constitutional Law 486–625 (16 ed. 2007); Alexandra Natapoff, Madisonian Multiculturalism, 45 Am. U.L. Rev. 751 (1996).

"By contrast, nothing in the Ninth Circuit panel's opinion. . . .": The closest the panel came to this issue was to state the concern that it may sometimes be difficult to distinguish the majority from the minority. That may be a reason for applying heightened judicial scrutiny to even benign-appearing racial or gender classifications. *See* Coalition for Economic Equity v. Wilson, 122 F.3d at 708 (citing Adarand Constructors v. Pena, 515 U.S. at 225 and City of Richmond v. J.A. Croson Co., 488 U.S. at 493). It is not, however, a reason for ignoring discrimination.

The Supreme Court Six Years and Ten Years Later

"Grutter v. Bollinger": 539 U.S. 306 (2003).

"'the narrowly tailored use. . . .'": *Id.* at 316. Stressing the importance of a "narrowly tailored" policy, the Court noted that race was only one factor in the admissions decision and that each applicant was evaluated individually. *Id.* at 315–16, 335–39. Moreover, the Court expressed its expectation that there would be no need for such a policy 25 years hence. *Id.* at 343.

"strict scrutiny [and by analogy. . . .": *Id.* at 327.

"Context matters when reviewing. . . .": Id. at 327, 333 (emphasis added)

"may not be limited to educational institutions.": *See* John C. Jeffries, Jr., Bakke Revisited, 2003 Sup. Ct. Rev. 1, 14–15.

"'Effective participation by members. . . .'": *See* Grutter v. Bollinger, 539 U.S. at 332.

"'Major American businesses. . . .'": *Id.* at 330–31.

"Parents Involved in Community Schools v. Seattle School Dist. No. 1": 551 U.S. 701 (2007).

"'in practical application . . . is fatal. . . .'": *Id.* at 834 (Breyer, J., dissenting).

"even *less* emphasis on race": *Id.* at 857 (Breyer, J., dissenting).

A Rejection of the Hunter/Seattle *Doctrine but Vindication for Judge Henderson*

"Three years after. . . .": *See* Schuette v. Coalition to Defend Affirmative Action, Integration and Immigration Rights and Fight for Equality by Any Means Necessary (BAMN), 134 S.Ct. 1623, 1629 (2014) [**hereinafter Schutte v. BAMN**].

"Prior to the enactment. . . .": *Id.* at 1652–53 (Sotomayor, J., dissenting).

"The district court. . . .": *See* Coalition to Defend Affirmative Action v. Regents of University of Michigan, 539 F. Supp. 2d 924 (2008).

"Relying on *Hunter* and *Seattle*": *See* Coalition to Defend Affirmative Action, Integration and Immigration Rights and Fight for Equality by Any Means Necessary (BAMN) v. Regents of Univ. of Michigan, 652 F.3d 607 (6th Cir. 2011), *aff'd en banc*, 701 F.3d 466 (6th Cir. 2012).

"The case. . . .": *See* Schuette v. BAMN, 134 S.Ct. 1623 (2014).

"Chief Justice Roberts . . . joined by Justices Alito, Scalia, and Thomas": Some of Justices Scalia's and Thomas' statements had predated Proposition 209. *See* Adarand Constructors, Inc. v. Pena, 515 U.S. at 230 (Scalia, J., concurring); *id.* at 240–41 (Thomas, J., concurring); City of Richmond v. J.A. Croson Co., 488 U.S. at 520–28 (Scalia, J., concurring).

"Chief Justice Roberts . . . maintained that using race. . . .": *See* Parents Involved in Community Schools v. Seattle School Dist. No. 1, 551 U.S. at 746–47.

"widely quoted passage": *E.g.*, Jeffrey Toobin, Chief Justice Roberts, Meet Bundy and Sterling, Daily Comment (New Yorker blog), April 29, 2014; Joan Biscupic, In U.S. Top Court Race Case, John Roberts Is Chief Phrasemaker, Reuters, October 15, 2013.

"'The way to stop discrimination. . . .'": Parents Involved in Community Schools v. Seattle School Dist. No. 1, 551 U.S. at 748. Justice Thomas made the same point in his *Parents Involved* concurrence:

> The plans before us base school assignment decisions on students' race. Because "[o]ur Constitution is color-blind, and neither knows nor tolerates classes among citizens," such race-based decisionmaking is unconstitutional. [quoting Justice Harlan's dissent in Plessy v. Ferguson]

Id. at 782 (Thomas, J., concurring). By contrast, Justice Kennedy expressed a more nuanced view in his *Parents Involved* concurrence:

> The statement by Justice Harlan that "[o]ur Constitution is color-blind" was most certainly justified in the context of his dissent in Plessy v. Ferguson. The Court's decision in that case was a grievous error it took far too long to overrule. *Plessy*, of course, concerned official classification by race applicable to all persons who sought to use railway carriages. And, as an aspiration, Justice Harlan's axiom must command our assent. In the real world, it is regrettable to say, it cannot be a universal constitutional principle.

Id. at 788 (Kennedy, J., concurring).
"My colleagues are of the view. . . .": Schuette v. BAMN, 134 S.Ct. at 1675–76 (Sotomayor, J., dissenting).
"Justice Sotomayor's dissent, which relied on. . . .": *See id.* at 1653–54 (Sotomayor, J., dissenting).
"Justices Scalia and Thomas . . . wanted to overrule. . . .": *See id.* at 1640–43 (Scalia, J., concurring).
"Justice Kennedy . . . offered a new rationale. . . .": *See id.* at 1631–36.
"This case . . . is about who may resolve. . . .": *Id.* at 1638.
"'reinterpret[ed]' . . . 'beyond recognition.'": *Id.* at 1642 (Scalia, J., concurring).
"'We ordinarily understand our precedents. . . .'": *Id.* at 1663 (Sotomayor, J., dissenting)
"reflect an important principle. . . .": *Id.* at 1650 (Breyer, J., concurring).
"First, the policy was designed. . . .": *See id.* at 1649.
"Second,. . . 'an administrative process. . . .'": *See id.* at 1650–51 (quotation at 1651).

Chapter Twenty-Two
The Ninth Circuit?

"[H]e is a man. . . .": Oral History at iii.
"He was one of five individuals. . . .": *See* Region: Boxer Nominates 5 for Appeals Court, San Francisco Chronicle, August 2, 1993, page A19.
"I won't mention the attorney's name. . . .": Oral History at 175.
"[W]hat you have to worry about. . . .": *Id.*
"The court to which Thelton goes. . . .": United States District Court, Northern District of California, Induction Ceremony: Honorable Thelton E. Henderson, San Francisco, California, July 30, 1980, at 24–25 (copy in author's possession).

Appendix A
The Legal Framework

An Elaboration on the Fact–Law Distinction

On the rule that isolated acts of sexual harassment are not "sufficiently severe or pervasive" to create an "abusive work environment," *see* AMTRAK v. Morgan, 536 U.S. 101, 115–16 (2002); Meritor Savings Bank, FSB v. Vinson, 477 U.S. 57, 67 (1986).

On the "compelling governmental interest" test, *see* Adarand Constructors, Inc. v. Pena, 515 U.S. 200 (1995).

"while rarely fully articulated": *But see* Schuette v. Coalition to Defend Affirmative Action, Integration and Immigration Rights and Fight for Equality by Any Means Necessary (BAMN), 134 S.Ct. 1623 (2014) (Sotomayor, J., dissenting).

Binding Precedent and Stare Decisis

On the question whether warrants are required for code inspections, *see* Camera v. Municipal Court of the City and County of San Francisco, 387 U.S. 523 (1967).

"Brown v. Board of Education": 347 U.S. 483 (1954).

On *Brown's* progeny, *see, e.g.,* Jack Bass, Unlikely Heroes (1981).

"Plessy v. Ferguson": 163 U.S. 537 (1896).

"Gideon v. Wainwright": 372 U.S. 335 (1963).

"Betts v. Brady": 316 U.S. 455 (1942).

"Lawrence v. Texas": 539 U.S. 558 (2003).

"Bowers v. Hardwick": 478 U.S. 186 (1986).

"that it is returning to sounder, preexisting precedent.": *See* Gideon v. Wainwright, 372 U.S. at 344.

"Or perhaps a court will say. . . .": *See id.* at 349–52 (Harlan, J., concurring); Gerald H. Israel, Gideon v. Wainwright: The "Art" of Overruling, 1963 Sup. Ct. Rev. 211.

Appendix B
High Tech Gays in the Ninth Circuit

"the appeal from Judge Henderson's *High Tech Gays* decision": *See* High Tech Gays v. Defense Indus. Sec. Clearance Office, 895 F.2d 563 (9th Cir. 1990).

" 'The Supreme Court has ruled. . . .' ": *Id.* at 571.

"Initially, the panel identified. . . .": The panel cited Bowen v. Gilliard, 483 U.S. 587, 602–03 (1987), and Lyng v. Castillo, 477 U.S. 635, 638 (1986), for the proposition that a suspect or quasi-suspect class "must (1) have suffered a history of discrimination; (2) exhibit obvious, immutable, *or* distinguishing characteristics that define them as a discrete group; and (3) show that they are a minority *or* politically powerless." High Tech Gays v. Defense Indus. Sec. Clearance Office, 895 F.2d at 573 (emphasis added). The panel concluded that gays and lesbians satisfied only the first criterion. *Id.*

"[First,] homosexuality is not. . . .": *Id.* at 573–74.

"There is every reason. . . .": High Tech Gays v. Defense Indus. Sec. Clearance Office, 909 F.2d at 377 (Canby, J., dissenting) (citing Gay Rights Coalition v. Georgetown University, 536 A.2d 1, 34 (D.C.App.1987); A. Bell, M. Weinberg, & F. Hammersmith, Sexual Preference-Its Development in Men and Women 166–67, 190, 211, 222 (1981); L. Tribe, American Constitutional Law 944–45 n. 17 (1978)). Furthermore, Judge Canby observed, the panel's own description of this criterion for suspect classification is phrased in terms of "immutable *or* other distinguishing characteristics," High Tech Gays v. Defense Indus. Sec. Clearance Office, 909 F.2d at 377 (emphasis by Judge Canby), and the Supreme Court "has more than once recited the characteristics of a suspect class without mentioning immutability. . . ." *Id.* (citing Cleburne v. Cleburne Living Center, Inc., 473 U.S. 432, 440–41 (1985); Massachusetts Bd. of Retirement v. Murgia, 427 U.S. 307, 313 (1976); San Antonio School Dist. v. Rodriguez, 411 U.S. 1, 28 (1973); and Graham v Richardson, 403 U.S. 365, 372 (1971) ("classifications based on alienage [not an immutable characteristic], like those based on nationality or race, are inherently suspect and subject to close judicial scrutiny")). "The real question is whether discrimination on the basis of the class's distinguishing characteristic amounts to an unfair branding or resort to prejudice, not necessarily whether the characteristic is immutable." High Tech Gays v. Defense Indus. Sec. Clearance Office, 909. F.2d at 377 (Canby, J. dissenting)

"[The panel's] support. . . .": High Tech Gays v. Defense Indus. Sec. Clearance Office, 909 F.2d at 377–78 (Canby, J., dissenting).

"Since 'the Constitution confers. . . .' ": High Tech Gays v. Defense Indus. Sec. Clearance Office, 895 U.S. at 571.

"Fn. 1 . . . the panel at one point suggested. . . .": *See* High Tech Gays v. Defense Indus. Sec. Clearance Office, 895 F.2d at 571.

"Fn 1. . . . '[t]his Court's approach. . . .' ": *Id. See also* High Tech Gays v. Defense Indus. Sec. Clearance Office, 909 F.2d at 379 (Canby, J., dissenting).

"Similarly, one can characterize. . . .": *See, e.g.,* Reva Siegal, Reasoning from the Body: A Historical Perspective on Abortion Regulations and Equal Protection, 44 Stan. L. Rev. 261 (1992); Sylvia Law, Rethinking Sex and the Constitution, 132 U. Pa. L. Rev. 995 (1984).

" 'great resistance to expand. . . .' ": High Tech Gays v. Defense Indus. Sec. Clearance Office, 895 F.2d at 571 (quoting Bowers v. Hardwick).

". . . The unwillingness to read. . . .": *Cf.* Cass Sunstein, Sexual Orientation and the Constitution: A Note on the Relationship between Due Process and Equal Protection, 55 U. Chi. L. Rev. 1161 (1988) ("[T]he Due Process Clause has been interpreted largely (though not exclusively) to protect traditional practices against short-run departures. The clause has therefore been associated with a particular conception of judicial review, one that sees courts as safeguards against novel developments brought about temporary majorities who are insufficiently sensitive to the claims of history. The Equal Protection Clause, by contrast, has been understood as an attempt to protect disadvantaged groups from discriminatory practices, however deeply engrained and longstanding.")

"cited *Cleburne* several times": *See* High Tech Gays v. Defense Indus. Sec. Clearance Office 895 F.2d at 570, 571, 573, 574, & 575.

"relying on *Cleburne*": *See id.* at 575.

"whether they may be 'susceptible. . . .' ": *See* High Tech Gays v. Defense Indus. Sec. Clearance Office, 895 F.2d at 576.

"The government had made this claim. . . .": *See* High Tech Gays v. Defense Indus. Sec. Clearance Office, 909 F.2d at 381 (Canby, J., dissenting).

"As the panel pointed out. . . .": *See* High Tech Gays v. Defense Indus. Sec. Clearance Office, 895 F.2d at 576–77.

"no evidence suggesting. . . .": *See* High Tech Gays v. Defense Indus. Sec. Clearance Office, 668 F. Supp. at 1375.

" 'helps to perpetuate. . . .' ": High Tech Gays v. Defense Indus. Sec. Clearance Office, 909 F.2d at 381 (Canby, J., dissenting).

" 'The counterintelligence agencies' reasons. . . .' ": High Tech Gays v. Defense Indus. Sec. Clearance Office, 895 F.2d at 895 (emphasis added).

Appendix C
Rush to Judgment: The Ninth Circuit's Proposition 209 Opinion

"Coalition for Economic Equity v. Wilson": 946 F. Supp. 692 (N.D. Cal. 1996), *rev'd*, 122 F.3d 692 (9th Cir. 1997).

"By contrast, the entire time. . . .": *See* Coalition for Economic Equity v. Wilson, 122 F.3d at 697.

"the balance of hardships. . . .": Coalition for Economic Equity v. Wilson, 946 F. Supp. at 1520.

The Motions Panel's Decision to Consider the Preliminary Injunction Appeal

"Monterey Mechanical Co. v. Wilson": 125 F.3d 702 (9th Cir. 1997).

"Both of these factual matters are relevant. . . .": *See* Monterey Mechanical Co. v. Wilson, 138 F.3d 1270, 1274, 1276, 1278 (9th Cir. 1997) (Reinhardt, J., dissenting from order rejecting suggestion for rehearing *en banc*).

"I . . . believe the motions panel. . . .": *Id.* at 1274 n.3 (Reinhardt, J., dissenting from order rejecting suggestion for rehearing *en banc*).

"Judge Kleinfeld . . . responded. . . .": *See id.* at 1271 (Klenifeld, J., concurring in order rejecting suggestion for rehearing *en banc*).

" 'focused primarily on the merits. . . .' ": Coalition for Economic Equity v. Wilson, 122 F.3d at 699.

" 'We *thus* deferred. . . .' ": *Id.* (emphasis added).

"CADAP filed its application. . . .": *See* Petition for Rehearing at 3. Judge Henderson denied the stay motion on February 7, 1997. Coalition for Economic Equity v. Wilson, 1997 W.L. 70641.

The Motions Panel's Decision to Consider the Merits of Proposition 209

"the usual role. . . .": *See* Zepeda v. U.S.I.N.S., 753 F.2d 719, 724 (9th Cir. 1984) ("Review of an order granting or denying a preliminary injunction is much more limited than review of an order granting or denying a permanent injunction. At the preliminary injunction stage, the substantive law aspects of the district court's order will be reversed only if the order rests on an erroneous legal premise and, thus, constitutes an abuse of discretion; at the permanent injunction stage, we freely review all conclusions of law."); Sports Form, Inc. v. United Press Int'l, 686 F.2d. 750, 752 (9th Cir. 1982) ("[U]nless the district court's decision [to grant or deny a preliminary injunction] rests on an erroneous legal premise, it will not be reversed simply because the appellate court would have arrived at a different result if it had applied the law to the facts of the case. Rather, the appellate court will reverse only if the district court abused its discretion.")

"Gregorio T. v. Wilson, the case upon which. . . .": *See* Coalition for Economic Equity v. Wilson, 122 F.3d at 699 n.5 (citing Gregorio T. v. Wilson, 59 F.3d 1002 (9th Cir. 1995) and Gregorio T. v. Wilson, 54 F.3d 599 (9th Cir. 1995)).

"In *Gregorio T.*, the court refused. . . .": *See* Gregorio T. v. Wilson, 59 F.3d at 1004–05.

"to declare, as the motions panel did,. . . .": *See* Coalition for Economic Equity v. Wilson, 122 F.3d at 707.

"Detailed consideration of the merits. . . .": Associated General Contractors of California, Inc. v. Coalition for Economic Equity, 950 F.2d 1401, 1419 (9th Cir. 1991) (O'Scannlain, J., concurring).

"'all facts alleged in the complaint. . . .'": Coalition for Economic Equity v. Willson, 122 F.3d at 710–11.

"They were the motions panel's actual findings. . . .": *See id.* at 707, 710–11.

"only if he applied 'an erroneous legal premise'. . . .": *See id.* at 699.

"or had 'abuse[d his] discretion.'": *See id.* at 700.

"Mere disagreement about how to apply the law. . . .": *See id.* at 701 n.9.

"the panel's conclusory statements. . . .": *See id.* at 701 ("As a matter of 'conventional' equal protection analysis, there is simply no doubt that proposition 209 is constitutional."), 702 ("If merely stating this alleged equal protection violation does not suffice to refute it, the central tenet of the Equal Protection Clause teeters on the brink of incoherence."), 708 ("The controlling words we must remember are 'equal' and 'protection.' Impediments to preferential treatment do not deny equal protection."), and 708 ("The alleged 'equal protection' burden that Proposition 209 imposes on those who would seek race and gender preferences is a burden the Constitution itself imposes.").

"Conventional" Equal Protection Analysis

"'the so-called *"Hunter"* doctrine'": Coalition for Economic Equity v. Wilson, 122 F.3d at 703).

"Courts have regularly invoked. . . .": *See id.* at 712–14 (Norris, J. dissenting from denial of rehearing en banc).

"'do not create some paradoxical exception'": Coalition for Economic Equity v. Wilson, 122 F.3d at 707.

"'As a matter of. . . .'": *Id.* at 701.

". . . [A]ny individual suffers an injury. . . .": *Id.* at 702.

"Proposition 209 *prohibits*. . . .": *Id.* (emphasis in original).

A Bizarre Detour

"Noting that. . . .": *Id.* at 704.

"Perhaps . . . the answer to its question should be 'no.'": *See* John Hart Ely, Democracy and Distrust: A Theory of Judicial Review 170–71 (1980).

"Fn. 1. . . . 'The majority needs no protection. . . .' ": Coalition for Economic Equity v. Wilson, 122 F.3d at 704 (quoting Hunter v. Erickson, 393 U.S. 385, 391 (1969)).

"Moreover, in other cases. . . .": *E.g.,* Adarand Constructors v. Pena, 515 U.S. 200 (1995) (Department of Transportation's policy giving preference to minority contractors); Wygant v. Jackson Board of Education, 476 U.S. 267 (1986) (board of education layoff policy giving preference to minorities); University of California Regents v. Bakke, 438 U.S. 265 (1978) (medical school admissions quota for minorities).

"Fn. 2. . . . City of Richmond v. J.A. Croson Co.": 488 U.S. 469 (1989).

"In any event. . . .": *See* Coalition for Economic Equity v. Wilson, 946 F. Supp. 1480, 1495 (N.D. Cal. 1996).

" 'Proposition 209 burdens. . . .' ": Coalition for Economic Equity v. Wilson, 122 F.3d at 705.

"[T]he panel would have us believe. . . .": Coalition for Economic Equity v. Wilson, 122 F.3d at 716 (Norris, J., dissenting from denial of rehearing en banc) (quoting and citing, and noting that the panel did not cite, Romer v. Evans, 517 U.S. 620, 639 (1996) (Scalia, J., dissenting)).

"if only Judge Henderson had made a finding. . . .": *See* Coalition for Economic Equity v. Wilson, 122 F.3d at 705 n.13.

"could have taken judicial notice. . . .": *See* Fed. R. Evid. 201.

The Effort to Distinguish Hunter *and* Seattle

"accurately set forth the holdings of *Hunter* and *Seattle*.": *See* Coalition for Economic Equity v. Wilson, 122 F.3d at 703.

" 'does not isolate race and gender. . . .' ": *Id.* at 707.

" 'treat race and gender antidiscrimination laws. . . .' ": *Id.*

" 'Neither *Hunter* nor *Seattle* — nor common sense. . . .' ": *Id.* at 715 (Norris, J., dissenting from denial of rehearing en banc) (emphasis in original).

The "Au Contraire!" *Argument*

"When people enact a law. . . .": *Id.* at 708–09 (emphasis in original).

"only if the *courts* conclude. . . .": *See* Adarand Constructors v. Pena, 515 U.S. 200, 230 (1995) (determining the validity of any law implicating race "is the job of the court applying strict scrutiny").

"but nothing that it said here. . . .": *See* Girardeau A. Spann, Proposition 209, 47 Duke L.J. 187 (1997).

But Elderly Women and Disabled Minorities Can Seek Preferences

" '[i]mpediments to preferential treatment. . . .' ": Coalition for Economic Equity v. Wilson, 122 F.3d at 708.

"Proposition 209 only prohibits. . . .": *Id.* at 708 n.17 (quoting Judge Henderson's opinion).

The Supposed Inapplicability of Hunter *and* Seattle *to Protect Affirmative Action Interests*

"When the government. . . .": *Id.* at 702, 708 & n16.

"To hold that a democratically enacted. . . .": *Id.* at 709.

"[T]he district court did not hold. . . .": *Id.* at 715 (Norris, J., dissenting from denial of rehearing en banc).

"'whether the particular *method*. . . .'": Coalition for Economic Equity v. Wilson, 946 F. Supp. at 1490.

"The panel justifies its result. . . .": Coalition for Economic Equity v. Wilson, 122 F.3d at 713–14 (Norris, J., dissenting from denial of rehearing en banc).